BAYONETS IN PARADISE

PUBLISHED WITH THE SUPPORT OF THE
MAURICE J. SULLIVAN & FAMILY FUND
IN THE UNIVERSITY OF HAWAI'I FOUNDATION

BAYONETS IN PARADISE

Martial Law in Hawai'i during World War II

Harry N. Scheiber and Jane L. Scheiber

UNIVERSITY OF HAWAI'I PRESS
Honolulu

21 20 19 18 17 16   6 5 4 3 2 1

Library of Congress Cataloging-in-Publication Data
Scheiber, Harry N., author.
Bayonets in paradise : martial law in Hawaiʻi during World War II / Harry N. Scheiber
and Jane L. Scheiber.
pages cm
Includes bibliographical references and index.
ISBN 978-0-8248-5288-7 (hardcover : alk. paper)
1. Martial law—Hawaii—History—20th century.   2. Japanese Americans—Legal status, laws, etc.—
Hawaii—History—20th century.   3. World War, 1939–1945—Law and legislation—United States.
4. World War, 1939–1945—Hawaii.   5. Hawaii—History—1900–1959.
I. Scheiber, Jane L., author.   II. Title.
KFH496.S34 2016
342.73′06280996909044—dc23   2015017664

University of Hawaiʻi Press books are printed on acid-free
paper and meet the guidelines for permanence and
durability of the Council on Library Resources.

Designed by Milenda Nan Ok Lee

For Our Family

Inter arma silent leges
(In time of war laws are silent)

CONTENTS

PREFACE

The current war on terror has highlighted for Americans today the inherent tension between individual freedoms protected by the Constitution and the government's obligations to provide for national security. Three days after terrorist attacks struck the United States on September 11, 2001, President George W. Bush declared a state of emergency, and on September 18, Congress gave the president sweeping authorization "to use all necessary and appropriate force" against nations, organizations, and individuals to prevent future terrorist attacks. Presidents Bush and Obama have used this authorization to justify a range of actions from indefinite detention to drone strikes to electronic surveillance.[1]

President Bush also signed an executive order announcing that military tribunals would be established to conduct secret trials of foreign nationals who were "terrorists or suspected terrorists." In authorizing the military tribunals, Bush declared that an emergency existed for national defense purposes, and that "issuance of this order is necessary to meet the emergency."[2] The executive order stated that "it is not practicable to apply in military commissions under this order the principles of law and the rules of evidence generally recognized in the trial of criminal cases in the United States district courts."[3] This application of military justice represented a major departure from the long-held American policy that condemned secret trials of any kind, let alone by military courts not bound by the accepted rules of due process to which civilian courts were held. Although the Supreme Court subsequently upheld the rights to the writ of habeas corpus of detainees being held in the American base at Guantanamo—even those who were classified as enemy combatants—the use of military tribunals and indefinite detention in the war on terror continues and has deeply divided American public opinion.[4]

Yet neither military tribunals nor the denial of habeas corpus rights was entirely without precedent. President Lincoln's suspension of the writ of habeas corpus and his use of military trials of civilians in the Civil War is relatively well known. Less familiar is the fact that sixty years before the 9/11 crisis, in another national emergency, military justice supplanted civilian justice in the territory of Hawai'i, not just for aliens suspected of acting in the interests of the enemy, but for an entire civilian population of more than 423,000, of whom 89 percent were citizens. For throughout most of World War II, Hawai'i was under the full control of the military; the privilege of the writ of habeas corpus was suspended, and the authority of the civilian government was subordinated so fully that the army officially termed the federal judges "agents" of the military.

This clash between American constitutional guarantees of liberty and the need for national security, as it played out during World War II in the Hawaiian Islands—involving the military command, the territorial civilian government, and the Roosevelt administration in Washington, DC—is the subject of this book. The authors hope not only to tell the story of this crisis in the history of American democracy, but also to place that crisis in the context of the continuing struggle to protect our freedoms.

ACKNOWLEDGMENTS

This book is the product of many years, in fact several decades, of research on a topic that was largely obscure for historians, constitutional scholars, and the public outside of Hawai'i when we began our work on it. In the course of reconstructing and interpreting the history of martial law in Hawai'i, we have become indebted to an honored company of "keepers of the tradition"—to the archivists, librarians, and administrators of the several institutions in which we have done our research. Hence we extend our thanks first to the professional staffs of the University of California, Berkeley, School of Law Library, and especially to Prof. Kathleen Vanden Heuvel; the Bancroft Library, UC Berkeley; the Franklin D. Roosevelt Library, Hyde Park; the National Archives at College Park and at San Bruno; the Manuscripts Division of the Library of Congress; the Bentley Historical Library, University of Michigan; and the Hoover Institution Archives of Stanford University.

For assistance during our hundreds of hours of research in Hawai'i, we thank the staff of the King Kamehameha V Judiciary History Center; the Hawai'i State Archives; the Japanese Cultural Center of Hawai'i, especially Marcia Kemble, Jane Kurahara, Brian Niiya, and Betsy Young; and the reference librarians and archivists of the Hamilton Library, University of Hawai'i at Manoa, with thanks particularly to Sherman Seki, who has lent unstinting help with our work in the Japanese Internment and Relocation collection and with the illustrations.

Having the advice and guidance of professional colleagues has been of essential importance to us in writing this book. We wish to thank, above all, Professor Emeritus Roger Daniels of the University of Cincinnati, who for more than fifty years has been the preeminent scholar on the ethnic Japanese and their travails in World War II. He has provided us with detailed, constructive criticisms and suggestions, reflecting his uniquely learned perspective. We also want to express our gratitude to the late Jon Van Dyke, professor of law in the Richardson School of Law, University of Hawai'i, whose insights and keen interest in the project were incredibly important to us. Jon and his wife, Sherry Broder, Esq., have regularly extended to us their hospitality, counsel, and above all, a warm and sustaining friendship.

Other colleagues who contributed supportively at different stages of the research, and to whom we are similarly grateful, are our friends Lawrence M. Friedman of Stanford University, Maeva Marcus of George Washington University, Laura Kalman of UC Santa Barbara, Jonathan Lurie of Rutgers University, Sandra VanBurkleo of Wayne State University, and the late Paul Murphy of the University of Minnesota. We also owe special thanks to Dean Avi Soifer and Professor Williamson Chang of the Richardson School of Law, University of Hawai'i, and to many other individuals in Hawai'i, including the late Chief Justice William S. Richardson of the Hawai'i Supreme Court and also members of the Japanese-American community who have shared their reminiscences and offered comments on our work. Formal interviews were kindly accorded us by the late Senator Hiram Fong, the late Mrs. Garner Anthony, and the late John P. Frank, Esq. Any errors of fact and all interpretations in this book are, of course, entirely our responsibility.

A number of American and foreign institutions generously hosted lectures or seminars at which we have presented our research in various phases of the work: the American Society for Legal History; the American Historical Association's Pacific Coast Branch; the Center for the Study of Law and Society at UC Berkeley; the Richardson School of Law, University of Hawai'i and its Jon Van Dyke Institute; the Hawai'i Judiciary History Center; the Ninth Judicial Circuit annual meeting; Stanford Law School; Yale History Department and Law School; the Center for Constitutional Studies at Utah Valley University; the Law Faculty of Uppsala University, Sweden; and the Japan Federation of Bar Associations, Tokyo. Articles of ours on subthemes of the main work have been published in the *University of Hawai'i Law Review, Western Legal History,* and *Legal Affairs,* and we extend thanks to their editors.

We gratefully acknowledge the partial funding of research that has been provided by the Stefan Riesenfeld Chair Professorship endowment and by the Office of the Dean, School of Law, UC Berkeley. Benjamin Jones and James Phillips served ably as research assistants while engaged in doctoral and law studies at UC Berkeley. Finally, we are also much indebted to Toni Mendicino of the Institute for Legal Research, UC Berkeley Law School staff, for her skilled technical support.

A NOTE ON TERMINOLOGY

There is considerable controversy today among scholars and political activists with regard to nomenclature concerning what was long routinely (if loosely) termed the "Japanese-American internments" in World War II. We therefore wish to clarify our use of terms.

We use the terms "Japanese Americans," "Nikkei," and "ethnic Japanese" interchangeably to refer to all persons of Japanese descent living in the United States or its territories, including Hawai'i. Where appropriate to distinguish among the Japanese Americans, we have used the following terms: "Issei"—first-generation immigrants who, except for a few World War I veterans, were prevented by legislation from becoming citizens prior to 1952; "Nisei"—second-generation Japanese Americans, born on U.S. soil and therefore American citizens; "Sansei"—third-generation Japanese Americans; and "Kibei"—those Nisei who went to Japan for an extended period, usually for part or all of their education, before returning to the territory of Hawai'i or the United States.

We use the term "detainees" to describe generally all the persons who were arrested on suspicion of being dangerous to the security of the United States and denied their freedom, whether in War Relocation Authority camps, internment camps run by the army or the Department of Justice, or temporary custodial facilities. The term "internees" refers to a subset of detainees: (1) enemy aliens—including Japanese, Germans, and Italians—who were incarcerated in camps run by the Department of Justice or the army, in Hawai'i or on the mainland; and (2) citizens and aliens who were arrested and incarcerated in Hawai'i as security threats under the terms of martial law.

The army and civilian authorities used the term "evacuees" to categorize the many Hawai'i Nikkei who were sent by the army from Hawaii in late 1942 and early 1943 and placed in mainland relocation camps run by the War Relocation Authority. "Excludees" refers to those persons who were suspected of being a security threat and were sent to the WRA camp at Tule Lake after martial law was terminated in October 1944. Both evacuees and excludees, like the internees, were, in fact, incarcerated.

Because of the cruel way in which the mainland Nikkei were forcibly removed en masse from their homes and essentially held as prisoners behind barbed wire (although with families intact, and provisions for children's schooling and community activities), numerous activists and scholars have used the term "concentration camps" to describe the facilities in which they were incarcerated. In fact, during the prewar period and well into the war years, the term was occasionally used by President Roosevelt and was frequently employed by civilian and military leaders. Because of its association with the Nazi death camps, however, we have used the term "concentration camps" in this study only when quoting directly from documents of the war period or from historians who have adopted that nomenclature.

We use "internment camps" to refer to the facilities that housed internees: (1) the camps on the mainland, run by the army or the Department of Justice's Immigration and Naturalization Service, in which enemy aliens were incarcerated; and (2) the facilities in Hawai'i in which several hundred aliens and citizens were confined by the army under the terms of martial law. We use the terms "relocation camps" and "WRA camps" to refer to the incarceration facilities that were run by the War Relocation Authority. Regardless of terminology, all of the facilities deprived those detained of their liberty.

ABBREVIATIONS

ACLU	American Civil Liberties Union
AFL	American Federation of Labor
CIC	Counter-Intelligence Corps (U.S. Army)
CIO	Congress of Industrial Organizations
CWIRC	Commission on Wartime Relocation and Internment of Civilians
DOJ	Department of Justice
ESC	Emergency Service Committee
FBI	Federal Bureau of Investigation
FDRL	Franklin D. Roosevelt Library
G-2	Army Intelligence
HSA	Hawaiʻi State Archives
HSPA	Hawaii Sugar Planters' Association
HTG	Hawaii Territorial Guard
HWRD	Hawaii War Records Depository, Hamilton Library, University of Hawaiʻi
ILWU	International Longshore and Warehouse Union
JAERR	Japanese American Evacuation and Resettlement Records, Bancroft Library, University of California, Berkeley
JAGSL	Judge Advocate General School Library
JAJB	Japanese American Joint Board
JCCH	Japanese Cultural Center of Hawaiʻi
JIR	Japanese Internment and Relocation Files—The Hawaiʻi Experience, Hamilton Library, University of Hawaiʻi
LC	Library of Congress
MID	Military Intelligence Division
MIS	Military Intelligence Service
NA	National Archives
NARA	National Archives and Records Administration
NASB	National Archives, San Bruno
OCD	Office of Civilian Defense

OIS   Office of Internal Security
OMG   Office of the Military Governor
ONI   Office of Naval Intelligence
OPA   Office of Price Administration
RG   Record Group
WLB   War Labor Board
WMC   War Manpower Commission
WRA   War Relocation Authority

BAYONETS IN PARADISE

INTRODUCTION

Wartime Emergency Powers and Martial Law

O n only a few occasions in the history of the United States have American citizens been placed for a substantial period of time under a rule of martial law—the imposition of military rule by military authorities—with the suspension of constitutional rights that this extreme form of military control over civilian life entails. The best-known such episode came in the Civil War years, when President Abraham Lincoln, believing the safety of the armies was at stake, approved a suspension of the writ of habeas corpus and ordered military trials of civilians behind the lines. By the time the United States Supreme Court ruled in 1866 on the constitutionality of these measures, in the famous decision of *Ex parte Milligan*,[1] the war had ended. Despite the fact that Congress had passed the Habeas Corpus Act of 1863 legitimizing Lincoln's suspension of the writ of habeas corpus,[2] the Court's ruling went against the government. The Court declared that constitutional rights must be respected in wartime unless there were conditions of actual, not merely anticipated, invasion; and unless the civilian courts were closed and unable to function owing to the war emergency.[3]

So stood the law at the outbreak of World War II.[4] Although a line of twentieth-century cases in the nation's high court had dealt with martial law in various situations, all of them concerned the invocation of emergency military power by state governors in times of labor strikes or other civil turmoil.[5] Not until after the Pearl Harbor disaster of December 7, 1941, would the *Milligan* doctrine be tested in the crucible of wartime conditions.

Meanwhile, when Congress established Hawai'i as a territory of the United States in 1900, it provided by statute for the territorial governor to declare martial law in cases when invasion was "imminent" as well as actual—a noteworthy departure from the *Milligan* standard. Thus, Section 67 of Hawai'i's Organic Act provided that the territorial governor "may, in case of rebellion or invasion, or imminent danger thereof, when the public safety requires it, suspend the privilege of the writ of habeas corpus, or place the Territory or any part thereof, under martial law until communication can be had with the President and his decision thereon made known."[6]

But how far the powers of military authorities under martial law would run, under this language, if American territory should actually be threatened with attack—and whether the federal courts would permit the army to curtail, at its own discretion, the jurisdiction of civilian courts—remained only theoretical questions until planes from the Japanese Imperial Navy launched their infamous air raid on Pearl Harbor and the surrounding American bases on Oʻahu on December 7, 1941.[7]

With rescue work and firefighting in Honolulu still frantically underway, once the last of Japan's attack planes had departed on that fateful day, the civilian territorial governor, Joseph Poindexter, placed the entire population of the Hawaiian Islands under martial law. He suspended the writ of habeas corpus and turned over his own powers, as well as those normally exercised by the territory's judicial officers, to the U.S. Army commanding general, Walter C. Short. The army stated that, with fears of impending land invasion and subversion well justified throughout the Islands, it was taking complete control of the territory and its civilian population of over 423,000 persons, of whom some 158,000, or 37 percent, were of Japanese birth or of Japanese descent.[8]

There followed nearly three years of military government in Hawaiʻi, covering almost every important aspect of civilian life—all in the name of "military necessity." In both its scope and duration, martial law in Hawaiʻi in World War II was entirely without precedent in American history. "All discussions of the workings of martial law in this country," the army recognized at the end of the war, "have emphasized its use in the control of insurrections, strikes, and civil strife. . . . The concept [of martial law] was not a new one, but its modern development was unique."[9]

As had occurred during the Civil War, there were legal challenges to this regime. And as had also occurred in past wars generally, the federal courts did hear such challenges—but their proceedings typically went on over many months as appeals were taken, and the issue did not reach the U.S. Supreme Court for a definitive ruling until after the fighting had ended. Consistent with that record, the only appeal challenging military rule in Hawaiʻi that reached the U.S. Supreme Court was the long-nearly-forgotten case of *Duncan v. Kahanamoku*.[10] This appeal was heard, ironically enough, on December 7, 1945, exactly four years to the day after the Pearl Harbor bombing. The *Duncan* majority decision finally came down in a 6–2 divided Supreme Court decision only in February 1946, many months after Japan's surrender.[11] The Court's majority in *Duncan* handed a stinging rebuke to the government. Although the majority opinion was technically focused upon the terms of the Hawaiʻi Organic Act, that is, interpreting the statute rather than terms of the Constitution itself, the Court reaffirmed in powerful terms the more general proposition that the judiciary has an obligation to protect citizens' constitutional rights even under the conditions of modern warfare. In that sense, *Duncan* stands in dramatic contrast to the two most notorious "Japanese-American cases" of the World War II era, *Hirabayashi* and *Korematsu,* in which the Court's majority upheld an extraordinary discretionary authority exercised by the government in the incarceration of Japanese Americans living on the West Coast of the United States.[12] By casting the mantle of constitutional legitimacy over the tragic fate visited by the government upon these 110,000 mainland detainees, the great majority of whom were American citizens, the Court had held itself fairly open to comparisons with the judicial role in advancing detested pro-slavery doctrines in the *Dred Scott* case of 1857.

The judgment of history has subsequently repudiated the Court's decisions in regard to the doctrines of the Japanese-American cases. The two decisions were termed "a disaster" by the earliest of the academic commentators, and they have been almost entirely without respectable defenders in the scholarly and professional literature of recent decades.[13]

In 1976, President Gerald Ford, declaring the wartime treatment of Americans of Japanese ancestry a "tragedy" and a "setback to fundamental American principles," officially repealed Executive Order 9066, which had authorized the evacuation and relocation.[14] In 1983, a report by the Congressional Commission on Wartime Internment and Relocation of Citizens cited "grave injustices" and urged a policy of redress for the survivors of the relocation camps; and the following year, a federal district court overturned Fred Korematsu's conviction.[15] A few years later, the Civil Liberties Act of 1988 acknowledged the "injustice of the evacuation, relocation, and internment of United States citizens and permanent resident aliens of Japanese ancestry during World War II," formally apologized on behalf of the people of the United States, and provided reparations of $20,000 for each survivor of the relocation camps.[16] Thus, after the passage of many years, both Congress and the federal courts finally acknowledged that tragic errors had been made and injustices done; and nominal restitution has now been paid from the national treasury as conscience money to living survivors of the camps.[17] Both Gordon Hirabayashi and Fred Korematsu were subsequently recognized with the Presidential Medal of Freedom for their stand against injustice.[18]

Ironically, critics of the Court's decisions in the Japanese-American cases frequently have cited the wartime experience in the Hawaiian Islands as compelling evidence that the mainland internments were totally unnecessary even had they been somehow justifiable constitutionally. In Hawai'i, this argument runs, except for fewer than 1,500 persons who were interned, the very populous community of American residents of Japanese ancestry—50 percent greater in number than were interned on the mainland, and constituting more than one-third of the Islands' civilian population—were not incarcerated or detained, let alone evacuated from their home area. And yet there were no proven instances whatsoever of espionage, sabotage, or other overt antiwar activity by Americans of Japanese descent in Hawai'i during the war.[19] Whatever disloyalty there may conceivably have been in the community had no perceivable effects. Indeed, there was extensive positive evidence of the Japanese Americans' patriotic support of the war, most dramatically in the oversubscribing by thousands of men to the call for enlistment when the army finally agreed to a Nisei unit in 1943.[20] An obvious question arises from this evidence in relation to the "military necessity" argument for interning the mainland ethnic Japanese: If Americans of Japanese ancestry in Hawai'i, thus on the whole freely conducting their activities and working in the larger wartime community, posed no danger in a location closer by more than two thousand miles to the combat areas, what possible reason existed for the internment of the mainland's Japanese Americans?[21]

The irony of Hawai'i's being cited in such a comparison as exemplary of a liberal policy respectful of civilians' constitutional rights, with no danger to security, lies in the fact that throughout most of the war period, the U.S. government actually suspended the constitutional liberties not only of Hawai'i's ethnic Japanese but of the entire civilian population of the Islands—people of every ancestry—when the army imposed a comprehensive and harshly restrictive military regime just after Pearl Harbor. As we shall argue in this book, it was also largely an arbitrary and capricious regime: Hawai'i's civilians were subjected to what the Supreme Court's majority in *Duncan* would deplore as a wholesale and wanton violation of constitutional liberties.[22]

Nearly every civil liberty guaranteed in the Bill of Rights of the Constitution and in subsequent amendments was set aside for some or all of the civilian population of Hawai'i, including the First Amendment rights of freedom of religion, of speech, of press, and of assembly; the Fourth Amendment guarantee of freedom from unreasonable search and seizure; the Fifth Amendment's guarantee of due process; the Sixth and Seventh Amendments' rights to trial by jury, confrontation of witnesses, and right to counsel; and the Fourteenth Amendment's right to equal protection of the laws.[23]

Reflecting in 1957 on the history of army rule under martial law, Garner Anthony—Hawai'i's wartime territorial attorney general, who had been a consistent champion of constitutional values and a prominent critic of the army's regime in Hawai'i—concluded that much of the record was "not understandable." The difficulty in providing an explanation for it, he wrote, lay partly in the fact that the army's suppression of traditional liberties of the citizenry had been so sweeping and so blatant—especially so, because he regarded it as "inconceivable that those in high places in the War Department were not cognizant" that they were sanctioning grievous violations of constitutional rights. Not only was the martial law regime illegal, as the Supreme Court affirmed in the *Duncan* case decision, Anthony wrote, but in a broader sense it was "contrary to our most cherished traditions of the supremacy of the law." The most puzzling thing of all, for him, was that the army should have so intransigently maintained its hold on government and the administration of justice in the Islands long after any realistic prospect of a further attack by Japanese forces had passed. "It will probably be years," he wrote, "before the historian of the future can clearly appraise the motives and causes that led the army to pursue the course it did in Hawaii."[24]

In this book, we take up the challenge that Anthony laid down for future historians. A progressive release of extensive archival materials in recent years has afforded us the opportunity to conduct research on martial law in wartime Hawai'i on a much richer evidentiary basis than was possible previously. These materials cast new light on the motives and the dynamics by which the military—backed by President Roosevelt and his War Department—so callously cast aside the inherited constitutional tradition of American law.

The army operated in wartime Hawai'i on a view of legitimate wartime powers that ran directly contrary to the basic constitutional precept expressed by Justice Sandra Day O'Connor in a modern-day "war on terror" case in which the Court reaffirmed the right of due process for a prisoner: "A state of war," O'Connor declared, "is not a blank check for the president when it comes to the rights of the American citizen."[25] In wartime Hawai'i, the army command, backed by the White House and the War Department, took for itself that "blank check" and used it as its charter for exercising absolute authority over the entire civilian population.

Fully as applicable today—as the nation engages in an apparently open-ended "war on terror"—as it was more than sixty-five years ago is Garner Anthony's admonition that the history of Hawai'i's experience in World War II with martial law, especially with regard to the dramatic constitutional and legal questions that this history produced, is "not only of particular interest to lawyers, political scientists and historians," but also must be "of general interest to every thoughtful citizen who believes that the constitutional safeguards of civil liberties are as important in time of war as in time of peace."[26]

PART I

Martial Law and Military Government

Chapter One

PRELUDE TO MARTIAL LAW

Security and the "Japanese Problem"

Only a few hours after Japanese planes rained destruction on Pearl Harbor on December 7, 1941, Joseph P. Poindexter, the territorial governor of Hawai'i, issued a proclamation placing the entire territory under martial law. He suspended the writ of habeas corpus and requested the commanding general of the Hawaiian Department to exercise all governmental functions, including judicial powers, "until the danger of invasion is removed."[1] In a separate but simultaneous proclamation, the commanding general, Lieutenant General Walter C. Short, declared himself the "Military Governor" of Hawai'i—a self-assumed title that was to become a point of great controversy in later months—and announced that he had "taken charge of the government of the Territory." Citing the necessity of stricter controls than would otherwise be proper because of the "imminence of attack by the enemy and the possibility of invasion," he warned that citizens who disobeyed his orders would be "severely punished by military tribunals" or held in custody until the civil courts were once again able to function.[2]

In this way the entire civilian population of the Hawaiian Islands was placed under the control of a military governor whose discretionary powers were virtually absolute. This comprehensive suspension of constitutional guarantees was destined to last until October 1944, with only slight modifications of military rule implemented in March 1943.

The martial law regime came forth full-blown on December 7, rather than incrementally, largely as the result of the efforts of Lieutenant Colonel Thomas H. Green, the army's chief legal officer in Hawai'i. Green had been working at the Fort Shafter headquarters for nearly a year to prepare detailed plans for military control of Hawai'i in the event of an acute war emergency. In pursuing this task, Green had drafted a set of detailed "general orders" not only for martial law as a temporary emergency measure, but also for the complete takeover by the army of the territory's civilian authority—executive, legislative, and judicial—and the creation of a comprehensive military government.[3]

Green's detailed plans for martial law and military government were the culmination of nearly two decades of discussions, by both military and civilian leaders in Honolulu and in Washington, regarding the use of martial law in the event of war with Japan. From the start, martial law in Hawai'i was regarded as a measure for internal security and a way to deal with the presence of large numbers of ethnic Japanese who might side with the enemy in the case of war. A provision for declaring martial law was included in the Organic Act of 1900, establishing the Territory of Hawai'i.[4] The first serious discussions of its implementation in Hawai'i, however, occurred in the early 1920s, when it was cited by its advocates as a way to manage "the Japanese problem."[5]

Early Japanese Immigration

The "Japanese problem" had its origins in the growth of Japanese immigration into the Hawaiian Islands, which paralleled the growth of the sugar plantations in the second half of the nineteenth century. A reciprocity treaty between the United States and the Kingdom of Hawai'i, signed in 1876, allowed duty-free sales of Hawaiian sugar in the United States, thereby reinforcing the dominance of the sugar industry in the social and economic life of the Islands until World War II. When the treaty was renewed in 1887, the United States insisted upon—and received—access to Pearl Bay, later to be known as Pearl Harbor.

The plantation economy created a seemingly endless demand for cheap labor. As the indigenous Hawaiian population declined, largely as the result of diseases that had been introduced into the Islands, the plantation owners looked to Asia—first China, then Japan, and finally the Philippines—for contract workers to meet their labor needs.[6] By 1884, there were more than 18,000 Chinese in Hawai'i, constituting more than one-fifth of the population. Concerned that the Chinese were gaining too strong a foothold, the Hawaiian Cabinet Council adopted a series of restrictive measures in the late 1880s and early 1890s, effectively ending the immigration of Chinese contract labor.[7]

The Hawaiian planters then turned to Japan as a likely source for cheap labor. Japanese laborers began arriving in Hawai'i in significant numbers beginning in 1886.[8] The planters were initially enthusiastic about the new wave of Japanese immigrants: thus a planters' journal editorial declared early in 1888, "These people assume so readily the customs and habits of the country, that there does not exist the same prejudice against them that there is with the Chinese, while as laborers they seem to give as much satisfaction as any others."[9] Several thousand Japanese workers emigrated to Hawai'i each succeeding year, with 64,000 arriving in the four years 1894 to 1898 alone.[10] Indeed, when in 1897 the United States prepared to annex Hawai'i, the Japanese government filed a formal protest with the U.S. Department of State, claiming that the annexation would deprive 25,000 Japanese, who would be eligible for Hawaiian citizenship but not citizenship in the United States, of their rights.[11]

Japanese immigrant laborers landing from sailing ship, on causeway to Quarantine Island, Honolulu Harbor. Date: ca. 1893. Credit: Courtesy of the Hawai'i State Archives.

By 1900, the year that Hawai'i became a U.S. Territory, there were more than 60,000 Japanese in Hawai'i, constituting nearly 40 percent of the total Hawaiian population.[12] The Japanese had replaced Chinese workers as the dominant labor force on the plantations, and there were significant numbers in business, the professions, and the various trades, where one of every five skilled workers was Japanese.[13] In keeping with Japanese government policy—and in contrast to Chinese immigration—about 20 percent of the Japanese immigrants were women. The resulting family structure contributed to a relatively stable community, evidenced by the establishment of Japanese language schools, Buddhist temples, and other mainstays of Japanese culture.[14]

Anti-Japanese Sentiment, 1900–1930

The numbers and success of the Japanese, both in Hawai'i and on the mainland, combined with widespread racial prejudice and fears of the "yellow peril" to create a wave of anti-Japanese sentiment in the United States early in the twentieth century, especially after the 1905 Russo-Japanese War.[15] In Hawai'i, these factors were exacerbated by the importation of more than 10,000 Japanese "picture brides" and by the continued movement of Japanese plantation workers into skilled and semiskilled occupations in the towns.[16] "It is not easy to give an adequate idea of the resentment and the bitterness felt by the white mechanic and white merchant who see themselves steadily forced to the wall and even driven out of the Territory, by Asiatic competition," stated a Department of Labor report in 1905.[17]

Anti-Japanese sentiment culminated in the Immigration Act of 1924, which finally halted Japanese immigration to the United States and its territories. Also known as the "Asian Exclusion Act," this legislation prohibited immigration of persons ineligible for citizenship; and since only "whites" and "blacks" could become citizens, Asians (considered "yellow" at the time) were ineligible. While the Organic Act of 1900 extended constitutional protections to citizens in the Territory of Hawai'i, it also meant that the Japanese immigrants were subjected to American laws restricting naturalization. Two Supreme Court cases—a 1922 decision rejecting Takao Ozawa's attempt to become naturalized as a "white" person, and a 1925 decision denying naturalization for Hidemitsu Toyota, a World War I veteran—ended any Japanese hopes for naturalization.[18] Indeed, the citizenship of more than 450 Hawai'i Japanese immigrants who had been naturalized by a federal court following their military service in World War I was revoked in 1927.[19] In 1935, President Roosevelt did sign into law the Lea-Nye Bill, which conferred citizenship on approximately 500 World War I U.S. Army veterans from "oriental" countries. The denial of citizenship to the vast majority of Japanese immigrants (the Issei) was later to become a significant factor, however, during the loyalty hearings under martial law.[20]

Despite the anti-Japanese legislation, the ethnic Japanese population in Hawai'i continued to grow, as the 1910s and 1920s were marked by a baby boom. By 1930, their numbers had swelled to nearly 140,000, or more than 42 percent of the population of Hawai'i. Unlike their immigrant parents, who were prohibited from becoming naturalized, these Hawai'i-born children (the Nisei) were American citizens—a fact that was viewed with increasing alarm by the existing white power structure as the Nisei reached voting age.

Once so eagerly welcomed to the Islands, the Japanese and their American-born children were increasingly viewed by the Hawaiian Sugar Planters' Association (HSPA) and *haole* (white) elite not only as an economic, political, and social threat, but also as a security threat, especially after 1908, when U.S. defense plans against the Japanese fleet began to center on Pearl Harbor.[21] In 1917, a naval officer in Pearl Harbor gave voice to a theme that was to dominate U.S. military thinking through the early years of World War II:

> For the defense of Oahu, the present greatest menace to our security is the large proportion of population of foreign birth and sympathies who are very liable to turn against this country.... There are fair hopes of making good citizens of all of the white population, but with the Japanese this can probably never be done.[22]

The following year, Major H. C. Merriam, an intelligence officer in the army's Hawaiian Department, reported to the chief of military intelligence in Washington on

"The Increase of Japanese Population in the Hawaiian Islands and What It Means."
Even if the Nisei were to side with the United States in case of a confrontation with
Japan, he wrote, the small American Caucasian population of about 15,000 would be
outnumbered four to one. Furthermore, he warned, the Nisei could eventually use their
voting rights to control the political fate of the territory. Merriam identified the main
sources of anti-Americanism: the Japanese government, the Japanese language schools,
and the Buddhist churches—the very elements that would be singled out as prime suspects for disloyalty when war finally erupted in 1941. The Japanese language schools in
particular became the objects of suspicion and of restrictive regulatory measures by
the territorial legislature between 1920 and 1925, but the legislation was struck down
in 1927 by the U.S. Supreme Court as a denial of the due process clause of the U.S. Constitution.[23] Thereafter the schools continued to operate until the war, free of legal obstacles but not of distrust by the military and many prominent *haole.*

A series of strikes by the Japanese sugar-cane workers against low wages and poor
working conditions broke out soon after the turn of the century, as the Organic Act
abolished the labor contracts that had held the laborers in virtual slavery. These strikes,
as well as the movement of the Japanese workers away from the plantations, heightened both the fears and the anti-Japanese sentiment of the plantation owners.[24] The
HSPA, which had been organized in 1895, acted in concert to suppress the strikes.[25]
The great strike of 1920, which involved some 8,300 Filipino and Japanese workers—
more than three-fourths of the plantation workforce then employed on O'ahu—in particular triggered a rise in virulent anti-Japanese feelings.[26] Despite their protestations
to the contrary, the strikers were accused by the minority white population, and especially by the sugar planters and the press, of being racially motivated and desirous of
seizing economic control of the Islands. There was some sentiment to use military force
to put down the strike, but the acting governor, Curtis Iaukea, refused to succumb to
political pressure. Nevertheless, Army Intelligence formed a close working alliance with
the plantation owners that would last through the war years, using the HSPA's industrial spy system to keep them informed of any emergency situations arising from labor
unrest.

Claiming that the strike was "an attempt on the part of an alien race to cripple
our principal industry and to gain dominance of the American territory of Hawaii,"
the *Honolulu Advertiser* denounced not only the strikers but also the Buddhist priests,
Japanese newspaper editors, and "other subjects of the Mikado."[27] The *Honolulu Star-
Bulletin* similarly urged its readers to stay focused on the main issue: "Is Hawaii to remain American or become Japanese? A compromise of any nature or any degree with
the alien agitators would be . . . an indirect but nevertheless deadly invasion of American sovereignty in Hawaii."[28] Such sentiments resonated broadly with public officials
and popular opinion on the mainland, where a nativist, white-supremacy movement
was in full sway.[29]

In 1923, a federal commission appointed to investigate the labor situation in Hawai'i
warned of the "Japanese menace" and reported:

Hawaii may have its labor problems . . . , but we believe that the question of National Defense and the necessity to curtail the domination of the alien Japanese in every phase of the Hawaiian life is more important than all the other problems combined.[30]

What was initially a labor problem had come to be viewed as a military problem as well. The chief of Army Intelligence in Hawai'i, Lieutenant Colonel George Brooke, stated that the workers were really interested in supporting Japanese nationalist interests and that Japanese religious, social, and cultural organizations were promoting Japanese imperialism. It was only a matter of time, he warned in 1921, before the Japanese would control the affairs of the territory through the ballot, exerting their influence for the benefit of the Japanese Empire rather than of the United States.[31]

The Bureau of Investigation, later to become the FBI, also became alarmed about the "Japanese situation," and J. Edgar Hoover, then a young special assistant to the attorney general, proposed to the chief of military intelligence that they share their reports. By the end of 1921, an intelligence network linked the Bureau, the Military Intelligence Division (MID), the Office of Naval Intelligence (ONI), and the HSPA, providing weekly situation reports, which typically pointed to the threat of Japanese domination of the Islands. The following year, the Bureau filed a report entitled "Japanese Espionage—Hawaii," which for the first time listed 157 Japanese persons who were regarded as subversive or potentially dangerous by military or civilian intelligence agencies.[32]

Subsequent military reports in the 1920s echoed the same themes. In 1929, the MID declared that the Japanese race in the Hawaiian Islands was "a military liability"; its report that year listed leaders in the Japanese community (not only those suspected of espionage) simply based on their positions of influence, and concluded: "In the event of war with Japan all Japanese, alien and Hawaii-born, of all ranks, should be considered as enemy aliens *ab initio.*"[33]

Planning for War and Martial Law, 1921–1938

While the intelligence offices were reporting on such potential dangers, the army's War Plans Division (WPD) was shaping strategies that presaged the actual measures taken when Pearl Harbor was bombed, including the declaration of martial law. Major General Charles P. Summerall, who became commander of the army's Hawai'i Department in 1921, immediately directed his staff to prepare plans for war with Japan.[34] "We expected the Japanese population to cooperate with the enemy at the time of attack," he wrote in his memoir. Therefore, "[a]s soon as invasion became imminent, all dangerous leaders were to be arrested," and troops were to cordon off the Japanese population. "We expected to declare martial law, and the proclamation and orders were prepared. The territorial authorities were to control the civilian population."[35] These plans, refined over the next twenty years, set forth the basic policies that would be implemented in

1941—with the notable exception, as we shall see, that the military also wrested control of the civilian institutions from the territorial authorities.

In 1923, Colonel John L. DeWitt, then acting assistant chief of staff in the War Plans Division, elaborated plans that foreshadowed in explicit detail what was actually to befall the Hawaiian Islands, including selective detention. (DeWitt was later to become commander in charge of the Western Defense Command [WDC] during World War II and, notoriously, to play a key role in the mass incarceration of ethnic Japanese from the West Coast.) His 1923 proposed procedures for Hawai'i included the registration of all enemy aliens, the internment of anyone deemed a security risk, and the imposition of military control over labor and information. Martial law, according to DeWitt's plan, would include the suspension of the writ of habeas corpus and the subservience of both the judiciary and civil officials to the military governor. Further, it would impose a curfew, prohibit assemblies, control radios, close the foreign-language press, and regulate liquor.

DeWitt asked the army's judge advocate general in May 1923 to rule on the legality of a proposed general order that would declare martial law on the grounds of military necessity. In his response, the judge advocate general, W. A. Bethel, reviewed the Supreme Court's ruling in the Civil War case of *ex parte Milligan;* he pointed out that civilians could not be tried in military courts when civil courts were functioning, and that martial law could be adopted only when what he termed the "necessity of national self-preservation" demanded it. If the United States were at war with "a strong Asiatic naval power many of whose nationals reside in Hawaii and such persons should be liable to obstruct the measures adopted by our military forces in Hawaii for its prosecution, the civil courts not being able to restrain them, the exercise of military authority over them to whatever extent might be necessary to thwart their acts or intentions would be justified."[36] The "military necessity" argument was to be invoked when war actually came, and it was to be used as justification for continuing martial law until 1944.

Concerned about constitutional issues and the respective roles of the president, the army commander, and the governor of Hawai'i, the WPD requested a second opinion on martial law in 1931. The acting judge advocate general, Colonel A. W. Brown, agreed that the commanding general of the Hawaiian Department, in the event of an attack, would have authority to take whatever measures were necessary with regard to the civilian population to fulfill his military mission. Brown warned, however, that the commander would be personally liable for any measures not demanded by true necessity. Exactly this issue of personal liability did, in fact, come to the fore in the postwar period in a series of lawsuits against the army.[37]

Although the WPD preferred to leave vague the precise manner in which martial law would be declared, there was no doubting the delineation of authority. "Whatever be the means by which it [martial law] is brought about," wrote the head of the WPD to the chief of staff, "the military commander becomes the supreme authority in the locality, responsible only to the Commander-in-Chief." This delineation of the line of command was detailed in "Responsibility for the Defense of Oahu," approved by the secretary of war in 1931.[38]

The likelihood of war with Japan appeared to increase with its aggression in Manchuria in 1931 and its bombing of Shanghai in 1932. At about the same time, racial prejudice was heightened by the press's sensationalized coverage of two local criminal trials, one for rape in 1931 and one for murder in 1932, in the so-called Massie Affair. Mrs. Massie, the Caucasian wife of a naval officer, claimed that she had been gang-raped by a group of Hawaiian youths. Five young men were arrested, but there was little evidence that they were guilty of the alleged crime, or even that Mrs. Massie had been raped. The mixed-race jury was unable to reach a verdict. The lack of a conviction in the case was followed by increased tensions and small-scale riots between whites and nonwhites—including a near-fatal beating of one of the defendants.

Mrs. Massie's husband and her mother then decided to take the law into their own hands. With the help of two servicemen, they kidnapped one of the defendants in an attempt to get him to confess; when he refused, he was killed. The four white citizens were put on trial for the murder of this native Hawaiian, with the renowned Clarence Darrow representing the defendants, thus assuring widespread press coverage. The four were found guilty of manslaughter, but the governor of the territory, Lawrence M. Judd, pressured by the *haole* oligarchy and perhaps fearing outraged public opinion that would damage the image of Hawai'i, commuted their sentences from ten years to one hour. Judd's action was in marked contrast to his refusal to grant clemency to a deranged Japanese-American youth, Myles Fukunaga, who was hanged for killing the son of a prominent *haole* businessman in 1928.[39]

Although all charges were eventually dropped against the youths charged with the rape of Mrs. Massie, the Massie Affair had long-lasting consequences for race relations in Hawai'i, exacerbating the divisions between the *haoles,* on the one hand, and the ethnic Japanese, Chinese, and Hawaiians, on the other. It further led to calls in Congress to strip Hawai'i of its territorial status and place it under some form of commission government.

The following year, in 1933, the Hawaiian branch of Army Intelligence, at the request of the head of the WPD, produced another of its periodic reports, warning of the threat posed by the increasing population of ethnic Japanese in Hawai'i. The fifteen-volume report, *Estimate of the Situation—Japanese Population in Hawaii,* stated: "There are definite indications that the resident Japanese, by peaceful conquest and the use of American methods are creating under the American flag, a situation, which, in the course of time, unless halted will, in fact, produce a Territory Japanese and not American controlled."[40] The report cited the opinion of many whites in Hawai'i that in case of a war with Japan, the majority of the population of Japanese descent would prove disloyal, and it concluded that sabotage could "seriously interfere" with the defense of O'ahu.[41]

President Roosevelt and Hawai'i's Japanese Americans

President Roosevelt visited Hawaii in the summer of 1934, becoming the first sitting president to travel to the territory. He met with the commanding general of the army's Hawaiian Department, the commandant of the Fourteenth Naval District at Pearl Harbor, and with Governor Poindexter. He publicly praised the multiethnic nature of the Hawaiian population, which he had personally witnessed in a parade in his honor in Honolulu. Assuring the people of Hawai'i that they were "in very truth an integral part of the Nation," Roosevelt continued: "In a fine old prayer for our country are found these words: 'Fashion into one happy people those brought hither out of many kindreds and tongues.' That prayer is being answered in the Territory of Hawaii. . . . [T]oday men and women and children from many lands are united in loyalty to and understanding of the high purposes of America."[42]

Privately, however, Roosevelt, too, became concerned about sabotage, especially about pro-Japanese fifth-columnists and Japanese Americans being hosted on visiting Japanese naval vessels that docked in Hawai'i. In 1936, he wrote to Admiral W. H. Standley of the military's Joint Board in Washington:

> One obvious thought occurs to me—that every Japanese citizen or non-citizen on the Island of Oahu who meets these Japanese ships or has any connection with their officers or men should be secretly but definitely identified and his or her name placed on a special list of those who would be the first to be placed in a *concentration camp* in the event of trouble.
>
> . . . I think a Joint Board should consider and adopt plans relating to the Japanese population of all the islands.[43]

His failure to draw any distinction between the Issei and Nisei in suggesting swift internment, as well as his disregard for the Nisei's constitutional rights as U.S. citizens, is noteworthy in light of his actions once the nation was actually at war.[44]

Responding to Roosevelt's memo, Acting Secretary of War Harry Woodring assured the president that the Joint Defense Plan assigned control of aliens and alien sympathizers in all the islands to the army, which would exercise its control through the recently established Service Command. Presaging the army control of civilians that would eventually be imposed under martial law, Woodring wrote: "In war that Command . . . will be charged with the control of the civil population and the prevention of sabotage, of civil disturbances, or of local uprisings."[45]

The administration in Washington continued its involvement with the Hawaiian situation at the highest level. In the fall of 1937, a cabinet-level committee met to "study the problem of pernicious activities of Japanese naval and civil personnel in Hawaii." They proposed measures, which Roosevelt approved, to control Japanese vessels in American waters.[46] Meanwhile, the army's intelligence division, G-2, increased its staff in Hawai'i and expanded its efforts in counterintelligence.[47]

Amidst these discussions of espionage and the need to revise defense plans, the idea of martial law was once again revived, this time by Lieutenant Colonel George S. Patton—then serving as chief of military intelligence in Hawaiʻi and subsequently to achieve fame as the army commander in the African and European campaigns in World War II. In a plan that he entitled "The Initial Seizure of Orange [Japanese] Nationals," he suggested that 128 members of "the Orange race," with "position and influence in the Orange community," be taken and held as hostages at the outbreak of the war. Ninety-five of those on his list were Japanese citizens, and thirty-three were American citizens; they included religious, political, and educational leaders in the ethnic Japanese community, along with publishers, businessmen, doctors, and others who were highly regarded. Although Patton did not specify what would happen to the hostages, it may be surmised that he hoped to cripple any resistance by the Japanese community by seizing its leaders, not only those who were suspected of espionage. That he had little concern for the rights of civilian individuals may be inferred from his recommendation at the time of the war veterans' Bonus March on Washington in 1932: "If you have captured a dangerous agitator and some misguided judge issues a write [sic] of Habeas Corpus . . . there is always danger that the man might try to escape. If he does see that he at least falls out of ranks before you shoot [him]."[48]

Although Patton's plan was shelved in 1940, certain of its elements were in fact implemented when the war began. These included proclaiming martial law and establishing military commissions to try those accused of "military offenses"; closing the Japanese language schools; confiscating all amateur radio sets from the Japanese; closing all waters to Japanese vessels; seizing Japanese banks and certain businesses; excluding all Japanese, including domestics, from military bases; and imposing censorship on mail, radio, and the press.[49]

The Ethnic Japanese in Hawaiian Society

The focus on "the Japanese problem" in Hawaiʻi was sharpened by the debates in the 1930s over statehood.[50] The statehood movement gained impetus in the mid-thirties from opposition to proposals for a commission form of government following the Massie Affair, and from the passage of the Jones Costigan Act, which put quotas on the amount of sugar that could be imported to the United States by foreign countries and territories.

In early 1935, Hawaiʻi Delegate Samuel Wilder King introduced into Congress a new version of a bill that would enable Hawaiʻi to form a state government, and a congressional subcommittee held hearings in Hawaiʻi. Much of the testimony favored statehood, which meant persuading the visiting congressmen that the Japanese did not pose a serious threat. Governor Poindexter, for example, celebrating the fiftieth anniversary of the immigration of the first Japanese contract workers, had remarked that those of Japanese ancestry were a "very part and parcel" of the community and American institutions.[51] University professors, social workers, and teachers testified that the Japanese problem was really just "five parts pure imagination and five parts misunderstanding," leading one historian to characterize them as "the enthusiastic priests of the melting pot."[52] The congressional committee, however, postponed action.

In 1937, when a joint congressional committee took up the issue of statehood and held two weeks of public hearings in the Islands, the tensions between the United States and Japan had increased, and the "Japanese question" assumed new urgency. The committee asked hard questions about the number of ethnic Japanese, their citizenship status, their age, and their allegiance to the Japanese emperor. By this time, open racial bigotry, while not unknown, was less accepted in Hawai'i than in some other parts of the United States. Thus one of Hawai'i's leading sociologists wrote: "So strong has this Island ritual of racial equality—sometimes confused with the local 'Aloha-spirit'—been that few public avowals of a contrary attitude have occurred."[53] The hearings on statehood, however, brought to the surface some of the animosity toward the ethnic Japanese that ran as an undercurrent through many segments of society in Hawai'i in the late 1930s, even though it was no longer generally publicly sanctioned.[54] Most outspoken on the issue of a Japanese conspiracy was John F. G. Stokes, a naturalized citizen from Australia who had been an ethnographer and archaeologist at the Bishop Museum in Honolulu. Viewing all Hawai'i residents of Japanese descent as instruments of the Japanese emperor, engaged in a conspiracy to use Hawai'i as a stepping-stone to world domination, Stokes concluded: "[I]t seems that statehood for Hawaii at the present time might become dangerous to the United States in the near future. At best it would be risky, so why place Hawaiian control in the hands of an unproven group, especially one descended from subjects of an aggressive and ambitious nation which at any moment may become an active enemy?"[55]

Most of the testimony, however, supported statehood, and a number of social, educational, and political leaders testified that the Nikkei, and especially the Nisei, were loyal Americans. Representative of this group was Frank Midkiff, who had taught at the exclusive Punahou private school, then had headed Kamehameha Schools, a private educational trust for the education of children of Hawaiian ancestry, and would soon become head of the Honolulu Chamber of Commerce. Not only were Japanese-American citizens loyal, Midkiff testified, but Japanese customs "add to and enrich the culture of America." Even the contemplation of earlier war plans of "impounding within a stockade or on an island all persons of Japanese ancestry, whether American-born or not," would have harmful results, he stated. "In case of war, disloyal individuals could be dealt with on the merits of each case," he advised.[56]

Although some members of Congress were vehemently opposed to statehood, as a result of the hearings the congressional committee recommended a plebiscite, which was held in 1940.[57] Despite a heated debate in the local press that included opposition to a state that would be dominated by Japanese Americans, two-thirds of the votes cast favored statehood; but by that time war with Japan seemed all but inevitable, and Congress took no action.[58]

The Joint Congressional Committee had raised important issues regarding the ethnic Japanese population, emphasizing that they were the largest single ethnic group in the territory, outnumbering Caucasians by about 50 percent.[59] By the time war with Japan was imminent, persons of Japanese ancestry constituted about 37 percent of Hawai'i's total population of 423,000.[60] They made up a significant percentage of the plantation labor force; and thousands were numbered among the skilled and semi-skilled working force in the shipyards (which were vital to U.S. Navy operations), in transportation and other public utilities operations, in postal facilities, and in many other civilian government offices. There was also a substantial Nikkei presence in the trades, in retail and wholesale commerce, in education, and even in elected political office. Furthermore, they constituted nearly the entirety of the fishing fleet workers—a matter of particular concern to the military, who feared that men in fishing vessels could spy on naval operations. The Nikkei community thus obviously played a vital role in the Hawaiian economy.[61]

About one-fourth of the ethnic Japanese, or some 37,000, were first-generation immigrants (Issei), ineligible for citizenship and thus considered aliens. Most of these Issei were older, having come to Hawai'i to work on the sugar plantations in the years before the Immigration Act of 1924 excluded "all aliens ineligible to citizenship." The majority of them remained culturally Japanese, and some spoke little or no English. The military was particularly troubled by what they regarded as "influences from Japan" among the Issei: Japanese-language radio broadcasts, which were carried daily on the major stations; Japanese-language newspapers, which had a circulation of 30,000 in 1941; and Japanese cultural and social organizations, including societies based on place of origin in Japan, sports associations, and the United Japanese Society—an umbrella organization for some 150 groups, including professional societies, in Hawai'i.[62]

Far more numerous than the Issei were their children and grandchildren, totaling some 121,000, and constituting more than 75 percent of Hawai'i's population of Japanese descent. The Nisei, or second generation, were regarded by the army as a potential security problem; the Sansei, or third generation, were too young to be considered a security risk. By dint of their birth on American soil, they were citizens of the United States, although some of them had been registered by their families with the Japanese consulate and so held status as dual citizens under both U.S. and Japanese law. (Prior to 1924, Japan considered all children born to Japanese citizens overseas to be subjects of the Japanese emperor; after that date, only those children of Japanese born overseas who were registered with a Japanese consulate within fourteen days of their birth would be considered Japanese.)[63] The process for expatriation from Japan for those born prior to 1924 was complex, and it was not known how many Nisei whose allegiance was to the United States persevered in seeking such formal expatriation.[64]

Many of the Nisei—more than 80 percent—attended Japanese language schools after regular school hours, if for no other reason than to be able to communicate better with their families.[65] By 1940 there were more than 230 Japanese language schools in Hawai'i, enrolling nearly 43,000 students and employing more than 700 teachers. The army and navy intelligence services and the FBI all viewed these schools not only as obstacles to Americanization, but also as centers of pro-Japanese indoctrination and "a very real menace to American security. . . . The Japanese language school instructs its youth in the nobility of courage and glory of patriotism: for the benefit of the Island Empire and His Imperial Highness."[66]

Many of those who held dual citizenship were Kibei, a subset of the Nisei.[67] The word "Kibei" comes from *ki,* to return to, and *bei,* America. For economic or cultural reasons or both, the Kibeis' families had sent them back to Japan at some point in their younger years to live temporarily with grandparents or other relatives (the duration of their residency in Japan varying considerably) and to receive schooling there.[68] They had then returned to the Islands to rejoin their families and resume their lives in American society as best they could, some speaking little English and many of them ostracized by the larger group of much more Americanized Nisei.[69]

The total number of Kibei in Hawai'i was estimated by Office of the Military Governor (OMG) officers in November 1943 to be "over 3,000,"[70] but other estimates run as high as 5,000.[71] Despite their small numbers, they were regarded by both the FBI and the army and navy intelligence services as likely harboring disloyal sentiments and thus representing a significant danger to internal security because of their Japanese education, which included emperor worship and, for the older youth, military training. A small fraction of the Kibei had even served in the Japanese armed forces, and it is likely that at least some of the Kibei had been indoctrinated with notions of Japanese superiority and destiny to rule the world—a concept generally not shared by their relatives living in Hawai'i.[72]

The diversity in legal status of citizenship within the Nikkei community in Hawai'i was not the only dimension of subgroup pluralism, for there were also significant social and cultural elements that posed some perplexities for the military and other officials charged with shaping security policy. There was a social distance, often a dramatic gulf, between the generations—especially between the Japanese-speaking Issei and the Nisei, who (with the exception of the Kibei) used mainly English in their daily activities and who were taking advantage of educational opportunities up to the college and university level, thereby establishing themselves in the professions, in the commercial sector, and in politics.[73] In addition, there were differences in socio economic status and in affiliations based on regions of origin in Japan. All of these factors had to be considered by the FBI and the military and intelligence officers responsible for the security of the Hawaiian Islands, which had become the western outpost for military operations as war with Japan loomed ever closer.

Chapter Two

FINAL WAR PLANNING FOR HAWAI'I,

1939–1941

Martial Law and Selective Internment

In the years leading up to the war, the Chief of Staff for Military Intelligence (G-2) had been specifically charged both with efforts (including counterintelligence) among the civilian population, especially aliens, to guard against subversion, and with propaganda to encourage loyalty to the United States. The Provost Marshal's Office was similarly engaged in protecting Pearl Harbor and Honolulu from internal disturbance as well as external attack.[1]

President Roosevelt nonetheless remained concerned about espionage, and in September 1939 he instructed the Justice Department and FBI to assume responsibility for domestic surveillance and investigations of all subversive activities.[2] Consequently, FBI Director J. Edgar Hoover handpicked Robert L. Shivers to reestablish the FBI office in Honolulu, which, with the exception of a few months in late 1937 and early 1938, had been closed since 1934.[3] Born in Tennessee in 1894, Shivers had already demonstrated his leadership skills as head of the FBI field offices in Pittsburgh, Buffalo, and Miami. In Hawai'i, he took it upon himself to forge strong relations with the army, the navy, the local police, and even with leaders of the very community whose loyalty he was to assess: the Japanese Americans. Although he had never personally known an individual of Asian descent prior to coming to Hawai'i, he and his wife were persuaded to provide room and board for a young Japanese-American student, Shizue Kobatake, who answered his many questions about her culture and who eventually became essentially a family member. Shivers, who soon became the dominant member of the army-navy-FBI-police intelligence networks, was to play a major role in the formation of the 442nd combat unit and, importantly, in preventing in Hawai'i the kind of mass removal and incarceration of Japanese Americans that took place on the West Coast of the mainland.[4]

Shivers received from the army's Military Intelligence Division (MID) and the Office of Naval Intelligence (ONI) in early 1940 "the names and addresses of all persons whom they considered dangerous to the internal security of these islands and who should be picked up for custodial detention in the event of war."[5] The ONI, under the direction of Captain Irving H. Mayfield, had been carrying out surveillance on

Special Agent Robert Shivers, FBI Bureau
Chief, Honolulu.
Credit: Federal Bureau of Investigation.

several hundred Japanese suspects and Japanese consular officers, including tapping
the telephone lines of the latter.[6] The three agencies continued to cooperate in the
months ahead, holding weekly meetings, with the FBI sharing information on all fifth-
column activities, investigating all names submitted by army and navy intelligence,
and preparing custodial detention memoranda where warranted. The MID, in turn,
would be responsible for the security of all army establishments and their civilian
employees, with the ONI assuming similar duties for all naval bases and their civilian
workers.[7]

The FBI, which was short of funds and personnel to conduct all the investigative
work, asked the Honolulu Police Department to form its own espionage unit in December 1940. This unit was directed by John A. Burns, then head of the vice squad,
who would later become the territorial delegate to Congress and subsequently serve as
governor of Hawai'i from 1962 to 1974. Burns and the four other men in his unit—a
Korean, a Nisei, a Japanese-*haole,* and a Hawaiian—engaged in undercover operations and advised both the FBI and military intelligence on "the background, general
reputation and activities" of individuals named by the FBI "to ascertain whether in the
event of hostilities between this country and Japan" their interests "would be inimical
to those of the United states."[8] According to Burns, "We had this massive investigation going on during the whole of the year [1941] and that's all my men did." Burns had
lived in Hawai'i since the age of four and had had considerable experience in dealing
with the Nikkei population. He did not share the popular anti-Japanese sentiment of

Honolulu Police Captain John Burns, with three fellow "War Bond Drive Canvassers," December 7, 1943. L–r: Tatsuro Matsuo, Y. B. Goto, Burns, Dr. Ernest Murai. Credit: *Honolulu Star-Bulletin* photo, courtesy of HWRD, University of Hawai'i.

the time, and he thought it unfair that those who had been brought over as plantation labor were not eligible to become citizens. The ethnic Japanese, he stated later, "were just as good Americans, they tried to be, and we were the ones that were not being fair. . . . It's a wonder they were loyal to the United States, as they were."[9] In November 1941, Burns wrote a guest editorial in the *Honolulu Star-Bulletin* that defended the Nisei as "good, law-abiding citizens" and pointed out that there was no evidence showing the Japanese aliens to be disloyal.[10]

In contrast to the MID, which continued to receive information from the Hawaiian Sugar Planters' Association and other prominent white citizens, as it had been doing for nearly two decades, the FBI established a network of confidential informants, mainly "reliable and trustworthy second-generation Japanese" residing in communities with a preponderance of Japanese aliens and citizens of Japanese ancestry.[11] As a result, the FBI developed a strikingly different picture from that of the MID of the danger of espionage. According to the report of one FBI agent in September 1940, confidential informants stated that the second-generation (Nisei) were predominantly loyal to the United States; and even the alien Japanese were not to be feared, for they were elderly, not organized for sabotage, and loyal to their children. The report attributed the reluctance of the Nisei to give up their dual citizenship—which was to become a significant factor in loyalty hearings during the war—as a practical matter of owning property in Japan or as a safety net in case they were either forced to leave Hawai'i or racism made their lives intolerable.[12]

The FBI issued a long memorandum on the ethnic Japanese in Hawai'i in November 1940, denying the military's charges that most of that population would be disloyal in the event of war. Reporting that there was an inner circle of some one thousand "consular agents," Japanese language school teachers and Shinto and Buddhist priests who were at risk for espionage, the memorandum proposed that this group be interned at the outbreak of war. "Upon the interning of the Japanese leaders in the community, there need be no fear of the reaction of the local Japanese population in the event of a war with Japan," the memorandum stated.[13] As for the rest of the ethnic Japanese in Hawai'i, the memo declared that there was much less pro-Japanese sentiment among either "the local born Japanese or the alien Japanese who have been residing in the Hawaiian Islands for the greater part of their life-time."[14] The memo also suggested a pro-American campaign aimed at the Nisei youth to counteract the influence of pro-Japanese propaganda.

Military Intelligence agreed with the FBI's strategy. They had carefully considered "mass deportation of Japanese to the mainland, segregation of all Japanese on one of the smaller islands of the Hawaiian group, or the establishment of large-scale detention camps in the valleys of Oahu," but they concluded that none of these options was practical.[15] Despairing of their ability to determine the loyalty of 160,000 ethnic Japanese, MID assumed that the Issei would be disloyal and focused attention, instead, on Americanizing the Nisei. Toward that end, Military Intelligence established an advisory committee of carefully screened Nisei; the committee, in turn, launched a series of mass rallies at which the Nisei were told of the advantages of the American way of life—and were warned of "prompt punitive action" for any acts hostile to the United States.[16] Naval Intelligence, working with Army Intelligence and the FBI in keeping a close watch on organizations controlled by alien Japanese but including Nisei members, also reported "no tangible evidence of a subversive nature involving Hawaiian nisei."[17] The intelligence establishment concluded that active disloyalty on the part of the ethnic Japanese community was unlikely except in the case of a Japanese landing and occupation of Hawai'i.[18]

As a result of their combined efforts, the FBI and the G-2 division of the army had gathered "records on every citizen of doubtful loyalty." They had compiled two lists, each of approximately 300 persons: those on the first list were to be apprehended immediately on the outbreak of war, while those on the second list were to be placed under surveillance and have their activities curtailed.[19]

The Americanization campaign included, in addition to propaganda, efforts to get the Nisei to renounce their dual citizenship.[20] In the fall of 1940, under the leadership of the Hawaiian Japanese Civic Association, more than 30,000 Nisei, or about three-fourths of adult dual citizens in Hawai'i, had petitioned Secretary of State Cordell

Hull to negotiate a simple way for them to renounce their Japanese citizenship. Because of the strained relations with Japan, Hull was unable to take action, but the U.S. government subsequently accepted their declarations as renunciation of Japanese citizenship. The Japanese government, however, did not accept this arrangement.[21] The War Department, too, was eager for dual citizens to be able to renounce their foreign allegiance, and thought that those who refused to do so should be deported; the army was particularly concerned about the possibilities for espionage by dual citizens being included in the draft. The War Department therefore recommended in summer 1941 that Congress amend the Nationality Act of 1940 accordingly—an effort that finally culminated in legislation in 1944.[22]

Continuing Fears of Sabotage

Meanwhile, the military continued to prepare for widespread fifth-column activity. The army maneuvers in 1940 envisioned sabotage, street riots, and an attempt to take over the territorial government of Hawaiʻi. According to the script outlining the maneuvers, martial law was declared, and the commander of the Hawaiian Department was appointed military governor.[23]

Civilians, too, were concerned about the danger of sabotage. In July 1940, led by Honolulu's mayor and chief of police, as well as several plantation managers, they organized the "Provisional Police" to help defend Hawaiʻi against possible sabotage or attack. This all-civilian paramilitary organization, formed at the army's request, consisted of plantation employees, American Legionnaires, and workers specially trained in guard duty. They were divided into districts that closely coincided with plantation lines. They were trained and equipped by the army, which appreciated the savings in its own manpower requirements.[24]

As war appeared ever more likely in late 1940 and early 1941, anti-Japanese sentiment became more vocal, both in Hawaiʻi and on the mainland. For example, the *New York Post* reported that Hawaiʻi could become the Achilles' heel of U.S. defenses because of "the dubious loyalty of some 40 percent of the territory's residents," arguing that a possible Hawaiʻi fifth column was among "the foremost of the nation's defense problems."[25] There were calls both in the U.S. government and among elements of the civilian population for action against the Nikkei, especially the alien Japanese. In July 1940, the navy and the FBI, fearing espionage, urged legislation that would curb the activities of Japanese-owned sampans operating in Hawaiian waters.[26] A year later, the *Hawaii Sentinel,* which was stridently anti-Japanese, carried a large headline: "PURGE SPIES HAWAII DEMANDED BY LEGION." The story went on to detail the American Legion's demands that the Justice Department deport "all actual and potential shinto subversive elements in Hawaii," including all Japanese school teachers and Shinto priests.[27]

Rumors of disloyalty among ethnic Japanese persisted in Congress. In summer 1940, Representative William Schulte of Indiana said he had evidence of the existence of a "considerable element" in Hawaiʻi that was engaged in fifth-column activities.[28]

In January 1941, Senator Guy Gillette of Iowa accused Japan of conscripting 50,000 Nisei in Hawai'i.[29] The subject of the loyalty of Hawai'i's Japanese was again raised in summer 1941, this time in the House Naval Affairs Committee. When one member questioned the wisdom of putting an air base in O'ahu in light of the nearby Japanese population, Committee Chair Carl Vinson responded, "If necessary we can segregate a few or a few thousand Japanese. I think the Navy is trying to protect its property against all subversive elements."[30] In August, when Japan refused to let an American ship enter a Japanese port to pick up U.S. citizens wishing to leave that country, Representative John D. Dingell of Michigan called on the United States to "order the imprisonment in concentration camps in Hawaii of 10,000 alien Japanese," a one hundred to one reprisal against taking Americans hostage.[31] And in October, Senator Gillette again raised the specter of disloyalty, calling for a special committee to investigate the extent to which Axis powers were organizing and disseminating propaganda among alien residents of the United States, particularly on the West Coast and in Hawai'i. Although the text of the resolution did not single out the Japanese, his discussion of the measure clearly did.[32]

Countering Anti-Japanese Prejudice

Calmer voices tried to reassure both the public and the Hawai'i residents of Japanese ancestry, who were becoming increasingly fearful that they would be put in concentration camps. Those leaders who boldly advocated racial tolerance in Hawai'i—whether for moral or purely practical considerations—did much to ensure that most Japanese Americans in the Islands did not suffer the mass incarcerations to which the West Coast Nikkei would be subjected.

Prominent among those speaking out against racial prejudice was Delegate Samuel King, who was disdainfully given the moniker of "Sampan Sam" by the anti-Japanese weekly, the *Hawaii Sentinel*.[33] In a letter to Representative Vinson, King wrote, "The people [of Hawaii] as a whole are intensely patriotic and completely accept the obligations of their American citizenship. This is true of our citizens of Japanese ancestry as it is of all other racial groups. . . . Aliens in Hawaii—in large part an elderly group of long residence in the Territory—are no more dangerous to our defense program than aliens of the United States as a whole."[34] King, who was himself part native Hawaiian, further stated that allowing suspicion of any one group of the population "would only lead to disunity."[35] Convinced of the loyalty of Hawai'i's population, King subsequently declared that what he called the "sixth column" fomenters of racial prejudice posed a greater danger than any alleged fifth columnists.[36]

In August 1941, prompted by reports from the Hawaiian Chamber of Commerce of "considerable fear" and "rumors widespread" about treatment of aliens, King sought statements from senior administration officials to reassure the Japanese alien population that they would be treated fairly.[37] Secretary of State Hull did not think such a statement advisable at that time, but Attorney General Francis Biddle quoted a previous statement from his predecessor, Robert Jackson: "It would be a tragic blunder, as well as an unforgivable injustice, to assume that foreign birth means lack of loyalty to America. . . . I am convinced that the overwhelming number of resident aliens and naturalized citizens are loyal Americans."[38] Privately, Biddle told King that he agreed with his condemnation of "persecution against innocent people merely because of a geographical accident of birth or because of their ineligibility to citizenship due to causes beyond their control."[39]

Secretary Harold Ickes, whose Department of the Interior was responsible for the administration of the Territory of Hawai'i, gave King precisely what he wanted—a statement, for public release, attesting to the loyalties of the ethnic Japanese:

> I consider it a serious injustice to assume that these persons, although of foreign birth and ineligible for citizenship, are therefore disloyal to our government. On the contrary, the fact that they have established their home in the Islands and have accepted the protection of our laws, is a strong indication that they are devoted to the ideals of this country.

Ickes appealed to public opinion to treat the Japanese aliens fairly "unless they individually are found guilty of wrong doing."[40]

Meanwhile, a group of community leaders was working to counter anti-Japanese sentiment among the civilian population, which included significant numbers of Chinese and Koreans, whose homelands had been occupied by Japan, as well as Filipinos, whose country was in immediate danger from Japan. This group included Hung Wai Ching, a YMCA executive who was the son of Chinese immigrants; Charles Hemenway, one of the founders of the University of Hawai'i, a former attorney general of the territory, and president of the Hawai'i Trust Company; and Shigeo Yoshida, an educator and writer who was descended from Japanese samurai. Joined by Robert Shivers of the FBI, the chiefs of army and navy intelligence, civilian officials, and business and professional leaders, the group became the Council for Inter-Racial Unity. Shivers headed its steering committee, which met bi-weekly during the year prior to the Japanese attack on Pearl Harbor. (Indeed, Ching, Yoshida, and some others were on their way to have breakfast with Shivers on the morning of December 7 when Pearl Harbor was attacked.)[41] Recognizing that a united citizenry was essential for defense, the council members worked through meetings, public speeches, education, and personal networks to promote racial harmony. According to Shivers, the council "contributed much toward conditioning the civilian populace toward the idea of working together in the event of war and trusting the constituted authorities to handle the task of dealing with any subversive groups."[42]

Two other groups of Nisei met with the FBI regularly—at least weekly—to advise Shivers and his agents on matters of internal security regarding the ethnic Japanese population and to develop plans to control any potentially subversive groups or individuals. One outgrowth of these meetings was the formation of the O'ahu Citizens

Committee for Home Defense, organized in early 1941, which assumed responsibility "to work with the constituted authorities in the continuing task of evaluating what went on in the Japanese community," and to bring "out more positively the inherent loyalty of the Americans of Japanese Ancestry toward the United States."[43]

Encouraged by such groups and the newspapers, the Nisei made a concerted effort to demonstrate their loyalty. Thousands of Japanese Americans turned out for a rally at McKinley High School, sponsored by the Oʻahu Citizens' Committee for Home Defense in June 1941. There they unanimously pledged their "unreserved loyalty to the United States of America."[44] A few days later, the annual conference of the New Americans—a movement of *haole* and Nikkei elite founded in 1927 to benefit Nisei leaders—took as their theme "Our Present Patriotic Responsibilities." The delegates pledged anew their loyalty to the United States and resolved "that we consider expatriation from Japan and the eradication of a dual national status a duty of the individual and the group."[45]

Yet another group was organized in 1941 by John Burns of the Honolulu Police Department to serve as a liaison between the Nikkei community and the police and other official agencies responsible for security. Consisting of some sixty or more loyal Nisei, whose names were screened by the FBI, this Police Contact Group had as its purpose to disseminate "American principles and practices" among the ethnic Japanese and to obtain "information from within the community of the activities of Japan and her agents."[46] In the first year of the war, it provided much valuable information to Burns's espionage unit and helped with morale among the Nikkei by keeping them informed of matters concerning them. Because of its delicate mission, however, some Issei, especially, scorned its members and other Nisei informants.

Perhaps most important in calming prewar racism was the stance of the FBI and of the army itself, both of which regarded intolerance as harmful to the defense of the Islands. FBI bureau chief Robert L. Shivers emphasized in June that the citizens of Hawaiʻi had a primary responsibility to promote understanding among the racial groups and to combat the effects of war hysteria. He went on to assure aliens and others that they had nothing to fear unless they proved themselves unworthy of the trust placed in them.[47] "We guarantee to every person who conducts himself in a proper, law-abiding manner that he will not be molested, persecuted, or prosecuted," Shivers told a Maui audience.[48]

While the War Department was opposed to including citizens of Japanese descent in the military draft—a position that was overridden by actions in both the Senate and the House Military Affairs committees—the commanders on the ground in Hawaiʻi expressed confidence in the large majority of the Nikkei.[49] "The army is not worried about the Japanese in Hawaii," said Lieutenant General Charles D. Herron, who commanded the Hawaiian Department from 1938 until his mandatory retirement in March 1941. "Among them there may be a small hostile alien group, but we can handle that situation." He continued, in what seemed like a pointed remark, "It seems people who know least about Hawaii and live farthest away are most disturbed over this matter.

People who know the islands are not worried over possible sabotage."[50] Herron himself had advocated integrating the Nisei into the Organized Reserve, and in August, after he had retired, he tried to reassure the ethnic Japanese that it would be "the height of folly" to consider placing all aliens in a concentration camp.[51]

Such sentiments were echoed by other army officials in Hawai'i. Addressing the June 1941 rally of Nisei citizens on behalf of General Short, Herron's successor, assistant chief of staff for military intelligence in Hawai'i, Lieutenant Colonel M. W. Marston, stated, "The fact that more than half of the first group of selective service men were of Japanese ancestry illustrates the fine way in which our citizens of Japanese ancestry are meeting their responsibilities. . . . You people of Japanese ancestry are potentially one of our greatest assets whether in peace or war."[52] And a month later, another army staff officer, again speaking on behalf of General Short, told a largely Japanese-American audience: "The Army feels it can depend upon the people of the Japanese race in Hawaii for full support. . . . [T]he army in an emergency does not intend to treat the people of the Japanese race in Hawaii any different from those of any other race."[53] At the same time, however, he urged the audience "to search out from among their number" anyone who was not acting in the best interests of America, and report them immediately to the police. In addition, he warned,

> if acts of sabotage or attempts to injure our national defense in any way, are committed by any member of a particular group, all members of that group will be under suspicion until the guilty party is apprehended, and proof is given that his acts were not supported or condoned by others of the group.
>
> Further, while this suspicion exists, many innocent members of the group may, through error, be accused falsely of disloyal acts, and may suffer unjustly before their innocence can be established.[54]

It is likely that the Nikkei took such warnings seriously; it is certain that no cases of sabotage were ever brought against any Nikkei resident of Hawai'i.

While thus expressing his confidence in the Japanese Americans through his staff's statements, General Short nevertheless worried about the "large percentage of aliens and citizens of doubtful loyalty on Oahu," and in May 1941 he requested funding from the War Department to reinforce key military facilities.[55] He hoped to encourage the loyalty of the ethnic Japanese population in Hawai'i through a counterpropaganda campaign. He also urged the War Department to oppose the Justice Department's plans to prosecute certain Japanese consular agents who had failed to register and thus had technically violated U.S. law. Short argued that they were, in fact, not spies but largely residents in outlying communities whose main functions were to assist Japanese residents in registering births, deaths, and requests for exemption from Japanese military service. "Prosecution at this time," Short argued, "would unduly alarm entire population and jeopardize success [of] our current campaign to secure loyalty [of the] Japanese population."[56] Nevertheless, Short continued to fear sabotage by the alien Japanese in

Honolulu. Ironically, among the measures he took to act against sabotage was closely bunching the planes on the various airfields on the Island "so that they might be carefully guarded against possible subversive action by Japanese agents."[57] This action, of course, made the planes an easy target for the Japanese bombers on December 7.

Detention Lists and Internment Plans

The navy's personnel took a less sanguine view of the Japanese population than did the army's, trusting neither the aliens nor the Nisei. Disregarding civil service regulations, the Pearl Harbor Naval Shipyard blatantly discriminated against Japanese Americans in its hiring practices, always putting them at the bottom of the list, a practice that President Roosevelt knew about but did not oppose.[58] The anti-Japanese tone was set by Secretary of the Navy Frank Knox, who consistently advocated the incarceration or forced removal of all ethnic Japanese in O'ahu. In October 1940, he urged President Roosevelt to take a series of measures to "impress the Japanese with the seriousness of our preparations for war." Among Knox's recommendations was to "[p]repare plans for concentration camps (Army-Justice.)"[59]

Despite the somewhat reassuring reports from the FBI, the Roosevelt administration continued to prepare for the possibility of sabotage by fifth-columnists. In February 1941, the separate lists of suspects to be arrested in case of war that had been drawn up by Army Intelligence, the ONI, and the FBI were combined into a master list of some 2,000 Japanese from Hawai'i and the mainland. Subsequently expanded, this "ABC list," as it was informally called, was controlled by the Department of Justice's Special Defense Unit; it was limited to aliens, because in the absence of martial law, the Nisei could not be summarily detained. The "A" section, like its earlier Hawaiian counterpart, listed consular officials, Shinto and Buddhist priests, community leaders, and fishermen who were considered "immediately dangerous." "Potentially dangerous" people, whose loyalty was yet to be determined by the FBI, constituted the "B" list, and the "C" section consisted of those suspected of sympathizing with Japan.[60] While promising "fair treatment" of enemy aliens in the event of war, Attorney General Francis Biddle admitted the administration had plans that ranged from "paroling of those persons not suspected of subversive activity to those whose detainment would be necessary."[61]

It is a certainty that the Roosevelt administration was considering interning all enemy aliens. In early March 1941, Secretary of War Henry Stimson was coordinating plans for the custody of enemy aliens who would be turned over by the Justice Department to the War Department in the event of a declaration of war. Stimson requested of Attorney General Biddle that any such declaration by the president include provisions that would prohibit the movement of all enemy aliens in and out of the Territory of Hawai'i, and would confine movement of enemy aliens within the Islands to "such restricted areas as may be locally prescribed. It is further requested that you delegate to the Federal District Attorney in Hawaii the authority to intern all alien enemies in that territory."[62]

Later in March, however, the Department of Justice and the Department of War reached a tentative agreement, limiting internment to persons deemed "dangerous": "only those persons whose removal from society is consistent with the public interest" would be interned. The plans outlined in the draft agreement were specifically designed to avoid problems resulting from "over-internment," internment of infirm persons or minors, "the reckless internment of labor leaders," and the internment of persons for statements made prior to the outbreak of war. Thus the two departments had agreed on a policy of selective detention rather than incarceration of all enemy aliens as early as March 1941, and these same provisions were incorporated in the final document, signed in July of that year. The Justice Department would prepare the necessary presidential proclamations to control enemy aliens, and it would delegate to Biddle's representative in Hawai'i the authority to arrest and confine enemy aliens there. However, the War Department would assume responsibility for "permanent custodial detention" of those persons selected for internment.[63] By mid-April, General Short had identified the Immigration Station in Honolulu and the Quarantine Station on Sand Island, at the entrance to Honolulu Harbor, as the most suitable locations to hold enemy alien internees, although the Public Health Service objected to turning over the Quarantine Station, insisting that its operation there was vital to the health of both civilian and military personnel.[64] Based on what would prove to be quite accurate military intelligence, Short estimated the persons to be interned as approximately 500 enemy aliens and 1,000 others identified as "suspects to be watched and apprehended upon the first indication of disloyal acts."[65]

Visiting Hawai'i in August 1941, Biddle's assistant attorney general, Norman M. Littell, noted: "The head of the FBI, military authorities, lawyers, judges and others confirmed that the great mass of the Japanese would not go back to Japan if they could." They feared intervention by Japan, and "only a small minority of them, who are being watched and are allegedly detectable, would be Japanese fifth columnists or representatives."[66] President Roosevelt, however, continued to worry about the danger of sabotage. In the fall of 1941, not content to rely solely on the FBI and military intelligence, he hired his advisor and speechwriter, John Franklin Carter, to undertake a secret study of the Japanese on the West Coast and in Hawai'i to determine if Japanese agents were engaged in espionage and to gauge the extent of support for Japan among the ethnic Japanese community in the event of war. Carter selected Curtis B. Munson, a Detroit businessman who was given investigative powers as a special agent of the State Department, to perform this mission.

Opposing the proposals for concentration camps, Munson reported that in case of war, the vast majority of the Japanese Americans on the West Coast "will be quiet, very quiet." There are, he noted, "still Japanese in the United States who will tie dynamite around their waist and make a human bomb out of themselves . . . but today they are few." The allegiance of the Issei to Japan, he reported, was weakened by the fact that they had chosen to bring up their children in America, and they were attached to the land that they worked. They feared being put in a concentration camp, and "[m]any would take out American citizenship if allowed to do so."

"The weakest from a Japanese standpoint," Munson reported, "are the Nisei. They are universally estimated from 90 to 98% loyal to the United States if the Japanese educated element of the Kibei is excluded. They are pathetically eager to show this loyalty."[67] Indeed, Munson reported he was more concerned about violence *against* the ethnic Japanese than about subversion by them on the West Coast, and that the Communists posed a greater threat to the United States than persons of Japanese ancestry.

Regarding the Kibei, however, Munson reported:

> The Kibei are considered the most dangerous element and closer to the *Issei* with special reference to those who received their early education in Japan. It must be noted, however, that many of those who visited Japan subsequent to their early American education come back with added loyalty to the United States. In fact it is a saying that all a Nisei needs is a trip to Japan to make a loyal American out of him. The American educated Japanese is a boor in Japan and treated as a foreigner.[68]

Nevertheless, the mainland Kibei were "still the element most to be watched." Writing that "There is no Japanese 'problem' on the Coast," Munson concluded: "For the most part the local Japanese are loyal to the United States or, at worst, hope that by remaining quiet they can avoid concentration camps or irresponsible mobs." The real danger, Munson noted, was that the United States was wide open to sabotage, having left dams, bridges, harbors and power stations unguarded.[69]

Reporting on Hawai'i, where he spent nine days in November with the full cooperation of army and navy intelligence and the FBI, Munson pointed out that the ethnic Japanese constitute a "vital labor supply" in the Islands. He concluded:

> The consensus of opinion is that there will be no racial uprising of the Japanese in Honolulu. The first generation, as on the Coast, are ideologically and culturally closest to Japan. Though many of them speak no English, or at best only pigeon [*sic*]-English, it is considered that the big bulk of them will be loyal. This is especially so, for in Hawaii the first generation is largely on the land and devoted to it. . . . The second generation is estimated as approximately ninety-eight percent loyal. However, with the large Japanese population in the Hawaiian Islands, giving this the best interpretation possible, it would mean that fifteen hundred were disloyal. However, the F.B.I. state that there are only about four hundred suspects, and the F.B.I.'s private estimate is that only fifty or sixty of these are sinister.[70]

Noting that the Japanese were not discriminated against in Hawai'i as they were on the mainland, Munson stated: "In a word, Hawaii is more of a melting pot because there are more brown skins to melt—Japanese, Hawaiian, Chinese and Filipino. It is interesting to note that there has been absolutely no bad feeling between the Japanese and the Chinese in the islands due to the Japanese-Chinese war. Why should they be any worse toward us?" He concluded that even if the Japanese fleet were to appear off Hawai'i, the "big majority [of ethnic Japanese in Hawaii] . . . would be neutral or even actively loyal."[71] Nevertheless, Munson warned Washington, "The best consensus of opinion seemed to agree that martial law should be proclaimed now in Hawaii."[72]

Roosevelt was far from reassured by Munson's report, perhaps because in transmitting it, on November 7, Carter emphasized the concerns about the potentially dangerous 2 percent rather than the overall loyalty of the 98 percent of Japanese Americans, especially of the majority Nisei.[73] In any case, as Munson had made clear, the FBI and the military and naval intelligence services in Hawai'i had been working diligently to identify those who should be arrested in case of war. By December 1, 1941, plans and arrangements had already been completed for the apprehension of Japanese aliens as well as German and Italian aliens in the Territory of Hawai'i.[74]

In a memo written just three days before the Pearl Harbor attack, FBI bureau chief Shivers outlined the plan that the three intelligence agencies had agreed upon and that would soon be put into action:

> Since there are over 41,000 Japanese aliens in the Territory of Hawaii, it is obvious that the War Department would not and could not seize approximately a tenth of the population of the Hawaiian Islands and place that number in concentration camps. Furthermore, there are approximately 115,000 American citizens of Japanese ancestry which makes a total of, in round figures, 155,000 people in the Territory of Hawaii of Japanese ancestry against a total population of 430,000. Therefore the seizure of Japanese aliens in Hawaii is a matter of *selectivity*. . . .
>
> [I]t is the considered opinion of this office and the Office of Military Intelligence in Hawaii that if the leadership of the Japanese alien population is seized, that, of itself, will break the backbone of any Japanese alien resistance. . . . Those aliens who have been listed for custodial detention comprise the alien leadership in Hawaii in every branch of alien activity, namely: businessmen, consular agents, Japanese language school teachers and principals, Buddhist and Shinto priests, and others of no particular affiliation who by reason of their extreme nationalistic sentiments would be a danger to our security as well as others who have seen Japanese military service.[75]

In designing these plans, Shivers went on, the commanding general of the Hawaiian Department and military intelligence sought "to preserve and maintain the respect of the alien populace in the constituted authorities and to maintain the loyalty of the vast majority of the second and third generation Japanese without alienating this group."[76]

Shivers sent separately to FBI director Hoover a list of those for whom detention memoranda had been submitted; the list named 212 consular agents, 53 Shinto and Buddhist priests, and 82 others (including businessmen, editors of Japanese publications, physicians, and engineers) "linked with the furtherance of Japanese national policies to the disadvantage of the United States," for a total of 337. Also listed for detention were 80 German aliens and 29 Italian aliens.[77]

Administrative and Legal Measures: The M-Day Bill and Martial Law

Meanwhile, as the Americanization campaign among the Japanese Americans in Hawai'i continued in the year leading up to the war, General Herron, then commander of the Hawaiian Department, instructed the new judge advocate in his headquarters, Lieutenant Colonel Thomas H. Green, to develop the administrative and legal measures for security in case of an emergency.[78] According to Green's memoir, "The decision as to the form of such measures was not part of my duty at the time but a determination of what legal remedies were available was wholly within my province."[79] Indeed, there was not much that Green did not consider to be in his province. He had practiced law briefly in Boston before being called into federal service with the Massachusetts National Guard for action on the Mexican border in 1916. Green had then served as a cavalry officer in France during World War I, becoming commanding officer of his regiment. In 1924, after further legal training, he transferred to the Judge Advocate General's Department, where he "liberalized the scope of the office's work."[80] He was a man of broad ambition and small inclination for compromises. Green would play a major role in the history of martial law in Hawai'i.

Green had arrived in Hawai'i in August 1940. After studying the situation, he "began to outline changes in the law" that would "permit immediate action to be taken by existing authorities in the event of an emergency."[81] In other words, he asserted, he was looking for an alternative to martial law that would keep the civilian authorities in control. Written years after the war, the memoir perhaps exaggerates Green's professed effort to avoid martial law, but it is nevertheless informative as to the thinking in army headquarters in Hawai'i. Green states that his proposed plan would place control "in the hands of the Governor, but that he could, if he so desired, confer upon subordinate officials extraordinary powers which could clothe them with authority to meet whatever difficulties the situation might require." By early 1941, Green had concluded:

1. Under the existing state of the law, in case of war with Japan, internal security would require either martial law or military intervention.
2. This might be avoided if the civil authorities could be authorized to take immediate action to accomplish the same purpose.
3. If this could be done, it would remove any onus of martial law from the military and would release a full complement of troops for combat duty.
4. The civil authorities are now unable to undertake any such program, and legislation would be necessary to accomplish the desired result.

5. The matter should be taken up with the Governor through his Attorney General.

6. If the existing state of the law continued, steps should be taken and agreements made with the Governor relative to declaring martial law. Failure to do so might consume valuable time in controversy in time of an emergency.

7. Thought should be given to the situation wherein the existing law continues and the Governor declines to declare martial law.[82]

By February 7, 1941, when General Short, replacing Herron, assumed office as commanding general of the Hawaiian Department, Green stated that he had "an outline of proposed legislation, together with some rough drafts of martial law proclamations." Green referred to the legislation as an "'M-Day Bill,' the letter 'M' standing for mobilization." According to the official army history, Short was not convinced that martial law would be needed, but if it became necessary, Short wanted its administration to be vested as much as possible in the civilian authorities, assisted by the armed forces.[83] At Short's instruction, Green arranged a meeting with Joseph Hodgson, the territorial attorney general, and Governor Poindexter. While recognizing that the granting of extraordinary powers to him would not be politically popular, Poindexter apparently asked Hodgson to draft a bill along these lines for the legislature's consideration. According to Green, he himself, together with Hodgson and two staff lawyers in the territorial adjutant general's office, drafted the bill, "which was the first proposed legislation of its kind."[84]

The Hawai'i Defense Act of 1941, which became known popularly as the "M-Day Bill," was introduced into the legislature in February 1941. The bill authorized the governor, in case of an extreme emergency, to exercise unprecedented, broad powers without the requirement for normal deliberation, including regulation of food and supplies, price control, and the registration of all residents of the territory. As Poindexter had anticipated, there was strong opposition to granting so much power to a single individual, and the legislature adjourned in April without adopting the measure.[85] On September 15, with war clouds gathering, Governor Poindexter called a special session of the legislature to consider a slightly modified version of the bill. Addressing the legislature, he warned: "That we will be drawn into actual hostilities is an apprehension which all of us share, but which we must face with courage and determination. . . . I recommend the enactment of a measure which will make suitable and adequate provision for the immediate and comprehensive designation and delegation of powers which under normal times would be unnecessary in a democratic form of government."[86] Two days later, in an unusual step, General Short similarly urged its passage, testifying to the territorial senate:

Many of these things can be done better by the civil authorities than by the military authorities, even after we possess the necessary powers to execute them. Many of them even after the declaration of martial law the military authorities would call on the civil authorities to perform. *The proper action at this time might do much to delay or even render unnecessary a declaration of martial law. . . .*

The essential legislation to provide this protection is entirely a function of the government and the legislature. *The military authorities have no place in such action.* If we tried to prescribe action we would be invading the public affairs of the civil authorities.[87]

Even if the army did have to impose martial law, Short continued, he anticipated that many of the ordinary functions of civilian governance would remain with the governor, under the broad powers the act afforded him.[88]

This time the legislature acted quickly, and the Hawai'i Defense Act passed both houses and was signed into law on October 3, 1941. The measure vested authority to exercise unparalleled, virtually dictatorial powers in the governor in case of a military emergency, with only minimal safeguards for individual rights. Enforcement of the law, however, was to remain in civilian courts, with certain standards of due process preserved.[89]

Secretary of War Henry L. Stimson, nevertheless, was not content to rely on the territorial governor and the M-Day bill. He therefore submitted a draft of a martial law bill that was introduced into Congress in early November. Designed to bypass the governor, the bill would authorize the president to suspend the privilege of the writ of habeas corpus, to place the territories of Hawai'i and Puerto Rico under martial law "in case of rebellion or invasion or imminent danger thereof," and to direct the commanders of the U.S. military and naval forces to prevent or suppress violence or invasion without going through any civilian authorities. In arguing for the bill, Stimson cited the danger of sabotage or other subversive activities prior to the outbreak of war "due to the fact that approximately one tenth of the population of Hawaii are aliens," and the likely necessity to have martial law in place before any attempted invasion—an imposition that the Supreme Court had disallowed under its *Milligan* ruling.[90]

The bill was vigorously opposed by both Governor Poindexter, who thought it superfluous, and Delegate Samuel King, who called it "entirely unnecessary" and "an affront to the loyalty and patriotism of citizens of Hawaii." King further pointed out that General Short was in favor of the M-Day bill and that the territorial governor, no less than the military commanders, reports directly to the president. King also feared that the proposed legislation, which was not limited to the current situation, could become permanent and serve as "an opening wedge for the replacement of civil government by military rule."[91] Supported by civic leaders in Honolulu as well as by members of the Senate Military Affairs Committee, King drafted an amendment to the proposed bill that would give the president the same emergency powers as those of the governor but would not stigmatize the Hawaiian people or government. On December 3, however, the chairman of the House Military Affairs Committee, not wishing to antagonize the citizens of a primary defense area, rendered the whole matter of the martial bill mute by refusing to hold hearings.[92] Thus the bill died, but not before the War Department had revealed its lack of faith in both the civilian population of Hawai'i and the governor.

Meanwhile Colonel Green, who also doubted that the passage of the Hawai'i Defense Act, or "M-Day Bill," was sufficient preparation for war, continued to develop his plan for martial law. According to his memoir, he "drafted a form of proclamation for declaring martial law by the Governor under the provisions of the Organic Act. . . . I went further and drafted a proclamation of martial law for use by General Short in the event that all else failed."[93] He also busied himself preparing general orders to handle any emergency in case martial law should be declared, as will be seen in the next chapter. As it turned out, Green himself would be responsible for implementing those general orders.

Thus, on the eve of war with Japan, all the elements for martial law were in place. The list of persons who should be interned on the outbreak of war—largely leaders of the Japanese community rather than known subversives—had been compiled after years of surveillance by the FBI and the intelligence officers of the army and navy. Martial law had been viewed as a probable military necessity since at least the 1920s. The M-Day Bill had been passed, giving the governor extraordinary emergency powers. And both the proclamation of martial law and the measures to implement it were lying in readiness.

Chapter Three

IMPLEMENTATION OF MARTIAL LAW
AND MILITARY GOVERNMENT

The Japanese air attack on Pearl Harbor began at 7:55 a.m. on December 7, 1941. By 11:30 a.m., Governor Poindexter had invoked the M-Day Act. And just four hours after that, the decision was made to place the territory under martial law, which was proclaimed simultaneously but separately by Poindexter and General Short. Exactly who made the decision, and under what circumstances, is a matter of some controversy.

According to later recollections of Governor Poindexter, immediately after the air raid on Pearl Harbor had ended, General Walter Short came to his office to inform him that the security of the Islands urgently required immediate declaration of comprehensive martial law and the suspension of the writ of habeas corpus.[1] Although General Short had urged the territorial legislature to prepare for a war emergency by enacting the Hawai'i Defense (or M-Day or Mobilization-Day) Act just three months earlier, arguing that many government functions could be done better by civil than military authorities, he now apparently regarded the M-Day provisions for vesting virtually dictatorial powers in the territorial governor as inadequate. According to Poindexter's later sworn testimony, as well as the recollections of Acting Attorney General Kai, who was present at the meeting, Short informed the governor that he anticipated a Japanese invasion of O'ahu that very night, and he persuaded Poindexter that martial law was absolutely necessary.[2] Robert Shivers, Honolulu bureau chief of the FBI, also urged the governor to declare martial law.[3]

Governor Poindexter telephoned President Roosevelt at 12:40 p.m. As noted in the diary of Secretary of the Territory Charles Hite, who listened in on the governor's calls on December 7, Poindexter informed Roosevelt of the extent of the attack and "said Short had asked for martial law and he thought he should invoke it. President replied he approved. Gov. said main danger from local Japs."[4] The diary continues: "When Short left Gov. said never hated doing anything so much in all his life."[5] Governor Poindexter would later testify that he had been reluctant to declare martial law but had done so only because General Short had insisted that it was "absolutely essential" to the defense of the islands.[6] Poindexter cited "the large Japanese population we have in

Hawaii" as the main reason for martial law.[7] He further testified, however, that he "probably never would have signed the proclamation" for martial law if he had been given sufficient time to study the matter thoroughly.[8] In Poindexter's recollection, the army insisted upon the absolute necessity of full power, though also promising that there would be at least a partial restoration of civilian authority at an early date, "once the danger of invasion has passed."[9]

Secretary of the Interior Harold Ickes, the governor's superior in the civilian chain of authority, wrote in 1942 that Poindexter had told him personally "that he was coerced by General Short" to turn over all authority to the army because Short had said he could not otherwise guarantee the security of the civilian population; and that Short predicted a substantial restoration of the civilian government within thirty days.[10] Ickes recorded in his manuscript diaries that "Governor Poindexter reported to me that he had surrendered all civilian power practically under duress at the hands of the commanding general. Green [who was present] did not argue about this."[11]

The army command consistently denied, however, that any such commitment as to restoration of control had been offered, contending that Poindexter had agreed fully and willingly with the proposition that an entire and unqualified transfer of authority over judicial and executive as well as legislative functions was an absolute necessity. According to Colonel Green, who claimed he was the only witness at the meeting with Poindexter and Short, the governor said, in essence, "I feel that the situation is beyond me and the civil authorities and I think the safety of the Territory and its citizens require me to declare martial law." Green's memoir goes on to state that General Short then concurred with Governor Poindexter's decision.[12] Green maintained that there was "not a word of truth" in Hite's account, denouncing it as a "figment of the imagination."[13]

This apparent disagreement between Governor Poindexter and General Short proved to be but the opening salvo in a struggle for control between the civil and military authorities, both in Hawai'i and in Washington—a struggle that was to last through most of the war. Neither Short, who was summarily removed and replaced by General Delos C. Emmons on December 17, 1941, nor Poindexter, who was succeeded by Ingram Stainback in August 1942, would remain principal actors, but the tension continued under their successors.[14]

Martial Law Declared

Whatever the accuracy of Poindexter's account of his meeting with General Short, when war thundered down from the skies over O'ahu on December 7, the army—thanks to Colonel Green's earlier efforts—was fully prepared to place the entire governance of the population under its own control. Acting Attorney General Ernie Kai recalled that the governor, during the meeting with Short, pulled from a safe the draft of a proclamation of martial law; he asked Kai to make sure it complied with the Territorial

Organic Act and to put it in proper form for the governor's signature. Kai did so, and both Governor Poindexter and General Short signed the proclamation of martial law early in the afternoon.[15]

At 3:30 p.m., Poindexter, citing the Hawai'i Organic Act, placed the territory under martial law, suspended the writ of habeas corpus, and asked the commanding general to exercise *all the powers normally exercised by the governor and "by judicial officers and employees" of the territory, counties and cities of Hawai'i.*[16] In a simultaneous proclamation, Short accepted the transfer of power, "assumed the position of military governor," and took "charge of the government of the Territory."[17] He verbally designated Colonel Green as his Executive in carrying out those functions, and that very afternoon, the Office of the Military Governor (OMG) was established in Iolani Palace, the seat of government for the Territory of Hawai'i.[18] Poindexter informed President Roosevelt by telegram of his actions, and two days later, by reply telegram, the president approved the suspension of the writ of habeas corpus and placing the territory under martial law. There is no indication that he ever saw the proclamations themselves, although it is important to note that Attorney General Biddle advised the president that the action taken—including the declaration of martial law, the suspension of the privilege of the writ of habeas corpus, the appointment of a military governor, and the suspension of civil courts—"is appropriate."[19]

In turning over the judicial and legislative powers of the civilian government, as well as the executive powers, Poindexter went well beyond the invocation of martial law: he in effect instituted military government. Military government is, according to the army's own manual, "exercised by a belligerent in occupying an enemy's territory,"[20] whereas martial law is used in domestic situations in defense of the civil power and is subordinate to it. Similarly, the title "Military Governor" had previously been used only in conquered or rebellious territories.[21] Nevertheless, it was both military government and martial law that were imposed—illegally, as its critics would claim—in Hawai'i.[22] The military government in quick order closed the civil courts, issued its own rules and regulations in the form of general orders, and assumed control not only of defense, but also of communications and much of the economic and social lives of the population of Hawai'i.

Although the wide scope of martial law brought the activities of all civilians in the Islands under army rule, the declaration of martial law and the actual administration of military government had some uniquely harsh consequences for residents of Japanese ancestry—both alien residents and citizens—in Hawai'i, and to some degree for other residents of Asian ancestry. In marked contrast, however, to the drastic policy applied in May 1942 of forcibly removing and then incarcerating all 110,000 Nikkei residents of western California, Washington, Oregon, Alaska, and a portion of Arizona, the army instituted a policy in Hawai'i of "selective internment," leaving most Japanese Americans in the territory free to continue their lives in their own homes (and in most cases, their prewar employment), as best they could—but, like the rest of Hawai'i's

Front page of December 7, 1941, *Star-Bulletin* "Extra." Credit: Courtesy of HWRD, University of Hawai'i.

civilian population, under army rule.[23] Eventually 1,569 persons would be detained on suspicion of disloyalty or as "potentially dangerous." Of these, 1,466—less than 1 percent of their ethnic group in Hawai'i—were of Japanese descent.[24]

The individual who was largely responsible for the policies in Hawai'i was General Delos Emmons, who succeeded Short as commanding general and military governor ten days after the attack on Pearl Harbor. A graduate of the U.S. Military Academy, he had subsequently taken flight training and attended the Air Corps Tactical School and the Command and General Staff School. He rose rapidly through the ranks, and in 1939 Roosevelt appointed Emmons as chief of the General Headquarters (GHQ) Air Force, where he became a strong advocate of the offensive capabilities of bomber aircraft. Following the attack on Pearl Harbor by the Japanese navy's aircraft, General George Marshall, chief of staff of the army, wanted an air officer to command the Hawaiian Department, and he selected Emmons.

Emmons was no stranger to Hawai'i. He had served as Air Officer of the Hawaiian Department at Fort Shafter from 1934 to 1936, and he understood the multiethnic nature of the Islands' population and the important role of the Nikkei in the economy. Almost immediately upon taking office, Emmons issued several important public statements asking for racial and ethnic tolerance. He also lent his support to the activities of a civilian agency under the territorial governor, the Public Morale Section, which was sanctioned by the military and worked actively against discrimination in counterpoint with its conduct of a propaganda campaign for "Americanism" in the Japanese-American community.[25] Of great importance, too, was Emmons's support of allowing Japanese Americans to enter combat units. Thus, after being prevented from enlistment in the armed forces in early 1942, Japanese-American citizens were finally invited in early 1943 to form a Hawai'i fighting unit; and, as is well known, their combat team became one of the most decorated units in American military history.[26] By war's end, more than 12,000 Hawai'i Nisei had served in the armed forces.

Initial Security Measures and Detentions

This is not to say that Hawai'i residents of Japanese ancestry were regarded by the military—or civilian—government as beyond suspicion. On the contrary, as discussed above, the presence of such large numbers of ethnic Japanese in Hawai'i was the reason for the years of planning for martial law before December 7, 1941, and the justification for its immediate imposition following the Pearl Harbor attack.

Of particular concern to both military and civilian security officials was the potential danger of fifth-column activity from within this group if the Islands were invaded by Japan; and after the Pearl Harbor attack, such an invasion appeared to be an immediate danger. On December 7, shortly after the bombing raid on Pearl Harbor, President Roosevelt signed Presidential Proclamation No. 2525, declaring "all natives, citizens or subjects of the Empire of Japan" living in the United States and not naturalized to be "liable to be apprehended, restrained, secured, and removed as alien enemies."[27] Similar proclamations were issued regarding German and Italian aliens. The secretary of war, through the commanding general, was charged with responsibility for all enemy aliens in the Territory of Hawai'i, including the arrest, detention, and internment of those considered dangerous.

As soon as Governor Poindexter and General Short declared martial law—and even before the United States had formally declared war—General Short directed that "all enemy alien Japanese and citizens of that ancestry" on whom the FBI had submitted custodial detention letters were to be "apprehended and interned."[28] The FBI plans for persons on their detention lists that had been completed days earlier were immediately implemented. As happened on the mainland, and in accordance with the plans detailed by FBI bureau chief Shivers, the army and the FBI moved quickly to round up aliens and other individuals who previously had been investigated and were suspected of being disloyal or dangerous in a war situation.[29] The detainees included almost all Shinto and Buddhist priests, teachers of Japanese language schools, consular agents and other leaders of the Nikkei community, and many Issei fishermen, whose offshore activities had long been the subject of unsubstantiated rumors and suspicions.[30]

The arrests were accomplished with the assistance of the police department, whose espionage bureau's head, John Burns, reported directly to Shivers when the war broke out.[31] The FBI plans had been based on the locations of police beats, with one three-person squad assigned to each beat. Each squad was to be headed by an FBI special agent, typically assisted by a military intelligence officer and a police officer. Seven squads were to operate within Honolulu, and six squads outside the city. The army was supposed to provide the transportation, but in the chaos following the Pearl Harbor attack, the vehicles were not available; consequently, the FBI agent in charge, Robert Shivers, directed his agents to use FBI cars or their personal automobiles. Shivers also called on the Honolulu police to provide men and vehicles as necessary to carry out the apprehension of the suspected Japanese. In all, some fifty agents and policemen participated in the arrests.[32]

According to FBI Special Agent Shivers, "the apprehension of these aliens went off . . . smoothly."[33] Prior to the outbreak of the war, his FBI bureau had prepared three-by-five cards on each subject who was to be detained, showing name, address, and citizenship status. The back of the card had been stamped with the statement, "Received custody of the person named on the reverse side." On the afternoon and evening of December 7, Shivers personally assigned the squads to the precincts on O'ahu, gave them instructions to deliver the apprehended individuals to the Honolulu Immigration Station, and distributed the cards for the detainees. As Shivers reported, "As the individuals were picked up by the various squads, they were taken to the Immigration Station, where they were receipted for on the reverse side of the card by the Military Police. The cards were then returned to this office."[34]

Similar operations took place on the other islands of the Territory of Hawai'i. The names of the persons to be detained were telephoned by the MID to their representatives on those islands. On the Island of Hawai'i, the arrests were made by the military authorities in conjunction with the local police, under the supervision of three FBI special agents; those apprehended were taken to the Kilauea Military Camp for detention. On Kaua'i, two FBI special agents, assisted by the local police, apprehended the persons on the detention list. On Maui, Moloka'i, and Lana'i, where there were no FBI agents, Military Intelligence (G-2) apprehended fifty-one, four, and two persons, respectively. Additional persons of Japanese ancestry were arrested later on December 7 and on December 8 on the basis of new information furnished by the Nisei who had been serving as FBI informants, as well as information gleaned by the FBI and military intelligence.[35]

On December 7, the president had authorized the Department of Justice to take into custody all enemy aliens deemed dangerous to the safety of the United States. The FBI and the army command in Hawai'i interpreted this authorization as applicable, ad hoc, not only to aliens but also to dual citizens, including, of course, all Kibei and other ethnic Japanese who were deemed dual citizens. The authorization was subsequently formally amended specifically to include dual citizens.[36] Within two days, OMG and its legal staff had overseen the arrest and internment of Japanese-American citizens, treating them identically as they did enemy aliens, as a prerogative that they exercised under the authority of martial law. By the morning of December 8, a total of 391 persons of Japanese descent had been apprehended.[37]

Enemy aliens from other countries were also to be caught in the net. Although war was not officially declared against Germany and Italy until December 11, the Office of the Provost Marshal General in Washington sent the following radiogram for the commanding general in the Hawaiian Department on December 8: "Second Presidential Proclamation dated December eighth classifies German and Italian aliens as enemy aliens. Secretary of War directs immediate apprehension of all German and Italian alien enemies on the A, B, and C lists. Instructions on hearing procedures will follow."[38] Consequently, at the direction of the military governor, the FBI acted on December 8, in a similar manner as with the Japanese, to apprehend *all* German and Italian aliens, and citizens of those ancestries who were on the detention lists.[39] A perfunctory entry in the FBI log for December 9 noted: "Suspected German and Italian aliens were taken into temporary detention together with a few German and Italian-born naturalized citizens last night."[40] A separate FBI report placed the total numbers arrested through December 9 at 473:[41]

TABLE 1
Persons Detained in Hawai'i, December 7–9, 1941

Japanese aliens (Issei)	345
Japanese-American citizens (Nisei)	22
German aliens	74
German-American citizens	19
Italian aliens	11
Italian-American citizens	2
Total	473

Source: FBI Memorandum, C. H. Carson to Ladd, December 9, 1941, File No. 100–2-20, Section 1, www.foitimes.com/internment/Honolulu1.pdf.

Thus on the afternoons and evenings of December 7 and December 8, the FBI, assisted by the military and local police, had quickly apprehended all the persons on the FBI custodial detention lists. They did so without presenting any charges or explanations or, in some cases, even warrants. Although responsibility for the enemy alien program was vested in the War Department, the arrests were actually made under the auspices of the FBI. Validating warrants were therefore subsequently submitted for the secretary of war's signature "in order that there may be no question raised as to the validity of the arrests."[42] The initial raids that picked up persons of Japanese ancestry had taken only three hours; the raids that apprehended the Italians and Germans, or those of that ancestry, had taken even less time.[43]

These raids, conducted with such efficiency from the perspective of the military authorities and the FBI, struck terror in the hearts of the individuals who were apprehended and, equally, of their families and communities. Frequently, suspects were not even given time to say goodbye to their families or to secure warm clothing. Yasutaro Soga, the editor of a Japanese language newspaper, recounts his arrest:

> While the evening dusk was gathering, a car with blue lights suddenly stopped in front of our yard. My son, Shigeo, went to the entrance hall to meet the visitors, three military policemen. They were six feet tall and young and wore MP armbands. They said they were taking me to the Immigration Office. I immediately answered, "All right." . . . I was escorted out of the house. My wife came with me as far as the entrance hall and whispered, "Please be careful not to catch a cold." I tried to say something but could not utter a word and silently went to the car. Two of the MPs sat in the front, and one sat beside me in the back with a pistol in his hand.[44]

Similar stories can be found in an increasingly available literature. For example, the grandson of a Kibei, a Mr. Kubota, who owned a general store in a sugar plantation village on Oʻahu's north shore, wrote that there was a "rattling knock" on his grandfather's home on the evening of December 8. Two FBI agents identified themselves and took his grandfather to Honolulu for questioning. "No one knew what had happened or what was wrong. . . ." Because his grandfather had entertained Japanese nationals in his own home and had a radio, he was suspected of espionage. Following the attack on Pearl Harbor, the grandson wrote, "Circumstances and an undertone of racial resentment had combined with wartime hysteria . . . to cast suspicion on the loyalties of my grandfather and all other Japanese Americans." His grandfather was one of the lucky ones; he was released after a few days.[45]

And a Hawaiʻi Kibei recalls:

> [The] FBI asked me to go with them to the Department of Immigration for a little while to answer a few questions. When we reached the Department of Immigration building I was put behind bars for several weeks and no questions were asked

of me. We had our meals out in the yard enclosed by walls under armed guards with their rifles drawn. All the time I was there I was not told why I was being held behind bars and neither the FBI nor the Immigration officer asked me any questions.[46]

The raids affected many who lived on the other Hawaiian islands, as well. One Issei on the west coast of Hawai'i recounts that a Japanese policeman arrived at his home on the night of December 7, and said,

"Mister, Get dressed."
"Where are we going?"
"I don't know; just get dressed. You won't be there long."
"[J]ust like that they took me . . . [and] I didn't return home for the whole 4 years."[47]

He was taken to the Kilauea Military Camp near the volcano, where there were already 105 detainees.

In many cases, the head of the family simply disappeared, and several weeks passed before his family learned he had been interned. For example, the family of an Issei Buddhist minister who was arrested on December 7 did not learn until late summer 1942 that he had been taken to the mainland.[48] In other cases, children were left unattended when both parents were interned.[49] For example, Joe Pacific, an Italian American who owned a shoe repair shop, was putting black paper on his windows with his daughter when the FBI picked him up at 2:00 in the afternoon of December 8. The FBI agent told him he would be home in fifteen minutes, but he was detained for four months. His German-born wife was picked up a few hours later, leaving their nine-year-old daughter unattended. One of his customers, a judge, finally arranged for the girl to go to a convent school.[50]

Similarly, Doris Berg Nye, whose German-American father worked for Sears, Roebuck & Co. and, with his wife, ran a nursing home in Honolulu, recounted how her parents were interned in Honolulu on December 8, and her eighteen-year-old sister was taken away five days later. At age eleven, Doris and her younger sister, nine, were "left as abandoned children." All five family members were U.S. citizens. "The internment and all of its ramifications was not supposed to happen to us. After all, as U.S. citizens, we were protected by the Federal Constitution, its freedoms, civil liberties and certain 'inalienable rights.' That was not the case. On Dec. 7, 1941, all of that went out the window."[51] The Berg family was not reunited until summer of 1943.

The sweep teams searched homes and business properties; they regarded the possession of Japanese flags, patriotic literature, swords or other Japanese treasures, or even board games in the Japanese language as ample reason to detain the owners. Firearms and radio sets were confiscated, as dozens of tips about short-wave radios poured into the FBI from ordinary citizens as well as FBI informants in the days immediately following Pearl Harbor.[52]

Apprehended in this initial sweep operation, as had been planned, were several dozen Buddhist and Shinto priests, officers of community social and charitable organizations, Japanese language school teachers and principals, journalists, and others who held influential positions. Included were most of the 234 Japanese consular agents, whom the FBI described as "individuals of some influence in their local Japanese circles. . . . Generally their duties consisted of aiding Japanese individuals, taking the Japanese census, and filling out many forms required by the Japanese government of its Japanese nationals when they desired to transfer properties, claim estates in Japan, and other similar activities. They also aided in the registering of Japanese babies with the Consulate."[53] Ironically, some of the individuals connected with the Japanese Consulate, including several Christian ministers, had been helping dual citizens to expatriate from Japan.[54] For example, Hisashi Fukuhara, who had come from Japan in 1916 and was helping dual citizens expatriate from Japan so they could get American teaching jobs, recalled, "It was for this reason that I was taken. I was doing consul's job, that's why. . . . I was helping people who didn't know Japanese. They can't write anything because they don't know. . . . I didn't receive even five cents from the consulate, but I was helping the people for their sake."[55] Fukuhara, a barber on the island of Hawai'i who also wrote haiku poetry, was arrested on December 7 and was sent to Sand Island and then to mainland internment camps, where he spent the entire war. His wife, a Nisei, was left to tend the barbershop—better off than the wives of the priests, who were left with no livelihood.

Targeting the elite of the Nikkei community was explicitly designed as a way of undermining the strength of leadership in the various sectors of community life, and not coincidentally it had an intimidating effect on others because of the prominence of the people targeted. However, the "temporary" mass arrests of all Japanese living in Hawai'i, which Attorney General Francis Biddle had said in November would be likely in the event of war, did not take place.[56]

The FBI, local police, and military patrols also picked up specific persons, including German Americans and Italian Americans, who were not necessarily leaders of any sort but had been identified by investigations conducted before December 1941 as possibly holding disloyal views or as engaged in suspect activities.[57] Among those detained was Hans Zimmerman, a naturalized citizen from Germany who had served for more than two years in the U.S. Army. A successful naturopathic doctor, he had offered his clinic and his services to the army on December 7. The following day, he was asked to accompany two men to army headquarters for ten to twenty minutes. He was immediately imprisoned at the Immigration Station, with no charges filed against him. The testimony in his favor of Joseph Farrington, Hawai'i's delegate to Congress, and other prominent Honolulu citizens failed to secure his release. Despite the fact that he was a citizen, he was identified in a presidential warrant as being an enemy alien. Over the next months and years, Zimmerman would file a series of suits against the government for denial of his civil liberties; his final challenge was not decided until well after the war had ended.[58]

In the days following December 7, reinforcements of personnel for both the FBI and G-2 arrived from the mainland, enabling the two agencies, often working together in teams, to expand greatly their investigations. As a result, according to G-2 officer George Bicknell, "more and more individuals were apprehended and placed in detention. This process also worked in reverse as further checks indicated that some of those detained could be released in custody of responsible American citizens."[59] Nearly all of the Kibei living in Hawai'i were investigated during the first year of the war.[60]

Some persons taken into custody in the initial sweeps were, very simply, the victims of undocumented rumor or gossip. In the immediate aftermath of the attack on Pearl Harbor, many civilian residents called the FBI to report "suspicious behavior," or "pro-Japanese," or "pro-Nazi" sympathies, often with few if any specifics; in at least some of these cases, the FBI or military intelligence brought the suspect individuals in for questioning.[61] Others were arrested on the basis of information, regardless of how vague it was, from the FBI's confidential informants. For example, the detention memoranda for two Italians noted, "Confidential Informant A advised that Subject was an individual who would be inimical to the welfare and internal security of the United States in the event of a national emergency."[62]

The army command decided to credit such undocumented reports as being accurate rather than risk overlooking a serious potential danger. One individual who was the object of such rumors was a New York–born citizen—the son of a Finnish father and a Swedish mother—who had served in the U.S. Army and was on duty as chief of communications of the Office of Civilian Defense in Honolulu on December 8 when he was taken away by car.

> The officer in the rear seat held a tommy gun pointed at me. . . . I was driven directly to the immigration station in Honolulu. . . . In due course an Army officer asked my name which I gave [Carl Armfelt], whereupon he asked, German or Italian. I replied, American. He then said, Don't get funny are you a German or an Italian and I answered, I am an American . . . and I would like to know what's going on, whereupon he ordered an Army enlisted man to put down German on the record. . . .
>
> I was led by two guards to a cell door, was pushed in. The cell was dark and there were about 175 others in there. We were kept for a period of approximately 12 days, although there were beds for only 30. The rest of us slept on the floor without mattress, blankets or other coverings. We were not provided with soap, towels, or razors or facilities for taking a bath.[63]

Armfelt was charged with being an enemy alien and was interned for two years, despite having served for two years in the U.S. Army.

Additional arrests were made in the ensuing weeks, in at least some cases with similar results.[64] For example, Gunther and Anna Walther, German-born American citizens, had contacted the FBI in late 1940 and early 1941 to offer their language services, which

were accepted on a part-time basis. They were questioned in May 1941 by the FBI because Walther appeared in a photo with some Nazis on board a ship when he visited
Germany in 1939. On February 8, 1942, the Walthers were again approached by the FBI
and brought to the Immigration Station for questioning. They were told it would take
only twenty minutes, but they were held for twenty-one months, first on Sand Island
and then at Honouliuli. Gunther Walther and his wife were separated, and he was
coerced into signing a paper saying he was an enemy alien. He had a second hearing
in February 1943, and, for the first time, was presented with the charge against him:
"Not loyal to the United States." He was denied legal assistance, he was not permitted
to cross-examine witnesses, and he was not released on parole until August 1943.[65]

Grievous procedural errors had been made, and the issue of the legality of the summary arrests and internment of U.S. citizens led to court challenges and an internal
investigation by the Inspector General of the War Department in June 1943. He found
a "succession of errors and oversights in the arrest, hearing, and internment of citizens," particularly the failure to specify in their records "that they were being held
under the authority of martial law rather than the War Department directives which
made no provision for citizen internees." The Inspector General recommended a review of the cases of all citizen internees, a recommendation that was implemented by
the Military Governor's Reviewing Board.[66] Several months later, when the legality of
internment of American citizens was before the courts, Assistant Secretary of War John
McCloy also suggested to General Richardson, Emmons's successor as military governor, that "it may prove desirable" to correct the language in dockets of citizen internees to show that they were confined under martial law and not in accordance with the
presidential proclamations of December 7 and 8, 1941.[67]

After being arrested, the majority by the FBI but many by the police or the army,
most of the suspects were taken into custody by the 810th Military Police Company at
the Immigration and Naturalization Service (INS) immigration station in Honolulu,
where they were temporarily detained.[68] As recounted by Soga, the journalist who was
arrested in the initial sweep, at the immigration station those who had been apprehended
were ordered about "like dogs" at the point of a bayonet by military guards, "packed like
sushi" into a space designed for half their number, and made to eat outside on the
ground, regardless of the weather.[69]

Others were locked up in the Kalaheo Stockade and county jails in Kaua'i, at the
Kilauea Military Camp on the Big Island of Hawai'i, or an internment camp in Haiku,
Maui.[70] All suffered the fears that came with not knowing how long they would be held,
where they might be sent, or, as some testified they thought, whether they were to be
killed.[71] One Japanese language school teacher and poet from Hilo tells of his arrest on
the night of December 7, when he was taken to Kilauea. The following morning he was
subjected to a second search in front of the barracks, where he was surrounded by dozens of armed soldiers. "[T]heir guns glittered ominously in the rain. It flashed across
my mind that they were preparing to execute us. We were ordered to walk. So we started
walking in the cold rain, . . . fearing that we would be killed."[72] Another Japanese lan-

guage school teacher from Kaua'i recalled similar fears following his arrest on December 8 and imprisonment in a local jail: "On the third day, we were placed on a dump truck and taken away without a word. . . . We were wondering where they were going to execute us. Some thought the graveyard that we were nearing was going to be the place."[73]

By mid-December, some 300 Japanese being held at the Immigration Station had been transferred by ship, under heavy military guard, to Sand Island—a camp in Honolulu harbor formerly used for quarantined immigrants that had been taken over by the army as a detention camp.[74] It would be weeks before the internees or their families would know their fate. Not informing the detainees of the final disposition of their cases was a matter of policy in the early months of the war.[75] At Sand Island, the prisoners were held, in extremely primitive facilities under tight security, under an intimidating regime of discipline that reinforced their apprehension as to their future.

As stated in the official report from the Office of the Chief of Military History, which was issued after the conclusion of the war, the procedures for the "Collection and Custody of Enemy Aliens" were very carefully planned. In the period immediately following the attack on Pearl Harbor, "no single chance could be taken with a possible act of sabotage or with any form of espionage which might give aid to Japan." It was not surprising, therefore, that "[f]irst priority in the system called for the immediate detention of everyone who was already suspected of [possible] enemy allegiance or sympathy, and prompt apprehension of those who fell into such a category. . . . Second priority . . . [was to give] fair impartial treatment to everyone temporarily detained."[76] The extent to which the military authorities honored this second priority—to afford prisoners fair treatment—is discussed in chapter 9, below.

PART II

Civilians under Army Rule

"The Iron Grasp of Martial Law"

Chapter Four

LIFE UNDER GENERAL ORDERS

In the early weeks of the war, there was no public challenge to martial law. It was accepted as an emergency measure with practically no resistance in Hawai'i, and indeed it was received with obvious relief and enthusiasm in many segments of the civilian population.[1] According to one reporter on the scene, "The change from the fullest of liberty to the iron grasp of martial law overnight was not easy, but it was negotiated willingly and eagerly by a population that has received the most sincere compliments from Army and Navy commanders on its hearty cooperation."[2]

Most residents of the Islands apparently also believed that the civilian courts and the civilian government would resume their basic functions as soon as the acute emergency situation had passed—in a few months at most. But any assumption that the army would willingly relinquish its control over civilian life proved wholly unwarranted. For more than fifteen months—until March 1943, when a portion of the civilian government's authority and individual civil liberties were restored—the military would rule Hawai'i with virtually an unchecked authority, acting as executive, legislature, and judiciary and suspending constitutional guarantees on a wholesale basis. Martial law was not lifted entirely until October 1944, more than two years after the Battle of Midway had ended any real danger of invasion or massive strike against Hawai'i.

Although the army did permit the civil courts to reopen for noncriminal, nonjury cases early in 1942, the jurisdiction of those courts was strictly limited; hence, nearly all misdemeanors and all felonies continued to be tried before military tribunals. The general orders issued by the army recognized no residual or controlling powers in the governor, the legislative officers of the territory or its municipalities, or the civilian courts at any level. Indeed, the army thereafter formally regarded the civilian courts, when they were allowed to resume functioning in a limited way, as "agents of the Military Governor."[3]

General Emmons did not mince words about the sacrifices that military necessity demanded of the civilian population or about the authoritarian nature of martial law: "The sole purpose of martial law and the military government now in effect," he stated in a public address in January 1942, "is to better defend these islands. . . . [I]t is vital that full responsibility and complete authority shall be invested in one head." While promising to disrupt the community's business as little as possible, Emmons said that "neither life in general, business nor politics can go on as usual." Wartime conditions necessitated "immediate and positive action," and everyone had a "duty to obey instantly and unqualifiedly the orders of competent authority. The invaluable democratic process of peacetime debate and discussion does not fit into the picture of frontline battle efficiency."[4] Emmons would maintain this position throughout the period of his command, arguing that Hawai'i was "under an expected and constant threat" that necessitated martial law, a regime "purposely designed to meet war conditions of military and civil necessity which were forced upon these fair islands by a new type of fast, long range invasion warfare."[5]

During the period of most comprehensive military rule in Hawai'i, from the attack on Pearl Harbor to March 1943, some 181 general orders were issued over the name of the military governor—31 of them in the first 10 days—affecting virtually every aspect of civilian life. From March 1943, when some powers were returned to the civilian government, until the end of martial law in October 1944, an additional 70 general orders were issued by the military governor, and even after martial law was ended, some two dozen "security orders" and "special orders" would regulate the daily lives of the residents of Hawai'i.[6] Violators of the general orders were subject to arrest by the regular civilian police, the military police, or the shore patrol.

As the territorial attorney general, J. Garner Anthony, recounted at the time, these general orders represented a "military regime with . . . stringent controls over the civilian population."[7] Even Lieutenant General Richardson, who became military governor in June 1943, acknowledged that martial law resulted in "a sudden readjustment of civilian life."[8]

Control was administered by the person who had planned the army's takeover of the government, Lieutenant Colonel Green, who assumed the title of "Executive, Office of the Military Governor" and appropriated the territorial government offices in Iolani Palace. According to Green, at the outset of the military regime "Emmons indicated I was to run the show."[9] Green undoubtedly exaggerated his autonomy; official army records indicate that Emmons, and later his successor, General Robert C. Richardson, made "daily visits" from their commanding general's office in Fort Shafter, from which they directed military operations, to "their Military Governor's Office in order to direct its activities." The Executive, this source continues, was "a steward" for the military governor; "all policies emanated from the Military Governor himself," although Green would often suggest both policies and courses of action.[10] Certainly Green was responsible for the general orders that effected the policies. As Green stated: "Substantially all of these General Orders were verbatim copies of drafts I had prepared long prior to the outbreak of hostilities."[11]

Despite the army's assertion of control, the territorial and county civilian governments continued to coexist—not always harmoniously—with the military government.[12] Elections were held as usual (although candidates of Japanese ancestry were

OMG mascot "Sgt. Toughie" and army private
keep guard at headquarters. Credit: U.S. Army
Signal Corps photo, courtesy of HWRD,
University of Hawai'i.

discouraged from running), and the legislature met in its regular biennial sessions in 1943 and 1945.[13]

Most notably, the Office of Civilian Defense (OCD), created by Poindexter on December 7, functioned as a special department of the territorial government under the authority granted to the governor by the M-Day Act. The OCD immediately absorbed the various committees of Honolulu's Major Disaster Council, which had developed plans in the months leading up to the war to handle emergency requirements of vital functions such as engineering, burial, power, communications, transportation, and water supply. Among these functions, the OCD assumed, with the approval of the Office of the Military Governor (OMG), the registration and fingerprinting of all civilians, ordered under Defense Act Rule No. 14.[14]

The OCD successfully resisted subjecting itself to the Office of the Military Governor. Staffed initially by volunteers, it soon acquired a full-time staff, who were paid by a special appropriation from the federal government.[15] On O'ahu, the OCD's work consisted of protecting the civilian population through such measures as the construction of bomb shelters and instruction in the use of gas masks, administering to medical needs, and providing information to civilians. On the other islands, the OCD served as the main administrative organization of the military governor. In the eyes of the military, the OCD's main, and indispensable, function was "relieving the military for combat duty and providing protection for civilians by civilians."[16]

With the territorial governor issuing more than 150 "defense act rules" in addition to the military governor's general orders, there was considerable confusion in the administration of government, and civilians had to find their way through a maze of military and civilian bureaucracies. But it was the military governor's regulation of their daily lives—from curfews and blackouts to control of labor, supplies, and judicial proceedings—that most deeply affected civilians.

Thus Governor Stainback complained to Ickes in late October 1942: "The so-called 'Military Governor' is still exercising his complete and unrestrained authority over the citizens of the Territory in matters that can have little bearing upon military subjects." He cited, as examples, new general orders regulating speed limits and the numbering of houses in Honolulu.[17] He decried not only the loss of constitutional safeguards of civil liberty but also the incompetence of the military in handling civil matters.[18]

Stainback's newly appointed territorial attorney general, Garner Anthony, detailed the full extent of the military government's reach in a report to the governor one year after the bombing of Pearl Harbor: "At the present time, the 'military governor' exercises control over almost every civilian activity whether governmental or private" with the exception of taxation. Anthony summarized these fields, in addition to military matters, as follows:

(1) The courts, civil and criminal
(2) Municipal affairs, operation of taxi cabs, rent control, rubbish and garbage disposal, house numbering, traffic regulations, one-way streets, no parking zones, and control over police
(3) Labor
(4) The press
(5) The Office of Civilian Defense
(6) Public health, civilian hospitals, and water works
(7) Prisons, jails and insane asylum
(8) Price control
(9) Liquor
(10) Food control and production
(11) Land transportation
(12) Gasoline rationing
(13) Materials and supplies, including all WPB [war production board] functions
(14) Fiscal matters, including the collection and disposition of fines and receipts from liquor commissions
(15) Use of territorial and county properties and institutions
(16) Incarceration of military prisoners in territorial prisons and county jails.[19]

The costs of the military government's operation were borne by the simple expedient of the army's arbitrary takeover of $15 million in emergency funds that were allotted by the president to the territorial governor and the Department of the Interior in February 1942 "for the protection, care and relief of the civilian population."[20] In addition, the Office of the Military Governor held onto all income from the purchase of individual liquor permits as well as fines and forfeitures imposed by the provost courts, applying these funds to meet court costs and general administrative expenses. Deprived of its major sources of revenues, the civilian government complained to the military government, and after protracted negotiations involving the secretary of war and the secretary of the interior, an agreement was finally reached in 1943 by which revenues not needed for the operation of the military government would be returned to the Territory of Hawaii and to the county governments.[21]

And so Lieutenant Colonel Green (soon to be promoted to colonel, then in May 1942 to brigadier general) became, in terms of day-to-day administration, the czar of Hawai'i's civilian life, including civil and criminal law enforcement. He wielded vast power, overseeing every aspect of comprehensive military government, both administrative and judicial. "My authority was substantially unlimited," Green wrote in his recollections of his Hawai'i assignment.[22] It was, Green mused, "very simple to get into an autocratic state in which we believe ourselves infallible. We're not, and it takes a blast now and then [in staff meetings] to keep us in line. . . ."[23]

The scope of the army's general orders reached into every corner of daily life, often with the imposition of policies that deviated dramatically from the norms of peacetime American communities and—in many ways—from the rules that were established during the wartime emergency in the forty-eight mainland states. Japanese alien residents were subjected to additional special regulations to guard against subversion, and for the first two years of the war, these special restrictions applied to residents of Korean ancestry as well.[24]

The army controlled not only the civil and criminal law, but nearly the entire range of federal administrative law that on the mainland was under jurisdiction of the War Production Board, the Office of Price Administration (OPA), the War Labor Board, and other "alphabet agencies."[25] The Office of the Military Governor exercised this control through section heads and administrators who were mainly army officers, albeit many of them had been civilians with reserve officer status that had recently been activated. However, a majority of their staffs were civilians, according to Commanding General Richardson, who also held the title of military governor from 1943 until martial law was ended.[26] Indeed, as stated by one reporter on the scene, "Although final decisions on civilian control measures are up to the military governor, civilian directors have been appointed in all possible categories."[27]

Among the immediate measures taken that profoundly affected daily life were the closing of all schools, both private and public. This action was taken in part to prevent massive loss of life in the event of another air attack and in part to make the school facilities available for emergency work. Boy Scouts, Girl Scouts and other youth groups were pressed into service as messengers, first aid and food workers, and road patrols.[28] Many of the teachers—some 1,100 in O'ahu—were put to work registering and fingerprinting the civilian population, which was compulsory for all civilians except

Commanding General Delos Emmons (seated) with Brigadier General Thomas H. Green, who served under Emmons until mid-1943 as "Executive." Credit: U.S. Army Signal Corps photo, courtesy of HWRD, University of Hawai'i.

infants—the first mass fingerprinting of civilians in U.S. history.[29] Other teachers were pressed into work as censors and civilian enrollment clerks.

The schools remained shuttered for one to two months. When the schools reopened in February, they held classes for four days per week instead of five, as there was soon a shortage of teachers, and older students were needed for harvesting crops or other work deemed essential to the war effort.[30] Students were assigned to such work on the

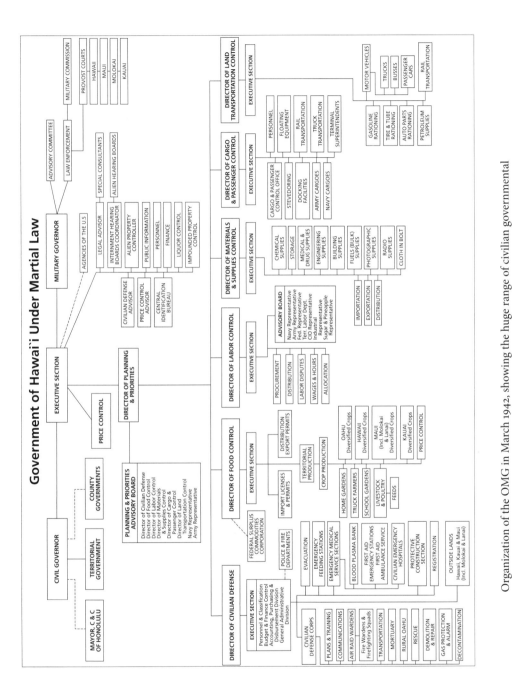

Organization of the OMG in March 1942, showing the huge range of civilian governmental functions under military control of the "Executive Section." N.B. The chart erroneously shows the OCD as reporting directly to the Executive Section; in fact, it resisted direction by the OMG. Credit: Chart is based on General Order 56, Section 3, March 1, 1942, revision, reproduced from Gwenfread Allen, *Hawaii's War Years, 1941–45* (Honolulu: University of Hawai'i Press, 1950).

All civilians in the Islands were required to be fingerprinted—even Mrs. Eleanor Roosevelt, shown in her Red Cross volunteer's uniform while visiting Hawai'i in September 1943. Credit: U.S. Army Signal Corps photo, courtesy of HWRD, University of Hawai'i.

fifth day; it was not a matter of choice. As Richard Chun, a Chinese American who was a student at the time, later recalled, once a week, "All students worked in the pineapple field [or the sugar cane fields or farms vital to the war effort]. . . . And you get graded, too, because there's teachers in the fields."[31] His local school was converted into a hospital, and he had to travel several miles to school. Like many others who had a chance to make good money, he dropped out of school before graduating to work in the defense industry.

Indeed, the Superintendent of Schools encouraged all high-school seniors who were not planning to go on to higher education to "drop out and enter upon regular employment,"[32] and general orders permitted children from twelve to sixteen years of age to work up to forty-hour weeks.[33] These factors, combined with the evacuation of thousands of women and children to the mainland, resulted in a radical drop in school enrollments.[34]

The army also temporarily closed all saloons and prohibited the sale of alcoholic beverages, but pressure from liquor dealers, war workers, and other civilians led to the

Training maneuvers in 1942 on the McKinley High School fields, one indication of how the enormous wartime buildup of army forces made its presence felt in the community.
Credit: U.S. Army Signal Corps photo, courtesy of HWRD, University of Hawaiʻi.

reopening of the bars in February. Enemy aliens, however, were not allowed to buy or sell liquor. Rationing was implemented for liquor sales under army regulations, with each purchaser having to buy a permit from the OMG at a cost of one dollar per permit for sixty days. Dealers violating the law were fined $5,000.[35]

Within a few months of the outbreak of war, the army was also busily regulating gambling (forbidding use of marked cards and dice), traffic and parking, prostitution, and even dog-leash requirements. In addition, hospitals and other emergency facilities were placed under direct military control.[36] Fearing that the enemy might seize cash in case of an invasion, the military government also controlled currency, limiting the amount of cash that individuals could hold to $200 and businesses to $500. In addition, civilians had to surrender their U.S. currency, which was replaced with a new issue bearing a "HAWAII" imprint; the old bills were burned in a crematorium and at the Aiea sugar mills.[37]

Among the most intrusive, and, in the long run, most resented, incursions on freedom were a curfew and blackout that were instituted beginning on the evening of December 7. Initially carried out by the Office of Civilian Defense, the curfew and blackout were controlled by the military governor starting on December 11, when he issued General Orders No. 16. With the exception of military patrols, all cars and busses had

Military guard challenging a civilian who was out after dark. The army's strict curfew continued throughout most of the war. Credit: U.S. Army Signal Corps photo, courtesy of HWRD, University of Hawaiʻi.

to be off the streets by 6:00 p.m., and all civilians were to be off the streets by 6:30. In order to comply with these regulations, most businesses had to close by 3:00 p.m., and restaurants had to stop serving by 4:00 p.m. so their workers could get home before the curfew.[38] The blackout also went into effect by 6:00, although the hours varied according to the time of sunset. Even lighted cigarettes and cigars were prohibited outdoors for the first year of the war. Eventually, the population learned to cover their windows with black cloth or tarpaper, but ventilation in the warm summer nights remained a problem. The curfew was extended in February 1942 until 9:00 p.m., and, a few months later, until 10 o'clock. In summer 1942, a "dimout" replaced the required complete blackout, with the military regulating not only the kind of bulb that could be used, but also the minimum distance between bulbs and the number of square feet to be covered by a single bulb.[39] Following a survey from the ground and the air, the OMG relaxed some of the restrictions: dimout hours were modified by late 1943 and lights were permitted until 10 p.m. in rooms that did not face the ocean.[40] The blackout was lifted entirely in May 1944; vehicles were permitted on the streets only with special blackout headlights until July of that year.

Violations of the curfew and blackout rules constituted a substantial number of the cases that were brought before the provost courts. In the early months of the war, the majority of the violators were of Japanese descent; they were subjected to heavy fines and often jail sentences.[41]

Censorship

Other orders promulgated in the first weeks of the war dramatically abridged the First Amendment rights to freedom of speech and freedom of the press. Individual speech and writing, as well as that of the public media, were regulated by the military. General Orders No. 31 made the use of language that "discourages the vigorous prosecution of the war" a misdemeanor, punishable by up to $1,000 in fines or a year in prison or both; and rigorous censorship was imposed on the press, radio, telephones, cables, and mail.[42]

The army intelligence organization, G-2, under Lieutenant Colonel Kendall J. Fielder, chief of Army Intelligence, was responsible for military censorship, with separate agencies to handle press and radio censorship, postal censorship (civilian mail), theater censorship (army mail), and cable and radio censorship.[43] According to Fielder, "There was no question about the necessity of censorship. If we hadn't had some type of censorship we certainly would have left a loophole for information to leak out."[44]

As early as January 1941, Secretary of the Navy Frank Knox had enlisted the cooperation of the press in abstaining from publicizing ship movements or naval construction.[45] Once the war actually began, however, army censorship in Hawai'i was in marked contrast to civilian censorship on the mainland. National censorship was authorized by Congress in the First War Powers Act of December 18, and the following day President Roosevelt signed Executive Order 8985, creating the Office of Censorship. But Roosevelt had already set the guidelines for censorship at a press conference two days earlier. Noting that "All Americans abhor censorship, just as they abhor war," Roosevelt urged that "such forms of censorship as are necessary shall be administered effectively and in harmony with the best interests of our free institutions." The president also called upon "a patriotic press and radio to abstain *voluntarily* from the dissemination of detailed information of certain kinds, such as reports of the movements of vessels and troops."[46] Byron Price, the executive news editor of the Associated Press, directed the Office of Censorship throughout the war, with army and navy personnel working under his supervision. This office issued its first Voluntary Censorship Code on January 15, 1942, and on the mainland the press remained under a system of voluntary self-censorship throughout the war years.

In contrast, censorship in Hawai'i—a war zone—actually began within a couple of hours of the attack on Pearl Harbor, even before martial law was declared, and military control of the media persisted throughout the war. Anxious to prevent the transmission of any unauthorized information about the attack or its aftermath, the army intelligence organization, in cooperation with the navy, immediately cracked down on telephone, radio, and cable communications. They even cut off General Poindexter's radio announcement that he had invoked the M-Day powers, lest the Japanese home in on the radio signal.[47] Army and navy censors also moved into the newspaper offices and post offices, where they supervised civilian censors for the first few weeks of the war.

The Press

The *Honolulu Star-Bulletin,* one of the territory's two major newspapers, issued its first "extra" on the bombing of Pearl Harbor within two hours of the attack. In that edition and several other "extras" printed throughout the day, they exercised self-restraint in reporting damage and casualties, "perhaps from an intuitive knowledge that it would be giving information and possibly aid and comfort to the enemy," according to its editor, Riley Allen.[48] The other leading paper, the *Honolulu Advertiser,* was less restrained. Under its banner headlines on December 8, "Saboteurs Land Here," it warned of an impending invasion and reported on several unconfirmed acts of sabotage.[49] This brought an immediate summons by Lieutenant Colonel Fielder, of G-2, to Lorrin Thurston, president and general manager of the *Advertiser,* to come to his office. Told that they had better comply with the military's requests "or else," the *Advertiser's* leadership agreed that they would publish no further stories regarding military matters without first checking with G-2. According to Fielder, all reporters and personnel were quickly briefed, and "throughout the war there was no real friction."[50] Their policy was spelled out in a December 13 editorial: "The Military Governor has deemed it in the best interest of the Territory that newspapers and radio stations submit to censorship. The *Advertiser,* fully cognizant of the necessity for such action for the duration of military rule, is happy to comply."[51]

Fielder similarly approached Allen of the *Star Bulletin,* who understood the need for censorship but was less enthusiastic about self-censorship. Concerned that he would "lean over backward and refrain from publishing matters which . . . might be considered certainly publishable," he recommended two external censors, who took up their post in the *Star Bulletin's* offices.[52] The censors were appointed by the military intelligence division, and they worked in close cooperation with the Office of the Military Governor. Subsequently, however, they were withdrawn, and the managing editor of the *Star Bulletin,* Vern Hinkley, was designated as the G-2 censor.[53]

The military did not leave compliance only to such verbal understandings. On December 10, General Green issued General Orders No. 14, which prohibited "the publication, printing, or circulation of all newspapers, magazines, periodicals, the dissemination of news or information by means of any unauthorized printed matter, or by wireless, radio, or press association." Exceptions were made for six newspapers: the *Honolulu Star-Bulletin,* the *Honolulu Advertiser,* the Hilo *Tribune-Herald,* the *Hawaii Press,* the *Maui News,* and the *Garden Isle.* Even these papers were restricted to "such conditions and regulations as shall be prescribed from time to time by the Military Governor."[54] This extraordinary limitation on First Amendment rights was virtually without precedent since colonial days, but because OMG controlled shipping allocations and newsprint, editors had little choice but to comply.[55]

Before the month was out, a number of other newspapers and magazines, including two Chinese papers with translations, were permitted to resume publication, again subject to such restrictions as prescribed by the military governor, and their number was further expanded in January and May of 1942.[56] The two Korean weeklies, which were shut down by General Orders No. 14, merged into the *Korean National Herald–Pacific Weekly;* it was granted permission to start publishing, with an English-language section, in January 1942.[57] For all publications, in any language, any military news was subject to scrutiny by the OMG.

The publication of all foreign language newspapers and of "weekly labor and communistic papers and other uncertain publications" was suspended on December 12, leaving the Japanese-speaking Issei without a news source.[58] Two Japanese-language papers, the *Nippu Jiji* and the *Hochi* (which changed their names to the *Hawaii Times* and the *Hawaii Herald,* respectively, during the war years) were permitted to resume publication in early January 1942, although several leaders of the Japanese-language press, including *Nippu Jiji*'s editor Yasutaro Soga, were among those rounded up in the first FBI sweeps of aliens on December 7.[59] Even before the war, territorial law had required that English translations of all articles in the Japanese language be filed with the territorial attorney general.[60] Once the papers resumed publication, the military censors from the *Star Bulletin* were transferred to the Japanese-language press.[61] The censors made certain that the two Japanese-language papers supported the Americanization movement, and they urged reference to the enemy (as opposed to the local ethnic Japanese community) as "Japs," a word that the Nikkei disliked (and that the *Star Bulletin* resisted using). According to one reporter of the *Nippu Jiji/Hawaii Times,* "We had to write like a mouthpiece all the directives indicated by the U.S. Army, not unlike a phonograph."[62]

Indeed, there was a Counter-Propaganda Section within the army's G-2 intelligence branch that fed editorials to the English-Japanese press and "slanted the treatment of news stories to the end that Allied claims are given perfect credence and Tokyo claims are ridiculed."[63] The Counter Propaganda Section also "coached" some radio commentators and directly controlled others, who were encouraged to issue "stern warnings" to the ethnic Japanese population to speak English, to adhere to the letter and the spirit of martial law, and to demonstrate "loyalty to America for the good of the local Japanese community as well as for the success of the Allied war effort."[64] Such control of the foreign language press was authorized by martial law, although Congress passed an act in 1942 that permitted military control of foreign language papers "whenever necessary to prevent espionage and sabotage."[65] This act allowed the army to control the foreign-language press in Hawai'i even after martial law was terminated in 1944.

Censorship of all the press was particularly strict on matters relating to the conduct of martial law and the military government. To further ensure that the military regime was viewed favorably, the military governor maintained a public relations office to distribute positive press releases. In addition, in November 1942, Thurston, the president and general manager of the *Honolulu Advertiser,* was named "public relations adviser to the military governor," thus effectively silencing any criticism of martial law from this prominent newspaper.[66] Even prior to his official appointment, however, Thurston was a strong proponent for martial law—a stance that he maintained throughout the war.[67] In an editorial on September 4, 1942, after the Battle of Midway had eased fears of invasion, he wrote that Hawai'i was proud to serve as "a test tube and guinea pig" for martial law. "The public has accepted military rule as a fact that is to be with us for no short time," the editorial stated. "It does not ask for its abolition or that Washington turn over all the duties of the military government to civilian authority."[68]

That Thurston did not speak for everyone, let alone Governor Poindexter's successor, Ingram Stainback, would soon become apparent. The *Star Bulletin*'s publisher, Joseph Farrington (scion of an influential political family who was elected in 1942 as Hawai'i's delegate to Congress), and his editor, Riley Allen, chafed at the censorship, claiming that it limited their ability to keep their readers informed. Farrington tried to persuade Congress to restrict martial law, while Allen openly criticized some of the military government's actions, drawing a warning from the authorities.[69]

One year after the war began, the solicitor of the Department of the Interior, Warner Gardner, reported from Hawai'i that he found the press being "rigidly censored" under the licensing system imposed by the army. An editor had been warned, he wrote, against publishing any outright criticism of army rule. The extent of control was made manifest when the *Hilo Tribune Herald*'s offices were briefly padlocked in February 1943 following an editorial that was critical of pressures to get young Nisei men to join the armed forces. Gardner's report continued: "The press cannot report murders and rapes, and cannot discuss prostitution, and cannot even say that prostitution is under Army control. A complete, rigid and entirely illegal [*sic*] censorship is imposed over all mail to the mainland. Telephones are tapped, and recordings made, at will."[70]

A month later, in March 1943, there was a partial restoration of civilian government in Hawai'i,[71] and strict military censorship formally ended. The media in Hawai'i then came under the same voluntary press censorship as existed on the mainland under the federal Office of Censorship. In Hawai'i, however, military personnel maintained a presence and worked closely with the civilian censors throughout the war.[72] According to Allen of the *Star Bulletin*, the press remained "under definite and extensive restrictions as to publication of certain classes and items of news, this through direct requests which in some cases amount[ed] to directives of the Army and Navy commands."[73] Information about number of troops stationed, numbers of military units and their addresses, arrivals of ships and planes, construction of military facilities, military accidents, and travel of prominent civilian officials was all prohibited.[74]

Such control of military news, sometimes in the form of moral suasion, persisted throughout the war. For example, in early 1944, following the publication of stories about Japanese atrocities, there were incidents of Filipinos assaulting Japanese Americans. The JAG officer in charge of the Kaua'i District, where the incidents occurred, "caused the informal suggestion to be made to the local radio station, the local newspaper, and the Filipino weekly, that it might be better if these atrocity releases were not further emphasized at this time."[75] And as late as June 1944, Riley Allen wrote: "Although censorship is described as voluntary, it actually is very rigid in the Hawaiian Islands, with a very tight grip being kept by Navy PRO [Public Relations Office] and Army G-2 on all sorts of matters."[76] The reality of military control was confirmed by Harry Albright, a former *Advertiser* reporter who became a colonel in Fielder's G-2 office: "The restoration [of civilian control in 1943] did not change our operations at all."[77]

Radio

Censorship of radio broadcasts was even stricter than that of the newspapers. The two main stations, KGU and KGMB on Oʻahu, carried immediate reports of the attack on Pearl Harbor. They also cooperated with the military authorities and broadcast calls for all military personnel to report to duty as well as other official bulletins, including the declarations of an emergency and the proclamation of martial law. However, within two hours of the bombings, the military censors ordered them to desist from giving details about the size or exact locations of the attacks.[78] Radio stations did not resume regular broadcasts until December 10, when General Orders No. 14 permitted four radio stations (KGU and KGMB on Oʻahu, and one each on Kauaʻi and Hawaiʻi) and four press associations (Associated Press, United Press, International News Service, and Transradio Press) to operate.[79] They were subject to conditions that were prescribed by the military governor, including the submission of radio scripts in advance. No revisions of text or spontaneous commentary were permitted.[80] Military censors sat in the broadcast control room, making sure—on occasion even at gunpoint—that there were no deviations from the script.[81] Radio was important both for instant communication and as a means of keeping people occupied during the blackout, but Japanese-language broadcasts were prohibited throughout the war.

Mail

The censorship of mail, like the curfew and the blackout, was particularly intrusive in the daily lives of Hawaiian residents under martial law, leading one commentator to call the office of mail censorship the "snip and snoop department."[82] Mail censorship had been carefully planned by the War and Navy departments in advance of hostilities.[83] It began immediately after the Pearl Harbor attack, with an embargo on all mail then in Honolulu, and it grew to involve a staff of several hundred civilian workers. The mail censorship office operated under direct instructions from the War Department to prevent any information of military importance from leaving the Islands. It was initially led by Captain Harold Shaw, an army reserve officer who had graduated from the University of Hawaiʻi and had just returned from specialized censorship training in Washington, DC.

Although the top staff members were army officers, most of the work was done by civilian censors whose ranks included a broad cross section of Hawaiʻi businessmen, professionals, retired teachers, and housewives, including wives of men in the armed services, whose employment as censors allowed them to remain in Hawaiʻi. A special effort was made to recruit those with foreign-language skills, and translators for more than fifty languages were involved in censorship work.[84] For a brief period in 1943, when Shaw was called to Washington, the censorship office was entirely under the civilian control of the National Office of Censorship. Indeed, the censorship of mail from civilians in the territory was among the functions that were returned to the civilian government under the partial restoration of March 10, 1943. In 1944, however, postal censorship reverted to the control of General Richardson and the Office of Internal Security, although its director, Willard Wilson, was a civilian professor at the University of Hawai'i.[85]

Executive Order 9489, issued in October 1944 in conjunction with the end of martial law, specifically authorized the military's regulation of "transmission of information" between Hawai'i and points outside the territory, and as late as July 1945 there were still 250 people working in the Postal Censor's Office.[86] By that time General Richardson, well aware of the public resentment of mail censorship, was fearful of criticism in the local press. He therefore considered switching to a system of "spot-checking" the mail; however, he was persuaded by his staff that censorship was still necessary for local and national security. General Fielder of G-2 thereupon promised to contact the editors of the local papers and point out the continued need for censorship, indicating that he expected the cooperation of the press.[87]

The volume of the censors' work was enormous. In one two-week period, for example, more than 156,000 personal communications had been reviewed, of which 60 percent had been written by war workers. The tally for a single day exceeded 10,000.[88] Sensitive information was carefully excised or blacked out, and a wide variety of materials, from bills of lading to children's drawings, were withheld.[89] The information gleaned by the censors was also used to judge morale among civilians and among war workers, in particular.[90]

Although official government mail was not supposed to be censored, even top civilian administrators, including Governor-Elect Stainback, Department of Justice officials, and Congressional Delegate Joseph Farrington had their communications intercepted, giving the military the upper hand in its struggle with the civilian authorities.[91] As late as December 1944, the censors, now under civilian control but cooperating with the army command, were still opening correspondence between civilian officials in Hawai'i and their superiors in Washington, leading Under Secretary of the Interior Fortas to complain that this was "a serious violation of the right of free and confidential communication."[92] Nor was General Green himself exempt: letters to him from his wife were also censored.[93]

Information deemed of value was passed along by the censors to the intelligence agencies, much to the annoyance of private citizens and business firms, although the censors claimed that they had carried on their work "without intrusion into the American heritage of free thought and free expression," allowing highly unflattering personal assessments of even Roosevelt and the military governor to go forward as long as they contained no sensitive military information.[94] However unpopular censorship was, the military regarded it as absolutely essential when "any householder from his lanai could observe each task force as it steamed from Pearl Harbor, . . . when any schoolboy knew that the roar overhead came from the new B-29s which were poised on Oahu before their breakthrough to Japan."[95] For similar reasons, long-distance telephone calls, too, were monitored, and only English could be spoken.

Whether because of necessity and fear of reprisals or because of a genuine desire not to hurt the war effort, the media on the whole had a cooperative relationship with the military, and censorship was not contested in the courts.

Other Economic and Social Regulations

Among the most urgent matters facing the army command on December 7 was that of supplying the necessities for the civilian and military population, as well as for the defense of the territory. Hawai'i depended on the mainland for vital supplies, and in the immediate aftermath of the attack on Pearl Harbor, the shipping lanes were closed. The Islands imported more than 60 percent of their food, including 95 percent of their rice—basic food for most Hawai'i residents—from the U.S. mainland on a week-to-week basis.[96] Fish, another staple of the diet in Hawai'i, was also in limited supply, since the multi million-dollar commercial fishing industry, which was controlled almost entirely by the Nikkei, was curtailed just on the eve of the war by anti-Japanese legislation that restricted licensing of fishing vessels of five tons or more to U.S. citizens.[97]

General Green's plan to meet this crisis required, in his words, "joint operation by the military and the civilian businessmen together with the civil authorities. The theory behind it was that the military had the power and skill to procure supplies, and the businessmen and the civil authorities had the skill and experience to operate a supply system."[98] The theory, however, did not always work in practice.

As noted earlier, the army assumed control during 1942 of all the wartime functions that were handled on the mainland by the "alphabet agencies," including key administrative units such as the War Production Board, the War Labor Board, and the Office of Price Administration. General Orders No. 56, issued on January 26, 1942, established a Director of Planning and Priorities, who, in turn, supervised six directorships: Civilian Defense, Food Control, Labor Control, Materials and Supplies Control, Cargo and Passenger Control, and Land Transportation Control. Colonel Morrill Marston, the Department of Hawai'i Supply Officer, was appointed the Director of Planning and Priorities. The other positions were filled by prominent civilians.[99] Simply put, the Office of the Military Governor directly supervised, and more generally assumed final oversight of, all the minutiae as well as general functions of administration in the civilian territorial agencies.[100]

Food Production

The military officers in charge were often not familiar with local conditions, nor were they necessarily experts in the areas under their supervision. For example, in an effort

to make the Islands more self-sufficient in food production, the army ordered that po-
tatoes and other vegetables be planted on sugar and pineapple plantations where soil
and weather conditions were ill-suited for such use; the result was described by one
government official as "grotesque, futile and expensive."[101] Following this abortive attempt, the military authorities appointed an advisory committee of civilians, which
recommended smaller plantings with intensive cultivation. The advice was rejected,
and the committee was told, "It must be thoroughly understood that the policies as set
forth by the Military Governor must govern in all instances where practicable."[102] Other
examples of inept management included importing enough carrot seed to plant a significant portion of Oʻahu, despite the fact that the germinating life of the seed was only
six months, and importing enough cheese to last for ten years.[103] The army gradually
gave the growers more discretion, and food production increased. As one agriculturist
quipped, "The Generals don't know that you can't order a plant to grow the way you
can order a soldier to march."[104] A new Office of Food Production was created in November 1942 under the direction of Walter Dillingham, a major local business leader;
he intervened successfully with the military command to allow Nikkei farmers to
remain on their farms and to raise the prices that farmers obtained for food—both
critical measures in increasing food production. In achieving these goals, Dillingham relied heavily on the expertise of Yasuo Baron Goto, a Japanese-born graduate
of the University of Hawaiʻi who had become an agricultural expert with its Extension Service.[105]

Despite shortages of feed, poultry and beef production were sustained, and hog
production thrived as the number of war workers—and their garbage—increased. Restrictions on fishing, and the exclusion of aliens from the offshore fishing waters, greatly
reduced the catches for the war period. In general, however, Hawaiʻi's residents were
not subjected to the food rationing that prevailed on the mainland, and the food supply was adequate, if lacking in the variety that was enjoyed in peacetime. By spring
1943, a visiting member of Ickes's staff reported: "The islands are at present in a most
favorable position compared to most mainland communities in matters of food, clothing and various materials and supplies used by the civilian population."[106] Indeed, the
relative abundance of foodstuffs and other supplies (combined, of course, with censorship) probably contributed to the general acceptance of the military regime by the
civilian population. As Territorial Attorney General Garner Anthony later wrote, "In
short, the Army deprived the citizen of his most cherished possession—the inheritance
of free men—which the founders of this country had waged bloody battles to secure,
and these were supinely exchanged for meat, butter, Kleenex, and liquor."[107]

Price Control

Price control, like food production, was initially placed under the management of the
military governor, with the director of Food Control in charge of regulating sales and
prices of food. The combination of the large civilian and military payrolls brought on

by the war and the limitations on supplies created by the shortage of shipping soon led to inflationary pressures. In May, a Price Control Section was created within the OMG, with the Hawai'i representative of the national OPA serving as its director.[108] Following the lead of the mainland OPA, which in April 1942 froze prices, using March prices to set maximum limits, the military governor in Hawai'i froze prices in May, based on April's prices. The April 1942 price level soon proved unrealistic, however, and there were hundreds of appeals from various industries and providers that were unable to make a reasonable profit.

On March 10, 1943, when civilian authority was restored to many administrative functions, control over prices in the Hawaiian Islands was finally relinquished to the national OPA. The OPA appointed advisory committees of industry and business leaders, and also war price and rationing boards. Gasoline and liquor were rationed, but, in contrast to the mainland, food was not. The OPA gradually adopted specific price schedules to replace the April 1942 price ceilings, adjusting them as conditions warranted to permit a reasonable markup. Although there were the usual complaints about the OPA, it successfully kept prices in check.[109]

Prostitution

The regulation of prostitution, like that of other aspects of economic and social life, became the focus of a struggle for control between the military and civilian governments during the war.[110] Prostitution, although illegal in Hawai'i under both territorial and federal law, had long flourished in the Islands.[111] Its existence was not necessarily regarded as a "social evil" by all elements of Hawai'i's multicultural population; furthermore, its necessity to service the predominantly male plantation workforce as well as soldiers, sailors, and defense workers was widely accepted. As Riley Allen, editor of the *Honolulu Star-Bulletin,* noted, "Acceptance of commercial prostitution had become a *habit.* It was a habit of officials and of the public—a settled frame of mind." The presence in Hawai'i of "hundreds of thousands of members of the armed forces and war workers," Allen said, "in the minds of many men, makes it necessary to have an 'outlet' in the form of houses of prostitution."[112]

Rather than rigorously enforce the laws against it, the Honolulu police department strictly controlled prostitution itself in the years before the war, limiting it to some twenty brothels in which more than two hundred of the prostitutes were compelled to live as well as to work. Each prostitute was registered as an "entertainer" by the police, who charged a license fee of one dollar per year. The prostitutes were medically examined every week, and their lives outside work were tightly regulated: Waikiki beach and fashionable areas of the city were off-limits, they were forbidden to own real property or an automobile, and they could not marry service personnel. Police vice squad members fingerprinted each arriving "entertainer" and enforced—sometimes brutally—residential requirements, curfews, and prohibitions on pimps, on streetwalking, on patronizing bars, and on drugs and alcohol.[113]

As hundreds of thousands of men entered Hawaiʻi just before and during the war, prostitution became a very lucrative business, both for the prostitutes, who sometimes serviced more than one hundred men a day at three dollars for three minutes, and for the madams, who reportedly cleared more than $150,000 each annually. Payoffs, according to some sources, enriched the police, as well.[114] Victor Houston, a former delegate to Congress and a member of the Honolulu Police Commission, tried in vain in the summer of 1941 to close the brothels; his efforts fell on deaf ears in the territorial legislature and in the police commission itself.

By the time the war began, General Green would later recall, prostitution "had reached the proportions where it was a menace to public health, morals and decency. . . . At the outset of the war, this prostitution problem was one of many which were dumped into the lap of the Military Governor."[115] When martial law was declared following the attack on Pearl Harbor, the brothels, like the saloons, were initially closed. Many of the brothels were used to house the wounded, and prostitutes helped to care for the injured. With their living quarters occupied, some of the prostitutes used the closure to defy the rigid police control, move into residences outside the red-light district, and enjoy the freedoms of ordinary civilians. When the brothels were permitted to reopen, not all of the prostitutes returned to their madams.

Both the military governor and Colonel Frank Steer, who as provost marshal was responsible for the military police and law enforcement, were more concerned about preventing venereal disease and keeping up the morale of the servicemen than they were about keeping the prostitutes out of sight. Therefore they initially moved only to clean up the sanitary conditions of the brothels.[116] According to Green, army and navy officials regarded prostitution as "a purely civilian matter, and . . . if the military venereal rate was kept low, they would make no objection nor interfere."[117] On the other hand, the civilian chief of police, William Gabrielson, was determined to keep the prostitutes confined, as before the war, to the Hotel Street red-light district.

The inevitable clash between the OMG and the civilian police came in April 1942, when the police acted on the complaint of local residents and moved to evict four prostitutes from a house in Waikiki. OMG ordered the police to cease their attempts to return the women to the brothels forcibly, maintaining that if the women violated the law, they should be brought before the provost courts. An infuriated Gabrielson leaked an administrative memo to the press, placing control of the vice district directly in the hands of the military, but Emmons refused to relieve the police of their responsibility for civil law enforcement.[118]

The civilian police continued to harass the prostitutes, who were increasingly taking up residence outside the red-light district, and the military police continued to assure the women that they had the right to resist. Finally, in summer of 1942, the prostitutes went on a three-week strike, picketing outside the police department and demanding the right to live where they wished, entertain relatives in their homes, and enjoy the same rights as other citizens. (The newspapers, which were being censored, were not allowed to cover the strike.) More than eighty of the prostitutes presented a signed petition to the OMG—a plea, in the words of General Green's memoir, "for relief from what they considered unjust restrictions which actually amounted to slavery." Although he had shown scant regard for the civil liberties of Hawai'i's citizenry when it came to the restrictions of martial law, Green took up the cause of the prostitutes: "[T]he treatment of these citizens was an extreme case" of the infringement of civil rights, Green wrote after the war, and despite the fact that "[t]here was no glory or favorable publicity in taking care of the rights of these wretches," the OMG moved in to straighten out the matter.[119] While Green's account may be viewed with some skepticism, in fact Emmons and Gabrielson finally worked out a compromise by which the prostitutes could live where they wished and appear in public, but their business had to be confined to the brothels. The military, aided by the Hawai'i Board of Health, would be responsible for maintaining sanitary conditions in the brothels and making sure the women received their regular medical checkups, but other regulations were under police control.[120]

In early 1943, when civil government was partially restored, General Emmons tried to persuade Governor Stainback to take over the regulation of prostitution, but the governor refused.[121] By then, the increasingly blatant activities of some of the "entertainers" were drawing protests from citizens of various neighborhoods, and the Honolulu Council of Social Agencies established a "Social Protection Committee" to work toward the elimination of the houses of prostitution. The committee issued its report, "Prostitution in Honolulu," on August 1, 1944, detailing all the particulars of the brothel system and showing on a map that prostitutes lived in many of the city's neighborhoods. The Honolulu Council of Social Agencies demanded to know where Admiral Nimitz and the military governor stood on the enforcement of territorial laws against prostitution. The military thus had little choice but to abandon its habit of looking the other way regarding the illicit activities of the prostitutes.[122] It is possible that the military's acquiescence to closing the brothels was also influenced by the advent of penicillin, which could cure venereal disease.[123]

Governor Stainback, eager to diminish military control, now became actively involved. In September 1944, he asked the Police Commission to close permanently the houses of prostitution in Honolulu, noting that this action could not have succeeded as long as the military had been unwilling to cooperate.[124] In separate but identical letters to General Richardson and Admiral Nimitz, Stainback wrote that he had been assured by federal and territorial health authorities that the "segregation and control of open prostitution" did not minimize the spread of venereal disease—the only reason that it had been tolerated—and he was sure he could count on the army's and navy's support in enforcing the laws against prostitution.[125] The police vice squad closed the brothels on September 22 with little opposition from the prostitutes, the madams, or their clients.[126] Riley Allen was among those who voiced approval of the fact that "we finally waked up" and ceased "this scandalous violation of the law."[127] Thus the struggle over the control of prostitution—if not prostitution itself—came to a close.[128]

Shipping and Housing

Not surprisingly, given Hawai'i's status as the staging area for the entire Pacific war, regulation of shipping and housing became urgent matters for the military government. In the initial months of the war, the army ordered army and navy dependents to leave the Islands and encouraged women and children in civilian families to relocate to the mainland both for their safety and to reduce the demand for housing, food, and other supplies. Consequently, some thirty thousand were evacuated from the Islands and took up temporary homes, mainly in California and the state of Washington. (One unintentional but significant consequence of this evacuation was that it used up shipping that might otherwise have been allocated to removing many thousands of Japanese Americans from O'ahu.)[129] When months went by and they were unable to return to their homes, the increasingly difficult circumstances—including severe economic deprivation—in which many of these "strandees" found themselves had become a severe embarrassment for the army. Finding places for passage on ships going eastward from Hawai'i was one thing; it was another matter to make space available for their return when thousands of troops and military equipment were being loaded on every available vessel departing the West Coast for the Islands.

Delegate King and Governor Stainback took up their cause, as well as that of a number of Islanders who were caught on the West Coast when war broke out. Among the latter group were seamen of Japanese ancestry, who were denied passage on American vessels.[130] Reporting to the Interior Department on the "exile of numerous Hawaii residents on the mainland" nine months after the attack on Pearl Harbor, Stainback pointed out that many of these women thought they would be gone for a period of a few months only, but the military authorities had decided that anyone who had left the island voluntarily, with few exceptions, could not return. The separation, he said, was causing great hardships on the families and demoralization of the men.[131]

A sympathetic Interior Secretary Ickes approached the War Department about allowing the return of Hawai'i residents, as well as transportation for the wives of war workers, pointing out that with the curtailment of private life resulting from the curfew, "it is in the interest of island morale and defense that men have the companionship which the presence of their wives provides."[132] His efforts, however, were flatly rejected; he was told: "The Department Commander has carefully weighed the advantages of allowing dependents in Hawaii against the disadvantages of committing the necessary shipping to transport and supply these people. He found the latter course not only inadvisable, but impossible."[133] Nevertheless, Governor Stainback, joined by the Citizens Council, continued to urge the return of the strandees, arguing that they would contribute to the war effort and improve morale.[134]

Finally, in November 1942, Emmons announced priorities for transportation from the mainland to Hawai'i. First priority was to be given to personnel of the armed services, male essential government workers, male war workers under contract, and nurses and other female technicians. Second priority was to go to female civil service employ-

Civilians crowd a steamship office seeking transportation to the mainland, a movement encouraged by General Emmons and the OMG, December 31, 1941. Credit: *Honolulu Star-Bulletin* photo, courtesy of HWRD, University of Hawai'i.

ees (without children), businessmen, and other male residents with jobs, and third priority to other women without children.[135] A few months later, in April 1943, the army and the navy issued a joint policy governing transportation to the Hawaiian area from the mainland. Similar in most respects to Emmons's earlier statement, the joint policy gave third priority to residents who had left the Islands prior to the war and who had definite promise of essential war employment; and fourth, "only after all other priority groups have been given passage," to wives and other dependents of island residents.[136] Some 5,000 Hawai'i residents in this last category still remained on the West Coast in late 1943, denied places on Pacific-bound ships and focusing their anger on General Green and the army command in Honolulu, which controlled space allocations. Ickes continued to make it a policy priority to press for return of the civilian strandees, but his office reported in March 1944 that after repeated appeals to the War Department, the Navy Department, and the War Shipping Agency, "the upshot was flat failure."[137]

What made the strandee issue particularly volatile politically was the increasing public recognition that the army was giving priority to the wives of civilian laborers who had been newly recruited from the mainland—contributing, incidentally, to a serious housing shortage in O'ahu—while denying passage to residents who had been evacuated. Moreover, civilian employees of the military and naval services and their contractors apparently were given passage space for vacations on the mainland and return, while the "exiles" remained stranded. As late as February 1944, a frustrated Stainback complained to the Interior Department about the "entertainers" who were being given priority over the strandees: "I am . . . reliably informed that a great number of the so-called defense workers and 'entertainers' who have come down during the past couple of years are merely prostitutes in disguise."[138]

The fact that a significant proportion of the workers being recruited for dockyard and other heavy work in the navy and other military facilities were African Americans may well have added to the resentment that strandees were given such short shrift. Hawai'i was generally regarded as more racially tolerant than the mainland, and in 1939 Samuel Wilder King, Hawai'i's delegate to Congress, wrote an article for *Asia* magazine titled, "Hawaii Has No Race Problem."[139] Nevertheless, bias against African Americans was hardly unknown. Prior to the war, there had been evidence of strong feeling among some elements of the Islands' population, including the nascent unions, against an influx of black labor. Thus, when the army had planned to replace Americans of Japanese ancestry with imported "Negro labor" battalions in security-sensitive areas such as dockyards, an OMG officer recalled, "an immediate protest had arisen from civilian organizations that such action would create a new racial problem," and so the plan was abandoned.[140] The opposition was not exclusively on racial grounds, however; at least some of it was based on opposition to military labor replacing civilian labor. Thus, the same Delegate King who had extolled racial harmony in the Islands successfully urged both the U.S. House of Representatives and the Senate to pass resolutions in April 1941 opposing the use of black labor battalions in the Islands.[141]

After civilian rule was partially restored in early 1943, the governor established an Office of Island Resident Return to deal with the strandee problem. Former governor Lawrence M. Judd Sr. was named administrator of this agency. At year's end, Judd filed a lengthy report complaining of the counterpart military agency, the Travel Section of the OMG, stating that the "general attitude" of the army unit was to act arbitrarily and in violation of terms of a joint policy agreed to by the army and the navy in April 1943, which had stipulated that applications for civilians' return would be submitted to the civilian governor for concurrence after approval by the military governor. Applications for passage from the mainland were not being treated on their merits, Judd averred; information was not being shared with Judd's agency; and priorities were being established and issued to individual applicants without the army's obtaining concurrence of the civilian agency.[142] Among the decisions by the navy that led to friction with the civilian government was the arbitrary establishment of three months' residence in Hawai'i prior to evacuation to the mainland as prerequisite for an individual even to be considered for passage back to the Islands. Ironically, the families of many army personnel, some of them the families of men stationed in combat areas, were among those affected.[143] The last of the strandees were unable to get passage back to Hawai'i until 1945.[144] At a minimum, the strandee or "exiles" issue was a public relations night-mare for the army command.[145]

The housing crisis, like the strandee problem, was in part the result of the lack of shipping. Tens of thousands of defense workers—far outnumbering the evacuees—were imported from the mainland to meet the labor shortage on O'ahu. Many of them in-sisted on bringing their families as a condition of coming to Hawai'i.[146] The housing crisis worsened as the war continued, as more defense workers arrived and some of the evacuees and veterans began to return to Hawai'i. The civilian population of O'ahu increased from 258,000 in 1940 to 348,000 in 1945, with much of the increase attribut-able to defense workers from the mainland. By 1945, less than half of the newcomers to Hawai'i had been provided for, and as many as eighteen men, sleeping in three shifts, shared a single room in "hot bed apartments."[147] The *Honolulu Advertiser,* which un-dertook an advertising campaign in Washington to call attention to the dire state of affairs, summed up the situation: "The ship that brought the man [war worker] failed to bring the materials to house him."[148]

Lack of coordination among the bureaucracies exacerbated the situation: materi-als for new housing were in short supply, and the navy was reluctant to allocate ship-ping until the lumber had been secured; conversely, authorities in Washington would not allocate building materials until the shipping was available.[149] The Interior Depart-ment placed the blame on the army and navy for failing to endorse the urgent recom-mendations of the civilian agencies; without such support from the armed services, the National Housing Agency and the Federal Works Agency refused to act.[150] Finally, in March 1945, a House of Representatives subcommittee came to Honolulu to investi-gate the housing crisis. It concluded that the army and navy had failed to accept re-sponsibility for the housing and health of the community. In addition, the committee found, a lack of coordination among the local and territorial civilian agencies and between the civilian agencies and the military had frustrated rather than expedited a solution to the situation.[151] Officials of the National Housing Administration and the Federal Public Housing Authority came to Hawai'i following the congressional com-mittee hearings, but arguments over the sites for proposed development and shortages of labor and material continued to frustrate their best efforts. Housing remained an intractable problem through the war's end and well beyond.

The housing crisis clearly was an area of policy—similar in that regard to the ar-my's failure to deal well with the strandee issue—in which the military's performance in regulating Hawai'i's civilian life was less than even minimally effective.

Chapter Five

CONTROL OF LABOR

A particularly onerous and eventually much-criticized aspect of martial law— and the source of one of the greatest curtailments of individual liberty—was the army's control over labor, including wartime wages, working conditions, and allocations of workers to industries and firms. Shortages of manpower, and especially of skilled labor, were of major concern to the army command, and the necessity of military regulation of labor was broadly accepted in the early months of the war. Once the threat of a Japanese invasion had receded, however, the control of labor became a focal point of the debate between the military and big business interests on the one side, who insisted on maintaining martial law, and the labor unions, the civilian governor, and the Department of the Interior, who argued for its elimination.

In 1940, there were some 152,000 men and 37,000 women in the civilian labor force in Hawaiʻi, many of them having been imported from the mainland in the buildup of defenses prior to the war. These numbers represented more than 80 percent of the male population and more than 30 percent of the females over fourteen years of age. More than a third of the men and 14 percent of the women were involved with the sugar industry and other forms of agriculture and fishing. The second-largest sector was national defense, which employed more than 29,000 persons, mostly men, working either directly for the army and navy or for army and navy contractors, engaged largely in construction work. Manufacturing (other than sugar refining) and the wholesale and retail trade were the other large sectors, with personal services accounting for nearly one-third of women's work.[1]

The war created acute labor shortages in many fields, and, as noted earlier, women and children were quickly added to the workforce, although their numbers were offset in part by the thousands who evacuated to the mainland. The labor shortage for war work was so severe in early January that several hundred skilled workers were brought in from the New York Navy Yard to repair the damaged ships in Pearl Harbor, and Emmons said he would not hesitate to force labor to work on the Honolulu docks, if necessary.[2]

With the armed services and civilian employers competing frantically for available workers, manpower controls became a matter of urgency. A series of general orders, issued in the name of military security by the Office of the Military Governor (OMG), sought to bring order out of the confusion and ensure that wartime priorities were met, but they also impinged deeply on personal freedoms and contributed to blatant inequities. Less than two weeks after the attack on Pearl Harbor, the military suspended all labor contracts and froze prevailing wages. It also required all civilians working for public utilities, local or federal government agencies, or government contractors and subcontractors—an estimated total of 90,000 workers, or nearly half the workforce—to remain in their positions unless released by their employer. Persons to be employed in the future were required to "report to the job for which they are ordered by the Military Governor."[3] Green admitted that "the freeze order worked a tremendous hardship" on certain lower-paid categories of workers who could have filled higher-paid jobs, but he was convinced that the war emergency demanded a stable labor force.[4] Garner Anthony, then the attorney general of Hawai'i, took a less benign view, reporting to Governor Stainback in December 1942: "Those in command here seem to lose sight of the fact that the Civil War and the Thirteenth Amendment are generally considered to have put at rest involuntary servitude."[5]

To administer the urgent labor situation, General Orders No. 56, issued in late January 1942, established a Director of Labor Control, who reported to the Director of Planning and Priorities in the Office of the Military Governor.[6] Green also established a "Labor Control Board" to advise the Director of Labor Control; its membership consisted of one representative each from industry, the plantations, the AFL, the CIO, the federal U.S. Employment Service, the Territorial Hawai'i Labor Board, the Army Engineers, and the Naval Construction Corps. The labor representatives urged an easing of the military's restrictions on labor, including the return to collective bargaining and the unfreezing of labor in nondefense industries, but their pleas fell on deaf ears—those of the Director of Labor Control, J. Douglas Bond, manager of the Ewa plantation, one of the Big Five's plantations.[7] The appointment of Bond as Director of the Section of Labor Control actually had its origins before the war began, when Lieutenant Colonel Green and two of his assistants in the office of the Judge Advocate General (JAG), Major William R. C. Morrison (later to succeed Green) and Major James F. Hanley, drove through the Ewa plantation and determined that "if ever martial law were declared personnel would be drawn from the plantations to administer labor control, since the example set by Ewa Plantation reflected astute labor policies and relationships."[8]

The same general orders required all able-bodied unemployed men over the age of eighteen to register with the U.S. Employment Service, and all businesses and public agencies were ordered to notify the Employment Service of any persons added to or dropped from their payroll. Failure to comply with these orders carried a fine of $1,000 or up to a year's imprisonment, or both. The U.S. Employment Service, with offices in Honolulu, Maui, Kaua'i, and the Big Island, thus became the central agency for allocating

The military government required the registration of all women over sixteen years of age. Albert Waterhouse, director of the Office of Civilian Defense, and the OCD's registration division staff at work in the basement of Kawaiahao Church. Credit: *Honolulu Star-Bulletin* photo, courtesy of HWRD, University of Hawai'i.

all civilian labor for both public and private payrolls. Such allocations, however, were to be in accordance with the priorities established by the Director of Labor Control in the OMG. Not surprisingly, the army and navy, defense contractors, civilian defense, and public utilities had priority over nondefense industry.[9]

Registration for all women over the age of sixteen was mandated in November 1942. Women who were not working were not compelled to work, but those already employed had to register with the U.S. Employment Service and accept assignment to new jobs within seventy-two hours of losing a job. More than half of women were soon working outside the home, some having taken employment for fear they would otherwise be evacuated, with others volunteering for the Red Cross and other service agencies.[10] As a result of these and other measures—including the large importation of defense workers from the mainland—there was an eight-fold expansion in the number of workers employed by the federal government between 1940 and 1944.[11]

Much more sweeping control of labor was instituted under the terms of General Orders No. 91 in late March 1942, when stevedores and hospital workers were added to the categories of labor under control of the military governor, that is, public utility workers, all government workers, and all those working for government subcontractors. General Orders No. 91 also regulated hours of work and wages, and established an appeal mechanism for workers. Job-switching and absenteeism from work without an employer's permission were now made criminal offenses: workers in the designated categories were made subject to prosecution in the provost courts and to fines or imprisonment of up to two months' time for unauthorized absences from work or attempts to change jobs without permission.[12]

According to civilian leaders on the Islands, absenteeism was one of the crimes most frequently punished with jail sentences. In the early days of the war, individual employers filed charges against absent employees directly with the provost courts, but the procedure was soon regularized, with reports going to the Labor Control Office in the OMG. The Director of Labor Control stated that 96 percent of workers reported for absenteeism were returned to their jobs without being brought before the provost courts. On their first offense, they received a warning letter; on their second offense, they were summoned for an interview and an "investigation" of their case. Violators were prosecuted only on their third offense, by which time they were regarded as "extreme incorrigibles." What the general orders termed a "failure to report to work" was interpreted by the provost judges as giving them authority to convict and punish for absences of even only a few hours. Most of those offenders being prosecuted for absenteeism for the first time were given fines of $150 to $200 (about two weeks' wages) and suspended sentences, although sentences of two months were fairly common.[13] Even those sentences were suspended, and the absentee was placed on probation for six months if he agreed to return to work. Nearly 1,350 cases (in which only about 11 percent of the defendants were ethnic Japanese workers) came before the provost courts involving the violation of labor laws, with absenteeism on the waterfront posing a particularly intractable problem.[14]

The harsh treatment received by "flagrant absentees" before the military courts was probably encouraged by the top army legal officers, as evidenced by the advice given the provost officers at a May 1944 conference of all the provost judges: because his office sought to "rehabilitate" such delinquents, the supervisor of the provost courts advised the judges, the typical defendant had already "had every chance" to correct his work habits before being prosecuted. "When all patience is exhausted, he is brought up before you for prosecution. To the best of my knowledge, we never lost a case in Provost Court."[15] Furthermore, he suggested that in every labor case the provost court should sentence the defendant to hard labor: "When they get to the places of incarceration," he explained, "they will be put on HARD LABOR anyway."[16]

Under pressure from the Department of the Interior, General Robert Richardson Jr., who succeeded Emmons as military governor on June 1, 1943, amended the general orders shortly after this May 1944 conference to abolish jail sentences for absentees unless the convicted party could not pay the fine. But even that move, as Under Secretary of Interior Abe Fortas pointed out, could be fairly characterized as "still a far cry from restoration of an American system of values in Hawaii."[17]

A particularly disturbing aspect of the labor policy was the way in which it was administered against the stevedores and other workers on the docks in Honolulu: it was they who were most often prosecuted for absenteeism. The contracts that the International Longshore and Warehouse Union had negotiated on behalf of the dockworkers in 1941 were set aside by general orders that froze the men in their jobs and froze wages.[18] The exigencies of tight shipping schedules and sensitive military and naval operations in the harbor facilities, the army contended, meant that there was an "absolute necessity of keeping the men on the job. . . ."[19] In 1943 alone, there were some 680 prosecutions for "flagrant absenteeism," of which 44 percent were on the waterfront. General Richardson attributed the high absentee rate in part to what he termed the "traditional laxity here of the work habits of the Filipinos" who had replaced Japanese Americans on the waterfront, and in part to the seventy-hour work weeks that were necessitated by labor shortages and the urgency of moving the cargo.[20] The absentees themselves usually cited poor health or, in the cases of the many defense workers brought under contract from the mainland, an inability to adjust to the living conditions of Hawai'i.[21]

The Army and Big Business

Among other aspects of military control of labor that received much criticism were the "sweetheart deals" with the large plantations. The close relationship between the military and the Hawaiian Sugar Planters' Association (HSPA) that had developed in the 1930s continued during the war years, and went far beyond the appointment of Bond as director of the Section of Labor Control. Some district army commanders in the outer islands froze plantation workers to their jobs and denied them permits to travel to higher-paying jobs in O'ahu. On O'ahu, there was an informal but effective agreement that the army and navy and their contractors would not hire plantation field hands directly, but the pineapple and sugar companies contracted out the same workers to the army for military construction projects and for work on the docks.[22] The plantations supplied more than 200,000 man-days of labor to the Army Engineers during the war.[23] The army defended this effective conscription of civilian workers because the arrangement assured that construction deadlines would be met, while compensation to the plantation companies was consistent with cost-plus contracting rules then in effect.

The plantation companies, not the workers, pocketed the difference between the going rate for field labor—forty-two cents per hour, plus nine cents for perquisites—and the sixty-two cents per hour paid to labor contractors.[24] By the end of the war, the plantations had received some $6 million for their loans of labor and equipment.[25] Although defense workers were forbidden by the U.S. Engineering Department from discussing hours and wages with the loaned plantation workers, it was impossible to keep such matters quiet. The plantation workers, early in the war, could only look enviously at those who worked directly for defense contractors at much higher wages, but their pent-up resentment helped speed union organization on the plantations later in the war.[26] The close relationship between the planters and the army was not all one-way, however; under a directive from President Roosevelt, soldiers were to be released to salvage crops, and dozens of volunteer soldiers earned 45 cents per hour in addition to their military pay to harvest pineapple in Kaua'i.[27]

Other industries, too, benefited from special relationships with the army. For example, cannery workers and stevedores were transferred to the army between shifts, and then returned to private industry when needed there.[28] Army and navy construction workers were also loaned to several civilian projects, including a new wing for Queen's Hospital in Honolulu, the completion of a power plant for the Hawaiian Electric Company, and the construction of housing units. General Richardson, in taking credit for such arrangements, noted the private sector's "inability to obtain necessary labor from civilian sources," without, of course, acknowledging that the army's own allocation of labor was at least partially responsible for the unavailability of labor in the private sector.[29] The powerful corporate interests in the Islands were given significant incentives by such measures to line up in support of the army when the military encountered criticism for martial law; and when labor threatened to sponsor job actions, as happened very late in the war, the army could be relied upon to weigh in on the employers' side in the name of sustaining the Islands' security and readiness.[30]

The business community's general support for the army was reflected in the way that the Honolulu Chamber of Commerce became a reliable ally of the military governor. Thus, in December 1942, the vice president of the Chamber assured General Emmons that "most persons [in Hawai'i] appreciate and concur in the policies regarding martial law versus civil authority."[31] And a few days later, when rumors from Washington indicated that army control of the Islands' economy might be curtailed, the Chamber's leadership issued statements of public support for the commanding general and sent cables to Washington urging that the military be left with all its powers intact—asserting, for good measure, that "our Military Governor has been eminently fair and considerate of our civil rights this past year."[32] Garner Anthony, then territorial attorney general, confronted Frank Midkiff, president of the Chamber and one of the giants of the territory's business and education communities, and asked why the cables had made such claims concerning civil liberties. "Midkiff told me that the Chamber was not interested in the courts or the rights of civilians," Anthony reported to the delegate in Congress, "but was only interested in the obtaining of priorities and the freezing of labor."[33] According to Delegate Farrington, the action of the Chamber of Commerce had "seriously prejudiced" its position with important officials in Interior and Justice, with potentially far-reaching consequences.[34]

Although doubtless there were shades and variations of opinion in the business community, the prevailing interpretation of such incidents in the Department of the Interior was that the army and the major corporate interests were working in tandem, under the banner of patriotism and wartime loyalty, to maintain a tight hold on the working people of the Islands. Perhaps the harshest expression of this view—which had an important impact on the position of the Interior Department in policy negotiations over Hawai'i[35]—came from the director of the Division of Territories and Island Possessions, who advised Secretary Ickes in May 1944 that "a small number of fascist-minded business men" were mainly responsible for the way in which the rights of laborers were being handled so abusively in Hawai'i. "They are influential with the 'Office of the Military Governor,'" he wrote:

> This group favor the military regime with all its stringent controls of labor, severe and arbitrary penalties for infractions of orders. To be sure, they want to win this war, but they are also interested in profits and find it extremely convenient to obtain whatsoever they desire in the form of an order from the military authorities. They are not hampered either by democratic processes, such as legislation, or by territorial civil servants who, as a rule, are far more able to deal with the shrewd men of business than the average army officer.[36]

The Labor Unions under Military Government

The labor unions, led mainly by leftist organizers, had enjoyed some success in unionizing workers on the docks and the plantations just before the war; indeed, the stevedores had won their first union contract in Honolulu in June 1941. The unions had also made inroads with hotel workers, the transit workers, brewers, and the Dairymen's Association. As thousands of defense workers entered Hawai'i in 1940 and 1941, union membership swelled from 3,500 to 10,000 just before the war.[37] The labor controls of the military government, however, virtually halted unskilled labor union activity, at least temporarily.

The unions showed little inclination to resist army control until 1943. While the American Federation of Labor (AFL) continued to organize skilled workers, especially the tradesmen who flocked from the mainland to highly paid defense work in Hawai'i, the International Longshore and Warehouse Union (ILWU) and other Congress of Industrial Organizations (CIO) unions saw their membership drop precipitously in the early years of the war. Stevedores of Japanese ancestry were excluded from military areas, including port facilities, and their leaders were intimidated by the fear of internment or of the provost courts—or worse. For example, in at least one instance, an informer for military intelligence actively tried to dissuade Nikkei plantation workers near Hilo from participating in union activities, which he claimed were "subversive of the war effort."[38] Jack Kawano, a Nisei who had organized the longshoremen and was president of ILWU Local 137, was barred from the docks by the army, and his counterpart in Kaua'i, Ichiro Izuka, was arrested and detained for four months. And when labor organizer Arthur Rutledge planned to picket a restaurant that had broken its contract with the union, the military officer in charge of labor threatened him with "a bayonet up his arse."[39]

Although some union leaders privately referred to the Office of the Military Governor (OMG) as "One Mighty God,"[40] far from pressing for removal of absenteeism as an offense triable in provost courts, the top union brass typically adopted a posture of "supine acquiescence," and, as a patriotic act, the unions followed a "no strike" policy until the fighting in the Pacific theater had nearly come to an end. Indeed, for the entire year of 1942, labor gave up holidays and surrendered its collective bargaining powers.[41] As one longshoreman's union official reported, the war had left the largely Japanese membership of Local 135 "confused and dispirited, and fearful of activity. Being of Japanese extraction, whether citizens or not, . . . they were not only made to feel suspect, but were in fact suspected, and in many cases, openly so." As a result, he reported, they will pitch in and do their part for the war effort and the community as asked, but "as individuals and not as Union men."[42]

The OMG, of course, denied it was antiunion, and in at least one case, that of the Stevedores Union, the military government actively enlisted union support. Efficient operations on the docks were critical to the entire war effort, yet the docks were in disrepair and highly flammable, "presenting a paradise of opportunity for saboteurs," in the words of an army intelligence officer.[43] Many of the stevedores were Japanese Americans, but there were also Filipinos, Chinese, Hawaiians, Portuguese, and Caucasians among the dockworkers, creating considerable racial tensions. Army Intelligence, after a thorough investigation of the union leaders, summoned the leadership to a meeting in late December 1941 and placed responsibility on the union to provide security and efficiency on the waterfront. This co-optation tactic worked: the union undertook investigations of its own membership, formed safety committees and fire brigades, and urged increased effort on the docks, thereby earning the praise of the OMG.[44]

Possibly the relative cooperation of the unions was also attributable to the curious fact that the military government—with the full approval, apparently, of the major employers—generally pursued a more liberal policy toward wage increases and misgrading of employees so as to allow higher pay scales than would have been permissible by strict application of the War Labor Board (WLB) standards imposed on the mainland. Contrary to this pattern, on the other hand, the army regulations mandated work weeks of six days of eight hours each on all war projects, and a mandatory seventy-hour week was not unusual on the docks or on the bus lines; nevertheless, overtime pay became effective only after forty-four hours' work, despite provisions of the Fair Labor Standards Act of 1938 that explicitly required overtime scales on work in excess of forty hours.[45] Indeed, Hawai'i was largely exempt, at least in the first year of the war, from most of the national regulations of wage and price controls, and there was a real increase in the purchasing power of wages.[46]

Military vs. Civilian Control of Labor

The importance of a stable labor supply to the successful prosecution of the war, which had been a central tenet of the military regime, was not lost on those who wished to see an end to martial law. Nevertheless, Interior Secretary Ickes was steadfast in his opinion that "[n]either labor shortage nor military interest can, in a democratic nation, justify a regimentation of free labor by military edict and enforced by punishment by a military tribunal."[47] While the departments of Interior and Justice wanted the military to relinquish all control of labor, the War Department adamantly refused. Following a series of talks that began in Washington in December 1942 among cabinet officials, Governor Stainback, Territorial Attorney General Garner Anthony, General Green, and others, a compromise agreement was reached for partial restoration of civilian controls.[48] The resulting proclamation, issued on February 8 and effective on March 10, 1943, returned to the governor and territorial, federal, and local civilian agencies "control of the supply, employment, hours, wages, and working conditions of labor" *except* as to employees of the army and navy and their contractors, stevedores and other dock workers, and public utilities workers.[49] These very large exceptions remained under the control of the military.

Ickes was anxious to know which functions Governor Stainback proposed would be exercised by the governor and territorial authorities and which would be exercised by federal agencies with the partial restoration of civilian control.[50] Indeed, the control of labor in Hawai'i was confusing at best: The national War Manpower Commission (WMC), the federal agency that had been created in April 1942 to oversee the allocation of manpower, had named Newton Holcomb as its Hawaiian territorial director. At the same time, Holcomb was appointed by the army as manpower adviser to the military governor, but most of the real power was being exercised by J. D. Bond, the director of Labor Control within the OMG.[51]

"The most important single issue confronting us March Tenth," Governor Stainback replied, "is labor control by reason of the fact that many groups will be unfrozen who may seek change of employment."[52] Stainback therefore proposed a temporary measure that would prevent worker flight from critical industries. Acting under the powers of the Hawai'i Defense Act, Stainback issued Rule No. 42 for control over labor not still under jurisdiction of the OMG. The civilian regulations required all persons over the age of eighteen who were not employed to register with the U.S. Employment Service, which had to be notified of all additions to and separations from employment; thus, the U.S. Employment Service remained the central clearinghouse for all labor—for the workers controlled by the military as well as for those under the civilian government. Rule No. 42 also provided for a seven-member Hawaii Manpower Board, with representation from both industry and labor unions, to oversee the implementation of civilian labor policy; and the governor appointed a new Director of Labor, L. Q. McComas. Certain industries, including dairy and hospital operations, were designated as "essential." A small three-person board was appointed for each of these designated industries to establish fair labor standards of wages and hours, and employees of those industries were not permitted to leave their jobs except on appeal to the Director or the Board.[53]

Governor Stainback's appointees to the new territorial Hawaii War Manpower Board included three management members and three labor representatives—among them Arthur Rutledge and Jack Kawano, both militant organizers who were solicitous of the welfare of Nikkei workers and who were regarded with deep suspicion by the army brass. An impartial chairman, Robert Beasley, and Newton Holcomb, the national

War Manpower Commission's director for Hawai'i, were the other members. Garner Anthony, the prominent critic of the martial law regime who was then serving as the territory's attorney general, sat in on meetings to advise on legal issues, provide guidance on devising procedural rules, and represent the governor's views on major policy issues.[54] As with labor under military control, "a high incidence of absenteeism" soon became a problem, with the chairman of the Hawaii War Manpower Board reporting to Stainback that it constituted "a serious threat to the war effort."[55]

In accordance with the division of control over labor, a new General Orders No. 10 was issued on March 10, 1943, which narrowed the range of the military's control of labor to include only workers directly involved with defense—those in the employ of the army, the navy, their contractors, and workers on the docks and in public utilities. Close to 100,000 workers were thus affected.[56] The regulations regarding registration, job freezes, and wages and hours of work were similar to those in earlier general orders; so, too, were the criticisms of their fairness and efficacy.[57]

The freezes on jobs that were continued under General Orders No. 10 apparently failed to prevent turnover in vital employment. Of the tens of thousands of workers who had poured into Hawai'i in 1942 to work on defense contracts, a high percentage returned to the mainland after their contracts expired rather than be "re-frozen" into another lengthy contract. Local workers were able to escape job freezes by the simple tactic of provoking their own discharges. Although such workers would then be discharged "with prejudice," they were readily able to find other employment. From the worker's standpoint, the system, which gave total discretion to the employer, resulted in inequitable and arbitrary decisions: some employers released their workers freely and others set harsh conditions, especially since employers were not even required to show cause for discharging a worker. In any case, the Section of Labor Control in the OMG, which was responsible for the quasi-judicial function of handling appeals, was allegedly staffed by personnel with few qualifications for the job.[58]

Absenteeism continued to be widespread. Although the provost courts remained ready to prosecute cases brought to their attention, several separate reports, each covering a separate absence, had to be filed before an individual could be brought into court. One of the supervisors involved in employment administration under General Orders No. 10 warned Stainback that "the OMG labor controls—loosely set up, loosely administered—have proved disruptive rather than stabilizing. Oahu would not now have a labor shortage if only 25% of the Mainland workers here within the past two years had remained. From very close contact with these workers, the fact emerged that many of them would have remained had it not been for what they considered the inequalities of the labor controls in force."[59]

In an effort to address the labor shortage, Stainback launched the "Governor's Work to Win Campaign," enlisting the business community's support in increasing efficiency, reducing absenteeism, and encouraging individuals not currently employed to join the labor force.[60] The problems persisted, however, and the governor's Hawaii War Manpower Board became increasingly frustrated, over the course of six months following its establishment in March 1943, in its efforts to devise an effective stabilization program affecting wages, movement of workers among jobs, and interisland migration. The basic problem that was confounding their intentions, it had became clear, was what members referred to as the "hydra-headed" nature of the Islands' labor regime—or, rather, *labor regimes,* in the plural—in which the army and territorial authorities controlled distinct segments of the labor force.

Holcomb, now wearing three hats—as director of the Hawai'i office of the federal War Manpower Commission (WMC), as labor adviser to the OMG, and as member of the Hawaii War Manpower Board—pressed hard for a "unified" regime, in which the army would coordinate with, but not have final authority over, a comprehensive program regulating the entire workforce of the territory.[61] At first cautiously, but after a few weeks, more outspokenly, Anthony lined up with Holcomb. He was thus recorded in the May 17 meeting as doubting outright "if any effective program could be worked out unless it were to revoke the authority of the Military over labor."[62] Anthony made clear that this was also Governor Stainback's position. By that time, the national emergency agencies in Washington were also intervening directly. Thus in April, Paul McNutt, the director of the federal WMC, weighed in on the side of Holcomb and Anthony, declaring the need for a unified program.

The union representatives on the Hawaii War Manpower Board also favored a unified plan and cutting back on the army's authority. These labor members advocated that a "rule of reason" should be applied in the hearing of appeals from workers who might otherwise face stringent penalties for absenteeism or job-changing that affected the war effort—a concern that Anthony promised to address in drafting new regulations.[63] Despite the conviction of General Richardson and his staff that Rutledge was an extremist bent on bringing the army and the business community to their knees at any cost, in fact during the board's deliberations Rutledge did not object to the continuation of comprehensive regulatory controls, so long as the enforcement power was not vested in the provost courts (as it was under the military's labor regime). Determined as Rutledge and the other labor leaders undoubtedly were to bring a union shop regime to Hawai'i, they thus adopted a compromise position and aligned themselves with the Stainback administration and with Holcomb on the basic issues of labor controls during 1943 and 1944.[64]

The board's management representatives, on the whole, did not raise serious objections to the concept of a unified regime; yet, it is worth recalling, these businessmen enjoyed a comforting reliance that the OMG would resist excessive concessions to the interests of labor.[65] The military, however, continued to cling tenaciously to control of its sector of the labor force, and in this they did have the support of at least some of the larger business interests in the territory. In June 1943, the Central Labor Council of the AFL requested of General Richardson that the military give up *all* control of labor, stating that "the continuing of Military rule, however enlightened or paternal, is incompatible with the rights of a free people in a democracy."[66] In response, Richardson asserted that control needed to remain with the army and navy, and that the importance of such control was a primary reason for maintaining martial law.[67] Far from agreeing to reduce his role, Richardson suggested to the governor that the Hawai'i War Manpower Board survey all labor that was not currently working on military and naval projects with an eye toward channeling such labor toward defense projects, since a shortage of labor was on the horizon.[68] Backed by Admiral Nimitz, who was commander in chief of the Pacific Ocean Areas, and by McCloy, Richardson was able to forestall any efforts to eliminate military controls of labor.[69]

As these conflicts over policy continued, some seventy companies in Hawai'i, led by the Big Five, joined together in August 1943 to form the Hawaii Employers Council to work out plans for relations between employers and employees.[70] Although labor was given a seat at the conference table, the Employers Council was widely viewed as an organization created specifically to counter the strength of organized labor.[71] Writing to Secretary of the Interior Ickes, Governor Stainback warned that the employers intended to keep Honolulu an open shop town and would shut their doors "rather than submit to union domination." The pro-military and antilabor groups were creating a serious situation, Stainback wrote. "These people, seeing that the dock worker who for any reason fails to show up on his job is given a severe prison sentence by a provost judge, would like to have such proceedings available to them in dealing with their labor. So the pro-military and the anti-labor have this point in common." Some of the employers who had labor problems, Stainback noted, would "welcome the assistance of the armed forces in settling them." He worried that the antilabor business leaders would work with the military "to effect a complete restoration of military government here"—a contention that McCloy would vigorously deny.[72]

Amidst this turmoil over labor—and the concomitant, deeper issue of continuing martial law—the U.S. Department of Labor sent its own representative, John Ring, to investigate the situation in Hawai'i in the summer of 1943. He reported late that year that the military and the administrative agencies it had created were operating systematically in favor of management interests over the interests of labor—a claim hotly denied by General Richardson, who denounced the report as a "scurrilous libel upon the War Department and my administration here." Defending his management of labor as having met the needs of the army, the navy, and "responsible" labor and business leaders, Richardson condemned the criticism as nurtured only by the "radical element of labor in the territory" that was expressing a view "not concurred in by the established stable element of labor in this community." While he acknowledged that the Director of Labor Control in the military government was a former plantation manager, Richardson asserted that "the labor on plantations is not under the jurisdiction of the Military here"—rather disingenuously overlooking the sweetheart deals that made plantation labor available for defense projects.[73]

Richardson further insisted on the fairness of the appeals machinery for handling grievances and transfers of workers between jobs. He denied charges that he had tried to stop union organization and noted the gains in union membership since partial restoration of the civilian government in March. However, contrasting the "recognized leaders of responsible organized labor" with the radical leadership that was concentrating its organizing efforts upon ethnic Japanese workers, he attested that the latter's real objective was to have "the army divested [of] control of labor[,] . . . a forerunner of another direct attack on martial law itself." No doubt Richardson's verbal attack on the radical leadership was prompted by a slowdown by the largely Nikkei bus drivers on the Honolulu transit system in July, and by a walkout in August by predominantly Nikkei workers of Theo. H. Davies, one of the Big Five. Withal, Richardson concluded, the radical element was trying "to organize labor *along subversive lines,* which then becomes a matter of military security," and thus, implicitly, a justification for the continuation of martial law.[74]

For Richardson, the control of labor remained a key issue in discussions about relinquishing martial law. In late January 1944, he wrote confidentially to McCloy: "I am studying the local situation with a view to proposing the elimination of martial law." If martial law were terminated, he wrote, "Some sort of control of labor would appear to be necessary in the prosecution of the Army and Navy contracts, particularly the operations at Pearl Harbor."[75] Taking a directly opposing view, L. Q. McComas, the Hawai'i Director of Labor and Industrial Relations, could "see no reasonable excuse" for the continuation of military control of labor, which, he argued, had been imposed to assure the proper prosecution of the war in a combat zone. But since the territory "is no longer considered a combat zone," he contended, "then with civil control established," with the federal War Manpower Commission and the federal War Labor Board, "the need for military control of labor falls of its own weight."[76]

Continuing tensions over labor controls were exacerbated by a background of admitted inefficiencies and predictable complexities that a fragmented labor plan involved. Any hopes that the workforce controls imposed under the M-Day Act powers, as exercised through the recommendations of the territorial labor committee, would quickly produce an efficient labor regime were soon disappointed.

In counterpoint with these developments, the governor's War Manpower Board continued its debate of basic policy. By May of 1943, the board had coalesced in general support of the plan advocated by Holcomb and his allies—a plan that was consistent with Stainback's ideas—for a unified labor regime. The plan called for administration by the civilian authorities, under the framework of national regulations to be instituted by the federal War Manpower Commission for purposes of labor stabilization, including allocation of workforce having high priority for the war effort, work rules, and inter-island travel. Regulations would be formulated and implemented with the army and navy in a "liaison" relationship with the new regime.[77] Pursuing the same general strategy of re-asserting national rules and national agency regulations, Rutledge and his labor union colleague Jack Owens were pressing also for the assertion of authority in Hawai'i by the National War Labor Board, an agency whose regulation of union organization and industrial relations predictably would be more favorable to the unions than either the OMG policies or even the M-Day law's application up to that time.[78]

General Richardson and his legal staff in the OMG wanted no part of a mere "liaison" relationship that would involve surrendering one iota of its authority over labor. Persistence of the stalemate over many months was assured by the posture of Colonel William R. C. Morrison. A veteran of World War I, he had arrived in Hawai'i in January 1941 and was General Green's assistant in preparing the detailed plans that permitted martial law to be implemented immediately on December 7. Morrison had then replaced Green as the Executive to the military governor in April 1943. Morrison flatly refused even to meet with the labor board or other territorial officers to discuss giving up the "hydra-headed" concept and substituting a unified regime.[79] Any discussions regarding Hawai'i's labor regime with a view toward compromise, in the official view of the OMG from March 1943 to mid-1944, would be giving in to a sedulous Trojan Horse tactic, opening this island "fortress" to a devastating undermining of control over security.[80]

Richardson viewed the governor's labor board as an instrument being used at the forefront of a "campaign" by Stainback, Anthony, and Farrington, "the prime instigators of the fight against the military," to do away with martial law. As for Holcomb's role, Richardson deplored his "decided inclination to play along with the radical union element," which the general regarded as a self-interested tactic; Holcolmb's longer-term goal, he charged, was to win for himself the role of director in the proposed new unified labor regime that would subordinate military and security interests. Although Richardson conceded that the OMG regime was "labor regimentation of the strictest order," he claimed that it was generally admired in Hawai'i and was being opposed mainly by the radical unionists. "The honest defense worker" had proven entirely willing to accept the Army's regulations. Any essential defense worker who was an absentee illegally, under these rules, was "in effect on the same footing as any soldier in this theater who goes AWOL," Richardson asserted; moreover, the swift process and heavy hand of the provost courts was essential for maintaining "this control and discipline."[81]

Sidestepping the OMG resistance to the emergent plan, however, Director McNutt of the national War Manpower Commission had begun to take action following his May 1943 announcement that he would designate Honolulu as a "critical labor area." Thus he was setting the stage for his imposition of a federal Employment Stabilization Program, with authority over all sectors, including what the army and navy had marked out under their own control as workforces "vital" to the war effort. In October, this plan became official, as McNutt's commission extended to all workers not covered by OMG jurisdiction in Hawai'i the same rules for stabilization of labor that applied in areas of critical manpower shortages on the mainland. Although workers still were required to obtain a release from their job in order to accept alternative employment, and such employment had to be referred by the U.S. Employment Service, the appeals process took into account personal factors such as working conditions and skill utilization. Shortly thereafter, the OMG amended General Orders No. 10 so that it applied only to O'ahu, thus effectively ending the military control of labor on the other islands.[82]

The military controls over nearly 100,000 essential workers on Oʻahu, however, continued to outrage Governor Stainback. He noted that despite the harsh penalties meted out by the provost courts for absenteeism, the continuing absentee rate for labor under military control exceeded that for labor under civilian control. Stainback was convinced, he wrote to Secretary Ickes in early 1944, that if existing federal regulations of wages and manpower were fully applied to Hawaiʻi,

> the war program here would benefit thereby; that there would be a better spirit among labor, a wiser use of labor, and a decrease in absenteeism. *Labor under military control here is a form of involuntary servitude enforced as it were at the point of a bayonet.* . . . [F]urthermore, it is, as stated above, not effective control.[83]

In particular, Stainback and the Hawaiʻi War Manpower Board wanted the federal War Labor Board to extend both its wage stabilization and dispute resolution controls to Hawaiʻi; so, too, did the national WMC.[84] By May, the OMG, no doubt foreseeing the inevitable, suggested to McCloy that it would be advisable to "explore immediately" the possibility of having the War Labor Board establish an office in the territory; it also suggested that the army be credited with bringing the WLB to Hawaiʻi in any publicity that might be issued.[85] The following month, the OMG relinquished its role in settling labor disputes to the WLB, much to the satisfaction of labor, but it did not give up its overall role in administering labor.[86]

Union Resistance to Military Controls

The unions were significant players in bringing Hawaiʻi under the jurisdiction of the War Labor Board. By early 1943, after a year of cooperation and a no-strike policy despite mandatory long workweeks, labor was becoming restive under the military's control. A series of impasses between the unions and management were resolved through mediation or by the Central Labor Council, but labor was clearly not satisfied.[87] In the year following the partial curbing of the military governor's reach and the return of the courts to civil jurisdiction, labor leaders, no longer fearing arbitrary military justice, resumed their organizing efforts with considerable success. The plantation workers especially, seething with anger at the pro-management policies of the military government that froze them to their work and denied them access to high-paying defense industry jobs, were ready for unionization, and tens of thousands flocked into the unions.[88]

Yet as late as March 1944, the unions were still made to feel the arbitrary power of the military governor. When the ILWU attempted to organize workers on Maui, the provost marshal summarily arrested the union organizers for allegedly entering a restricted area at Kahului Harbor; they were interrogated by the military authorities and were then sent back to Honolulu to "make sure their credentials were in order."[89] Although the union complained to President Roosevelt, the War Labor Board, the National Labor Relations Board, and the secretaries of war and the interior, Richardson defended the military's actions. In a letter to the ILWU, he claimed authority to "take whatever measures may be necessary to assure complete internal security for the proper protection of all military and naval installations."[90] Nevertheless, the labor leaders were permitted to return to Maui to continue their organizing activities.

Finally, in spring 1944, there was a formal union protest against the military's jurisdiction over labor and the OMG's handling of labor disputes that could not be resolved by collective bargaining. In March, in a "Memorandum on Military Control of Hawaiian Labor" that charged the OMG with being "biased against unions and negligent of labor," a local of the AFL Teamsters' Union, headed by Rutledge, challenged the military governor's continued jurisdiction over labor. The memorandum attributed the decline in union membership to military policy and intimidation, including arranging the arrest of the head of the Kaua'i Longshoremen's Union, who was jailed for six months with no charges filed against him. The military did "little or nothing" to settle labor disputes or to supply the mechanisms for settling grievances, according to the memo. It charged that the "military government is in the hands of the businessmen of the Islands who are not only anti-union but are also unsympathetic to opportunities for the non-white population." It objected to the rejection by the newly created Waterfront Board of the union's choices for representation. Far from addressing the inequities of wage differentials, the memo stated, the military governor's freezing orders perpetuated the unfairness.[91]

The memorandum also cited the decision of the Labor Control Board in the "Tuna Packers case," which pitted the Marine Engineering and Dry Dock Workers Union (a forerunner of the ILWU) against the management of the Hawaiian Tuna Packers' shipping company; the dispute was resolved by a three-man panel representing labor, industry, and the military government. The panel ruled that the jurisdiction of the military governor over employee-employer relationships was "complete and unlimited";[92] it rejected union claims and ruled that management had the basic responsibility for the war program which "can neither be divided between a company and a union, nor can it be abridged by reason of existence of a management-labor committee or by anything else." The union's memo continued: "We consider the military incompetent to administer labor in Hawaii." Whatever "fancied need for this arbitrary subjugation of a free people that might once have existed," the memorandum stated, had long since ceased to exist. Emphasizing labor's acceptance of the military regime so long as it was necessary in furthering the U.S. offensive, the memo called for an end to "this illegal military control over patriotic citizens."[93] The union urged that the military's control of labor in Hawai'i be replaced by the War Manpower Commission and the War Labor Board, the federal agencies that were operating in this sphere on the mainland.

The Department of the Interior, which had long urged an end to military rule, sided with the union and with Governor Stainback.[94] John Frank, an Interior Department attorney, transmitted the union memorandum to Interior Under Secretary Abe Fortas, writing: "The attached memorandum reflects an outrageous condition and supports

Governor Stainback's oft-repeated statement that martial law in Hawai'i is a carefully planned pretext for anti-labor activities."[95] Frank drafted a letter that Interior Secretary Ickes sent to Secretary of War Stimson, stating: "Recent events in Hawaii bring the martial law situation to a head. I have received a report from labor union officials in Hawaii, showing that martial law is adversely and unnecessarily affecting the unions and preventing the sound development of employer-employee relations."[96]

Labor and the Continuation of Martial Law

Within the War Department, too, there was at least a tacit recognition that control of labor had become the central justification for the continuation of martial law. Thus one member of the War Department staff complained in late spring 1944 that "the major arguments used under martial law have not dealt with the question of the military necessity for such martial law but have tended to become arguments for the maintenance of control of the labor forces in Hawaii."[97]

Finally, in June 1944, William H. Davis, the chairman of the National War Labor Board, visited Hawai'i to assess the labor situation firsthand. Once again, control of labor was linked with the continuation of martial law. Fortas wrote Davis in strict confidence that he and McCloy, whom Secretary of War Stimson had put in charge of the "security problem" in Hawai'i and the West Coast following the Pearl Harbor attack, had met to consider "the possibility of terminating martial law subject to the working out of local legislation or regulations to control the labor situation," and he hoped that Davis could advise him and McCloy "of the best means of handling the labor problems in Hawai'i, without martial law controls."[98]

Upon returning to Washington, DC, Davis met with McCloy and Fortas to discuss a proposal "that the military be relieved of its jurisdiction over civilian labor and that martial law be lifted." The plan called for the War Labor Board to establish a six-person panel representing labor, industry (or the military), and the public; the civilian governor would outlaw strikes and work stoppages under his M-Day powers; and War Labor Board rulings would be enforced as on the mainland, with the president ultimately backing up its orders. The War Manpower Commission would act to direct labor where it was most critically needed, and both the WMC and the governor would act to discourage absenteeism. In transmitting the plan to Ickes, Fortas emphasized: "It is fundamental that our agreement to any plan be contingent upon concurrent or immediately subsequent lifting of martial law."[99]

McCloy and Fortas agreed to the plan, and a few days later McCloy cabled Richardson, urging the soundness of the proposal and suggesting that "we go the whole way and at the same time terminate the General Order provisions pertaining to absenteeism" and let the civil authorities take over all labor functions. Assuring Richardson that military control could always be restored if necessary, McCloy wrote, *"Acceptance by all interested parties of this would in effect eliminate the final justification for continuance of martial law. . . . Secretary [of War Stimson] concurs."*[100]

Richardson, however, was adamantly opposed to McCloy's plan. He denied the efficacy of the Hawaiʻi Defense Act to deal with absenteeism, especially since the civil governor was "sensitive to the cry of 'involuntary servitude.'" Richardson recognized all too well the link between martial law and the control of labor, but he reached a different conclusion from McCloy's, justifying his long-standing refusal to open talks and warning:

> Any approach to the Governor or the Department of the Interior at this time would merely place them in a bargaining position to ask for the complete elimination of the very limited martial law that exists here and which covers security subjects which are the most important matters involving my responsibilities.[101]

Far from loosening General Orders No. 10, Richardson wanted to increase the military's control over some 35,000 workers who were rated as non-essential. He proposed that the War Manpower Commission and its director, Holcomb, "remain in the position of administrator of the program *subject to the determining policy of the Army and Navy*."[102] Richardson urged McCloy to "wait until we sink the remaining Jap carriers" before relinquishing military control of security.[103]

And so for the following month, McCloy insisted on continuing martial law while promising his Washington colleagues to continue to try to persuade Richardson and Admiral King of the navy to agree to its termination. While Richardson professed that "the Army should take the initiative in getting rid of martial law," he was not satisfied with the proposed measures to punish violations of the OMG's security regulations, and especially of the labor regulations.[104] A disappointed Abe Fortas told Secretary Ickes that he was going to request that the president terminate martial law simultaneously with the implementation of a return of labor to civilian control.[105] In this, too, the Interior Department was to be frustrated, as martial law continued for another three months until October 24, 1944.

By August, it was apparent even to Richardson that he was fighting a losing battle over labor control. Making it appear that he was seizing the initiative, he released to the press a copy of a letter to WMC director Holcomb, warning that the stepped-up Selective Service program would lead to critical manpower shortages and urging the importance of a "closer integration of labor controls in a manner now most desirable."[106] Under his proposal, both the OMG's labor control board and the WMC's labor-management board would continue their functions, but their efforts would be coordinated through a joint manpower priorities committee. Having refused for months to negotiate with the civilian labor officials, Richardson now "suggested" to Holcomb that he should "confer with the Director of Labor Control [in the OMG] at the earliest possible time to complete necessary details."[107]

Finally, with the approval of the army and the navy, the plan for a unified manpower commission was implemented on August 21, 1944. It applied to the island of Oʻahu only; the labor shortage was not considered as critical on the other islands. The civil authorities reasserted full jurisdiction and brought Hawai'i's wage and hour policies into line with congressionally mandated standards.[108] A special priorities committee, including representatives of the army and navy as well as the WMC (but not of the territorial governor) would set manpower priorities, and all hiring would be handled through the U.S. Employment Commission and the U.S. Civil Service Commission.[109] In essence, those seeking employment were restricted to jobs supporting the war effort.

Although the War Manpower Commission formally replaced the controls of General Orders No. 10 of March 1943, thus establishing the principle of civilian control, in practice the military continued to wield considerable power through army representation on WMC committees. The army also continued to control wage and salary issues for its own civilian employees in government-owned, government-operated facilities.[110] For his part, General Richardson took the occasion to stress the increased need for manpower "at this great base" as the American combat forces were closing in on the enemy.[111]

And so the struggle between the military and civilian authorities for control of labor was seemingly put to rest, two-and-a half years after the war began. With labor placed back under civilian jurisdiction in August, a turning point had been reached, and it was clearly only a matter of time before civilian government would be fully restored.

Even after martial law ended in October 1944, however, the battles over labor between the civilian and military authorities continued. Charges of inefficiency and arbitrariness were traded between the WMC and the army, and the struggle reached the cabinet level in the nation's capital on several occasions. The fight over the control of labor finally ended only with the surrender of Japan.[112]

Chapter Six

"DRUM-HEAD JUSTICE"?

The Military Courts and the Suspension of Habeas Corpus

A key legal and constitutional issue in wartime Hawai'i was the suspension of the writ of habeas corpus—a fundamental constitutional right by which persons taken into custody can seek to have a court of law determine the legality of the proceedings that had led to their detention. Article I of the Constitution guarantees that "[t]he privilege of the writ of habeas corpus shall not be suspended, unless when in cases of rebellion or invasion, the public safety may require it." In proclaiming martial law on the afternoon of December 7, Governor Poindexter, acting on provisions in the Hawai'i Organic Act of 1900, specifically "suspend[ed] the privilege of the writ of habeas corpus until further notice." As noted earlier, he further called on the Commanding General, Hawaiian Department, "during the present emergency and until the danger of invasion is removed, to exercise the powers normally exercised by judicial officers and employees of this territory."[1]

Commanding General Walter Short, in his proclamation of the same date, warned that those who did not obey the proclamation of martial law and the subsequent ordinances would be "severely punished by military tribunals" or "held in custody until such time as the civil courts are able to function."[2] General Orders No. 4, issued on December 7, specified that "[m]ilitary commissions and provost courts shall have power to try and determine any case" involving a breach of the laws of the United States, of Hawai'i, or of the orders of the military authorities, with the exception of crimes committed by officers or enlisted men in the army and navy, whose cases would be disposed of by their respective services. The provost courts were to have full sentencing authority, imposing up to five years' imprisonment or a fine not to exceed $5,000, and there was no appeal except to the Office of the Military Governor. More serious offenses were to be tried before a military commission. Penalties were to "be guided by, but not limited to," penalties authorized by courts martial or civilian laws of the territory or of the United States. Procedures before the military commissions and provost courts were to be similar to those before a court martial.[3]

Thus, with one sweeping general order, the military cast aside the civilian statutes and legal procedures of Hawai'i and the United States, and took over the functions of

the civilian courts. Military personnel also took over the courtrooms and judicial facilities throughout the Territory of Hawai'i, displacing the civilian judges in an action that was without precedent except in the case of American occupation of enemy
lands. Those civilians found guilty of offenses of any kind were denied the privilege
of petitioning for a habeas corpus hearing that would permit a court to evaluate the legality of their arrest and incarceration. The army was adamant with regard to control of
the courts: "The administration of criminal justice is an essential element of martial law,
as this is a theater of operations," wrote General Emmons in July 1942. "The police power
is not sufficient as it must have with it the power to punish the offender speedily."[4]

Emmons also justified military control of the justice system with the argument
that any restoration of right to trial by jury in civilian courts would require use of pan-
els reflecting the demographic fact that "the Caucasian population is only about one
third of the total"—and that it was impossible to imagine "substantial justice" being
obtained by juries, given "the racial setup" in the Islands.[5] With citizens of Chinese,
Korean, and Philippine ethnic minorities, as well as Japanese Americans, eligible for
juries under the law, General Green declared, "all the racial hatred, and there is plenty
of it here under cover, will come to the fore, and justice, whether it be criminal or civil,
is simply out of the window."[6] The Office of Internal Security, in a 1945 review of "Wartime Security Controls in Hawaii: 1941–1945," justified a military judicial system rather
starkly:

> [Under martial law] the military commander makes the laws, executes the laws,
> and punishes for violation of the laws. No system of martial law could be effec-
> tive without vesting in the military commander the power to enforce his laws by
> means of punishment for their violation. . . . Consequently, a judicial system to
> carry out and effectuate the commander's orders is of prime importance to mar-
> tial law. . . . An independent judiciary would be able to nullify the act of the mili-
> tary completely.[7]

Military Commissions

At the outbreak of the war, when the civilian courts were first suspended in this way,
the army created a "military commission" of three civilians and four army officers to
try serious criminal offenses, including capital crimes, and to try crimes of war such
as sabotage.[8] This military commission had the power to impose sentences, including
the death penalty, "commensurate with the offense committed," although no one was
to be executed without approval of the military governor.

The commission met in this form only once, on December 10, when Colonel Green
called a meeting of the commission to establish procedures. Exactly what occurred at
that meeting has been recounted, with somewhat different particulars, by Green and
by Garner Anthony, a partner in one of the Islands' leading law firms and a former
president of the Hawai'i Bar Association, who attended the meeting at the request of

Judge Steadman, the senior civilian member of the commission. According to Green, Anthony raised the question of the personal liability of civilians who served on the commission, and he asked for assurances of indemnity from the U.S. attorney general. Green, who observed that people in all walks of life were giving their services without such indemnity, was outraged, and he adjourned the meeting.[9] In Anthony's version of the events, two of the civilian members of the commission asked about who would appoint them as military judges, and on what basis of authority; an army major answered that General Short's order was sufficient.

"But what," the civilian member asked, "if General Short is wrong?"

"A commanding general is never wrong," replied the major.[10]

In either case, that one meeting revealed the attitude of the military toward civilians who had the temerity to question army authority—an attitude that was perhaps understandable in the immediate aftermath of the attack on Pearl Harbor, but one that persisted throughout the war. The meeting also aroused in Green an antagonism toward Anthony that proved undiminished throughout the ensuing period of Green's service as Executive, marking out Anthony for him (as Green confided to his diaries) as a personal enemy, a man of bad judgment, and at best a misguided foe of army rule.[11] Ironically, years later, as the war's end approached, Green and his military-lawyer colleagues would themselves worry about nothing more than the possibility of civil suits for their own roles in administering the army's regime in Hawai'i.[12]

The commission, as originally constituted, never did hear a case, for the army soon decided to drop the civilian members. On December 14, it was replaced by an all-military commission.[13] This reconstituted commission, which began operation in late January, proceeded along the lines of an army court-martial; its verdicts and sentences were reviewed by three Judge Advocate General officers, who constituted the Military Governor's Board of Review, which in turn made recommendations to the military governor himself. The commission operated in such secrecy that the Department of the Interior, seeking further information, was told by the governor's office that "the list of cases and the nature of the offenses proposed to be tried before this Commission are kept secret. . . . Whether or not the officers assigned as defense counsel have legal backgrounds is not known, nor can we ascertain whether an accused person is permitted to be represented by counsel of his own choosing."[14]

The military commission tried only eight cases during the entire war period and so was of small significance as measured by the number of individuals its operations touched, but two of the cases it did try were of considerable significance.[15]

The Otto Kuehn Case

The first case was the trial of Bernard Julius Otto Kuehn, a German immigrant who was arrested with his wife and two children as enemy aliens on December 8. The case—the only espionage case to come to trial in Hawai'i during the entire war—provides a study of military justice at work. It highlights complex questions of jurisdiction and the legality of the military commission as well as the involvement of several cabinet officials and of President Roosevelt himself.

Kuehn had been under investigation by the FBI for two years, and following his detention he admitted to being a paid agent of the Japanese consulate in Hawai'i. He was charged with illegally obtaining and transmitting to the Japanese consulate information regarding the national defense of the United States. On January 7, 1942, FBI agent Robert Shivers wrote to J. Edgar Hoover, director of the FBI, laying out several issues: first, asking whether jurisdiction should be in the U.S. District Court, which was not then functioning in criminal cases, or before the military commission, even though Kuehn's alleged espionage activities were committed before December 7, when martial law was declared; and second, warning that the evidence necessary to convict Kuehn would necessarily involve members of the Japanese Consulate who enjoyed diplomatic immunity. Shivers predicted that if Kuehn were tried before the military commission, he would be sentenced to death. "A public prosecution of Kuehn and public dissemination of the evidence on which the conviction was obtained would have a good, wholesome effect on the public morale," Shivers wrote.[16] Hoover instructed Shivers to discuss the matter with the military governor and the U.S. Attorney in Hawai'i, and the FBI would abide by their decision.[17]

Meanwhile, Hoover brought the matter to the attention of Attorney General Biddle.[18] The attorney general's office advised Hoover that the military commission should proceed with the trial, but because the State Department wished to exchange the Japanese consular agents in Hawai'i for American consular agents being held in Japan, there should be no prosecution of the Japanese agents involved with Kuehn.[19] Pending their prosecution on espionage charges, Kuehn and his wife were brought before a civilian Internee Hearing Board, established by the War Department to determine whether enemy aliens and dual citizens posed a potential threat to security; the board recommended in early February that the Kuehns be interned for the duration of the war.[20]

Kuehn went on trial before the military commission in Honolulu on February 19, 1942; ironically, the trial was held in the courtroom of United States Federal Judge Ingram Stainback (soon to be appointed governor of the territory), since his civilian court had been ordered closed. Two days later, Kuehn was found guilty and sentenced to be shot. At Colonel Green's instructions, the trial and verdict were kept secret while he awaited advice from the War Department, State Department, and the White House before carrying out the execution; both Green and officials in Washington feared reprisals against U.S. nationals being held in Japan and Germany. In relaying this information to FBI Director Hoover, Shivers added, "I might state that relations with Colonel Green and his office have been extremely cordial . . . and every effort should be made to protect the confidence."[21]

Once again, Hoover brought the information to the attention of the attorney general, as it was the first death sentence imposed for espionage since the war began.[22] The conviction was also reviewed in Washington by the judge advocate general, Colonel Myron C. Cramer, who upheld the validity of the martial law regime in Hawai'i and the decision of the military commission. Secretary of War Stimson then referred the matter to the State Department, which replied that they would defer to the War Department, and the matter was then sent to Attorney General Biddle for his advice.[23]

The attorney general, however, delayed ruling on the legality of the military commission for several months; his office was waiting for a decision from the Supreme Court on a saboteur case involving eight Germans on the East Coast of the United States, as "undoubtedly, the Supreme Court will express some views about the powers and jurisdiction of military commissions."[24] Like Kuehn, the eight alleged saboteurs, two of whom were U.S. citizens, were tried before a military commission, in this case one appointed by President Roosevelt, who issued a proclamation on July 2, 1942, denying access to the civil courts by enemies who had entered the country to commit sabotage or espionage. Regarding the Nazi saboteurs, Roosevelt declared: "I won't give them up. . . . I won't hand them over to any United States Marshal armed with a writ of habeas corpus."[25] The Supreme Court ruled on July 31 that the military commission had jurisdiction to try the case and that the saboteurs' petition for a writ of habeas corpus had been denied, but the Court's opinion, in *Ex parte Quirin,* was not delivered until October 29, 1942, twelve weeks after six of the saboteurs had been executed.[26] The Court unanimously upheld the right of a military commission to try offenders against the law of war, but at the same time it implicitly rejected the president's assertion of alleged executive power to bar habeas corpus and judicial review in the case.

As late as November 24—nine months after the military commission sentenced Kuehn to death—the FBI was still seeking action from the attorney general on his case.[27] But unbeknownst to the FBI, General Emmons on October 26 had commuted Kuehn's sentence to fifty years at hard labor, and Kuehn had been transferred to Fort Leavenworth on November 20.[28] His family remained interned in Hawai'i for the rest of the war. General Green, reflecting on the case in his memoir, noted: "Clearly, the delay incident to final disposition in this case is one further reason why civil courts and procedures would not have been adequate in the administration of martial law in Hawaii."[29]

The Case of Saffery Brown

The second important case tried by the military commission proved to be of critical importance politically: It tried and convicted for murder, which the army had designated a capital crime, a part-Hawaiian Maui laborer named Saffery Brown.[30] In February 1942, Brown—the thirty-one-year-old father of seven children—was arrested by the authorities after shooting his wife during a domestic dispute. His seventeen-year marriage had been troubled from the start: Brown testified that his wife squandered his money on alcohol, neglected the children, and frequently became violent. He also suspected his wife of cheating on him, and she admitted she would rather have another man than him. "She done all things she could to me, but I still remained her husband, because the Lord said, he who divorces his wife, and marry another, commits adultery." According to his statement, on the day of the shooting, his wife had thrown him and the children out of the house; Brown returned to the house to beg her to try to work out their differences, threatening her with a shotgun, and somehow the gun went off. "I don't know how the shot went off. . . . I lost my head and didn't know what I was doing. Everything mixed up in my mind. I saw darkness, then I shot myself." Brown survived, but his wife died shortly later at the hospital.[31]

Local civilian officials in Maui believed that Brown's gun had gone off during a struggle set off by "a fit of jealousy," and there was some testimony that the gun might even have been set off when one of the children hit Brown's hand.[32] They did not believe that premeditated murder was at issue. They were therefore outraged when, in May 1942, a military commission passed a death sentence after denying Brown the right to a jury trial, reportedly permitting him to be represented by a nonlawyer (against a highly qualified judge advocate general lawyer for the army's prosecution team), and failing to recognize explicitly any distinction between first and second degree murder. None of the five army officers who constituted the military commission was a lawyer. "This is the first time that the death sentence has ever been inflicted upon anyone living in the County of Maui," the county treasurer wrote to the Hawai'i territorial delegate to Congress, Samuel Wilder King. (It was also the first time that the death sentence had been imposed by American courts on an individual of Hawaiian extraction anywhere in the Territory.) He asked King to intercede if for no other reason than that all who had attended the trial felt that premeditation had never been considered as a factor and that Brown's counsel had been unqualified.[33]

Delegate King was appalled by the information that came to him from trusted political associates concerning what seemed a serious abuse of army authority. He promptly called upon Secretary of the Interior Harold Ickes to ask the War Department to head off the prisoner's impending execution. After study of the record by the judge advocate general, Secretary of War Stimson decided to order General Emmons to hold the execution order "in abeyance." Within a month's time, under continuing political pressure from Washington, Emmons formally commuted Brown's sentence to a life term at hard labor,[34] but not before the case had roused the fears of civil libertarians and civilian leaders, who perceived the trial as an example of drumhead justice and an ominous portent of what future trials in military courts might produce for civilians in Hawai'i.[35] By September, a sampling of public opinion drawn from letters reviewed by the censorship office showed that martial law was still approved by 80 percent of the populace, but there was increasing pressure for a return of civil courts.[36]

The controversy over the Saffery Brown trial dramatized the extent to which the army had taken control of civilian governance and justice—and had set aside normal constitutional guarantees. It thus precipitated the martial law issue in a dramatic way, helping to influence the opinions about army rule that were taking form in the minds of key political actors such as Secretary Ickes, Delegate King, and members of the territorial civilian officialdom and the Hawai'i bar, many of whom would take the lead in seeking an end to martial law. Even Frank Midkiff, a prominent civic leader who would soon become head of the Honolulu Chamber of Commerce and who had generally been supportive of the army's authority, informed Ickes that "the governor [Poindexter] is now desirous of restoring civil government to all except essentially military affairs." Further, Midkiff stated that while General Short had intended "to operate on this basis but a short time," the military government under General Emmons showed no signs of turning functions back—and had even been "extended to many items that belong to and could be dealt with by the usual civil government."[37]

The attorney Garner Anthony, who, as has been noted, had been skeptical of the legality of the army's initiatives even on Pearl Harbor day, was more than ever convinced that changes of policy must be sought. While the commutation of Brown's sentence "answers the immediate question, *i.e.,* whether the man should hang," Anthony wrote, "it is no solution of the problem." Anthony regarded the army's conduct of trials, whether by the military commission or any other court, for those charged with purely civilian offenses as being clearly "illegal." He wanted immediate action in Washington to assure restoration of proper civilian control of ordinary justice.[38] Anthony's view was of special importance, for not long after expressing these opinions he would take leave from the Robertson, Castle and Anthony law firm and accept appointment as the territorial attorney general.

The Provost Courts

Far more important institutionally than the military commission were the provost courts, established to enforce the whole range of military regulations; they also conducted trials for felonies and misdemeanors under territorial and federal laws, which were continued in effect by military orders. Two provost courts were immediately established in Oʻahu on December 7, 1941, with one court established on each of the other main islands in the ensuing weeks. Additional courts were appointed on Oʻahu in 1942 and 1943.[39]

Although civil courts were permitted to reopen, under a general order of December 16, 1941, their functions were limited to such matters as land settlements and takings of land needed by the army or navy; filing of probates, trusts, and other matters of equity; and domestic relations and custody of juveniles. In January 1942, the various civilian courts were authorized "*as agents of the Military Governor* to exercise their respective functions" as they existed before martial law, but with very major exceptions: there could be no jury trials or writs of habeas corpus; no suits could be permitted against members of the armed forces or anyone engaged in any occupation or activity under the direction of the military governor or essential to the national defense, nor could any such persons be subpoenaed; and the only criminal cases that could be heard were those that were pending on December 7 and did not require a jury.[40]

By the summer of 1942, following the decisive American victory at Midway, Secretary Ickes and some members of the Justice Department and even of the War Department were beginning to call for a modification of the martial law regime. The new nominee for governor, Ingram Stainback, had been insistently urging them to restore civilian government, and especially to restore the functions of the civilian courts. General Green was therefore summoned to Washington for talks with members of the cabinet departments, which resulted in a "delineation" agreement.[41] In August, Abe Fortas, acting secretary of the interior, sent the newly confirmed Governor Stainback a draft of a new general order that the Department of the Interior was proposing. He noted:

> I hope that the proposed action will clarify the status of the courts, which should function not as agents of the military but as courts of the civilian government, acting, to be sure, as other agencies and individuals must act, under such restrictions as the military necessities of the situation may justify and the military authorities may impose.[42]

As a result of these talks, a limited further expansion of civilian court functions was permitted under general orders issued in the late summer of 1942, but the key restrictions remained: the suspension of the privilege of the writ of habeas corpus, no suits against members of the armed forces or civilian defense workers (nearly half the workforce), and no prosecutions for violation of general orders (including those regarding the curfew) or offenses against the war effort. The provost courts also maintained jurisdiction over public drunkenness, prostitution, vagrancy, flag desecration, and riots and unlawful assemblies, despite objections from Stainback. Furthermore, the military governor was the sole and final judge of the jurisdiction of the federal, territorial, and military courts.[43]

Given these severe limitations on the civil courts, the provost courts were, de facto, for nearly three years the principal institutions of justice in Hawaiʻi. As we have seen already, the provost judges were also the harsh enforcers of the notorious general orders against "chronic absenteeism" and job-switching by workers.[44]

Even though the army's prewar plans called for these courts to operate under the procedural rules of summary courts-martial, the prevailing conditions once war began induced the provost courts to create their own procedures, allowing them to hear more serious cases than summary courts-martial.[45] Civilians brought before the provost courts were denied virtually all of the basic constitutional guarantees of due process contained in the Bill of Rights, including the right to trial by jury and freedom from unreasonable searches and seizures without a warrant. Often no written charges were presented, and defendants were not permitted to cross-examine witnesses against them. Even the length of the statement the accused could make on his or her own behalf was frequently limited.

A single officer (often wearing a sidearm) presided in the provost court, and he directly examined prisoners and any witnesses. Many of the judges were without legal training, at least in the first year of the war. A notable exception was the chief judge of the Honolulu provost courts, Neal Franklin, who had been a Maryland lawyer and army judge advocate. Franklin used the magistrates of the civilian district courts, which were then closed, to sit with him and advise him on territorial laws and customary sentences. Most of the provost judges, however, simply used their own discretion in the early weeks, assigning penalties of up to $5,000 in fines or up to five years of imprisonment, since there were no specific penalties for violation of general orders issued prior to mid-January 1942. Thereafter, maximum penalties were generally included with general orders, but the provost judges still had broad discretion in sentencing.[46]

Although defendants were formally allowed the right to counsel, the provost judges commonly told them that lawyers were neither necessary nor desirable. Word soon spread that contrite acceptance of the court's verdict was likely to yield a lighter sentence than appearing with counsel—an important piece of common wisdom, since the verdict could be appealed only to the military governor.[47] In the few trials that were appealed, the trial record that was kept often proved to be crude and inaccurate.[48] Members of the Hawaiʻi bar who had represented defendants who decided to risk appearance with counsel recounted some memorable experiences before the provost judges. For example, one Honolulu lawyer reported that a provost judge threatened him with contempt simply because he had requested reduction of a client's bail.[49]

Authors of the army's own official history of military government in Hawaiʻi would later conclude that "an orderly trial was practically unknown" and the method of trial was "hasty and inadequate": "When the judge felt he had heard sufficient evidence, he would render an immediate decision, impose a sentence, and turn to the next case. . . . [M]any lawyers felt that they were helpless to assist their clients. Some judges had indicated in open court that they did not desire the attorney to participate in the trial."[50] This official history further remarked upon serious "excesses" in the abusive way that hapless defendants were treated by the provost judges and other personnel of the provost courts, especially during the first year of the war, when the provost court judges were disposing of as many as 150 cases per day.[51] Even General Richardson acknowledged that "legal procedure was geared to wartime tempo."[52] Not until early 1944 were procedures regularized with the publication of a manual of practices and procedures to be followed by provost court judges.[53]

In a few documented instances, the army appointed plantation managers to serve as provost judges, even though they were not military officers, and these men presided over trials of their own employees. The army saw nothing wrong with this practice; as General Green asserted: "With reference to [one] plantation employee being a provost court [judge], the job is not an enviable one in Hawaii. . . . No Army officer was available and the number of white civilians was small. Plantation managers, generally, are of a high type and in normal times exercise considerable control over plantation personnel. There is no legal or other objection to such a person serving as Provost Court."[54] His explanation clearly reflected the assumption, made explicit in several military communications out of Honolulu, that only Caucasians "of a high type" could be trusted with such authority. Similarly, the army rationalized that it could not tolerate the prospect of restoring the right to trial by jury in civilian courts because it would mean that citizens of Asian ancestry would serve, leading to questions of loyalty and security as well as risking vengeful decisions taken out of ethnic hostility—a risk that the army apparently did not fear would come into play when all-white juries deliberated.[55]

As a result of these practices, trial in a provost court only superficially resembled a civil court trial operating under constitutional rules of procedure. The average trial in provost courts took five minutes or less, and it was customarily held on the same day as the offense was committed, giving defendants little time to prepare their cases. The sentences were carried out immediately, before any review or appeal of the case was possible. The official army history acknowledges that many defendants were convicted without sufficient evidence.[56]

According to Ernest Kai, who was attorney general for Hawai'i in 1942 and then secretary of the territory under Governor Stainback, "The military knew nothing about the law. . . . Traffic accidents were a farce. If you got into a traffic accident, it [the sentence] depended on who was sitting up there at the desk and whether he had a headache. . . . There was no rule by which he was governed."[57] These trials were "among the worst features of the military conquest of the civilian government," amounting to nothing more than "drum-head justice," an Interior Department lawyer charged in a report written just a year after Pearl Harbor.[58] If the jurisdiction of the courts was challenged by a defendant, the provost judges were advised by the command, they should "arbitrarily deny the claim, and if they want to contest the matter let them get out a writ of habeas corpus."[59] This was bizarre advice, of course, since the military was engaged in

Wahiawa District Court, which became a provost court after the start of the war when the military government closed civilian courts. Credit: *Honolulu Star-Bulletin* photo, courtesy of HWRD.

denying, consistently, the jurisdiction of the federal courts to hear any habeas petitions that might come forward!

Because records were minimal or garbled in many provost court proceedings, particularly at the beginning of the war, fully reliable data on verdicts and sentences is lacking. Thus Lieutenant Colonel Slattery, one of the two top legal aides in OMG, spoke in 1944 to the provost judges about the difficulties of documenting cases. "The court is extremely busy. If the court does like I do, I sign almost anything that is presented to me by the staff. We have men that are experienced. When they say sign here, we do." Given the pace of work and the possibilities of oversights and error, he stated, there were many charge sheets that did not establish the basis of jurisdiction or cite correctly (if at all) the general order that was involved in the violation. Also, the proper signatures were often missing from the records.[60]

The most reliable estimate is that the provost courts tried in all some 55,000 to 60,000 civilian cases during the war, with traffic violations, curfew and blackout violations, and absenteeism accounting for most of them.[61] In early 1942, the provost courts held night sessions and met on Saturday afternoons and Sundays to handle the huge caseload. Approximately 95 percent of those charged with violations were prosecuted, and conviction was almost certain.[62] Of the 22,480 trials conducted in Honolulu's provost court in 1942–1943, some 99 percent resulted in convictions.[63] Indeed, one Hawai'i attorney reported a 100 percent conviction rate for 819 people who pleaded "not guilty" during one period of time in the provost courts.[64] Several hundred persons were sentenced to prison under martial law, including some of those who were found guilty of being absent from vital war jobs—despite the fact that such sentences exacerbated the manpower shortage that the harsh sentences were designed to prevent. According to the army, these sentences were for chronic absenteeism only, or, as General Richardson stated, for "the extreme incorrigibles who in effect refused to work after a series of notices given to them over a period of weeks"; and such sentences were often suspended on condition that the individual would report regularly for work.[65]

Of the 55,000–60,000 civilian cases tried by the provost courts, approximately 200 convictions resulted in a prison term of one year or more, the army reported, and about 90 of those individuals served their full terms. They were incarcerated at Oahu Prison. These sentences of a year or more were meted out for crimes of violence, sex offenses, burglaries, robberies, embezzlement, and violations of security measures, including failure to report previous service in the armed forces of Germany and Japan.[66] Fines amounting to more than $500,000 total were imposed in the first eight months of the war alone. No distinction was made between juveniles and adults, and defendants as young as fourteen years of age were tried by provost judges.[67]

Sentencing Policy

Sentencing policy was an especially egregious feature of military justice. In the early months of the war, there was wide variation in the sentences imposed by different provost judges for the same offense. In the summer of 1942, General Emmons appointed a provost court commissioner, whose job was to regularize sentences by setting guidelines. Because these were guidelines only and not rigid standards, however, the individual judges retained broad discretion.[68] The provost court commissioner was nevertheless able to regularize provost court procedures and make them more uniform, eliminating the basis of some complaints against procedures, but not against the existence of the courts themselves.[69]

Punishments by provost courts were almost invariably stiffer than those prescribed by civil law on conviction for similar offenses, especially in the first two years of the war. For example, a taxi driver was sentenced to three months at hard labor for selling three quarts of whiskey on a Sunday; a liquor dealer who had violated regulations was sentenced to five years at hard labor and his $20,000 stock of liquor was confiscated; and fines of $50 to $100 or a jail sentence of thirty days were customary for repeat offenders of blackout regulations.[70] Although the Legal Section of the OMG at least cursorily reviewed every case and on occasion recommended to the military governor a reduced sentence, a new trial, or clemency, no review was instituted before a prisoner had been incarcerated for three months or more (six months in the case of those sentenced for terms of a year or longer). Inexplicably, many persons who were jailed were forced to do hard labor, whether or not the sentence had specifically required it. The army also authorized the provost courts to exact purchases of war bonds from prisoners in lieu of fines (a practice that the Treasury Department later disallowed), and often persons convicted by these courts were required to donate blood, or else were given a choice between serving time or donating blood, with each donation being worth fifteen days' credit against a prison sentence or $30 credit against a fine. This practice was later discontinued when the public began referring to being fined "a bucket of blood."[71]

Although the provost courts meted out the sentences, the military government turned to the civil authorities for executing the sentences. Because the provost courts often mandated jail terms for offenses that would have been punished with fines in the civil courts, the territorial prisons and county jails experienced a sharp increase in their populations. Compounding problems for the wardens in the first weeks of the war was the fact that there were frequently no commitment papers accompanying the prisoners delivered to them. This situation was remedied in 1942 when the deputy attorney general of Hawaiʻi devised a commitment form, which was then printed and prepared by the prisoners themselves! The cost of housing these prisoners was also borne by the territory, despite the fact that they were not convicted by the territorial judiciary, since the federal government refused to pay the bill for prisoners who were convicted in a provost court and not in a federal court.[72]

An investigation in Hawaiʻi conducted by the solicitor of the Department of the Interior in late 1942 reported instances of "defendants . . . [who were] convicted of violating 'the spirit of martial law' or 'the spirit' of general orders when the text has been found inadequate"; and he averred that the sentences meted out were much more se-

vere than those handed down by military courts against uniformed personnel for identical violations.[73] Even General Green conceded, in August 1942, that "the Provost
Courts may have been more severe than was necessary in the beginning, but the
severity applied to all alike." He went on to defend the system, however, saying, "No
Provost Court was admonished, and there has been no modification of attitude, namely,
equal justice to all. The severity of the punishments has been reduced because [it is] no
longer necessary."[74] Eighteen months later, in February 1944, General Richardson similarly admitted that some of the sentencing had been excessive, but he reported that a
review of the provost courts and military commissions was then under way: "The early
operations of these courts undoubtedly justified some criticism. . . . A Board has been
established and is presently reviewing all earlier cases where the accused is presently
in confinement, with a view to granting clemency or parole consistent with Territorial
practice."[75]

Indeed, Richardson appointed a Military Commission and Provost Court Reviewing and Parole Board in November 1943. However, he did not report the results of the
board's reviews to the War Department until more than a year later, in December 1944,
by which time martial law had officially been terminated and the board had released
as many prisoners as possible "consistent with the exercise of sound discretion."[76]
Richardson wrote that when the board started its review, there were eighty-three prisoners, and review resulted in adjustments and paroles of many. "Sentences generally
were adjusted," he stated, "to make them consistent with penalties imposed by the
Federal and territorial courts for similar crimes." As a result, Richardson wrote, only
eighteen prisoners would remain in the Oʻahu penitentiary by January 1, 1945, with all
but four expected to be released by the end of the year.[77]

General Richardson and the review board wished to use the existing civilian Territorial Board of Pardons to process the paroles; Governor Stainback, however, questioned the validity per se of the provost courts and therefore refused to participate in
any aspect of detention or parole of prisoners convicted by the military courts. Paroles
were therefore handled by a member of the review board itself, with some prisoners
being granted parole on the condition that they leave Hawaiʻi, thereby avoiding possible habeas corpus challenges to martial law. The cases of prisoners of Japanese ancestry were sent to the Counter Intelligence Division for review to determine if they
should be held as internees; unless the prisoner was thought to be potentially dangerous, he was generally released from jail and considered to have "probably paid his debt
to society for that offense."[78]

The army command was not insensitive to the possibility that racism might come
into play in the enforcement, especially by military police, of the OMG's general orders when violations were charged against any of the approximately 6,000 African-
American troops and more than 20,000 African-American civilian workers on the Islands. Thus at the 1944 conference of provost judges, one of the senior officers recounted
a case in which a military policeman had arbitrarily singled out a "colored boy" for a
speeding ticket, so that the case was ordered to be dropped. But a higher-ranking officer,

Colonel William F. Steer, the provost marshal, stepped in quickly to cast the story in an entirely different light: "Probably if you check up," Steer declared, "he was from Alabama. There are a certain class of negroes who are race conscious fighting for their rights." He went on to say that giving such activists a traffic citation "isn't race discrimination."[79]

The provost court trials were held in closed session, with the public excluded, a practice that General Green defended on the grounds that it served the purpose of "avoid[ing] public curiosity."[80] The press, however, was allowed to attend; indeed, according to Neal Franklin, chief judge of the Honolulu provost courts for the army, "newspaper reporters from all Honolulu papers . . . were in constant attendance."[81] Little wonder, then, that the provost court commissioner, Captain John Wickham, advised the judges at a 1944 conference that they should avoid publicity: "I would be very careful [about] getting into the papers under any circumstances. . . . If there are any reporters in your courtroom, edit their stories. Establish a relationship with the reporter. If something pops up of unusual interest with dynamite in it request to see the story before [it is] published."[82]

Perhaps because of such policies, public criticism of the provost courts was muted for most of the war period. In addition, as noted earlier, private mail was censored by the army, as were newspapers and radio broadcasts. To be critical of army rule was to risk a suspicion of "disloyalty" that could all too easily lead to summary arrest. Thus Governor Stainback complained in fall of 1942: "The military authorities take the attitude that any slightest suggestion or criticism of any move is disloyal. They use as a club the threat of 'failure to cooperate.' Regardless of the stupidity of their demands and the fact that they [their general orders] may have no relation to public defense, they must not be questioned under penalty of 'failure to cooperate.'"[83]

Doubtless many (perhaps most) civilians in Hawai'i were at least initially thoroughly convinced that the army's control of the justice system was justified, and that sacrifice of some traditional liberties was a reasonable price to pay for military security. Memories of the devastating Pearl Harbor attack did not fade quickly. The army's decision to try nearly all civilians charged with significant civil and criminal violations in the provost courts was based in the first instance on the premise that "civil judges could not be sufficiently severe under existing civil law, and they could not be given appropriate powers [to exercise sanctions] by us."[84] But in the early days of the war, civilian leaders apparently approved the ban on jury trials. According to General Green, Judge Ingram Stainback of the U.S. District Court in Honolulu (later governor), U.S. District Attorney Angus Taylor, and several other important figures in the justice system all advised the army against permitting jury trials or relaxing other restrictions on the civilian courts. Stainback, Green contended, warned that "juries here were even worse than those on the mainland" and so might cause problems for administration of the army's emergency measures.[85]

Furthermore, the fear of the provost courts' quick trials and harsh sentences, combined with the curfew and blackout regulations, were presumably responsible for a reduction of 31 percent in major criminal offenses in Honolulu in the first year of the war. This drop in crime occurred despite a major increase in the population as military personnel and defense workers flooded into Hawai'i, leading the chief of police for Honolulu to assert: "The operation of Provost Courts was effective."[86]

By December 1942, however, with the threat of another Japanese attack on Hawai'i receding, an increasingly vocal civilian leadership had become outraged by the continuing substitution of military justice for civilian justice. We have already noted the characterization by the solicitor of the Department of the Interior of military trials as "drum-head justice." At about the same time, Attorney General Biddle and Under Secretary of the Interior Fortas protested to the War Department: "[T]he provost courts, in disregard of the safeguards of our judicial tradition and of the Constitution, impose punitive and lawless discipline upon the civilian population."[87]

There followed a series of negotiations in Washington, with the Departments of Justice and Interior, joined by Governor Stainback and Territorial Attorney General Anthony, advocating the return of the courts to civil authority, and the War Department, joined by General Emmons and General Green, advocating the continuation of military courts. A compromise was finally reached in early 1943, whereby jurisdiction over most civil and criminal cases, except those involving military personnel or a violation of general orders, was returned to the civil courts.[88]

Yet even as late as July 1944, when several cases challenging the very validity of the provost courts were on appeal in the federal courts, the military governor was still insisting on trying absenteeism and curfew and blackout violations in the provost courts. To allow such cases to be tried by civilian courts, the territorial attorney general was told, "would be considered as an admission of weakness by the military and hence was out of the question."[89]

When the full record of the provost courts was reviewed in 1946 by a leading authority on military law who was then serving as special counsel to the army, he concluded:

> From all I have been able to learn, they were unfair, unjudicial, and unmilitary. If any officer ever ran a summary court the way these people ran a provost court you would fire them out to Canton Island or a little farther. . . . It's a very, very nasty, unpleasant picture, and you just cannot justify it in any way.[90]

The federal district court judge in Hawai'i, Delbert Metzger, put it rather more bluntly, characterizing the military regime in Hawai'i as simply "the antithesis of Americanism."[91]

PART III

Japanese Americans under Martial Law

Chapter Seven

"AN EXTREME DEGREE OF FEAR"

In the immediate aftermath of the attack on Pearl Harbor, there was widespread fear and confusion among both the civilian population of Hawai'i and some of its military leaders. There was fear that the air attack would be followed by a Japanese invasion, and fear that the local ethnic Japanese would aid the invaders or at least participate in sabotage.[1] News of the outrages committed by Japan's troops in Asia fueled concerns of another kind. Japanese Americans feared both punitive measures against them by the authorities and reprisals against them by other ethnic groups, especially the Filipinos—something that the army command also feared.[2]

It is not surprising, in this atmosphere, that Japanese aliens in Hawai'i, and in some cases U.S. citizens of Japanese descent, were subjected to particularly harsh regulations to guard against possible subversion, in addition to suffering the curtailment of civil liberties imposed on all residents by martial law. Indeed, as we have noted, the large Japanese-American population was cited as the principal justification for the imposition and continuance of martial law in Hawai'i. General Orders No. 5, issued on December 8, assured Hawai'i's ethnic Japanese population that

> so long as they shall conduct themselves in accordance with law, they shall be undisturbed in the peaceful pursuit of their lives and their occupations and be accorded the consideration due all peaceful and law abiding persons, *except so far as restrictions may be necessary for their own protection and for the safety of the United States.*[3]

The measure also called on all citizens "to preserve the peace" and treat persons of Japanese ancestry "with all such friendliness as may be compatible with loyalty and allegiance to the United States."[4]

Even as discriminatory regulations were thus justified by the martial law regime from the very start of the war, the assurances to the vast majority of persons of Japanese ancestry were also honored by the military, in striking contrast to army policies central to the incarceration of all persons of Japanese ancestry on the West Coast of the mainland. Although the ethnic Japanese were regarded as a potential security threat—both as to sabotage or espionage, and as to the possibility of their undermining defense in the event of a Japanese invasion—in Hawai'i the army instituted only *selective* arrests and internments or other categories of incarceration.[5]

During the course of the war, some 10,000 Japanese-American residents in the Islands—approximately one in eleven ethnic Japanese adults—were identified and investigated as to their loyalty. These numbers included all Kibei as well as some 6,000 Nisei who had volunteered for the armed services or were potential draftees.[6] Hundreds of them were picked up for interrogation and loyalty assessments by hearing boards and the military authorities.

Approximately 2,000 persons—one-third of them American citizens, mostly Kibei—were incarcerated, either in Hawai'i or in Department of Justice or War Relocation Authority camps on the mainland.[7] Somewhat less than half of the persons taken into custody were held by the army as internees, under authority of martial law, losing their freedom for the duration of the war; others were evacuated to mainland relocation centers and/or internment camps in the formal status of "evacuees" or "excludees" rather than "internees."[8]

The length of detention varied; some were incarcerated for the duration of the war, while others were released following review hearings in 1943 and 1944. Some were permitted to leave the mainland centers in "released" status and to take up jobs and residence outside the western U.S. area under control of the Western Defense Command, where the army had conducted the mass exclusion program. Even those so released were kept under control of the War Relocation Authority (WRA) and the Hawai'i Army Command, however, and they were not permitted to return to Hawai'i until after the war's end. All of the detainees lived behind barbed wire fences, patrolled by armed guards and under surveillance from guard towers, in tents or in barracks with few comforts. They were deprived of liberty, privacy, and their normal livelihoods, and often of unification with their families.

Although only a small percentage of the ethnic Japanese in Hawai'i were thus actually interned or relocated, the policy of selective detention, which continued throughout the war, had a chilling effect on the others. From the army's point of view,

> The arrest and detention of suspicious Japanese was having a most salutary effect upon other members of the Japanese community. Many of these people learned of neighbors or acquaintances being interned. . . . This caused them concern over the loyalty of other individuals and they became much more cautious in their contacts with any Japanese whose antecedents were not well known to them and their families.[9]

The news of the exclusion and forced relocation of all Nikkei from the West Coast of the United States in early 1942 had a further intimidating effect on Hawai'i's Japanese Americans. The population of Japanese descent thus lived in constant fear of searches, investigations, arrests, interrogations, and incarceration. Combined with the more general restrictions of martial law and the specific regulations that applied to the Nikkei, this policy of selective detention became an effective instrument of control over the population of Japanese ancestry.

Race-Based Regulations

On the day after the Pearl Harbor attack, general orders required Japanese alien residents in Hawai'i to turn in to the nearest police station all firearms, ammunition, explosives, flashlights, portable radios and cameras, radio transmitters and other items, even road maps, that could be used in espionage. Some fearful aliens complied without waiting for receipts for their valuables or giving their names; others were subjected to house-to-house searches by the Army Signal Corps, and contraband articles were often confiscated with inadequate receipts for claiming goods after the war. Although the military governor appointed an alien property custodian, in fact many of the items confiscated simply disappeared or were made available for the use of the armed services.[10] In addition, although they were not on the list of specifically prohibited items, the Military Intelligence Division confiscated all Japanese phonograph records of a "propagandistic nature" from dealers, radio stations, and some individuals.[11]

Areas of O'ahu, especially in and near the military bases and airfields, were declared off-limits for all enemy aliens. Japanese farmers who were evacuated from the area suffered heavy financial losses. More than 1,500 Japanese were evacuated with less than a day's notice from an area near Honolulu harbor and the railroad terminal, with no chance to dispose of their furniture or make arrangements for the sick and elderly. A year later some of them were still homeless. Although the civic leader Frank Midkiff, who was chairman of the Evacuation Committee in the Office of Civilian Defense, brought the matter of the welfare of these residents to the attention of Colonel Green, the shortage of labor and materials prevented the construction of suitable shelters, and the army recommended that these individuals be shipped to the mainland, away from potential combat zones.[12]

Some seven hundred Japanese fishermen also suffered unusual hardships because they were prohibited from going to sea, lest they commit espionage, and they lacked the skills for other employment. Military authorities seized the entire sampan fleet and placed it under military guard. Fishermen who had been at sea on December 7 and knew nothing of the attack on Pearl Harbor were fired upon when they approached land; at least six were killed, others were wounded, and still others were interned. Japanese-American workers in the shipyards or other government installations were required to wear large badges that set them apart from others on those jobs, and Japanese aliens were prohibited from employment on defense projects.[13]

Other Nikkei who suffered unusual hardships included hundreds of Japanese-American flower growers, whose livelihood was undermined by the collapse of tourism. Ethnic Japanese domestic employees in many cases were dismissed or were too afraid to report for work. And when the Japanese teahouses of Honolulu were closed on December 7, the elderly Issei women who worked, and lived, in these establishments, and most of whom spoke no English, were left on their own. The International Institute of the YWCA and other social agencies provided guidance and service programs, such as sewing groups, first-aid classes, and cooking instruction for these women and other Issei, providing new social networks and encouraging their participation in the war effort.[14]

Thus many permanent residents who had been born in Japan, and who therefore were legally ineligible for U.S. citizenship, lost their jobs after literally decades of working in Hawai'i. A year after the war started, there was still evidence of increasing discrimination against the Nikkei, especially in skilled trades.[15] Adding to their difficulties were the OMG's general orders that prohibited them from being at large during blackout (which was earlier than the curfew), from changing occupations or place of residence without the approval of the provost marshal, and from traveling outside their home island without permission. Meeting in groups of ten or more (even for religious ceremonies) was also banned, thus crippling the social organizations that were the basis of the Issei's community. Weddings and funerals could be held only with special permits.[16] The freezing of all Japanese assets by presidential proclamation in July 1941 also resulted in financial difficulties for many of the alien Japanese, especially importers and retailers.

Other government actions also discriminated against Japanese Americans. For example, as late as 1944, the regional director of the Farm Security Administration of the U.S. Department of Agriculture directed that "No loans of any kind shall be made to Japanese regardless of citizenship status, and any funds on hand for such loans already closed shall not be disbursed." This directive drew an outraged protest from the president of the Territorial Senate, who called it "the most un-American directive" that he had ever seen, and one that would inhibit efforts both to Americanize the Japanese-American farmers and to increase food production during the war.[17]

No doubt the hardships experienced by the Japanese Americans would have been much greater if not for President Roosevelt's Executive Order of June 1941, prohibiting discrimination based on race, color, creed, and national origin in the federal government and defense industries. This policy helped many persons of Japanese ancestry to find employment in the booming wartime economy, and although they did not share in economic gains to the same extent as Caucasians, the majority of the Nikkei were better off financially in 1945 than they had been in 1941.[18] And in many key aspects of wartime administration in Hawai'i, such as the distribution of gas masks and the rationing of food and gasoline, the Japanese-American community was given equal treatment with the rest of the population.

Furthermore, some territorial officials specifically called for fair treatment of Japanese Americans. For example, the superintendent of public instruction told his teachers in January 1942: "The position of loyal American citizens of Japanese ancestry and of aliens who are unable to become naturalized, is certainly not enviable. Teachers must do everything to help the morale of these people." Similarly, the chairman of the commissioners of public instruction cautioned against showing prejudice to fellow teachers of children because of their ancestry. "They did not select their ancestors. They certainly have no responsibility for the conduct of the axis powers."[19]

Korean Americans

Residents of Korean ancestry, ironically, found themselves subjected to the same restrictions that applied to the residents of Japanese ancestry. Although General Orders No. 5 did not specifically mention Koreans, they were subjects of Japan as the result of Japan's forced annexation of Korea in 1910, and they were therefore made to feel the sting of the measures against enemy aliens in Hawai'i. On the mainland, Attorney General Biddle, indirectly acknowledging the status of Koreans as involuntary subjects rather than citizens of Japan, exempted them in February 1942 from the restrictions that applied to enemy aliens. No such exemptions were officially granted, however, by the OMG in Hawai'i, where army police and sentries claimed to be unable to differentiate them by appearance from the Japanese.[20] Unofficially, however, certain restrictions against alien enemies, such as possession of cameras and short-wave radios, were not enforced against Koreans, leading Secretary of War Stimson to point out: "As a consequence of the spirit of cooperation of the Korean nationals in Hawai'i, many privileges have been granted to them not generally granted to alien Japanese."[21]

Nearly 2,400 of the approximately 7,000 ethnic Koreans in Hawai'i were first-generation immigrants who, like the Issei, were ineligible for citizenship; however, they were leaders in anti-Japanese movements in the Korean community in Hawai'i, and they saw the war between the United States and Japan as a path for Korean independence.[22] Being treated as enemy aliens and subjected to race-based restrictions—even if those restrictions were not always enforced as vigorously against the Koreans as against the Japanese—was therefore particularly galling for these residents whose native country had endured so much at the hands of the Japanese.[23] Their American-born children were equally offended. As one of them expressed it, "I act, speak and think like an American. . . . I never thought of myself as anything but an American. My parents . . . always thought of the United States as their liberator." He was outraged that alien Koreans were classified as enemies "when they hate the Japs and taught their children to hate the Japs."[24]

Local Korean leaders, as well as officials of the self-designated Korean government in exile, located in Washington, conducted an intensive publicity campaign to persuade the army to recognize the distinction between residents of Korean ancestry and those of Japanese ancestry, winning some outspoken support from Senator Guy Gillette of Iowa.[25] In Honolulu, the *Korean National Herald–Pacific Weekly* pointed out that "every Korean born is an enemy born for Japan,"[26] and the *Star-Bulletin* (owned by the family of the territorial delegate to Congress, Joseph R. Farrington, and the only newspaper in the Islands to question the legitimacy of army rule) also lent forceful support to the Korean cause, calling the stigmatization of Koreans as enemy aliens an "injustice and a tragedy."[27] The army, however, remained intransigent, and Koreans were not exempted from the new enemy-alien restrictions issued in March 1943 after partial restoration of the civil government.

The issue came to a head in May 1943, when a Korean was arrested for violating the curfew. The provost court ruling by Lieutenant Colonel Moe Baroff, while recognizing their predicament, declared Koreans to be enemy aliens for purposes of enforcing regulations directed at Americans of Japanese ancestry. The conviction was appealed to General Emmons by a civilian counsel.[28] Emmons tersely rejected counsel's arguments—unimpressed by the plea that the Korean people had endured harsh treatment at the hands of Japan's militarist regime since 1910, and that Europeans whose countries had been conquered by Nazi Germany were not considered to be enemy aliens. Emmons simply stated that after consideration "the findings and judgment of the provost court are sustained."[29] His decision was clearly a particularly stinging insult, of course, to a people whose country and kin had so long suffered under the hand of Japanese imperialism, and it prompted further efforts for a change in the status of Korean aliens.

Appeals through Korean lobbyists (including future Korean President Syngman Rhee) to President Roosevelt and to Secretary of War Stimson resulted in an investigation by the Military Intelligence Division, which in June 1943 justified the designation of Koreans as enemy aliens on the basis of the oft-used argument of military necessity.[30] In preparing a policy statement for the War Department, General Richardson— following consultation with military and naval intelligence and the FBI—cited several reasons for denying "friendly alien" status for Koreans, including:

(1) Many alien Koreans were believed to have ties to Japan (including relatives living in Korea and Japan) and had traveled to Japan and Korea.

(2) Some Koreans were said to "have connections which might allow them to sell their services to the highest bidder."

(3) Korean leaders were said to "appear to be opportunists who are more interested in personal aggrandizement than they are in organizing a movement representing a sincere expression of a people who desire to maintain their own national integrity."

(4) "It is almost impossible to distinguish between Koreans and Japanese by sight alone, and Japanese who speak Korean might try to represent themselves as Koreans." Language problems would add to the work of intelligence officers if alien Koreans were classified as friendly aliens.

(5) Changing the status for Koreans "might provide an opening wedge for the Formosans, Okinawans, and other colonists not of pure Japanese blood"; and

(6) Existing restrictions were not a major inconvenience and they affected only about 2,500 people, whereas exempting these people would necessitate processing them through alien hearing boards; this, in turn, would invite "further unrest and give their leaders a stronger platform for protest."[31]

In setting forth its policy, the military government exhibited the same reliance on stereotypes that consistently marked its treatment of the ethnic Japanese.

The status of Korean aliens was finally and quietly resolved in December 1943. Following a meeting of President Roosevelt, Prime Minister Churchill, and Generalissimo Chiang Kai-shek in Cairo, at which the three world leaders agreed, among other things, that Korea should be a free and independent country, the military governor in Hawai'i reversed his position on the restrictions on Koreans. General Orders No. 45, issued on December 4, exempted Koreans from enemy-alien curfew restrictions.

Despite their early classification as enemy aliens, however, no Koreans were ever detained or brought up before hearing boards as being dangerous to the security of the United States.[32]

Fear and Confusion among Japanese Americans

Many times more numerous than the Koreans, the Islands' ethnic Japanese—deprived of their cultural, religious, and community leaders by the initial sweep of arrests and internments—lived in "an extreme degree of fear."[33] The military authorities closed the Shinto temples and Japanese language schools, and they discouraged the practice of Buddhism by denying petitions for meetings. For example, a petition to hold Buddhist prayer services for Nisei soldiers who had been killed in action or were fighting on the front was met with the following statement from Colonel William R. C. Morrison, the Executive in the OMG: "The general policy in this office is to discourage the resumption of Japanese religious activities other than Christian. This attempt to revive Buddhist services should not be approved at this time. . . . Once religious services are permitted to be resumed by the Japanese, opportunities are presented for subversive gatherings." Morrison acknowledged that Christian services also presented opportunities for gatherings, but "Japanese espousing the Christian religion are less likely to promulgate Japanese matters."[34]

The Issei especially, who were also deprived of their news sources by the early suspension of foreign language broadcasts and newspapers, were increasingly isolated. Since public use of the Japanese language was banned and many Issei had no other language, they were, according to one observer, "filled with fear and chose to remain inside their homes."[35] Another observer noted, "Fear became the dominant emotion in the lives of most of the Issei in particular."[36] Afraid of saying or doing the wrong thing, of associating with the wrong people, of losing their livelihoods, or of being spied upon by the FBI's Nikkei informants, the Issei withdrew. Ironically, the Issei's withdrawn behavior increased the misgivings of the anti-Japanese elements in Hawai'i, who pointed to their sullenness as evidence of their untrustworthy nature.[37] The Issei also tended to obey very scrupulously all military orders, such as carrying gas masks—thereby incurring further suspicion that they had advance notice of another attack by Japan.[38]

The ethnic Japanese were afraid not only of being suspected of disloyalty and of internment by the military authorities, but also of reprisals from the authorities and from other Hawai'i residents. "It must be remembered," General Green asserted after the war, "that there were 55,000 Filipinos, many of whom—armed with the weapon of their trade, the machete—were ready, willing, and even anxious to annihilate all those of Japanese blood; and there were thousands of Chinese who would be glad to see it done."[39]

The Issei abandoned their traditional Japanese clothing, and most families of Japanese descent destroyed not only Japanese flags, but books, photos, family shrines, and memorabilia.[40] As one plantation worker recalled: "I knew they would come to my house and search my place when the war started. Thus, I burned my Japanese textbooks and some pictures. . . . Unfortunately, some of my friends who kept their Japanese books and pictures were arrested."[41] According to FBI testimony before the Roberts Commission— the special commission appointed by President Roosevelt to investigate the Pearl Harbor attack—the local Japanese-American population "was well afraid, pretty well afraid" by the show of military force in the weeks following December 7.[42]

The families of the alien Japanese who had been arrested were especially fearful and confused. In many cases, the families did not know for weeks where the detainees were being held or even if they were alive. Their friends did not dare to visit them, for fear that they, too, would be arrested. As one detainee sadly recalled, "The Japanese . . . were scared to associate with us. They thought they would be arrested themselves. They just avoided us. . . . They wouldn't even talk to us. . . . Even my friends would separate themselves from us and cut their ties. That was the harshest."[43]

It was particularly difficult for the ethnic Japanese who lived in plantation communities. The Hawai'i Sugar Planters Association, always eager to cooperate with the military and the FBI, submitted a list of Japanese aliens with "pro-Japanese tendencies" to the FBI on December 12.[44] Exacerbating the fears of the Nikkei plantation workers was the large percentage of Filipino workers. As the daughter of an Issei shopkeeper in Kohala wrote: "With father's internment, Mother was left with seven young children without any means of support. Because of the dark cloud of suspicion hovering over our heads, the people did not patronize our store. . . . We lived in perpetual fear, for our community had many Filipino laborers and the war between Japan and the Philippines was especially bitter."[45]

Most of the wives of the alien internees were themselves also aliens, but their children were, for the most part, American-born citizens. The dilemma faced by these families was poignantly recalled by a former language school teacher: "My first and foremost concern was how my internment affected my children. . . . I wanted them to understand that my internment was due to the war and not to any subversive activities on my part. I wanted them to think and behave as proud American citizens."[46] And the wife of an internee stated in an interview:

My husband sent me a note from the Immigration Detention Quarter where he was interned, telling me that from that time on I must forget completely that I was the wife of an enemy alien and concentrate on being the mother of American children. He wanted me to sever all my connection with him and Japan and devote myself to helping our children to serve their country. . . . One of our sons was already in the Army, stationed at Schofield, when the war broke out.[47]

In January 1942, the army asked the territorial civilian Department of Public Welfare to assist the families of the detainees, and social workers were initially able to look after most of their needs. This agency cooperated with the Territorial Office of Defense Health and Welfare Services and other community agencies, including the American Friends Service Committee, to provide services and assistance as needed.[48] In addition, after March 31, 1942, the OMG arranged for the American Red Cross to receive information on the families of the detainees; Red Cross representatives then visited the families to ascertain their need for assistance, including financial relief, medical help, or employment assistance, then referring them to appropriate agencies.[49]

However, by summer of 1942, as the United States and Japanese governments were negotiating for an "exchange repatriation" of their nationals, there was a state of substantial confusion. Many of the Hawai'i aliens interned on the mainland wrote to their families that the internees were going to be repatriated to Japan, along with their wives and children, and so advised their families in Hawai'i to make preparations to leave immediately. These families sought further information from the social workers in Hawai'i, but no firm answers were forthcoming from the Red Cross or the Department of Justice.[50]

Some of the Japanese aliens' families thereupon sought help from the Swedish consulate, which was handling affairs for Japanese nationals after the closure of the Japanese consulate. After inquiring at the Military Intelligence Office, the Swedish consulate reported that the exchange repatriation would apply only to "Japanese residing on the Mainland and to men from Hawaii without families."[51] This information directly contradicted that which came from the Provost Marshal General, who informed the Welfare Department that the enemy aliens who were interned on the mainland could apply for repatriation for themselves and their families, but the final decision rested with the State Department.[52] In early August, a member of the Welfare Department implored Samuel Wilder King, Hawai'i's delegate to Congress, to seek immediate clarification, writing:

> The need for a clearly stated policy and plan of procedure is urgent, as there are business affairs which these families need to settle. Also, there are families in which the wife and younger children wish to join the head of the family in Japan while older children will refuse to leave Hawaii, which to them is home. The constant flow of letters from the internees in which the families are told to make plans to go to Japan keep many of these women and children in a state of emotional conflict, especially in light of the conflicting reports from other sources.[53]

Attributing "the apparent confusion in regard to repatriation of families of Japanese aliens in Hawaii" to "ill-founded rumors emanating from unknown sources prior to a definite decision on the matter," the Provost Marshal General confirmed to Delegate King that the State Department ultimately would decide on whether or not an internee would be repatriated.[54]

Rampant Rumors

The initial roundups of individuals on the FBI's detention list and of other ethnic Japanese in the first days and weeks following the attack on Pearl Harbor were deemed insufficient by some prominent *haole* and by many junior uniformed officers and their families in the Islands, who were a principal source of what a confidential FBI report dismissed as "the million false and fantastic rumors" of disloyalty among the Japanese Americans in Hawai'i.[55] Such rumors regarding alleged sabotage and espionage by persons of Japanese ancestry in connection with the Pearl Harbor debacle ran rampant in December 1941 and early 1942, both in Hawai'i and on the mainland, especially after the arrival there of the thousands of women who had been evacuated from the Islands.[56] The precision of Japan's attack and Japan's knowledge of the U.S. strategic locations suggested that there had been espionage. Even General Emmons, commenting in early January on the successful espionage by Japan, said, "They knew everything," although he went on to reassure the public that the espionage had successfully been smashed.[57] According to the myths put into circulation by these rumors, the ethnic Japanese in Hawai'i knew in advance of the attack; Japanese-American drivers deliberately obstructed the roads to Pearl Harbor; Nikkei plantation workers had cut arrows in the cane fields to guide the air attack; Japanese pilots were former residents of Hawai'i, wearing McKinley High School and University of Hawai'i rings; fishing sampans operated by Japanese Americans had been in touch with the Japanese Imperial Navy's warships; signal lights had been flashed to enemy ships and planes; Nikkei merchants had kept detailed records of purchases of naval supplies to gauge fleet movements, and so forth.

Highly placed officials gave credence to these rumors. For example, on December 12, 1941, Rear Admiral Kimmel wrote: "Fifth column activities added great confusion" on December 7.[58] Especially damaging in this regard was a press conference statement on December 15 by Secretary of the Navy Knox, who, undoubtedly trying to deflect blame for the Pearl Harbor debacle from the navy, declared: "I think the most effective 'fifth column' work of the entire war was done in Hawaii, with the possible exception of Norway."[59] Similarly, despite the lack of evidence of subversive activities among the Japanese Americans who had been detained in the initial sweeps, the War Department reported to the press on December 22 that 273 "Fifth Columnists" had been arrested from among the 35,000 Japanese aliens living in Hawai'i. While noting that most of Hawai'i's population of Japanese ancestry had given no evidence of disloyalty, some had "provided the enemy with valuable information." The report stated that "all known Japanese leaders of subversive activities" had been detained, but that the military and civil authorities would continue to seek out dangerous individuals.[60] Lieutenant Commander

Kenneth Ringle of the Office of Naval Intelligence, the Navy's leading expert on the mainland Nikkei community, added his own negative assessment of the ethnic Japanese living in America. Ringle, reporting in January 1942, opposed the mass internment of Japanese aliens and citizens of Japanese extraction, but only for practical reasons:

[Mass internment would] undoubtedly alienate their loyalty to the United States, would add the extra burden of supporting and guarding these people to the war effort, would disrupt many essential businesses, notably that of the growing and supplying of food stuffs, and would probably cause a widespread outbreak of sabotage and riot.[61]

However, he recommended the custodial detention of potentially dangerous citizens, especially the Japanese-educated Kibei:

[T]there are among the Japanese both alien and United States citizens, certain individuals, *either deliberately placed by the Japanese government or actuated by a fanatical loyalty to that country who would act as saboteurs or agents.* This number is estimated to be less than three per cent of the total, or about 3500 in the entire United States. . . .

[T]he most potentially dangerous element of all are those American citizens of Japanese ancestry who have spent the formative years of their lives, from 10 to 20, in Japan and have returned to the United States to claim their legal American citizenship within the last few years. These people are essentially and inherently Japanese and may have been deliberately sent back to the United States by the Japanese government to act as agents. In spite of their legal citizenship and the protection afforded them by the Bill of Rights, they should be looked upon as enemy aliens and many of them placed in custodial detention.[62]

In his assessment of the Kibei, Ringle echoed the statements made by Curtis Munson just before the outbreak of war.[63] Munson, however, had little patience for the navy's anti-Japanese stance, noting that in Honolulu "the seagoing Navy was inclined to consider everybody with slant eyes bad," an attitude he attributed to "self-interest, largely in the economic field, and in the Navy usually from pure lack of knowledge and the good old 'eat 'em up alive' school. It is not the measured judgment of 98% of the intelligence services or the knowing citizenry either on the mainland or in Honolulu," wrote Munson.[64]

The FBI, Governor Poindexter, Mayor Lester Petrie of Honolulu, and others in Hawai'i vigorously denied the rumors of espionage and sabotage in their testimony to a congressional investigating committee.[65] Shivers, FBI chief in Honolulu, emphatically contradicted Admiral Kimmel: "There was no confusion in Hawai'i as a result of fifth column activities. . . . I speak with authority when I say that the confusion in Hawaii [during and after the Pearl Harbor attack] was in the minds of the confused, and not because of fifth column activities."[66] Similarly, Shivers testified before the Roberts Commission that he was "satisfied that [Japanese espionage] was centered in the Japanese consulate."[67] And FBI Director J. Edgar Hoover wrote in March 1942, "Relative to the question of whether there had been any sabotage committed in Hawaii, I desire to advise that no sabotage was committed there prior to Dec. 7 [1941], on December 7, or subsequent to that time." Only the Japanese consular officials, Hoover asserted, had been found to have engaged in espionage prior to the Pearl Harbor attack.[68]

Nevertheless, the rumors persisted both in Hawai'i and on the mainland. In Hawai'i, these "false and untrue fantasies" increased anti-Japanese sentiment. "There was no means available to check the rapid spread of this mis-information," wrote G-2's Colonel Bicknell, "until such damage had been done that a mere denial of the facts would be brushed aside by the avalanche of adverse material."[69] The findings of the Roberts Commission on the Pearl Harbor debacle, which were released in late January 1942, further contributed to fears of Japanese subversion.[70] Along with mixed testimony on the issue of Japanese-American loyalty, the commission included in its documents accounts of the "Ni'ihau incident," in which a downed Japanese pilot was helped by a single Nisei on the isolated island of Ni'ihau. Although the residents of Ni'ihau did not even know that the United States and Japan were at war, the episode on Ni'ihau was cited in a January 1942 navy intelligence report as indicative of the "likelihood that Japanese residents previously believed loyal to the United States may aid Japan if further Japanese attacks appear successful," and it may well have influenced the administration's thinking on the need to intern Japanese Americans on the West Coast.[71]

Similarly, the FBI reported that following the Ni'ihau incident, its informants thought many of the ethnic Japanese in Hawai'i "will aid and abet Japan." The FBI had also discovered significant quantities of Japanese flags, samurai swords, and other material that the agents regarded as indicative of a "patriotic attitude toward Japan." Although there had been "no open expression of hostility to the United States" among the alien Japanese community in Hawai'i, the FBI nevertheless concluded in early January 1942 that "the alien Japanese will undoubtedly follow the Japanese Government should it appear that . . . they may occupy these islands." Japanese propaganda, the FBI report stated, had kindled "the flame of loyalty and Japanism" that had been somewhat dormant prior to the war, and that might well break out in case of Japanese victories. Recognizing that many second- and third-generation Japanese Americans were loyal to the United States, the FBI wanted to "take advantage of that loyalty and utilize it for the purpose of immobilizing the super-patriotic alien Japanese."[72] Thus, while they denounced the rumors of espionage or sabotage by Japanese Americans at the time of the Pearl Harbor attack, the intelligence agencies were guarded in their evaluation of the allegiance of the ethnic Japanese, especially the Issei.

Shortly thereafter, the "Tolan Committee" (The House Select Committee Investigating National Defense Migration) held hearings on the removal of persons of Japanese ancestry from the West Coast of the United States, and some of the committee members were convinced of widespread sabotage by the Nikkei in Hawai'i.[73] In the

Senate, Senator Gillette of Iowa also warned of the potential danger of fifth-column activities, emphasizing the alleged indoctrination of Japanese-American children by priests and Japanese consuls, and the pride of dual citizens in Japan's ambitions in Asia.[74]

The rumors and resulting widespread distrust of Japanese Americans, combined with the detention of both aliens and Nisei, had an intimidating effect on the entire ethnic Japanese community. As the pastor of a Japanese Christian church in Kaua'i lamented, with citizens being interned arbitrarily, everyone feared it would happen to them, too. "Knowing it can happen, the sensible thing would be to keep quiet and live a meaningful life while it lasted," he said. "Being an American citizen now has no meaning in the eyes of the authorities. . . . [E]very Japanese is discredited to begin with," the pastor stated.[75]

Colonel Green confided to his diary in February, not quite two months after the Pearl Harbor attack, that the Japanese-American residents had "simply shut up" and were "scared to death," in fear of "a local uprising and a slaughter."[76] Green added, ominously: "I am afraid of it too."[77]

The Right to Serve

The presence of armed individuals of Japanese descent on O'ahu hardly quieted the unease and suspicion that persisted in the early weeks of the war. On the morning of December 7, immediately following the Pearl Harbor attack, Japanese-American members of the University of Hawai'i ROTC had sprung into action beside their fellow students to defend key installations on O'ahu, and a few hours later they were asked to join the Hawai'i Territorial Guard (HTG), formed that day by Governor Poindexter in response to Japan's attack. Most enlisted, soon joined by other young Nisei, and by the end of December more than 1,300 men were guarding some 150 outposts. In the initial weeks following the Pearl Harbor attack, the several hundred Japanese Americans who had volunteered for service constituted a plurality of the multiethnic Hawai'i Territorial Guard.[78]

General Short was aware of the largely Japanese-American composition of the ROTC at the time, and he was confident of their loyalty. They were given arms to guard schools, wells, bridges, pumping stations, fuel and gas storage facilities, government offices, the governor's residence, and other vital facilities. At least one of the volunteers was the son of a man on the FBI detention list who had been arrested the day of the attack. According to one young Nisei ROTC member, Ted Tsukiyama, there was no screening or hesitancy in calling up the ROTC members. "There was no question about what we were supposed to do or what our duty was or where our loyalty lay. . . . They just said turn out, and we turned out. And then HTG [Hawai'i Territorial Guard]—same thing. They just automatically swore us in."[79]

On January 19, however, Emmons—without explanation, but following a War Department directive that all Japanese Americans be classified as enemy aliens ineligible for the draft—disbanded the Hawai'i Territorial Guard. He re-formed the unit the following day, after discharging the Nisei. Tsukiyama described the feelings of the Japanese Americans who had been summarily dismissed: "complete rejection, abandonment and repudiation . . . , only because our faces and our names resembled that of the enemy. . . . The very bottom had dropped out of our existence."[80] Frustrated and angry, the Japanese-American community dared not complain. They did, however, successfully petition the military governor, offering their services in whatever way they could be used, and in February the group of 169 men was reorganized as the Varsity Victory Volunteers (VVV).[81] Assigned as a labor battalion to the 34th Combat Engineers regiment at Schofield barracks, the VVV worked for the following year on quarrying and construction projects vital to defense. The significance of their efforts went beyond direct contributions to the war effort, for their dedication and loyalty likely helped persuade the administration in January 1943 to allow Japanese Americans to volunteer for a segregated regimental combat team—the 442nd. Assistant Secretary of War John McCloy, who had seen the VVV at work when he visited Hawai'i in December 1942, was among the advocates of forming a Japanese-American combat unit.[82] The VVV was disbanded in January 1943 so its members could volunteer for military service.

In addition to the Japanese Americans in the ROTC unit that became the Hawai'i Territorial Guard, there were 1,432 Nisei volunteers and draftees already in the U.S. Army when war erupted, since the 1940 Selective Training and Service Act, which created the country's first peacetime draft, did not bar their service. Some 200 belonged to the 1399th Engineering Construction Battalion; the remainder were members of the 298th and 299th Infantry Regiments of the Hawai'i National Guard, which were federalized and assigned to guard the shorelines.[83] The War Department suggested in February 1942 that all the Japanese-American soldiers be discharged or transferred, but Emmons resisted, citing the shortage of troops.[84] In May 1942, military intelligence learned that Japan was preparing to launch a major attack on Midway which, if successful, could serve as the launching point for an attempted invasion of the Hawaiian Islands. It is not clear what prompted the army at this point quietly to ship the Nisei infantrymen to Camp McCoy, in Wisconsin, on June 5. It may have been done from fear that in case of invasion some of these Nisei troops might prove disloyal, but there was also concern that it would be impossible to distinguish them from the enemy forces in combat. Other possible explanations are that the army was seeking to appease the anti-Japanese elements in Hawai'i—or that it was influenced by a petition from the Hawaiian Japanese Civic Association, endorsed by General Emmons, requesting that Nisei be allowed to form a combat unit. Now named the 100th Infantry Battalion, they were moved from Camp McCoy to Camp Shelby, Mississippi, in early 1943 and then in September to the European theater of war.[85]

The question of Japanese Americans serving in combat units remained problematic, however, throughout 1942. The Selective Service Board in O'ahu complained to Governor Stainback that the policy of discontinuing the induction of registrants of Japanese ancestry was in conflict with the law. Further, the policy threatened to cause resentment among other racial groups whose men were being drafted—especially since Japanese Americans were taking the high-paid jobs of the inductees; at the same time, it was destructive of the morale of Japanese Americans who wanted a chance to prove their loyalty.[86] Another government official reported that there was "much antagonism" toward the young Japanese Americans who, unable to enlist, were attending the University of Hawai'i, earning high wages, or, in some cases, profiteering from the war.[87] Governor Stainback called the matter to Secretary Ickes's attention, but no action was immediately taken.[88] In fact, a special board consisting of five high-ranking army officers and Dillon Myer, director of the WRA, had been considering the matter of "Military Utilization of U.S. Citizens of Japanese Ancestry" over the summer. Among those testifying in favor of a combat unit were General Emmons and Admiral Nimitz. However, in mid-September the special board recommended against such a unit "because of the universal distrust in which they [Japanese Americans] are held."[89]

Emmons and Colonel Fielder, head of Army Intelligence in Hawai'i, continued to press upon McCloy the importance of letting the Nisei serve—and the danger of their injured pride turning to alienation if they were not allowed to demonstrate their loyalty. As 1942 drew to a close, General Marshall called attention to the positive propaganda value of a Nisei fighting unit with America's allies. By January 1943, McCloy's mind was made up. He had been heavily influenced by General Emmons, "who feels very strongly that these fellows will make grand soldiers," McCloy told General DeWitt, the commanding general of the Western Defense Command.[90] Then, finally, on February 1, 1943, President Roosevelt issued a call for volunteers for the 442nd Infantry Regiment.[91] In Hawai'i, some 9,500 Nisei—more than six times the quota that the army initially assigned to the Islands—answered the call for volunteers.

The 100th Infantry Battalion, which had been training on the mainland, was later combined with the 442nd Infantry Regiment. With "Go for Broke" as their slogan, they fought with legendary bravery, first in Italy and then with the invading forces following D-Day in northern Europe. They became one of the most decorated units of the war, receiving more than nine thousand Purple Heart medals and seven Presidential Unit Citations.[92] Less decorated than the 442nd, but invaluable for the war effort, were the more than six hundred Nisei who answered the calls for volunteers, in June and November 1943, from the army's school for interpreters. Following their training in Minnesota, they were attached to fighting units throughout the Pacific, and they served with distinction in China, Burma, the Philippines, the Solomons and the Marianas, New Guinea, and Okinawa.[93]

Yet even as the well-publicized heroism of the Nisei in the armed forces was gaining praise and helping to change the image of Japanese Americans among the American population as a whole, large numbers of their fellow Japanese Americans—and in many cases the parents of those wearing the American uniform—were being held in internment or WRA camps in Hawai'i and on the mainland.

Chapter Eight

SELECTIVE DETENTION AND REMOVAL

Although General Emmons dismissed the Japanese Americans from the Hawai'i Territorial Guard in January 1942, he was to prove a determined and largely effective opponent of the more racist elements in Hawaiian society and in the Washington administration, the latter including Secretary of the Navy Frank Knox. Emmons would even stonewall President Roosevelt himself on the issue of forced removal of all Japanese Americans. Indeed, his was a voice for calm and for confidence in the loyalty of the vast majority of Nikkei.

In his first public statement to the people of Hawai'i following his appointment as commanding general, widely broadcast and published in the Honolulu papers on December 22, 1941, Emmons deplored the "fear and suspicion on the part of employers" that had led to the dismissal of ethnic Japanese workers. "If the courage of the people in the island is to be maintained and the morale sustained," Emmons stated, "we cannot afford unnecessarily and indiscriminately to keep any number of loyal workers from useful employment." Reminding his audience that "This is America and we must do things the American way," he urged the need to "distinguish between loyalty and disloyalty among our people," although he recognized that "[s]ometimes this is difficult to do, especially under the stress of war." He warned that "additional investigation and apprehensions will be made and possibly additional suspects will be placed in custodial detention," but "these people are not prisoners of war and will not be treated as such. . . . There is no intention on the part of the Federal authorities to operate mass concentration camps. No person, be he citizen or alien, need worry, provided he is not connected with subversive elements."[1] In this, he echoed the radio address of Colonel Kendall J. Fielder, head of Army Intelligence (G-2), who on December 11 had commended the people of Hawai'i for their cooperation with the authorities during the first week of the war, urged the "loyal citizens of all racial ancestries" to "work and fight together to the end," and declared: "There is no desire on the part of the authorities to organize mass concentration camps."[2]

Pressures for Mass Removal

Yet, despite the army's reassurances of fair play for the Japanese Americans in Hawai'i, it was precisely "concentration camps" that were being considered in Washington.[3] When Emmons pledged fair treatment, he was undoubtedly unaware that just two days earlier, Roosevelt's cabinet had discussed the matter of removing all ethnic Japanese from O'ahu. Secretary of the Navy Frank Knox urged that not only aliens but also citizens of Japanese ancestry should be removed from O'ahu, ignoring the constitutional issues involved.[4] Secretary of War Stimson, however, recommended that only enemy aliens be removed, and President Roosevelt concurred.[5] The special assistant to the secretary of war, Harvey Hollister Bundy, reported to the FBI a few days later that Roosevelt declared at the cabinet meeting that he wanted all Japanese aliens in Hawai'i interned immediately; the War Department, however, intended to leave matters in the hands of the commanding general of the Hawaiian Islands.[6] On January 10, Knox requested information about the "practicability of concentration of local Japanese nationals" on an island other than O'ahu, and how they might be housed and fed; in transmitting the request to Emmons, the Office of the Provost Marshal General was at pains to explain that "this inquiry is prompted entirely by the Secretary of the Navy."[7]

Emmons made clear in no uncertain words his opposition to such a plan. He replied that "[m]ost families contain alien parents or grandparents mixed with young citizens and numerous small children"; that "there are as many dangerous elements among the [Japanese-American] *citizens* as among the aliens"; and that only "wholesale evacuation of all Japanese and many others" could absolutely protect the flow of information. Such an evacuation, he cautioned, would be "dangerous and highly impractical" and would result in shortages of shipping, of construction supplies, and of labor. Nor were the troops necessary to guard such a concentration of ethnic Japanese available. Emmons further warned, "Any evacuation plan would have serious repercussions on loyalty of citizens of Japanese ancestry." If the War Department nevertheless decided on evacuation, Emmons urged, it should be to the mainland.[8]

While resisting pressures from Washington for the mass removal of Japanese aliens, Emmons also sought to contain anti-Japanese sentiment in Hawai'i. "We must hold a close check upon our emotions and our tongues," Emmons told the Honolulu Chamber of Commerce on January 15. "There will be no witch-hunting or vigilante action against those suspected of disloyalty," he said; any dangerous persons would be dealt with by the "regularly constituted authorities." Even as he promised individual treatment, however, Emmons also warned against disloyal actions and kept his options open:

> Aliens in Hawaii, as well as citizens, will in every instance be judged by the military government on the basis of their individual conduct. There has been and will be no mass condemnation or mass punishment unless it is forced by military necessity. Those disloyal in design, words or action will be dealt with swiftly and severely.[9]

Nor did General Emmons ignore or rebuff entirely the pressures for special measures against the population of Japanese descent. Concerning the fate of the four hundred ethnic Japanese already being held as internees by the army only five weeks after the air assault, Emmons requested that his authority to remove them to the mainland "should be approved at once and broadened to include any suspected Japanese who are now in confinement or who may be apprehended in the future."[10]

On January 17, Emmons was granted this authorization,[11] but still he dragged his feet. At the end of the month, the cabinet, responding in part to the report of the Roberts Commission, again discussed the subject of evacuating from O'ahu residents of Japanese descent, and Emmons was again asked for his opinion.[12] While conceding that it would be "desirable for health, supply and security reasons to evacuate as many Japanese as practical, and as soon as practical," he again cited labor shortages and urged that priority be given to evacuating some 20,000 women and children, other than ethnic Japanese, and the approximately 500 enemy aliens already interned. Second priority was to go to "as many Japanese with their families as can be transported." Until a large reinforcement of army troops could be sent, Emmons warned, it was "absolutely necessary" that no publicity be given to plans for evacuation or other security action; but "in the event of an assault on Oahu prior to evacuation of large numbers of Japanese," he continued, "plans are ready to immobilize all Japanese in place."[13]

Emmons insisted that his command must have full discretion as to which individuals or groups should be evacuated. He specified further that he wanted that authority to make selections *without regard to nationality or citizenship,* [though] giving normal priority of evacuation to aliens."[14] His reference to authority to treat citizens in the same way as aliens was an ominous portent for the Nisei population at large (not only the small number already picked up and being held as internees) as well as for German-American and Italian-American U.S. citizens who had been arrested and interned along with the ethnic Japanese detainees.[15]

While assigning high priority to security measures specifically targeted at the Japanese-American population—U.S. citizens and aliens alike—Emmons succeeded in turning aside the pressures to remove all Hawai'i residents of Japanese descent to Moloka'i or some other location remote from Honolulu. These pressures were coming, in part, from segments of the civilian population in Hawai'i. Thus Army Intelligence reported in early January 1942: "There are those individuals who are strongly anti-Japanese, and their influence must be countered whenever possible. Some citizens do not understand the impracticability of internment of a quarter of our entire population."[16] Of greater importance, however, were the pressures that were coming repeatedly from the navy, the White House, Acting U.S. Attorney Angus Taylor, and even some of Emmons's army superiors. Army and navy officers in the Islands, no less than the civilian leadership in Washington, were deeply fearful—not without good reason, as captured Japanese war plans documents would later reveal—that the air attack on Honolulu would be followed by an invasion force launched from the Imperial Japanese

Navy carrier fleet.[17] Hence the focus of much of the secret radio traffic between the army command in Hawai'i and the War Department concerned the invasion threat.

An immediate augmentation of the army forces on the Islands was needed, Emmons stated, not only to repulse an invasion force but also to deal with "any Japanese civilian uprising combined with organized sabotage." These latter dangers, he radioed, "will most likely occur simultaneously, particularly if [the Nikkei] population thinks attack will be successful."[18] To eliminate the possibilities of any disloyal ethnic Japanese remaining on O'ahu, it would be necessary to evacuate as many as 100,000 persons, Emmons estimated.[19] However, he continued to oppose firing Japanese workers en masse from defense and other public projects, as directed by the War Department, as well as mass evacuation of persons of Japanese ancestry, pending the arrival of such army troops. Citing the fact that the ethnic Japanese constituted 95 percent of the skilled workforce in Hawai'i, he warned: "The discharge of these workers in a body will stop almost all high priority and non defense [sic] construction and work, or will cause pro-Japanese sentiment, disloyalty, a feeling of desperation, and encourage sabotage." Emmons went on to urge that the "handling of the Japanese question here should be done by those in direct contact with it."[20]

Nevertheless, on February 12, 1942, General George C. Marshall, army chief of staff, recommended to the Joint Chiefs that "[a]ll Japanese residents of the Hawaiian Islands (whether U.S. citizens or aliens) be transported to the U.S. mainland and placed under guard at a concentration camp in such locality as is most suitable."[21] A few days later, while Marshall's proposal was still under consideration, Knox personally wrote to President Roosevelt that "our forces in Oahu are practically operating now in what is, in effect, enemy country . . . in the presence of a population predominately with enemy sympathies and affiliations." He urged on the president the need for mass evacuation and internment of Hawai'i's Japanese, "no matter what it costs or how much effort it takes."[22] Roosevelt replied on February 26:

> Like you, I have long felt that most of the Japanese should be removed from Oahu to one of the other islands. . . . *I do not worry about the constitutional question—* first, because of my recent order [Executive Order 9066] and, second, because Hawaii is under martial law. The whole matter is one of immediate and present war emergency.
>
> I think you and Stimson can agree and then go ahead and do it as a military project.[23]

Japanese Americans in Hawai'i thus came perilously close to forced removal and relocation: Roosevelt authorized Knox and Stimson to make the necessary arrangements for evacuation from O'ahu. Although the president had urged evacuation to Moloka'i, on March 11 he was informed that the joint chiefs of staff recommended that "such Japanese (either U.S. citizens or aliens) as are considered by appropriate authority in the Hawaiian Islands *to constitute a source of danger* be transported to the U.S. mainland and placed under guard in concentration camps."[24] This recommendation represented a significant modification from Marshall's earlier draft that had provided for the mass removal from Oʻahu of *all* ethnic Japanese.[25] Two days later, the president approved the joint chiefs' recommendation. Stimson by then had concluded that mass evacuation was impractical, and Emmons was left to decide on whom to evacuate, with the number 20,000 being accepted by the president.[26]

Conceding that Emmons should have the final authority, Assistant Chief of Staff Dwight D. Eisenhower wrote to Emmons, "Only, *repeat only,* those persons ordered interned by you will be evacuated."[27] Emmons replied that it was impossible to state definitely the number of Japanese to be interned and sent to the mainland, as continuing investigations were necessary to clarify the status of the suspects. His estimate of the number of ethnic Japanese to be evacuated and interned was 1,500 men and 50 women. "However," he cautioned, "circumstances may arise at any time making it advisable to raise this estimate to much larger figures."[28]

Fearing that the loss of Japanese-American labor would result in the collapse of agricultural, dockyard, and commercial operations vital to the war effort, Emmons would remain steadfast in his opposition to any mass removal and internment policy comparable to that which the army instituted on the West Coast of the mainland under Executive Order 9066, confirmed by congressional legislation.[29] His position was supported by Army Intelligence, which assured Emmons that in an emergency the majority of persons of Japanese ancestry would follow orders to confine themselves to their homes, if necessary.[30]

By late 1942, most, though not all, of the influential leaders in Hawaiʻi supported Emmons in his opposition to mass removals. In the first few months of the war, Frank Midkiff, chairman of the Evacuation Committee of the Office of Civilian Defense (OCD), had suggested to Emmons that because placing all ethnic Japanese in concentration camps was impractical, all enemy aliens and dual citizens should be immobilized in their homes if Emmons deemed it necessary. American citizens of enemy alien descent who were not dual citizens should be given an opportunity to renew their oath of allegiance to the United States, and, if they passed a review, should be permitted to go about their work. Such a plan, Midkiff pointed out, would provide other Asians with positive identification, would provide government clearance for all civilians who were entitled to liberty, and would avoid classifying all those of alien ancestry as enemies. He also suggested that those who were cleared might be of service as agents and observers among enemy aliens.[31] No action appears to have been taken, however, on his recommendation.

As the months wore on, other voices were raised against mass evacuation or incarceration. For example, in May 1942 the Territorial Office of Defense Health and Welfare Services issued a confidential report on "The Japanese Population of the Territory of Hawaii—Its Relationship to the War Effort." It acknowledged that "there are evidences of fears, resentment, distrust and other similar reactions," especially among the older Issei who could not understand what was happening. The report also recognized that some Nisei resented the discrepancy between the ideals of democracy that they had been taught and the realities of their discriminatory treatment. And even when Nisei identified completely with America, there were often strong conflicts with the older generation. "For these and other reasons," the report concluded, "the ultimate loyalty of the Japanese population in the Territory is an unknown quantity." However, the experience of the last five months had failed to prove the necessity of wholesale evacuation of the ethnic Japanese to "safeguard against the activities of a few potential saboteurs."[32]

Of more significance, those who thought that the evacuation of several thousand would suffice to remove potentially dangerous ethnic Japanese included the heads of Military Intelligence (Lieutenant Colonel Bicknell and Captain Blake), of Navy Intelligence (Captain Mayfield), and of the FBI (Robert Shivers). Both Samuel King, Hawai'i's delegate to Congress, and the delegate-elect, Joseph Farrington, were also opposed to a large-scale evacuation. Not surprisingly, the Hawaiian Sugar Planters' Association (HSPA), the Oahu Railway, and other large employers of Japanese Americans were also against it.[33] Indeed, some of those who favored more stringent measures against the ethnic Japanese accused the army of succumbing to the pressures of big business and the HSPA, "who use the Japs for gathering the pineapples and crops. . . . [T]he crops possibly should be sacrificed rather than take the chances."[34] The administration in Washington, however, was confident that the army could handle the situation: "Since martial law prevails," wrote Edward Ennis, head of the Alien Enemy Control Unit, "I would leave it to the Army, particularly if the FBI is satisfied."[35]

Moreover, as the months passed after the December 7 attack and not a single act of espionage or sabotage by a Hawai'i resident of Japanese descent was discovered, the president's removal order increasingly seemed misguided to the army command in Honolulu and to the War Department. "It was a calculated risk" to resist the idea of a mass internment or evacuation, General Green later recalled, "but there was very little choice in the matter" since it would have been impossible to fill the places of thousands of ethnic Japanese who worked as skilled mechanics and artisans. Hence Emmons and Green decided that "all things considered our best policy would be to hold the local Japanese in place under very strict control."[36]

Pro-America Campaign among Japanese Americans

Influential members of the Japanese-American community itself meanwhile sought to work with the Office of the Military Governor (OMG) to allay the fears of those calling for forced removals. In early January, Jack Wakayama, the president of the Hawaiian-Japanese Civic Association, a leadership group composed primarily of Nisei, wrote to his fellow Japanese-American citizens: "Let us accept the challenge to prove beyond all doubt that we are Americans and can do our share as Americans in a common cause." Warning that the manner in which they conducted themselves would determine their relationship with the rest of the people of Hawai'i not only during the war but in the future, he encouraged them to volunteer their services for the armed forces, to contribute to the Red Cross and the blood bank, and to speak English whenever possible. "Report to the F.B.I. any information we may discover concerning subversive activities," he wrote. Further, they should "assume active and aggressive leadership in controlling the thoughts and activities of our alien parents and in directing their lives in conformity with the American Way."[37]

Also working to alleviate racial tensions was the Public Morale Division, created within the Office of Civilian Defense on December 18, 1941. The group initially included YMCA secretary Hung Wai Ching and writer and school administrator Shigeo Yoshida, both of whom had served on the prewar Council for Inter-racial Unity, as well as YMCA leader Charles Loomis.[38] Slightly more than a month later, they were brought into the Office of the Military Governor as the Morale Section, working under the immediate supervision of the Assistant Chief of Staff for Military Intelligence, Colonel Kendall Fielder. They were charged with serving as a liaison between the civilian community and the army on matters relating to public morale, and with promoting a "unified and cooperative community."[39] Their work was to be carried out through various racial and advisory committees, the schools, churches, media, and various civic organizations and clubs, as well as through government agencies.[40]

The Morale Section was particularly concerned with anti-Japanese sentiment among the Filipinos, Koreans, and Chinese in Hawai'i.[41] It was also convinced that most of the Issei were "still loyal at heart to the emperor" and that a propaganda campaign aimed at stressing Issei obligations to America and the importance of an American victory for their children would be the most effective way to neutralize pro-Japanese sentiment. The Morale Section therefore adopted a strategy of working quietly but effectively behind the scenes, using several ethnic subcommittees to implement its aims.[42]

These committees included, most importantly, the Emergency Service Committee (ESC), a group of Nisei that was formed in February 1942 on O'ahu, and similar groups that were appointed on the other islands in the following months.[43] The ESC comprised thirteen Nisei men, with Loomis and Ching as ex officio members; it also had an advisory board of nearly fifty Japanese Americans who were leaders in their districts, as well as a number of *haole* businessmen and educational leaders. The ESC's main purpose was to "channel the inherent loyalty of the people of Japanese ancestry into a program of active participation in the war effort" and to overcome their insecurity and fear following the attack on Pearl Harbor.[44] From its formation until the end of the war, the ESC and its parallel organizations on the other islands served as the chief liaison between the army and the Japanese-American community, receiving guidance from the OMG but acting independently.[45]

With the Issei priests and language school teachers interned, the ESC and the morale committees on the other islands took on leadership roles among the Japanese Americans. In mid-1942, the ESC merged with the Hawaiian-Japanese Civic Association.[46] They held hundreds of meetings, in Japanese and in English, to alleviate confusion and fear and to explain the military's general orders and the mainland evacuation policy. They also urged the ethnic Japanese community to engage in volunteer efforts such as clearing *kiawe* thickets, constructing trails, stringing barbed wire, and otherwise participating in construction and demolition projects needed by the military. Encouraged by slogans such as "If you can't shoulder a gun, you can get behind the men who are carrying the guns," volunteers on Kaua'i alone contributed nearly 10,000 man-hours to such projects.[47]

With the support of the OMG, the members of the ESC undertook campaigns for blood donations and for the purchase of war bonds and the Bombs on Tokyo campaign. They also launched a "Speak American" campaign, with the morale committees offering English classes to thousands of students in conjunction with the University of Hawai'i's adult education program. In addition, the ESC encouraged the Issei to mute their cultural identification with Japan, thereby helping to deflect some of the anti-Japanese sentiment during the war. The Issei were reminded of the old Japanese saying regarding divided loyalties: "When you have two mothers, one who brought you into this world and one who brought you up, you owe much more towards the mother who brought you up."[48] At least one of the Morale Committees petitioned the army to let Japanese Americans volunteer for the armed services, and once Japanese Americans were permitted to enlist for combat duty in early 1943, the ESC led a drive to encourage the call to arms.[49]

In pursuit of their overall goal of enabling and encouraging the full participation of the Japanese-American community in the war effort, the morale committees on the islands other than O'ahu assumed additional tasks for the OMG. For example, in Kaua'i, the Morale Committee was appointed as the liaison office to look after the welfare of the detainees and their families, and it also took legal steps for the liquidation and subsequent distribution of assets of Japanese language schools, temples, and other institutions that were closed by the OMG. Later the Kaua'i Morale Committee assisted veterans and their families with such matters as the GI Bill of Rights and insurance.[50]

Among the ESC's activities was sponsorship of two conferences of Americans of Japanese Ancestry. The first was held in Honolulu in September 1943, as the offensive against the Japanese in the Pacific intensified and the casualties were returning to Hawai'i, increasing anti-Japanese sentiment. The conferees discussed problems confronted by the Nisei as they assumed leadership of their community, including the disruptive impact of the war on family structure, economic problems, the problem of relationships between servicemen and young Nisei women, the need to disregard perceived slights, and the importance of both aliens' and citizens' supporting the war effort more actively. The delegates also urged the creation—under the army's guidance—of new youth organizations to address the behavior of younger Nisei and to replace the Buddhist clubs that were closed with the outbreak of war. Of particular significance was an address on "Problems of the People of Japanese Ancestry in Hawaii as Seen from the Military Point of View," by Lieutenant Colonel Charles Selby. Selby sternly told the conferees that it was up to them to "take aggressive action" to demonstrate their Americanism and speak out against the Axis leaders (even the Japanese emperor); at the same time, the Nisei must minimize behaviors that resulted in adverse criticism, such as use of the Japanese language and acting "cocky."[51]

The second conference was held in late January 1945 and was concerned in part with the postwar period and the future of the Nikkei community. Like the first conference, it promoted assimilation as a way to ensure that the Japanese Americans would fit into the broader society. And, like other ESC programs, it included practical information, such as a discussion of benefits to which servicemen were entitled.[52]

The Morale Committees and the ESC continued to function throughout the war, even after martial law was terminated in October 1944. It was not until the end of September 1945 that they were finally dissolved, and even then some of the committee leaders engaged in other forms of cooperative work to promote inter-racial harmony and improve democracy.[53]

Internment of Alleged Security Risks

General Emmons, meanwhile, approved the continued internment of nearly all the ethnic Japanese picked up in the first wave of arrests. He assured Washington that all persons of Japanese descent who were considered loyalty or security risks were either being held in a camp on Sand Island in O'ahu or else transferred to camps on the mainland. As of February 8, 1942, the army held 518 citizens and enemy aliens in Hawai'i, in legal status designated as "internees," under army control as an exercise of martial law policies.[54] On February 21, 1942—just two days after the president signed Executive Order 9066, authorizing the exclusion of "any or all persons" from prescribed military areas—the army began sending the Sand Island internees to camps on the mainland.[55]

While OMG supervised the evacuation of the internees, the G-2 Counter Intelligence Division actually selected which internees should be evacuated. Colonel Walker, of the Alien Processing Center, devised the detailed plan for evacuation and was responsible for actually processing these individuals.[56]

Army officers at the OMG were soon made to realize that the military regime lacked formal legal authority to remove citizens; they had received no authorization comparable to what the president and Congress had given to the Western Defense Command to carry out the mass removal and detention from the West Coast mainland states. On March 3, 1942, Colonel Archer Lerch, deputy provost marshal general, therefore advised the adjutant general:

> It is believed advisable that hereafter no United States citizens be transferred to the Mainland. Legal status of internees under martial law probably cannot be successfully questioned so long as individuals are detained in Territory. Legality of detention of citizens under internment order issued in Hawaii questionable when internees transferred to Mainland.[57]

Detainees waiting to be fingerprinted and recorded by the FBI on February 17, 1942, at the Immigration Station, Honolulu, which was used as a detention center in the first weeks of the war. Credit: U.S. Army Signal Corps photo, courtesy of the National Archives, Photo #111 SC 137268.

Apparently the concerns of the Adjutant General's office had not reached the president before March 13, when Roosevelt approved the joint chiefs' recommendation to place "in concentration camps" Japanese-American residents of Hawai'i, both aliens and citizens, who were deemed dangerous. Secretary of War Stimson, however, soon brought the matter of incarcerating citizens from Hawai'i to the president's attention. Protesting that he had not seen the joint chiefs' proposal, Stimson warned the president that the cases of a few such citizens from Hawai'i had been taken up by the American Civil Liberties Union, and "habeas corpus writs are contemplated." The War Department, Stimson continued, had looked at the evidence (or lack thereof) and "was satisfied that they cannot be held in confinement under the present legal situation in this country." Stimson was therefore "considering returning them to Hawaii where martial law exists and they can be detained."[58]

In order to implement the evacuation as proposed in the March 13 memo, Stimson told the president, he would have "to suspend in some degree the writ of habeas corpus" (which was still in effect on the mainland) and institute something comparable to Great Britain's Defense of the Realm Act—a measure passed in 1939 and modeled on World War I legislation that gave the government extraordinary executive powers to censor publications, to imprison individuals without trial, and to commandeer resources needed for the war effort. Stimson was apparently less concerned with the civil liberties of the Nisei than he was with the need to control potential saboteurs and with legal requirements to avoid challenges to incarceration. Indeed, Stimson's memorandum continued, if there were to be a concerted sabotage campaign from within in combination with an attack on American frontiers from without, "such a legal step as the Defense of the Realm Act must be taken."[59]

Stimson confided to his diary:

> As the thing stands at present, a number of them have been arrested in Hawaii without very much evidence of disloyalty, have been shipped to the United States, and are interned there. McCloy and I are both agreed that this was contrary to law; that while we have a perfect right to move them away from defenses for the purpose of protecting our war effort, that does not carry with it the right to imprison them without convincing evidence.[60]

In fact, McCloy, fearing that if the citizens were released on writs of habeas corpus on the mainland they could be dangerous, had already written to Emmons about the possibility of returning them to Hawai'i. Emmons, who considered all the evacuees dangerous and opposed releasing any of them, agreed to have them returned for internment in Hawai'i.[61]

Only through its general authority under martial law in Hawai'i did the army have the legal power to intern citizens or dual citizens. Consequently, the army returned the Nisei—a total of nineteen—from the mainland to the Sand Island Detention Station in August 1942.[62] One Nisei, a physician, was part of a group of 170 Japanese, 19 Germans and Italians, and a captured Japanese Navy officer who were sent to the mainland in March 1942. He recalled his ordeal:

> When I led the Oahu internees on March 1942 to San Francisco, we received cruel and inhuman treatment. We were taken to Camp McCoy in Wisconsin. Then after two months, we were transferred to Camp Forest, Tennessee. After one month, we went to Camp Livingston in Louisiana. The authorities then discovered it was a mistake to intern U.S. citizens in areas not under martial law so about 17 of us were shipped back to Hawaii because we were U.S. Citizens.
>
> When we landed, we were rearrested and taken back to Sand Island. We had made a circuit of 9,000 miles from Sand Island to the mainland camps and back again to Sand Island.[63]

Thus, although some Nisei citizens or dual citizens were transported to the mainland in the first year of the war, because the Department of Justice refused to accept citizens in 1942, only aliens were sent as internees thereafter.[64] Nisei internees would be held instead in the Territory of Hawai'i, most of them initially at Sand Island. In March 1943, most of the Nisei still in custody there would be transferred to a newly opened internment camp that was hastily built at Honouliuli, about twenty-five miles from Honolulu near the town of Ewa.[65]

However, as we describe below, scores of Nisei internees continued to be transferred to the mainland. Technically designated as "evacuees," they were "released" into the custody of the War Relocation Authority (WRA), rather than sent as internees in the Justice Department camps. They were incarcerated nonetheless.[66] Those detainees requesting repatriation to Japan were subsequently transferred to the Tule Lake camp, which in 1943 became a segregation center for those with pro-Japanese sympathies.[67]

What was important to the War Department as a priority in the early months of the war was that the army appeared to be pursuing strong security measures against the ethnic Japanese. Assistant Secretary of War John McCloy visited Hawai'i in March 1942. McCloy had been a principal architect of the policy of mass removal and incarceration of the West-Coast Japanese Americans on the mainland. Nevertheless, he came away from Hawai'i, where he had direct authority over the Office of the Military Governor, convinced that both the army and the top navy officers on the scene were justified in opposing mass evacuation of the Nikkei. He further acknowledged that any such mass evacuation to either an outlying island or the mainland was impractical because of the lack of shipping, the importance of the Japanese labor force, the lack of facilities on the mainland, and "the political repercussions on the West Coast and in the United States generally to the introduction of 150,000 more Japanese." He also noted the "grave legal difficulties in placing American citizens, even of Japanese ancestry, in concentration camps."[68]

McCloy publicly stated for the Honolulu newspapers of March 27 and 28 that mass evacuation of the ethnic Japanese was impractical and was not contemplated, and he provided strong affirmation of the military's view of selective internment only in the highest policy circles.[69] Privately, he reported to the secretary of war that army and navy officials in Hawai'i opposed mass evacuation and preferred "to treat the Japanese in Hawaii as citizens of an occupied foreign country."[70] By April 3, McCloy and the army's Operations Division seemed to have accepted Emmons's recommendation for evacuating only the 1,500 men considered dangerous.[71]

Neither Secretary Knox nor President Roosevelt himself, however, was willing to abandon the idea of large-scale removals. On April 20, Knox again advocated "taking all of the Japs out of Oahu and putting them in a concentration camp on some other island."[72] Roosevelt was not persuaded that labor needs had to be given a high priority—especially so as he had been warned repeatedly by Secretary Knox of a continuing security threat posed by the presence of ethnic Japanese, a view reinforced by special intelligence reports claiming that 600 or more "active agents [were] still loose" in O'ahu and engaged in spying and possible espionage.[73]

A month later, McCloy, feeling the political pressure, wrote to General Emmons: "Both the President and the Secretary of the Navy continuously refer to the desirability of moving Japanese from the Island of Oahu to some other Island rather than to bring any numbers of them to the United States." McCloy said he was resisting any such change because of the difficulties involved. However, he wrote, "[T]he matter has not come to rest and the thought now is that if the number that were to be moved were to be limited, say, 10,000 or 15,000, the practicability of moving them to Hawaii [the Big Island] would be apparent.... I feel I should send you warning that this subject may crop up again and that you might be thinking of it."[74] Emmons was unswayed. "I think we can counteract any such suggestions by logic when the time comes," he replied to McCloy.[75]

Additional Removals: "Relocation"

Nevertheless, Emmons and his staff did begin working on plans that would remove some additional ethnic Japanese from the Territory of Hawai'i. In late June 1942, Emmons proposed that those who constituted an economic drain on the war effort, as well as families of internees already on the mainland, be *voluntarily* evacuated to the mainland.[76] The War Department assured Emmons that it had now abandoned the idea of mass evacuations of aliens and citizens of Japanese extraction. "It is realized, however, that there are certain groups of Japanese in Hawaii who are either believed to be dangerous or are most likely to become so during any period of invasion or immediate threat of invasion." Thus, Emmons was told, the War Relocation Authority had made provision for up to 15,000 evacuees from Hawai'i in relocation centers on the mainland. "These centers are not, repeat not, internment camps but instead are resettlement areas with housing facilities and opportunities to work provided by the government."[77]

The distinction between internment camps and the relocation centers was made explicit in a War Department memorandum of July 17, which also rescinded Roosevelt's order of March 13 to place dangerous U.S. citizens as well as aliens from Hawai'i in mainland concentration camps:

> No United States citizen of any derivation whatsoever, either naturalized or native-born, now residing in Hawaii, and considered . . . to constitute a source of danger to our national security, will be transferred to the continental United States for internment. Such individuals will be interned in the Hawaiian Islands under authority vested in the Military Governor.[78]

The same memo authorized Emmons to evacuate for *resettlement* in WRA facilities (not for internment) "up to 15,000 persons, in family groups, from among the United States citizens of Japanese ancestry who may be considered as potentially dangerous to national security."[79]

This change in policy was the result of a joint memorandum, sent just two days earlier, in which Army Chief of Staff Marshall and the chief of naval operations, Admiral Ernest J. King, had advised President Roosevelt of the danger of U.S. citizens obtaining release from custody on the mainland by applying for a writ of habeas corpus. Accordingly, they had urged him to rescind his March 13 order in favor of the new policy as incorporated in the memo to Emmons: citizens from Hawai'i who were considered an actual danger to national security were to be interned in Hawai'i under martial law; citizens considered a potential danger were to be relocated, with their families, to the mainland. Faced with this united front by the military and naval chiefs, Roosevelt personally approved the new language and rescinded the earlier order.[80] Thus by mid-1942, it was clear that Emmons and the army had prevailed in opposing Roosevelt's (and Knox's) earlier plans for mass removals and detention of the Nikkei from O'ahu.

The first families actually to be evacuated left Hawai'i in August 1942. They constituted a group of 133 persons—37 women and 96 children—whose husbands or fathers were interned on the mainland and had requested repatriation to Japan. Some parents left without their children, who chose to remain in Hawai'i.[81] They were part of an exchange arranged with Japan through the services of the Swedish vice consul.

Meanwhile, Emmons continued to refine his plans for selective evacuation into the fall months, maintaining his focus on the families of internees and those who were a drain on the economy.[82] In October, he wrote that he wished the evacuation to be "ostensibly on a voluntary basis." Apparently concerned about the welfare of the evacuees, he requested information on the availability of schools and hospitals, the type of employment and types of shelter that would be available, and the location of the relocation centers.[83] A few days later, Emmons was authorized to proceed with an evacuation of up to 3,000 initially, although a total of 15,000 was approved for the long run. He was assured by General Marshall that he had full authority as military governor and by presidential order to evacuate "any alien or citizen Japanese you deem potentially dangerous." However, Marshall deemed it "undesirable and unnecessary" to make the evacuation voluntary. At the same time, Marshall reassured Emmons that there were grade schools and high schools, as well as hospital facilities, available at the relocation centers; that housing consisted of cantonment type, family units; and that employment was primarily agricultural. He did warn, however, that subsequent movement of the evacuees would be by permit only, after they had reached the relocation centers.[84]

Although as late as October 1942 the Hawai'i command clearly was being made aware that "Washington is [still] pressing" for evacuation of more Japanese Americans, General Emmons's policy, as reported by Green, was: "Agree but stall."[85] A high-ranking army officer summarized for the War Department how Emmons was handling the "Japanese Problem in Hawaii":

(a) Actively dangerous citizens are interned in Hawaii to avoid any possibilities of release on the mainland because of writ of habeas corpus proceedings (Military government).

(b) Actively dangerous enemy aliens are returned to the mainland for internment (Presidential decree).

(c) Potentially dangerous citizens and aliens alike are being returned to the mainland in family groups for settlement in relocation centers (Presidential decree).[86]

In late October, Secretary of War Stimson formally certified to President Roosevelt that
no persons of Japanese descent "known to be hostile to the United States" any longer
remained free in Hawai'i and outside the internment camps.[87]

Roosevelt nevertheless remained concerned about the army's attitude, and on November 2 he personally sent a memorandum of his views to the army chief of staff,
General Marshall, and to Secretary of War Stimson. "I think that General Emmons
should be told," the president asserted, "that the only consideration is that of the safety
of the Islands and that the labor situation is not only not a secondary matter but should
not be given any consideration whatsoever. General Emmons and Admiral Nimitz
should be advised of this. Military and naval safety is absolutely paramount."[88]

On the very day that FDR sent off these instructions, General Emmons assured
the War Department that he was continuing to plan the evacuation of some five thousand residents of Japanese descent—but he left little doubt that the reason was the need
to respond to orders from the White House, and not any objective security danger:

> The five thousand to be evacuated . . . , when and if transportation becomes avail-
> able, are not necessarily disloyal to the United States. This group will comprise
> those residents who might be potentially dangerous in the event of a crisis, yet
> they have committed no suspicious acts. It is impossible to determine whether or
> not they are loyal. In general the evacuation will remove persons who are least
> desirable in the territory and who are contributing nothing to the war effort.[89]

Despite the explicit directive of November 2 from the White House, the decision
to initiate a comprehensive removal or internment was successfully resisted by the army
and the highest-ranking War Department officials. In effect, FDR's initiative died from
suffocation by bureaucratic resistance. The fact that no hard evidence of any espionage
or sabotage was ever discovered apparently served, in the end, to validate the army's
policy of giving labor needs first priority.

The OMG never conceived of the selective evacuation policy as a first step for mass
detention or removals. In formal terms, the program as announced was intended to
transfer out of Hawai'i, in a series of removals, groups of individuals selected for evacuation "who are either non-productive [to the wartime economy] or who are potentially
dangerous in the Islands but not dangerous on the Mainland."[90] On the mainland,
it was explained, the people removed would no longer be able to conduct espionage or
engage in sabotage near the sites of sensitive military and naval operations such as
were located in Hawai'i.

The initial detailed evacuation plan, dated December 1, 1942 (just short of a year
after the attack on Pearl Harbor), anticipated that some 3,250 persons would be transferred to mainland relocation centers. The largest group selected for removal consisted

Sampans in Honolulu harbor, some flying Japanese colors. The army banned the sampans and removed many of the fishermen, mainly Issei, to the mainland. Credit: Hawai'i State Archives.

of fishermen (mostly Issei), now banned by the military from going out to sea lest they conduct surveillance for the enemy. Because the fishermen had specialized skills, not readily adaptable to other employment on the Islands, OMG staff feared that they would need public relief and thus become a financial burden for the military government. This group, including families (with an average of six children), would number an estimated 2,000; thus it was nearly two-thirds of the projected total to be evacuated.[91]

The second largest group in the plan was to comprise Kibei and their "small families," for a total of 475. The Kibei, who were U.S. citizens, had been detained and then interned in Hawai'i; they were included in the broad category of security risks because of their recent close ties to Japan.[92] According to one official source, *all* Kibei who had returned from Japan in the three years prior to the war were rounded up for evacuation, irrespective of their individual loyalty.[93] In most cases, prior to being evacuated, each citizen internee was given a chance to meet with his wife to reach a joint decision on evacuation; the chief of internal security then reviewed each case for suitability for release on the mainland.[94]

Among the others targeted for removal were a small number of individual Kibei and 225 aliens who had requested repatriation to Japan; all Japanese aliens (legally, enemy aliens) who were interned in Hawai'i, and these aliens' families; and the families of selected Japanese aliens who had previously been removed and were interned on the mainland. The families, in both these latter categories, were formally designated "voluntary evacuees."[95]

Before being evacuated, they were given a form to sign, "Consent to Internment in Family Internment Camp." The form acknowledged that they were petitioning to be placed in a family internment camp, that they consented to "all restrictions and regulations applicable to interned enemy aliens," and that they understood they could not leave the camp as long as the order of internment affecting their family member remained in effect. At the same time, the form made clear that the petition did not imply in any way that they had been engaged in subversive activities, nor did it affect their rights and privileges except regarding the restrictions of the camp.[96]

The removals based on this plan took place in four embarkation groups, beginning in November 1942 and ending in March 1943. According to army records, "313 persons formerly interned in the Territory of Hawai'i, who together with their families and 26 other family units, numbering 1,040 in all, were evacuated."[97] Of those transferred, 88 percent were Nisei citizens, including most of the Kibei who had been targeted. More than two-thirds of the evacuees were women and children.[98] Actual evacuations, however, fell far short of the initial goal of 3,250. The program ended in March 1943, when the evacuations were abruptly halted.[99]

This evacuation to the mainland was, according to one army official, "primarily for the purpose of removing non-productive and undesirable Japanese and their families from the Islands" and "largely a token evacuation to satisfy certain interests which have strongly advocated movement of Japanese from the Hawaiian Islands."[100] Token though it may have been, this evacuation wrought severe financial and psychological hardships to those affected. As one young evacuee, the daughter of a storekeeper on the Big Island of Hawai'i, recalled:

> In November, almost a year after Pearl Harbor, we were told to prepare for evacuation. In panic, we packed our personal belongings and few household items. We left behind all the store goods, large household items, car, father's journal of his family that he traced to the 1500s and his treasured stamp collection. . . . It was part of his life . . . lost forever.
>
> All the Big Island evacuees were taken to Hilo and later to Honolulu on a cattle ship. . . . We were given numbers for personal and family identification; our human dignity had been stripped away. We were faceless individuals with numbers.[101]

It was two and a half years before her father, detained in Camp Livingston in Louisiana, joined his family at Camp Jerome in Arkansas. They returned to Hawai'i after the war, only to find that they had no home to return to; it had been taken over, along with their store, by the plantation.[102] Their story was hardly atypical.

At a later time, during late 1944 and into 1945, OMG would inaugurate another removal program, but with a different legal template and under the rubric "exclusion" rather than "evacuation."[103]

Pressures for Further Removals

Stringent as the evacuation policy was, especially for the Kibei and their relatives, the army's program did not satisfy the top Naval Intelligence officers in Hawai'i, nor did it appease others pressing for a stronger policy of removals. Reporting in December 1942, one government official observed that "influential white Americans" in Hawai'i feared that

> it may not be long before the Japanese Americans will have economic and politi-
> cal control of the Territory of Hawaii. Men like J. A. Balch, chairman of the board
> of directors of the Mutual Telephone Co. of Honolulu, and Angus Taylor, U.S. At-
> torney, feel that this is the time to rid the Islands permanently of this dangerous
> Japanese influence. . . . [T]here is a substantial pressure group working to secure
> mass evacuation.[104]

A Special Assistant to the Secretary of the Interior, reporting on conditions in Hawai'i in spring 1943, also noted: "There is considerable anti-Japanese sentiment through-out the Territory, much of it long standing and one frequently hears expressions of impatience about the Government's 'failure' to evacuate many more Japanese to the mainland."[105]

Throughout the spring of 1943, Balch in particular campaigned in the media and through public officials to evacuate at least 100,000 Japanese Americans to the main-land and turn their jobs over to white laborers from the mainland.[106] Balch argued that no nation could exist safely with so large a minority "consisting of a race as unassimi-lable as the Japanese," but his motives were openly economic as well as xenophobic: unless such a removal was effected, he contended, "these people [will] gain even greater political and economic control" than they already enjoyed. The "Japanese race," he claimed, was making economic gains at the expense of other citizens whose sons "were being slaughtered by these sadistic people in the Solomons and elsewhere in the Pacific."[107]

As late as April 1943, U.S. District Attorney Angus Taylor, too, was still pressing the Justice Department to crack down on the Japanese Americans in Hawai'i on grounds that there was extensive espionage and sabotage; he condemned the army regime for being too inattentive to the threat.[108] Justice officials viewed his reports with great skepticism, especially as the FBI reportedly regarded Taylor as "unreliable and unin-formed."[109] In fact, the FBI flatly rejected Taylor's information as being "incorrect, fanciful, and farfetched. These charges have been answered time and time again."[110] Four months later, in September 1943, Taylor had also become a major annoyance for

McCloy, who noted in his diary the need for a meeting with General Cramer on "busting Taylor and substitution of Crozier."[111]

The navy—which was not responsible, as the army was, for maintaining production, for the logistics of removal, and for civilian morale—consistently demanded a more rigorous policy of removal of the Japanese from Oʻahu, especially from broad areas around the naval bases. Thus in August 1942, Secretary Knox wrote to the president that he was still "gravely concerned over the menace which is presented in Oahu by the very large number of unquestionably pro-Japanese who are still at large on that Island."[112] Writing some weeks after the Battle of Midway, he decried the view that "the war in the Pacific is practically won" as "extremely dangerous and unjustified."[113]

In December 1942, as Emmons's evacuation policy was underway, the army's chief intelligence officer in Hawaiʻi, Colonel Fielder, defended the army's policy. While acknowledging that "[i]t has long been recognized from a security standpoint it would be desirable to remove all persons of Japanese extraction from the Territory of Hawaii," Fielder stated that the shortage of transport ships and the importance of 160,000 ethnic Japanese to the economy made such measures impractical. Persons of Japanese ancestry, he pointed out, constituted 24 percent of agricultural laborers, 80 percent of dairy employees and food handlers, 45 percent of the workers in manufacturing and industry, 45 percent in trades, 30 percent in transportation and commerce, 60 percent of Oahu Railway's laborers, and 56 percent in domestic and personal service. Further, they operated more than 90 percent of the truck farms on Oʻahu. Fielder concluded: "We have a delicate situation on our hands and must avoid mass discrimination against the Japanese residents, and any move which will alienate what loyalty that exists."[114]

A few months later, Fielder made public his position regarding the ethnic Japanese, which was in sharp contrast to the policies pursued on the West Coast of the mainland. Addressing the University of Hawaiʻi's convocation in April 1943, he stated: "We have removed, and shall continue to remove—for national and local security—that minority of aliens and citizens here who are considered dangerous or potentially dangerous in time of war. We did not impugn, because of race, the good name of the rest of them, alien or citizen." The army's policy was not one of mere sentimentality, but rather a "sane, reasonable, democratic and SAFE judgment." If accepted, Fielder contended, the "Japanese element of the population . . . is an asset to the community. Yet rejected and treated as potential enemies they would constitute a burden, even a danger, to our security."[115]

Despite such arguments from the army, the navy remained intransigent in its views. Secretary Knox was still agitating the question of whether the ethnic Japanese in Hawaiʻi posed a palpable security threat in March 1943.[116] The navy's security and intelligence staffs in Hawaiʻi took a similar stance. Their position was illustrated in stark form when in late 1943 Navy Security demanded the evacuation of "thousands and thousands" of Nikkei from three major coastal areas of Oʻahu in which important naval logistical and operational activities were centered.[117] Fielder scorned the idea, warning that if the navy's local Security Officer were permitted any control over policy, "The minute he moves in, three years of effort to promote racial harmony, economic status quo, and domestic tranquility will go by the boards."[118] Similar concerns about racism and potential economic damage were expressed by Congressional Delegate Samuel King and his successor-elect, Joseph R. Farrington, who was president and general manager of the *Honolulu Star-Bulletin,* and by the Oahu Sugar Planters Association and the Oahu Railway.[119]

There is every indication, however, that OMG intended to continue to expand— albeit on a modest and gradual basis—the evacuation program. Thus it is necessary to ask why so many fewer persons were removed than had been planned, and why the program ended so suddenly. The answer seems to lie in part in Emmons's concerns that the Hawaiian evacuees be separated from any Japanese aliens in the camps who were about to be repatriated, lest they pass on information about the Islands' installations. The Japanese from Hawai'i were "fully aware," Emmons wrote, "of the Hawaiian situation and might be a source of useful information for the enemy."[120] Indeed, Emmons opposed repatriation of any Japanese from Hawai'i, but in this he was overruled because of existing agreements between Japan and the United States.[121] Assistant Secretary of War McCloy pointed out to Emmons the difficulties posed by requesting separation of the evacuees from Hawai'i, including adverse reactions both in Hawai'i and on the part of the evacuees; the need to construct additional facilities; and the "severe discrimination" against the Hawai'i evacuees. He suggested, instead, that the evacuation be discontinued if doing so would not impair security in Hawai'i.[122]

But the termination of the evacuation program was due also, in part, to inter-bureaucracy conflicts that owed much to the heavy-handed manner in which OMG implemented the evacuation procedure—especially with regard to a firestorm of criticism that it drew from Dillon Myer, director of the War Relocation Authority, and his staff.[123] Relocation center officials were complaining internally that the Hawaiian evacuation was creating problems within their organization.[124] As Myer wrote to Assistant Secretary of War McCloy: "Our experience at Jerome, where the Hawaiian evacuees are located, has not been good. They have proved to be unwilling workers and about half of them have answered no to the loyalty question number 28 in the selective service registration form. They definitely are not the kind of people who should be scattered among the West Coast evacuees."[125]

The relocation centers were becoming overcrowded, and the newly arrived evacuees from Hawai'i were running into frictions with the mainland Japanese Americans who were already being held in these facilities. It should be noted, however, that Myer's account of the experience at Jerome was contrary to a report that was sent to him the very next day by Paul Taylor, director of the Jerome WRA facility. Remarking that 820 evacuees from Hawai'i had arrived at Jerome, Taylor reported that they "had not presented any particular problem to date." The mainland Nikkei had "accepted the Hawaiian group in good grace," although they complained about their English and their pro-Japanese attitudes. Taylor also explained that about half the men from Hawai'i had qualified their answers to Question 28, saying they could not answer "yes" because of having been interned with no reason given and their previous assertions of loyalty having been ignored.[126]

Although Director Myer may have exaggerated the difficulties with the detainees from Hawai'i, there were other problems as well. Legal issues remained troubling: the WRA lacked formal authority to place Nisei in internment camps or to effect their parole, since, as noted earlier, the citizen evacuees were in custody under authority only of martial law and therefore remained the legal and administrative responsibility of the OMG in Hawai'i. Moreover, the WRA officials had begun to suspect that evacuation had less to do with protecting Hawai'i's military security than with OMG unburdening itself at the expense of mainland authorities. And so Myer and others registered increasingly urgent complaints about the program. On February 27, Myer requested that the War Department ask Emmons to suspend altogether any further evacuations to the mainland.[127]

By the end of March 1943, the bureaucratic tensions that were mounting so dramatically finally forced Emmons to halt the evacuation program. It was officially suspended on April 2, unless the number of internees exceeded Hawai'i's capacity for housing them.[128] (Eight voluntary evacuees from Hawai'i—family members seeking to reunite with spouses or parents taken to the mainland earlier—entered the WRA centers between May 1943 and September 1944.)[129] And so the army legal staff and the security officials in Hawai'i went back to the drawing board in their offices at Iolani Palace to reconsider the policies for removal of internees and for internal security control. As before, the Kibei—being citizens, hence potentially a source of habeas corpus litigation that could undermine the army's powerful hold on both security and general civilian affairs—remained the focus of attention for the OMG and its legal officers.

Acting by its authority under martial law, the army continued to detain both Issei and Nisei during the remainder of the war. Rather than being sent to the mainland, they were now interned mainly in the newly constructed internment camp at Honouliuli on O'ahu. By May 1943, this camp housed 84 Issei and 154 Nisei.[130] Others were held in smaller numbers in Kalaheo in Kaua'i, Waiakea on the Big Island of Hawai'i, Haiku on Maui, and on Moloka'i and Lana'i.

Exclusion

By 1944, however, with the threat of an invasion by Japan having receded, pressures mounted in both Washington and Hawai'i to terminate martial law. A series of legal challenges to martial law also raised the possibility of American citizens of Japanese ancestry being held in Hawai'i suing for their release in the courts. In summer 1943, the federal district court in Honolulu agreed to hear a habeas petition, and in spring 1944 three more test cases of martial law came before the courts.[131] Although none of these cases involved Japanese Americans, the door to legal challenges to martial law had been opened.

Thus, early in 1944, General Richardson again tried to transfer a group of Kibei to the mainland. Writing to McCloy in February 1944, Richardson reported that there were 135 Kibei still interned in Hawaiʻi, of whom 100 had professed loyalty to the United States or made no statements of loyalty either way. Believing them nevertheless to be dangerous, Richardson proposed to transfer them to a WRA center on the mainland, "for the reason that if any of them should institute habeas corpus proceedings in the local United States District Court, we might not be able to present a strong case against them."[132] The director of the WRA, Dillon Myer, had already made clear to Richardson, however, that "he found it very undesirable to accept additional residents at the Tule Lake Segregation Center." Indeed, he had requested General William R. Morrison, who had succeeded Green as Executive in the OMG, to "dissuade voluntary evacuees from applying to join their families in mainland relocation centers."[133] Aware of Myer's position, McCloy's office replied to Richardson that there was insufficient housing available at the Tule Lake Center, the logical place to receive the Kibei, and that the legal case for detaining them in Hawaiʻi was stronger than if they were transferred to the mainland. He suggested that Richardson, instead, try paroling the least dangerous.[134]

Insisting on the continued necessity of its security policy as long as the war was still raging in the Pacific, but fearing both the possibility of habeas suits and the end of martial law, the army was faced with the challenge of devising a new strategy to detain Nisei. As the pressures for ending martial law increased in the summer of 1944, the army was still holding, as internees under martial law, more than one hundred persons of Japanese ancestry. Of that hundred, Morrison said, "at least seventy of them are people that we, under no circumstances . . . would consider letting loose on the streets anywhere. They are persons who are of the opinion that they want Japan to win the war."[135]

Richardson and his legal staff therefore wanted an executive order that would grant them authority to intern citizens of Japanese ancestry in the absence of martial law. He regarded reliance on Executive Order 9066, which Garner Anthony had suggested as an alternative to martial law, as unacceptable because it would deprive the military of "our right of apprehension and internment of citizen Japanese deemed dangerous" by the intelligence authorities. Each exclusion order would be reviewable by the courts, and Richardson did not want security to be "subject to determination in every single case of a local judge."[136] Several months later, Richardson was still registering the same objections to Executive Order 9066, adding to its list of shortcomings that it did not provide adequately for censorship.[137] Both Ickes and Biddle, however, rejected as "inadvisable" and "perhaps illegal" the inclusion in the executive order of the power to intern American citizens (including dual citizens). McCloy therefore told Richardson that the only solution was to send such citizens to the mainland, "where Interior and Justice agree to adopt [a] liberal policy relative to their internment at Tule Lake."[138] Satisfied that the ability to incarcerate suspects on the mainland would provide adequate control of Japanese-American citizens whose loyalty they doubted but against whom there were no real charges that would hold up in a court of law, the army thus decided on a policy of "exclusion."

Exclusion, at its core, was little more than the forced removal of Nisei citizens, including Kibei, to the mainland, but with one fundamental legal difference from internment. Since mainland authorities lacked the legal power to intern Hawai'i Kibei or to monitor their parole, OMG was unable to evacuate Kibei without facing severe criticism for sending a purportedly dangerous population group potentially to roam freely on the mainland. With considerable input from OMG as well as from his cabinet, the president issued Executive Order No. 9489, signed on October 18, 1944, which authorized the secretary of war to designate a military commander who could declare the Territory of Hawai'i or any part thereof to be a military area, over which he would possess authority as the military commander. This authority included the power to order the "evacuation, exclusion, and detention incident thereto" of individuals from the designated military area to prevent espionage or sabotage; the right of any individuals to enter, remain in or leave the military area was subject to whatever restrictions the military commander might impose.[139]

In essence, Executive Order 9489 thus gave to the Hawaiian Command the same authority that Executive Order 9066 had given to the Western Defense Command and that had resulted in the mass removals of the ethnic Japanese population from the West Coast. Its result, however, was far less disastrous for Hawai'i's ethnic Japanese than Executive Order 9066 had been for the mainland Nikkei, for Richardson, like Emmons, continued the policy of *selective* detention.

On October 24, 1944—the very day that martial law in Hawai'i was formally terminated—General Richardson issued Public Proclamation Number One of the Military Commander of the Territory of Hawai'i Military Area, designating the entire Territory of Hawai'i as a military area. He declared that "any or all such persons will be ordered excluded or evacuated from the Territory of Hawaii Military Area or from any part thereof by the Military Commander whenever such exclusion is necessary to prevent espionage or sabotage."[140]

In the months preceding this proclamation, officials in the Legal Section of OMG had compiled lists of Kibei and other dual citizens to be excluded from the territory, and the first seventy Kibei selected for exclusion were already identified the day before Richardson's proclamation.[141] A new hearing procedure was established that differed from that previously instituted under martial law: the suspects now were unable to present any evidence on their own behalf, or to bring witnesses or counsel; and the hearing review board consisted solely of army officers, with no civilian representation.[142] Following such hearings, the results of which were apparently a foregone conclusion, the Hawai'i Command shipped the first group of excludees from the Port of Honolulu to the mainland on November 8, 1944, just two weeks after the proclamation went into effect.[143] By war's end, a total of seventy-three excludees had been sent to Tule Lake, including a group of thirty-four Kibei being held at Honouliuli who, in the summer of 1944, had requested repatriation to Japan.[144]

The army's insistence on exclusion resulted from its continued fears of threats to internal security. Indeed, as late as March 1945 the Counter Intelligence Division (CID) was worried about sabotage—ironically, because now their fears were based on Japan's diminished capacity to wage effective war. "What will [be] the reaction among the local Japanese when they realize Japan truly is in danger and that country and its people truly are suffering? That has been the question in the back of the mind with the CID for more than a year now. . . . [I]t was felt there might well be a time, a kind of occasion, which would bring on one or many acts inimical to the internal security. Sabotage, for example."[145] And so the CID was motivated to "concentrate on ferreting out and apprehending Japanese of proven or suspected loyalty to Nippon."[146] The investigations of both aliens and citizens continued, with some being interned even as others were cleared or released, until the final months of the war.

Chapter Nine

DETERMINING LOYALTY

Review Boards, Questionnaires, and Racial Profiling

The need for security and defense of the Islands—and hence the corollary need for selective internments—remained paramount in the thinking of the Office of the Military Governor (OMG) throughout the war. Having initially decided that detention, internment, and evacuation of residents of Japanese and other enemy ancestry would be selective, Emmons (and after June 1, 1943, his successor, Robert C. Richardson) and the OMG staff had to determine how best to make that selection. Thus, from the earliest days of the war, the basis for determining the loyalty of the ethnic Japanese—and the potential security risk they posed—became a central, complex, and highly controversial issue for security policy. Although similar issues for determining loyalty applied to the much smaller number of German and Italian detainees, the focus was, for the most part, on those of Japanese extraction, both because of their numbers and because of the fear of a Japanese invasion.

The intelligence officers of the army, navy, and civilian security units had all recognized the importance of citizenship status as well as other factors of diversity in Hawaiʻi's Nikkei community as a social (and legal) reality, relevant to security policy. They therefore sought to design policies that would take account of the unique characteristics of each subgroup, and even within subgroups, to separate the loyal from those who were potential security threats. This effort was in sharp contrast to the policy on the West Coast of the mainland, where race alone was sufficient basis for removal and incarceration. The task in Hawaiʻi was made all the more difficult by the fact that the outbreak of the war had created a wide diversity of reactions among Japanese Americans themselves, ranging from those who took principled stands on their obligations and rights as Americans, to those who—though not necessarily dangerous—either were neutral or quietly favored a Japanese victory. The reactions of many were far too complex to be simply classified as "loyal" or "disloyal."[1] Furthermore, the attitudes of some of Hawaiʻi's Japanese Americans changed during the course of the war as they were stripped of their civil liberties, separated from their families, and subjected to incarceration.

Dealing with this challenge of determining loyalty, the bureaucracy—consisting in the Islands entirely of Caucasians, none of whom had expert knowledge of Japanese culture—devised an elaborately rationalized template for what today is termed "profiling." A nuanced interrogatory protocol would eventually be formulated, based on experience in handling ethnic Japanese who were taken into custody in the initial weeks of the war in December 1941 and early 1942.[2]

Hearing Boards

The army was assigned final responsibility for security and internments under martial law, augmented by an interservice agreement on unified command. The initial procedures regarding aliens—Japanese, Italians, and Germans—were set forth in the first days following the attack on Pearl Harbor in a radiogram from the War Department to the commanding general. The commanding general was given responsibility to "apprehend all alien enemies deemed dangers [sic] to safety of U- S-, including Japanese, Italian and German citizens." The following day this was amended to include dual citizens. Those arrested were to be detained "until [the] necessity for internment has been determined following recommendation of a hearing board." The number of hearing boards that the Commanding General was authorized to appoint was left to his discretion, but each board was "to comprise three civilian citizens, one of whom should be an attorney if available." One member of the board was to present the case, act as executive, and submit appropriate reports. The instructions continued:

> Hearings shall be informal and expeditious. Hearings are not accorded as a matter of right but are allowed in order to avoid injustice and to obtain all available information concerning citizenship, loyalty and activities of alien enemies apprehended. Aliens may appear personally or by counsel, testify in own behalf and bring witnesses to testify as to activities and loyalty.[3]

Those apprehended were to be provided with basic housing in barracks, including basic necessities such as bedding and clothing. The commanding general was further admonished: "Alien enemies apprehended concerning whom there is no showing of violation of a criminal statute are not criminals and may not *repeat not* be treated as such. . . . Detention or internment in jails or prison except where no other facilities are available is not permissible."[4]

Overall responsibility for the hearings was assigned to Major Edward E. Walker. A retired army officer who served as high sheriff of the Territory of Hawai'i for seven years, Walker was recalled to active duty on December 12, 1941, and designated as the provost marshal's liaison officer at the OMG. One day later, General Green handed him the radiogram from the War Department that authorized the internment of enemy aliens and the establishment of hearing boards, together with a list of names from which to select the members of three hearing boards. Green told Walker to get to work, reporting to G-2. Thus was Walker charged with designing and implementing a procedure for hearings and processing of enemy aliens, with no written directives and, indeed, with no name given to his organization. Walker himself suggested the name "Hawaiian Department Alien Processing Center."

In the spring of 1942, Walker and the Alien Processing Center were transferred from the provost marshal's office to the OMG, although custody of the detainees remained the responsibility of the provost marshal.[5] According to official army records, the Alien Processing Center served in "an intermediate position between the various intelligence agencies and the civilian population of the Territory."[6] The Alien Processing Center's functions were purely operational; the executive section and the military governor continued to formulate policies. Despite its name, the Alien Processing Center was responsible for processing all those who were apprehended by the investigative agencies—citizens and aliens alike—as well as all those who were sent to the mainland or repatriated to Japan.[7]

Prior to arrest, each suspect had been the subject of an investigation by, and usually an interview with, one of the three intelligence agencies–the ONI, MID, or FBI. If the agency believed the subject should be detained, his or her case was reviewed by a panel consisting of representatives of at least two of the three intelligence agencies prior to an arrest warrant being issued.[8]

Following arrest, each detainee was brought before a hearing board. Three boards were established on December 14 and were ready to start work the following day. By that time, there were already several hundred suspects—mostly aliens, but some citizens—in custody at the Immigration Station, all of whom had been rounded up, without any warrants of any kind, by the FBI, MID, ONI, and the local police.[9] Walker outlined to the board members their functions and informed the boards that their role was advisory, with final action to be taken by the commanding general. However, Walker could give few detailed instructions—mainly because his attempts to secure them from the executive section of the OMG met with little satisfaction, despite the fact that there were published procedures in use by the Immigration and Naturalization Service (INS) on the mainland.[10]

In addition to the hearing boards on Oʻahu, which began operations on December 16, Walker established hearing boards on Hawaiʻi, Maui, and Kauaʻi. On these outer islands, the executive officer of the hearing board was responsible not only for the hearing itself, but also for the detention and care of the persons and property of those brought before them—functions handled by the provost marshal on Oʻahu.[11] Their recommendations were sent for review and final decision in Honolulu.[12]

According to the OMG, the hearing boards consisted of "three civilians and a recorder, who is an Army officer. One of the three civilian members is designated the president of the Board, and is usually an attorney."[13] In fact, however, there appears to have been considerable latitude in the composition of the hearing boards, with some boards having at least two military officers.[14]

The hearing board recommended to the commanding general, for every suspect who was taken into custody, whether to release, parole, or intern the individual on security grounds. All hearings were confidential, and in the case of aliens, the recommendations of the hearing board were to be kept confidential. When the hearing on a case was completed, the board's recommendation and a record of the proceedings were forwarded to an Intelligence Review Board, consisting of representatives of Military Intelligence, Naval Intelligence, and the FBI. In reviewing many dozens of cases of internees, the authors have found that the military board of intelligence officers often overruled a civilian board's recommendations for parole or release—even when, to cite one example, the civilian board had concluded that an individual had "maintained . . . in the manner expected of the highest grade of alien in the United States" the allegiance owed by an alien, and there was "no evidence whatsoever of any subversive activities, or any anti-American statements, or any anti-American activities."[15]

The intelligence officers' recommendations, in turn, were forwarded to the military governor. General Emmons issued orders that no person was to be interned or released from internment without the personal approval of FBI Special Agent Shivers, as well as his own approval, regardless of the findings of the hearing board.[16] Asked after the war if he relied on the recommendations of Colonel Fielder of G-2 and the intelligence review board, Emmons replied, "I relied on myself. I certainly gave the recommendations of these various boards and the recommendations of Colonel Fielder great weight, but I made the decisions."[17] He did, however, admit that he "had great confidence" in Shivers, whose word thus was important in Emmons's decisions.[18]

In the spring of 1943, a new Military Governor's Reviewing Board was created at the suggestion of Colonel William R. C. Morrison, Green's successor as Executive in the Office of the Military Governor, to review all cases before final action by the Commanding General.[19] Morrison served as chair, and its members included Colonel Fielder of Military Intelligence (G-2); Major L. F. Springer, who succeeded Walker as head of the Hawaiian Department Alien Processing Center; Lieutenant Colonel E. V. Slattery of the Judge Advocate General Division, who was chief of the Legal Section of the OMG; Major F. C. Blake of the Counter Intelligence Division; and Major R. B. Griffith, of the Executive Section of the OMG. In addition to reviewing new cases, the Military Governor's Reviewing Board constantly reviewed the cases of those who had already been interned, granting rehearings.[20] The board met weekly and generally considered twelve to fifteen cases each week; an internee could request a rehearing by writing to the military governor, professing his loyalty. In addition, General Richardson, shortly after taking office in June 1943, ordered the review of some two hundred dual citizens who were then interned in Hawai'i, and the cases of detainees confined on the mainland were also reviewed in due course. The process for the rehearings was similar to that of the original hearings, except that the earlier proceedings became part of the record presented.[21]

The provost marshal's office set forth general guidelines for the hearing boards:

> It is desired that the hearing be confined to the pertinent issues involved in the internment, and cover three subjects contained in the War Department Directive, i.e., CITIZENSHIP, LOYALTY, and the INTERNEE'S ACTIVITIES.... The question of the internee's character is not particularly pertinent to these hearings.
>
> Keep in mind that these hearings are informal; that the Internee is not heard as a matter of his rights and that it is desired that these records be expedited.[22]

At the hearings—the first of several to which the detainees would be subjected during the course of the war—a government agent presented the case against the detainee, which usually included a summary of the reports of FBI informants and of intelligence agencies' findings, to the hearing board. The detainee was not permitted to be present during this presentation, nor was he permitted to examine the evidence; he was informed only in the most general, summary way of the charges against him, with no details or explanations provided. The board then questioned the detainee. Although detainees were permitted to have an attorney present (at their own expense), and in some cases attorneys did appear, in fact access to legal counsel was limited.[23] According to one detainee, who was accused of being German although he was a U.S. citizen of Swedish and Finnish extraction,

> [An] officer said we would be given a hearing and would be permitted to call four witnesses in our behalf. We were given a pencil and a piece of paper on which to write the names.... I asked if I might have a council [sic] of my own choice and at my own expense at the hearing but was told that I could not and it would do me no good even if council should appear. I then asked to be represented by military council [sic] but Captain X replied that they did not have time.[24]

Such attorneys as did appear, as well as some internees and the American Civil Liberties Union, tried, without success, to obtain information about specific charges.[25] In 1943, Samuel Wilder King, Hawai'i's delegate to Congress, complained to the Department of Justice:

> Upon submitting the matter to the War Department I am referred to the Department of Justice and upon taking these cases with the Department of Justice I am referred back to the War Department. My only feeling is that some agency of the United States Government should accept the responsibility of safeguarding our principles of equity and justice by reviewing the circumstances under which they were placed in custody.[26]

Detainees were allowed to submit the names of witnesses they wished to be called, and Japanese interpreters were provided for those who did not speak English. The witnesses included some of Honolulu's business and political leaders, among them Joseph Farrington, then a member of the Territorial Senate and later to become Hawai'i's delegate to Congress.[27]

Walker raised the problem of jurisdiction over U.S. citizens on the first day of the hearings. Some of the suspects were naturalized U.S. citizens (as noted above) with no dual citizenship in enemy countries, and others were aliens of friendly countries. Although the hearing boards had been empowered to hear cases of enemy aliens and dual citizens only, Green instructed Walker to proceed with hearings on all suspected citizens.[28]

The hearings varied considerably in scope and in the manner of proceedings; they could last fifteen to twenty minutes or several days, during which time many detainees were unable to contact their families or even to obtain basic necessities for comfort. The recommendations of the hearing boards varied, as well. For example, in Maui, the board at one point recommended that 35 percent of the suspects be released or paroled—a much larger percentage than from any other board—prompting one army staff member to remark on the "lack of '*kokua*' [help, or cooperation]" between the investigating officers and the board.[29]

Some hearings were conducted in an atmosphere that was, in the words of one internee, "more like a group meeting than a court session," with the commissioners, the suspect, and a stenographer sitting around a table. Despite the outwardly friendly atmosphere, the questioning was hostile.

"Did you buy Japanese government bonds?"

"No."

"Did you buy American bonds?"

"No."

"Why didn't you buy them?"

". . . I had no money at the time."

"You could have bought them if you wanted to."[30]

Other hearings were far more intimidating. One Hawai'i Kibei recounted:

After this [the Immigration Station] I was sent to Sand Island and remained there for six months. It was during my stay at Sand Island [that] the FBI [took] me to the Federal Building [in Honolulu] where the FBI and military officers question[ed] me. They put their guns on the table in plain view, like a threat. I felt they were interrogating me as though I were a spy—but I was not. The FBI and military officers told me that since America was at war with Japan and because I was raised in Okinawa, Japan and regardless that I was an American citizen, I was an internee (P.O.W.).[31]

Another Japanese American, who took a job as a defense worker when he was no longer permitted to fish for a living, was picked up on January 9, 1942. He later recalled:

They took me to the Dillingham building, . . . where they had the FBI office. No matter what they asked me, I did not know or was not familiar with. . . . They had a pistol placed in front of the questioning man. They had 2 of them with guns asking me all sorts of questions. . . . Those 2–3 hours, I really suffered from the questioning. Especially when I had no information or knowledge in what they were asking.[32]

It is little wonder, then, that many of the detainees felt that the hearings were, at best, pro forma. Another internee testified:

The hearings were in reality, merely individual interrogation of suspected "bad Japs." The officer asked several pointed questions which required a yes/ no answer. If I answered affirmatively when asked whether I am loyal to the United States, they would accuse me of being a liar. But if I had said no, then I would be thrown in jail. I felt there was no way I could be considered a loyal American.[33]

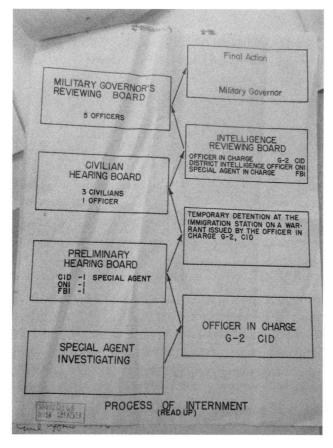

Flowchart showing the process used in determining whether to order internment of a suspect. Photocopy; original is in the records of the OMG.

Many of those who were interned would subsequently complain at their loyalty hearings of the way they were detained and interrogated, with their protestations of loyalty being disregarded.[34] Not a single one of the internees was found guilty of overt acts against U.S. laws, no one was investigated for sabotage, and only a few were suspected of espionage. Rather, according to a U.S. congressional investigation following the war, the internees were judged "on personalities and their utterances, criminal and credit records, and probably nationalistic sympathies."[35]

Factors Considered in Investigations

The Nikkei detainees were questioned about place of birth, education, frequency of travel to Japan, friends and relatives in Japan, any participation in Japanese consular activities or social events, and whether they had made donations of money, food, or clothing to Japan. They were asked what they thought of the Great East Asia Co-Prosperity Sphere, and if they were pro-Japanese—a particularly difficult question for Japanese aliens who were ineligible for American citizenship. Comparable questions were asked of the German and Italian detainees.

Among the "adverse factors" the hearing boards considered in determining whether to intern an individual were leadership roles in the Japanese community, membership in Japanese organizations (including martial arts and religious organizations), visits to Japan (regardless of family or business reasons for such visits), and education in Japan. Other negative factors included registration (for example, the birth of a child) with the Japanese consulate, service in the Japanese military or application for deferment from service in the Japanese army, property in Japan, money in Japanese banks, donations to Japanese causes, entertainment of visiting Japanese naval personnel in Hawai'i, and failure to learn English or adopt American ways. Literate Japanese had often helped their illiterate neighbors to fill out paperwork to register births and deaths; some had helped Nisei to expatriate from Japan and declare sole loyalty to the United States. Nonetheless, they were usually considered of doubtful loyalty because they had been "consular agents."

Factors working in favor of the detainee were purchase of U.S. war bonds, donations to the Red Cross or war effort, civilian defense activities, relative fluency in English and attempts to Americanize. Other positive factors were "being an adherent of the Christian religion . . . and baptized as a child," children's membership in American organizations such as the Boy Scouts, naturalization as a U.S. citizen (for Japanese who had served in World War I, as well as for German Americans and Italian Americans), and stated willingness to serve the United States in any capacity, including an invasion of Japan.[36]

In our examination of numerous records of loyalty/security hearing boards before which both alien residents and citizens of Japanese ancestry were brought for questioning—and to face the possibility of detention—we found that completely unsubstantiated allegations were quite consistently made the basis for decisions. Also evident was the extent to which any expression by an internee of outrage or resistance based on a notion of his constitutional rights would be interpreted by the examiners as evidence of his disloyalty or untrustworthiness.[37] Yet the records clearly show that some detainees had lost their sense of loyalty to America precisely because of their treatment by the army. For example, one Kibei was asked, under oath:

Q: If you were released from Sand Island, would you be willing to volunteer and serve in the Armed Forces of the United States?
A: It is too late to ask such questions.
Q: In other words you are not a loyal American citizen. Is that correct?
A: After being detained here, I don't think there is anyone who would volunteer in the United States Army.

And another Kibei, upon being asked if he wanted to see Japan or the United States win the war, replied: "I was born in America; I returned to America, because I wanted to be an American; but since I have been detained in this detention camp, my feelings have changed." Asked if he wanted to cut off his American citizenship because of the government's action in detaining him, he stated: "I don't feel that I am an American citizen if I am treated in this way, and I can't believe that I will ever be an American citizen, even if I am let out; so I think in that case it is better that I return to Japan, and I will cut off my American citizenship." And yet another Kibei who had been willing to volunteer for the American army, stated, "My feelings have changed now because I have been taken in here and detained." The hearing board in each case recommended internment because the subject's "embittered feelings would make him a potentially dangerous person to be at large."[38]

Illustrative of the way in which internments were handled in the early weeks of the war was an incident originating in Kaua'i, where the local district commanding officer received reports that three postmasters of Japanese ancestry "[were] suspected of pro-Japanese sentiments." One, the district commander informed Green at the Military Government headquarters, was "a confirmed *haole* hater" who had visited the Japanese-occupied areas of China and returned "with glowing tales about the might of the Japanese Empire." A second was "supposed to have voiced publicly his sympathy with the Japanese cause." The last, he wrote, "also is supposed to have voiced pro-Japanese sentiments; however so far I know very little about him."[39] This communication brought an immediate response from Green, who in February 1942 wrote tersely but definitively: "With reference to your letter of February 13 . . . pertaining to certain postmasters, I understand that the whole matter has been taken care of by arresting the individuals mentioned in your letter and that you have no further problem in this matter. Keep up the good work."[40] With this letter, Green also forwarded to Kaua'i a formal memorandum entitled "Disloyal Citizens," carrying the following instructions: "In all instances where individuals of Japanese ancestry have been apprehended for publicly voicing any opinion against the United States, they should be interned for the duration of the war."[41]

Some detainees were released immediately following their hearings, while others were placed on parole, either immediately after the hearing or following a period of internment. The provost marshal and the district commanders were responsible for parolees. Each parolee had to report weekly to a sponsor, who was to be selected by the parole officer and who was to "observe and report the Parolee's conduct, activities and whereabouts" and report periodically to the parole officer. Parolees were subject to further detention if at any time they were deemed dangerous to internal security. No parolee could travel, change residence, or be released from parole without the written approval of the OMG.[42] Most Caucasian parolees were released after six months; ethnic Japanese parolees remained in parole status for a year.[43]

As the war progressed, the intelligence services—especially Navy Intelligence—tried to systematize the bases for determining loyalty. A memo prepared by Navy Intelligence in early 1943 to guide agents in assessing the loyalty of Japanese employed on naval projects lays out in detail the "Factors to Be Considered in Investigations of Japanese Subjects." Most of the memo deals with "Citizen Japanese." Dated February 25, 1943, the memo declares, "Every individual of Japanese ancestry in Hawaii has been exposed to some Japanese influence," so that a distinction must be recognized between actions by an individual and an "exposure to influences over which he had no control."[44] According to the memo, an individual does not need to be proven *disloyal* to be considered a threat to internal security; if his loyalty is doubtful, even if he has demonstrated no pro-Japanese sentiments, he is to be considered dangerous and undesirable for naval work. "Determination of loyalty is a difficult procedure; it cannot be made by use of mathematical formulas," the memo states. "In evaluating the Japanese in Hawaii, numerous factors should be taken into consideration, but no single factor should be given undue weight (except, of course, admission of disloyalty by the individual)." Judicious evaluation of the factors bearing on loyalty had not always been carried out in the interrogations previously conducted, the authors of the report had found.

The factors to be considered were similar to those addressed by the hearing boards and in previous interrogations of Japanese Americans applying for certain defense jobs, but the guidelines called for more subtle evaluations. For example, "current reading habits" and efforts at "self-education" could possibly offset Japanese schooling, and motives and location should be considered in assessing visits to Japan. The memo also cautioned against stereotyping, as it had been used in some earlier evaluations of loyalty:

> Often a report contains the phrase, "Subject is typically Japanese in reaction," or something similar. The "typical Japanese" is as much a piece of fiction as is the "typical American," and this office should concern itself with facts rather than

with fiction. "Americanization" is a loose term; to say an individual is "not Americanized" is to damn him without specification.

Having thus declaimed against stereotyping, the memo nevertheless went on to say, "It should be remembered that many Nisei are extremely immature in their political concepts."

Turning to the alien Japanese, the memo stated that many of the same factors should be considered, but it emphasized that these individuals "have specifically been denied the privilege of becoming United States citizens," no matter how much they would have liked to be naturalized. Drawing a sharp line between behaviors expected of a Japanese-American citizen and those expected of an alien, the memo stated that the "preliminary hearing board in Honolulu has taken the position that *passive loyalty* on the part of an alien Japanese is sufficient, and any active display of pro-Americanism is just so much more to his credit." The criteria for "passive loyalty" included long residence in Hawai'i; a predominance of financial, property and family interests in Hawai'i; few or no return trips to Japan; lack of participation in pro-Japanese activity before the war; and no display of pro-Japanese sympathies before or since the outbreak of the war. Of particular importance was the subject's attitude toward the emperor—not as to his divinity, which had been a criterion in the past, but as to his authority. These standards, the memo asserted, were the only practical solution to the problem of determining loyalty, since both mass evacuation and mass internment of the 35,000 alien Japanese in Hawai'i would be impractical.[45]

The cautionary tone and *relatively* moderate content of this navy document are noteworthy on two counts. First, the memo advised intelligence personnel to take a measured, balanced view of the background and beliefs of subjects being investigated or questioned. And second, inferred or explicitly stated in the text is the fact that actual practice had not conformed to these standards, and that serious errors of judgment had been made.

Several months later, the Navy Intelligence office in Hawai'i shifted its attitude and issued a new manual, taking a much harsher line in its guidance for investigators and interrogators.[46] Whereas the earlier document had systematically expressed caveats about assumptions that could easily be made too hastily and with unfair results, the new manual set forth its recommendations in the template of a racial and cultural stereotype of the Japanese, emphasizing that positive evidences of loyalty associated with a suspect should be discounted for a variety of reasons.

Assumptions of Kibei Disloyalty

Especially significant were statements suggesting the high likelihood of a Kibei suspect's being disloyal to the United States and dangerous to security. Although the new manual, like the earlier one, counseled that there was no more reality in the concept of a "typical Kibei" than of that of a "typical American," the substantive content of the document ran counter to this notion that stereotyping be abandoned.

The new manual's analysis of Kibei culture and disloyalty was especially illuminating with regard to the invocation of stereotypes intended to guide intelligence and security officers more generally.[47] The manual contained, for example, lengthy quotations from a book published in 1907, *Japan: An Attempt at Interpretation,* by Lafcadio Hearn, the Irish-American humorist and ethnographic writer. Hearn is quoted to the effect that "the extraordinary capacity of the Japanese for communal organization, is the strongest possible evidence of their unfitness for any modern democratic form of government."[48]

Restricting its attention to those Kibei who spent three or more years in Japan following their twelfth birthday, the manual asserted that on the whole, "Kibei will display far more pro-Japanese sentiment than will other Nisei. It is of interest to note that the Japanese community itself considers the Kibei to be the most dangerous class in their midst." The manual also asserted that the District Intelligence Office of the Navy considered those Kibei with long periods of residence in Japan to be "dangerous to the internal security of the United States," having received "most, if not all, of their formal education in Japan, with the concomitant indoctrination of emperor worship and other phases of Japanese nationalism." Family ties, significant period of residency, educational experience, and other aspects of their former residence in Japan, according to the manual, should serve as evidentiary support for a *presumption of disloyalty.* "Protestations of loyalty to the United States made by Japanese," according to the manual, "should be weighed in the light of the speaker's background and tested by the motives he may have for making such statements."[49]

According to the manual's bias and instructions, the Kibei were likely to be conflicted in loyalty by the duties traditionally owed to family and the Japanese state. Therefore, the loyalty interrogation protocol, as set forth in the manual, was calibrated to uncover "potential" disloyalty by testing the subject's willingness to disregard parents or country, rather than simply asking whether the subject wanted the United States to prevail in military conflict. For example, subjects who professed loyalty to the American cause should be asked whether they would agree to enlist and take up arms against Japan—and if so, whether they would be willing to kill in combat any relatives who were serving in the Japanese armed forces. Some suspects were asked whether they would assassinate Emperor Hirohito, if given the chance. The manual warned interrogators, on this point, that many who worshiped the emperor—and thereby were to be deemed faithful to the "theocratic-militaristic-totalitarian state that is Japan"—would give false replies to such questions, being "realistic enough to compromise their scruples in order to remain at liberty."[50] One question often put to Kibei that posed an especially serious moral dilemma for them was whether they would be willing to broadcast antiemperor propaganda on the radio, even though it might jeopardize the safety or lives of the family members living in Japan with whom they were likely to have kept in touch.

Although the navy manual was designed specifically as a guide for screening Japanese-American applicants for jobs on naval defense projects, similar questions were used by all the review boards in determining whether an individual Nikkei was a security risk to the safety of the United States—and thus subject to what today would be called preventive detention. In the end, it was a virtually no-win game for the persons under interrogation, especially the Kibei, because intelligence officers began to assess positive answers to such questions not as evidence of loyalty to America but rather as evidence of "typical" Japanese deviousness: that is, persons actually disloyal had simply learned to give the "right" answers and thus mask their anti-American views.

The plight of the Kibei being subjected to such questioning was articulated by one of them who was not released until after the war's end:

> He asked me if my parents were attacking, would I shoot them. I told him I couldn't do it. Sitting at the next desk over was a Japanese FBI agent. He told me that it was because of people like me that rest of the Japanese in Hawaii would suffer.... It was enough that they asked me if I would shoot my parents, but to tell me I was wrong in saying that I would not, was too much.... If I said I would shoot my parents you would know it was a lie. I think they used that kind of questioning as a trick to send us to Sand Island.[51]

Indeed, from the start, in both investigative processes and their interrogations in custody, the Kibei had to bear a greater burden than was borne by other Japanese Americans if they were to avoid internment. This was evidenced by the deeply prejudiced profile that was applied to them by administrators, the officers conducting arrests, interrogators, and the personnel of review boards. Although the navy manual may have cautioned against the notion of a "typical Kibei," in the reports of interrogations and board proceedings, one repeatedly finds the revealing phrase, "No evidence of any subversive activities was presented. However, this is a typical Kibei case."[52] When a subject was described as "a typical Kibei," it was a shorthand way of saying that this person was not to be trusted—was at worst disloyal and possibly actively subversive, at best "potentially disloyal." This last phrase was applied routinely, capturing many undoubtedly innocent and loyal suspects in the web of incarceration and evacuation and/or internment.

The attitude and stereotyping that had characterized the early-war security operations and were embodied in the navy manual were also often explicitly exhibited by officers at the highest levels of the military hierarchy. For example, in 1942, General DeWitt—the obsessively anti-Japanese-American officer in charge of the Western Defense Command, and the leading army proponent for the internment of Nikkei on the West Coast—had argued that *all* Kibei were, ipso facto, loyal to Japan; he favored interning all Kibei for the duration of the war, nullifying their U.S. citizenship, and deporting them to Japan after the war had ended.[53] In December 1943, Major Louis Springer, head of the Alien Processing Center, similarly lamented "the absence of adequate machinery" to deprive many of the Kibei of their United States citizenship. Summarizing the cases of twenty-five Kibei being held in internment in Hawai'i, he wrote to the Executive of the OMG: "It may be said that birth in the United States in these cases, as well as others, is unfortunate for . . . they are actually at heart citizens of Japan."[54] Springer similarly told a conference of provost court judges: "The particular cases of subversive activities are found particularly in citizens who spent the majority of their young life in Japan. They are definitely pro-Japanese. . . . The General feels that in this regard those Japanese should be definitely locked up."[55]

When the War Department reevaluated internment policy in 1944, General Richardson would advise McCloy that among the 135 Kibei then interned in Hawai'i, some had admitted loyalty to Japan, but about 100 of them

> have either made statements of loyalty to the United States or have made no statements to indicate their loyalty either way, or have made evasive statements. . . . Despite the fact that so many have made statements of loyalty to the United States, it is my opinion based on findings of Hearing Boards and intelligence reports that they are dangerous to the security of the United States and that their utterances of loyalty are inconsistent with their backgrounds and training in Japan.[56]

It is telling that Colonel Slattery, chief of the legal section of the OMG and the officer in charge of many of the assessments of loyalty, proposed as late as September 1944 that federal legislation should be passed that would strip Kibei of their American nationality by virtue of years spent in Japan.[57]

In summarizing wartime security controls in Hawai'i, the Office of Internal Security, which replaced the Office of Military Governor shortly before martial law was terminated in 1944, wrote:

> It can be stated generally that the Kibei . . . returned to Hawai'i [from Japan] more alien in thought, attitude and reaction than the many alien residents in the Islands. It was quite natural to assume, therefore, that those Japanese who would most likely be disloyal to the United States, and thus be a constant and ever-present threat to the public peace, safety and security of the nation, would be the kibei.[58]

The OMG staff officers in charge of policy toward the ethnic Japanese in Hawai'i would systematically continue to cast doubt upon the loyalty of the Kibei down to the last day of the war in 1945, and even beyond.

The attitude of these officers was rooted, no doubt, partly in unvarnished racial prejudice. But their conviction that the Kibei constituted a uniquely dangerous potential threat to security had also been fueled by the viral spread of rumors in December 1941 and early 1942 about alleged sabotage and espionage by persons of Japanese ancestry in connection with the Pearl Harbor debacle. As noted above, these rumors persisted, despite vigorous denial by the FBI and the testimony to the Roberts Commission.

Hostile racial attitudes were given further strength, as the war went on, by the extraordinary expansion of security-sensitive military and naval installations and activities in Hawai'i, which was the base of logistic operations for the entire Pacific theater of war; by the reports of the atrocities committed by Japanese forces against Allied prisoners of war; and, perhaps above all, by the news of mounting Allied casualties that filtered back to Hawai'i from the western Pacific combat areas, and the arrival of hospital ships carrying the wounded and bodies of the fallen.

General Emmons, but even more so his successor after mid-1943, General Richardson, adamantly contended that the stringent control exercised by the army over civilian life through martial law—and especially the internments and other security measures targeted at the Nikkei community in the martial law context—were responsible for the successful maintenance of internal security. Richardson and his subordinate officers in OMG presented Washington with all the arguments and political influence they could muster in their intransigent resistance to pressures that they relax any policies that were directed at Kibei or other groups suspected of disloyalty and possible subversion. Emphasizing the danger presented by Kibei who admitted to hearing boards that they were loyal to Japan, the OMG argued in late 1943 and early 1944 that only martial law "permits the internment of dangerous persons, regardless of their citizenship."[59] Even as late as April 1945, when the detainees from the West Coast mainland states were being released from the camps and the government was beginning to wind down security operations, some of Richardson's staff officers in Hawai'i were still asserting that the ethnic Japanese population "would *unanimously* prefer Oriental control [of the Territory] and are sentimentally if not actively loyal to Japan."[60] Such reports conveniently ignored the fact that the Hawai'i Nisei had volunteered in great numbers for active military service and had achieved an exceptional record for valor, with Kibei in particular serving as translators and interpreters.[61]

Loyalty Questionnaires

The matter of determining the loyalty of the Nikkei population, and especially of the Kibei, gained striking new importance in early 1943. Despite an earlier War Department study urging that "the military potential of the United States citizens of Japanese ancestry be considered as negative because of the universal distrust in which they are held,"[62] Assistant Secretary of War McCloy, Secretary of War Stimson, and Chief of Staff General George C. Marshall all argued in October 1942 in favor of a Nisei fighting unit. The following month, General Emmons, impressed by the training record of the 100th Battalion, lent his endorsement, stating that the Nisei would make "grand soldiers."[63] Also in November, the Japanese American Citizens League, a Nisei organization that encouraged cooperation with the government, petitioned the president to allow Japanese Americans to serve in the military. Roosevelt was finally persuaded (in part because of the propaganda value), and the administration decided in January 1943 to create an all-Nisei combat unit and to allow Nisei to volunteer for the military.[64]

In order to effect this dramatic reversal of policy, the army devised a loyalty questionnaire to be completed by all Nisei of draft age that would reveal "tendencies of loyalty or disloyalty to the United States."[65] Each applicant's loyalty would then be reviewed by military intelligence and the FBI, with a joint military board making the final decision. Thus the Nisei would have two ways to demonstrate their loyalty: by volunteering for military service and by answering the loyalty questions in the affirmative. The army, aware that the call for volunteers might cause resentment among those who had been deprived of their liberty, explained at each of the WRA centers that "The fundamental purpose [of registration] is to put your situation on a plane which is consistent with the dignity of American citizenship." While acknowledging that "the best solution has not been found for you . . . in your relation to the United States, which is the land of your birth and your residence," the army spokespersons also promised: "Your government would not take these steps unless it intended to go further in restoring you to a normal place in the life of the country, with the privileges and obligations of other American citizens."[66]

In February 1943, the WRA, which had been looking for a means to give leave clearance to some of the evacuees so they could work outside the camps, seized upon this procedure to determine the loyalty of *all* the evacuees over the age of seventeen being held in their camps, from Hawai'i and the mainland, men and women, Issei and Nisei alike. The WRA accordingly designed a companion questionnaire, "Application for Leave Clearance," that differed only slightly from the army's.[67] Thus all the Hawai'i residents who had been sent to the mainland WRA centers were subjected to these questionnaires.

The WRA questionnaire, forced upon the residents of the camps without notice or coherent explanation, created a crisis for many of the confined Nikkei, who did not know why they were made to answer the questionnaire or how the information would be used. Some Issei were afraid of being cast out of the camps and into hostile environments where they could not survive; why else were they being forced to fill out an application for leave clearance? Some Nisei thought the questionnaire was designed to force them to volunteer to fight for the country that had stripped them of their civil liberties and imprisoned them without cause. The racially segregated all-Nisei combat unit was cited by some as further evidence of continued discrimination. Still others feared that the questionnaire would result in their being separated from their families.[68]

The questionnaires, like previous hearings, sought biographical information as well as information on such subjects as education in Japan; relatives in, and trips to, Japan; dual citizenship; and memberships in organizations. Particularly troublesome were Questions 27 and 28, which demanded a simple "yes" or "no" answer. The first, Question 27, asked of draft-age Nisei, "Are you willing to serve in the Armed Forces of the United States on combat duty, wherever ordered?" Question 28 was even more problematic: "Will you swear unqualified allegiance to the United States of America and faithfully defend the United States from any and all attack by foreign or domestic forces, and foreswear any form of allegiance or obedience to the Japanese emperor, or any other foreign government, power or organization?" Some of the Nisei feared that a "yes" answer to this question would indicate that they had once held allegiance to the Japan. The Issei, for their part, were being asked to give up allegiance to the only country of which they could be citizens, rendering them stateless; and that question was later changed for them, to ask if they would "swear to abide by the laws of the United States and to take no action which would in any way interfere with the war effort of the United States."[69]

As the Commission on Wartime Relocation and Internment of Civilians would conclude in 1982, in its analysis supporting a policy of reparations for detainees,

> the loyalty questionnaire demanded a personal expression of position from each evacuee. . . . Most evacuees probably had deeply ambiguous feelings about a government in whose rhetorical values of liberty and equality they wanted to believe, but who found their present treatment a painful contradiction of those values. The loyalty questionnaire left little room to express that ambiguity.[70]

A significant number of the detainees—including those from Hawai'i—originally answered "no" to Question 28 or refused to answer as a protest against their removal and incarceration. Of a group of 138 detainees from Hawai'i who were not subsequently sent to Tule Lake for being pro-Japanese but who were still confined in mainland camps in 1945, 26—all of them citizens or dual citizens—refused to answer Question 28 or answered negatively because they had been interned. Others gave a qualified "yes," citing their uncertainty because of their internment.[71] The report on one dual citizen, K. M., was fairly typical of the findings on detainees who were not overtly pro-Japanese:

> Did not answer Question 28, but appended the following statement, "Has been loyal to US and was willing to pledge allegiance to US but having been suspected and accused by the Govt. of being pro-Japanese and having been interned and retained as an internee after having stated his loyalty to the US and his willingness to defend the US, although he will abide by the laws of the US and will in no way interfere with the war effort it will be impossible to swear allegiance when the Govt. will not recognize it.[72]

The plight of the Kibei was particularly poignant. As one mainland Kibei explained, for those who were American citizens but who had lived and studied in Japan, "It was hardly a simple yes-or-no matter." They shared more than ethnic and family ties with the Japanese people: "To pledge our loyalty to America meant collaborating in the killing and wounding of people who lived in Japan, the denial of a personal connection based on a shared culture. This denial was a source of particular anguish for Kibei."[73] For the Kibei who were asked to volunteer for the armed services, there was the very personal dilemma: "My big concern was, what if I meet up with someone I know at the warfront? My relative, my classmate, my good friends, you know. What am I supposed to react? That was my biggest concern."[74]

For some, renouncing the Japanese emperor, who was regarded as a deity, was especially troubling. As one investigative report on a Kibei from Hawai'i stated, "His religious beliefs reveal that he believes Hirohito to be a descendant of the sun Goddess . . . and that anything he does must be right." Therefore, the report continued, internees would view Japan as justified in attacking Pearl Harbor if the emperor approved; and if the emperor broadcast that he should not aid the American war effort, he would obey that order.[75]

Some families had one relative fighting in the Japanese army and another in the U.S. Army. While some Nisei were genuinely confused as to how to answer the loyalty questions, and others were pressured to say "no" by radical pro-Japanese elements in the camps, others may be assumed to have answered in a manner that would best promote their self-interests and gain them release from incarceration. It is also likely that some Kibei had returned to Hawai'i just prior to the war in order to avoid conscription by the Japanese army; by answering "no" to Question 28, they could also avoid military service for the United States.[76]

The results of the questionnaire varied from camp to camp, with the Tule Lake camp being the most extreme. Some 3,000 detainees there—approximately one-third of those eligible to register—refused to complete the questionnaire.[77] In total, of nearly 78,000 male and female residents of the WRA camps who were eligible to register, 87 percent responded to the loyalty question with an unqualified "yes." The remainder, including more than 20 percent of the Nisei men, answered "no," refused to answer, or qualified their answer.[78] Those who answered "no" to Questions 27 and 28 and were suspected by the authorities of being pro-Japanese were subsequently sent to the Tule Lake internment camp, often being separated from their families in the process.[79] The questionnaire had the further effect of sharply increasing the number of Issei who requested repatriation and of Nisei who requested expatriation to Japan.[80]

To process the mass of data from the questionnaires, the War Department and the WRA had agreed to an interdepartmental Japanese American Joint Board (JAJB), with representatives from the WRA, the Office of Naval Intelligence, the Army Intelligence (G-2), the FBI, and the War Department General Staff.[81] The board established a detailed, if simplistic, system of "plus" or "minus" point values for each answer on the questionnaire. The values assigned were similar to the "adverse" and "positive" factors on earlier evaluations. No interviews were involved. This system was soon replaced by a checklist that would result in assigning the detainees to one of three categories: "white" (cleared for war work or for indefinite leave); "black" (rejected for leave); and "brown" (all other cases). By May 1944, when the JAJB was dissolved, it had processed questionnaires from nearly 40,000 Nisei and found adverse findings in nearly one-third of them.

A comparable point system was used in Hawai'i to determine fitness to serve in the army's segregated Nisei unit. Positive points were assigned to each individual for being a graduate of an American high school or college, for being registered to vote, for being married to an American citizen, for using an Anglicized first name, or for being an agricultural worker. Points were subtracted for having attended a Japanese language school, for being married to a citizen of Japan, for using a Japanese first name, or for having been a fisherman.[82]

The results of the loyalty questionnaires helped tip the balance in favor of those political and military leaders in the armed services, Congress, and the administration who advocated segregating the "loyal" from the "disloyal" Nikkei. In May, Secretary of War Stimson instructed Myer that the WRA should immediately "screen out from the centers and segregate in close confinement all individuals appearing to have pro-Japanese sympathies," including those who had requested repatriation, as well as the "troublemakers."[83] Although the WRA had earlier objected to the proposal of General DeWitt, head of the Western Defense Command, to segregate all Kibei, regardless of findings of loyalty, Myer now agreed to the new policy. He did, however, point out the "constitutional problems inherent in the confinement of American citizens . . . without leave privileges in segregation centers."[84]

Tule Lake was selected as the segregation center. The segregants included (1) those who had applied for repatriation to Japan and had not withdrawn their applications by July 1, 1943; (2) those who had answered "no" or had refused to answer the loyalty question; (3) those who had been denied leave clearance because of adverse findings; (4) aliens from the Department of Justice camps who had been recommended for detention; and (5) family members of segregants who elected to remain with the family.[85]

Because of the confusion over Question 28, a new set of hearings was offered to those who had answered "no" or refused to answer. A number of the detainees from Hawai'i changed their answers to an unqualified "yes" when given a second chance, citing, as the reasons for their original answers, confusion, frustration at having been interned, acting under pressure, or fear of being separated from their families. Most of this group were not segregated.[86] Others, however, adhered to their original answers, many expressing anger at the way they had been treated, and asking to be repatriated to Japan. Of the total of 1,040 Hawai'i residents who had been evacuated to the mainland in late 1942 and early 1943 and had been confined at WRA camps, 340—approximately one-third—were transferred to the Tule Lake Segregation Center. Of this number, 131 requested repatriation or expatriation to Japan, 180 were sent because of their answers to the loyalty question, and 9 "for other reasons." Ninety-six percent of the transfers from Hawai'i were U.S. citizens, presumably mainly Kibei and their families.[87] Additional transfers of Japanese Americans from Hawai'i to Tule Lake brought the total to 656 by July 1944.[88] Their fate is discussed below.

From the detailed archival records of the government's evaluations of these segregants, it is clear that the great majority had declared themselves loyal to the United States in earlier screenings. Their attestations of loyalty had been deemed spurious, however, by the review boards and intelligence officers, leading not only to their internment at Tule Lake, but also to the loss of their personal sense of loyalty. For example, one Kibei, S. K., had been taken to Japan in 1897, aged eight, and returned to O'ahu in 1912. Despite having served in the Hawai'i National Guard and in the U.S. Army in 1918–1919, he was deemed a security risk in part because he ran a hotel that was frequented by military personnel so that he could have overheard their conversations. Although he affirmed his loyalty as an American citizen, he testified that he was "interned for fifteen months for no reason . . . and I lost my pride as an American citizen. They should not intern any American citizen, so I am quite confused." He stated that he preferred continued internment to going back to Japan. The hearing board concluded: "Despite the fact that the internee professes loyalty to the United States it is the opinion of this office that subject's loyalty statements are merely self-serving."[89]

The detainees' pleas for confrontation of the witnesses and evidence being used against them had been ignored, and they had been subjected to what they viewed as arbitrary and degrading treatment during their forcible removal to the mainland. In some of the reports, the officials explicitly stated that no tangible evidence of disloyal or dangerous activity had been found.[90] The hearing boards' condemnation of many suspects had been based heavily on the fact that these persons were Kibei; more generally, if interrogators or review boards were unconvinced of a Nisei's sincerity, or found the individual's answers "evasive," then little or nothing more was needed to warrant internment.[91] For example, in a June 1944 review of one Kibei who had been interned the previous year, Slattery wrote, "I am of the opinion that subject has attempted to give answers favorable to his cause but has not expressed his true feelings. He is in my opinion still dangerous . . . and I therefore recommend his continued internment for the duration of the war."[92]

The situation for the Kibei was poignantly described by one of them, who emphasized that his parents, not he, had made the decision that he be educated in Japan. He had been given no reason for his arrest:

> Just that I received my education in Japan. But I didn't have a choice in receiving my education in Japan. My parents returned to Japan and took me with them. I told them [the Hearing Board] that but they said didn't you receive military training while attending school there? That military training was compulsory. . . . Wasn't that the same as taking ROTC here? Yet they said I received military indoctrination.[93]

His protestations were ignored, and he was incarcerated until April 1946—eight months after the war had ended.

It must be remembered that all of the incarcerated Japanese Americans, including those who were steadfast in declaring loyalty, had undergone the physical and psychological hardships of removal and transfer—often multiple transfers—over a period of two to four years. They had also been subjected to repeated interrogations and loyalty interviews—first, for the group from Hawai'i, on initial arrest and incarceration; again when the government ordered loyalty determinations in 1943 for all persons held in the relocation centers, so as to implement the combined leave clearance/military service volunteer registration program; and yet again for the "segregation" to Tule Lake of those found disloyal or potentially dangerous.

Yet the government's attempt to determine the loyalty of the ethnic Japanese did not end there, for in January 1944, the military draft was extended to citizens of Japanese ancestry, including those in the WRA camps. Once again, men of draft age being held in detention—including the Hawai'i Nisei who had been paroled and sent to the WRA camps—were subjected to further scrutiny, with the focus on the infamous questionnaire, and especially on Questions 27 and 28. Those who answered "no" to both were deemed disloyal. Even many who answered "yes" to both questions, however, were often kept in detention either because they were Kibei, and therefore suspect, or because of other factors considered "adverse" in the highly subjective evaluations.[94]

The underlying premise of the entire intelligence operation that led to the loss of liberty for nearly two thousand Nikkei in Hawai'i (as it did for 110,000 Nikkei from the West Coast of the mainland) was that to be of Japanese descent was to be suspect. This was profiling in raw and unvarnished form. In the case of Hawai'i, that premise was vastly less devastating in its effects than it was as applied by the army on the mainland, for in Hawai'i, it was the basis for "selective" investigation and potential detention rather than for mass removal and incarceration. The military intelligence and FBI operations in the Islands were geared to the investigation of individual suspects' personal behaviors (presumed to reveal cultural proclivities and hence primary loyalties), in light of educational background, religious beliefs and practices, business or organizational associations, and other factors regarded as relevant to assessing loyalty. To that degree, the determination of loyalty rested at least superficially on an evaluation of a range of relevant facts and factors, rather than beginning and ending, as it did on the mainland, with the single criterion of race.[95]

Presumption of Guilt

Nevertheless, far from being presumed innocent until proven guilty, the detainees were, in many cases, presumed guilty and had to prove their innocence. This was especially true of aliens. As Major Louis F. Springer, who had been in command at Sand Island and then became head of the Alien Processing Center, stated, "[A]n alien does not owe loyalty in a strict sense to the United States, but it is felt that an alien owes a temporary loyalty, or must prove by his actions or expressions that he is not inimical to the interest of this country."[96] The present authors' examination of cases brought before the Military Governor's Internee Review Board shows that such proof was often hard for the detainee to establish.

Many particulars of the substantive criteria that were formulated to separate the "loyal" from the "disloyal" appear in retrospect to have been insupportable. For example, questions were posed to suspects for which almost any answer would be evidence of disloyalty or "potential disloyalty." The perduring assumptions that anyone of Japanese descent would be ready to lie, would be at best evasive, was untrustworthy, and the like clearly prejudiced the decisions that led to many incarcerations. And worst of all, with regard to the general investigative and decision-making procedures, decisions often turned on evidence of questionable relevance to whether a suspect was actually a security risk. Such evidence included membership in specified organizations, cultural lifestyle, religious affiliation, style of dress, possession of religious materials, use of the English language, relatives living in Japan, and contributions to suspect organizations (the contributions in some cases literally less than a dollar).

The highly subjective determination of attitude was often key to a decision on whether to parole an individual. Resentment over their treatment was almost sure to work against the internees. For example, a list of fifteen internment cases from Hawai'i that the army reviewed in March 1944 included two decisions for "*parole if no resentment shown.*" Similarly, in mid-April, two of the internees being reviewed were "to be interviewed by Major Springer and paroled if no resentment shown," and two weeks later, two more cases were "to be interviewed to determine attitude, loyalty and resentment."[97] On the other hand, lack of resentment about having been interned could override such presumably negative factors as visits to Japan and having relatives in the Japanese army.[98]

The "no win" situation for the internee was spelled out explicitly in a memo from Lieutenant Colonel Eugene V. Slattery, chief of the legal section in the OMG, to the Military Governor's Reviewing Board in June 15, 1944: "For several months past, this office and the office of G-2, CID, have been conducting interviews of internees in Hawai'i, in order to determine their present attitude and loyalty," Slattery wrote. However, the interviews were not entirely satisfactory, in his view. He wrote:

> We have been able by the method of interviews to sift the potentially good internees from those who are avowedly dangerous to our internal security. These interviews were alright when we were only interviewing a few of the internees whose cases merited special consideration. Of late, however, we have interviewed so many of them, and from present indications it appears as if we shall interview all of the internees, that the purpose of the interview has been defeated. The internees at the camp know now, and expect to be interviewed. Accordingly, those who have family ties in Hawaii and are therefore anxious to be released from the camp are prepared to give the desired answers to questions concerning their attitude and loyalty. Those who are unmarried and who do not care to be released openly admit their disloyalty to the United States.[99]

Noting that many are now giving "the right answers," he predicted that "future interviews will not prove satisfactory" and recommended formal hearings. In effect, if the answers are right, the system for determining the answers must be wrong.

Equally revealing is Slattery's concern that the questioning they had used would not stand up in a court of law.

> It appears to me also that the interviews are not satisfactory from another standpoint, to wit, how much weight would a Court of Law give to these interviews. If

these men were granted rehearings, then we have an official record of their expressions and there appears to be no doubt that a Court would take such a record
into consideration. Furthermore, it is submitted that an internee appearing before a regularly constituted Hearing board would not likely give answers which
would not display their true feelings. A Hearing board has more dignity and authority than our informal interviews have and the internees respecting such authority would be inclined to show their really true feelings.[100]

Ironically, in the formal review hearings in subsequent months, outcomes depended
heavily on findings of attitude and loyalty based upon the evidence submitted in the
form of reports and/or transcripts of these earlier "interviews."

Yet it was on the basis of "facts" and findings such as these that persons were taken
away from their families and their homes, faced, as many of them understandably believed, with the possibility of never seeing loved ones again. General Emmons admitted
as much when being deposed under oath for a postwar civil liability trial: "In Hawaii, we
were taking no chances," he said, "and we used the expression 'potentially dangerous'
in a very liberal way, . . . a very broad way. . . . In the case of any doubt of any kind, we
had the man interned."[101] For many who were interned, Emmons readily conceded,
there was no evidence that the person interned would likely do any harm. In making
his decisions, Emmons admitted, it did not matter whether the person in question was
an American citizen or not, and he did not hesitate to approve arrest, internment, or
evacuation of individuals even in the absence of any "real evidence that they were
dangerous." And he stated further:

> We had information in the form of gossip, hearsay and conclusions, and so on,
> that I would distinguish from evidence. What I mean is that had we presented in
> court what we had, and what the FBI had, on these people, the court would not
> [have] accepted it. . . . At least, I never saw any [such tangible evidence]. . . . Had
> we had such evidence, we would have tried them before a military commission.[102]

Colonel Bicknell of Hawai'i's G-2 put it another way. In describing the army's
security measures, he explained that in the case of a Japanese invasion, some local Japanese Americans would be afraid of the invading forces, some would remain neutral,
some would fight to repel the enemy, and some "would aid their blood brothers from
Japan. It was not difficult to reach these general conclusions but to determine the class
into which each individual would eventually fall was quite impossible." The real danger,
according to Bicknell, was that there were "many who, under normal conditions would
be loyal to the United States but under the influence of battle hysteria and with a display of the flag of Nippon on the rifles of the landing troops . . . might easily revert to
type in spite of newly acquired convictions. For these reasons it was only fair to assume
that every person of Japanese ancestry must be closely guarded for our own protection as well as to protect him from his inner self."[103]

Three common themes that emerged in the hearings of Japanese-American suspects—internment without any substantiated evidence, suspicion of Kibei, and the importance of the suspect's attitude in determining his or her fate—are dramatically illustrated in a particularly egregious case that originated in Kaua'i. H. T. T., a Nisei, attended elementary school and two years of high school in Hawai'i, in addition to studying telegraphy in Philadelphia. He had spent fifteen months in a preparatory school in Japan, where he also attended Waseda University for three years. After the attack on Pearl Harbor, he had served in Hawai'i as a special police officer without remuneration until mid-January 1942. He was detained and interned, following a hearing by the hearing review board in June 1942, as a result of a report by a police captain in Kaua'i who claimed that H. T. T. was the head of Japanese espionage on that island. Asked about the source of his information, the police captain told the MID "that *he had gotten it from his wife who prayed to God and had gotten this information from heaven.*"[104]

Although a trap set by the army and designed to catch the suspect transmitting information to the enemy failed to produce any evidence of espionage, H. T. T. spent twenty-three months in internment on the basis of this "information from heaven," reinforced by the fact that he had been partially educated in Japan. An MID memo of September 1943 stated that "this case was mushroomed from a mere suspicion to a very serious charge, but was not based on sufficient fact."[105] Nevertheless, H. T. T. was not paroled until May 18, 1944, following another hearing at which he showed "no resentment" and "impressed the agents as being thoroughly loyal and philosophical about his predicament."[106]

The adjudication procedure thus was explicitly based on crediting even mere undocumented gossip or suspicion. The process of loyalty determination was nontransparent; it gave unlimited discretion to the military commander, who was free to accept or reject the decisions of formal review boards (and he regularly accepted the advice of intelligence officers when they recommended that he override review boards' findings that a particular individual was loyal and should be released).[107] If specific documentation of behavior allegedly warranting internment was available to the army, it was not revealed to the person under investigation or interrogation, and permission was never granted to confront accusers. The case files for those sentenced to internment or removal typically would be closed with the prescribed stock phrase, "dangerous or potentially dangerous to the security of the United States."[108]

By this process were hundreds of U.S. citizens deemed "disloyal" or "potentially disloyal," and therefore subjected to incarceration. For some, including hundreds of the detained Kibei from Hawai'i, the final result was exposure to the terrifying chaos and coercion that prevailed at the Tule Lake camp. Entrapment in the processes of investigation, interrogation, transfer, and incarceration was compounded at Tule Lake by confusion, duress, and violence—with the result that several thousand detainees and their kin from the mainland, plus a reported 136 from Hawai'i, signed papers renouncing their U.S. citizenship and asking for return to Japan.[109]

For anyone suspected of a role in the disruptions, there was further questioning by the camp officials, the FBI, or army officers; and for those who were the victims of disruption or violence, there was interrogation in the effort to identify those who should be apprehended. With what degree of fairness these procedures were conducted—and how frightening or confusing, or at a minimum how offensive to their sense of dignity, they must have been for these people undergoing such reiterated evaluations—is an issue that must be given weight in any accounting of the government's and army's record on the home front in the World War II years.

Chapter Ten

THE FATE OF THE DETAINEES

Residents in Hawaiʻi of Japanese descent, and to a far lesser degree those of German and Italian descent, were investigated, arrested, interned, paroled, and released throughout the war. Some were enemy aliens, some were U.S. citizens; some were detained on the mainland, some were incarcerated in Hawaiʻi; some were detained for a few days, most were held for the duration of the war. Although their fates differed in particulars, all of the detainees were deprived of their liberty, often on the basis of flimsy or hearsay evidence with no formal charges filed against them.

Most of those arrested in the first weeks of the war were enemy aliens. Their detention and internment were in accord with congressional legislation dating back to 1798, which made enemy aliens "liable to be apprehended, restrained, secured, and removed."[1] By the end of March 1942, nearly 500 Japanese nationals, all but 7 of them men, had been interned. Of this number, two-thirds had been sent to internment camps on the mainland, in accordance with Emmons's policies of selective removal; the rest were interned in Hawaiʻi, mainly at Sand Island.[2] (It should be noted that the Geneva Convention calls for enemy aliens to be evacuated from combat zones, which further justified their deportation to the mainland.) As mentioned earlier, the Japanese aliens detained in this early period were mainly leaders of the community, Japanese language teachers and religious leaders, and consular agents.

In contrast, only seventy-two Nisei were in custody by the end of March 1942, being held as citizens under the provisions of martial law. Fifty-five of the Nisei were interned in Hawaiʻi and the remainder had been transported to the mainland, only to be returned to Hawaiʻi in August 1942.[3] Lesser numbers of residents of German and Italian ancestry, both aliens and citizens, had also been detained. In addition, more than eighty persons had been interrogated and released. According to Shivers, several of the German and Italian aliens were released "because of their sex, age and other circumstances which make such action necessary and imperative."[4]

TABLE 2

Persons of Enemy Ethnicity Detained in Hawai'i, December 7, 1941–March 30, 1942

	Interned in Hawai'i	Sent to Mainland	Total Incarcerated	Released
Japanese Ancestry				
Nationals (Issei)	166	323	489	26
U.S. citizens (Nisei)	55	17	72	21
	221	*340*	*561*	*47*
German Ancestry				
Nationals	29	12	41	27
U.S. Citizens	25	14	39	1
	54	*26*	*80*	*28*
Italian Ancestry				
Nationals	7		7	8
U.S. Citizens	0	2	2	0
	7	*2*	*9*	*8*
TOTALS	282	368	650	83

Source: Data from R. L. Shivers to Hoover, Director, FBI, March 30, 1942, FBI File No. 100-2-20. Also summarized in Tetsuden Kashima, *Judgment without Trial: Japanese American Imprisonment during World War II* (Seattle: University of Washington, 2003), 78.

Since martial law was the only basis for the detention of citizens in the absence of actual charges of sabotage or espionage, the military regarded the continuance of martial law as essential to the security and defense of the islands.

As the war continued, the proportion of Japanese aliens who were detained declined, and after April 1944, by which time Hawai'i was no longer considered to be an active combat zone, no more enemy aliens were removed to the mainland.[5] In contrast, the Nisei population—and especially the Kibei—were subjected to increasing arrests and internments (see charts 1–4).

As shown in table 3 below, by the end of the war, a total of 712 aliens (plus a few Kibei who wanted to renounce U.S. citizenship) had been sent to internment camps on the mainland under the terms of the Enemy Aliens Act. Held at first in Department of Justice camps, some of them were subsequently paroled to camps run by the War Relocation Authority, in part to permit reunification of families. Also sent to the mainland, under the provisions of martial law, were 306 formerly interned or detained U.S. citizens—mainly Kibei—who had been paroled from internment in Hawai'i and assigned to Relocation Centers on the mainland between November 1942 and March 1943. In addition, 783 civilians, both citizens and aliens, including more than 200 women

CHART 1
Orders Issued, U.S. Citizens*

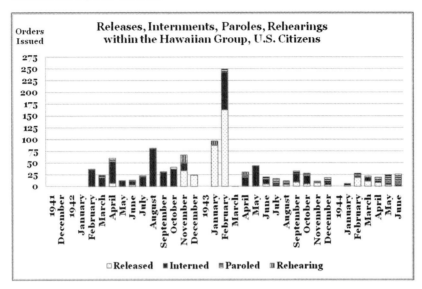

CHART 2

Aggregate Distribution, U.S. Citizens*

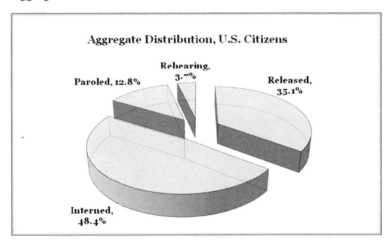

*From document entitled "Ordered by the commanding general, Central Pacific Area. Declassified 6 June 2008, Authority NND927556 [JG NARA]. Approved for Publication: E. P. Hardenbergh, Major T C." NB: The category "releases" includes the so-called gangplank releases in January and February 1943. See p. 195.

Source: Office of Military Governor, USAFICPA G-4, National Archives (Charts reconstructed from their original.) Period: December 7, 1941 to June 30, 1944.

CHART 3

Orders Issued, Non–U.S. Citizens*

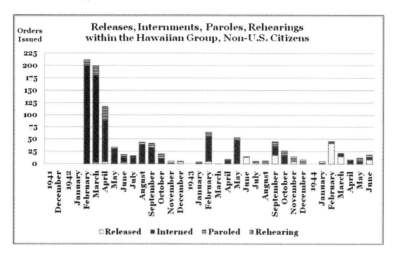

CHART 4

Aggregate Distribution, Non-U.S. Citizens*

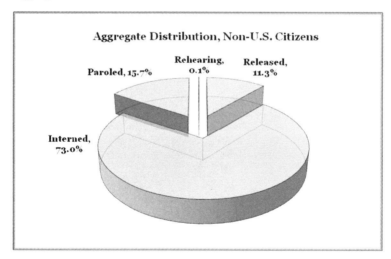

*Source the same as for Charts 1 and 2.

and nearly 500 persons under 19 years of age, who presumably were family members of internees or former internees and were designated as "voluntary evacuees," had been evacuated, mostly with the previous group. After martial law was terminated in 1944, an additional 73 U.S. citizens, again mainly Kibei, were "excluded" from the Territory of Hawai'i Military Area and sent to the WRA centers.[6]

TABLE 3

Japanese Americans Sent to Mainland from Hawai'i

---

1) 712 Issei (aliens), sent to internment camps.

2) 306 Nisei (mainly Kibei), paroled from internment in Hawai'i, sent to WRA camps (November 1942–March 1943).

3) 783 Issei, Nisei, and Sansei (about 90 percent women and children), family members of groups (1) and (2), plus some who were a "drain on the economy," sent to Army and WRA camps (mainly November 1942–March 1943).

4) 73 Nisei (mainly Kibei) "excluded" from the Territory of Hawai'i Military Area after martial law ended (November 1944), sent to Tule Lake.

Source: Based on data in A. M. Tollefson, Provost Marshal General's Office, "Persons Evacuated from the Territory of Hawaii Military Area Presently Residing on the Mainland," October 9, 1945, RG 494, NA.

Sand Island and Other Detention Camps in Hawai'i

The processes by which the detainees were arrested, and the hearings that determined their fate, have been described above. Also described were the conditions in the initial stop for most of them, the Immigration Station in Honolulu. Conditions at the next stop for most, Sand Island, were impersonal and initially extremely primitive, according to some firsthand accounts. The detainees had to erect their own tents—one tent for each eight people—for the first six months, until barracks were completed.[7] The internees also participated—voluntarily and "willingly . . . for the exercise," according to an army official—in erecting the fences that surrounded their compounds until the army engineer construction groups were available to complete the job. One compound was for prisoners of war, one for internees of German and Italian descent, one for males of Japanese descent, and one for female internees.[8]

The provost marshal was ultimately responsible for the operation of the internment camp, but the day-to-day administration of the camp fell to his appointee, the camp commander. Security was the responsibility of a military police company. At Sand Island, the internees were subjected to strip searches upon arrival and, in one case, simply because a spoon was supposedly missing. Otokichi Ozaki, a language school teacher and poet, reported after the war that he was interned in five different camps, but he was "never treated as unreasonably" as he was at Sand Island.[9] The internees were kept incommunicado from their families and others for the first weeks of the war, and their loved ones did not even know if they were alive. The internees, too, feared for their lives. According to one of them, "This internment camp was under . . . a great hulk of a man, profane and given to abusive language. . . . For approximately one month [he] addressed us daily to the effect that as soon as he got orders we would all be machine-gunned, that he had soldiers trained for that purpose."[10] The Issei journalist Soga described the camp director as "fat and arrogant," someone who "intentionally made mountains out of molehills and deliberately presented a defiant attitude to irritate us."[11] And another internee, a Japanese language school teacher, recalled: "The boss there [Sand Island] made us, us men, really cry. . . . This boss would make us stand in the rain, practically naked, in our undershirt and underpants."[12]

The individual so described was Carl F. Eifler, a six-foot, two-inch former Los Angeles police officer who had also served as a U.S. Customs Officer on the Mexican border before being transferred to Hawai'i. Called up from Army Reserve status early in 1941, he was a company commander in Hawai'i when Pearl Harbor was attacked. He was immediately placed in charge of the Sand Island camp, but a month later he was ordered to report to the Coordinator of Information in Washington, DC, the forerunner of the Office of Strategic Services. He went on to become known as the "deadliest colonel" for his daring exploits behind the lines in Burma.[13]

With Eifler's departure, the situation for those being held at Sand Island improved somewhat. Eifler's successor was Louis F. Springer, later to become head of the Hawaiian Department Alien Processing Center. By mid-March, the provost marshal had decided that the detainee "may feel more comfortable if he were to have some of his own clothes," and he invited the nearest relative of those being held to supply the detainee with a suitcase filled with an approved list of warm clothing and toiletries. Each detainee was also permitted an account of $100.[14]

Six months later, in September 1942, conditions seemed significantly better, at least according to John Sulzer, who visited the detention camp on behalf of the International Red Cross Committee.[15] Sulzer painted a far more benign picture than had prevailed earlier: He found the barracks well built, ventilated and supplied with electricity, with married couples being permitted to live in "well-constructed tents." The food was abundant; comfort items such as cigarettes and magazines were available in the canteen "at reasonable prices"; and the detainees had access to laundry facilities and good latrines and showers. The internees were allowed to write two letters and one postcard per week, although mail was censored. In contrast to Soga, Sulzer reported no incidents of disciplinary action up to the time of his visit. He concluded, "We think the camp is most excellent from all viewpoints. For the most part, the internees appear to agree on this, particularly the white races. . . . All the internees are unanimous in affirming that the authorities treat them well." His only real criticism was that the internees were held too long before being transferred to permanent camps.[16] Reports from the detainees, too, indicate that restrictions had been relaxed by summer of 1942, with family visits permitted on weekends and children of married detainees allowed to share their parents' tent on the weekends.[17]

According to Springer, the internees were also allowed to grow vegetables for their own consumption, as the rations provided by the army did not accommodate the typical diet of the Japanese Americans being incarcerated. And after the first few months of the war, internees who worked in the laundry, barbershop, tailor shop, or as clerks for the camp administration could earn a small wage (less than a dollar per day).[18]

The detainees were initially told they were prisoners of war, but two days after Emmons became commanding general, they were informed, "You are neither criminals nor prisoners of war, but merely detainees. Thus you are not governed by military rules."[19] The internees were divided into squads and companies, with some degree of conditional autonomy. But they were subjected to strict controls, they were surrounded by ten-foot high electric fences, and they were guarded by soldiers with fixed bayonets.

Beginning in February 1942, the detainees at Sand Island were transferred to camps on the mainland. In the spring and summer of 1942, their places were taken by detainees from the other islands, most of whom, in turn, also were transferred to the mainland until the end of the evacuation program in March 1943. By that time, more than 630 detainees had been sent to mainland centers.[20]

The temporary detainment sites on the other islands were similarly guarded.[21] On the island of Hawai'i (the Big Island), the Kilauea Military Camp, built in 1916 as a training ground for the National Guard and a vacation site for the army, was used as an internment center. Some 185 aliens and citizens were detained there, housed in barracks measuring fifty feet by one hundred feet. Not only were the physical facilities superior to those on Sand Island, but food was plentiful. On the other hand, the internees had to march between rows of soldiers with fixed bayonets in order to get to the mess hall. According to one internee, "The dignity of the people was taken away. Internees were constantly accompanied by soldiers, even to the latrine."[22] In mid-February, immediate families were permitted to visit the detainees. The families were instructed to provide each internee with $50 and warm clothes, in anticipation of shipment away from Kilauea. All of the detainees at Kilauea were transferred to Sand Island or the mainland before the summer of 1942, freeing the Kilauea site for other military uses—including a prisoner of war camp, which was added in 1944.[23] Smaller numbers of detainees on the Big Island were temporarily held at the Hilo Independent Language School, which became a headquarters for a company of military police.[24]

In Kaua'i, the internees were first held in the Waimea jail in the southwestern part of the island and in the Wailua County Jail, on the east side of the island. A two-story dormitory was soon constructed in Wailua to separate the internees from the regular inmates and to alleviate overcrowding. The detainees were permitted to enter and leave the building at will, and they engaged in cooking, gardening, carpentry, knitting for the Red Cross, English classes, and other activities. Families were permitted twice-weekly visits.[25] Other internees were held at the Kalaheo Stockade.[26] Most of the detainees from Kaua'i, including Umeno Harada, who had been involved in the Ni'ihau incident, were subsequently transferred to Sand Island.[27]

On Maui, the detainees were held in the Maui County jail in Wailuku, which also temporarily housed seven detainees from Moloka'i and Lana'i, and in the Haiku Military

Camp. The treatment of the detainees was the most relaxed on Maui, with family visits and Japanese-language publications permitted. Nearly eighty persons of Japanese descent were detained in Maui, with most of them also later transferred to Sand Island.[28]

By late spring of 1942, morale at Sand Island was deteriorating. Deprived of their freedom and uncertain of their fate, some of the detainees, particularly the Caucasians, demanded directly or through their attorneys or family members to know why they were being held. Finally, in June 1942, the Office of the Military Governor changed its policy and started notifying each detainee in writing of the disposition of his or her case. The commanding officer of the camp, Louis Springer, distributed the notifications, which, he reported, resulted in hysteria among the internees, with some of them asking to be shot rather than being confined in indefinite detention in an internment camp.[29] They had little choice, however, but to accept their fate—shipment to the mainland or continued incarceration in Hawai'i.

On March 1, 1943, Sand Island was closed, the OMG having decided that the detention camp should be located further inland, where it would not be subjected to the possibility of a direct attack from an enemy landing.[30] All the remaining internees were sent to the newly constructed Honouliuli Camp in Honouliuli Gulch, built in sugar-cane fields.[31] (Noting that "Honouliuli serves as a powerful reminder of the need to protect civil liberties in times of conflict, and the effects of martial law on civil society," President Obama designated the site as a National Monument in February 2015.)[32]

The internees called the camp "Hell Valley" because of the intense heat that characterized the weather in the local area. Honouliuli, like Sand Island, was heavily patrolled by armed guards and ringed with barbed wire, but the conditions were an improvement over Sand Island. In contrast to Sand Island and other detention facilities in Hawai'i, the Honouliuli camp had been built during World War II expressly to house internees and prisoners of war. The camp's 160 acres were divided into seven barbed wire enclosures, separating some 3,000 Japanese and Italian prisoners of war from the civilian internees, those of European ancestry from those of Japanese ancestry, and the men from the women. The whole complex was surrounded by fourteen guard towers. The internees lived in frame barracks, which, within two months, had electricity, permitting the use of radios; modern plumbing was available in the latrines; and the internees had access to a post exchange, a recreation field, and movies twice weekly. In addition, internees were allowed family visits twice per month. The internees planted trees, shrubs, and flower and vegetable gardens, and no complaints were registered with the Swedish vice-consul—the internees' liaison with the military government—who visited the camp. At his request, the internees were permitted to receive the two Japanese-language dailies published in Honolulu starting in June 1943.[33]

Two of the Kibei interned at Honouliuli later recollected that their treatment was not unduly harsh; one of them "took English classes, played his violin and attended Christian services on Sundays, when he prayed for the war to end."[34] Despite this some-

Honouliuli Internment Camp, Oʻahu. Internees' housing is shown here behind the barbed-wire fencing. Credit: R. H. Lodge photo, Hawaii's Plantation Village Collection, courtesy of the Japanese Cultural Center of Hawaiʻi.

what more relaxed atmosphere, however, requests by the internees for temporary furloughs to attend to business matters were routinely denied.[35] Some of the internees at Honouliuli also requested the establishment of a family internment camp similar to the WRA camps on the mainland, but the OMG and the director of the Alien Processing Center denied the request both because of the complexities of running a family camp with its need for schools and recreational facilities, and because the space was needed to house anticipated increased numbers of prisoners of war.[36] However, several alien Japanese children, who were very young or who had no one to look after them, became residents in 1944. Although its total capacity was 3,000, at its peak Honouliuli held only some 320 Nikkei internees, mostly Kibei and other Nisei who had been transferred from Sand Island or detained after Sand Island closed.[37] All but several dozen of the citizens of Japanese ancestry were released from internment during 1942 and 1943, with many of them being sent to WRA camps on the mainland. In late 1944, with the end of martial law, seventy of the Kibei were "excluded" from the territory and sent to the mainland, and many others were paroled. In the spring of 1945, however, the camp

Honouliuli Internment Camp, Oʻahu. Internees' housing shown here in foreground, with tents in separate compound behind used for confinement of POWs. Credit: R. H. Lodge photo, Hawaii's Plantation Village Collection, courtesy of the Japanese Cultural Center of Hawaiʻi.

still held thirty-four male Japanese aliens, including four minors; ten female Japanese aliens, including five minors; and six Nisei.[38] Even as late as September, after the war had ended, twenty-two Issei and Kibei were still being held.[39] By then, Honouliuli was occupied mainly by nearly 4,000 prisoners of war from both the European and Pacific theaters of war.[40]

During the course of the war, a total of more than 600 U.S. citizens, of whom more than 90 percent were Nisei, were interned in camps in Hawaiʻi.[41]

The Case of Sanji Abe

One of the most prominent Nisei to be interned in Honouliuli was Sanji Abe, who had been born in Hawaiʻi in 1895 to alien Japanese parents. His case is illustrative both of the workings of the military government charged with security and of the fate of many of the citizen internees. Abe, a dual citizen, was educated in the public schools of Hawaiʻi as well as in Japanese language schools. With the exception of two years' service in the U.S. Army during World War I, he was a member of the police department in

Hawai'i from 1916 until October 1940, when he became the first Nisei to be elected to the Senate of the Territory of Hawai'i. He expatriated from Japan during his election campaign. He had visited Japan twice: once, in 1921, as manager of a local baseball team that was touring Japan, and again in the summer of 1940, a trip he stated was for business. He held leadership positions in the Society of American Citizens of Japanese Ancestry. In addition to being a police officer, he had been associated with several other business enterprises and had accumulated nearly $73,000 in assets. One of those enterprises was a theater, and he was arrested in August 1942 for possession of a Japanese flag that was found among the stage props. He was released about ten days later because, as he pointed out, the military had not made possession of the Japanese flag a crime until after his arrest.[42]

Abe was re-arrested in September, this time without charge, and placed in custodial detention. The hearing board found that although he was exclusively a citizen of the United States, his loyalty was questionable. "His activities have been both pro-American and pro-Japanese and although the latter have not been shown to be subversive, they have been in some instances highly suspicious."[43] The hearing board accordingly recommended internment for the duration of the war, a recommendation in which the Intelligence Reviewing Board concurred, and Abe was officially interned on February 19, 1943.

The case against Abe cited his leadership of the Nikkei community; his entertainment of visiting Japanese naval personnel; his leadership in drives for Japanese war relief; the "suspicious circumstances" of his 1940 trip to Japan; his role as president of the International Theater Company, which showed only Japanese movies; the "unusual circumstances" of his expatriation from Japan; his association with the Japanese consulates in Honolulu and San Francisco; his involvement with a Japanese radio program that featured patriotic Japanese music; and his presidency of a company that published the bilingual newspaper *Hawaii Mainichi,* "which has been notorious for its pro-Japanese activities." In addition, he was "reported to have behaved mysteriously at a wedding on December 6, 1941." That mysterious behavior turned out to be conversing with the president of a Japanese language school and going outside, "looking at the sky, and generally act[ing] strangely." Abe denied involvement with either the Japanese fund drives of the newspaper or with the martial music on the radio station, and claimed he merely paid his respects to the consul. He submitted in his defense newspaper articles and legislation that he had supported as a territorial senator.

Abe applied for parole, and his case was reviewed by the Military Governor's Reviewing Board in January 1944. Lieutenant Colonel Slattery, Chief of the Legal Section, admitted that "no acts of a subversive nature were proved." Nevertheless, he wrote, "the circumstances surrounding many of his activities were suspicious. . . . It may well be that a person can be engaged in an activity and be unaware of the subversive elements in it. But Abe was engaged in such various activities, all of which are suspicious, that it seems highly improbable to me that he knew not of their questionable nature. There is no doubt that he is one of the outstanding leaders on Hawaii."[44] Slattery recommended he "be continued in internment to safeguard the public peace, safety, and security of the United States." Three months later, at which time Abe had a son serving in the U.S. Army, Slattery again thought he should be continued in internment, but he deferred to the Military Governor's Reviewing Board.[45] Abe was finally paroled on March 22, 1944, but he was not released from parole for nearly another year, in February 1945.[46] Clearly Abe's case, like that of so many of the internees, was one in which there was no specific evidence that he was dangerous, but one in which, as Emmons admitted, the military government was "taking no chances."[47] After the war, Abe resumed his business of importing and promoting Japanese films, but he never returned to politics.

Shipment to the Mainland

A different fate faced the nearly 1,900 enemy aliens and citizens who were removed to the mainland. Unlike the ethnic Japanese on the West Coast of the United States who were forcibly relocated in family groups, most of the individuals from Hawai'i who were detained and sent to the mainland had to leave their families behind.[48] At first, those leaving Sand Island thought they were being returned to Honolulu for release; when they learned that they were, instead, being shipped to the mainland, "they felt as if a bomb had been dropped on them." Most were not even given a chance to say goodbye to their families.[49] All endured a difficult sea voyage, in cramped quarters with poor sanitation facilities, facing enemy attack, uncertainty about their fate, and, in most cases, seasickness. Once they arrived in San Francisco, they were transferred to trains with covered windows, again not knowing where they were going. According to one detainee, "It was just spiritual despair. We didn't know how long we were going to be there or when the war was going to end. . . . If they told me I was going to be there so many months, it would have been bearable."[50]

Deprived of their liberty, separated from their homes and their families, unsure of their fate, the detainees also had to cope with "unbearable monotony." Although the detention camps were highly structured and the detainees were allowed to earn minimal wages for such jobs as laundrymen, yardmen, cooks and teachers, ennui proved to be a major enemy: "Eat. Sleep. Wake up. Eat. Sleep. Wake up. A life cut off from everything in the world. . . . I feel we are becoming addlebrained," wrote one. "If we continue to live like this for another two or three years, we will become living corpses. . . . Are we not becoming like leaking balloons—ambitionless, lethargic and apathetic?"[51]

The first group of detainees, mainly enemy aliens, was initially sent to Camp Mc-Coy in Wisconsin, where they were totally unprepared for the freezing winter temperatures. Like subsequent groups of detainees from Hawai'i, they were frequently transferred—often to other camps with extreme temperatures, both hot and cold. For example, one Japanese-born internee, Otokichi Ozaki, a poet who had lived in Hawai'i since 1915 and had worked for a Japanese-language newspaper and a Japanese school in Hilo, was arrested on December 7, 1941. He penned a remembrance of the first night of his arrest and incarceration:

A silent farewell
For sleeping children.
Into the dark cold I go.
The rain gently falling.

.   .   .   .

Scattered among us
Many a Nikkei
Taken prisoner.
Why?[52]

By December 1945, he had been detained in eight camps: the Kilauea Military Camp; Sand Island; Angel Island, California; Fort Sill, Oklahoma; Camp Livingston, Louisiana; Santa Fe, New Mexico; Jerome, Arkansas; and Tule Lake, California. He was a block manager at Tule Lake, and in 1945 he coordinated the return home of the Hawai'i group. His family had finally caught up with him in Jerome.[53]

The Hawai'i internees held on the mainland were permitted to request that their wives be brought to the mainland and that they be transferred together to a family camp. However, some internees, although they were lonely, did not want their wives to suffer the experience of being uprooted and living in confinement.[54] The families of the alien internees faced difficult times as well, having to decide whether to try to join their husbands, and then being given short notice before departure. There is some evidence that women who could support themselves chose to remain in Hawai'i, while those who had no source of livelihood opted (or were selected) for transfer to the mainland. Letters from Ozaki's wife Hideko, a Kibei who also taught at the Japanese language school, illustrate their dilemma. In May 1942, her husband had asked her to be ready to leave with their four children to join him on the mainland. She replied in June,

> I would like to go where you go, and I would like the children to come with me, for I believe that a family belongs together. Grandfather and Grandmother say they will remain in Hawaii; they have no desire to go back to Japan.
>
> It is true that I prefer to live here and have the children grow up where they were born. If there is any possibility that you would be allowed to return, I would wait for you here. . . . Our friends strongly urged me to remain. They feel the best things for the children and us is to wait until this awful war ends. . . . I shall do whatever you wish me to do.[55]

Six months later, in January 1943, Hideko Ozaki again wrote to her husband. She and the children had arrived in Arkansas; they were disappointed not to be reunited immediately with Otokichi, and they were unprepared for the cold weather.

> The children feel that I made a foolish decision in coming here, and I cannot disagree. It would have been so much simpler if we had remained in Hawaii. . . .

What a difficult time we had in disposing of our assets on 3-days' notice. We begged for an extension but were told that everyone, even the elderly, had to leave. The bulky items were sold and the rest given away or destroyed.[56]

The Ozakis were not reunited until 1944, more than a year later.

A similar case involved the family of the Reverend Kyojo Naitoh, a Buddhist priest who was arrested in Kaua'i on December 7 and was detained in Wailua prison, Kaua'i. He was then moved, successively, to the Immigration Station in Honolulu; Sand Island; Angel Island, California; Lowton City, Oklahoma; Camp Livingston, Louisiana; Santa Fe, New Mexico; Jerome, Arkansas; and Tule Lake, California. His wife and daughter left Kaua'i in December 1942 and arrived in Jerome in January 1943; they waited there for fifteen months before Reverend Naitoh was reunited with them.[57]

Some families were involuntarily evacuated. One internee, the daughter of a Buddhist minister and principal of a Japanese school who had been arrested on December 7, 1941, and detained in Kilauea Military Camp, recalled, "In late summer [1942], my mother received an official government notice saying that she and all children under 18 must pack some clothing and be sent to the mainland. We had no choice. . . . [T]here was no explanation or reason given to us. We were under the jurisdiction of the Department of Immigration and Naturalization Services. Others who were relocated were under the jurisdiction of the Department of War."[58] They were fingerprinted and given ID numbers at the Honolulu Immigration Station. "The officials only then told us that our fathers were sent somewhere on the mainland. . . . As young children, we did not know what was happening. 'Not knowing' is one of the most depressing feelings one gets."[59] They left Honolulu in August 1942; the family was finally reunited in Crystal City, Texas, in May 1943.[60]

As these examples illustrate, the policy for reuniting internees with their families, no matter how well intended, was a mixed picture in its implementation. The families were typically shipped out from Honolulu to the mainland weeks, often months, after the internees had been taken away; and there are many stories of family members who were taken first in the crowded holds of ships and then on darkened railroad cars and transported, hapless itinerants, from camp to camp on the mainland, a step behind the internees' transfers among camps in the South and northwestern states. Actual family reunification was seldom quickly achieved, as the request for the transfer of each internee went from Army Intelligence (G-2) in Hawai'i to the Alien Processing Center, through the OMG to the Provost Marshal General and finally to the Department of Justice, which had to approve the internee's transfer to the family internment camp or his parole to a WRA camp. The consequent uncertainties of their fate created painful anxiety for the people so affected.[61] Eventually, most of them were brought to the Department of Justice Camp in Crystal City, Texas (administered by the Immigration and Naturalization Service as a family camp), or to the WRA camps in Jerome, Arkansas; Topaz, Utah; or Tule Lake, California.[62]

The family members of the internees who sought reunification on the mainland with their husbands and fathers, including Hideko Ozaki and Mrs. Naitoh, were among the total of 1,040 persons who were evacuated in late 1942 and early 1943. This group also included Nisei citizens who had been interned in Hawai'i.

The Hawai'i internees who chose evacuation to the mainland rather than continued internment in late 1942 and early 1943 were mainly dual-citizen Kibei.[63] They had been promised they would be released, and, as an army official later stated, they were "under the impression that [they] . . . would be free of all restrictions except as to residence within the west coast area." The summaries of their files read, in most cases, "Released from internment at the time of his departure from the Territory of Hawaii to the Mainland of the United States"—hence the name "gangplank releases."[64]

These Japanese-American citizens were released without any consideration of the merits of their cases; it was, according to an official source, "purely a matter of expediency" in order to evacuate from the territory "certain undesirable elements in the Japanese population."[65] Before being released from internment, each one had to sign a waiver of the right to sue the government for detention.[66] "In consideration of being released as herein requested," the release form read, "and of being *detained, confined, or interned no longer,*" the internee and his heirs and executors agreed to "release . . . and forever discharge the United States of America" and all departments, officers, agents, and representatives thereof, from any actions, claims, suits or demands arising from apprehension, arrest, detention, and confinement.[67]

Not wanting to waive their rights for reimbursements for loss of personal property, many parolees were reluctant to sign these statements. Emmons, the commanding general and military governor, was questioned about these release forms after the war in a civil suit brought by one of the internees, Hans Zimmerman, who had refused to sign the waiver. Ironically, asked if he had directed Zimmerman to sign such a release, Emmons replied that he would not have been so foolish; he knew Zimmerman would not sign it. "I would not have signed it," Emmons replied, "and I don't think anybody else would have signed it."[68] Writing in 1946, a special investigator for the Justice Department pointed out (accurately, as events proved) that such a signed letter of release would have no standing in court: "It's just as though your hosts in Manchuria had asked you to sign a paper that you were well treated and well fed, and then on advice of a physician were told to stop eating because you were putting on too much weight. It's on a par with that sort of thing."[69]

Zimmerman, however, was one of only a very few persons who refused to sign the waiver. As the army's official history states, "They [the parolees] did sign it, however, as the only means of obtaining their freedom, but were left with a feeling that they had received injustice not only by being interned but even in the manner of release from internment."[70] According to one personal account, "I was coerced—intimidated—into signing that statement. I was told that if I didn't sign, I would again lose my freedom."[71] Another Hawai'i Kibei recalled in an interview:

One day a Caucasian who talked fluent Japanese came into the [Sand Island] center and told them that they had good news for them. He said the citizens could evacuate to the mainland with their families and that they would be free over here . . . and would get employment. Most of them anticipated doing some farm work. Women and children were told they would be united with their husbands who were interned on the mainland.[72]

The evacuees must indeed have been shocked, given these assurances that they would be "confined no longer," when they arrived at the mainland WRA centers to find themselves in enclosures surrounded by barbed wire and armed guards, with work permits strictly controlled by the authorities and leave to work outside the camps limited to those who passed a security clearance. As the WRA subsequently reported in regard to one such evacuee: "At the hearing he stated when they shipped him from de-

TABLE 4
Selective Detention Program, 1941–1945

Detained on suspicion of disloyalty or as potentially dangerous			Interned in Hawai'i	Sent to Mainland	Totals
Aliens					
	Japanese	896	184	712	
	German and Italian	56	44	12	
					(952)
U.S. Citizens					
	Japanese Ancestry (includes 468 Kibei)	570	191	(as parolees) 306 (as excludees) 73	
	German Ancestry	42	42		
	Italian Ancestry	2	2		
	Other Caucasian	3	3		
					(617)
Subtotal		1,569	(466)	(1,103)	1,569
"Evacuated" to mainland to join family or for economic reasons; sent to WRA camps				783	783
Total Incarcerated				1,886	2,352

Source: Compiled from data contained in Office of Internal Security (Honolulu), Memorandum to War Department No. R73740, November 30, 1945, RG 338, NA, and A. M. Tollefson, Office of Provost Marshal General, "Persons Evacuated from the Territory of Hawaii Military Area Presently Residing on the Mainland," October 9, 1945, RG 338, NA.
Note: Statistics vary from source to source.

tention in Hawaii to the Mainland, he understood they were to be free and was trying to find out at time of registration why he was placed in a camp."[73]

One prominent critic of the entire internment policy has called the evacuation from Hawai'i "a surrealistic tale of chicanery and duress, deplorable for its official use of mendacity to abrogate the rights of ordinary citizens blameless of wrongdoing."[74]

Indeed, the exact status of these paroled evacuees was not clear even to the intelligence branch of the army's Hawaiian Department that had approved their release. Thus in early February 1943, Colonel Bicknell of Hawai'i's G-2 section sought clarification from the assistant chief of staff of the Wartime Civil Control Administration in San Francisco, Colonel Bendetsen: "What is an evacuee—a citizen or resident moved for the benefit of the government but free to conduct his [business] affairs as he wishes within the limits of his mobility, or a suspect whose actions should be somewhat controlled? Are our evacuees considered to be equal to yours, or does their previous internment make them suspects, if so, to what degree?"[75] Bendetsen, who had been a principal architect of Executive Order 9066 and the policy of mass removal of Nikkei from the West Coast, replied that in his personal opinion, evacuees were, indeed, free to conduct their affairs "within the limits necessarily imposed" on their mobility. He did not "consider an evacuee as being a suspect merely because he is an evacuee. Certainly all evacuees, both on the mainland and from Hawai'i, are considered as the same and they are all accorded the same treatment."[76] He did not address the question of why, if these individuals were not suspect, their mobility should be so tightly circumscribed.

Tule Lake

Additional severe hardships confronted the individual detainees and their families who were transferred in 1944 to the Tule Lake Segregation Center, along with the seventy-three "excludees" who were sent there from Hawai'i following the termination of martial law in October 1944. At this center, the segregants were subjected to life in a situation of chaos and intimidation, both from pro-Japanese gangs of detainees and from the officials running the camp. According to the Reverend Naitoh, who was at Tule Lake from May 1944 to the end of November 1945,

> Trouble? There were a big trouble. The HOSHI-DAN movement, the disloyalty party . . . organized in the camp and they shout AntiAmerica. The HOSHI-Dan means Mental Service to Mother Country. The Japanese there was strong just like Communist leader and forced to every KIBEI-NISEI those who want join U.S. Army service, and the other followers, men and women and kids, they becoming the members and special meeting in hide places . . . and every Sunday they marched just like Japanese Soldiers with bald head men and pigtailed hairdressed women and kids all over the main roads especially near the Sunday service church or by hospital. . . . The free men and Hoshidan members were no-talk with together.

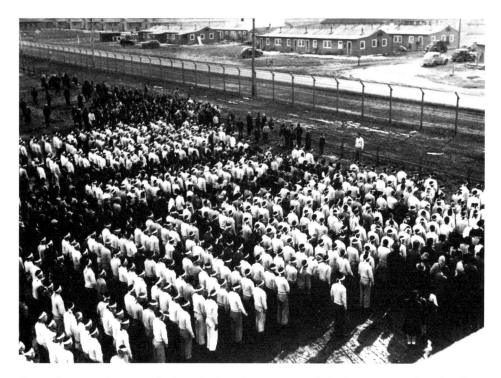

A mass demonstration staged by the radical pro-Japan group Hokoku Seinen Dan at the Tule Lake camp. Credit: U.S. Army Signal Corps photo, courtesy of the National Archives.

Naitoh goes on to describe how the leaders forced the Nisei to "throw away" their American citizenship.[77]

A large number of those segregated at Tule Lake did, indeed, decide in 1944 and early 1945 to renounce their American citizenship.[78] Hence the course of events at Tule Lake requires brief examination and appraisal. Such an appraisal can usefully begin with the fact that by August 1945 at least fifty-five, possibly many more, of the detainees from Hawaiʻi at Tule Lake had formally renounced American citizenship.[79] Such renunciation was made possible by the Nationality Act of June 1944, enacted by Congress in response to wartime anti-Japanese sentiment (much of it focused specifically on events at Tule Lake itself). This legislation created a procedure for U.S. citizens in times of war to renounce their citizenship in writing.[80]

To various government leaders and intelligence officers at the time, the fact that several thousand of those being held at Tule Lake, including these Hawaiʻi Japanese Americans, had chosen to return to Japan when afforded this opportunity was evidence that these renunciants were thoroughly disloyal, and hence that they had posed a tangible potential danger to wartime security. Such a view was advanced, of course, to justify the entire removal and internment program.

To other contemporary observers, including some officials closest to the situation on the ground, the Tule Lake story was far more complex. In their view, events were driven only in part by the disloyalty and pro-Japanese sentiments truly harbored by some detainees, including those organized into militant pro-Japanese gangs such as Hoshi-Dan. When the army announced in late December 1944 that the mass exclusion order was being rescinded, army officers gave the detainees a choice of resettlement outside Tule Lake or renunciation. Fearing for their livelihoods if not their lives if they were "resettled" in a hostile community with the war still going on, many of the detainees chose renunciation as a way of remaining at Tule Lake.[81]

Other factors were equally important, not least of which were the confusion, fear, and hostility that were inspired by government actions and, more generally, the lack of respect and the harsh treatment to which the detainees had been subjected. One of the most damaging missteps made by the WRA director's office and camp administrators involved giving out incorrect information as to criminal penalties that officials asserted would be risked by those not filling in the questionnaires. The resulting reaction from detainees escalated into a cycle of resistance and coercion, and eventually into resistance by those who were incarcerated to all supervisory efforts.[82]

Contributing to the disillusionment of those who said they had once been loyal— including some who had sought in vain to volunteer for combat service with the U.S. forces—were the conditions of pathological social disorder and breakdown of rules enforcement at the Tule Lake Center. In an affidavit placed on record in later legal proceedings, for example, the former assistant project director of the Tule Lake Center recalled that the detainees' morale and their sense of loyalty had been eroded by "the frustration and depression" induced, as he wrote,

> by living abnormal, regimented lives in an abnormal, regimented government center; the crowded, dismal barracks; the unpalatable food . . . ; lack of privacy in the community lavatories and laundry rooms; the "concentration camp" atmosphere of the daily routine; and the feeling that the "rights of man" as applied to other citizens and other aliens did not apply to them.[83]

Similarly, Attorney General Biddle stated in his notes of a cabinet meeting on December 22, 1944 (a time when the implications of the term as used to describe the Nazi operations was fully understood) that the Tule Lake center was "a dismal place—nothing but a concentration camp."[84] And in a landmark case in which the Ninth Circuit Court of Appeals would later accept the renunciants' claims that they had given up their citizenship under duress at Tule Lake, Chief Judge William Denman stated that "the oppressive conditions prevailing there . . . were in large part caused or made possible by the action and inaction of those government officials" whom he deemed responsible for "the oppressiveness of this imprisonment."[85] Indeed, the conditions, demonstrations, and violence became so bad that martial law was imposed on Tule Lake from early November 1943 to mid-January 1944.

Together with mainland detainees (or "colonists," as the WRA euphemistically termed these prisoners), a number of the Nikkei from Hawai'i became prominent in a determined resistance to disciplinary rule in the camp, in a movement that had begun during the 1943 registration campaign and become progressively more militant.[86] For example, the director of the Jerome WRA center reported in late February 1943 that "a group of the men from Hawaii attended at least three of the meetings [in preparation for general registration]." One of the men made "quite a lengthy speech against registration."[87] This resistance included an organized campaign to undermine the government's loyalty reviews during the registration campaign preliminary to instituting the Selective Service draft of citizen and dual citizen detainees in 1944. Their resistance also included violent action. Scores of young men were disciplined by the guards—and in one instance thrown into a stockade, then shipped off to a local civilian jail—for being members of pro-Japanese gangs that had beaten fellow detainees. These beatings were inflicted on supposed informers and others who had cooperated with the authorities, especially if they had attested to their loyalty to the United States by filling out registration forms that included the notorious Questions 27 and 28.[88]

Officials and security personnel in several of the WRA camps and centers, not only at Tule Lake, had reported from the outset of their operations that Kibei were often prominent in the ranks of "troublemakers," forming the core of support for disloyal, pro-Japanese activities. These actions included marches and demonstrations, denunciation of government rules, circulation of rumors often said to be based on propaganda broadcasts from Tokyo, strikes against job assignments and pay, and various types of spontaneous disruptions. Indeed, in his recollections of his WRA experience, former director Myer contended that the Hawai'i detainees had proven especially rebellious. General Emmons had misled him, he complained, as to the character of the persons evacuated from Hawai'i and sent to the WRA facilities. After these evacuees had arrived at the Jerome and Topaz camps, Myer wrote, "We soon realized . . . that we had a bunch of very tough young men." Following the "segregation" interviews for assessment of loyalty conducted in 1943, "these hard-nosed toughs" were transferred to Tule Lake and became "the nucleus for the strong-armed squad that served the purposes of the group in power" (the latter consisting of earlier-interned mainland Nisei, Issei, and some Kibei) during the height of violent outbreaks in November 1943.[89] Myer also recounted later an uprising at the Manzanar camp in which a Hawai'i-born World War I veteran, Joseph Kurihara, took a prominent role. Kurihara, Myer wrote, "turned his back on America because he thought America had turned its back on him"—a familiar theme, running through the personal histories of many detainees, as reflected in their testimony in loyalty investigations and interviews.[90]

Another WRA official noted after a disruption at a Tule Lake dance: "The members of the gang are reported to be Hawaiian-kibei . . . who probably knew each other in Hawaii before evacuation. . . . The feeling is that they will not shy from violent methods.

They are extremely bitter over evacuation since they alone were taken from Hawaii. All those who had returned from Japan within three years prior to the declaration of war were rounded up regardless of personal histories."[91] Initially sent to several different relocation centers, they were shunned by the other evacuees in those centers. In one center, several hundred sent from Hawai'i were quartered together, becoming a "tight group running their own affairs to suit themselves and feeling themselves not subordinate to the rules and customs of the community as a whole."[92]

On similar lines, a WRA attorney at Tule Lake reported that the younger Kibei, presumably including some from Hawai'i, had often done "the dirty work" of beatings and other actions aimed at intimidating other Tule Lake detainees—though they did so under control of an "insider" group of gang leaders who kept themselves under cover.[93] Precise numbers are impossible to come by in any attempt to assess the degree to which Hawai'i detainees were involved as foot soldiers, let alone as "inside" leaders, of resistance and violence at Tule Lake. It should be noted, however, that Japanese Americans from Hawai'i were only a small proportion—656, in mid-1944—of the total of 18,599 persons confined at Tule Lake.[94]

For the Hawai'i Nikkei and other detainees who played no part in subversion or violence and became the unfortunate victims of intimidation and disorder, their incarceration at Tule Lake was a nightmare. For those in the relocation center who reasserted their loyalty to the United States, including those who accepted conscription into the army, it required extraordinary courage to endure.

Release from Incarceration

Most of the detainees from Hawai'i were released on parole from the internment and WRA camps on the mainland but not returned to Hawai'i until war's end;[95] but for some who had been in Tule Lake, their ordeal would last for years after the war.

Those detainees with sons in the armed forces were among the first to be paroled. The reopening of the armed services to Nisei volunteers in January 1943, followed by the draft of Americans of Japanese descent a year later, created a poignant situation for families kept behind barbed wire under suspicion of disloyalty while their sons were fighting and dying in combat. By late 1943, the military began to acknowledge the sacrifices being made by these families and became more lenient in its policy of paroling such families on the mainland—although still not permitting their return to Hawai'i.

The case of a fifty-five-year-old enemy alien who owned a grocery store, K. T., is illustrative. K. T. had lived in Hawai'i since 1906 and had visited Japan only once to see his family. He had been a consular agent and admitted to possessing a picture of the Japanese emperor and a Japanese flag. The Hearing Board found that he was "loyal to Japan; and that he is not engaged in subversive activities." Intelligence agencies and the board unanimously recommended his internment in February 1942. In September of 1943, he wrote from Missoula, Montana, to General Richardson in Honolulu, requesting "modification of my status as an internee."

Shiroku "Whitey" Yamamoto (on right) and three other Nisei soldiers serving in the U.S. Army visiting family and friends still being detained in the Rohwer Relocation Center in Arkansas, 1944. Reproduced with permission of Shiroku Yamamoto. Photo # 8769, in U.S. Army Museum of History, Honolulu.

> I have done nothing contradictory to the laws and regulations of the United States and nothing injurious to this country. . . . In order to bring up my three children to be loyal and good citizen [*sic*] of the United States, I have done my best to give them high education. In April 1941 I subscribed [to] the first U.S. Defense bonds and have continued to subscribe to the subsequent issues. My son, Theodore, in order to perm[it] his highest duty to his country had volunteered to join the Army in June 1943. . . . Is now serving as . . . [in] Ann Arbor, Michigan. *As the father of a loyal American soldier, I feel it rather sad and inconsistent to remain as an internee and my present status is a dishonor to my son who is performing his duty to his country.*

The Military Governor's Reviewing Board decided that "In view of the policy concerning intern [*sic*] having sons in the United States Army," it is recommended "that subject be paroled on the Mainland upon the condition that he does not return to the Territory of Hawaii for the duration of the war."[96] A few exceptions to the parole policy were made, however, in cases of internees where there were "many adverse factors" or where, for example, a subject had been found to be "sly, slippery, shifty, and evasive," not to mention "tricky and dishonest."[97]

The irony of Japanese Americans in the army risking their lives to defend the country that imprisoned their parents did not escape the soldiers, who in some cases petitioned—not always successfully—for their parents' release. "For the past year," one Nisei soldier wrote,

> I have been troubled by this unusual situation—I in the Army—my father in internment. . . . I was born and raised in Hawaii; I believe in the government and the democracy for which it stands. I am ready to give my life for its preservation. But my conscience is clouded by one thought—my father in internment. How could a man who sends his son to the services of his country, a man who has 8 children, possibly attempt to harm the country of his children?[98]

By late 1944, even as the Hawai'i Command was still sending excludees to Tule Lake, consensus had formed in Washington against the continued internment and exclusion of Japanese Americans. Indeed, in January 1945, the Western Defense Command rescinded its mass exclusion orders against West Coast Nikkei from the mainland. In the OMG in Hawai'i, too, discussion began in earnest by late 1944, as the war entered its final phase, concerning policy for the return of the Hawai'i Nikkei evacuees and internees to the Territory of Hawai'i. On December 18, 1944, the U.S. Supreme Court had ruled, in the *Endo* case, that it was unconstitutional to continue to detain a citizen who had been certified as loyal by the internment authorities. This ruling was in the background as the military considered the release and return of Hawai'i Nisei and Kibei who were still in custody.[99] Even before the ruling, in early December 1944, William Morrison, who had been promoted to brigadier general and whose office was now in the Office of Internal Security (OIS) in Hawai'i,[100] declared that the commanding general found it "proper at this time to permit Japanese civilian internees from the Territory of Hawaii presently on parole in the mainland who have sons or daughters in the armed forces of the United States to return to the Territory of Hawaii." He requested that the provost marshal general's office furnish him with a list of such individuals and make the necessary arrangements for their transport.[101] More than 160 persons from Hawai'i who had been detained on the mainland had children serving in the armed forces.[102] The army outlined a point system for determining priority return status for those who had been removed from Hawai'i, which favored elderly individuals, persons who were evacuated before January 1, 1943, and persons with sons or daughters in the U.S. Armed Forces. The initial policy shift toward the return of the Hawai'i Nikkei thus was inspired in part by recognition of the contributions being made by some of these evacuees and their families toward the war effort.[103]

This sentiment for returning the Hawai'i internees and evacuees was echoed in Washington and among the Hawai'i Nikkei evacuee population itself. In February 1945, Secretary of the Interior Harold Ickes wrote to Secretary of War Stimson, contrasting the relaxation of restrictions on mainland Nikkei with the evacuation and exclusionary orders that were still in place against the Hawai'i Nikkei. Ickes was particularly concerned that "many of the Hawaiians who were voluntarily evacuated in 1943 agreed to being evacuated to the United States, in part at least, as a matter of patriotic cooperation with the authorities," while others, who had declined to evacuate the Territory of Hawai'i, had subsequently been released from the Honouliuli internment camp and returned to their homes in Hawai'i. A sense of injustice was rising among the voluntary evacuee population, who "feel that their cooperation with the Army authorities has resulted in a worse situation for themselves than for those who elected not to cooperate."[104]

General Richardson, asked to comment on Ickes's proposal to initiate a return procedure for the Hawai'i Nikkei, proposed that a board of officers review the case of each evacuee and assign priority status for return.[105] Richardson recognized, however, that the army's ability to bring all of the evacuees home by the end of 1945—nine months off—was contingent on available shipping. Shipping from the mainland to Hawai'i was in short supply for at least two reasons: first, the army of necessity gave priority to the flow of troops and supplies to the combat zones, for which Hawai'i was the mid-Pacific staging area; and, second, Secretary Ickes, Governor Stainback, and other elective officials pressed the army to use what space did become available to expedite the return of some 5,000 *haole* and other civilian "strandees" who (fearful of a Japanese invasion) had heeded army warnings after the Pearl Harbor raid and voluntarily left Hawai'i for the mainland.[106] Richardson also expressed the caveat that "there may be some individuals among these evacuees whose return . . . will not be recommended for security reasons," specifically including the sixty-seven Nisei who were excluded from Hawai'i in 1944.[107] Richardson's memorandum indicates that his headquarters was continuing to plan for the exclusion from Hawai'i of some Japanese Americans late into the war, and indeed he did order a small group of excludees from Hawai'i to be sent to Tule Lake as late as July 1945.[108]

The shortage of shipping was not the only obstacle, however, to the return of the Hawai'i detainees. When the Hawai'i Nikkei were transferred to the mainland, the Western Defense Command had issued nearly 500 *individual* orders excluding many of them (like other ethnic Japanese) from the West Coast. These individual orders against the Nikkei from Hawai'i remained in place, even when tens of thousands of Nikkei from California, Washington, Oregon, and Arizona were allowed to return home. Many of the Nikkei from Hawai'i thus found themselves in a bizarre legal limbo.[109] For example, one Nisei, who had volunteered for the army as a translator and had been serving in the Pacific combat theater, recalled: "As the war was ending, I received a letter from my sister [in the Rohwer Relocation Center] saying that they were being released but that my father could not go back to Hawaii because no alien was allowed to pass through the west coast. . . . I was real mad. My Commanding Officer said that if I wrote a letter, he would get it to General MacArthur's Headquarters for approval. I wrote the letter . . . and my father was allowed to travel across California and back to Hawaii."[110]

By spring of 1945, it had become imperative that these individual exclusion orders be lifted; otherwise the released detainees from Hawai'i could not return through West Coast ports.[111] Captain Stanley D. Arnold of the Japanese-American Branch was assigned by the Western Defense Command to travel to Honolulu, review the files, and summarize the relevant facts.[112] In addition to gathering information from the review board documents, Arnold was tasked with gathering information more generally on OMG's security program.[113] In his candid report to the Western Defense Command, Arnold declared that the ostensible success of the Hawaiian security program owed less to OMG's administrative talents than to the flexibility and privilege afforded it by the duration and scope of martial law in the territory. At the same time, Arnold asserted that "the Hawaiian Department made no mistake in ridding themselves" of the evacuees and internees, and that "security agencies in continental United States were exercising sound discretion when as a matter of policy they regarded every Hawaiian Japanese evacuee or internee with considerable doubt as to his loyalty."[114] Arnold was struck in particular by the insularity of the Kibei population, who, as we have seen, had been consistently singled out as a unique problem by security and intelligence officers.[115]

Meanwhile, Richardson's staff proceeded to implement a policy aimed at granting return to the large majority of voluntary evacuees and their families, against whom there were no orders excluding them from the West Coast. The review procedure that they developed, however, was slow, individualized, and discretionary. Hence, it resulted in considerable delay, even though the Department of the Interior was eager to complete the process before the relocation camps were shuttered by the end of 1945. By late May, the Commanding General's Review Board had approved the return of almost 400 Hawai'i Nikkei—fewer than one-fourth of the individuals who had been sent to internment camps or WRA camps on the mainland.[116] Dillon S. Myer, the director of the WRA, warned that unless the return procedure could be expedited substantially, many evacuees would need to take up temporary residence somewhere on the mainland once the relocation camps closed. Moreover, Myer cautioned, the WRA would soon be unable to cover the costs of ocean transportation, requiring a greater financial contribution from the army.[117]

This seeming impasse between the Hawai'i Command and the mainland authorities was suddenly broken only by the abrupt conclusion of hostilities between the United States and Japan on August 15, 1945—known as V-J Day (Victory in Japan)—following the atomic bomb attacks on Hiroshima and Nagasaki. On August 27, 1945, General Richardson accordingly notified the War Department that he had rescinded all orders that had been issued by OMG or the Hawai'i Command under which Japanese aliens and Japanese-American citizens had been sent to the mainland, there being no further military necessity for them.[118] With the War Department's approval, soon after V-J Day Richardson also released all alien enemies in internment in Hawai'i or on parole from internment.[119] As of August 29, there remained only eighteen aliens and four Kibei interned in Honouliuli Internment Camp.[120] In addition, 119 individuals in the Territory of Hawai'i were free on parole status.[121]

The surrender agreement between the United States and Japan on September 2, 1945, emboldened the mainland authorities to push for greatly accelerated procedures

for the return of the internees and evacuees from Hawai'i. In September, the Hawai'i
Command and the Provost Marshal General's Office gathered information on those
Kibei excludees who had renounced their U.S. citizenship and were seeking repatriation.[122] Within a month, the Hawai'i Command and the Provost Marshal General's Office had agreed on the priorities for shipping the detainees back to Hawai'i.[123] With
the closing of the WRA camps, the Hawai'i Japanese Americans were moved to the
West Coast to await transportation, and there was more bureaucratic jousting as to
which agency would pay for their food and housing.[124] The availability of shipping,
however, then became a critical issue, with the mainly *haole* "strandees" who had left
Hawai'i in early 1942 competing with the Japanese Americans for space.[125]

Finally, departure orders were issued in November for the transport back to Hawai'i
of the Nikkei who had been sent to the mainland. Nearly 450 left from Seattle on November 7 aboard the SS *Yarmouth,* and more than 900 others, plus 40 Nisei soldiers,
left from Los Angeles aboard the USAT *Shawnee* on November 30, 1945. They were
joyously greeted by relatives and friends bearing leis.[126] However, it was not until mid-
April 1946 that the last of the detainees and evacuees—except for the former Tule Lake
prisoners still being held on the mainland—left for home.[127] Close to 1,500 of the nearly
2,000 who had been sent to internment camps or relocation centers returned to Hawai'i,
bringing with them almost 100 new children and family members. Eighteen persons

Hawai'i Nikkei family who had been detained on the mainland boarding the army troop transport USAT *Shawnee* in Los Angeles, November 30, 1945, for their return to Hawai'i. Credit:
Charles E. Mace photo, courtesy of the Bancroft Library, University of California, Berkeley.

had died, and 241 chose to remain on the mainland; 248 Hawaiʻi Nikkei—about one in eight detainees—chose repatriation to Japan.[128]

"They Really Aren't Dangerous"

As to the hundreds of individuals who were interned in Hawaiʻi under martial law, most were unquestionably the victims of serious injustices. Many of them had been taken into custody—and even held for nearly the entire period of the war—on flimsy or nonexistent evidence. None had been able to see specific charges, confront accusers, or defend themselves with counsel before special screening boards controlled by the military. Many individuals were treated badly in the Sand Island encampment where they were held, and the families of many of the earliest internees were rounded up, given misleading information of what would happen to them, and then evacuated on a bogus "voluntary" basis to the mainland. Army officers in charge conceded that many individuals who were interned in those early months were regarded only as "troublemakers," and that others were picked up on the basis of entirely unsubstantiated complaints or rumor; hence, a great many of the people thus held hostage for larger policy purposes were in fact admittedly "harmless."[129]

Apart from the harsh treatment given them, many internees were incarcerated illegally in the first place, because the War Department had authorized the arrest and detention only of enemy aliens and dual citizens; but the army command in Honolulu had decided on its own to arrest and intern all who came under suspicion, including both naturalized and native-born citizens. Not until June 1943 did the inspector general of the War Department discover this error, leading the army to review all cases and to amend the records retroactively to specify that confinements had been authorized under the general terms of martial law.[130]

Some degree of alarm, even if dangers were only imagined, was certainly to be expected in the immediate aftermath of the Pearl Harbor disaster. But the offhand way in which Japanese Americans, both citizens and alien residents, were still being rounded up six months or more after Pearl Harbor, either to appease public sentiment or else in response to White House pressure, was epitomized in a trans-Pacific telephone comment by the army's chief security and intelligence officer in Hawaiʻi: "The evacuation [of selected internees] is merely a matter of relieving pressure. . . . They really aren't dangerous and not bad at all."[131]

The military nevertheless would make the continued presence of the large population of persons of Japanese ancestry in Hawaiʻi a key argument for the prolonged continuation of martial law. While this policy represented a serious injustice to countless detainees and their families, keeping them incarcerated with no real evidence that they were dangerous to internal security, the continuance of the policy did operate to underscore the military's two-part argument before public opinion and with the civilian government in Washington: it signified, first, that a continuing threat to internal security could be assumed to exist in the Islands and, second, that the army was alert to it. Thus in reporting to Assistant Secretary McCloy in February 1944, General Richardson stated: "In carrying out the parole policy the release of large numbers at any one time is avoided so as not to create an inference that the military authorities are relaxing their vigilance."[132] For the same reason, Richardson continued, "the release of prominent Japanese leaders of known Japanese tendencies is avoided[,] although in the record of many of these cases it appears that no overt acts have been committed by them."[133] And a few months later Richardson told the War Department that selective internment had served to warn and to intimidate the potentially disloyal ethnic Japanese, declaring:

> This method of handling the Japanese population has worked. The much-needed manpower has been utilized, and dangerous individuals interned while security demands for this [Military Area] have been met. . . . Martial law and the internments . . . have without doubt exerted a continuing pressure upon the Japanese community and acted as a deterrent on the Japanese community.[134]

This contention, that the Americans of Japanese ancestry constituted a serious and continuing threat to security in the Islands, would be cited repeatedly by the government in legal arguments when martial law was challenged in the courts; and, as applied to the mainland ethnic Japanese, it was one of the most important arguments upon which the Supreme Court's decisions upholding arrest and internment were based.[135]

Although the ethnic Japanese community, even more than any other segment of Hawai'i's population, thus suffered manifest deprivation of constitutional liberties as the result of army rule, the fact remains—and must be credited—that 99 percent of the Nikkei were at least spared the fate of so many on the West Coast: evacuation to prison-like camps, and a humiliating, extended incarceration along with the loss of their homes, their businesses, and in many instances their health and the very fabric of their family lives.

PART IV

Political Challenges

Chapter Eleven

ALARMS AND RESPONSES

As the months wore on, and especially after the decisive American victory in the Battle of Midway in June 1942, the threat of a Japanese invasion seemed to recede. So, too, in the minds of many civilians and their leaders, did the need for martial law. The military regime was openly challenged in the courts beginning in early 1942, and by 1943–1944 the army's role in governing Hawai'i was also emerging as a major issue in the national political arena. No longer could anyone responsibly say, as did the prominent Hawai'i business leader Walter Dillingham before a joint congressional committee in the period immediately following Pearl Harbor, that civil liberties and "the rights of American citizens" were seen as "hooey that nobody cared a damn about" in the Islands.[1]

The attempt to restore civilian rule to Hawai'i featured a struggle over control of policy between the military on the one side, and, on the other side, the Interior and Justice Departments, joined by the territorial governor and delegate to Congress. At the heart of this political struggle was the question of whether martial law and the suspension of the writ of habeas corpus were in fact necessary for the security of the Islands. The necessity for martial law must be judged, of course, in the context of the situation in the territory in December 1941. While the actual attack on Pearl Harbor came as a stunning surprise to both the military and civilian authorities, in fact both had been preparing for months for war with Japan. As we have noted, the territorial legislature—with the full support of the commanding general, Walter Short—had passed the Hawai'i Defense Act (the M-Day Act) in October.[2] This statute authorized the governor to assume more sweeping legislative and administrative powers than had ever before been delegated by any state of the Union to its executive in war emergencies, but with significant elements of standard due process in civilian courts for any person accused of violations.[3]

Governor Poindexter declared the M-Day Act to be in effect within hours of the attack on Pearl Harbor. Although the M-Day Act would remain in force throughout the war, Poindexter in fact relinquished his extraordinary M-Day powers later that day in favor of a military regime that would take over supervision of the entire government, including the courts. Whether he did so on his own judgment, or because General Short had persuaded him that only full army authority could protect Hawai'i, would later become a matter of dispute.[4]

From that day forward, until martial law was fully lifted in October 1944, nearly three years later, the army remained faithful to its basic position as to the legal and practical rationalization for martial law; that is, that martial law was essential for the security of Hawai'i. The army and navy commanders in Hawai'i insisted that the presence of a large population of Japanese alien residents and Japanese-American citizens constituted per se a security risk that could be handled only by martial law. And as late as the summer of 1944, the army was still contending that there was a strong possibility of another Japanese air strike, for which the Islands had to be prepared.[5]

Throughout the war, the cornerstone of the army's argument—which was supported, as we have seen, by the Navy and the War Departments—was that Hawai'i was a "fortress," and that every aspect of civilian life must be regarded as part of the military effort and vital to the efficiency of military operations. Thus General Emmons wrote to the assistant secretary of war of the importance of retaining military control over the "overlapping and closely integrated war functions of this Fortress."[6] In light of the internal and external threats to security, Emmons argued, he alone, as military governor, "must be the one to determine what functions can be returned to the civilian authorities and the courts."[7]

A premise underlying the army commanders' position was that civilian government, and especially the administration of justice, was subject to "politics" and was therefore unstable, unreliable, and incapable of swift action.[8] Just a month after he took command, General Emmons told the Chamber of Commerce:

> The sole purpose of martial law and military government now in effect is to better defend these islands. . . . Divided responsibility and diffused authority is not consistent with the swift and decisive action which emergency conditions require. This is no reflection upon your civil authorities or upon the people of Hawaii. . . . We Americans, naturally and properly, do not like martial law or military government. In normal times we would not accept it; but conditions are far from normal, as you all well know. The change back to normal will be made, of course, when conditions permit.[9]

Nearly a year later, in December 1942, General Emmons was still pressing on the War Department his argument that "in time of war the Hawaiian Islands, in spite of the fact that there is large and highly organized [*sic*] civilian community within them, are predominantly military in all their aspects."[10] Further, Emmons wrote,

> It is essential that civil authority be unified in Hawaii, which is not only in a theater of operations, but is an acutely confined area and of vitally [*sic*] strategic im-

portance. *I therefore recommend that the Governor of Hawaii be informed that he will be subordinate to the Military Governor* and that he should accept this situation as his duty arising from the consequence of the war and the importance of Hawaii in the strategy of the Pacific.[11]

Green, the Executive of the Office of the Military Governor (OMG), similarly urged the necessity of unified military control of civilian life. Thus in mid-1942, an Interior Department official reported a statement by Green to the effect that "direct administration of all controls over civilian life by the military authorities is necessary [and] that *the powers of the Military Governor under martial law are absolute and all-inclusive*."[12] In Green's view,

> The present setup was built entirely upon Army plans and it is held in place by Army cooperation and the faith that the local public has in the Army for honesty and integrity. If turned over to the civil authorities, it would lack public confidence, would be less efficient, and might even fail. . . . The safety of the civilian population is not the function of the Secretary of the Interior; it is that of the Military Commander. . . . The public there know this and are dreading the possibility that the Military may be ousted in a time of peril.[13]

Particularly reprehensible to Green was what he regarded as the arrogance of the civilian territorial governor, Ingram Stainback, who, Green complained, "feels he should be the Number 1 man here."[14]

In a memoir written after the war, General Green insisted that the leading civilian judges in Hawai'i supported the army's view as to the necessity for comprehensive control of civilian life, even including reducing their courts to the status of agencies of the military governor and commander.[15] An intriguing item of evidence in corroboration of Green's claim is a letter to him from Judge Delbert Metzger of the U.S. District Court, written in March 1943, commending Green and the army for their administration of the Islands: "There were times," Judge Metzger wrote, "when I thought you could have received much valuable and safe aid from the civil courts, but I realized that the army trained men, such as you had to work with, are more familiar with the workings of provost and military courts—which are certainly speedier—and that the use of civil courts might have tended to introduce a division of responsibility."[16] How the army command's formal legal view of its authority translated into practice is encapsulated in a retrospective comment by General Green, who, as noted earlier, claimed that his "authority was substantially unlimited."[17]

After the war, it is worth remarking, when the Supreme Court ruled in *Duncan* that army rule had been illegal, so that Green faced the prospect of civil damage suits, Green took a very different line: He had acted only as the agent of the president, the secretary of war, and the army command, he would contend, and should not be held responsible for the army's record.[18]

During the war itself, however—and indeed until the very last months of the fighting—the army command in Hawai'i continued to insist upon the legitimacy of its "absolute and all-inclusive" powers. Even the federal courts could not be trusted to enforce the law consistent with the requirements of military necessity, General Richardson argued as late as February 1944. To rely on the federal judiciary, he contended, would make the military "dependent upon the civilian authorities and the discretion of the prosecutors and the usual political factors that pervade civil enforcement agencies."[19] Indeed, the legal division of the OMG was even pushing the idea of transferring all Interior Department responsibilities to the War Department, a plan designed to solidify army control and insulate it against lateral attack at the Cabinet level.[20]

The Interior Department and the "Liberation" of Hawai'i

A very different view was taken, however, by officials of the Interior Department, which formally retained jurisdiction over the territory. As early as June 1942, the department's solicitor presented Secretary Ickes with an advisory memorandum arguing that the army's takeover of all judicial functions was manifestly unconstitutional. "The extension of martial law in Hawai'i is not conclusive of the necessity therefore," he wrote. "Moreover, such facts as are of public record tend to establish that the closing of civil courts to persons accused of crime is not legally justified."[21]

Meanwhile, Interior's first assistant secretary, E. K. Burlew, had set forth formally the legal position to which the department would steadily adhere in future discussions. The mere fact that the army had declared martial law in Hawai'i, Burlew contended, did not constitute a sufficient factual basis for regarding it as a "necessity" and thus as a legally or constitutionally justified measure. "The duly constituted civil authorities," he stated,

> are ready and able to perform not only their ordinary functions, but also to undertake the administration of any emergency controls of civilian activities which may be necessary, such as rationing, price controls, food production and so forth.
>
> It is felt that while the responsibility for the security of the islands rests with the Commanding General, the actual administrative functions should be carried out to the greatest extent possible by the civil government. Moreover, although military necessity may require the establishment of military tribunals to try civilians for offenses against the security of the territory and the military forces, there is every reason to restore the jurisdiction of the criminal courts in all other cases and to infringe as little as possible on constitutional guarantees.[22]

Although Secretary Ickes had been fully supportive of martial law in Hawai'i in the weeks immediately following the Pearl Harbor attack, as the war progressed he grew increasingly uncomfortable with the prospect of prolonged military rule in the Islands. The issue soon had become for him what he termed the liberation of "the American 'conquered territory' of Hawaii"![23] Beyond that, however, Ickes harbored a robust principled view about the effects of militarism; and if President Roosevelt seemed quite un-concerned about "the constitutional question," Ickes was deeply concerned about it.[24]

This is not to say that Ickes had been satisfied with the prewar social and economic regimes in the Islands. As an old-line Progressive, he had long considered Hawai'i to be in need of deep reforms because of the extraordinary concentration of power that the famed "Five Companies" exercised over the plantation economy and the financial, commercial, and public-utilities sectors. His concerns about militarism and concen-trated power merged in his views of army rule in Hawai'i during the war. Thus Ickes wrote in June 1942 that information reaching him from the Islands confirmed that the Big Five—"as tight a little oligarchy as ever existed"—had formed under the OMG re-gime an unholy alliance with the army that potentially threatened "what may remain of the rights, privileges, and liberties of the Hawaiian people."[25] Even conceding that the Big Five oligarchy had perhaps created "a more or less benevolent despotism," Ickes said, their close ties to the army command and martial law made the military govern-ment all the more insidious.[26]

Secretary of the Interior Harold Ickes (right) at swearing in of Abe Fortas (center) as new general counsel of the Federal Emergency Administration of Public Works in 1939. Fortas later served as under secretary under Ickes. Credit: Courtesy of Library of Congress, photo LC-H22-D-6480.

For Ickes, the danger posed by military control was exacerbated because, in his view, Poindexter was ineffectual and not able to stand up to the army. Accordingly, in February 1942, Ickes had sent an aide, Benjamin Thoron, to Hawaiʻi as his special representative, reporting directly to him.[27] As Ickes recorded in his diary, he wanted Thoron "to take over the duties of the Governor but to do it tactfully, and allow Poindexter to feel that he is really functioning. I told him also that he was to resist any improper demands on the part of the Army."[28] Thoron expressed his concern that there had never been "any serious effort to define the proper limits of the operations of the office of the Military Governor under Martial Law."[29] He reported to Ickes that he had found that while Poindexter "does not approve of all the measures taken by the military authorities, . . . he [Poindexter] feels that when the Commanding General makes a decision that military necessity requires that a certain thing be done in a certain way, he cannot and should not take the responsibility of insisting that it be done otherwise or that it not be done."[30] That Poindexter's fate was already sealed was made clear when Thoron made reference to his governorship as an "interregnum": "It is my opinion . . . that it is not too early to try to develop in the War Department here an attitude favorable to the return of administrative and judicial responsibility to the civil authorities, so that when the present interregnum in the Governorship is ended, the civil executive may be in a position to function more effectively."[31] Thoron, however, could not resist the army any more successfully than could the governor.[32] Thoron nevertheless impressed Green as sufficiently threatening to army interests that Green thought it "[m]ight be a good idea to appoint him Advisor."[33]

Whether because of Governor Poindexter's apparent inability to resist the army's takeover of civilian government functions, or simply because Poindexter was then weak from illness, as the end of his term approached in spring 1942, the Department of the Interior decided to replace him. The leading candidate to succeed him by presidential appointment was Ingram Stainback, then one of the two federal district court judges in Hawaiʻi, a liberal Democrat and former U.S. District Attorney for the territory. Stainback had been recommended by Assistant Attorney General Norman Littell as a man who was "able, fearless, unshakable, and forthright, . . . a good tough lawyer, faithful to the Democratic ideal and to the President." Stainback, he wrote, had never been intimidated by the Big Five companies, had demonstrated an "understanding of the native problems," and had reliably progressive views on the issues of land tenure in the Islands.[34] On Ickes's advice, Stainback interviewed for the job at the capital in June 1942, and, again on Ickes's advice, the president appointed him; he took up his position in Honolulu after confirmation by the Senate two months later.[35]

Stainback and the Constitutional Limits on Martial Law

If Secretary Ickes's purpose was to find a governor who would staunchly resist any prolongation of army rule, Stainback fit the bill perfectly—just as the command in Hawaiʻi feared. From the time of his interview forward, Stainback kept Ickes apprised of a long list of complaints about the military's policies under martial law; and he aligned himself firmly with the Department of the Interior view—insisting that the civil courts should be reopened and that the scope of army jurisdiction over civilian activities should be cut back at once.

While in Washington, Stainback also was boldly forthright in putting the War Department on notice directly as to his views of the legality of army rule. In a face-to-face meeting with Colonel Archibald King, a high-ranking Judge Advocate General officer, he contended that Governor Poindexter had lacked the authority under the martial law provision (Section 67) of the Hawai'i Organic Act to abrogate civilian authority altogether. The U.S. Constitution applied to Hawai'i no less than to the states of the Union, Stainback declared; and although emergency authority obviously had to be exercised by the military, there were limits upon how far that authority could go. It must be for national security alone, Stainback said, and could not be extended so far as was being done in Hawai'i. Trials in the provost courts of civilians for neighborhood disputes, drunkenness, or other such offenses "[had] no relation to national defense and . . . therefore [were] not justiciable as an exercise of martial law."[36]

When Colonel King asked Judge Stainback whether the presence of "a large number of aliens of doubtful loyalty," in islands located in a combat theater, did not justify the extraordinary measure of "full martial law," Stainback stood firm. Even under such conditions, he contended, "the whole civilian government does not fall within [army control]," and the military could not assume the power to bring civilians into its courts for all offenses.[37] It was an ominous further portent, from the army's standpoint, that Stainback also advanced the argument that because Governor Poindexter, acting alone, had turned over the territory to the army, it was in a successor governor's power—again acting alone—to "revoke his call upon the commanding general to take charge and [to revoke] his declaration of martial law."[38] What made this exchange particularly striking is the fact that Stainback had been serving as legal advisor to the military governor since early December 1941, assigned a cubicle adjacent to General Green's office—a position from which he seems to have made keen observations rather than rendered much advice.[39]

Shortly after becoming governor, Stainback drafted a proclamation whereby martial law would continue, habeas corpus would remain suspended, and the commanding general would continue to control matters directly affecting the security of the Islands, while all other functions would be reserved to the civil government. The Interior Department, however, rejected the proclamation, pending the outcome of negotiations for the military's voluntary return of powers to the civilian government.[40] And so Stainback was left with little choice but continually to implore Ickes to work at the cabinet level for the immediate restoration of civilian governmental functions. Like Ickes, Stainback was especially outraged by the army's use of the terms "Military Governor" and "Military Government"—terminology that had historically been used only in conquered territories. Stainback also complained bitterly of the army's handling of shipping priorities, its labor policies, and General Green's detailed administration of the most trivial subjects of local government. He also continued to denounce the operations of the provost courts, citing in detail for Ickes their irregular procedures and denial of due process.[41] Stainback's signature message as governor, during his service from June 1942 to the war's end, would be the maxim: "War does not abolish the Constitution."[42]

Delegates King and Farrington

Governor Stainback's views on these matters had been presaged and, indeed, been set out in almost identical terms by Hawai'i's territorial delegate to Congress, Samuel Wilder King. As discussed above, King, along with many other political leaders in the Islands, had initially become alarmed about army rule when the record of the military commission's procedures in the Saffery Brown murder trial came to light. By mid-1942, King had become convinced that both martial law and military government had lasted too long and gone too far. Calling upon members of the Roosevelt cabinet to support restoration of civilian government functions, just about the time that Stainback was summoned to Washington in June for interviews, King wrote to Ickes: "For a civilian community to live for months under what is in effect a military government is detrimental to the maintenance of self-government and repugnant to every principle for which we are fighting."[43]

It is noteworthy that King went to the cabinet secretaries rather than seeking to obtain redress from Congress in the form of legislation that would restore key elements of civilian rule in Hawai'i. Having encountered bitter opposition in Congress to Hawai'i statehood proposals that had prompted senators and representatives to vent overtly racist sentiments against Hawai'i's plural ethnic society, King feared the legislative path. "Any legislation sponsored at this time to clarify the situation might be used as a vehicle for more drastic measures than [were] actually needed" and could so result in legitimating the army's extreme position. It was far more desirable, he believed, for the executive branch to formulate a plan that would establish a new and clear-cut division of authority between the army and civilian officers in Hawai'i.[44]

Delegate King was especially courageous in publicizing his criticism of the military regime in mid-1942, because at this time he was also speaking out prominently in defense of Hawai'i's Japanese Americans against loose charges of disloyalty. Informed by a political associate in the Islands that King was suffering politically for his willingness to attest to the loyalty of the Japanese Americans in the Islands, the delegate replied with a succinct statement of his faith: "Our entire American democracy," King wrote, "is based on the assumption that every person is entitled to a square deal, regardless of race, creed, color or class."[45] Moreover, when Garner Anthony stepped forward to criticize the army policies in a major law review article published in May 1942, King encouraged him to stand firm: "Despite those who question your raising the issue at this time," he told Anthony, "I agree with you that we are not meeting our responsibilities if we dodge the issue."[46]

Samuel Wilder King, Hawai'i territorial delegate in Congress
from 1935 to the end of 1942. He later served as governor of the
Territory. Credit: Photo courtesy of the Hawai'i State Archives.

There is little doubt that King—who was of part native-Hawaiian descent, had grad-uated from the Naval Academy and served in World War I, and was a scion of one of the Islands' best-known families—suffered anguish as the result of his outspoken stand. He defended residents of Japanese ancestry, he wrote, "solely as a matter of principle, knowing that my position would be misunderstood and severely criticized even by many of my best friends. Once racial intolerance is permitted, there is no saying where it will end."[47] Eager to play an active role in the war effort, but also manifestly weary of the vicious political attacks that began to focus on him both at home and in Washing-ton, King initiated reactivation of his navy commission prior to the November 1942 elections and was subsequently assigned to active duty in the Pacific combat zone.

Elected to succeed him in November 1942 as Hawai'i's delegate in Congress was Joseph Farrington Jr., the son of a former governor and publisher of the *Honolulu Star-Bulletin,* the more liberal of the two leading newspapers in the Islands.[48] The new delegate lost little time after his election in assuming a public stance similar to Samuel King's, critical of the army's governance in Hawai'i. Not only did Farrington call for

Joseph R. Farrington, president and general manager of the *Honolulu Star-Bulletin,* was elected in 1942 to succeed Samuel Wilder King as Hawai'i territorial delegate in Congress, serving in that position until his death in 1957. Credit: Photo courtesy of the Hawai'i State Archives.

restoration of the civilian courts' ordinary jurisdiction, he also intensified the public debate by focusing upon the army's use of the terms "military government" and "military governor" in its administration of the Islands. In a statement issued in December 1942, Farrington condemned the military regime under martial law as being "without constitutional or legal foundation," and "contrary to every tradition of America."[49] The question of nomenclature was thus made symbolic of the issues regarding the basic legitimacy of army rule. As was indicated by the military's adamant refusal to consider giving up the title that the commanding general had assumed, the army embraced the notion that this nomenclature was an assertion of martial law's legitimacy.[50]

A few months earlier, a former territorial governor, Lawrence M. Judd, had added his influence to that of others in the Islands' elite who were expressing concern about the reach of army rule. Questioning whether so great a suspension of civilian judicial institutions as the army had instituted in Hawai'i could be justified, and declaring flatly that "civilian activities should be in the hands of civilians," Judd wrote: "The uncertainties are not healthy in a Democracy. The situation presents a profound problem. No obstacle should be placed in the path of the military commander. . . . Yet an American community such as ours is entitled to a 'practical reign of law' with the substance of the Bill of Rights preserved."[51]

Like Delegate King and Garner Anthony, who served as territorial attorney general under Stainback in 1942–1943, Farrington did not call for a complete return of all governing power to civilian officials, nor did he completely deny the validity of martial law. On key points, his critique of the military stopped far short of that. Thus his objections were not to the vesting of extraordinary emergency powers in the army by order of the president, nor to martial law by authority of the governor and/or the president. His criticisms were directed in the first instance to the army's capacious definition of martial law's legal reach. He objected in particular to the closing of the courts to habeas petitions, to the displacement of civilian government's authority in purely civilian matters, and to the army's policy of reducing the territorial courts to the status of "agents" of the military regime.

Farrington thus demanded as the bedrock minimum an acknowledgment of the federal courts' authority to rule independently on whether or not a "military necessity" argument should prevail and thereby warrant the military's takeover of all control. In this regard, Farrington advocated limiting the army's power by a strict application of the standard of constitutionality that was declared by the Supreme Court in the 1866 *Milligan* decision, under which military tribunals could not constitutionally supplant civilian courts so long as the civilian courts were open and were able to function. If applied properly in Hawai'i, the *Milligan* standard would make the habeas privilege available to citizens. Further, it would mean that the army could not define its own powers of law enforcement affecting civilian citizens, thereby immunizing its general orders and implementation policies from review in the federal courts.

Beyond the issue of judicial authority, however, Farrington and the other prominent political figures in Hawai'i who aligned with him desired restoration to Hawai'i's civilian government of all executive and legislative powers other than those clearly related to defense and security. They acknowledged, nonetheless, that changes in the authentic military needs and in the security status of the Islands could never be excluded from the calculus that defined the legal boundary line between civilian and military authority.[52]

While some of the most outspoken members in the territory's political elite were thus demanding a reduction of the military's powers, back in Washington they had a prominent ally in Secretary Ickes, who was sending the War Department a constant flow of letters similarly urging restoration of civilian government in the Islands. Writing two months after the decisive American victory in the June 1942 Battle of Midway, Ickes denied that security considerations any longer warranted comprehensive martial law. Any trials in military courts—whose procedures, as he wrote, "do violence to American concepts of civil rights"—should be very rigidly restricted to security cases alone.[53] Under the Hawai'i Defense Act, Ickes argued, the territorial governor and the civilian courts had been given more than adequate powers to handle all ordinary matters of criminal justice. If prosecuted under the Defense Act's terms, at least Hawai'i's citizens would have the benefit of trial by jury—an institution which, Ickes sternly reminded the War Department, was "fundamental to the concept of liberty which we are fighting to defend."[54]

In these arguments, Ickes had the full support of the solicitor of the Department of the Interior, W. W. Gardner, who reported in December 1942:

> No one can examine the evidence available as to government in the Hawaiian Islands without noting a basic element of totalitarian government: *unlimited authority without direct responsibility to the people governed.* While fighting for democracy on a dozen fronts, we have dictatorship, quite needlessly—almost by accident, in one vital part of the United States of America.... The authority of the "Military Governor," exercised through his executive officer in civilian matters, has grown in a Frankenstein displacement of civilian functions ... reducing the legal government, under the title of "Civil Governor," to a negligible appendage.[55]

Although as a lawyer and as a politician he had long been a strongly principled civil libertarian, the irascible Ickes was also a master bureaucrat. Thus he was also irritated, no doubt, that control of the territory, which in peacetime was under his Interior Department's supervision, had passed summarily to the army; and he frequently expressed frustration that President Roosevelt seemed little interested in ending "military usurpation" and returning these "occupied" Islands back under working control of his department.[56] Ickes repeatedly raised the issue with the president personally and in cabinet meetings throughout 1942, but with little result. Roosevelt could not be persuaded that the issue of martial law in Hawai'i should be given priority over his more urgent wartime responsibilities.[57]

Academic Debate

Meanwhile the questions surrounding the legality of army rule and the constitutional issues it implied became the focus of an emerging academic debate. The opening shot in the academic arena was fired by Garner Anthony, in an article entitled "Martial Law in Hawaii" in the May 1942 issue of the *California Law Review.* Anthony contended that under the principles of the *Milligan* case, the army was not competent to perpetuate martial law without submitting its determinations to review by the federal courts. While "political rights" were enjoyed by residents of a federal territory such as Hawai'i, albeit "[as] privileges held in the discretion of Congress," Anthony averred, "[their] personal and civil rights . . . are secured to them irrevocably by the Federal Constitution."[58] The Bill of Rights and the Constitution were intended, he wrote, to serve "for all exigencies," and not simply to provide a framework of government for "a fair-weather ship of state," as "some well-meaning but overzealous persons" might believe when they justi-fied suspension of the Constitution because a state of war existed.[59]

For Anthony, the "necessity" of a suspension of the right to the writ of habeas cor-pus, the propriety of a continued closing of the civilian courts, and the need for mar-tial law so comprehensive as the army had undertaken, were all questions properly left to the judiciary—and not to the military itself. In fact, Anthony argued, the army it-self had reopened the civilian courts—albeit only for nonjury civil trials—so it was evident that these courts were able to function. Only insofar as it was the military government that had illegally restricted their jurisdiction and procedures, he asserted, were these courts "disabled," the condition that under the *Milligan* standard would warrant the military courts' conducting criminal trials and other actions in matters that were purely of a civilian character. Further, Anthony pointed out, the *Milligan* standard required that there must be conditions of actual, not merely anticipated, in-vasion of the territory to justify the position the army had arbitrarily assumed with respect to the administration of justice. Anthony quoted the opinion of the Court in the *Milligan* case: "Martial law cannot arise from a threatened invasion. The necessity must be actual and present; the invasion real, such as effectually closes the courts and de-poses the civil administration."[60]

It must be stressed that Anthony did not believe that the suspension of habeas cor-pus or other extraordinary measures were under all circumstances illegal or uncon-stitutional. He argued that instead of allowing the army to write its own charter of powers in Hawai'i, any emergency measures should be explicitly authorized by con-gressional statute and then be subject to review, as to their constitutionality, by the fed-eral courts.[61] And while Anthony conceded that Governor Poindexter, in suspending the privilege of the writ of habeas corpus and placing the territory under martial law, had acted within the terms of the Organic Act, he nonetheless argued that even the president's authority, as the immediate emergency passed and the military displaced civil government, was not without limitations: "[T]here is no legislative authority given to the President that authorizes him to erect military tribunals for the trial of citizens."[62]

Moreover, Anthony contended that there was no accepted definition of martial law and its legitimate reach: "While Congress has authorized in Hawai'i the declaration of martial law in case of a threatened invasion, it has not said what martial law is and has given no content to that elusive expression."[63] He was emphatic, however, that "we must not establish by law within our own borders the very tyranny that we are now pledged to destroy" on the battlefields of war.[64]

Colonel Archibald King, the highest-ranking officer on the judge advocate gen-eral's staff in Washington, published a rejoinder to Anthony's article in the same law journal's September 1942 issue. King, who earlier had exchanged views on martial law with Stainback when they met in Washington, set out systematically the case for the constitutionality and legality of army rule in the Islands.[65] He rested his argument, first, on the general grounds that Hawai'i was experiencing a military emergency requiring extraordinary action and, second, upon the specific terms of the Hawai'i Organic Act and its provisions for a declaration of martial law. Whether there was imminent danger of invasion was not a proper matter for speculation by legal commentators or even by elective civilian officials, King averred: "No one knows more about these matters than Lieutenant General Emmons"; and the general's entire pattern of decisions since taking command (e.g., the mass evacuations of *haole* women and children) bespoke Emmons's premise that there remained imminent danger of an invasion by the enemy. "The resident of that beautiful archipelago may live in a paradise," King asserted, "but if he thinks that there is no danger of its being invaded, his is a fool's paradise."[66]

Colonel King also downplayed the importance of the *Milligan* doctrine, contending that it had been controversial among lawyers since the day the decision first came down. Even if the doctrine had made good sense in the Civil War era, he argued, the new technologies of warfare—and especially the kind of air power that Japan had thrown against Pearl Harbor—provided strong reason to reconsider the meaning of concepts such as "imminent invasion."[67] Quite apart from questions of military necessity and constitutionality, King continued, there was ample evidence that the territory's political leaders themselves recognized that extraordinary measures—albeit temporary ones—were legitimate in time of war. For this proposition he cited the specific terms of the Hawai'i Defense Act (the M-Day law) of October 3, 1941, which had provided for suspension of ordinary legislation and vested sweeping powers in the governor to control the economic and social life of the population. Governor Poindexter's decision to devolve these powers on the army should therefore be seen as part of a valid process by which the people of Hawai'i adapted to the exigencies of modern warfare: They had surrendered "a large part of their ordinary rights and privileges," King stated, ". . . in order that prompt and effective action may be taken to protect the islands."[68]

Ironically, at the very time he was preparing his article for press, King was counseling his War Department superiors behind closed doors that it was advisable to permit a relaxation of the military's control over the jurisdiction and procedures of the territorial courts! In response to his advice and under increasing pressure from Secretary Ickes, the War Department did agree to bring Colonel Green back to Washington for conferral on whether any modifications of martial law should be formulated.[69]

Further legal support for Colonel King's position, meanwhile, came in an article in the June 1942 issue of the *Harvard Law Review* by Charles Fairman, a Stanford University professor who was author of one of the leading legal treatises on martial law in the United States and therefore a formidable protagonist in this debate. Fairman, who, like General Green, had served in the army's 1916 "Pershing expedition" into Mexico against Pancho Villa, was an officer in the Army Reserve; he had recently been called to active duty when he wrote his *Harvard Law Review* article. Entitled "The Law of Martial Rule and the National Emergency," it endorsed in wholesale terms the army's legal position.[70] Fairman's analysis defended the army's regime in Hawai'i on the broadest possible grounds: he contended (as Colonel King had done) that only military leaders were competent to determine whether an emergency in wartime required extraordinary measures; hence the civilian courts must defer. Fairman defended not only martial law in Hawai'i but also the army's removal and internment of the Japanese-American population, both citizens and aliens alike, from the West Coast—a public issue that had become, of course, much more prominent than martial law at that time.

Fairman asserted that simply as a matter of common reason, the comprehensive jurisdiction and arbitrary procedures of the military courts—including the virtually unlimited discretion that the army's provost courts in Hawai'i enjoyed to impose "appropriate sentence[s]"—were entirely warranted. This view might "sound startling," Fairman readily admitted, "but [it] . . . is about what one acquainted with such situations would expect." As to the West Coast internments, Fairman contended that the "circumstances surrounding [the war's] outbreak argued for security as against trustfulness," and that the matter was in the last analysis a military one, in which the commanding general necessarily had discretion to cope with possible dangers.[71]

Fairman's argument also endorsed the essentially racist premises on which the army had proceeded both in Hawai'i and on the mainland in regard to the ethnic Japanese. Although he admitted no one would contend that *every* Japanese American was potentially disloyal, still, he asserted, the Nikkei were a people apart, having "lived among us without becoming a part of us"; they were "inscrutable to us" because of "fundamental differences in mores." For a people thus inscrutable and unassimilated to be taken from their homes and placed in camps, citizen and alien alike, was, he laconically conceded, certainly "an inconvenience"; but it had to be accepted as "only one of the unavoidable hardships incident to the war."[72] It was a reasonable guess, Fairman believed, that the courts would ultimately rule in favor of entire administrative discretion for the army, both in Hawai'i and in the internment situation. Such a course, he wrote, would be consistent with the judiciary's tendency in the late 1930s to give constitutional approval to wide discretion of civilian administrative agencies—the New Deal agencies created by the Roosevelt administration—over regulatory matters.[73]

With regard to the contention advanced by Anthony and other critics of army rule that the term "martial law" had never been well defined in American law, Fairman retorted that one "essential truth" on the question was discernible "through [the] maze" of Anglo-American legal history: It was that "martial law, so far as now consistent with the English constitution, is simply an application of the common-law principle that *measures necessary to preserve the realm and resist the enemy are justified.*"[74] He wrapped this historical lesson, moreover, in the mantle of the legal realism that had become dominant recently in American jurisprudential theory and to an increasing degree in constitutional law: "Just as in the construction of the commerce clause and other grants of national power the Court of late has notably sought to make them adequate to the conditions which we face, almost certainly it would so construe the war power as to include all that is requisite 'to wage war successfully.'"[75]

The publication of Anthony's article of May 1942—which was circulated immediately in Hawai'i and also was reported in the *New York Times* and other mainland papers—served the important purpose of defining in sharp focus the constitutional questions surrounding martial law. It also prompted the army's best legal minds to reveal in the public forum their belief that the *Milligan* doctrine was no longer applicable, thus denying that any constitutional limitations could be imposed on the military's authority to define its own powers under martial law.

The attention being given to Anthony's article locally was predictably alarming to General Emmons and his legal staff, impelling Emmons to issue a press release in Honolulu that sought to refute Anthony's criticisms. Emmons declared in this statement that the Organic Act and the president's approval of the martial law decision, taken together, rendered fully legal all the army's measures to date in Hawai'i. Emmons did not address, however, Anthony's important argument that the president's consent to martial law did not authorize all the army's measures to control Hawai'i's civilian population by seizing control over the entire territorial government.

Emmons acknowledged, albeit grudgingly, the propriety of "academic discussion regarding the legal technicalities" of martial law: "No doubt the history and operation of martial law in Hawai'i," he stated, "will be the subject of many interesting legal debates in years to come."[76] However, such intellectual exercises, he warned, were inappropriate at a dangerous juncture; and he had no intention of permitting "academic" criticisms of army rule to prompt any changes in his administration of the Islands. "In this theater of operations," he declared, "we are not going to question the wisdom of our Congress in passing the Organic Act nor question the judgment of our President in approving the declaration of martial law by the civil governor."[77]

Anthony, commenting upon this reaction to his article, did not retreat from his published views, writing privately in a letter to Delegate Samuel King: "Some may say that this is no time to talk about martial law, that it should be postponed for the post-mortem examination of the legal historian, [but] I believe that straight thinking, together with intelligent and orderly action, is vital to success. Playing the ostrich simply because a problem is delicate or hard will not advance the war effort."[78]

The sweeping claims as to the army's authority made by General Emmons, Colonel King, and Professor Fairman lent additional urgency to the continuing concerns of the critics of martial law. Especially troubling to Anthony, Governor Stainback, and Delegates King and Farrington—and, increasingly, to the Department of the Interior and to civil liberties–minded officers of the Justice Department—was the fact that the army command in Hawai'i was also portraying its regime as being not only fair in its administration but highly popular with the civilian population. Martial law, Emmons insisted,

> has been highly successful in this community and it has the confidence of the people generally. Its success has been due to the fact that it has been administered with the utmost regard for the feelings, the civil rights and the interests of the local population. *In other words the administration of martial rule here has been in effect martial rule without a bayonet.* The fairness and impartiality of both the provost courts and the Military Commission and the treatment of the public under

martial rule generally is now well recognized in the territory, and the civil rights of the public have been interfered with as little as possible.[79]

Thus when the War Department, in response to immediate pressure from Secretary Ickes, queried General Emmons as to whether he thought martial law might be eased, Emmons—doubtless relying upon Green for much of his text—responded that even merely giving up the title "military governor" would dangerously undermine his authority to an unacccptablc dcgrcc. Rationing and price control, he continued, "would be wholly ineffective if left in the hands of civilians." Nor could the civil courts be entrusted with prosecution of criminal matters, Emmons wrote, reiterating his office's position that in a theater of operations, "the administration of criminal justice is an essential element of martial law." The army must therefore continue to administer a "police power covering all phases of economic life in the community," especially given the presence of so large a Japanese-American population.[80]

Emmons's most telling argument, however, was one based upon his military expertise and assessment of strategic and security considerations. "It would appear that the Interior Department considers that the danger to Hawai'i from attack has passed," he stated. "Such a feeling is unwarranted, as these islands are in danger from attack at any time, and as the situation develops in the Middle East [*sic*] and in Russia the situation here may become increasingly hazardous."[81] Nothing in Emmons's analysis indicated a willingness to relinquish even an iota of military control.

Chapter Twelve

"DELINEATION" AND RESTORATION,
1942–1943

The rising indications that the army was taking a hard line and would resist any concessions whatever on martial law led Ickes and his allies in Interior and Justice to step up the pressure on the War Department. They now proposed that (as a minimum) a timetable be agreed upon for the restoration of civilian rule. As noted earlier, in June 1942 Colonel Archibald King of the Office of the Judge Advocate General himself was counseling the War Department that moderation of the martial law regime should at least be considered.[1] Consequently General Green was ordered back to Washington from Honolulu in August 1942—just at the time when Stainback's appointment as governor was being approved in the Senate—with the understanding that Green must meet with civilian officials in formal discussions of whether and how army rule might be modified.[2]

Green regarded his mission in these meetings as achieving a complete victory in fending off any and all demands for a reduction in the military's authority. He was well briefed for that mission because the army censorship office that operated under his own direction in Honolulu had been turning over to him copies of Governor Stainback's correspondence with the Department of the Interior in which the governor's specific objectives and proposed negotiating tactics were set forth. Similarly, the censorship office had provided Green with copies of the outgoing correspondence of Justice Department and other government officials who were reporting from Hawai'i to their superiors in Washington after being sent out to the Islands to engage in fact-finding and make policy recommendations. (The copies passed to Green typically carried the notation that the addressee "is unaware of our possession of the letter"!)[3] Thus, by the simple expedient of reading the mail of his political and governmental opponents, Green obtained information that helped him prepare for the bureaucratic battles that lay ahead for him in Washington.

Once the June 1942 talks began in Washington, Green found himself confronted with a concerted effort by the Department of the Interior and members of the attorney general's top staff to forge a cabinet-level, interdepartmental agreement for a significant reduction in the army's powers in Hawai'i. Green early concluded that Interior's real motive in raising specific issues about martial law was to undermine army rule entirely. "The very purpose of the present controversy," he thus told his War Department superiors, "is to divest the Military from control."[4]

In talks with sub–cabinet level civilian officials of the War, Justice, and Interior departments, Green proved completely unyielding. He denied categorically that General Short had promised Governor Poindexter that martial law would be kept in effect for only a short time, and he defended the necessity of the provost courts' procedures, insisting that the military operated these tribunals with advice from local judges and other qualified civilians. Further, he averred that the military regime had broad popular support. "Every thinking citizen," Green asserted, fully recognized that if the army withdrew from civil governance, it would leave the Territory open to a "hard time."[5]

Doubtless Green's aggressive posture simply confirmed Secretary Ickes in his view, which already had become adamant, that in Hawai'i the army was systematically violating the very principles that he regarded as fundamental to the concept of constitutional liberty. Frustrated by the War Department's apparent unwillingness to curb the martial law regime, Ickes complained to Secretary Stimson that he could find no precedent in American history in which "an American 'Military Commander' in a martial law area . . . abolished jury trials, closed courts, and assumed various civil powers because, in his opinion, it was 'better for the people.' "[6] Benjamin Thoron, head of the Office of Territories in Interior and a participant in the conference in Washington, had anticipated Ickes's position earlier in the year, reporting in May after a visit to Honolulu that army rule in Hawai'i was evidencing a "drift to a complete military dictatorship." The comprehensive reach of martial law, Thoron declared, was scarcely justified, since the security situation had become fundamentally different from when martial law had been first imposed.[7] Thoron's report did full justice to describing the robust view of "military necessity" that Green had embraced:

> From my conversation with Colonel Green it became apparent to me that he has reached the conclusion that direct administration of all controls over civilian life by military authorities is necessary; that the powers of the Military Governor under martial law are absolute and all inclusive; and that the extent to which they shall be exercised lies in the sole discretion of the Commanding General. He maintains categorically, and it seems to me dogmatically, that the control of civilian life through the civil authorities acting with the approval and support of the military authorities is not feasible, even in phases which are not in any degree apparent to the layman related to military activities or the security of the Territory.[8]

Against this tense background, an interdepartmental agreement was reached in August 1942 among Green and the Justice, Interior, and War Department negotiators. It provided for restoration of the civilian courts' jurisdiction over criminal law matters, but only a partial one. The exceptions were highly significant. First, members of the armed forces and persons engaged in defense activities under the army's direction (numbering some 80,000, or about half the workforce outside homes) were to be tried only by military tribunals. Second, various specified violations of military general orders, bearing directly on security of fortifications and the like, would continue to be enforced only by the provost courts. And third, the writ of habeas corpus continued to be suspended. Importantly, the continued existence of martial law—now as modified by the agreement—was explicitly reaffirmed. General Green returned to Hawai'i with this agreement in hand, and the army announced the new division of jurisdiction on September 2, 1942, in General Orders No. 133.[9]

Storm over the Army's "Delineation" Policy

For two quiet days after promulgation of General Orders No. 133, it seemed that the long-discussed restoration of significant powers to the civilian government had been put in place effectively. But then Emmons and Green dropped a legal bombshell, issuing on September 4 General Orders No. 135, which became known as the army's "delineation order." The new order purported merely to clarify the terms of the civilian-military division of authority as embodied in General Orders No. 133. Green contended that this further so-called clarification, enumerating in detail the judicial and administrative jurisdictional boundaries and procedures, was necessary because the agreement that had been negotiated in Washington—and embodied in the general order of two days earlier—was merely an agreement on "general principles." As such, Green asserted, it left open too many uncertainties as to which specific activities were related to "security," and therefore it provided the courts (provost courts and civilian courts alike) inadequate guidance as to their respective jurisdictions.[10]

In fact, however, the "delineation" that the army now set forth in General Orders 135 reversed a substantial portion of the concessions that Green had made in the Washington negotiations. In this order, the army clarified the meaning of the "general principles" by specifying that the provost courts' jurisdiction would continue to include control of "any violations in connection with the war effort," including prostitution, all traffic violations on public roads after blackout hour, and a range of selected crimes such as drunkenness and vagrancy under the terms of federal and territorial law. The Order also specified that all judicial proceedings in the provost courts would continue to be conducted as before, that is, without normal due-process guarantees or right to a jury trial. Any appeals of procedure or jurisdictional questions—whether in cases from the federal courts, the territorial courts, or the provost courts—would be decided exclusively by the commanding general *qua* Military Governor, "whose decision shall be final."[11]

Green told the War Department that prior to issuing the new delineation order, he had consulted diligently with the federal district attorney and with various civilian judges as well as with Governor Stainback, and that he had encountered no opposition to his proposals for dividing jurisdiction.[12] Green wrote that he had originally "had in mind turning over to the civilian authorities for disposition such common crimes as drunkenness, drunken driving, prostitution, vagrancy, and the like," but that a senior civilian judge (who remained unnamed) had persuaded him to leave jurisdiction in these matters in the military courts:

> This judge advised me strongly against turning any of these over. In the case of drunkenness, he informed me that the civil courts would be entirely unable to cope with the situation among defense workers when the maximum penalty allowed by Territorial law was only a small fine. . . . He also pointed out to me that in the case of drunken driving, the civil courts were required by Territorial law to revoke the license of the person convicted, and that to do so in the case of a defense worker who happened to be a machine operator, would be contrary to the best interests of the war effort. He informed me that the control of prostitution under civil courts would be ineffective and that they would have no more control over the subject during wartime than they had in peacetime, which was just about nil. He pointed out that the subject of vagrancy would clearly be best handled by the Military courts. This is, of course, in line with our Labor Order No. 19, in which continual vagrancy is punishable by trial before a Provost Court.[13]

How accurate this account might be—and also the identity of the judge whom General Green found to provide a cloak of legitimacy for General Orders No. 135—remain matters for speculation.

What is not speculative, however, is that the terms of the new delineation order were a gross distortion of what the negotiators from Interior and Justice thought they had agreed upon in the Washington meeting. Governor Stainback was outraged, and he immediately denounced Green's moves as a blatant and unprincipled subversion of the Washington understanding.[14] Within the Justice Department, the top legal officers who had participated in the Washington talks were similarly appalled when the text of General Orders No. 135 reached them. The concessions that they had made to the army in order to achieve a compromise agreement in Washington, Assistant Attorney General James Rowe Jr. declared, had been seized upon by Green and Emmons "merely as an invitation to further encroachments upon civil jurisdiction." The delineation order was a clear indication, Rowe concluded, that any further reliance upon the army's good faith would be at best "unwise." He now advised Attorney General Biddle that the only effective solution to the problems being posed by the arrogance of army rule in the Islands would be to have General Green transferred to another post at once, so that a different style of legal counsel might be made available to General Emmons. But the ultimate solution, Rowe averred, was to carry the issue to the White House and to persuade the president to order a wholesale restoration of civilian authority.[15] The solicitor of the Department of the Interior similarly denounced General Orders No. 135. It represented, he concluded, "the violation of the premises which underlay the entire agreement," and it "in effect constitutes the Military Governor a fifth tribunal whose executive decision will replace the judicial processes."[16]

Even the army's top legal officers in Washington—who obviously had not been consulted by Green before the delineation order was issued—found it impossible to defend the document. When the text of the order reached Assistant Secretary McCloy, he called upon the judge advocate general, Major General Myron Cramer, for an opinion on it. Cramer, who must have felt that he had been ambushed by Green and the Hawai'i command, was unequivocal in his counsel. He advised McCloy that the terms of the order by which the military governor would have final authority over jurisdictional questions in all judicial proceedings, federal or territorial as well as military, was at best a serious affront to the courts, and in any event a claim "of doubtful legal validity."[17] Cramer's analysis continued:

> [T]he question whether a particular case falls within the jurisdiction of the civil court is, like all other jurisdictional issues, for determination by the court itself. For him [Emmons] to tell the court that it shall not exercise jurisdiction in a particular case, which otherwise would be triable by it, or of which it has decided that it has jurisdiction, is . . . inconsistent with the dignity of the court and amounts to the exercise of judicial power by the [Military] Governor himself.

Cramer pointed out to McCloy that if these provisions of doubtful legality were struck out, together with all other provisions that were in patent violation of the War-Justice-Interior agreement reached in Washington, then "very little indeed of General Orders 135" would be left standing.[18]

In light of these responses from the judge advocate general as well as from high-level civilian officials in two cabinet-level departments, and with Secretary Ickes in high dudgeon on the issue, the chances that the delineation order could survive intact seemed slim indeed.

The Campaign to Restore Civilian Control

Among the army's critics in Hawai'i, no less than in the nation's capital, the reaction to General Orders No. 135 was not only swift, it was angry.[19] Governor Stainback irately claimed that he had not been consulted, and he was now determined to make a full-scale effort to win back the gubernatorial powers that he believed had been essentially stolen from his office—first by the terms of martial law, and now by Green's deviousness. Stainback augmented his political firepower considerably when he persuaded Garner Anthony to accept appointment to the post of territorial attorney general. Anthony's eloquent scholarly writings had made clear his opposition to many aspects of martial law and army rule, and so the military command in Hawai'i was deeply concerned about his appointment. Rumors had circulated locally in earlier weeks that Anthony was being considered for a different appointment, as the U.S. District Attorney for Hawai'i, a position for which his credentials were impeccable. A veteran of army service in World War I, he was a graduate of Harvard Law School and had made a distinguished record as a partner in Hawai'i's most prestigious corporate law firm, being elected in 1937 as president of the territorial bar association.[20] Green urged the War Department to help scuttle the plan, contending that Anthony's legal critique in his May 1942 *California Law Review* article "disqualifies him from holding a position in which it would be his official duty" to defend the army's regime against any legal challenge in the courts.[21] Despite the army's concerns, Anthony's appointment as territorial attorney general went forward, and he immediately gave highest priority to the matter of how to restore civilian government.

Relations between Green and Anthony had been sour since the first hours of the war, when Anthony challenged the use of civilians on military judicial commissions.[22] Their relations were not improved when, immediately after Anthony took up his new post, they had a heated exchange over their diametrically opposed views of whether the territorial attorney general had an implicit obligation to adhere to the army's line on disputed legal and policy matters.[23] Further enraging Green, Anthony objected to the continuing use by the Office of the Military Governor of the civilian officials' offices in the magnificent Iolani Palace. Three months later, Anthony was successful in his demand that the army brass return the palace to the civilian governor and other territorial office holders. But it proved to be less than an unconditional surrender by the military, for the top army officers, including Green (by then promoted to Brigadier General) and his staff, as well as the commanding general, took up new office quarters within the palace grounds in a building that came to be locally known as the "Little White House."[24]

One of Anthony's first duties on assuming office was to prepare for Governor Stainback a lengthy analysis of the legality and operations of martial law. This document, which was transmitted on December 1, 1942, reiterated the legal and constitutional arguments that Anthony had published earlier in his academic writings on martial law.[25] He followed with a wholesale condemnation of the military's seizure of nearly all civilian governmental functions. In even sterner terms, he denounced the blanket suspension of the right to petition for a writ of habeas corpus, and he contended that the procedures and operations of the provost courts were a serious abuse of power. As to censorship, Anthony argued, there was no legal basis for the policies by which the army had overridden the fundamental rule of law that supported a free press, let alone the way in which it managed news on such issues as prostitution controls. "Perhaps the greatest inroad on the liberty of the individual, next to abrogation of the Bill of Rights," Anthony contended, however, was the way in which the military orders controlling labor had virtually set aside the Thirteenth Amendment and its prohibition of involuntary servitude.[26]

Anthony concluded that a four-point program restoring to civilian authorities their proper jurisdiction should be made the object of a new agreement among the relevant agencies in Washington. The first point called for "the restoration of the courts to their normal functions," leaving to the federal district court in Hawai'i the authority to determine what specific cases involved palpable questions of sabotage, espionage, or loyalty. Second, he recommended "relinquishment by the military of all the civil functions presently usurped under military rule, such as food, price, and liquor controls." Third, the army should give up the title and substantive claims of "military governorship." Finally, he proposed the immediate suspension of all general orders currently in effect that were not demonstrably "based upon military necessity." This also would involve agreement that "except in case of a real emergency which will not admit of delay," any new general orders purporting to deal with such security matters should be submitted to the civilian governor for review prior to being issued by the army. The only alternative to such an agreement on these points, Anthony concluded, would be the termination altogether of martial law, through formal action by the president.[27]

Anthony's report immediately became the agenda for Governor Stainback in a renewed campaign to obtain restoration of the civilian government's authority. That objective was, of course, anathema to the army; the point was not lost that Anthony's recommendations were based on a rejection of all the core premises that the Hawai'i command had repeatedly set forth since December 1941 as their rationale for military government and martial law.

Negotiations in Washington, December 1942–January 1943

Stainback, whose mood was reported as being now "restive and indignant," asked Secretary Ickes to support renewed negotiations in Washington that might lead to a more acceptable "delineation" of functions and meaningful restoration of civilian government.[28] Ickes not only arranged for such a meeting, but he was also determined that as part of a new agreement the War Department must find another position "for the 'estimable General Green.'" He told allies in the negotiations to follow that he was "not going to smile again until this happens, as I believe it will if we will allow time for a little face-saving delay. . . . There are a lot of faces in these parts that ought to be smashed rather than saved, but we go on saving them."[29]

The mood indicated by Ickes's rhetoric in this communication quickly came to pervade the new negotiations, which commenced in early December, one year after the war had started. The talks proved to be intense and difficult. Unlike the Washington meetings the previous summer, this second set of meetings involved two cabinet-level secretaries: Ickes (who was joined by Under Secretary Abe Fortas) and Attorney General Biddle, along with several aides. For the War Department, Stimson (who was home ill and unable to attend the talks) was represented by Assistant Secretary McCloy, to whom the army command in Hawai'i was directly reporting. In addition, Generals Emmons and Green were both recalled from Hawai'i to participate directly; and later in the month Governor Stainback and Garner Anthony also came to Washington to make their case personally for restoration of civilian functions.[30] In the immediate background, Joseph Farrington, the newly elected territorial delegate to Congress, made his own contribution to the discourse through press releases, correspondence with constituents, and later submission of personal comments upon the agreements—making clear his support for the position that Garner Anthony had set out, fully endorsed by Governor Stainback, which called for a severe curtailment of army controls.[31]

Green's arrogant and unyielding defense of the provost courts and all other aspects of martial law simply hardened the perception in the Interior and Justice departments that he was a rigid, undemocratic individual with a vested interest in maintaining the army's monopoly of power in Hawai'i. Green confided in his diary and personal notes that Ickes's staff in Interior were antimilitary to the core—he characterized them variously as "vermin," "pink," and otherwise deplorable in their character and political ideas, men who were "our enemies" and lacked any realistic conception of what it took to provide an adequate defense for the Islands.[32] Predictably, then, Green made no friends in the negotiations.

The antagonism clearly was mutual. Thus Ickes, before the Washington talks began, opened the preparatory correspondence with the War Department by announcing that he simply no longer trusted Green's motives or willingness to abide by any decision to return significant power to the civilian authorities. In a letter to Secretary Stimson, Ickes caustically referred to the problem of "the American 'conquered territory' of Hawaii."[33] He also charged that the "military usurpation" which persisted in Hawai'i "still exists there as a result of the bad faith of General Green."[34]

The atmosphere was not made any calmer by the fact that Secretary Stimson and his assistant secretary, McCloy, were thoroughly convinced that martial law was popular with the people of Hawai'i. They attributed the pressure for change—in Stimson's words—as coming from "starry-eyed departments in Washington," and not from civilians in the Islands.[35] Just before the Washington talks began, moreover, McCloy had visited Hawai'i personally to assess the situation. In a report to the White House, he acknowledged that there was "considerable agitation among the lawyers," but he concluded that there was general acceptance of martial law; and so he was prepared to support the army against its critics.[36] McCloy was also prepared, however, to make some important concessions if the army command would agree. What he suggested specifically—transferring most criminal jurisdiction to the civilian courts—eventually became one of the key compromises in the agreement worked out in the December talks.[37]

Attorney General Biddle, who, like Ickes, had long been associated with civil liberties causes, shared Ickes's opinion of the situation in Hawai'i. Initially Biddle had supported the president's decision to approve Poindexter's declaration of martial law. By late 1942, however, Biddle had run out of patience with the military's policies and, especially, with the operation of the provost courts. Finding that Green would never make a single concession of army authority without putting up a struggle, he concluded that the officers who were running Hawai'i "lock stock and barrel, don't want to give an inch."[38]

Biddle was so angry now that he took the matter directly to the president, declaring that the army's administration in Hawai'i had proven itself "autocratic, wasteful, and unjust." As to Green, Biddle described him as a "stuffy and overzealous" martinet who ought to be relieved of his post immediately.[39] Popular resentment of army rule in the Islands had not received much attention as yet, Biddle wrote, but only because "criticism is suppressed"; the generals were getting most of their information about citizens' attitudes from a handful of elite leaders in the "Big Five." Warning of the political implications, Biddle declared that it was "a situation [that] has the makings of a lurid Congressional investigation."[40] Biddle's high-level assistant, James Rowe, was a strong civil libertarian; and he, too, had now begun to take a highly critical view not only of General Orders No. 135 but also, more generally, of both the army's stalling tactics and of Stimson's and McCloy's excessive tolerance of what Rowe viewed as an American variant of totalitarianism in Hawai'i.[41]

The Justice and Interior departments thus joined formally to propose the restoration to civilian agencies not only of ordinary civilian governance but also of even such security-related functions as civil defense, price control, and censorship of the mail.[42] The Interior-Justice Department joint position in the matter was perfected in a December 9 meeting (only a few days before Biddle wrote to the president), at which Governor Stainback, Garner Anthony, Angus Taylor (the Acting U.S. Attorney for Hawai'i), James Rowe and Samuel O. Clark of the Justice Department, and Under Secretary of the Interior Abe Fortas were present. They all agreed on the following bargaining strategy: *First,* their optimal objective was to obtain "drastic modification of military control" by presidential order, restoring the territorial civilian government to its pre–Pearl Harbor status, with the M-Day legislation to be effective under the governor's direction. *Second,* failing agreement by the War Department to approve the optimal objective, "steps would be taken to assure that any violations of the Military Governor's general orders would be triable by the civilian courts." And *third,* the civilian courts would be restored in their jurisdiction at least over all crimes except those specified in the Articles of War; otherwise, only crimes specified in proclamations of the military governor—which must apply only to defense and security—would remain triable in military tribunals. "Under all plans," the group agreed, "it is essential that the civilian courts and not the military authorities be given the power to determine their own jurisdiction over the various classes of crimes which they are to try."[43]

The Justice-Interior memorandum conceded that some elements of martial law might need to be continued, including suspension of the writ of habeas corpus, and also the military's jurisdiction over violations of the Articles of War and criminal prosecutions of uniformed personnel. But the memorandum specified that civilian authorities, federal and territorial, should be reinstated in their jurisdiction in many vital areas of law and policy, including "(a) civil defense matters, (b) price control, (c) public health, (d) censorship of civilian mail, (e) selection of residents [stranded on the mainland] who may return to the Territory, (f) production and distribution of food, (g) rationing, (h) liquor control and prostitution, (i) schools, (j) rents, (k) banking, currency and securities, and (l) collection of garbage."[44]

The underlying principle of the changes thus advocated by Biddle and Fortas was expressed in their unequivocal rejection of General Emmons's view that civilian government must be subordinated in all particulars to the military. "No such proposition has ever before been advanced with respect to American territory," they told the War Department:

> If the military necessities do not forbid the operations of the civil government, there is no possible ground in a democratic nation upon which to subject those operations to military rule. . . . American institutions have no place for a military bureau whose task is to supervise and to [compete] with the regular civilian government in the latter's appropriate sphere of action.[45]

Biddle personally carried the memorandum to the White House, an action that was decisive for what followed.[46] Until that time, the president had shown little concern about the army's rule in Hawai'i, except for the tension with the army in early 1942 over whether Japanese Americans should be interned or removed en masse.[47] As Biddle later recalled, the president generally "thought that rights should yield to the necessities of war. Rights came after victory, not before."[48] When Roosevelt responded to Biddle's memorandum now, however, the president displayed an unmistakable impatience with the troublesome news coming out of the Islands—especially, he wrote, because he knew "from many other sources that Emmons gets most of his knowledge of conditions from The Big Five."[49]

Roosevelt therefore sent to the attorney general a memorandum, dated December 13, 1942, conveying his displeasure with the conflicts that were plaguing governance of the Islands and stating that he expected the War Department "to clean this thing up."[50] In addition, Roosevelt decided that the army must move quickly to transfer General Green out of Hawai'i, where his presence had become such a powerful magnet for controversy and the source of angry conflict with the civilian authorities.[51]

Ironically, as noted above, when Assistant Secretary McCloy had visited Hawai'i for briefings in October, he himself had concluded that—although he would not override the commanding general's view—it would be reasonable to return to the civilian courts jurisdiction over all criminal cases that did not clearly have "a military aspect." And he had so informed the White House.[52] McCloy thus apparently was finally ready to concede that Green and Emmons had gone too far in defining security-related and military-related crimes in their delineation of jurisdiction in General Orders No. 135.

Delineation Resolved: The Restoration Agreement, January 1943

Once the president's weight had been thrown so dramatically into the balance, the disputing parties moved in a serious way toward resolution. And so the accelerated talks, phone calls, and side conferences went on almost daily in January. They turned upon the intense confrontation over what Biddle and Fortas insisted was "the basic issue of military supremacy over civilian government."[53] McCloy's assessment of the army-civilian issue in Hawai'i was no different: "The new man [Governor Stainback] has a new platform and the military are not disposed to relinquish martial law. Accordingly there is a fundamental disagreement on which it is most difficult to build cooperation."[54]

General Emmons did not participate in January except by correspondence, having returned to the Islands. General Green, however, remained fully involved in the talks—and, true to form, he remained intransigently resistant to concessions. Continued personal antagonism was evident throughout the talks. Green, for his part, complained in a cable to Emmons that three developments were causing things to go badly for the army: "In the first place, the propaganda of our opponents has been severe and not refuted. In the second place, our opponents have worked hard to get the ear of the President, and it looks as if they had succeeded. In the third place Mr. McCloy seems to feel that the civilians should run civilian activities. . . . This you must admit is a tough outlook, and it now looks to me as if we are faced with the problem of salvaging whatever is possible."[55]

The army's political problems, meanwhile, were multiplying, for newspaper columnists had begun to pick up the Hawai'i story, denouncing the signs of alleged dictatorship that were to be found in the martial law regime.[56] The widely syndicated *Merry-Go-Round* column by Drew Pearson, a commentator generally supportive of the New Deal, focused on charges of "Big Five" connections with the military; and Pearson blasted the president for permitting a wholesale violation of civil liberties in the Islands—a column that Ickes stated in his diary "was exceptionally accurate and quite full" (adding, "I was glad to have it published," though he was also pleased that apparently Pearson had not come by his information through leaks from anyone in the Department of the Interior).[57]

Another matter that added new context for the Washington negotiations stemmed from the recent publication by the Supreme Court of its decision in the *Quirin* case,[58] a habeas corpus case raising the issues of whether captured Nazi saboteurs enjoyed any constitutional rights to due process when a presidential proclamation had apparently denied them access to the courts. Although the opinion upheld the jurisdiction of a military commission to try cases involving offenses against the law of war, the language of the Supreme Court was nevertheless ominous for the champions of the army's regime in Hawai'i: "The duty . . . rests on the courts in time of war as well as in time of peace," the Court declared, "to preserve unimpaired the constitutional safeguards of liberty."[59] Governor Stainback had leapt upon this language in the *Quirin* decision to press anew with Ickes for an end to the "stupidity and bungling" of army control of civilian life in Hawai'i, contending once again it was now time for a full restoration of civilian government. "For eleven months Hawai'i has cooperated with the military," he wrote, "and I believe endured the loss of civil rights such as no other community in the United States would endure! . . . It is difficult to locate any constitutional safeguards of civil liberty that remain unimpaired in Hawai'i."[60] In his self-assigned capacity as military governor, Emmons was exercising "complete and unrestrained authority over the citizens of the territory," Stainback continued: "He seems determined to regulate and rule everything."[61]

Meanwhile, Green was orchestrating a counterpropaganda campaign. He advised his office in Hawai'i that it "should put out appropriate information," encourage publication of newspaper articles by sympathetic journalists, and also organize a press conference that would stress "that the future of the Pacific revolves around Hawai'i."[62] Green also solicited support from the Navy Department, obtaining from Admiral Nimitz a cable stating his command's continued concern about the presence of the large Japanese-American population in O'ahu and about the possibility of further military action by Japanese forces. These concerns, Nimitz wrote, led him to oppose "any change in status quo or any limitation of the authority of the Military Governor."[63]

Once General Emmons returned to Honolulu in December, he raised objections by way of radio messages to the War Department whenever any real diminution of military authority was considered in the continuing negotiations in Washington. The foundation of his position remained, as always, that Hawai'i was a "fortress," so that every facet of civilian life was integral to the military effort. Also basic to his argument, echoing Nimitz's view, was Emmons's insistence that the potential threat posed by Japanese-American citizens and aliens required sweeping powers for the military.[64]

In fact, as we have seen, Emmons was a moderate, compared to many in the army leadership on the mainland, with respect to how residents of Japanese ancestry should be treated; indeed, he had spoken out on several occasions against mindless racism directed against them.[65] Emmons had also staunchly championed the formation of an army combat unit to be composed of Nisei volunteers.[66] Nevertheless, he consistently stressed privately that the Japanese-American residents of the Islands included "some . . . disloyal and many others of doubtful loyalty."[67] Emmons also insisted that further air attacks on Hawai'i were not only possible but were likely. Comprehensive authority over civilian society by the army was essential, Emmons stated, in order to avoid another Pearl Harbor–type disaster—or even to be adequately prepared for a Japanese invasion of O'ahu, which, he warned, "could mean loss of the war."[68]

Emmons thus found completely unacceptable the concept underlying the Justice and Interior proposals, that is, the notion that certain functions were purely civilian and irrelevant to security. Equally unacceptable to him was the corollary proposition, as espoused by Anthony and Stainback, that only with the governor's permission could he as commander continue to assume emergency powers except in the most extreme circumstances. Because civilian affairs in Hawai'i had military implications "in all their aspects," the General argued, it was essential that *the civil governor, in the last analysis, be subordinate to the Military Governor.*[69] "The Commanding General, being responsible for the security of the Islands," he averred,

> must be the one to determine what functions can be returned to the civil authorities and the courts. I promise to consider sympathetically every recommendation from the Governor of Hawaii for the return of such functions; but, on the other hand, I feel that he must leave to me the final determination . . . and that when I so determine he loyally accept that determination and cooperate with me

and the other personnel of the military government. . . . Furthermore, it is my firm opinion that a decision as to the distribution of functions between the military and civil government cannot wisely be made . . . in Washington by persons unfamiliar with the military situation or local conditions.

Martial law, according to the natural meaning of the words, means that the military commander controls and that his decision and orders are final. Otherwise the term is meaningless.[70]

Emmons's letter did not come in any particular as a surprise to Assistant Secretary McCloy; for in fact, it was actually drafted and signed in McCloy's War Department office on the day it was dated (December 15), in the course of two long conferences involving Emmons, Green, and Colonel Archibald King! Later the same day, McCloy telephoned Admiral William Leahy, who was President Roosevelt's chief of staff, to convey information of the objections to Emmons's position held by Stainback, Ickes, and Biddle. Immediately after Leahy contacted him, FDR assigned his close adviser William Bullitt (former ambassador to the Soviet Union and to France) to investigate the controversy.[71] By the end of the month—a hectic time on another count for the army and for the White House, since the American forces in North Africa had incurred heavy losses and the land and air campaigns were bogging down—Roosevelt had decided he must act decisively to end the impasse within his cabinet. Admiral Leahy phoned on December 30, McCloy's diary states, and he said "the President was tired of having Stainback 'on his neck' [and] wanted a successor designated for General Green." Less than an hour later, McCloy and Judge Advocate General Cramer were "going over names of candidates for Green's job."[72]

Despite the forceful demands that had been set forth by Emmons, a compromise agreement by which the military would have to surrender a significant range of powers was probably a foregone conclusion from the time Biddle had contacted Roosevelt personally with his recommendations. Green was unaware that his tenure in the Hawai'i command was fated to be terminated, writing to Emmons on New Year's Day: "I feel as if I am operating with both feet in a bear trap and my hands in handcuffs." The negotiations were winding down, he reported, offering disconsolately his estimate of the outcome: "It seems to me that we are destined to be compelled to let Stainback have his fling, and in the event he fails we must pick up the pieces."[73]

On January 3, McCloy informed General Emmons of the president's "impatience to get it settled." Nonetheless, it took another three weeks and a series of additional intensive conferences in McCloy's office and by telephone before a compromise plan was finally hammered out.[74] The standoff was finally resolved at the end of January, but only through personal interventions by Secretaries Ickes and Stimson. The document that was agreed upon moved the line of delineation, as it were, over to the civilian side and narrowed the range of functions designated as under military or security-related jurisdiction. Under the agreement's terms, the army was permitted to keep in force a modified form of martial law, and the privilege of the writ of habeas corpus would remain suspended. The army also retained its authority to regulate labor in those areas of employment under direct military control (i.e., in defense jobs of any kind), and to continue its administration of censorship of communications except within the territory. At its strong insistence, the army also retained its jurisdiction over prostitution. The administration of justice was returned to the civilian courts, however, for both civil cases and criminal cases not directly related to security—a category of cases now understood by all parties to cover the great majority of offenses specified in the territorial statutes. However, criminal prosecutions for violations of military orders remained in the provost courts.[75] Thus, with the extremely important exception of the writ of habeas corpus, due process was restored in non-defense-related cases. In other aspects, too, the Interior-Justice joint objectives were realized: food and price controls, significant (though not all) aspects of labor control, and the censorship of civilian mail within the territory all were to be transferred back to federal and territorial civilian agencies.[76]

The agreement also incorporated a "recapture" clause, however, authorizing the commanding general to reinstate full martial law in case of an acute military emergency. Its inclusion was critical in the final stages of negotiation: Green commented that, while the overall agreement "will hamper [the army] considerably," so long as recapture of full powers was possible "it will always be a club by which we can compel efficiency and fair dealing."[77] Hence this clause had become for Green "at the heart of the whole thing"; without it, he believed, the entire policy of martial law must collapse as unworkable.[78] Pushing in the same direction, McCloy asked Stimson to stand firm on the need for the commanding general to have power to reassert authority as he deemed necessary. "If any discussion arises in the Cabinet meeting," McCloy urged, "there is a fundamental principle to which the military properly adhere: namely, that one man must be the final authority in the Islands and that he should be military rather than civilian; that a scrambled jurisdiction violates the principle of unified command in a spot where it is most important to have it."[79]

Stimson fully concurred, and he made the question of "final authority" for the commanding general the linchpin for the War Department's approval of the agreement. "The main point we have been fighting for [in the negotiations]," he recorded in his private diary, "is that the commander, who is responsible for the successful defense of the fortress, necessarily must have the last say on defense measures and he must have at bottom power to determine what defense measures are necessary."[80] In the end, Stimson observed, once his department and the army had agreed to "all relaxations possible," a process of "patient discussion" with Ickes and Biddle had permitted the negotiators to produce the overall formula that won assent.[81]

Stainback was unhappy, of course, with the outcome of the talks. For him, the continuation of even a modified form of martial law was an unfortunate concession. His allies in Washington hoped that he could nonetheless respond to the new situation without any major political missteps, for, as Ickes worried, "A good deal will depend now on how Governor Stainback comports himself because the Army will undoubtedly be glad of any opportunity to slip in and try to take over power [entirely]."[82] For his part, General Emmons was no less unhappy than Stainback: he predicted "indecision, confusion, and endless and unhappy arguments" from divided authority.[83] An equally gloomy assessment came from Green, who, as the negotiations moved inexorably against him, reflected that if the Islands were ever again subject to Japanese attack, there would be chaos and possible disaster. "God help us if the Japs ever did take Hawaii," Green wrote to Colonel Morrison, his right-hand man in Honolulu; "They [Fortas, Biddle, and other critics] just do not understand, or if they do they won't believe the possible danger."[84]

The White House and the cabinet officials left no choice, however, except for Stainback and the army to cooperate in implementing the agreement. President Roosevelt formally instructed Secretary Stimson on February 1, 1943, to put the agreement into effect immediately, writing:

> In an area of such strategic importance as the Hawaiian Islands . . . , I can readily appreciate the difficulty in defining exactly the boundaries between civil and military functions. I think the formula which this proclamation applies meets the present needs.
>
> I know that General Emmons will do all that he can, consistent with his military responsibility, to refrain from exercising his authority over what are normally civil functions. I am confident that the military and civil authorities will cooperate fully. . . .
>
> I hope also that there will be a further restoration of civil authority as and when the situation permits.[85]

As soon as the agreement was cast in specific language, McCloy radioed the document to Emmons in the format of a formal proclamation for publication in Hawai'i. Consistent with the president's view, McCloy urged the general "to interpret the proclamation broadly in the direction of returning functions to the civil authorities"—even including functions beyond those specified for return under terms of the agreement. He directed Emmons to work toward having "the spirit of the proclamations carried out fully and to the end that further talk of conflicts between civil and military in Hawai'i will be put to rest." McCloy spelled out further what he expected:

> Although I am not on the ground, I have an idea that the secret of having the thing work effectively is more free consultation with the Governor than has taken place in the past. . . . Also, it was the spirit [of the agreement] that the military would do what it could to assist the civilian authorities in making the arrangement work. We should not take a stand-offish attitude, but on the contrary should make it our business to do all that we can to assist the civilian authorities to perform the returned functions efficiently.[86]

Having finally brought this resolution to the burdensome Hawai'i negotiations—what Secretary Stimson jocularly termed one of McCloy's "pet babies"—McCloy was on an airplane a few days later headed for North Africa, on a special assignment to help deal with myriad problems of inter-Allied coordination being faced there by General Eisenhower.[87]

Restoration

In accordance with the Washington agreement, on February 8, Governor Stainback and the commanding general issued for publication in the Islands identical proclamations embodying the agreement's terms.[88] Even the editors of the magazine *Hawaii,* which hewed to a solidly pro-army line on the martial law question to the very end of the war, found reason for optimism despite the coming turnover of power, declaring:

> Fortunately, behind the scenes, the military governing structure sits like an indulgent father giving his small son his first opportunity to drive the car—maintaining hands off as long as everything goes well, but ever alert and ready to take hold of the controls in time to prevent serious accidents. . . .
>
> If politicians want to play at running a war-zone community, they will be allowed to play—so long as their amusement does not jeopardize the strategic value of Hawaii as an advance base in the Pacific war zone.[89]

Power was officially transferred on March 10—termed "Restoration Day" in the accompanying publicity, though there was some sub rosa talk in the Islands about its being "E-Day," for "Emancipation Day." (Green called it "Confusion Day.")[90] The event was celebrated with a festive gala in the throne room of Iolani Palace, attended by the legislature and high-ranking military and civilian officials, and featuring Islands music and dancing. An ominous signal of continuing tension was sounded in the background, however, as the army scheduled an anti-aircraft gun drill for the same hour as the celebration.[91]

Between the time that the February proclamation was issued and the March implementation of the Restoration Agreement, the office of Territorial Attorney General Garner Anthony had analyzed all the general orders issued by the OMG relating to civilian affairs and determined "how much of each orders should be preserved in the form of rules and regulations issued under the Hawai'i Defense Act and how many should be discarded in their entirety."[92] Thus all was in readiness on March 10: the commanding general (*qua* military governor) revoked the 181 general orders relating to civilian affairs that had been issued under martial law, and these orders were replaced by regulations promulgated by the civilian governor, acting under the power invested in him by the Hawai'i Defense (M-Day) Act, and by a new series of military general orders.

At Restoration Day ceremonies, March 10, 1943, Governor Ingram Stainback greets Admiral Chester Nimitz, with territorial senate president Harold W. Rice shown at right. Credit: *Honolulu Star-Bulletin* photo, courtesy of HWRD, University of Hawaiʻi.

Despite President Roosevelt's instructions to the War Department in February to expedite "further restoration of civil authority as and when the situation permits," from Restoration Day in March 1943 until October 1944 there were only minor adjustments made to the new regime under the compromise agreement for modified martial law. It was not until the latter date, after additional debate in the cabinet, that a presidential order would finally restore full control over civil affairs in Hawaiʻi to the civilian authorities.[93]

A more immediate event of significance for army rule when the new agreement first went into effect in March 1943 was the War Department's response to the president's order for transfer and reassignment of General Green. He was made "to walk the plank," Green wrote privately, because he had to take the heat for his superiors—and also because unscrupulous politicians and lawyers in the other agencies hated him.[94] Green bitterly resented the compromises he had been required to accept. Of Ickes, Biddle, Fortas, and other civilian officials who had opposed him, Green declared: "I can't understand which side of the war they are on." He told Colonel Morrison, the man who would succeed him in the Hawaiʻi command structure, that "they seem to have a private war with the Army and Navy which seems to supplant completely the war with the Japs."[95] Green regularly termed the cabinet officers and other civilian officials "politicians," a term not meant as a compliment. "Our opponents are simply sold on the idea that the military is wrong and anything and any cost to throw off the yoke will be satisfactory to them," partly because of their own predispositions and partly because they had been so badly misinformed as to the facts of life under army rule in Hawai'i—misled mainly by Governor Stainback and by what Green regarded as a cabal of Interior Department ideologues and their bureaucratic underlings.[96]

Green's removal from Hawai'i was hardly damaging to his career, as it turned out: McCloy reassigned Green to Washington, and two years later, he was appointed judge advocate general for the army despite the rising public criticism of his record while administering the military government in Hawai'i.[97]

In what was apparently a routinely scheduled move, completely unrelated to the martial law issues, General Emmons was also reassigned, returning to the mainland where he succeeded the virulently anti-Japanese General DeWitt as commanding general of the Western Defense Command in the Presidio, San Francisco. Emmons was succeeded in June as commanding general of the Hawaiian Department by General Robert C. Richardson Jr. A graduate of West Point (where he served as commandant of cadets) and a cavalry officer, Richardson was a seasoned combat veteran. He had spent three tours of duty in the Philippines, where he was wounded in action, and he had served as a liaison officer with the American Expeditionary Force in France during World War I. He was familiar with Washington politics, having served as director of public relations for the War Department during the buildup to World War II. He was also one of the army's most experienced officers in implementing martial law plans

General Robert C. Richardson, left, conferring with General Delos Emmons in Honolulu, during the change of command upon Richardson's arrival from the mainland in June 1943. Credit: U.S. Army Signal Corps photo, courtesy of HWRD, University of Hawai'i.

and operations. He had been involved in military control in San Francisco following the great 1906 earthquake, and then in 1919 he commanded the army force deployed in Gary, Indiana, under "qualified martial law" to put down the threat of violence in a steel strike there. In early 1941, with a major strike in the nation's coal mines threatening, President Roosevelt became concerned that "communists and subversives" were agitating for strikes in other industries involved in war materiel buildup; hence, the War Department assigned Richardson, by then already a three-star general, to develop a detailed plan for possible army takeover and emergency operation of affected factories and mines. During 1942 and until his transfer to the Hawai'i command in mid-1943, Richardson had principal responsibility for the army forces concentrated in California to bolster the mainland defenses against possible attacks on the West Coast by Japan.[98]

Any expectation by the army's critics in Washington and Hawai'i that Richardson would be less insistent than Emmons in demanding fullest possible authority as well as retention of the "Military Governor" title was to be disappointed. Nor would Richardson be any less vigorous than Emmons in defending the legality of the provost courts. For as events would prove, Richardson was ready to confront civilian authorities directly, albeit on the basis of some sadly misguided advice from his legal advisors (Colonel Morrison and his staff), in more forceful and even inflammatory ways than Emmons had ever been moved to do.[99]

Opposed Mentalities

An intriguing insight into the conflicts of basic mentalities that were in play at the highest level of government during the Washington talks may be found in a candid exchange of views between Harold Ickes and Henry L. Stimson in late January. Only because he did not want to trouble the beleaguered president, Secretary Ickes asserted, had he reluctantly agreed to permit the army to continue to exercise certain powers in Hawai'i—such as licensing and censorship of the press—which "offend our most cherished traditions." He considered "unfortunate and unnecessary," and, more important, appropriate only to conquered territory, the continued use of the title "Military Governor" by the army's commander in Honolulu.[100] Ickes also objected to any kind of "regimentation of free labor by military edict," even in the face of military necessity, and especially if enforced by provost courts rather than the civilian judiciary.[101]

Secretary Stimson replied to Ickes immediately in terms that located him squarely in the tradition of American imperialist diplomacy and the ethos of an earlier era of history. "Some day I should like to sit down with you over the fire," Stimson wrote, "and discuss some of the historical cases of military government in our American history with which I happen to be personally familiar, namely the governments of Cuba, Puerto Rico, and the Spanish War."[102] His former law partner Elihu Root had been secretary of war during the time of those occupations, Stimson continued, and out of his close friendship with Root he had gained a thorough understanding of "his principles and accomplishments in the solution of those problems"—that is, the military occupation of the former Spanish possessions—which manifested "the American traditions of freedom." Thus Stimson found in the memory of the army's role in those occupations of conquered provinces reason to regard them as "one of the brightest pages of enlightened administration in all our American history."[103] Having once himself served as governor-general in the occupied Philippines, Stimson regretted the "fear and abhorrence" of military governance that Ickes seemed to harbor, he wrote, and he hoped for a chance at some future time "to try to remove it."[104]

It is difficult to imagine an intellectual and ideological impasse more intractable than was revealed in this exchange of views. Ickes, tenacious as always, drafted a courteous reply—one that stated eloquently his constitutionalism and the civil liberties creed that it embodied. "In some ways I suppose that I am an old-fashioned conservative," Ickes wrote, in that he could not accept that a military government could ever "be consistent with 'the American tradition of freedom.' "[105] He regarded "the very conception" of military government as dangerous:

> I have a deep and abiding faith in the principles, theories, and institutions which have resulted in the freedom and liberty that Americans have enjoyed. Among these is the theory of the supremacy of civilian officials, directly or indirectly elected by and responsible to the people, and I am particularly afraid of government which is not responsible and which is administered by men who have military traditions and training. In specific instances, these men may provide model government, but there is a fundamental danger that their desire for directness, efficiency, and obedience may lead them to secure these benefits at the price of sacrificing the laborious, inefficient but precious virtues of democracies. . . . By and large, it seems clear that any gain in efficiency must come from shortcutting those involved processes of democracy upon which our civilization is founded.[106]

Although Stimson kept himself well informed on the Hawai'i conflict, in fact he delegated to John McCloy as assistant secretary all the day-to-day responsibility of dealing with the army's administration there—just as he vested McCloy at that time with oversight of the army's Japanese-American removal and internment policy on the mainland.[107] Whether or not McCloy shared the depth of Stimson's profound admiration for the army's record as administrator of conquered civilian populations, it is not particularly relevant to our analysis, since he faithfully implemented Stimson's views. This translated, for McCloy, into a highly pragmatic and instrumental style of oversight. Even as he became enmeshed in the daily negotiations of a new delineation agreement in December, McCloy voiced his serious doubts about the wisdom of trying to reduce the division of authority to a written document. To do so, McCloy warned, would mean "an undesirable and dangerous inflexibility" in a situation that demanded broad discretionary power.[108] "General principles may certainly be outlined," he conceded, "but *you can't draft Magna Carta for the Hawaiian Islands in time of war in the Pacific*."[109]

McCloy's support of the army command's demands for final authority in the Islands was based principally upon his bedrock conviction that the commanding general in Hawai'i must be seen as "the man on the ground who is responsible for such a large element in the protection of this country," and who thus must be given deference so that "his abilities to defend the area [would not] be compromised."[110] The best approach, McCloy insisted both then and for nearly a year thereafter, was "to let them work out on the ground just what [powers] can be turned over, and when."[111] The seemingly benign and self-regulating process—pragmatically driven, as McCloy described it—was in fact not easy to put in motion when one of the parties "on the ground" was an army general and his legal staff who insisted nearly to the end of the combat in the Pacific war that Hawai'i was a "fortress" open to attack at any moment. The generals were, in these circumstances, unwilling to concede that any civilian activity of significance properly belonged under the control of anyone except themselves.

Although there was thus little likelihood that President Roosevelt's hopes of "further restoration of civil authority" would quickly be realized, the fact remained that the Restoration Agreement at least had returned the jurisdiction of several significant areas of governance to the civilian authorities.

PART V

Legal Challenges

Chapter Thirteen

THE HABEAS CORPUS CASES

Internment on Trial

While the political challenge to martial law was thus seemingly put to rest with the implementation of the Restoration Agreement in March 1943, a parallel legal challenge that had begun in early 1942 was still going forward. This challenge involved the federal courts as the locus of a continuing debate of profoundly important constitutional questions, surfacing in a series of petitions for the privilege of habeas corpus. At issue were (1) the legality of the internment of American citizens deemed to be "potentially dangerous"; and (2) the jurisdiction of the provost courts to sentence civilians for crimes that were, at least in the arguments of the petitioners for habeas, unrelated to the war effort.[1]

The command lived in constant fear that "a multitude of likely court injunctions which will delay military effort" could easily bedevil all the army's operations—not only in Hawai'i, but also in the entire Pacific theater of war, dependent as it was upon Pearl Harbor as a naval base and on Hawai'i as a launching point for American armed forces being moved out to join in the western Pacific islands campaign.[2] The military's determination to keep the courts out of its way greatly influenced the formal policy and legal positions that the army in Hawai'i took generally in its dealings with the civilian agencies of government. And that same determination to resist judicial oversight of its governing policies also dominated the army's litigation tactics, as became evident when the legal challenge to the military's administration and provost-court operations under martial law did inevitably arise in the courts.

Four distinctive features of the litigation history emerged at the outset and then prevailed throughout the entire period of the war:

First, the number of cases that sought judicial relief from internments or provost court judgments was small—six in total. Three cases were challenges to the legality of the provost courts' jurisdiction; two of these were later joined for purposes of appeal to the Supreme Court; they will be considered in more detail in the next chapter. The remaining cases were habeas actions initiated by petitioners who were being interned on loyalty or security grounds. None of the detainees had been permitted access to the evidence on which the hearing boards and army reviewing officers had recommended their incarceration. Their immediate objective was to force the army to justify their internments in a habeas proceeding in the U.S. District Court in Honolulu; and of course their core objective was to gain release altogether from imprisonment.

Second, to a striking degree, the army lawyers' large strategy amounted to an elaborate, continuous avoidance of habeas hearings—a devious practice that may fairly be termed a "flight from habeas." The first internee who in February 1942 presented a habeas petition to Judge Metzger was turned away, the judge having declared his court as "closed under duress" by the army's general orders. Other internees, however, were granted habeas relief by the district court in mid-1943, and in each case the army appealed to the Ninth Circuit federal appeals court in San Francisco. That court took the position in all of these cases, and adhered to it throughout the war period, that "military necessity" was a sufficient reason for the army to deny the rights of citizens to ordinary constitutional due process, including the privilege of the writ of habeas corpus. In responding to the Ninth Circuit decisions in each case involving an internee, the army terminated the case, however, by rendering it moot—simply by releasing the prisoner from custody, rather than risk a further appeal to the U.S. Supreme Court that could result in a final decision adverse to the military's powers under martial law.

Third, none of these six cases was initiated by a Japanese American. Until nearly the end of the war, the army command gave priority to keeping those Japanese-American internees and prisoners who were citizens located in a jurisdiction—varying, according to the situation, between Hawai'i and the mainland—where it would be difficult for them to exercise their right to petition for a writ of habeas corpus. This priority was motivated by the military lawyers' fear that a successful legal challenge by a Japanese American would undermine the army's entire program of selective incarceration—which is to say, that such a success might subvert the entire legal foundation on which the more comprehensive martial law regime was justified. Thus, in the summer of 1942 a group of Japanese-American citizens who had been sent as internees to the mainland were returned to Hawai'i to prevent their release on habeas petitions; and in 1944, the army "excluded" several dozen Japanese-American citizens from Hawai'i, in part explicitly to avoid habeas proceedings once martial law was lifted.[3]

Here again, the underlying theme was that the army manipulated the detainee placements and movements out of concern that habeas petitions might actually be successful in the federal courts. The main thread running through the fabric of policy was the "flight from habeas," first closing the U.S. District Court in Hawai'i to habeas petitions; then employing mooting tactics to avoid final appeal; and throughout, the cruel practice of physically moving internees thousands of miles back and forth to assure they would not have access to courts for submission of habeas petitions or for appeals of initial judgments.

Paradoxically, some evidence suggests that in the late months of the war, the fact that no Japanese Americans petitioned for habeas became a source of chagrin for the army lawyers in the Hawai'i command. For they believed, probably correctly, that a Japanese-American citizen litigant would have a slender chance at best of successfully challenging incarceration resulting from a provost court conviction, internment, or other legal actions leading to imprisonment without normal due process. Hence, the court's rejection of such a challenge would be a victory for the military.

Fourth, from the first year of the war, and increasingly so as the conflict wore on, the Justice Department lawyers who were serving as counsel to the military in Hawai'i were critical of the army's policy. They repeatedly called upon the commanding generals to give up tactics (such as systematic mooting of cases) that were regarded in the Justice Department as unwise at best, and as a flagrant abuse of the legal system at worst. The commanding generals and the army's lawyers in Honolulu were as intransigent in regard to the litigation tactic as they had been in the negotiations over the delineation of martial law powers; they never retreated from their position that defining "military necessity"—including internal security and measures for defense of the Islands from attack—was exclusively their prerogative. Whether the U.S. Supreme Court would validate or overturn their position with respect to the military's powers remained a contested and unresolved question until the army finally allowed an appeal by two white citizens, convicted for crimes and imprisoned by provost court actions, to go the highest court for final adjudication. The Supreme Court's judgment of the legality of the martial law regime finally came down, in *Duncan v. Kahanamoku,* in March 1946, nearly eight months after Japan surrendered to the Allied forces.[4]

The *Zimmerman* Case

Three cases involving German-born naturalized U.S. citizens, all of whom were imprisoned by the army as security risks and held as internees, were brought into federal court in Honolulu in 1942 and 1943. In each case, there had been no formal charges, no chance to see the evidence or cross-examine witnesses, and no access to the written record of administrative proceedings that led to the imprisonment. And in each case, the internee petitioned in the U.S. District Court in Honolulu for a writ of habeas corpus. As was predictable, the lawyers representing the army argued in all three hearings that the military must have the exclusive power to decide how far its own authority (and abridgement of citizens' rights) should be allowed to run under the martial law regime. Denying the jurisdiction of any civilian court—even a federal court—the army contended that the military commander must have absolute control over civilian affairs; his authority should include the power to intern anyone, whether a citizen or alien, whom he deemed to be a threat to security. Hence, in private discussion of one of these cases, a high-ranking legal officer in the Office of the Judge Advocate General advised Green that "insufficiency of evidence" was not of controlling importance; the lack of concrete evidence, in this official view, "[had] no bearing on our legal right" to hold a detainee in custody.[5] How this legal theory played out in practice, and with what effect on the individuals involved, is described in the pages that follow.

The first of three German-American internee cases was initiated in the early weeks of 1942 by Hans Zimmerman, then being held at Sand Island. Zimmerman was a "naturopathic physician" with a successful practice in Honolulu.[6] His patients and his local social contacts included many persons highly placed in Hawai'i's social elite. The hearing board inquired of witnesses whether Zimmerman spoke German in private conversations. He had done so, which was hardly remarkable, since it was his first language and some of his friends were German Americans. The board further inquired as to whether he had visited Germany after Hitler assumed power there; he had done so, to visit family, as he said (and as the FBI later verified). The board also heard testimony from an FBI agent, or perhaps was shown the actual FBI file on Zimmerman. Years later, the file was turned over in confidence to the federal judge in a postwar civil suit that Zimmerman pursued against the army, seeking damages for his imprisonment. The file rests today in the voluminous archives from the Hawai'i district court, and its content illustrates what the authorities deemed sufficient evidence to justify an internment. The record in Zimmerman's case is also pertinent to the larger issue considered in our present study—the fairness of the non-transparent security procedures administered by the army more generally under martial law—and so it warrants a summary of its contents here:[7]

- An FBI agent's report, dated April 2, 1941, of an interview in Honolulu with "Confidential Informant No. 37," who claimed that Zimmerman, in a social visit to the informant's home in March 1941 (ten months before the United States entered the war) expressed antipathy to the English and admiration for Hitler's Germany and the possibility of a "United States of Europe" emerging under German hegemony.
- A report of this same agent's additional interview in April 1941 with informant No. 37, who stated that Zimmerman had told him that "he himself was not for Hitler, but when [his wife] said anything at all against the Germans, that he was ready for argument."
- The report of a second FBI agent, interviewing an attorney of some prominence with offices in Honolulu, who declared that "in 1938 or 1939 Zimmerman had told him that what the United States needed was more Bunds. . . . At this time Zimmerman also spoke in very laudatory terms of Hitler and the German people."
- Yet a third FBI agent's report of his interview in October 1941 of George Coleman, the acting district director of the U.S. Immigration and Naturalization Station in Honolulu, who stated that "a lady friend of his family had informed him that she learned from one of her friends that Dr. Hans Zimmerman was very pro-Nazi," but that this friend declined to quote Zimmerman. Coleman "did not desire to make known the identity of his informant," whose thirdhand assertion was thus made of record.

In addition to presumably being told of the above items in the FBI's summary report, the internment board was probably made aware of a September 1940 FBI study entitled "German Activities in the United States." The entry on Zimmerman in that study quoted an unnamed person, designated as "Confidential Informant HO-1," stating that Zimmerman was "very pro-Nazi," and that he had a brother who was "commander in the Germany Navy" (a statement later proven to be completely untrue). In a further quotation from the September 1940 file, Zimmerman "was reported by [name deleted] . . . as being very active in Nazi circles; that she had been on [sic] many parties with him and he entered into political discussions and openly stated himself to be Nazi."[8]

Zimmerman, held at the Sand Island camp throughout the hearings period, was not permitted to see any of these allegations, nor was he permitted to confront the FBI agents or the informants. He and his wife, Clara Zimmerman, suspected that he had been denounced as disloyal by local physicians with the MD degree, who they thought were jealous of the success that Zimmerman, a naturopath lacking the medical degree, enjoyed in his local practice by treating patients with diet, exercise, and physical therapy.[9] Whether or not local physicians had weighed in by circulating rumors about Zimmerman, in fact the hearing board's formal findings, filed on December 20, 1941, made no specific reference to charges by identifiable medical personnel.

In any event, the board concluded "that the evidence presented by the FBI shows that the internee had pro-Axis leanings and at numerous [sic] times suggested that the greatness of Hitler would eventually make him ruler of the world," and "that the record of the FBI shows the internee to have been active in interests inimical to the United States Government."[10] Against these charges, on his attorney's initiative, the board had heard testimony from a number of citizens (some of them his patients) with regard to his personal character, citing his earlier service in the U.S. Army and lack of any knowledge that he was disloyal to the United States. The positive testimony before the hearing board was given by men of substantial reputation in Hawaiʻi. They included Attorney Frank E. Thompson, of the local bar; Nolle Smith, the territorial government's budget director; John Fleming, vice president of the Bishop Trust Company; and Alvah Scott, president of the Mutual Telephone Company. Most prominent of the witnesses giving positive testimony was Joseph R. Farrington Jr., publisher of the Star-Bulletin and soon to be elected as Hawaiʻi's territorial delegate in Congress.

The army's intelligence officers, who regularly reviewed all hearing board decisions, nonetheless concurred with the board's recommendation of internment, and then the head of the FBI office in Hawaiʻi, Robert L. Shivers, signed off on the internment papers. In a postwar indemnification suit in which Zimmerman would seek civil damages, General Emmons, who as military governor was the final authority in the internment decisions, would admit under oath that he relied on the judgment of those charged with review of internment cases. Moreover, as we have noted, he regarded it as entirely appropriate to approve decisions that were based merely on "information in the form of gossip, hearsay, and conclusions, and so on."[11] He did not personally read the papers in the internment files other than the final recommendations, Emmons affirmed. (In cases involving Nikkei internees, however, he did not personally review any files whatsoever.) In Zimmerman's case, Emmons admitted that he knew of nothing "that would justify his indictment before a civil court that would result in his arrest . . .

or prosecution."[12] In accord with routine procedure of the command in Hawai'i, at no point either in the hearing process, in General Emmons's review of the files, in the subsequent course of appeals in federal courts, or even in his postwar civil suit, was Zimmerman ever given access to the full FBI statements on which the hearing board and the army had relied.

For several weeks after the board's decision and his formal internment, Zimmerman continued to be detained in the Sand Island camp. He was a singularly difficult prisoner, often denouncing the camp's rules (for example, insisting on his right to communicate as often as he wished with his lawyer and others); he complained of his being thrown in with alien enemies whom he suspected of disloyalty; and he was rude to the guards. In his quest to obtain release from custody, he appealed to personal friends to use their influence with the army, while his wife was making similar efforts with the assistance of a local attorney whom she retained. Meanwhile Zimmerman, a naturalized citizen, refused to sign a routine printed form that incorrectly designated his status as "enemy alien." The army officers running the camp thus regarded him as a nuisance, and they responded accordingly to his demands. In addition to censoring all his correspondence, the prison command on at least one occasion sequestered and denied delivery of what in normal procedure would have been a privileged communication from his attorney; and apparently many of his letters to his wife were intercepted and similarly withheld. His wife's attorney, however, had admonished Zimmerman that he should bear with the indignities and restrain from obstreperous behavior or making "vituperative remarks" in dealing with his captors. "Unless you keep your mouth shut," he warned, "you'll be there until the end of [the] world no matter what happens."[13]

The attorney was meanwhile preparing a petition for a writ of habeas corpus that would require the army to produce the prisoner in court and justify his internment. This plan was well known to General Emmons's command, since the censors were privy to every detail of the Zimmermans' intentions by reading their mail. The army, for its part, was making preparations to remove Zimmerman from Sand Island and transfer him to the mainland—and in that way to get him out of Hawai'i before the habeas petition could be acted upon by the district court. In any event, on February 19, 1942, one month after Zimmerman's internment was formalized, the petition on his behalf was presented to Judge Delbert Metzger in the U.S. District Court in Honolulu. Judge Metzger considered the petition informally for two days, but then he announced that he must decline to accept jurisdiction. To the consternation of Delegate King, Garner Anthony, and many other leading political figures and members of the Hawai'i bar, Metzger declared explicitly that his court had been closed "under duress." He explained his position by referring to the army's General Orders No. 57, issued a month earlier, that had declared courts of the territory (with nothing in the language of the order exempting the federal district court) as "agents of the Military Governor" and specifically prohibited a writ of habeas corpus to be issued.[14]

The ink had hardly dried on Judge Metzger's pronouncement when the army acted precipitously to remove Zimmerman from Hawai'i; in fact, it was done on that same day. Together with five other German-American internees, he was taken from Sand Island and placed on board an army transport vessel then in harbor in Honolulu; and late on February 21, the ship departed for the mainland. Neither the internees nor their families were given information as to their ultimate destination, which, in fact, was Camp McCoy, Wisconsin.[15] Their removal took the prisoners outside the reach of Judge Metzger's court, in case Metzger should change his mind and later resist the army's order against hearing habeas petitions.

The decision to remove these German-American citizen internees set the model for what became a standard tactic to defeat judicial intervention: we have termed this tactic "the flight from habeas"—specifically, the moving of prisoners to and from the mainland, and even mooting cases altogether in order to avoid judicial proceedings that could result in their release, thereby potentially curbing the military's exercise of absolute control under the martial law regime.

Two rather bizarre aspects of the whole Zimmerman proceeding in early 1942 require special mention. First, the army correspondence for weeks continued to refer incorrectly to Zimmerman and the other naturalized German-American internees as "enemy aliens," a classification that even the War Department officials in Washington assumed was accurate.[16] At one point, Assistant Secretary McCloy even referred to the group that included Zimmerman and the others as "Jap deportees."[17] This confusion was not sorted out for months, owing to the blizzard of bureaucratic paperwork generated in connection with their incarceration and transfers.[18]

Second, Judge Metzger himself wrote in a private communication to Zimmerman at Camp McCoy, about two weeks after he arrived there, that he believed Zimmerman was manifestly the victim of an injustice. "It is hard to conceive of you in a detention camp," Metzger wrote:

> The naturalization papers you received from this court are without tarnish, and you are entitled to all the privileges and protection that any other citizen [enjoys]. . . . In a community such as Honolulu with martial law prevailing, vicious acts and injustices become prevalent. . . . The FBI and the Army and Navy intelligence departments were frenziedly searching for someone to accuse of subversive activities or sympathies and suspicion prompted by secret whispering, possibly prompted by malice and revenge, was all that was necessary to throw any foreign born person into a detention camp—and once in camp that was the end of it, with no trial hearing or judicial recourse. . . . It is a thing that may happen in any country when the force of arms is the highest of all authority. . . . I trust you will hold yourself aloof of the company of cut-throats you are thrown in with.[19]

Apparently Zimmerman long held in confidence this extraordinary letter, which was mailed on March 13, 1942. It was not made known to others, except for the censors and presumably the army command, until Metzger approved its release to a Chicago newspaper seventeen months later.[20]

Metzger's assessment of the martial law regime's excesses offers an important insight into why in mid-1943 he would reverse his position on whether or not his court must defer to the army's orders prohibiting him from entertaining petitions for the habeas corpus writ. His action in reopening his court to such petitions in mid-1943 would produce a dramatic confrontation between General Richardson and himself, an incident with far-reaching effects on the army's regime in Hawai'i.[21]

The ACLU Enters the Litigation Arena

Just at the time that Judge Metzger issued his statement that his court was closed under duress, the news was also breaking in both Hawai'i and the mainland press about the army's trial before a military tribunal, and its handing down of the death sentence, in the Saffery Brown Case.[22] The scandalous lack of fairness in the military tribunal's procedure in that case, prior to the War Department's reduction of the sentence, won the attention of the American Civil Liberties Union. The ACLU leadership began gathering information on the Brown case but, meanwhile also began to take an interest in Zimmerman and his fate. Replying to inquiries in these matters, Delegate Samuel King asked the ACLU to advise him on the legal issues and to consider taking legal action in either matter or both.[23]

By early May 1942, the ACLU was regularly in touch with both King and Garner Anthony, who had just published his *California Law Review* article criticizing the army command's legal position on martial law and military government.[24] Anthony's analysis of the legal issues, transcending the particulars of Zimmerman's case, captured the attention of the ACLU's director, Roger Baldwin. And Baldwin, who was then perhaps America's most prominent civil liberties advocate, sought Anthony's advice on what his organization might usefully accomplish. Reiterating his published view that the army had far exceeded its constitutional authority by taking over the civilian government, closing the courts, and subjecting civilians to provost court trials, Anthony responded that his eye was not as yet on litigation. His main recommendation to Baldwin was, rather, that the ACLU "make a lasting contribution to American democracy" by lobbying Congress and the Roosevelt administration to define by specific legislation the authority of the army in Hawai'i, and above all by ordering the army to permit reopening of the civilian courts. The Japanese-American citizen internees, he pointed out, were being granted court hearings on the mainland in challenges to their incarceration, so that it was not only unjustified but blatantly inconsistent to deny judicial recourse in the civilian courts to the citizens of Hawai'i of any ethnic background.[25]

Thus did Anthony reaffirm his liberal constitutionalist position: So long as the jurisdiction of the courts was restored to permit judicial review of army orders and to hear habeas petitions, the requirements of the Constitution would be met, even if the army's policy was misguided—or, as he believed, "fascist."[26]

Writing in May 1942 regarding the state of public opinion in Hawai'i, Anthony clearly was feeling the heat of the reactions of the army brass and some civilian leaders to his *California Law Review* article. "It is curious," he told Baldwin,

> how some people feel that a state of war is the signal that all thinking should forthwith cease, and that anyone who endeavors to analyze a problem with the view to getting on an efficient and proper basis is doing something that verges on sedition. No one feels more strongly than I do the necessity, if the world is to be a fit place to live, of destroying the Axis dictatorships. No reasonable sphere of power should be withheld from the military commander, but this does not require a wholesale junking of the Bill of Rights, particularly in the field of criminal law.[27]

The events that followed indicate that the ACLU was inclined to give priority to litigation that would test the large constitutional issues rather than confine itself, as Anthony suggested, to a probably futile course of lobbying. The ACLU did not mobilize for actions in court, however, without some soul-searching along the way by individuals and by its board of directors as a group. The first reaction of some ACLU board directors was to worry about the wisdom of representing Zimmerman and other internees who might prove to be Nazi spies, or at least might be demonstrably more loyal to Germany than to the United States. Upon learning that Zimmerman had been hustled off to Camp McCoy, the directors decided to ask Wade Boardman, an eminent attorney in Wisconsin, whether it was advisable to file a habeas petition in the federal district court there. Boardman's response was dismaying to Baldwin and his colleagues. The incumbent federal district judge, he warned, was a solid bet to uphold the army's powers wholesale—and probably would do so "with much free comment on the subject of treason." Boardman also sharply rebuffed the request that he take on the case. Internment issues in a time of war, he declared, were problems that ought to be "worked out through the War Department," and he could see no reason on the record to warrant "a hostile challenging of the military authorities."[28]

While these initial ACLU moves were going forward, the War Department became aware of the prospect of a habeas proceeding for the prisoners. The army lawyers did not share Mr. Boardman's confidence as to what the district court in Madison would do. The War Department leaders were afraid—as General Emmons later recalled—that "they could not resist a writ of habeas corpus if [the prisoners] filed in the United States."[29] Hence, as soon as the military learned that the ACLU was preparing a habeas petition, the provost marshal general asked the Hawai'i command if it was acceptable to return Zimmerman and the others from the mainland, to be held again in custody in the Islands, where the military officialdom hoped that Judge Metzger would continue to decline to accept a habeas petition. Whatever the validity of that reliance, it seemed clear that martial law could (at least potentially) provide a more powerful obstacle to a habeas writ than the army could hope for if habeas petitions were presented to the federal district courts on the mainland.[30] Zimmerman and the other German-American internees were therefore returned to Hawai'i to be held in custody by the army.

The War Department, meanwhile, went out of its way to throw its own administrative obstacle in the way of a habeas submission by refusing to provide to ACLU counsel information regarding even the simple facts as to Zimmerman's location. McCloy himself signed letters to the ACLU withholding the facts as to whether the prisoners were being removed from Camp McCoy, and if so when, and to what location.[31] In this way, the War Department had became actively complicit in what a federal district judge later termed the army's strategy of "bluffing, stalling, threatening, dodging and evading" in its determination to avoid habeas proceedings with the opportunities they offered for judicial review of the legality of the martial law regime.[32]

The *Zimmerman* Case on Appeal in the Ninth Circuit, 1942–1943

While being held again in Hawai'i, Zimmerman instituted an appeal to the U.S. Ninth Circuit Court of Appeals of Judge Metzger's decision not to hear the petition. The briefs of counsel and *amici* for the Ninth Circuit panel in the Zimmerman appeal, submitted on September 17, 1942, presented very ably the key legal and constitutional issues that would run through a line of subsequent cases testing martial law—including the issues that three years later would be at the core of arguments and the justices' opinions in the *Duncan* case in the Supreme Court. The government's defense of the army rested squarely on the arguments from "necessity" in emergencies threatening the public safety, but especially from "military necessity" in wartime. Asking the court to take judicial notice—that is, to acknowledge, without need for formal argument on the evidence, the emergency created by the Pearl Harbor attack—their brief stressed that when Metzger ruled, there was hard combat going on in the Pacific theater of war. Martial law had been declared in the context of these developments, the government's brief contended; and in light of these same circumstances, it would be improper for the appellate court to assume authority to review the military's judgment as to "necessity" for martial rule. The government further contended that the review board's determination that Zimmerman was a security risk should be taken as sufficient cause and justification for his internment, even though the procedure had been extraordinary.[33] In a word, the army wanted the court to stand back and leave it free to do whatever was deemed necessary in light of the war emergency.

Counsel for Zimmerman, supported by the American Civil Liberties Union in an impressively argued amicus brief, argued from the principles in the 1866 decision in *Milligan* that the constitutional conditions for imposition of martial law were not fulfilled in Hawai'i. The ACLU brief, written by A. L. Wirin, also contended that close scrutiny must be given, as mandated by the famous *Carolene* dictum by Chief Justice Stone, to any governmental suppression of individual liberties essential to the political process.[34] The briefs maintained that the government's "vague intimations" as to emergency conditions in Hawai'i, allegedly warranting incarceration of a United States citizen without even the most rudimentary kind of due process, constituted an entirely insufficient factual basis for a ruling. The court should indeed take "judicial notice" of actual conditions in Hawai'i, they declared, just as the government had contended; but here the argument went to the opposite conclusion: the judges should take notice of the factual context so that they might make independent judgments as to whether the "military necessity" was such as to actually warrant suspension of all traditional guarantees of due process. To accept without careful scrutiny the army's interpretation of the facts, the brief concluded, would be to abdicate the proper role of the court.[35]

A curious sidelight to the Ninth Circuit appeal was the submission—rather to the chagrin of the army lawyers, and presumably unwelcome to the ACLU and Zimmerman's counsel—of an amicus brief submitted by California's attorney general, Earl Warren, and his deputy attorney general, Herbert Wenig. Their brief argued for broad power of the executive branch and the military in times of emergency. Because of the dangers of espionage, sabotage, and more generally disloyalty that they averred were faced by California, located as it was at the edge of the Pacific combat area, their state's government was "directly interested" in having the court take judicial notice of the prevailing wartime conditions—and in having the court proceed from its assessment of these conditions to a decision that would clearly define the extent of the executive's emergency powers.

Warren and Wenig had been prominent in the mobilization of pressures on the Roosevelt administration to issue the Executive Order of 1942 that authorized removal of the Japanese Americans from the West Coast.[36] In this brief, they were concerned not solely with asserting the legitimacy of martial law as it was being imposed in Hawai'i, the immediate subject of the appeal, but also with the possibility that litigation then being pursued by Japanese-American citizens of California seeking redress from evacuation and imprisonment might be successful. It was important that the court provide an opinion of broad scope, they contended, so that it would uphold the legitimacy under the Constitution of suspension of due process guarantees and, not least, "the milder *precautionary measures* of evacuating and detaining persons to remove even a slight chance of their being an interference with the war effort." This was especially important, Warren and Wenig argued, since "some of the 161,000 Japanese in the Islands" might be evacuated to the mainland and presumably pose an increased security threat there.[37] If federal district judges should respond favorably to petitions for habeas corpus writs, as were then pending in several western courts (all of them within the Ninth Circuit's jurisdiction), then the military authorities would be "held powerless" to deal with the dangers posed to internal security and the war effort. If that happened, the brief warned, "then the State of California must attempt to meet the dangers, potential or actual, thus presented." Hence clarification of the principles under which the state's own authorities could legally invoke extraordinary measures, *including martial law,* was of crucial importance.[38]

Earl Warren had an obsessive fear of sabotage and espionage that might be committed by California's Japanese Americans, leading him to consider the possibility of imposing martial law under the state government's authority.[39] That he carried his campaign into the Ninth Circuit in this amicus effort, seeking *in advance* a judicial imprimatur for drastic measures by the State, has not been widely recognized as part of Warren's hard-line posture in the weeks that led up to the removal and incarceration policies instituted in early 1942. He called on the Ninth Circuit, however, to define explicitly "the principles of martial law" as a matter of vital potential interest to California state government, on the grounds that *"the courts must remain the final arbiter of what constitutes appropriate action"*—an argument that was in startling contrast with the army brief's position, which was, of course, that the courts ought not to presume to assume powers that could serve to override the military judgments of "necessity" in wartime.[40]

The Ninth Circuit rejected Zimmerman's appeal, ruling in favor of the army merely on the face of the petition itself—because, the court said, the facts showed that detention had been ordered "after an inquiry related in some way to the public safety" in an area legally under martial law.[41] The ACLU thereupon announced that it would represent Zimmerman in an appeal to the Supreme Court. This move prompted the army to consider whether it might be most prudent to avoid allowing this further appeal to go forward, and indeed soon afterward the decision was made to release Zimmerman on parole.[42]

One factor in the army's decision was doubtless an internal high-level review given to the secret administrative record on Zimmerman, conducted personally by Major General Myron C. Cramer, the judge advocate general, who flatly concluded that "the case is a very weak one on the facts."[43] Another factor was advice being given by the Department of Justice, whose lawyers believed that an appeal to the Supreme Court might well produce unintended consequences: specifically, they were concerned that it might result in an order sending the case back to the trial court—with the possibility that "the Court may without warrant incorporate some unfortunate language in their decision concerning martial law in general."[44]

After the war, Zimmerman filed suit for unlawful arrest against General Emmons and other military personnel. It was in this proceeding that Emmons admitted that the factual case against Zimmerman "relied on gossip, and that sort of thing." In the end, he said, he had deferred to the FBI for definitive evaluation of the file.[45] Similarly, years later General Green would write in a memoir that the case against Zimmerman had consisted entirely of "circumstantial evidence," which, he averred, the FBI had concluded was sufficient to justify his detention.[46]

In any event, alerted by the Justice Department's warnings that an appeal of this admittedly weak case might end up by diminishing or invalidating the martial law regime in Hawai'i, the army decided to give Zimmerman his freedom—not unconditionally, but rather on parole status. Hedging their bets against possible civil action against them, the army demanded—as they did of all parolees—that Zimmerman first sign a waiver of liability. Predictably, he refused. Outraged by how he had been treated, and still intransigent, Zimmerman wrote: "I don't see how an innocent and law-abiding citizen can accept parole for something that [he] hasn't committed" and thereby succumb to "Gestapo methods and supreme Dictatorship right now in Hawaii."[47] The army then backed down on the waiver question, and so, after having been shuttled back and forth between a Wisconsin internee camp and Hawai'i, Zimmerman was again transferred to the mainland.

The military authorities released him only one day before his attorneys presented his petition for a writ of certiorari to the Supreme Court. On the grounds that he was no longer incarcerated, so that the army had thereby rendered the case moot, the Supreme Court declined to hear his case.[48]

The *Glockner* and *Seifert* Cases: Confrontation of the General and the Federal Judge

A year and a half later, in July 1943, events took a different turn, for by this time Judge Metzger had changed his mind about the status of his court under martial law. Metzger had raised no objection when the army closed the courts, including his own, just after Pearl Harbor, and he himself had declined to hear the Zimmerman habeas petition in February. By July 1942, however, he was advising General Green that the federal courts should be permitted to resume jury trials within about three months.[49] His advice was rejected by the army at that time, but with the passage of another year Metzger was clearly prepared to undertake confrontation, if necessary, over the prerogatives of his court. Japan's armed forces were fully engaged thousands of miles away from Hawai'i, and so he no longer regarded the emergency as warranting suspension of the Constitution in the Islands. Thus, when the next two internee cases challenging martial law came before him in the summer of 1943—five months after the partial restoration of civilian government—Metzger ruled that the army must produce the two petitioners and accept his determination of the legality of their detention.[50] Metzger was a veteran of army service in the Spanish-American war, and even General Green would admit privately that he was tough-minded and "not antagonistic to soldiers."[51] The judge was moved not by antimilitary sentiment, Green acknowledged, but by constitutional principle.[52]

The two new cases, like the Zimmerman case, involved citizens of German ancestry: Walter Glockner, a forty-three-year-old former brewmaster in a Honolulu brewery, and Edwin Seifert, twenty-nine, a former defense worker. Both were being held as internees, with no charges against them, and they presented their habeas petitions to Judge Metzger in August 1943 in what the army lawyers termed "obviously a test case." Indeed, military intelligence contended further that Metzger himself "was eager to make a test case of it," as evidenced by his request to the petitioners' attorneys that they provide him with "helpful argument on the question of whether the threat of imminent invasion by the enemy is so great at this time as to constitute necessity for martial law."[53] Glockner claimed in his petition that he had been inaccurately reported as having made a Hitler salute in 1938 [*sic*] and had invited friends to join him aboard a German merchant ship in Honolulu; Seifert, for his part, declared that he had been held on the false and sole charge that he was anti-Semitic.[54] (It is worth noting that if anti-Semitism was reason enough for arrest and detention, a significant number of Hawaiʻi's social elite and naval officers would doubtless have qualified in 1942.)

The Glockner and Seifert cases triggered a dramatic clash between the army command and the federal judiciary that made national headlines.[55] First, Judge Metzger handed down his ruling on August 16, declaring that the suspension of habeas corpus had ceased to be in force starting on March 10, 1943, the effective date of the partial restoration of civilian authority. He therefore ordered General Richardson to bring before him the two prisoners within forty-eight hours, for a determination of whether they should be continued in custody or released. The general flatly refused to acknowledge the court's authority. "I could not recognize the jurisdiction of the court," Richardson wrote privately to a friend, declaring that the petition was nothing but a cynical ploy. A cabal of politicians, he said, hoped to get martial law invalidated.[56]

The general did not act without support from superiors in his defiance of the court's jurisdiction. The day after Metzger's decision, Richardson received a cable from the Chief of Staff, General Marshall, ordering him "not *repeat not* to produce the prisoners in Metzger's court." Marshall advised Richardson that the U.S. Attorney would "accept process on the general's behalf, and will litigate from there."[57] Thus, when a U.S. marshal attempted to serve the summons on Richardson, he was "manhandled" by the general's military guards, blocking his way in full view of Richardson.[58] This episode, reported fully in the press, was greeted with astonishment on nearly all sides. Garner Anthony wrote to Delegate Farrington that it was "incredible . . . that anyone could be so stupid as to advise the general to forcibly interfere with a United States Marshal in his endeavor to obey the federal statutes and the order of a federal court in his service of papers."[59] As it proved, Anthony's view was in large measure shared by the War Department when the news reached Washington.[60]

As for Judge Metzger, he decided that he had seen enough. He ordered the hearing held over for three days, giving Richardson the additional time to consult his superiors and to comply with his writ. When the proceedings resumed, the following exchange took place:

> THE COURT: I ruled the other day that there would be no proceedings in this case until the petitioners were produced in court.
>
> MR. TAYLOR [U.S. Attorney for Hawaiʻi]: Your Honor, that is what I want to inform the court. That General Richardson has advised me that under no circumstances will the petitioners be produced before this court for proceedings.
>
> THE COURT: All right.
>
> MR. TAYLOR: If your Honor will allow me, I would like to read this statement to your Honor.

THE COURT: No. The United States Attorney will then prepare a citation for contempt against General Richardson and bring him before this court.[61]

Richardson again refused to appear, issuing a statement on August 24 declaring that the Islands were in a theater of war, so that his judgment "as to what is necessary is conclusive and not subject to review by the court." Martial law was still lawfully in effect, he insisted, giving notice that his office fully intended to enforce it and would continue to forbid habeas petitions.[62] Meanwhile, the army's counterintelligence division was directed to conduct a discreet, general investigation of Metzger—an investigation that, relying on informants, alleged that Metzger and Zimmerman were "intimate" friends and that claimed (entirely falsely) that Metzger lacked formal legal training. This investigation led nowhere because both the War Department and the Justice Department were determined to defuse the sensational confrontation.[63]

Judge Metzger responded by finding General Richardson in contempt and fining him $5,000, while continuing to demand that the army produce the prisoners.[64] Richardson, in turn, immediately responded by issuing General Orders No. 31—a truly extraordinary document: The order expressly prohibited any court in Hawai'i from receiving a petition for a writ of habeas corpus; and, in a move without precedent in American military history since the War of 1812, it made Judge Metzger subject to trial by a military court or commission, with a sentence of up to five years at hard labor if his court did not terminate its orders on the habeas petitions![65] Judge J. Frank McLaughlin—a generally conservative Republican who had been appointed to the federal district court in March 1943 when Judge Stainback became governor—would later declare that General Orders No. 31 was "the most disgraceful threat ever made anywhere against the judicial branch of our government."[66]

The principal legal advisor to Richardson in this confrontation was Colonel William Morrison, the Executive in the Office of the Military Governor (OMG). Assessing Morrison's role in the unfolding drama, a Justice Department investigator, a leading scholar on martial law, would later conclude: "There isn't anyone in the Army who could defend him, no lawyer in the Department of Justice . . . who can defend it. From the point of view of a Congressional investigation, it is really probably the worst black eye of martial law."[67] General Morrison, the investigator continued, not only "showed himself to be a poor lawyer, which is bad, but that he acted like a damn fool, which is much worse."[68]

Morrison had served under Green, and he regularly deferred to Green, seeking advice from him in many aspects of his responsibilities; and so it is likely that Green played a role behind the scenes. In fact, when Richardson issued General Orders No. 31, Green wrote in a communication that an army response had been "prepared" in advance in Hawai'i, anticipating that one day Judge Metzger might take such a tough line on the habeas corpus issue.[69]

General Richardson stood firm in his position, explaining to his superiors that he felt that he "could not depend on any . . . verbal agreement" with Metzger, because he distrusted the judge's honesty. Richardson even stated that he might have found it necessary to "risk the scandal which would result from my seizing in open court the petitioners should Judge Metzger have ordered their release or let them out on bail." Richardson continued:

> We are either under martial law or we are not, and the President has approved the suspension of the privilege of the writ of Habeas Corpus in the Territory. What the Governor and the judge fail to appreciate is that this is a theater of operations in a combat zone, which is very distinct from conditions in the mainland.[70]

Richardson also was unyielding in his contention that it was improper for the court "to initiate and discuss the question of the necessity of martial law in a theater of operations for the reason that it had already been so decided by the President of the United States"—a position that would become one of the more salient legal issues in the course of appellate review that would go forward in later cases.[71]

Officials in Washington were alarmed at the startling turn of events that erupted after Richardson issued his new order. The War Department was sufficiently upset by General Orders No. 31 that it actually delayed its being printed in the *Federal Register*, "recognizing that its publication . . . might serve to operate against the public interest by agitating a controversial matter."[72] Even Assistant Secretary McCloy—who previously had been the reliable defender of the commanding general—confessed discomfiture with "the prospect of a federal judge held in military detention." This situation, he warned Richardson, "would be explosive."[73] McCloy urged Richardson to present to Metzger in court the argument for the necessity of martial law, giving evidence "in very general terms, pointing to the existence of the Japanese fleet and air force, the general sensitivity of the islands to raids, their vital importance in the Pacific war . . . , without disclosing any military information."[74]

Richardson, however, objected to McCloy's suggestion, saying that no matter what he might present to Metzger, the prisoners were going to be ordered released so that "every single general order that we have issued to date would simply go out of the window."[75] Indeed, the prospect of appellate review was appalling to Richardson and his legal staff, and fear that the case might go up to the appellate court doubtless hardened Richardson's stand against Judge Metzger. "If we lost" in Metzger's court, the general told the War Department, "and the cases were then appealed, the most serious consequences would result pending an appellate decision. Every person prosecuted for violation of my General Orders would have the right to apply for a writ of habeas corpus and go free[,] and all enforcement of internal security matters now covered by my General Orders would break down."[76] Richardson then proceeded to identify all the military controls over civilian life that would be jeopardized by an adverse court decision—perhaps inadvertently making clear, in the process, the extent to which the army impinged on the daily activities of Hawai'i's residents:

In other words the lifting of martial law by a court decision or by any other action would have a direct effect on the enforcement of the following items of security: control of [blackout] and curfew, control of restricted areas, waterfront areas and security, regulation of trans-Pacific travel control, control of civilian population during air raids, control of telephone and radio communications, control of the considerable alien population of these islands, . . . control and internment of citizens dangerous to the internal security of the United States, [and] control of all labor here vitally necessary to our war effort. Such labor is controlled by scales of wages and hours[,] and failure to work subjects violators to punishment in Provost Court.[77]

Secretary Ickes, for his part, was unpersuaded by this litany of cascading problems. He regarded Richardson's moves against Judge Metzger as bearing out the wisdom of the constitutional creed that mandated supremacy of civilian government over the military. "I would like to see the courts decide the habeas corpus issue," Ickes wrote to McCloy. "If we are still an orderly and constitutional government the courts are the place to settle that issue."[78] Ironically, Ickes, Garner Anthony, McCloy and other officials privately believed that Judge Metzger had misunderstood the Restoration Agreement as having restored the privilege of the habeas writ.[79] Yet they all sought to bring the controversy to a quick resolution. "I wish that the Judge had not granted the writ of habeas corpus," Ickes confessed, but he deplored the way in which Richardson had gone "completely overboard" in responding: "I shudder to think what some general might do to the President and the Supreme Court over here if he became berserk."[80]

The Justice Department (now enjoying McCloy's cooperation) worked arduously to formulate some kind of compromise that would end the embarrassing impasse. Although McCloy believed that Richardson's action had been unwarranted, he nonetheless asserted that for Richardson to back down without some *quid pro quo* from the judge would "seriously impair his [Richardson's] prestige and his ability to execute his mission."[81]

Ickes, however, was in no mood to compromise. Richardson's rationalizations simply fueled Ickes's already considerable outrage about the army's "takeover" of civilian government in the Islands. And so Ickes now went over McCloy's head, calling on Secretary Stimson to intervene personally. Ickes roundly denounced Richardson's actions. "I should suppose," Ickes wrote, "that no competent lawyer or high ranking officer of the armed forces would any longer question that civil courts, and not military officers, have authority to determine this jurisdiction" with regard to habeas corpus: "It has come to be accepted, in both our judicial and our military institutions that a commanding officer in time of war may feel constrained to defy an order of a civil court, but in so doing he takes his chances with the results of judicial review of his actions, as well as with history. There can be no doubt that the decision as to the validity of his conduct will, in the final reckoning, be determined by the civil courts."[82]

The Justice Department's top-ranking officials similarly regarded General Richardson's action as legally insupportable. The solicitor general, Charles Fahy, advised the War Department that Richardson's worries about his "prestige" deserved no consideration, and he urged McCloy to require an immediate withdrawal of General Orders 31.[83] The Department of the Interior's under secretary, Abe Fortas, declared that both his department and Justice were "absolutely firm" on their demand that the order must be rescinded.[84]

Fortas did not allow to go unnoticed a major irony manifest in the legal situation in which the army now found itself: When the Restoration Agreement had been worked out prior to being issued in March, the Interior officials had proposed that the civilian governor should issue an order explicitly continuing the suspension of the writ of habeas corpus. "The Army made objection to this on grounds that I considered to be fantastic," Fortas recalled, having rested its view on the "absurd proposition" that "once martial law had been declared, control [had] passed to the military government, and that the civilian governor had no further power to do anything in the premises."[85] In order to bring the Restoration negotiations to closure, the Department of the Interior had reluctantly yielded; consequently, the language of the proclamation restoring partial civilian rule had fudged the issue of where power to suspend the writ lay, in the military or, instead, in the civilian governor. "We pointed out to the Army that if legal difficulties arose, the Army would suffer," Fortas wrote; and the army "is now pretty sheepish about the point" as it faced the prospect of bearing entire responsibility for civil liability—or at a minimum, serious political damage—if Judge Metzger's ruling should prevail on an appeal.[86]

The Justice Department and the Army

While the departments back in Washington were exchanging views on General Richardson's actions, Edward Ennis, an attorney with the Justice Department and director of the Alien Enemy Control Unit, was in Honolulu, serving in this instance in the capacity of principal counsel to the army command there. Ennis, too, exerted pressure on Richardson and Morrison to back off from the confrontation with the court. In a lengthy memorandum to General Richardson, Ennis explained why the general's intransigent stand was unacceptable. The issues that had provoked the confrontation with Judge Metzger, he wrote, transcended the boundaries of "a narrow technical, legal problem in which the Commanding General might feel bound to rely on, or justified in relying on, technical legal advice alone."[87] (This was a polite but not subtle way of suggesting that Colonel Morrison's legal counsel should not be taken as a definitive guide to policy.) It was, rather, Ennis continued, a serious *constitutional* problem that Richardson's order had precipitated, involving issues that implicated "[the] long-maintained balance between the Executive and the Judicial branches." Hence the confrontation with Judge Metzger had the potential to blow up into a serious constitutional crisis; therefore, measured wisdom and "no little statesmanship," rather than narrow legal counsel, were required. "In such a situation," Ennis counseled, "a page of history is worth a volume of logic—as Justice Holmes said in another connection"—and "history as well as the law teaches us that G.O. 31 is in error."[88]

Ennis further reminded the general that even at the height of the Battle of Britain, when the military threat was far greater than in Hawai'i in late 1943, the privilege of petition for habeas corpus had not been suspended on a wholesale basis.[89] While Ennis thus founded his advice principally on the view that Richardson should recognize the gravity of long-term constitutional imperatives, he did not neglect to call attention to the shorter-range tactical issues. Although he assured Richardson that he personally was willing to represent the army in any appeal of Judge Metzger's decision—and while, like any lawyer, he would normally relish the opportunity "to conduct such important historical constitutional litigation"—he thought it was foolish to go forward. Besides, Ennis pointed out, the facts behind the decision to detain the two internees did not speak well for the army's chances at prevailing: Glockner, he wrote, had been interned by then "for the unprecedentedly long time of nearly two years, and the case against him is not a strong one." Nor was Seifert a person who posed a clear danger to security in Hawai'i. Hence, Ennis advised, it seemed better to release Glockner and Seifert, and simply remove them to the mainland, far away from the theater of war operations. Moreover, Ennis argued further, it was unwise to trouble the Supreme Court in time of war with issues that could so easily be avoided.[90]

Obviously concerned that legal and tactical counsel in this mild mode might fail to move Richardson and his legal staff to moderate their position, Ennis played a stronger card: In polite but unambiguous terms, he warned that if Richardson failed to rescind General Orders No. 31, it would bring about "a cause célèbre in the courts which could not be successfully defended." Attorney General Biddle himself was "most anxious," Ennis declared, "to avoid any situation in which it would not be possible to represent the military authorities, whom the Department of Justice wishes to represent where any defense is available"![91]

With Richardson and the War Department thus explicitly put on notice that the Justice Department might refuse representation for the army in appellate litigation, the machinery of compromise went into motion. Informal discussions between Ennis and Judge Metzger, with Garner Anthony joining in the process, were followed by Ennis's carrying a compromise proposal to Richardson. He laid out the general terms of an agreement—the details to be worked out by civilian officials in Washington—that would start with rescinding the objectionable order by Richardson. Judge Metzger, though not willing to agree to any implication that his contempt order had been unjustified, compromised by consenting to a reduction of the contempt fine to the nominal sum of $100.[92] Metzger also informally agreed that the prisoners could properly be transferred to the mainland (as Ennis had suggested), thus placing them outside the jurisdiction of Metzger's court in Hawai'i for purposes of ruling on their habeas petitions. It was apparently understood by all parties that the prisoners would then likely be released.[93]

Until the time of this episode, Justice Department lawyers had faithfully represented the Hawai'i command in the courts. But now they had become convinced that the continuation of martial law for such a long period after the Pearl Harbor attack—and especially after the fighting had moved far into the Western Pacific—would very likely be found unconstitutional if a case were to be carried to the Supreme Court for a final judgment.[94] Always lying just beneath the surface of internal discussion was the well-acknowledged fact that the weak or non-existent evidentiary case against the two internees represented a source of potential embarrassment for the army. Indeed, Ennis wrote directly to McCloy to remind him that the army had ordered Glockner to be interned indefinitely despite the fact that he had been fully cleared by the FBI. "There is almost nothing which would suggest that this man is dangerous," Ennis stated; and given the long duration of his internment the appellate courts would probably inquire searchingly into the facts of his case, and such judicial review "in that case might prove embarrassing."[95] The evidence for continuing to imprison Seifert was apparently considered only slightly, if at all, more defensible.

Whether Richardson and Morrison had finally grasped the import of what Ennis was telling them—or instead were ready to persist in their bizarre effort to bully a federal judge—became irrelevant once the War Department indicated agreement with Ennis's position. At this point, no options were left to Richardson other than to release both prisoners on the mainland in October, in order to moot the case. Even then, there was embarrassment for Richardson's command; for the prisoners' release contradicted his earlier public statements, as well as the army counsel's arguments before the district court, that Glockner and Seifert posed a serious danger to security. Now, however, as a judge advocate general officer told McCloy, the army had come to recognize that their release had "the advantage of . . . quick disposition of the case without [a] trial which might disclose sharp division in public opinion, and in any event would focus nation-wide attention on Hawai'i."[96] Both Richardson and Admiral Nimitz now concurred with the view, he reported, that any further proceedings in these two cases would involve "a substantial risk of the full-dress trial which all here [in Richardson's headquarters] consider highly undesirable."[97] The prisoners were thus given their freedom, although not before the army demanded that each of them sign the standard waiver that relieved the military of any liability for false arrest or other wrongful deprivation of the internees' rights.[98]

And so cool heads prevailed, while at the same time Richardson's subordination to civilian control from the War Department had been reasserted (at least on this issue), and misguided counsel from Richardson's legal officers in headquarters had been discredited. In the federal district courtroom in Honolulu, however, the memory of this effort to intimidate Judge Metzger did not fade. On the contrary, it became a vital element shaping the context of future proceedings in his court.

Continued Deadlock

Intensifying the anger of the army's civilian critics—including, not least of all, the top officials in the Justice Department and the Department of the Interior—was the way in which General Richardson and his legal advisers were still resisting any new concessions as to the restoration of civilian government. Writing to McCloy in the fall of 1943, however, Richardson defended both the necessity and the popularity of martial law: "Security measures now in effect could not be enforced under civil control. As a matter of fact, martial law imposes no hardship on anyone in this community. Nor does it really deprive the civil authorities of any [sic] of their real powers to administer the Territory. I feel certain that if a plebiscite could be taken, 95 per cent of the population would vote for martial law."[99]

Neither Governor Stainback nor Territorial Attorney General Anthony believed that the army was ever going to yield its prerogatives so long as the war went on. Moreover, they had even begun to worry about the prospects for a return to normal civilian control *after* the war. A special report prepared by Anthony in September set forth anew the legal arguments against the legitimacy of army rule; it also surveyed the factual situation in Hawai'i that bore on the issue of "military necessity" as a justification for suspension of civil liberties. Despite the president's instructions at the time the Restoration Agreement formally went into effect on March 10, there had "not been a single instance of such a move" toward accomplishing the "gradual and complete restoration of civil authority" that had been an explicit objective of the program, although the military situation had greatly improved.[100]

Anthony reiterated the argument that in approving the declaration of martial law just after Pearl Harbor, President Roosevelt had not approved "the transfer of the Government of the Territory to the Army and the appointment of a 'Military Governor'"—neither of which could have been done legally by the president in any event, Anthony contended, since it would have exceeded presidential authority under terms of the Hawai'i Organic Act.[101] This fact cast doubt on the legality of provost court decisions involving civilian defendants, Anthony asserted; and so he warned that some 123 prisoners, sentenced to terms from 6 months to life imprisonment and being held in the O'ahu Prison, might need to be freed altogether or at least retried. Moreover, the provost courts were continuing to operate under procedures and authority "[not] contemplated by the constitution or laws of the United States or the Territory." This situation was perpetuating a "needless invasion of the civil liberties of our people," he wrote, but it also suggested "the possibility of liability of our government officials in holding those incarcerated without a valid conviction."[102]

Anthony cited chapter and verse as to the invalidity of the army's claim that "military necessity" required continuance of army rule: the courts were open and functioning with wide jurisdiction already ceded, grand juries and trial juries were restored, and all the major agricultural and commercial enterprises of the Islands were in full operation. The territorial legislature and county boards of supervisors were meeting normally, he pointed out, while air and steamer schedules had been regularized, and emergency measures such as those requiring troops to carry side-arms had long ago been terminated. In sum, Anthony concluded, the standard for return to civilian governance, as prescribed in the *Milligan* case, had been fully met. This standard, he contended, was clearly "that the moment that order is restored the necessity for martial law (hence its justification) ceases to exist."[103]

Anthony believed that the decision in *Ex parte Quirin*[104]—reaffirming the doctrine that "the constitutional safeguards of civil liberty" applied in wartime emergencies, assuring access to procedural review in the federal courts—taken together with the *Milligan* precedent, absolutely required an end to army rule. It should be done, he contended, by a joint proclamation of Governor Stainback and the commanding general, and should include immediate abandonment of the self-assigned title "Military Governor." Any security concerns could easily be addressed, as they had been addressed on the mainland, by implementation of the president's Executive Order No. 9066, under which the Japanese-American population had been evacuated from prescribed military areas, and by the congressional legislation of March 1942 that had validated in statutory form this order's terms.

Thus, Hawai'i could be designated a military area, and citizens who were found dangerous on loyalty or security grounds, Anthony went on to contend in his report, could be excluded from Hawai'i, but with "basic requirements of due process" enforced in a federal court. Once excluded from Hawai'i, Anthony proposed, they "would be free to move about other parts of the United States, except other designated military areas"—in marked contrast to the incarceration of the West-Coast Japanese Americans, who were interned or held in camps run by the War Relocation Authority. Distinguishing his suggested plan from the procedures followed with the roundup of suspected Japanese Americans in Hawai'i, who were afforded no due process, Anthony wrote: "This would involve a minimum infringement on the liberties of the citizen and at the same time adequately secure the public safety." Aliens could be interned in Hawai'i as they were on the mainland—with actions against them, however, always subject to judicial oversight. In that way, any army orders that might be challenged as violating civil liberties would be reviewed in an orderly manner in the courts, in accord with constitutional procedures. If a genuine emergency should occur, "martial law . . . could be proclaimed in a moment."[105] In the longer run, Anthony predicted, the citizenry's acquiescence in suspension of constitutional liberty would weaken the dedication to self-government under a regime of rights and of consent. Such was the ultimate danger.[106]

Anthony's suggestion for exclusion and internment, if necessary, should not be taken as evidence that he treated such sanctions lightly. Indeed, in June 1943 Anthony had delivered a commencement address at the University of Hawai'i in which he forthrightly condemned the mass incarceration of Japanese Americans on the mainland as a policy "savor[ing] of fascism in one of its ugliest forms—the mass condemnation of people simply because of the accident of birth, their racial ancestry." He saw no place in a democratic society for "concentration camps" such as had been proposed for Hawai'i at the war's outset.[107]

In the months ahead, Anthony—who stepped down as territorial attorney general in December 1943, but would then serve as pro bono counsel in the *Duncan* litigation and appeals to plead his case against the army—had ample opportunity to argue his position in the courts. There is little doubt that the army's behavior in threatening coercive action against Judge Metzger did much to confirm Anthony's dedication to his cause and the zeal with which he would pursue his campaign against martial law, both in the academic journals and before the federal judiciary.[108] Similarly, the imbroglio that pitted Richardson against virtually the whole civil establishment, not only Judge Metzger, reaffirmed for Ickes and his circle in Washington the view that "democratic government is jeopardized by military encroachments on civil authority."[109] It was a controlling premise for Ickes that, "if the dignity of our civilian government institutions is not upheld during times of stress, constitutional government as we conceive it will be in more danger from our own neglect than from the efforts of our enemies."[110] Based on that canonical belief, the efforts of the Department of the Interior to end martial law and restore civilian supremacy were unremitting. This, too, formed part of the essential background to the drama that was going forward in the courts.

The army command in Hawai'i found it disconcerting that no Japanese-American internee had stepped forward to petition for a writ of habeas corpus during the war, for the military lawyers were confident that the federal courts would be strongly inclined to uphold the military's powers under martial law if the petitioner were of Japanese ancestry.[111] Accordingly, after accepting the decision to release Glockner and Seifert on the mainland, General Richardson ordered the two remaining foreign-born internees of European ancestry to be transferred there as well, outside the jurisdiction of Judge Metzger's court. This action would assure absolutely, the general explained to McCloy, that "in the event of another [internee] case arising in the courts it will have to be that of a Japanese."[112] In this respect, however, Richardson and his legal aides were to be disappointed.

Chapter Fourteen

NEW HABEAS CASES

The Provost Courts on Trial

The next phase of the legal challenge to army rule was initiated by three prisoners who had been convicted by the provost courts for ordinary crimes rather than having been taken into custody and interned as alleged loyalty or security risks.[1] Unlike the earlier petitioners for habeas—Zimmerman, Seifert, and Glockner, all of them naturalized German-American citizens—the three petitioners who came forward in this phase were native-born citizens. The sentences the new petitioners were serving had been imposed by the provost courts for criminal violations of territorial law committed just before the war, or for violations of the military government's general orders under martial law.

The *Duncan* Case

The first round of the new litigations came in March 1944 in the case of Lloyd Duncan, a civilian shipyard worker who had been convicted by a provost court the previous month for assault on two military sentries. He was given a six-month prison sentence. The prison authorities had forced him to engage in hard labor, though the sentence had not called for it.[2] Duncan's petition for a writ of habeas corpus was presented to Judge Metzger's court by Garner Anthony, who had recently resigned his post as territorial attorney general. He had taken on Duncan's case on a pro bono basis, in hopes of obtaining a definitive judgment on the legitimacy of the martial law regime as it affected criminal process. His petition contended that as a factual matter, a claim of "military necessity" could no longer justify denying a civilian citizen his right to a jury trial in a civil court; that the civil courts were open and capable of handling the case; and that, under the *Milligan* rule, the provost court's proceeding in Duncan's case was therefore unconstitutional.[3]

This time General Richardson recognized that he had no choice but to appear as respondent in Judge Metzger's court and to produce the prisoner. There ensued a full-dress trial over a week's time, producing the most voluminous transcript ever generated up to that time in the federal district court in Honolulu. The proceedings received wide publicity in the local press, and they also attracted significant attention from mainland newspapers and media commentators. Both Richardson and Admiral Chester Nimitz, the highly respected commander of the Pacific Fleet, testified under oath that martial law in its fullest reach needed to be upheld. Nimitz asserted that Hawai'i remained in "constant, continuous and imminent danger of invasion by Japanese forces from the air, as well as by Japanese commando raiders and espionage parties landing from submarines." In that situation, both command officers asserted, the determination of military necessity was the army's prerogative and no one else's, certainly not a federal judge's.[4]

The opposing view, embodied in Anthony's brief, was presented in lengthy testimony by Governor Stainback, who of course had been consistently opposed to army control of civil affairs since first taking office in 1942. He now stated once again his belief that civilian courts rather than provost courts should have jurisdiction over non-war-related crimes. He testified that the army's actions in the case were insupportable, and that under Hawai'i's own statutes covering war emergencies, his administration and the ordinary civilian courts had ample power and resources to deal effectively with any case involving crimes of this sort.[5] For his part, General Richardson was convinced that Stainback was bent on "harassing" him and wanted to undermine the military's prestige with the citizenry.

An especially awkward scene for the army occurred when three territorial judges gave sworn testimony, all in support of Duncan. Samuel Kemp, who had served since mid-1941 as chief justice of the Hawai'i Supreme Court, followed by the senior judge of the Honolulu District Court and a circuit court judge, all testified that the civilian courts on which they sat were "ready, willing, and prepared to perform their normal functions" months before Duncan was arrested and convicted by the military.[6]

In a moment of high drama during cross-examination, General Richardson glared at Garner Anthony from the witness stand and accused him of "trying to weaken my authority" by challenging the measures that Richardson insisted were essential to ensure the security of the Islands. Anthony quietly responded: "All I am trying to do, General, is to give this boy . . . a fair trial under the Constitution of the United States."[7] This incident might easily have caused Anthony endless trouble in the civilian community, as it reflected on his loyalty in support of the war effort—although he himself was a veteran who had volunteered for combat duty in World War I. The timing of this dramatic exchange was significant, for Richardson's top legal officer, General Morrison, had been covertly urging some of Anthony's most important business clients to drop his firm as their attorneys because of Anthony's criticism of the military regime. Anthony was aware of this effort as being intended to "intimidate" and silence him, as he termed it. An official postwar investigation confirmed the extent of Morrison's deviousness, documenting that he had urged local executives to boycott any attorney who represented a client in a habeas proceeding, and "to transfer their law business to other lawyers who wouldn't bring habeas corpus suits."[8]

Edward Ennis, the army's counsel in the trial (as he had been in the Glockner and Seifert trials), defused the situation in the courtroom immediately after Richardson's exchange with Anthony. Rising to his feet, Ennis declared forcefully:

> So far as the Department of Justice is concerned—*and I want to speak for the Department of Justice and the Attorney General in this respect*—that we, of course, do not feel that the bringing of an action of this kind is in any way an attempt to take an antagonistic or unpatriotic or improper attitude towards the Government. I would like to state for myself, and I know for the attorney general . . . , that we consider it a helpful thing for an attorney to have the courage of his convictions to present to the court the issues as he sees them. And we feel that the interest of a member of the bar, and of the bar generally, in pursuing these questions . . . is commendable and furthers the interest of all of us in living under a regime of law.[9]

Ennis thus affirmed, for the public no less than for those in the courtroom, that Anthony's vigorous representation of Duncan was consistent with the ethical obligation of an attorney properly seeking to clarify an important constitutional question. It is a fair presumption that this intervention also defused what might potentially have been a nasty public reaction to Anthony's criticisms of military rule.

Pictured, left to right, are: Edward J. Ennis, special assistant to the U.S. attorney general on assignment as counsel to the army; J. Garner Anthony, attorney for the petitioner Duncan; Nils Tavares, territorial attorney general (standing); and Governor Ingram Stainback, preparing for the historic habeas corpus proceeding, the Duncan trial. Credit: *Honolulu Star-Bulletin* photo, courtesy of HWRD, University of Hawai'i.

After extended testimony on both sides, Judge Metzger ruled on April 13 against the army and issued the writ, ordering Duncan to be released from custody. The text of Metzger's release order reiterated his view, in agreement with contentions made in the early habeas petitions, that the continued army prohibition on his court's hearing of any habeas petitions had been illegal under the terms of the Interior–Justice–War Department "restoration" agreement from the moment that it went into effect in March 1943.[10] The army had no authority either under the Restoration Agreement or under the prevailing statutes, Metzger ruled, for continuing to try civilians in the provost courts for ordinary crimes.

Metzger's ruling was an impassioned assertion of the primacy of civilian government even in wartime:

> Some countries in Europe have tried a dictator system where the dictator could peremptorily pronounce laws and the rights of the subject to life and liberty, as he and his self-appointed courts and executives might decide from time to time. Many views have been advanced that such is the correct and efficient system for successfully conducting war, but that system is now on its way out. It is the antithesis of Americanism, and nothing short of riotous conditions and dissolution of lawfully constituted government can justify it in civilian affairs of the land.
>
> Civil affairs and civil government extend, in operation of law, to the battle zone or military camps, even in time of war.[11]

While acknowledging Nimitz's and Richardson's arguments that "martial law is desirable and necessary" in some circumstances, Metzger declared himself bound "not by their opinions, but by the laws of the land, . . . primarily, the national Constitution, and secondarily, the laws enacted by the Congress."

Conceding that civilians engaged in war activities are subject to military law and court martial for certain offenses while serving in the field of battle, he nonetheless rejected the army's position on the continuing need for the provost courts: "No part of the Island of Oahu in the Territory of Hawaii is in a battle field today," Metzger declared, "nor has it been for over two years, nor was the petitioner serving the Army in the field."

Turning to the military's argument that martial law was necessary because of the presence of the large ethnic Japanese population, Metzger stated that the army and navy should, if necessary, ask Congress for additional legislation to provide "protection against subversive or suspicious Japanese aliens, or even native-born persons of alien parentage," rather than "holding by force of arms an entire population under a form of helpless and unappealable subjugation called martial law or military government." Only Congress—not the War Department, nor even the group of high-level cabinet officials that had crafted the Restoration Agreement—can lawfully give the Territory of Hawai'i its form of government, he declared. Under the Organic Act, the governor could declare martial law. But even at the time of the December 1942 meeting in Washington, all grounds for the army's claim of necessity had passed; by then, the civil government was fully capable of operating efficiently, and the governor "had no more authority to declare it [martial law] in part than in whole." Further, Judge Metzger ruled, Governor Poindexter could not legally transfer or abdicate his responsibilities to execute the laws of the Territory of Hawai'i, and its government could not be vested in the hands of the commanding general: "The right to establish martial law under Sec. 67 of the Organic Act springs from the necessity arising from disorders such as disrupt and make inoperative civil government and it ceases and becomes unlawful as soon as the civil government is capable and willing to resume its normal functions." And so, in a sweeping indictment of the whole system of military government, Metzger concluded: "[T]he office of Military Governor of the Territory of Hawaii is without lawful creation and, as such office, possesses no lawful authority over civilian affairs or persons."

Ironically, the judge's reading of the restoration proclamation's language on this particular point was probably in error, as the major actors in the negotiations that had produced the Restoration Agreement—including Ickes, Fortas, Farrington, McCloy, and Anthony himself—all interpreted it. For example, Secretary Ickes stated in a letter to McCloy: "We agree with you that it was our intention that martial law should be continued. We might disagree as to whether or not an end could be put now, or at least in the future, to martial law, but I have no disposition to set my judgment in that matter against that of the War Department."[12] Similarly, Under Secretary Fortas recognized that the preamble to the proclamation had expressly referred to continuation of the suspension of the writ of habeas corpus, at the same time restoring regular civilian governmental functions; and he indicated that Metzger had misunderstood the text when he adopted Governor Stainback's view of the document and its terms. "I don't see any way out of this thing except to litigate it," Fortas said. "I don't think we can very well get into a situation where the C[ommanding] G[eneral] is openly in defiance of a court order, even though the court order may be unsound."[13] And so Metzger's interpretation stood for the moment. It remained for the higher courts, on an appeal, to address that issue more definitively.[14]

The *White* Case

Compounding the army's problems was another case that came up immediately after the *Duncan* case before Metzger's colleague on the district court in Hawai'i, Judge J. Frank McLaughlin. The petitioner in this instance was Harry White, a Honolulu stockbroker who had been tried, convicted, and sentenced in August 1942 by a provost court of embezzling $3,240 from clients' funds. White had questioned the jurisdiction of the provost court over both his crime (a purely civil offense, in violation of Hawai'i statutes) and his person (as a civilian not engaged in military work), but he was overruled. He had also demanded—and been denied—both a jury trial and time to prepare his defense. Serving a five-year term for this civil offense, he, too, claimed in his first petition for habeas relief that no military necessity existed to justify military trials of civilians and that his trial by a military tribunal was a violation of his basic constitutional rights.[15]

Judge McLaughlin ruled against the government and ordered White freed. Like Metzger, McLaughlin based his decision on broad legal grounds. He declared that the civilian governor's transfer to the army of all power over civilian justice, dating from Pearl Harbor Day, December 7, 1941, had been "absolutely and wholly invalid" from the very start. Nothing in American law, he declared, gave a governor such authority. McLaughlin echoed Metzger's ruling, rejecting the army's claim that military necessity was a matter for the military's judgment exclusively. To proclaim a military emergency "does not make it so," McLaughlin wrote; "Necessity cannot be manufactured even by General Orders. It must be real, not artificial."[16]

The *Spurlock* Case

Meanwhile the army's authority was challenged in yet another habeas case, this one involving a civilian former war worker named Fred Spurlock. He was described by General Richardson as "a Negro, age 32 originally from the State of Alabama," who (the general claimed, apparently erroneously) had a record of previous arrests for "crimes of violence."[17] In fact, Spurlock had been in provost court on only two occasions. The first involved a charge of assaulting a police officer. In November 1941, Spurlock had run away from a bar where a "bouncer" had threatened him, and he accidently collided head-on with two military policemen, who turned him over to a civilian police officer. His case was continued until January, when he was brought before a provost court and sentenced to five years in prison. Thus Spurlock was tried by a provost court for an offense committed before the army had taken control of the courts; and like White, he was given a sentence far in excess of sentences customarily imposed by peacetime civilian courts in Hawai'i for the same crime. At Spurlock's pleading, his sentence was initially suspended, and he was awarded probation.

Soon afterward, however, he was arrested again, this time for a fight with another civilian that was described as "a cutting affair." Hauled into provost court in March 1942 and charged with assault with a weapon, he was allowed no chance to testify and given no time to call witnesses. The army officer sitting as provost judge summarily reinstituted the five-year sentence, and Spurlock was taken to prison immediately. The entire proceeding took five to ten minutes at most. While in prison, Spurlock was held in the prison's "incorrigible unit" because of "further misconduct," or so Richardson alleged.[18]

More than two years later, in May 1944, Spurlock, still incarcerated, petitioned for a habeas writ in a letter to Judge McLaughlin. Upon first receiving the petition, McLaughlin approved Spurlock's request for a court-ordered appointment of an attorney in recognition of the prisoner's lack of funds to employ counsel. General Morrison was outraged. This appointment of "pauper's counsel," he asserted, would set off a deluge of habeas petitions from other prisoners who had been convicted by the provost courts. Authorized by General Richardson, he requested the War Department's support for a plan to seek from the Ninth Circuit or the Supreme Court a writ of prohibition "which would terminate actions of this type . . . pending a decision in the Duncan and White Cases."[19] Morrison's plan found no support in the War Department. But after hearing argument by counsel, McLaughlin ordered the prisoner to be released, ruling that the provost court judge had dealt so summarily with Spurlock that a gross denial of due process was determinative.[20] And so the army appealed the decision in the Ninth Circuit, along with the appeals of the *White* and *Duncan* cases.

Judge McLaughlin's order freeing Spurlock carried significance beyond the case itself. A conservative Republican who had served as the chairman of the internment review board for the Big Island, McLaughlin did not share his colleague Judge Metzger's liberal, pro-labor record in politics and private practice prior to being elevated to the bench. Nonetheless, the two judges were agreed on the matter of whether the trial of civilians by military courts was permissible under martial law on the sole judgment of the military authorities and without recourse to judicial review of an alleged "military necessity." As he had done in his habeas order freeing White, McLaughlin in *Spurlock* again rejected that argument as contrary to the basic terms of the Constitution in its protection of individual liberties. To leave the determination of necessity exclusively in the hands of the commander, he declared, and to deny that the factual foundation on which the claim "necessity" rested must be immune from judicial review, was a "specious doctrine." By that very doctrine, McLaughlin said,

> did Hitler and his ilk rise to dictatorial power. . . . Under our form of government the military even in time of war is subordinate to the civil power, not superior to it. During war, the military to be sure is allowed a wide range of discretion, but whether it has abused that discretion is a judicial question.[21]

In granting habeas in Spurlock's case, McLaughlin also called attention to the lack of due process, stating that "even if it be said that thus to try civilians in provost courts was necessary because the General said so, Spurlock did not even receive a fair military trial. Surely the Constitution assures him that much."[22]

Thus did the two district court judges in Hawai'i lay down the gauntlet, resting their challenge to martial law and its military courts on terms that echoed the essential constitutional arguments regarding "necessity" that had been voiced from the first months of the war by Garner Anthony and had been subsequently reiterated in academic and political discourse by other critics of army rule. The army's stubborn resistance to this criticism continued undiminished, despite the fact that the site of intensive combat in the Pacific theater was now more than two thousand miles away from Hawai'i. It remained to be seen, however, whether the Ninth Circuit would uphold the army's intransigence in its review of the three cases coming before it now.

The confrontation over martial law meanwhile had come to a stalemate, both legally and politically. How long this situation could be held in equipoise was already a matter for speculation, since the army was now facing new and increasingly formidable challenges.

Strategy and Lawyering in the *Duncan* and *White* Appeals

The army's briefs appealing to the Ninth Circuit all three rulings were officially filed in June 1944. The military's lawyers in the Hawai'i command hoped, however, that the Ninth Circuit could be bypassed and that the Supreme Court would agree to take the cases directly. There was a far better chance, they believed, that the Supreme Court would uphold the validity of martial law while American troops were still in the field than if the case came up after victory had been won. Thus one of General Richardson's principal legal officers, Colonel E. V. Slattery, had predicted in a February 1944 memorandum:

> The military will have its strongest position politically before the Court while the war is on. After the war it is possible that the military may be relegated in our social system to the place where it was for many years following the last war and prior to the present war. Once the war is over the Courts will find it much easier to be critical of the actions of the military.[23]

Significantly, Slattery's memorandum went on to consider a different, more explicitly self-serving argument on behalf of the individual army officers who had administered martial law: that failure to prosecute the appeals vigorously "would act as an inducement for further actions or suits," and that such suits could result in civil damage judgments in favor of persons wronged by military courts or administration.[24] This concern was hardly new. Previously, as we have noted, the army had made a practice of demanding waivers of civil liability from internees whom it released.[25]

While the *Duncan* and *White* appeals were going forward, the judge advocate general's staff in Washington similarly became explicitly concerned about the possibility that an adverse judgment in the Supreme Court in these cases might lead to a rash of "civil damage suits against any and all, the General, the Admiral, and everybody else."[26] General Richardson himself admitted, in his correspondence with Washington, that the threat of civil suits—or even criminal actions against him and his subordinates— "has been paramount in our minds throughout the entire litigation of the Duncan and White cases."[27]

A particularly intriguing feature of the litigation at this juncture was the role of Edward Ennis, the Justice Department lawyer assigned by the solicitor general to represent the army both in the district court and in the Ninth Circuit. The archival evidence clearly shows that Ennis performed his duties as counsel with serious misgivings about the merits of the cases he was litigating. As early as October 1942, when the army was involved in the Zimmerman appeal in the Ninth Circuit, Ennis had expressed in private correspondence with army officials his doubts about the constitutionality of martial law in Hawai'i.[28] In April 1943, Ennis wrote to Attorney General Biddle that he regarded it as his role to represent the army as a matter of the Department's "legal duty in a doubtful legal situation," but his arguments in court were not to be taken as "a complete policy approval" of the army's views of its authority under martial law.[29] And a few months later, Ennis was quoted in a Honolulu newspaper as saying that denial of the right of the writ of habeas corpus was not appropriate in cases "involving . . . matters of no interest to the military authorities."[30] Ennis's statement certainly served to cast serious doubt on the propriety of the army's stand in the *White* case, which involved merely embezzlement by a stock broker—a civil offense that had no palpable connection to security or defense of the Islands. Subsequently, Ennis advised the solicitor general that more generally he regarded as "probably unconstitutional" the suspension of habeas corpus in Hawai'i.[31]

Ennis was not the only one who harbored doubts about the possibility of success for the government in defending the army in the *Duncan* and *White* appeals. For even among lawyers in the Army General Staff offices, the view was gaining strength that "the War Department position on martial law in Hawai'i is becoming indefensible" insofar as any arguments based upon military necessity were concerned.[32] Indeed, at the very time General Richardson and Admiral Nimitz were testifying in Judge Metzger's courtroom that the Islands remained in imminent danger of enemy attack, the War Department was in the process of reorganizing its Central Pacific command, downgrading Hawai'i from the status of a combat zone to that of a "communications zone."[33]

Still another unusual aspect of the litigation was a division within the cabinet departments as to the desirable outcome of the appeals in the *Duncan* and *White* cases. These differences led to the involvement of civilian government lawyers in quietly aiding the case for Duncan against the army. The Department of the Interior lawyers, supported by Ickes and his under secretary, Abe Fortas, had long regarded the military's regime in Hawai'i as of doubtful constitutionality (or worse, as simply a ruthless power grab by the generals). Now, anticipating a hearing before the Supreme Court, attorneys in the Interior Department's solicitor's office quietly cooperated with Garner Anthony, who was then preparing a brief for Duncan, in providing him with office space and with file materials that he and the legal team representing Duncan could use for the appellate briefs.[34]

In summary, by late 1944 the army itself was prepared to abandon its established tactic of repeatedly mooting habeas cases rather than permitting the Supreme Court to make a definitive ruling on martial law. Instead, there was now evident eagerness to have the Supreme Court decide the pending appeals while the war was still being fought in the Pacific. And in the background was the concern expressed by General Richardson and other officers about their exposure to civil indemnification suits, should martial law be found invalid. Meanwhile, the principal counsel in litigation for the army, Edward Ennis, was giving voice privately to his serious doubts as to the cause for which he was committed to argue; and in the Interior Department, legal talent was being devoted behind the scenes to helping Anthony prepare his case against the army.

The Ninth Circuit Decision

It was thus in a highly unstable political and legal context that the Supreme Court, to the army's dismay, declined to accept direct review of the *Duncan, White,* and *Spurlock* cases. The appeals therefore went ahead in the Ninth Circuit on July 1, 1944, and were heard there. In November 1944, the circuit court's opinion came down, as it had in the earlier habeas cases from Hawai'i, reversing Judges Metzger's and McLaughlin's orders.[35] The court's majority not only upheld in sweeping terms the military's authority to punish a criminal defendant such as Duncan because he had attacked a sentry or military policeman; but they also approved the provost courts' jurisdiction under martial law to embrace ordinary civil cases such as the case of White, the stockbroker who had embezzled private funds, and of Spurlock, who had assaulted another civilian. The "summary punishment of criminal offenders of every sort," one judge noted, "might conceivably serve to discourage the commission of offenses" dangerous to the general security.[36]

The majority also endorsed explicitly the army's argument that the continued presence in Hawai'i of Japanese Americans "of doubtful loyalty" in alarming (if unspecified) numbers "posed a continuous threat to public security" and warranted the extraordinary, long-extended suspension of constitutional liberties for all civilians there. That the civilian courts "were disabled from functioning," the majority stated, made military trials necessary in August 1942, and they were no less essential in March 1944.[37] (That the courts were "disabled" only because the army had decided to disable them—as counsel for the prisoners had pleaded, and as Judge McLaughlin had stressed in his habeas orders—was a point that the opinion did not address.)

In a concurring opinion, Judge Curtis D. Wilbur ruled that Roosevelt's letter of February 1, 1943, authorizing the War Department to partially restore civilian rule, implicitly continued martial law in areas not conceded to the civilian authorities.[38] Wilbur's opinion declared: "We hold that in view of the existence of a global war in which this nation is involved, and from the facts shown in evidence [by military and naval authorities] in the court below, the courts cannot say the decision of the military authorities or of the Governor of Hawaii to continue such suspension [of the habeas privilege] is so arbitrary, capricious or fraudulent as to justify the courts in ignoring the action of the military authorities."[39]

In the original district court hearing on White's petition, Judge McLaughlin had ruled that the legitimate reach of army authority under martial law must be understood according to the *Milligan* doctrine—that is, that "the necessity is determined upon and in relation to the then existing facts."[40] The evaluation of the "then existing facts," McLaughlin wrote, was in the last analysis always a matter for *judicial* determination;

the army's own statement of military necessity did not make it a fact.[41] The Ninth Circuit took an entirely different view on this key point of law. The majority asserted that the military itself had the authority to determine the extent of danger and the measures required to protect the "fortress" and its population.[42]

In this manner, then, the ground was marked out for the Supreme Court to rule on a question of central importance to the cases. In Spurlock's case, which turned more on the issue of due process than of jurisdiction, the Ninth Circuit court declared that in wartime, when habeas corpus has been suspended, *a civilian is not entitled even to a military trial:* a civilian can be charged in a military court and found guilty and sentenced summarily, and such action by the military is not subject to judicial inquiry.[43]

A dissenting opinion by Judge Albert Lee Stephens, who contended that the military had exceeded its authority, was distributed to the judges; but at Stephens's request his opinion was withheld from publication until 1946.[44] When Stephens did finally release his dissenting opinion in the circuit court's subsequent *Duncan* appeal, he explained that he had suppressed the document because he had feared in 1944 that open dissent "had more possibility of harm than of good" with the war still waging.

Duncan, White, and Spurlock all petitioned for the writ of certiorari, asking the Supreme Court to review the decision of the Ninth Circuit. The writ was granted in the *Duncan* and *White* cases, which went forward jointly. However, in the case of Spurlock, who had already served nearly three years without even having a legal trial, the army (with Ennis probably playing a major role) decided to moot the case by pardoning Spurlock, thus assuring that the Supreme Court would not hear a further appeal.[45] The decision in the *Spurlock* case was yet another instance of mooting a case in which army justice in Hawai'i had been based on an insupportable factual foundation; moreover, the provost judge had dealt so arbitrarily with the defendant that McLaughlin had ruled he could free the prisoner on that ground alone.

In summary, then, of the six habeas cases that had challenged martial law, four were mooted, while only *Duncan* and *White* would be taken to the highest court for final judgment on the legality of army rule.[46]

PART VI

The End of Martial Law

Chapter Fifteen

RISING PROTESTS

The dramatic *Duncan* case trial was given wide attention in the mainland press as well as locally during the spring months of 1944, focusing a bright political spotlight on army rule and on the constitutional issues that were being litigated. Criticism of the army came now not only from liberal commentators who were concerned about civil liberties, but also from some conservative Republicans who were eager to find soft spots in the political armor of the wartime Roosevelt presidency.

Critics from both political parties began to publish articles and editorials disapproving of the army's policies in Hawai'i. Indeed, the press criticism had emerged before the 1944 election year, most notably at the time of the confrontation between Judge Metzger and General Richardson. As early as August 1943, the fiercely conservative Republican *Chicago Daily Tribune* had run a Honolulu dispatch that gave publicity to Hawai'i lawyers' concerns about the suspension of civilian courts' jurisdiction; it also reported the sentiment in the Hawai'i bar that General Richardson's extraordinary executive order threatening Judge Metzger with imprisonment amounted to "bayonet rule"! The Chicago paper also quoted Dean Emeritus Roscoe Pound of the Harvard Law School as saying that Judge Metzger's actions against the general were consistent not only with what was permissible but what "was his duty" in regard to habeas corpus.[1]

The Duncan trial brought increased criticism of the continued restrictions on civilian life in Hawai'i, with many influential newspapers asserting the imperative of civil liberties. One important constant factor was the manifest absence of any direct threat of attack by Japan. Thus the *Louisville Courier-Journal* declared that martial law could be justified only in the face of "urgent danger from hostile forces" and when civilian government was unable to handle its ordinary functions properly, which was "obviously not" the situation in Hawai'i.[2] The *San Francisco Daily News* applauded the district court judges in Hawai'i for proving "so zealous in their tendency to protect the right of habeas corpus . . . [which is] the principal legal barrier that stands between civil authority and military dictatorship."[3] Another San Francisco paper, the *San Francisco*

Chronicle, also supported the rulings by Judges Metzger and McLaughlin, insisting that their decisions would "keep the principle of civil rights intact for after-war purposes," an objective that transcended immediate military expediency.[4] Similar approval of the district courts' vindication of civil liberties was voiced in a *Boston Herald* editorial declaring that if the *Duncan* habeas petition failed in the courts, it would amount to "a literal perversion of the Constitution."[5] Of special potential influence was a signed article in the *Washington Post* by the respected journalist and historian Merlo Pusey, who wrote:

> When the victory is won and the excitement of war subsides we are going to be very much ashamed of two policies now in effect. They are the mistreatment of loyal American citizens of Japanese origin and the prolongation of military government in Hawaii. In both instances the constitutional rights of citizens have been flagrantly violated, and even if we assume that those encroachments were necessary in the first place, they have been extended much longer than any military necessity seems to justify.[6]

The crowning blow amidst this mounting press criticism came when the Republican *Chicago Daily Tribune* published another editorial in July 1944 blasting the Roosevelt administration for tolerating a lawless regime of raw military power in Hawai'i.[7] Its publication came at a time when the Department of the Interior was stepping up its efforts to achieve further restoration of civilian powers in the Islands—and when Under Secretary Fortas was confronted with the usual, unyielding resistance from the army and from the War Department.[8] Fortas leapt upon the opportunity to sound an alarm, forwarding a copy of the *Tribune* editorial to John McCloy, commenting wryly: "Certainly, neither you nor I should tolerate the continuation of a situation which permits that great liberal journal, the *Chicago Tribune,* to attack us as violating a fundamental principle of our constitutional government"![9]

There were also stirrings of politically damaging criticism from some members of Congress, with one representative from Michigan, for example, charging that military rule in Hawai'i embodied "hateful ideals and the political methods of our enemies."[10] And in response to an Interior official's testimony that continuance of martial law in Hawai'i was "unnecessary under conditions as they exist now," the chairman of the House subcommittee considering appropriations for the territories in April 1944 expressed astonishment: "I am amazed at the statement here . . . that we still have martial law in the Hawaiian islands."[11]

Within Hawai'i, criticism of martial law was also coming from the territorial bar association, which was taking an increasingly assertive stance in favor of restoration of full normal jurisdiction for civil courts and reinstitution of jury trials. At a special meeting of the association at the time when the *Duncan* habeas trial was about to commence, a resolution calling for restoration of the civilian justice system won nearly unanimous consent.[12]

The War Department and the army command in Hawai'i tended, however, to dismiss the bar association's complaints as self-serving, on grounds that the lawyers had an economic interest in restoration of jury trials and the full operation of civilian justice. This had been the military's reaction for a long time. Thus, in mid-1942 General Green had reported to Washington that martial law was supported by the public, the only significant problem being "some local sniping at the theory of Military government, principally, I am ashamed to say, by brothers of the legal profession."[13] A few months later, following a brief visit to Hawai'i in 1942, Assistant Secretary of War McCloy gave the White House a similarly benign view of civilian approval of the army regime, writing that "the considerable agitation among the lawyers" was the only exception to public satisfaction with martial law in Hawai'i.[14] General Richardson later echoed this mantra: "It is very strange," he wrote in 1946, "that during the entire period of martial law it was rare that there was ever a complaint over its administration except from a few lawyers in the community."[15] Disingenuously or otherwise, neither the army command nor the War Department ever appeared willing to acknowledge the possibility that the public dissatisfaction might have been muted because of the intimidating effect of army rule (including censorship) and the provost courts' arbitrary judicial regime.

When the local organized bar adopted its 1944 resolution criticizing martial law, it drew fire not only from the army but also from some civilian leaders who condemned it as a hindrance to prosecution of the war; and so the potential for implications of lack of patriotism and for ugly recriminations was great. Once again, however, the Justice Department's Edward Ennis played a vital moderating role, just as he had done during the proceedings in Judge Metzger's court. Speaking before the bar association meeting that called for an end to martial law, Ennis declared that such robust discussion of civilian rights and military policy was entirely appropriate—indeed "a healthy sign in a democracy," no less in wartime than in normal times. "In every war there has been considerable difficulty in demarking the limits of civilian and military authority," Ennis averred; and he predicted—presciently, as it proved—that it was unlikely that even the justices of the Supreme Court would achieve unanimity on the issues being litigated in the *Duncan* case.[16]

Other voices had joined the bar association, however, in what soon became an open campaign to end army rule. The territory's Democratic Party convention in May 1944 adopted a declaration calling for termination of martial law, stating that military rule was "illegal" and was "contrary to every tradition of America from its beginning."[17] Information also circulated in mid-1944 that the labor unions in Hawai'i were considering lawsuits against the army to challenge the constitutionality of the military governor's control over labor relations and wages.[18] There was no let-up, either, by Governor Stainback in his campaign of continuous pressure, both through Ickes and Fortas in the Interior Department and directly with the White House, for moderation or complete termination of martial law. Stainback also shrewdly appealed to the political interest of the Roosevelt administration, warning that right wing Republicans would leap on events such as the *Duncan* case and use them to allege there were "dangers to liberty with the continuation of the President in office."[19]

Fears for the Future of Civilian Governance

An additional motivation behind Stainback's campaign was his conviction—which proved to be well founded—that the army and navy, as well as a few elements of the business elite in Hawai'i itself, would welcome a perpetuation of military authority even beyond the end of the war. "Plans for future control of Hawai'i by certain fascist-minded individuals must be considered," he was reported as warning. "This contemplates Army and Navy control; some high ups [*sic*] in both civil and military life are making plans along this line."[20] Others in the Islands shared Stainback's concern on this score, as indicated by an army intelligence report in 1942 that referred to "deep-rooted suspicion of many Islands people, particularly some business and professional leaders, that the Federal Government is using martial law as an excuse to foist a commission form of government on Hawai'i after the war."[21] Ironically, Delegate Farrington was worried in December 1943 that if the president issued an executive order to curb the army's wartime authority in Hawai'i, it might well lead to "a counter-proposal in Congress, emanating from War Department sources, to establish military government in the Islands by law."[22]

In a lengthy report to Governor Stainback in late 1943 on the legal status and political implications of martial law, Territorial Attorney General Garner Anthony referred to this problem. He was concerned, he wrote, that even without necessarily "imputing any sinister design" to the army brass, a loss of self-government could too easily occur.[23] Once citizens became accustomed to martial rule, especially when material comforts were abundant (as they were in the Islands then), "the authoritarian principle" would no longer seem alien. Public apathy, Anthony concluded, would easily lead to acceptance of the military government's bureaucracy—"which naturally enough, like any other bureaucracy, will resist change or inroads upon its jurisdiction, and finally Congress may conclude that a military government is more suitable to Hawai'i than our present government under the Organic Act."[24]

Anthony's concern about the integrity of democratic government in Hawai'i had another important focus. In one of his most notable public addresses, he linked the issue of whether the territory was threatened with becoming "simply a military garrison" with a sensitive related question: whether Hawai'i would be able to maintain its dedication to the "ideals of a prejudice-free, multi-racial community" such as was being achieved, he averred, in Islands society. "Can we demonstrate," Anthony asked, "that here the races of man can live in decency and dignity with equal opportunity for all?" With its multiracial citizenry, Hawai'i had a special mission to perform. It was "a miniature of the nation," and the survival and vigor of democratic self-government made it essential that it not become a vassal state of the military.[25]

Other leading figures among Hawai'i's political and social elite suspected in early 1944 that concrete plans to curb their political rights were being actively pursued. To cite one example, a prominent Honolulu attorney admonished Delegate Farrington that "we must all work very hard to prevent any possible attempt of the Army and the Navy, backed by [certain civilians in Hawai'i], to put the island of Oahu permanently under military control."[26]

Such worries about the long-term displacement of civilian self-government were well merited, for the army command's lawyers in Hawai'i were already working on plans much on the lines that their critics feared. In a January 1944 memorandum for General Richardson, Morrison had denounced Metzger and Stainback as "oblivious to the fact that we are fighting a war." He thus proposed that the "best strategy is to have ready a good defense and also to launch an offensive by suggesting a few audacious plans" to transfer control of the territory to the War Department. "If the military and naval authorities decide that they have a permanent stake in these Islands, now, in time of war, is the time to adopt a forthright and realistic attitude."[27] Richardson soon afterward proposed confidentially to the War Department that responsibility for administration of the Islands should be transferred from the Department of the Interior to the War Department. This change, Richardson wrote, would conveniently silence at a single stroke "the consistent complaining of the Territorial officials by making them responsible to the Secretary of War for the duration."[28] Apparently McCloy spared his government colleagues outside the War Department any information of this proposal, and it was held in strict secrecy for several months by McCloy and the army's legal staff. It did resurface briefly later, however, and it received serious consideration (before being buried again) in the War Department's legal staff discussions.[29]

Meanwhile, practical matters relating to the day-to-day administration of criminal justice were gaining prominence in the debates regarding both martial law generally and the army's tactics in the cases challenging the ban on petitions of habeas in particular. The territorial attorney general, Nils Tavares, who succeeded Garner Anthony in January 1944, foresaw difficulties for law enforcement if Judges Metzger and McLaughlin issued further releases in response to habeas petitions.[30] Such orders might possibly include the release of the few prisoners who had been convicted of serious crimes and who, when freed, might be a threat to the safety of the community. Tavares therefore advised the army that it had become important, as a simple matter of effective domestic security, to return immediately all civil and criminal jurisdiction to the civilian courts, rather than awaiting the result of the Ninth Circuit appeals. Comment from the OMG was hardly calculated to allay his concerns. Giving up provost court jurisdiction, the army replied to Tavares, would be seen by the public as "an admission of weakness" and on that basis alone was out of the question.[31]

Governor Stainback, for his part, complained that the army was creating new military justice districts throughout the Islands, with a consequent proliferation of provost courts. He forwarded to Ickes an editorial in the *Honolulu Star-Bulletin* that complained, "It would seem the Army could form at least a company, if not a regiment, out of the men that they have exercising legal authority throughout the Territory"—a situation that was deplorable not only because of the constitutional issue, but also because the provost courts' operations served as constant reminders to the citizenry of an unwarranted displacement of civilian authority.[32]

The Military Government's Strategies for Retaining Power

Concerned by information that Stainback and Ickes were pressing the War Department to accept Tavares's proposal, the OMG legal staff wrote a detailed memorandum in rejoinder. Their main contention was that the ongoing business of the provost courts was not seriously intrusive into civilian life and therefore did not require so radical a change. The actual composition of the provost courts' dockets, however, even as summarized in the memorandum itself, was hardly persuasive on this point. The principal category of prosecutions was for violations of the evening curfew and blackout orders—regulations that, in fact, were notoriously the target of the greatest public resentment then being voiced against martial law.[33] Also in the dockets, however, were numerous cases involving violations of the army's stringent labor regulations, including absenteeism from the job, and failure of persons (even juveniles) to accept employment. As we have noted, these labor rules, long in effect under general orders, were a major instrument of control for the powerful sugar plantations and many other employers. It was no surprise, therefore, that the territorial Chamber of Commerce strongly supported the army in its continued enforcement of these rules. Also on the summary list the OMG compiled were "censorship violations," a broad category that presumably included tight mail censorship and the monitoring of cables and private phone conversations.[34]

Tavares was undeterred by the army's contention that provost court justice was of relatively minor impact. He and Stainback continued pressing the case for the termination of martial law. It was important for termination to be accomplished by executive action of the president and the territorial governor, Tavares advised, rather than its being "kicked to death by court action" while leaving in question the validity of criminal sentences.[35]

In its public pronouncements, the army command in Hawai'i was steadfastly resisting its critics, justifying the continuation of martial law as essential to security. Privately, however, the legal officers in Richardson's headquarters were becoming concerned with some purely self-interested aspects of the process by which termination might occur. In early 1944, for example, they had worried that a sudden termination order might undermine the army's case against the appeals going forward in the appellate courts; but no less important to the generals, it might also cause the army to "lose face in the community." Another object of their concern, equally prominent in the legal staff's deliberation at that time, was to find ways to ensure that if forced to terminate martial law, "the Army should receive credit" for it, rather than allowing the public to credit the courts or the pressures from civilian political leaders.[36]

Richardson's chief legal officer, General Morrison, and the second-ranking army lawyer on his staff, Colonel Eugene V. Slattery, began weighing alternatives to the formal legal foundations of martial law as it had operated up to that time.[37] It is instructive that General Richardson and his legal staff were initially opposed to one option that might have provided ample power to the military while responding to the rising pressures for the restoration of federal courts' jurisdiction and the termination of martial law: This was the proposed application to Hawai'i of Executive Order 9066—the order under which the mainland's Japanese Americans had been excluded from the West Coast, forcibly relocated, and incarcerated. Anthony had earlier advocated such a plan as preferable to martial law.[38] Richardson, however, rejected this plan as leaving him with inadequate discretion in dealing with Japanese Americans whom his command deemed security risks. It would also have reduced his options in regard to censorship and to the control of travel and of the labor force. Most notably, Richardson feared that reliance on Executive Order 9066 would place him at the mercy of the federal courts, which would be in a position to interpret the terms both of his administrative jurisdiction and the conditions for hearing habeas corpus petitions.[39]

As of mid-1944, Richardson preferred to continue the process of fighting habeas actions in the district court, as in the *Duncan* case and others; mounting appeals to the Ninth Circuit; and implementing the large tactic of "flight from habeas" by the selective mooting of cases. Not long afterward, as we shall discuss below, Richardson changed his views entirely and threw his personal support to the idea of the president's creation of a new military area under his command. He also abandoned the mooting tactic, as his legal staff pushed hard to present the *Duncan* and *White* cases to the Supreme Court.

Doubtless responding in some measure to the rising public criticism while the habeas cases were on appeal, the army command suggested that it would make on-the-ground concessions by turning back to civilian agencies some of the less important regulatory powers over economic matters that the military regime had controlled since Pearl Harbor. Governor Stainback regarded these minor changes as being of trivial consequence.[40] Meanwhile, Stainback was also continuing to demand that Richardson relinquish the title "military governor," as it was a title that had been used only in situations—such as Cuba and the Philippines after the Spanish-American War—in which the military was ruling a conquered populace.[41] On this issue, too, Richardson, like Emmons before him, refused to budge. Abolition of the title, the two generals consistently argued, "would create confusion and destroy the uniformity of authority which now exists between civilians and the military."[42] In advancing this position, the two generals and their legal staffs never made even a pretense of justifying such alleged "uniformity" on constitutional grounds. Instead, they relied upon the different—and rather revealing—argument that abolition of the title "would seriously impair the vital power to regulate and obviously invite the growth of some competing power based on the will of local politics [sic] or rival business interests."[43]

Early in the war period, the War Department backed the commanding generals on this issue; but as early as July 1943, McCloy had finally begun to shift ground, advising the Hawaiʻi command that he believed there was merit to an objection Fortas had raised, that the title, "in the eyes of civilians," had become "an important symbol of military usurpation of civil government."[44] McCloy meanwhile told Ickes that he would "press for the elimination of the title," conceding that in actuality it contributed little to the commanding general's authority in Hawaiʻi.[45]

A few months later, the senior army brass became involved as well. Chief of Staff General George C. Marshall asked General Julius Ochs Adler, commander of the 77th Infantry Division, which was the unit responsible for the defense of Hawaiʻi, to confer with General Richardson on the martial law situation. Following his meeting with Richardson, Adler consulted with both Marshall and McCloy; he then advised Richardson confidentially to "quietly drop the title, 'Military Governor,'" and create a bureau for civilian affairs.[46] Adler also advised Richardson, then in the midst of the confrontation with Judge Metzger, to withdraw the offending General Orders No. 31 and proceed to resolve the controversy over habeas corpus on a less confrontational basis.[47] Although Richardson was forced to accept a compromise on the matter of the habeas altercation, still another year would pass before he finally yielded to the pressures from both the War Department and the army senior command and relinquished the "military governor" title.

Despite McCloy's verbal concessions, the War Department deferred to the views of its commanders in Hawaiʻi, reverting in early 1944 to the position that the generals knew best what was important to successful prosecution of the war in such matters, even if this meant holding on to the merely symbolic nomenclature of military government.[48] Not until July 1944—a full year after McCloy's first request—did General Richardson finally give up the title of Military Governor.

Chapter Sixteen

THE TERMINATION OF MARTIAL LAW

The army's ability stubbornly to resist direction from Washington, even from the War Department, can be attributed in part to the mind-set of President Roosevelt himself. As Attorney General Biddle recalled in his memoirs, Roosevelt "was never theoretical about things" in matters affecting the conduct of the war; he acted pragmatically: "What must be done to defend the country must be done. The decision was for his Secretary of War. . . . The military might be wrong. But they were fighting the war."[1]

Roosevelt was faced in the early months of the war with critical challenges for U.S. forces and the military's strategic plans in both the European and Pacific theaters—in no regard more critical than in relation to the protection of his Pacific fleet's base in Hawai'i.[2] However, he had become determined much earlier to mobilize as well against internal dangers to the national security. Thus in May 1941 he declared an "unlimited national emergency," warning Americans of the threat posed by the aggressive militarism of the Axis powers, and calling upon employers and labor to maintain industrial production amidst a buildup of military capacity. At the same time, his proclamation also highlighted the danger of threats to internal security from "foreign directed subversion."[3] This emergency declaration had followed, moreover, his earlier announcement in August 1940 that he was assigning to the FBI an expanded role in dealing with what he saw as urgent problems of "espionage, sabotage, [and] subversive activities."[4]

Thus, it was predictable that once the nation had been attacked, Roosevelt would subordinate civil liberties to the imperatives of security. The president, Biddle wrote, regarded the survival of national security and democratic government itself as being at stake, hence his posture on the constitutional issue: "If anything, he thought that rights should yield to the necessities of war. *Rights came after victory, not before.*"[5]

The president's posture in this regard goes far toward explaining why it was a long and tortuous road for the critics of martial law—including Secretary Ickes and Attorney General Biddle—to force the army to relinquish its authority over civilian affairs in Hawai'i. It will be recalled that Roosevelt at the start of the war had personally authorized an evacuation of Oʻahu's Japanese-American population to Molokai or the mainland; and in December 1942 he had instructed the War Department to transfer General Green out of Hawaiʻi and to conclude the agreement that resulted in the restoration of March 1943. Apart from those two interventions, Roosevelt seems to have remained generally aloof from the debates over army rule in Hawaiʻi that raged within his cabinet—at least until press criticism and expressions of rising concern in Congress in 1943–1944 demanded his attention. Besides, cabinet members, including even Ickes, were sensitive about the need to protect Roosevelt from unnecessary aggravation and distractions over martial law in Hawaiʻi at a time when the wartime summit conferences, large issues of strategy, and domestic politics were preoccupying him and (as many feared) were taking a toll on his health.[6] FDR seemed to maintain his posture of relative indifference so long as there were no high political costs to be paid—and, above all, so long as the naval and military operations supplying the Pacific war out of the Hawaiʻi port continued to operate smoothly.

A Turning Point: FDR Weighs In, Mid-1944

A significant turning point in the martial law controversy came in July 1944, however, when the president made a brief visit to Oʻahu to confer with General Douglas MacArthur, Admirals Nimitz and Halsey, General Richardson, and other top officers in the Pacific theater to plan the final campaign against Japan. While in Honolulu, Roosevelt also took steps toward giving a firmer personal direction to the Hawaiʻi martial law situation. Thus he met briefly with General Richardson to discuss the status of army rule in Hawaiʻi. Richardson told the president that he and his staff were working intensively on drafting a new executive order—one that would include formal termination of martial law, an initiative for which Richardson disingenuously took full credit. The plan he was preparing, Richardson said, "would give me as military commander all the necessary powers to ensure security," as it embraced the previously debated concept of creating a military district with authority such as Executive Order 9066 had given the army on the West Coast.[7] Remarking upon the prospect of getting the president to accept this plan, an obviously ebullient Richardson reported to McCloy that Roosevelt *"agreed that a rose by any other name smells as sweet."*[8]

One can easily picture Roosevelt thus reassuring the general and waving off the problem with his trademark smile, yet at the same time deciding that the issue needed further investigation. Apparently he did decide exactly that. Before leaving the Islands, the president instructed one of his most trusted advisers, Judge Samuel Rosenman, to stay on to get a first-hand reading on the conflicts that had surrounded the restoration issue and the prospective termination of martial law.[9]

Rosenman met first with Stainback, who—predictably—presented at length the arguments for prompt termination of military rule. To bolster his case, the governor also handed to Rosenman a report recently prepared for him by Territorial Attorney General Tavares that deplored how the martial law regime had developed into "the

President Roosevelt visited Honolulu in August 1944 to plan the final assault against
Japan. He is shown here aboard a navy cruiser in Pearl Harbor for briefings on the
martial law situation by Governor Stainback and General Richardson (seated with the
president). Other uniformed officers in the photo include, left to right, General Douglas
MacArthur, Admiral William D. Leahy, Vice Admiral Robert Ghormley, and Rear
Admiral William Furlong. Credit: U.S. Navy photo, courtesy of HWRD, University
of Hawai'i.

needless invasion of the civil liberties of our people."[10] Tavares also had catalogued reasons for urgency: a general malaise and decline in civilian morale; a constitutional
suit allegedly being planned by the labor unions for relief in the courts against continued army labor controls; and, not least important, the tenuous legal position in which
law enforcement was left by the series of U.S. District Court decisions in Honolulu in
which Judges Metzger and McLaughlin had held judgments of the provost courts and/
or martial law itself to be invalid.[11] Stainback also told Rosenman at this meeting that
he had just written to Secretary Ickes to warn that the widely circulated *Chicago Tribune* attack on martial law "is only the opening gun" of what might become a devastating Republican attack on FDR in a presidential election year, with army rule in
Hawai'i "as an example of the dangers to liberty that would be risked if Roosevelt were
to win another term in office."[12]

Subsequently, Rosenman conferred privately with General Richardson, who—also
predictably—gave him a very different account of both the objective situation and the
prescribed solutions. Glossing over the real issues, Richardson told Rosenman, as he

had told Roosevelt, "that it was the name 'martial law,' rather than any power exercised under it, that was annoying to a certain group of civilians"—thus implying that the ongoing controversies stemmed not from a deprivation of civil liberties or the army's flawed and arbitrary justice system, but rather from mere annoyance on the part of Stainback and his circle.[13] Uneasy because Rosenman had received a document from Stainback that he himself had not seen, Richardson "felt it necessary to fortify" Rosenman with a clear statement of his position on the hierarchy of authority: "I am absolutely and irrevocably opposed," the general declared, "to being placed in a position where the successful execution of my mission is dependent upon Governor Stainback or any of his subordinates."[14]

As he had done with the president, Richardson also sought to convey to Rosenman that he and his command's legal advisers had originated the initiative for termination of martial law and return of significant power to the civilian government. It must have been gratifying to Richardson that Roosevelt, as the general was at pains to report to the War Department, "*praised our initiative.*"[15] Richardson's professed interest in terminating martial law did not, however, tell the whole story. For as recently as a week earlier, the War Department and army lawyers in Washington were still actively considering Richardson's earlier proposal that the president issue an emergency order transferring the Interior Department's entire authority in Hawai'i to the War Department for the duration of the war![16] Concerned that Richardson was putting his own spin on the facts, Under Secretary Fortas wrote to Ickes, recommending that Ickes ask the president for an immediate executive order restoring full civilian powers (though with normal emergency restrictions) because the army had shown no signs of authentically accepting an end to martial law.[17]

In dealing with the War Department, too, Richardson pursued further his campaign to advance the fiction that he and his staff had been the ones to suggest the idea for terminating martial law. For example, he expressed to McCloy his gratification that "the integrated labor program *which was initiated in my office* meets with your approval and that of the Navy."[18] He also tried to persuade McCloy to press for the earliest possible agreement on his proposed order to end martial law: "Immediate action is urged," Richardson said, "*as the Army should receive credit for initiating steps to abolish martial law* and for proposing the security executive order regardless of the outcome of the Habeas Corpus cases," that is, the *Duncan* and *White* appeals.[19] And indeed, when termination did actually come in late October 1944, *Hawaii,* a news magazine that associated itself consistently with the army line on every major policy issue, declared the end of martial law to be "the fruit of nearly two years constant effort and negotiation, *instigated by the military.*"[20]

The prospect of the termination of martial law (on whatever terms were finally decided) was by this time also a highly salient factor in War Department strategizing about the habeas cases and their appeal. Thus, the top judge advocate general staff officers, now including General Green himself, were said to be worried that "termination of martial law prior to the decisions in these cases . . . [in] the Ninth Circuit . . . might prejudice the decisions in these cases and that the Army might lose face in the community by such action."[21]

Clearly, any lines that may once have separated a concern with law from the politics of bureaucratic turf claims, or the tactics of litigation in habeas corpus cases from plain face-saving, had become almost indiscernible in the War Department correspondence and in the army command's cables from Hawai'i. The judge advocate general officers had become so interested in micromanaging the situation that one of the senior army lawyers, Colonel William Hughes, proposed that if significant jurisdiction were to be returned to the civil courts, the president should be asked to send a confidential letter to the two district judges in Hawai'i: "[He should] in effect say to the civil courts, 'I will give you a chance to operate without martial law, but if you don't rise to the occasion, martial law will be re-instituted.' It is readily possible that upon receipt of such a letter the two judges would take on the new cases as a patriotic duty and might operate very efficiently."[22] His proposal quietly died.

The army lawyers had also begun to focus intensely on the ominous prospect of civil liability suits in the event that all the legal loose ends were not tied up carefully while the formal actions were being taken to terminate martial law. Lawyers for the Justice Department and the Interior Department had contended for more than a year that the termination proclamation should be issued by Governor Stainback, since under the Organic Act only the governor had the authority to declare martial law in the first place; alternatively, it should be issued jointly by Stainback and the president. The army had opposed this position, maintaining instead that all authority over martial law and its termination had legally passed to the military, leaving Stainback without jurisdiction in the matter.[23] Now, once it became clear that FDR was soon going to take action, the army's lawyers began to argue the urgency of having the president alone proclaim the termination. Their zeal was impelled by self-interest. If Roosevelt issued the proclamation, the judge advocate general's office advised, "it inferentially makes the President legally responsible for martial law from Pearl Harbor day to date. As many of Governor Stainback's supporters are threatening enormous civil suits for false imprisonment against General Richardson and others, it might be of some value later on to be able to plead *respondeat superior*[24] and to have the proof on record."[25] The Department of the Navy also weighed in, urging, for its own reasons, that the president, and not the secretary of war, issue the termination order; this would assure that the navy's prerogatives under the principle of "unity of command" would not be interpreted as abridged in the military area to be announced for Hawai'i.[26]

Meanwhile, Secretary Ickes's outrage with regard to the continued violation of constitutional liberties in Hawai'i remained unabated. He now also had in hand, and very much in mind, the evidence of intensifying newspaper editorial criticism of the Hawai'i martial law policy around the nation—and especially the notorious *Chicago Tribune* blast. Ickes thus abandoned hope that the negotiations would come to anything, and instead he decided to approach the White House directly for action. He told the president on August 5 that he no longer had the slightest confidence that the army and the War Department negotiators were interested in anything except cosmetic changes, noting their "persistent, although understandable, reluctance . . . to relinquish the power and authority over all activities in that theater of operations which they so long exercised."[27]

Ickes therefore called upon FDR to terminate immediately the military regime in the Islands and to order the writ of habeas corpus restored. Suggesting specific language, he proposed that the president announce to all departments involved that "there seems to be, from my personal inspection, complete law and order in Hawaii"—but he recommended, in addition, that FDR also state that "civil officers there must lean over backward to carry out reasonable recommendations by the military and naval commanders."[28] A declaration that Hawai'i was a military area, under the same terms as the executive orders and congressional legislation that had been applied on the mainland, would be more than enough, Ickes contended, to ensure that security would be maintained properly while restoring to citizens of the territory their access to the courts for protecting their rights.[29]

The exact language of the proposed executive order was the subject of weeks of negotiations and exchanges of drafts among Richardson and his legal advisers, McCloy, the judge advocate general, the Department of the Interior, and the Department of Justice throughout the late summer of 1944. At issue were the authority to detain Japanese-American citizens, censorship, enforcement of regulations in the courts, the continuation of blackouts and curfews, travel controls, and a "recapture clause" whereby martial law could again be imposed if military necessity so required.[30] At last, on October 18, the president issued Executive Order No. 9489, authorizing the secretary of war to designate a military commander for the Territory of Hawai'i, and giving the military commander the right to establish a military area, to exclude persons from that area, and to maintain certain controls deemed essential for security. The Executive Order also authorized the commanding general to take a variety of security measures, including establishment of a curfew and blackout, and the regulation of firearms, ports and harbors, travel, foreign-language newspapers, radio transmissions, and communications among the islands of the territory or between the military area and points outside.[31]

Having granted the military the control it deemed essential for security, on the next day, October 19, 1944, the president issued Proclamation 2627, terminating martial law and restoring the writ of habeas corpus. The effective date of the proclamation was October 24, the date on which Governor Stainback issued a proclamation to the same effect. Also on that date, Secretary of War Stimson designated General Richardson as military commander, and Richardson thereupon proclaimed the establishment of the Territory of Hawai'i as a military area.[32]

Ceremony at Iolani Palace, showing, left to right, General James Huey, Commander of Hawaiʻi National Guard; Admiral William F. Halsey; Governor Ingram Stainback; and General Robert Richardson, honoring a group of U.S. service personnel after liberation from Japanese POW camps. Credit: U.S. Navy photo, courtesy of HWRD, University of Hawaiʻi.

Successor to the Military Government: The Office of Internal Security

Compelled to give up the politically offensive terminology of "military government" to which the army had clung so tenaciously, Richardson nevertheless continued in operation the army's apparatus for control of civilian affairs. He renamed the Office of the Military Governor (OMG) as the Office of Internal Security (OIS) in July; but the OIS was indistinguishable from the old OMG in its structure and line of command, personnel, and range of jurisdiction, except for the territorial courts' jurisdiction in ordinary criminal cases.[33] Morrison, who formerly held the position of the OMG "Executive" (the office the army had created when martial law was first instituted in December 1941), continued to serve as Richardson's chief legal officer, with the new title of executive of the commanding general for internal security.[34] Now a brigadier general, Morrison retained his supervision of the military's role in regulating activities in the civilian sector. He and Richardson's other legal officers were to be disappointed, however, in their quest for the War Department's endorsement of their proposal to have the powers of the Interior Department transferred to the War Department and the military commander. Probably they were most surprised of all to find that General Green, who now served in the judge advocate general's office in Washington, was among those who expressed skepticism about the idea.[35]

Richardson did hold out the promise that some functions of governance, even including some aspects of labor controls, would gradually be returned to civilian authority.[36] In fact, as noted earlier, Richardson had enjoyed remarkable success, with McCloy's backing, in resisting even the explicit instructions from President Roosevelt in March 1943, at the time of the partial restoration, for "further restoration of civil authority as and when the situation permits."[37] The key, of course, is that it was left to the army itself to decide when the situation permitted such action. Especially with regard to keeping a firm, controlling hand over the Islands' labor force, as we have seen, Richardson gave up powers grudgingly and with explicit reservations that would assure the "recapture" of those powers whenever the army might deem it necessary.[38]

It is not surprising, then, that disputes continued to rage over implementation.[39] First, matters of nomenclature continued to bedevil the relations between the military and Stainback's administration. Thus the governor, seconded strongly by Under Secretary of the Interior Fortas, objected to the stratagem by which General Richardson was now issuing orders under the title "military commander of the territory"—a title that was in compliance with the statute granting him specified powers over the military area but one that his critics found no less offensive than the former title of "military governor."[40] Even McCloy wondered why simply using his title of "military commander" did not lend sufficient dignity and authority to Richardson's pronouncements. Whatever the merits of the question, this persistent sideshow inflamed further the relations between the governor's office and the army command. "I have never known such a petty man nor one so insincere," Richardson complained of Stainback; he also derided "the continued sniping by the Department of the Interior at our sincere efforts to do a good job."[41] Hoping to put the matter to rest, McCloy finally informed the Interior Department that the designation "Office of Internal Security" would be used thenceforth—a terminology that "tends to disavow any warlike intent or jurisdictionitis"—and that he had faith that Richardson would keep guard against any actions by his staff that exceeded their newly circumscribed authority.[42]

Of more substantial importance was rising civilian criticism of the continued curfew in the Islands. The curfew had been extended from 9:00 until 10:00 p.m. in May 1942, but it remained in effect even when blackout regulations were lifted in July 1944. Garner Anthony and other territorial officials had long maintained it no longer served a valid security function.[43] Not until July 1945 did General Richardson yield to such criticism, telling a press conference that he had himself personally "felt that way for many months" but had decided to consult the Honolulu Chamber of Commerce, whose leaders convinced him that the curfew policy should not be lifted despite his personal views.[44] This was a rare instance in which General Richardson deferred to civilian opinion from any source on the type of security matter which the army, in court and before the public, had always insisted was exclusively within its own competency and jurisdiction. One can presume that he consulted the Chamber of Commerce because its officers had been undeviatingly supportive of the army's wishes in all matters relating to martial law, and Richardson could be quite certain of obtaining the answer he wanted when he asked for their advice.[45]

Turmoil within the Roosevelt administration's highest circles broke out again when one of Richardson's first special security orders after the termination banned the possession of firearms by citizens of German or Italian descent, and by naturalized citizens who had once been German or Italian nationals, as well as by all Japanese Americans.[46] After the attorney general had raised the issue with him, Fortas urged Secretary Ickes to protest the order by complaining to Stimson. "Discrimination based solely upon nationality was bad enough in the case of persons of Japanese ancestry," Fortas wrote; but to extend discrimination still further in this way was "intolerable," in no way being justified by security concerns.[47] In language that Ickes approved and apparently adopted in writing to Stimson, Fortas's draft letter continued with a denunciation of racism as evidenced in the army's record throughout the war, not sparing from the indictment the military's internment policy imposed on the West Coast:

> In fact, [the order] indicates clearly that the virus of racial discrimination cannot be confined to the victimization of one class or group. Your officers in Hawaii and on the West coast started with the Japanese. Your officers in Hawaii have now expanded their prejudices to embrace American citizens whose sole distinction is that they are of German or Italian descent. . . .
>
> I cannot believe that this regulation, which is founded on a theory indistinguishable from the Nazi philosophy of contamination by race and ancestry, was adopted with your approval or that of Assistant Secretary McCloy. I hope that you will carefully consider this matter and that you will not only cause this regulation to be rescinded but that you will make an effort to ascertain whether the officers who are responsible for it are not so imbued with undemocratic prejudices that they should be transferred to duties in which their prejudices will have less opportunity to inflict injury upon American principles.[48]

There were yet other serious, persisting problems. As Executive, General Morrison, with his assistant, Major E. V. Slattery, had run the army's administrative and provost court operations affecting civilian affairs from the time of Green's departure in mid-1943 until the war's end. Protégés of Green, they were promoted to higher ranks and were then retained in their posts even after the war—arranged at Richardson's request and with Green's intervention. In the months following Japan's surrender, the OIS was busy with arrangements for bringing home both the Japanese Americans who had been removed to the mainland and the several thousand strandees who had left Hawai'i in the early months of the war and been unable to secure passage home.

Morrison's office was also responsible for returning thousands of dollars worth of property that had been confiscated for security reasons when war broke out.[49] Both Morrison and Slattery became prominent targets of criticism for their personal and official styles in conducting their duties. An investigation ordered by the War Department and conducted confidentially by Frederick Wiener, a Justice Department expert on martial law, came down hard on the record these two officers had made. Morrison in particular was the subject of a blistering critique. He was faulted for arbitrariness, arrogance, and deviousness; he was "discourteous to civilians, and discourteous to military men"; he attempted to keep the army's own historians out of his files, in what the investigator termed an outright "cover-up of his activities"; and he had given the commanding general incompetent legal advice, in particular with regard to the confrontation with Judge Metzger and General Orders No. 31.[50] If Congress ever undertook a full-scale public investigation of these activities as well as those of the Executive and the provost courts during General Green's regime in Hawai'i, the Wiener report stated, "it will be a twenty-five year setback for the Army."[51]

In fact, Morrison was about to be reduced in rank and probably given terminal leave, but extensions of their commissions and their Hawai'i assignment were arranged for Slattery and Morrison specifically (and apparently solely) so that they could assist in preparing a legal defense against the rash of civil liability suits that the army anticipated it would face in the event it lost the *Duncan* and *White* appeals.[52] Morrison was "perhaps more thoroughly familiar with what has transpired" under martial law in Hawai'i than anyone else, Richardson wrote to General MacArthur early in 1946, and he "is the man on whom I have to depend to answer the ever recurrent questions from the War Department and elsewhere now arising as an aftermath of martial law."[53] At the time, the behavior of the army lawyer-administrators, consistently supported and promoted by General Richardson, simply gave further reason for concern to those who were carrying responsibility as counsel in defending the army in the appeals going forward in the habeas corpus cases.

PART VII

The Supreme Court Rules

Chapter Seventeen

THE *DUNCAN* AND *WHITE* CASES

The Ninth Circuit court delivered its opinion in the *Duncan* and *White* cases on November 1, 1944. Although President Roosevelt had terminated martial law and restored the writ of habeas corpus in Hawai'i two weeks earlier, all parties concerned—the Justice Department's trial attorneys, the army lawyers, the lawyers for the plaintiffs, and the civilian officials—were nevertheless eager to appeal the two cases to the nation's highest court. Unlike in earlier years, when the army had mooted cases by releasing internees and convicted prisoners rather than risk an adverse decision on appeal to the Supreme Court, the military lawyers now sought an early ruling from the high court while fierce combat in the Pacific was still going on. For after the war was over, the army command officers still were convinced, the justices would have a much more critical view of the comprehensive suspension of civil liberties in Hawai'i than would be likely in a wartime setting.

Even though the Justice Department's trial attorneys continued to believe that the provost courts and internments were unconstitutional and that the army deserved to lose on any further appeal, they agreed with the army lawyers to appeal the cases. The Justice Department lawyers also ascertained that the civilian officials—Governor Stainback, Territorial Attorney General Tavares, and the two federal district judges in Honolulu—all remained consistent in their eagerness, for reasons different from the army's, to have the case go up for final judgment as soon as feasible.[1] Meanwhile the army legal staff in Hawai'i sought to petition for an extraordinary procedural measure from the Supreme Court—either a "writ of prohibition," by which the Court would order the federal trial judges in Honolulu to restrain from freeing on habeas corpus orders any army prisoners (including any Japanese-American internees who had allegedly expressed openly disloyal sentiments before military interviewers), or else an informal directive that would accomplish the same purpose.[2] The Justice Department declined to present such a petition to the Court.

Thus, the lawyers on both sides began their work of organizing their teams for preparation of briefs and, afterward, oral arguments on what they hoped would be a full hearing before the Supreme Court during the regular cycle of the Court's calendar.

At this point, national publicity in an entirely new dimension was given to Duke Kahanamoku—a man famed internationally for his several Olympic records in swimming, his career in popularization of the previously obscure sport of board surfing, and his prominence as a media personality and entrepreneur in the Hawai'i tourist industry. He was an iconic figure in Hawai'i, constantly pictured in the local newspapers in the company of visiting celebrities from the worlds of sports, the movies, and politics. In the 1930s, Kahanamoku had entered political life, capitalizing on the public adoration he enjoyed to win successive elections as sheriff of Honolulu, an office he held for twenty-six years, until 1961. Among his formal responsibilities was supervision of the city and county jails and prisons.[3] After Duncan's conviction in the provost court, he had been handed over to the sheriff's office for imprisonment, making Kahanamoku the official custodian of record of Duncan. Thus his name quite fortuitously became attached to this historic case in the jurisprudence of U.S. civil-military relations and constitutional history.

The case thus went up to the Supreme Court as *Lloyd C. Duncan v. Duke Paoa Kahanamoku, Sheriff of the City and County of Honolulu.* It was joined there with the *White* case, as had been done in the Ninth Circuit. Garner Anthony, counsel for Duncan, filed Duncan's petition for certiorari on December 29, 1944, and the Court agreed on February 12, 1945, to review the case. The actual management of the military's defense against Duncan's claim was entirely in the hands of the army and Justice Department lawyers, with the sheriff's office essentially invisible in the litigation. It is a matter of local lore in Hawai'i, however, that Duke Kahanamoku was dismayed to have his name associated with this case as the legal defender of provost court justice.

The parallel petition of the stockbroker White was also accepted by the Court. Unlike in the army's handling of Duncan's imprisonment, the Office of the Military Governor had ordered control of White to be held, as matter of custody of record, by the command's provost marshal, even though he was transferred for incarceration to the Honolulu civilian prison. Hence, his case went forward, twinned with Duncan's under the formal title *Harry E. White, Petitioner, against William F. Steer, Colonel, Infantry, U.S. Army, Provost Marshal, Central Pacific Area.*

Oral argument remained to be scheduled, but at last the stage was set in February for review by the Court of the passionately contested policies that had been pursued under the martial law regime in wartime Hawai'i.

The timing of the *Duncan* and *White* appeals worked against the army, as it turned out, since the Supreme Court did not hear argument until December 7, 1945—that is, three months after Japan's surrender, and, of course, the fourth anniversary, to the very day, of the Pearl Harbor attack. This was also more than a year after the president had formally terminated martial law and restored the privilege of the writ of habeas corpus in Hawai'i.

High-level policy developments in late 1944 and 1945 were also exerting a major influence in the political and legal milieu in which the appeal from the Ninth Circuit went forward. Very shortly after the Ninth Circuit ruling on *Duncan* and *White* in November 1944, Secretary of War Stimson had certified that the army's claims of "military necessity" were no longer plausible with respect to mainland internments of Japanese Americans.[4] And in the last weeks of 1944 the government had set into motion a release program justified by the War Department on the dual grounds, as Assistant Secretary McCloy asserted, that "it can no longer be said that the West Coast is in danger of large-scale invasion" and, in addition, that Japanese Americans in the armed forces had made a record of "courage and devotion to this country."[5]

Roosevelt had opposed the release of the mainland detainees prior to the November election, but once the president's unprecedented fourth term was secured, McCloy was free to move ahead with his announcement. The Supreme Court's impending decision in the *Endo* case was also no doubt relevant.[6] Mitsuye Endo had filed a habeas petition to obtain an unconditional release from her continued incarceration in a relocation camp, where she was being held even after having been cleared of any suspicion of disloyalty. Issuing its decision on December 18, 1944, the Court ruled against the government and required Endo's immediate release. It was the first Supreme Court case during World War II in which the Court rejected the government's arguments of military necessity in support of incarceration without due process of United States citizens.[7] Acting on inside information of the imminent decision in *Endo,* the War Department issued a Sunday morning press release—just a day before the Court's Monday announcement of decisions—to seize the initiative for the army by announcing it was immediately instituting a program to release those being held in the camps.[8]

Thus it was against this rapidly changing background that the *Duncan* and *White* appeals to the Supreme Court went forward. The War Department pressured the Justice Department to have Herbert Wechsler argue the cases. As assistant attorney general in charge of the War Division, Wechsler had overseen appellate litigation on the West Coast internments as well as martial law in Hawaiʻi, and he had helped argue *Korematsu* for the government before the Supreme Court. He was not only very familiar with the Hawaiʻi cases, but, unlike other top attorneys in the Justice Department, the War Department thought, he was also "confident of winning them."[9] Wechsler, however, had been assigned to the Nuremberg trials as chief technical adviser to the American judges, so he was unavailable.

The Justice Department chose to select Edward Ennis—who believed that "martial law was entirely wrong in Hawaii after the first year," and who had expressed that view fully to the army[10]—to play the key role in preparing the *Duncan* and *White* briefs for the appeals. This was consistent with the role that Ennis had recently played in the *Endo* case. Ennis believed that the decisions to relocate *en masse* the Japanese Americans from the West Coast of the United States but not from Hawaiʻi "were basically practical political decisions, rather than decisions of actual military necessity."[11] Moreover, he regarded the detention "of American citizens in concentration camps on the basis of race" for longer periods of time than absolutely necessary as being "dangerous and repugnant" to the principles of American government.[12]

It is not surprising, then, that Ennis had opposed a proposal to moot the *Endo* appeal by the release of Ms. Endo from the relocation center. To moot the case, he contended, would deprive the Justice Department of the opportunity to obtain a definitive constitutional ruling on a crucial civil liberties issue—but he also had explicitly in mind the relationship to "the present [January 1944] *probably unconstitutional suspension of habeas corpus in Hawaii.*"[13] Were the case to be mooted, he feared, the Justice Department could do nothing to see the larger interests of the law advanced. "The only way left to this Department to deal with the Japanese [internees] problem effectively," he reminded the solicitor general, "is on its own ground, in the courts."[14] In a case such as Endo's—in which the army and the internment camp administrators had plainly violated a citizen's rights—the Justice Department, Ennis advised, should "merely . . . present the relevant considerations" to the Court and not make an unqualified argument for constitutionality.[15] For Ennis, then, the *Duncan* and *White* cases—and the entire pattern of the army's policies in Hawai'i—presented much the same kind of opportunity: the appeal would give the Supreme Court an opportunity to establish correct precedent and strike a blow for constitutional liberties.[16]

At issue in the arguments before the Court in *Duncan* and *White* were the key questions that had been debated before Judges Metzger and McLaughlin in Honolulu: (1) whether the federal statutes in any way authorized trials of civilians by military courts when civilian courts could be opened and functioning; (2) whether the federal courts retained any authority to review a determination by the commander that "necessity" required suspension of civil liberties; and, (3) whether, if such extraordinary military authority was ever proper, it could be continued into 1944 in a territory far removed from the actual combat zones.

Because such extensive testimony had been given by General Richardson, Admiral Nimitz, Governor Stainback, and other territorial officials in the *Duncan* habeas hearings in the district court, the justices had the full range of issues spread before them on the record with respect to the vexed issue of "military necessity." Included were arguments regarding the degree to which the Japanese-American population was potentially dangerous, the likelihood of invasion (however defined), the relevance of the powers of civilian government as it actually functioned under various phases of martial law, and, withal, the degree to which progress of the American military and naval forces against Japan affected the legitimacy of continued army rule. All four of the opinions that finally came down—those of Justice Black for the Court, of Chief Justice Stone and Justice Murphy in concurring opinions, and of Justice Burton for himself and Justice Frankfurter in a vigorous dissent—would refer explicitly to that record of testimony in the district court.

The Briefs for the Plaintiffs and the Government

Garner Anthony, serving as Duncan's counsel, argued that even if martial law itself were sustainable on constitutional grounds, it could not be extended to include the arbitrary closing of civilian courts or the extension of the military tribunals' jurisdiction over civilians for such ordinary crimes as embezzlement or simple assault. Anthony contended that the Court must honor the *Milligan* criteria for validation of martial law; and he quoted the ruling in *Milligan* to the effect that even if habeas corpus were properly denied, the Constitution does not permit the army to order a citizen so denied to be tried "otherwise than by the course of common law." In any event, nothing in the Organic Act authorizing suspension of the writ, he argued, could be construed as empowering the army "to prescribe new crimes or offenses, or to create 'courts' or 'tribunals' to try offenses." The Court, he argued, should overturn the Ninth Circuit ruling, which he characterized as having held "in effect . . . that the will of the commander, not the Constitution and laws of the United States, is the supreme law of the land."[17] He asked the Court at a minimum to uphold the civilian citizen's right to judicial review or to issuance of a writ after being convicted by a provost court "for an offense of the class constitutionally triable only by jury."[18]

In preparing his brief, it is interesting to note, Anthony was given office space in the Department of the Interior and continued to work closely with John P. Frank and others in that department's legal staff. He was also given access to Interior's internal archives, including its correspondence with the War Department. Hence Anthony's appearance for oral argument in December was the culmination of an unusual scenario in which the legal resources and talents of one department of the federal government were mobilized to help a lawyer pursue his client's case against another department.[19]

In an amicus brief filed on behalf of the petitioners, the Bar Association of Hawai'i and Nils Tavares, territorial attorney general, similarly called upon the Court to rule that the declaration of martial law could not itself be cited as ample reason for closing the courts and subjecting civilian justice "to the will of the military commander."[20] Another amicus brief, by the American Civil Liberties Union, signed by seven of the nation's most distinguished constitutional lawyers, emphasized the fact that more than two years had elapsed prior to the arrest and conviction of Duncan, "during which no attempt had been made to get Congress to authorize military trials of any kind." This, the argument concluded, "show[ed] the absence of any real necessity for such trials" for such an extended period of time after the true emergency following the Pearl Harbor attack.[21]

The government's brief, led by Solicitor General Fahy and by Ennis, contended that an ample legislative basis for imposition of martial law had been provided by the Organic Act, Section 67. Going beyond the terms of the statute, however, their argument also invoked "the inherent power of self-defense and self-preservation possessed by this nation."[22] Having made this broad claim, the government nonetheless then effectively invited the Court to give judicial scrutiny to the army's determination as to "military necessity." If a civilian court were to subject the military's judgment to a test in such an instance of martial law, the brief stated, it should be only that of "determining whether all the circumstances afforded a reasonable basis for the action."[23]

This opening was one that the army lawyers had been resisting since the 1942 *Zimmerman* appeal.[24] They had never wanted to admit the validity of any kind of judicial review of their discretion in instituting or extending martial law. The Ninth Circuit had agreed fully with the army position, declaring that such judicial review would risk "idle or captious" wartime policies.[25] Now it remained to be seen if the Supreme Court would undertake a review of the army's "military necessity" rationale.

The Impact of the Japanese-American Cases

Anthony's strategy of underlining the arbitrariness of the army's claim to authority, together with emphasizing the lack of explicit statutory authority for the operation of provost courts in ordinary criminal and civil matters, proved to be highly effective. In the first place, it distinguished at a general level the facts of the two Hawai'i cases from those of the Japanese-American cases (*Hirabayashi* and *Korematsu*), the latter having involved actions by the army explicitly authorized initially by Executive Order and then by a congressional statute and appropriations bills that reinforced the executive's action.[26] This distinction brought the *Duncan* and *White* cases more within the ambit of the 1944 *Endo* case—*Endo* being the one major decision of the war period in which the high court released an internee, giving as its reason that the government lacked explicit statutory authority for denying the petitioner unconditional release from an internment camp and denying her constitutional due process once her loyalty had been affirmed by the government itself.[27]

Second, by pointing out so tellingly the lack of clear statutory authority for the extraordinary wartime discretionary power that the army had seized for itself in Hawai'i, Anthony's brief and the amici arguments in the *Duncan* appeal highlighted the *threat to civilian judicial power itself* that inhered in the army's view of "necessity" and its alleged legitimization of so sweeping a seizure of governmental authority. None of the Japanese-American cases had involved the specific question of martial law or army discretion to suspend civil liberties wholesale and to close the courts; instead, as noted above, they had come to the high court under terms of the executive order and an act of Congress, enforceable against citizens by the civilian courts. By contrast, General Richardson's position, set forth clearly in the trial record of *Duncan* in district court, was that the army's authority was superior to that of the entire civilian establishment, thus reducing the courts themselves to the status of its "agents" (a term specifically employed in the general orders issued by the commanding general/military governor).[28]

Still another cluster of facts in the *Duncan* and *White* appeals worked against the government's chances to win the case for the army. In both *Hirabayashi* in 1943 and *Korematsu* in 1944, the justices had given heavy weight to the explicit rationale in the president's Executive Order No. 9066 (authorizing creation of military areas and exclusion of residents from that area by order of the army) that invoked the need to guard against "espionage and . . . sabotage."[29] When the Court was called upon in 1944 to validate the government's continued incarceration of Ms. Endo, however, the irrelevance of that rationale became controlling for most of the justices. In internal Court memoranda, and also in Justice Douglas's majority opinion, members of the *Endo* majority held that there could be no rational concern about espionage or sabotage in connection with Ms. Endo, whose loyalty, after all, had been attested to by the government itself and was admitted by the government in the briefs. Thus Justice Reed reminded Douglas, while he was preparing the majority opinion in *Endo*, that "the entire program [of detention] is based on espionage"; and so, if that rationale for detention became irrelevant, Endo's appeal for a writ of habeas corpus must be honored.[30] The justices' increasing skepticism of claims to sweeping discretion by the military was further revealed in Reed's observation that "even where we have espionage and sabotage, . . . it is not permissible to restrain the loyal citizen . . . for a longer time than is necessary to determine loyalty."[31]

When a majority had finally formed in favor of Endo, Chief Justice Stone (anticipating that the army would shortly announce an end to the internment program) delayed the conclusion of deliberations and publication of the decision. Justice Douglas strongly objected to this delay: Endo was a loyal citizen posing no security risk, Douglas reminded the chief justice, and so she had an unquestioned constitutional right to her freedom immediately.[32] "The matter is at a standstill," Douglas stated, "[only] because officers of the government have indicated that some change in detention plans are under consideration." Such administrative or policy developments should not be permitted, Douglas insisted, to trump Endo's absolute right to be released: "I feel strongly that we should act promptly and not lend our aid in compounding the wrong by keeping her in unlawful confinement through our inaction a day longer than necessary to reach a decision."[33]

Justice Douglas's position on *Endo* was a signal that once the Court moved away from consideration of the wholesale evacuation and internment of an ethnic group at a time of extreme emergency—that is, the measures pursued soon after Pearl Harbor, with explicit executive and congressional authorization—and dealt instead with deprivation of the civil liberties of an individual citizen in a discrete situation clearly not an emergency, the justices would not be so solicitous of the army's prerogatives or the Executive's war powers. Thus, in language strikingly absent from the other Japanese-American cases, the draft majority opinion in *Endo* asserted that a balance must be struck between, on the one side, a need for the kind of extraordinary powers "sufficient to deal with the exigencies of war time problems," as had been affirmed in the earlier Japanese-American cases, and, on the other, the Constitution's safeguards of individual liberty against arbitrary power. The latter included "procedural safeguards surrounding the arrest, detention and conviction of individuals, compliance with which is essential if convictions are to be sustained."[34]

The *Endo* majority also cited the constitutional strictures of Article I, Section 9, which provided that the writ of habeas corpus might be suspended only in "cases of rebellion or invasion when the public safety may require it," offering, in addition, a dictum on a rule of interpretation: namely, that executive orders and acts of Congress (even war measures) should be narrowly construed when basic individual liberties were at stake "so as to avoid any possible conflict with specific guarantees of the

Constitution."[35] With the Court in *Endo* taking such a position on the war powers, so different from its posture when espionage and sabotage were alleged to be directly at issue in an extreme emergency, the prospects for the army in the *Duncan* appeal could not have looked very promising as the opposing briefs were being prepared in 1945.

Still further doubt was cast on the army's prospects for victory in *Duncan* by Justice Roberts's insistence, in his concurring opinion in *Endo,* that the Court should forthrightly face the constitutional issue instead of worrying (as the majority did in its opinion) whether or not the statute's language authorized the petitioner's detention after a formal finding of her loyalty. Guarantees of the Bill of Rights were at stake, Roberts declared; and "there can be but one answer" to the question of her right to be freed from detention immediately.[36] Justice Murphy, too, had already placed himself on record as forcefully denouncing the entire policy of detention as "an unconstitutional resort to racism."[37]

As one considers the portents that could be read from these cases that preceded the *Duncan* appeal, it seems obvious that any arguments (such as those the government made before the Court in *Duncan*) contending that the use of provost courts for ordinary civil and criminal justice matters was necessary to assure the security of the Islands had lost their logical force simply by the passage of time. For during the entire period from the Pearl Harbor attack to the submission of the habeas petitions in 1944, no acts of either sabotage or espionage by Japanese Americans or anyone else had occurred in Hawai'i.[38] To be sure, the army ascribed the successful record, in this respect, to the stringency and coercive potential of its martial law regime.[39] By the last months of the war, however, let alone in a retrospective postwar view, the justices had ample reason to conclude that espionage and sabotage were no longer a serious threat, and certainly not with reference to the prospect of an alleged "imminent invasion."

The *Duncan* and *White* Opinions

All these considerations became significant in the drama that played out in the justices' chambers prior to the announcement of the Court's decision in the Hawai'i cases. After the initial conference, with a majority lining up in favor of *Duncan* and *White,* Chief Justice Stone assigned the opinion to Justice Black, author of the majority opinion in 1944 upholding the government's internment program in the *Korematsu* case. The issue this time focused, however, on two Anglo-American petitioners; they were not members of the suspect, stigmatized ethnic group that Black had been willing to subject to exceptional deprivations of civil liberties because of the alleged security threat on the West Coast.

The chief justice hoped that the majority opinion would be narrowly based, with the Court finding that its analysis of the specific facts relating to the situation in Hawai'i did not support the army's claim that "necessity" justified the military regime's use of provost courts. Stone had no doubt that the army had acted wrongly in Hawai'i. But he counseled against a principled constitutional decision, as he hoped above all to avoid adoption of a comprehensive rule that would cripple the government in a future emergency with conditions that could not be known in advance. "I do not think we have to state what the constitutional limits of martial law are," Stone told Black, continuing:

> I should not be prepared to say that under no circumstances, when the public safety and order require it, the military, having authority to apply martial law, could not set up courts and try offenses. But it is enough for present purposes, even assuming danger of invasion, that there is no public necessity of creating military courts when the civil courts are open and able to function.[40]

Justice Black, however, was of a very different mind; indeed, the entire thrust of his effort, as he sought to bring his colleagues into the majority opinion, was based initially on the notion that the *Milligan* principle must be reaffirmed, placing the *Duncan* decision on solid constitutional, not merely statutory, grounds. Thus Black responded to the chief justice privately with a reaffirmation of the *Milligan* principle that denied the Executive exclusive discretionary authority in taking over civilian governmental functions.

Three underlying principles, pertaining to Black's understanding of *Milligan,* were revealed in his confidential exchanges with Stone. First, an emergency did not authorize an arbitrary departure from the principle of separation of powers. The Executive could not claim the power "to obliterate the Congress and the Courts," any more than one or both of the other branches could destroy the Executive.[41]

Second, Black contended, no military regime that went so far in its claims of authority as the one in Hawai'i had done could be justified under the Constitution. Even in an emergency that warranted extraordinary measures under martial law, including the detention of individuals on a temporary basis, there was no "necessity" that could justify how the army in Hawai'i "wiped out all previously enacted legislation, substituted military edicts, and set up military tribunals over the courts throughout the islands"—in sum, a "totalitarian program." Black was unwilling to accept Stone's suggestion that the majority opinion should stop with a statement that the circumstances in the Hawai'i situation—that is, the facts on which the claim of "necessity" was founded—did not justify what the army had done. To do so, Black feared, would imply that an allegedly more severe emergency might justify such a totalitarian approach in other times: "Judicial invalidation of the program on the limited ground that the circumstances did not justify it in this loyal territory could be accepted as a declaration that other circumstances could." This he was unwilling to propose, either explicitly or (as Stone suggested) by implication. Nor did Black, at least initially, wish to rest the opinion solely on a narrow reading of the Hawai'i Organic Act's provisions regarding martial law; if that was what others in the majority decided, he told Stone, "my present idea would be to rest my own vote squarely on the *Milligan* case."

Third, Black denied that the military's policies could be rationally tied to the effective performance of "military tasks," in the course of which there might be a temporary closing of buildings that housed even courts or the legislature. The army can, "of course, remove the obstructions which block its military progress," and even in "loyal territory" (as he spoke of Hawaiʻi) "civilian obstructionists of its imperative military functions" might be punished—but only under "the laws of war," in an exercise of martial law powers rather than total control and displacement of governmental authority. Here in Hawaiʻi was no slippery slope, no theoretical parade of horrors; here, for Black, was the ultimate outrage in a democratic society: the assertion by the army of such power that, say, in a dire emergency in the District of Columbia itself, it might act to "set up military tribunals to carry on the duties of this and other courts."[42]

Black's reference to "*this* and other courts" made his position unequivocally clear: the army's declarations that the civilian courts in Hawaiʻi were mere agents of the military government was a threat, ultimately, to the authority of the Supreme Court itself, no less than to trial courts on the ground. The courts were a sacred palladium, in Black's constitutional theology; and so the army had claimed too much. The military's claim against the authority of the judiciary itself was, in the end, thus decisive with Black. It probably was also influential in the forming of a majority on the Court to reverse the Ninth Circuit's finding, upholding the *Duncan* and *White* appeals.

In crafting the compromise draft that became the Court's majority opinion, published on February 25, 1946, Black did, in the end, adopt the tactic of focusing upon the statute and its interpretation, stating that the Organic Act could not be construed as giving sweeping authority to the army to supplant the civil government. In a narrow legal sense, then, his opinion did not reach the constitutional issue of whether Congress could ever properly authorize such a regime over a protracted period of war with a receding threat of invasion.[43]

Nonetheless, Black included in the opinion a long discourse on the history of habeas corpus in Anglo-American law, thus clothing the ruling in a mantle of constitutional rhetoric. He left no doubt that the army's regime in Hawaiʻi represented to him the very kind of tyranny that had made the habeas writ historically so vital to liberty. Nor did Black find any room for doubt that Congress understood the danger of such tyranny when it passed the 1900 Organic Act: "The phrase 'martial law' as employed in that Act, . . . while intended to authorize the military to act vigorously for the defense of the Islands against actual or threatened rebellion or invasion, was not intended to authorize the supplanting of courts by military tribunals."[44]

Chief Justice Stone wrote a separate concurring opinion: He remained convinced that Black's approach to the issue was dangerously constraining and could leave the government and the military powerless in some future emergency. His spare and eloquent concurring opinion thus focused upon the concept of emergency powers.[45] Unlike the majority, who asserted that the term "martial law" was of indefinite meaning, Stone insisted that it must be viewed in terms of the situation: "Its object, the preservation of the public safety and good order, defines its scope. . . . A law of necessity," Stone declared, can justify important sacrifices of constitutional liberty in order to avoid undermining military security and defense. He found, however, that the government's power to command sacrifice in this regard "may not extend beyond what is required by the exigency which calls it forth."[46] The civil courts, he wrote, operating under constitutional rules, and not the military commander's fiat, must be relied upon to make the final judgment of what was so "required" by the emergency.

In explaining his own findings as to the facts, Stone adverted to the testimony of the military authorities themselves in the district court, where they "advanced no reason which has any bearing on public safety or good order for closing the civil courts to the trial of these petitioners, or for trying them in military courts."[47] Bars and other places of public amusement were open when the petitioners were tried, he wrote, and the civil courts were open for other purposes. From these facts and related evidence of how the society and economy of the Islands were functioning (a matter of taking "judicial notice"), Stone found nothing that could support the government's contentions that the prosecution of these cases in the provost courts was a military necessity.

Justice Murphy was not content with Black's rehearsal of the history of habeas corpus in the jurisprudence of Anglo-American civil liberty, nor did he find sufficient the chief justice's terse references to the facts of everyday life in the Islands while the provost courts continued to operate despite normalization of civilian life in so many other respects. Instead, in his separate concurring opinion, Murphy went through the arguments of the government step by step. He commented on each contention with a sense of outrage that bespoke his concern to remove any impression of doctrinal ambiguity or judicial timidity that might invite a repetition of such military action in future times. Murphy especially abhorred General Richardson's contention, in trial court testimony, that the civilian courts could not be relied upon to maintain order because they were subject to "all sorts of influences, political and otherwise," so that to be effective, military rule must be absolute and not subject to challenge. "The mere fact that it may be more expedient and convenient for the military to try violators of its own orders before its own tribunals," Murphy declared, "does not and should not afford a constitutional basis for the jurisdiction of such tribunals when civil courts are in fact functioning or are capable of functioning."[48]

Even more offensive, Murphy wrote, was Richardson's assertion that security could not be achieved merely by proclaiming the Islands to be a military area, that is, by dealing with the emergency in the same way as the army had done on the West Coast, with its orders enforceable by the federal courts as provided in executive orders and congressional statutes. "That the military refrained from using the statutory framework which Congress erected," Murphy rejoined, "affords no constitutional justification for the creation of military tribunals to try such violators."[49]

Justice Murphy saved his strongest criticism, however, for the government's argument that the presence of large numbers of Americans of Japanese ancestry in Hawai'i was in itself a sufficient justification for army rule despite the complete absence of any documented sabotage or espionage. As he had done in previous dissents, Murphy characterized this classification of an entire ethnic or racial group, with resultant loss of liberty to them, as blatantly unconstitutional; and he denounced forthrightly the racism that was inherent in such an approach.

Racism has no place whatever in our civilization. The Constitution as well as the conscience of mankind disclaims its use for any purpose, military or otherwise. . . . We must be on constant guard against an excessive use of power . . . that results in the needless destruction of our rights and liberties.[50]

Justice Burton, joined by Frankfurter, filed a dissenting opinion. It endorsed wholesale the government's claims as to emergency powers and the need for the army itself to determine the issue of "military necessity" without being subject to review by civilian courts. In the initial conference, Frankfurter apparently spoke of the horrors of the Holocaust in Europe and the need to support the discretion of the military in order to assure national survival in a global war.[51] In his *Korematsu* opinion in 1944, Frankfurter had espoused what reads like a doctrine of total judicial self-restraint in wartime. Congress and the president, he wrote, should have full authority to decide how the Japanese Americans must be treated: "That is their business, not ours," he had declared.[52] This spirit of extreme deference was evident now in Burton's *Duncan* dissent. His opinion shrewdly suggested that the Court's vote on the Hawai'i appeals might have been quite different if war were still being waged; the Court in 1946 enjoyed the luxury of hindsight, in the wake of an overwhelming military victory. It was too easily forgotten, Burton asserted, that the Islands during the war were "like a frontier stockade under savage attack."[53] Frankfurter had made this argument in conference, stating (as Justice Murphy recorded his views): "Our job is that of historian. We sit here on Dec. 6th [*sic*] 1945. It is my duty to project myself into 1942. . . . What would this court have done in '42 and [an] injunction was sought? This is [the] President of the U.S. and he had [the] responsibility of conducting war. If I can't say I wouldn't vote for not enjoining [the] military in '42 I can't do it now."[54]

The executive must retain the option of permitting the military to exercise absolute control in such a situation, and especially so, Burton went on—echoing the premises and contentions of the majorities in *Hirabayashi* and in *Korematsu*—when "the possible presence . . . of many Japanese collaborators" rendered the fortress exceptionally vulnerable to "disastrous sabotage and terrorism among civilians."[55] Burton therefore concluded that the Organic Act should have been interpreted in the broad terms that would authorize complete military rule, leaving to the army itself the decision as to what powers were necessary for it to perform its functions.[56] For the two dissenters, the operations of the provost courts, and the complete takeover of Hawai'i's civil government as well, were thus justified by the emergency and by a doctrine of government's need to defend the nation against possible destruction.

Duncan (together with White) thus prevailed in the final 6–2 decision by the Court. (The Court's ninth Justice, Robert Jackson, was on leave as chief counsel at the Nuremberg war crimes trials and did not participate in the *Duncan* vote.) "The great lesson to be learned from the case," the legal scholar and martial law expert Charles Fairman commented shortly after publication of the decision in *Duncan*, is that the Court has rejected the theory that, in a situation of threatened invasion or comparable emergency, it is proper for the commander to take upon himself the position of 'military governor' of the entire community, bringing the whole field of government under his command and thereafter operating at will either through military subordinates or through civil functionaries acting as his 'agents.' This was the theory which General Richardson expounded, . . . and this is the theory which the Court definitively repelled.[57]

During the war years, as we have noted, Fairman had been supportive of the army's prerogatives in the Japanese-American exclusion and detention policies, and he had been critical of Garner Anthony's initial challenge to the military in Hawai'i. Moreover, as a legal officer in the army, Fairman had been associated actively with the defense of the military's regime in Hawai'i.[58] Hence it was especially telling that now even Fairman aligned himself against the absolutist view taken by the army and embodied in General Richardson's trial testimony in *Duncan*.

Fairman concluded that "the justification for trying Duncan and White by provost court really came to nothing more than the *ipse dixit* of the commander."[59] Unlike the evacuation and detention of the West Coast Japanese Americans—which Fairman was still prepared to defend on the grounds that at least such measures, "though drastic, had a clear relation to a permissible end"[60]—the takeover of civilian justice and the use of the provost courts in Hawai'i had no such relationship. Yet Fairman still remained in the camp of those who would give the commander exceptional powers in a true emergency: so long as the purpose be lawful, "then *pro tanto* the civil authority gives way."[61]

But even for Fairman, the determination of what purposes were "lawful" could not be left to the commander alone. Although he was unhappy with the absolutist tone and implications of Black's opinion, with its sweeping and resonant appeal to the entire tradition of Anglo-American legal history, Fairman declined to endorse the imperatives that naturally flow from "military thinking," which, as he now conceded, "runs to absolute solutions." The proper principle in military emergencies, he now concluded, was "that the commander's authority over civil affairs is limited to measures of demonstrable necessity."[62] This, he admitted, would require the army and the civilian governors to accept and live with "not an *absolute* but a *mixed* situation; not exclusive but *concurrent* authority. This is not congenial to the soldier's mind; but the alternative would obliterate interests of civil liberty and democratic government too valuable to be sacrificed more than is actually necessary."[63] The Court had now made clear, Fairman conceded, that— contrary to the burden of his own arguments in his earlier writings—it was the federal judiciary, and not the army itself, that would properly make the final judgment as to the necessity of extraordinary measures in a situation such as that of wartime Hawai'i.[64]

For some of the other actors in the constitutional drama set in motion by army rule in Hawai'i, it was difficult to assume the posture of cool reassessment that Fairman had taken.

Reflecting many years later on his role in the entire history of the martial law cases, Edward Ennis described the personal dilemma that he had faced from the conflict of values between constitutional principle and his obligations as government counsel: "I went out there [to Hawai'i] and defended General Richardson and Admiral Nimitz," he said, "and took those cases up to the U.S. Supreme Court and argued them, and lost them, I am glad to say. I thought they were wrong at the time."[65]

Judge McLaughlin was even harsher in his postwar assessment of martial law. He had presided in the federal district court in White's hearing, and he also had granted Spurlock's petition in a case (mooted by the army's release of the prisoner before it was heard by the Supreme Court) in which the procedures of the provost court in convicting an African-American laborer were so brutal and indefensible that even General Richardson admitted the dangers of pursuing the appeal.[66] Speaking before the Social Science Association of Honolulu, though asking that the presentation not be released to the press, Judge McLaughlin gave full vent to his personal views. What the army had done in Hawai'i was dangerous above all, he declared, because "if what they did here was right, it could be done at any time in any other part of the United States." In this sense, McLaughlin declared, America had been brought perilously close to authorizing "military dictatorship."[67]

McLaughlin found nothing in the record that would lead him to conclude, as, for example, Fairman had contended, that the army had acted in good faith.[67] Nor did he accept the contention in an editorial published days before in the *Honolulu Advertiser,* which—in keeping with the paper's consistent support of army rule during martial law—asserted that the *Duncan* majority failed to understand civilian opinion in the Islands: The editorial had been headlined "They Did It!—And We Liked It!"[68] Against such views, Judge McLaughlin denounced as unconscionable the military's policies and its manipulation of the law through mooting of cases and advancement of unconstitutional claims. "They did it intentionally," he concluded:

> They did it with design aforethought. They did it in knowing disregard of the Constitution. They did it because Hawaii is not a State. They did it because they did not have faith that Americanism transcends race, class and creed. So 'They Did It'—with a gun.[69]

Chapter Eighteen

WAR'S AFTERMATH AND THE COURTS

The army leaders had long been worried that an adverse decision on martial law by the Supreme Court could trigger civil liability suits directed against individual officers, and, as we have seen, they had prepared for such an eventuality. Indeed, men who had earlier shown little regard for considerations of due process or constitutional rights now became zealous champions of "fair play."

The first note of alarm on this score came from General Green in January 1943, when he anticipated his reassignment to a position on the mainland. Reminding his successor, General Morrison, that Governor Stainback "despised us," he advised Morrison to deny Stainback access to the military's office files. "We would never be able to see them once they were turned over," Green predicted.[1] From that time forward, Morrison and other legal staff in the Hawai'i command seem to have kept the possibility of civil liability in the forefront of discussion whenever future exigencies were discussed.

With Green's transfer to the office of the judge advocate general (JAG) in Washington, the same perspective began to surface there as well. Thus in September 1944, as noted earlier, a JAG office memorandum to Secretary Stimson advised that the president himself, rather than the commanding general in Hawai'i, should issue an executive order if martial law were to be terminated. In that way, the memorandum stated, military officers would "be able to plead *respondeat superior* and to have the proof on record" when and if lawsuits materialized.[2]

After the oral arguments in the *Duncan* case were completed in the Supreme Court, but before the Court had issued its ruling, the Justice Department authorized a full investigation of the martial law regime by Frederick Bernays Wiener. Wiener had been a government lawyer since 1933, serving in the Department of the Interior and then as special assistant to the attorney general in the Justice Department. He was an expert in military law: a reserve officer in the Judge Advocate General's Department, he went on active duty in 1941 and served throughout the war, returning to the Justice Department as assistant to the solicitor general in 1945.[3] Generals Green and Richardson, as we have seen, arranged for their legal advisers, Morrison and Slatterly, to remain in their OMG posts during the investigation.[4] The two men (Morrison, of course, himself a defendant in civil suits!) were the only ones "with a thorough knowledge of all the files," Richardson wrote; and so "to relieve them now . . . would be calamitous and certainly would be most prejudicial to my personal interests."[5]

Civil Suits: The Army in the Dock

General Green, newly appointed as judge advocate general, meanwhile was using his authority and the prestige of his office to mobilize an intensive effort to prepare his own defense in pending suits that were directed at him for his actions as Executive in the OMG. In this process, he drew heavily upon his subordinate staff in the JAG offices. "It is a comfort," he wrote to a confidante, "to know that I have 110 lawyers in my own shop whose services I would call on to the extent necessary. . . . I am taking no chances."[6] He assigned a team of legal officers of captain's rank to do research in the relevant records of the War Department (copies of which survive, in great volume, archived in Green's private papers) and to prepare an interpretive summary and report for him. No doubt well attuned to what their chief wanted from their efforts, the legal team submitted a statement of findings that could be incorporated into a legal brief and also used in other ways with Congress or for public relations purposes.

Their memorandum was in five parts. First, it set out the full *respondeat superior* rationale, declaring that Green had exercised no independent power as Executive, but rather had operated in a chain of command in which "both Mr. McCloy and General Emmons took an active, and, by virtue of their superior rank, a more authoritative part" than Green's. Second, it contended that any criticism directed at the martial law regime or its officers was not objective but must be seen as "part of the campaign" by Stainback and others to regain civilian control. Third, the memorandum averred that this "campaign" was not supported by the citizenry in Hawai'i, and in fact was "opposed by public opinion" regarding both the command's leadership and martial law more generally. Fourth, it asserted, there was an intentional pattern of "underhanded efforts . . . to discredit the military authorities"; however, it cited only one specific example, declaring it to have been "typical." The fifth—and most astonishing—assertion accused Governor Stainback of indifference to the cause of victory in the war effort. This contention was "documented" by reference to letters written by the governor that were intercepted by army censors, and then shared with the OMG and the War Department: "Governor Stainback's letters to Secretary Ickes revealed that the governor's 'chief objectives' were not to 'cooperate in the prosecution of the war, but to regain his peacetime jurisdiction and to injure, as much as possible, those men who had opposed him' in this attempt—principally yourself [Green] and to a somewhat less extent, General Emmons."[7]

The archival records in fact compel entirely different conclusions with regard to nearly all the crucial points. Most important, it was Green, Richardson, and Morrison who resorted to innuendo and often distorted facts in an effort to discredit the critics of martial law, just as the Wiener investigation would conclude. As to the notion that Stainback was not interested in "assisting" the OMG regime, moreover, the archival documentation clearly reveals that Green, Morrison, and Richardson all defined "cooperation" and "assistance" as the equivalent to absolute obedience to their orders and policies.[8]

The case of *Duncan v. Kahanamoku* was meanwhile receiving widespread publicity in the media, including a series of broadcasts by the popular conservative radio commentator Fulton Lewis Jr., that charged the army with having engaged in numerous gross abuses of power in the administration of martial law in the Islands.[9] When Stimson's successor as secretary of war, Robert Patterson, was asked by Congress for a response to the Lewis broadcasts, Green quickly prepared an extended defense of his position. Patterson signed on to this document and forwarded it to Congress almost verbatim as Green had written it; and it was read into the *Congressional Record* on March 26, 1946, just when the *Duncan* case decision was released. In this document, Patterson (quoting verbatim from Green's memorandum) contended that the Islands had been "exposed to dire peril" and that "the civil courts [were] ill adapted to cope with an emergency" such as Hawai'i experienced—a rehash of the argument about the incapacitation of the civilian courts that the Supreme Court majority had just explicitly rejected. Patterson denied that any person had been interned without a careful and fair hearing, or that any prisoner had ever been held in conditions that were less than comfortable.[10]

When restrictions on civilian life were progressively relaxed, Patterson asserted, it was on the army's own initiative. In a remarkable summing up that obscured and distorted the findings both of fact and of law as had just been stated in the Supreme Court's opinions in *Duncan,* Patterson declared: "The Army did not in any sense oust or overthrow the civil government of the Territory. *The civil authorities of the Territory continued for the most part to function as before, their authority supported and assured by martial law.*" Withal, he denied that the military had acted in any regard that would justify charges that it had behaved tyrannically or exceeded its legal authority.[11]

Garner Anthony would later comment that it was hard to understand how Patterson, "an able lawyer," would put his name to a document that patently demonstrated "a lack of familiarity with the opinion of the Supreme Court."[12] That the language and content of Patterson's statement were, in fact, Green's own makes this feature of the document much less puzzling.

How Green would later rely on the *respondeat superior* defense was made evident in a further memorandum from his hand, this one sent under his own name to the War Department's chief public relations officer. He demanded that a press release be issued that unambiguously absolved him of responsibility for the results of army policy and administration under martial law. "It is of course quite clear," he averred, "that I am not responsible for the proclamation of martial law which was issued by the Civilian Governor of the Territory, and was approved by the President of the United States. Likewise I am, of course, not responsible for the administration of martial law. It was a War Department activity from the start; the responsible head was the commanding general."[13]

It is understandable enough that Green should have insisted that the War Department's responsibility be recognized, given how McCloy and Stimson had generally been so dedicated to supporting the military's decisions in Hawai'i. In what surely was one of the most disingenuous statements to be found in all the archival records of martial law in Hawai'i, however, Green went much further: he presumed to implicate even his most implacable critics in the Roosevelt administration in Washington, Secretary Ickes and Attorney General Biddle. Green wrote: "Broad policies were passed on not only by [Stimson] but by the Secretary of the Interior, the Attorney General, and in some cases, the Navy Department. It is these policies which are really being attacked"![14]

The inner core of Green's character was revealed in this document as perhaps nowhere else in the records. The man who in later speeches and writing preened about his central role in the control of civilian life in the Islands—recording in his private diary, "My authority was substantially unlimited"—cowered, when facing law suits in this period, behind the shield of the notorious defense that he was only under the authority of his superiors. Ironically, in General Emmons's testimony in a civil indemnification suit such as Green was seeking to head off, he was asked by counsel to describe Green's position under his command. Whether unable to resist the opening for invoking some nuances, or possibly instead giving vent to personal resentment of Green's craven public stance, Emmons described Green's status in the OMG as that of merely a "superior type chief clerk."[15] He was himself the one in command, Emmons made clear, and he accepted entire responsibility for the policies pursued.

As Green and others had feared, several civil indemnification suits were filed by former internees throughout 1946 in federal trial courts in both Hawai'i and mainland locations.[16] Among others, Carl Magnus Armfelt, Gunther Herbert Walther, and Anna Walther—all of whom had been arrested on December 8, 1941 as being pro-German and interned for nearly two years—filed suits against Short, Emmons, Morrison, Richardson, and Green in the U.S. District Court in Hawai'i. The U.S. Marshal was unable to serve the summons against the defendants, and Armfelt's suit was dismissed in 1946.[17]

In early 1947, a bill was moved in Congress for a dollar-a-day compensation to be paid to any persons who had been "unlawfully interned."[18] The War Department opposed the legislation, since it would implicitly recognize its culpability for illegal actions; and for precisely the same reason, the Hawai'i territorial delegate in Congress, Garner Anthony, and others in Hawai'i political life voiced support for it.[19] In fact, Richardson himself had argued in favor of compensation. It "should be self-evident," he wrote to the secretary of war in spring 1946, that the government should give redress to any individual who had sustained legal injuries "as a result of a war activity, such as martial law in Hawaii," certain aspects of which the Supreme Court had declared illegal. "Long-range statesmanship," he continued, "requires (a) immunity of military commanders for their official acts done reasonably and in good faith in the course of their duties, [and] (b) confidence in the civilian population that if the Army does anything illegal under martial law, it will pay for it."[20]

The proposed legislation affected the civil suits because attorneys for the former internees may well have anticipated that the prospects of the bill's enactment might influence juries or judges in rendering judgments (or in setting damage award sums).[21] Whether for that reason, or owing to the statute of limitations, legal costs, or other grounds, potential plaintiffs were discouraged from going forward with their suits. Hence most of the litigation had disappeared from the dockets by the last months of 1947.

The withdrawal of most of the suits did not mean, however, that the military officers who were being sued were able to relax their vigilance or to think that they had prevailed without the bother of defending themselves in court. On the contrary, Green, Emmons, Morrison, and Richardson, who were the main targets of litigation, were outraged that they were being stranded (as they saw themselves), in effect abandoned by the government and now facing the possibility of enormous financial liabilities. For not only did the War Department oppose any congressional provisions for restitution to those who had been incarcerated, it also decided against asking Congress to enact legislation that would have guaranteed full compensation to any officer held liable for damages in the ongoing suits that remained. Having received the investigative report from Wiener, which advised the War Department to keep a low public profile because the army's record on martial law in Hawai'i was so indefensible, the department stood by while law suits were in their early stages.[22]

Richardson regarded this stance as a gross betrayal by the government, and one he did not deserve. He also contended for the purely military interest at stake. In future wartime emergencies, he argued, commanding generals such as himself "may hesitate to take the prompt decisive action that the interest of the nation requires."[23] In this regard, at least, the personal interest of the generals prevailed, as the government decided to assign Department of Justice counsel—including Wiener himself, another irony—to represent Emmons and Richardson in civil suits.

Only one of these suits actually went to a full trial; it was held in 1950, in the federal district court in Honolulu, with its daily proceedings reported in close detail by the Hawai'i press. It was no surprise—at least to anyone familiar with the record of the legal challenges to martial law in the war years—that this last remaining suit was pressed by that indefatigable litigant, Dr. Hans Zimmerman.[24] He had returned to Honolulu after the war's end and apparently revived a lucrative naturopathic practice (also enjoying the benefit of his wife's substantial stream of income from her own assets). To represent him as counsel, he engaged A. L. Wirin, the Los Angeles civil liberties attorney who had handled his habeas appeals for the ACLU in 1942. He also brought in several local attorneys to assist. In an initial filing in the federal court in Honolulu in 1946, Zimmerman entered a claim for $575,000 in damages against General Emmons, former governor Poindexter, General Morrison, former FBI Hawai'i Bureau Chief Robert Shivers, and the former Army Intelligence chief under Emmons's command, Colonel George W. Bicknell. Also named in the suit were Captain Irving H. Mayfield of the naval intelligence service, and several civilians who had served on the loyalty review board that recommended Zimmerman's internment in December 1941.[25] Federal Judge Paul J. McCormick, of the district court in Los Angeles, was assigned to the case when Judges Metzger and McLaughlin recused themselves because of their former involvement in ruling on internees' and provost court prisoners' habeas petitions. (In the case of McLaughlin, there was also the possible appearance of prejudice owing to his service in 1942 on the internment review board in Hilo.)[26]

When Zimmerman's case finally went to trial before a jury in December 1950, the lawyering took a turn that was probably fatally damaging to Zimmerman's chances of victory: his attorneys, stating that they had become convinced that the other defendants had acted "in good faith," dropped the action against all the persons named in the suit except General Emmons.[27] In the course of the trial proceedings, General Emmons conceded freely that the process accorded Zimmerman and other internees had fallen far short of constitutional standards as applied in normal times. He did not seek to contend that responsibility for decisions on the ground was anyone's but his own, but he insisted that he was acting under clear authority devolved on him with approval of the president.[28]

In addition to depositions taken from General Green and others involved in the internments decisions, selected extracts from the FBI records on Zimmerman were subpoenaed and made available to counsel. (In fact, so far as we can ascertain, this was the first time that a federal court had successfully obtained delivery of such confidential FBI files.) The die was cast, however, when Judge McCormick instructed the jury: "Even if you might find that General Emmons's acts exceeded his authority, he can not be held liable in damages if his actions represented a reasonable judgment exercised in good faith under the circumstances as he saw them at the time." Only if Emmons had acted "unnecessarily and arbitrarily," and the internment was "illegal," the judge stated, could the general be liable for damages.[29] The "good faith" defense was a difficult one to discredit, even more so than *respondeat superior,* and on December 22, after many hours of deliberation, the jury came down in favor of Emmons.[30]

In the view of at least one distinguished commentator, the late Senator Hiram Fong, the outcome was a virtually foregone conclusion. Reflecting many years later on the Zimmerman situation, Senator Fong asserted that no jury of Hawai'i civilians who remembered the fear of invasion by Japanese forces that had prevailed in the Islands during the war would have voted to hold Emmons or any other army or security officer liable for damages.[31] Undaunted, however, Zimmerman appealed to the Ninth Circuit, which denied his appeal in August 1955, and then to the Supreme Court, which issued a brief order rejecting his case with finality.[32] Informed of the Supreme Court's decision, Zimmerman said, "That's the end of it. But it was a good try."[33]

And so the issue of indemnification died out—as, indeed, for mainstream constitutional law experts and most historians, though not for Islands residents, the entire history of martial law in Hawai'i seemed almost to disappear from memory for several decades. Even Garner Anthony, who had been the sparkplug of informed criticism during much of the martial law period, declined to take a role in representation of any plaintiffs in the suits for indemnification. He explained in an oral history interview in 1971 that once the war had ended, the internments and other wartime civil liberties issues became for him *pau* (in the past), at least so far as litigation other than the *Duncan* case was concerned. He had rededicated himself to his prestigious law practice, and then in the 1950s he took a leading role in the campaign for Hawai'i statehood and in writing the state's constitution. In 1955, however, he published a book on the army's record in administering martial law, a work that stood for several decades as a unique reference of substantial scope on the history of this episode in the war years.[34]

The army generals came through the lawsuits unscathed financially, and once the legal turmoil subsided they moved smoothly on with their lives. Green became a professor of military law at the University of Arizona, giving numerous public addresses in which he reiterated his arguments about the legality of martial law during his period of service. His manuscripts of public addresses and lectures are intriguing for their progressively stronger emphasis on the theme that, in actuality, he had been in sole control of Hawai'i's civilian sector—a very different story from what he had told earlier, when law suits were threatening. Many of his retrospective notations in his diaries and correspondence are pungent, condescending dismissals of the intelligence,

Secretary of War Henry L. Stimson bestowing the Distinguished Service Medal on Lieutenant General Delos Emmons, July 1943. In background is Brigadier General H. B. Lewis. Credit: Library of Congress.

rectitude, and even loyalty of those who had been prominent wartime critics of his record.[35]

Emmons became, successively, commander of the Western Defense Command, then of the Alaskan Department, and finally of the new Armed Forces Staff College in Norfolk, Virginia, before retiring in 1948 after forty-three years of distinguished service. Richardson remained as commander of the U.S. Army in the Pacific until his retirement in 1946.[36] The command post that he built at Fort Shafter in 1944, the "Pineapple Pentagon," was named Richardson Hall in his honor and still serves as headquarters for the Pacific operations of the U.S. Army. Morrison became deputy chief of staff for General Douglas MacArthur, and then he served with the army in Japan and Korea from 1950 until his retirement in 1957.

As to those men and women who had been caught in the war years as victims in either the web of provost court trials or the opaque and often cruel processes of internment and incarceration, it seems that generally they simply sought to move on with their lives. From scattered press reports, it appears that many of them—including Zimmerman—whose names had attracted public notice in fact rebuilt their lives successfully once the war had ended.[37]

The Postwar Years in Hawai'i

For the Japanese Americans who had been interned or incarcerated in camps run by the War Relocation Authority, the challenges were far greater than for others who had suffered. Many of them lost businesses and their homes; and they endured for many years the social stigma of having been *selectively* incarcerated. Many were silent about the war years, not wishing to recall painful memories and not mentioning their incarceration to their grandchildren. Some who had been shopkeepers or language school teachers took more menial jobs upon their return in order to support their families. Most of them, however, were able to resume some semblance of their prewar lives or find new ways of moving forward. The community and religious leaders who had been rounded up at the start of the war returned to find their temples and Japanese language schools closed, and they endured hard times; but many of these institutions were reopened within a few years of the war's end. Issei newspapermen and businessmen also resumed their leadership positions in the community.[38]

Other internees whose families were able to keep their businesses going were accepted back into the community and were also able to resume their lives as before the war, although many families suffered financial losses. In 1948, Congress passed the Japanese American Evacuation Claims Act to compensate losses of property suffered by those who had been evacuated or excluded from Hawai'i and the West Coast,[39] but because of the difficulty of proving property losses, few claimants received anything like full compensation. Nor was there any attempt to compensate individuals for the loss of liberty, loss of income, and psychological suffering that they endured; these were among the casualties of war.[40]

For the large Hawaiʻi Nikkei population, the war had resulted in profound social changes. The internment of their leaders, combined with fear of their own arrest and of anti-Japanese popular sentiment, induced many of the Issei to abandon outward manifestations of Japanese culture. At the same time, hundreds of Issei women became involved in service clubs (special permission having allowed such meetings, which were otherwise banned by martial law), welcoming a chance to prove they were trustworthy.[41] In 1952, Congress passed the Immigration and Nationality Act of 1952; reluctantly vetoed by President Truman but then overridden, the measure made the Issei eligible for the first time to become naturalized citizens, thus removing a major barrier to full participation in the larger society.[42]

For many Nisei, too, the war was an opportunity to prove anew their loyalty. Their disproportionally high enlistment in the armed services, the distinction in combat and sacrifices of the famous 442nd Regiment, and their contributions to military intelligence and on the home front won wide respect nationally. But their service to the nation had also raised their sights and their determination to be treated as equal citizens, while the GI Bill brought new opportunities for their advancement.[43]

For Hawaiʻi's civilian population more generally, the war had brought an improvement in their economic status as the scarcity of labor drove up wages and allowed laborers on the lower rungs of the economic ladder to rise a step or two into jobs vacated by workers who took the highest-paying defense jobs. The war's end opened the way to a period of rapid economic transformation (accompanied by unionization and turmoil in labor relations), an influx of new residents, a boom in tourism, and, in 1959, the vindication of its peoples' claims to full rights of citizenship by the granting of statehood.

Another face of vindication was manifested in the new politics of the new state: Three Asian Americans were elected from 1959 to 1963 to serve in the Congress: Hiram Fong and Daniel Inouye to the Senate and Spark Matsunaga to the House. Samuel King, who as delegate had been one of the first leaders to sound an alert against the damage to civil liberties that threatened in Hawaiʻi when martial law was declared, became a member of the Hawaii Statehood Commission and then the new state's first governor of native Hawaiian descent. John Burns, who, as head of the espionage division in the Honolulu Police Department, had called for fair play toward the Japanese Americans, became the second governor of the newly admitted state, a position he held for a dozen years. Neil Tavares, the outspoken territorial attorney general, chaired the Hawaii Statehood Commission and then was appointed a U.S. District Judge. Robert Shivers, who had done so much as head of the Honolulu branch of the FBI to promote racial harmony and to limit the arrests of the Nikkei in Hawaiʻi, was prominently discussed in the postwar years as a possible appointment to the position of territorial governor—a position made impossible by his declining health.[44] That they, along with Garner Anthony, were cast in positions of such important public trust represented a popular commitment to advancing both a robust multiracial culture and a democratic government in what had been a troubled community under harsh military control in the recent years of war.

The Renunciants and the Courts

For one group of Japanese Americans, however—including several dozen from Hawaiʻi—who had opted, for varying reasons, to renounce their U.S. citizenship and were held at the Tule Lake camp, the end of the war did not mean an end to their ordeal of incarceration. Their return to their homes was long delayed, and, for a few, it was literally decades before the last of their legal entanglement had been cleared up and their citizenship status clarified.

With Japan's surrender, the WRA was preparing to close the Tule Lake camp early in 1946. This plan was well known to the prisoners, and rumors circulated that families would be broken up with forced relocation in North America or deportation to Japan. Compounding the plight of many renunciants was the WRA's intransigent refusal in early 1945 to permit any further transfers to the Tule Lake facility of persons not already in relocation camps, even to enable families to reunite there despite the uncertainties of pending decisions on a detainee's fate.[45]

At the time of Japan's surrender, several hundred of the more than 5,000 renunciants were already in the process of petitioning the government for permission to revoke their renunciations. They cited duress, coercion by the gangs in the camps, and confusion as to their options at the time they had formally renounced. The Department of Justice (DOJ) flatly rejected their appeals, asserting that once a renunciation was filed, no reversal was possible. The government lawyers even contended that once having renounced their American citizenship, the renunciants were no longer dual citizens, but legally were now citizens only of Japan and hence "enemy aliens." As such, they were not eligible for redress against deportation. (A few individuals who had never fulfilled formal requirements for Japanese citizenship actually were now legally stateless.)[46] The DOJ adopted this bizarre legal stance on grounds that the surrender itself did not mark an official end to the war.

As events proved, the DOJ adhered doggedly to its hard-line stand on the irrevocability of renunciations throughout a long, complex period of litigation over the status of the Tule Lake prisoners.[47] The opening shot of the litigation was sounded in federal district court in San Francisco in November 1945, in a suit filed for an injunction to stop the deportation process; it was filed exactly two days before the ships carrying hundreds of renunciants to Japan were scheduled to leave port. A San Francisco civil liberties attorney, Wayne Collins, represented 987 citizen or dual-citizen plaintiffs in this suit, but he also filed a petition for habeas corpus on behalf of another group being held at Tule Lake pending their deportation as well.

Accepting jurisdiction, District Court Judge Louis Goodman, of the Northern District of California, acted immediately, heading off the impending ship boarding and placing a hold on the deportation process. His order required the government to submit evidence pertaining to individual plaintiffs' loyalty or disloyalty; until receiving such submissions, he would continue the injunction in force.[48] The DOJ responded by announcing that it would conduct a "mitigation hearing" for each individual renunciant, in order to review the evidence in files and then recommend disposition of the individual case. Even at this late stage in their ordeal of removal and imprisonment, the Kibei, both from the mainland and from Hawaiʻi, found themselves uniquely at risk: for in the mitigation hearings that followed, the government examiners apparently treated the mere fact that a renunciant was a Kibei as strong evidence of disloyalty, and thus prima facie reason to deny the petition for restoration of U.S. citizenship.[49]

As the files on individuals were submitted to him, Judge Goodman rejected this unsupported contention of disloyalty regarding the Kibei, and he also threw out other evidence that the government lawyers presented to deny the great majority of the litigants their claims. He ordered that citizenship should be restored wholesale to the renunciants involved in the suit. There was no constitutional authority, he wrote, "to detain and imprison American Nisei citizens . . . when they were not charged with criminality."[50] Goodman's final order in the case, announced in April 1949, fully three and a half years after the surrender of Japan, declared that the renunciants' state of mind at the time they signed away their U.S. citizenship had inevitably been affected by a congeries of factors: the "fear, anxiety, resentment, uncertainty," and sense of "hopelessness" to which they had been reduced by oppressive physical conditions and pervasive violence at Tule Lake, and by the government's confusing administrative policies at the camp.[51] His order acknowledged the accuracy of the contentions of counsel in argument and of affidavits submitted later by the litigants, namely, that they had been given no time to prepare for the interviews that had been conducted at the camp; they had been afforded no opportunity to summon witnesses or obtain depositions, nor to see the secret dossiers held by their interrogators; and they had been denied the right to engage legal counsel prior to their arrival at Tule Lake and the proactive role assumed by Collins. The template affidavit text, prepared by Collins, charged that the renunciants had been subject to a procedure "neither full, complete, nor adequate, . . . and neither fair nor impartial."[52]

The government immediately filed an appeal in the Ninth Circuit for reversal of Judge Goodman's order. And so once again the status of the renunciants' citizenship was in question. Deportation was still threatened, and their lives were cast in a fog of uncertainty. The proceedings in the case on appeal, *McGrath v. Abo,* were joined by other prisoners, almost all from Tule Lake, so now 4,315 renunciants were parties to the suit. Not until January 1951 did the Ninth Circuit decision come down.[53] Judge William Denman wrote the opinion for the court, accepting the lower court's factual conclusions holding that the voluntariness of individual renunciations was questionable in light of conditions at Tule Lake. Rather than restore citizenship outright to the renunciants on that basis, however, the *Abo* court held instead that there was only a "rebuttable presumption" that individual renunciants had been coerced or improperly influenced. In such a large group, the court ruled, it was logical to expect that there were in fact some disloyal persons who should not be allowed to regain citizenship, for the "state of mind" rationale would not apply to them. The court expressed similar skepticism regarding those detainees who applied for restoration of citizenship only after the bombings of Hiroshima and Nagasaki had made it evident that Japan would lose the war. Nonetheless, the Ninth Circuit decision at least held the door open for the renunciants to resume a free life once again as citizens in their land of birth.

It was thus a victory for the renunciants, but a severely qualified one—for the appeal had failed to restore their citizenship without delay, as Judge Goodman had ruled two years earlier was their firm constitutional right. Instead, thousands of affidavits and petitions would have to be filed in the district court by individual renunciants; and the government would review and submit to the court its own judgment, including any rebuttal of presumption, as the court had framed the issue, in each individual case. If the court approved the individual's eligibility for restoration of citizenship, it would be granted—but one case at a time.[54]

Disappointment felt on this score by Collins and his clients in the *Abo* case was especially keen because Judge Denman, in a case decided two years earlier, *Acheson v. Murakami,* had written for the Ninth Circuit court in a decision upholding judgment in favor of three citizens (all of them wives of Issei) who had renounced at Tule Lake. In that case, the court had ruled that their U.S. citizenship be restored forthwith. Moreover, in his *Murakami* opinion, Denman had harshly denounced almost every aspect of the government's policies for relocation and internment. He deplored "General DeWitt's doctrine of enemy racism" and his record of "inflam[ing] the existing anti-Japanese sentiment," exemplified by DeWitt's assurances to the public "that a race of such enemy blood strain must commit sabotage." The same mentality, Denman wrote, was responsible for the officialdom's crediting of rumors about sabotage by Japanese Americans in Hawai'i in connection with the Pearl Harbor raid: "The Army high command knew all these stories were false," Denman declared. The internment policy, together with knowledge of rampant anti-Japanese racism in the country, necessarily affected "the minds of our fellow citizens as to the value of their citizenship," he wrote.

Denman's opinion in *Murakami* also referred in detail to the armed turrets on corners of the stockade at Tule Lake, the cramped dormitory-style quarters that packed multiple families into crowded spaces with no hope of privacy, the lack of protection against dust storms and winter cold, and the terrifying effects of violence by the pro-Japanese groups and the gangs, all affecting prisoners' state of mind. No federal court would have permitted such conditions in any penitentiary holding convicted criminals, Denman asserted. He also offered explicit comparisons with the Nazi regime and the race hatred that it had generated. In sum, the court in *Murakami* was unremitting in criticism of the army and the WRA, and it was broadly sympathetic to the plight of the renunciants.[55]

But that decision was in 1949. The evidence that Judge Denman and his court then found sufficient in *Murakami* to restore citizenship immediately to the three women was found insufficient to justify immediate relief for the more than 4,000 litigants in the *Abo* appeal two years later. The Cold War's effect on the judicial mind in the Ninth Circuit was now at work. Thus Denman wrote in *Abo* that against the Cold War background, "with the hot war in Korea, the federal courts should be more vigilant than ever [about disloyalty]," making it important to identify "enemy minded renun-ciants," who should be denied restoration of citizenship. He went on to focus on the Kibei renunciants, citing the fact that more than half the native-born citizens held at Tule Lake were Kibei, and that the record in district court in *Murakami* had con-tended that many Kibei were "permanently pro Japanese." Thus the court assumed a new posture of "judicial vigilance," as it mandated the submission of the several thou-sand individual affidavits and the subsequent administrative reviews prior to final in-dividual determinations.[56]

In further negotiations between Collins and Justice Department officers, includ-ing Assistant Attorney General (and future Chief Justice) Warren E. Burger, arrange-ments were agreed upon for expediting the process for the government's review of affidavits. Collins worked with a majority of the named plaintiffs to frame their state-ments and oversee processing. At least fifty-five renunciants from Hawai'i submitted affidavits to the district court following the 1951 Ninth Circuit decision in *Abo*. What the total number of renunciants from Hawai'i may have been, what proportion of them were Kibei, and other interesting questions about the Hawai'i prisoners remain unresolved. What is certain is that the fifty-five plaintiffs we have identified constituted at minimum one in eleven of all the Hawai'i prisoners held at Tule Lake; it is uncertain how many of the prisoners from Hawai'i had been among the 1,327 detainees already deported to Japan in 1945–1946 who later submitted affidavits for the administrative review ordered in the *Abo* decision.[57]

Of the 5,589 applications from renunciants, citizenship was restored to 4,978.[58] The *Abo* case went on for fully twenty-three years; thus, as one scholar has noted, Collins "battled eight different attorneys general" over that time. The final district court ac-tion, a "Withdrawal and Dismissal" by the government that was filed in the sole re-maining renunciant's case, did not occur until November 13, 1968.[59]

One can easily imagine the joy of the family when a Hawai'i renunciant won res-toration; the numbers of such returnees and the timing, however, are unknown. There had been emotional public ceremonies and reunions of loved ones in Honolulu in No-vember and December 1945, when the *Yarmouth* and the *Shawnee* brought into port the mass return of hundreds of Hawai'i's imprisoned Japanese Americans, as well as dozens of Nisei soldiers. The renunciants who came back from Tule Lake were the last remnant of that coerced exodus. Their return was a series of individual events, joyous to their families, to be sure, but largely private matters. The music of the celebrations had faded; the history of the evacuations, exclusions, and internments came to a poi-gnantly quiet ending; and for them, too, at last, the war experience was ended.

CONCLUSION

W hile the military serves the vital function of preserving the existence of the nation," Chief Justice Earl Warren once wrote, "it is, at the same time, the one element of government that exercises a type of authority not easily assimilated in a free society." In order to protect the citizenry's constitutional liberties, the need to subordinate the military to the civilian authority had become what Warren termed an "axiom" in the American constitutional canon. "It is so deeply rooted in our national experience," Warren stated, "that it must be regarded as an essential constituent of the fabric of our political life. But sometimes competing with this principle . . . is the claim of military necessity."[1]

Thus in periods of great emergencies, and in response to urgent claims of "military necessity," the Supreme Court has been called upon to define the limits of extraordinary incursions on the liberties of citizens that are protected by the Bill of Rights. The case of *Duncan v. Kahanamoku* was a landmark in that history.[2] Indeed, Chief Justice Warren's reference to supremacy of civilian authority echoed both the tone and the thrust of Justice Black's exposition, in his majority opinion in *Duncan,* on the spirit of Anglo-American tradition.

In Hawai'i, the army's takeover of government, with its extraordinary curtailment of the jurisdiction of the federal and territorial courts and its extended suspension of habeas corpus, challenged head-on the concept that Earl Warren deemed to be axiomatic: the supremacy of civilian authority over the military's power. President Roosevelt and his War Department officialdom fully supported the commanders in Hawai'i, accepting the army's "military necessity" rationale to curtail constitutional guarantees in Hawai'i so radically and to defend the military's assault on Bill of Rights liberties in the litigation over habeas corpus. The *ipse dixit* of the military commander, who consistently denied the judiciary's authority to review the validity of his decisions as to what "military necessity" required, was substituted for rule of law as provided by the Constitution. The military regime, the Supreme Court found in *Duncan,* had gone "beyond what [was] required by the exigency" that had called it forth.

In the same way as the *Milligan* decision came down after the end of the Civil War, however, and as a brace of important World War I cases on wartime infringements of freedom of speech and press were decided only after the war had ended, the Supreme Court's ruling in *Duncan* on the legality of the army's trials of civilians under martial law similarly came too late to benefit the actual victims of arbitrary "justice" in the provost courts.[3] Moreover, large numbers of Hawai'i's citizens and aliens of Japanese ethnicity were arrested under martial law, often held in dreadful conditions, many of them then repeatedly moved great distances while being separated from their families, and interned or otherwise incarcerated for the entire period of the war. The survivors of these ordeals would never have the chance to hear their rights affirmed by the high court. More than four decades passed before they would share in receiving a 1988 presidential apology and financial redress of $20,000 each; but the Supreme Court never explicitly revisited the constitutional rulings that had denied them relief.[4]

It was not until 1944 in the *Endo* decision, and then in the postwar *Duncan* decision of 1946, that the Supreme Court finally weighed in to affirm citizens' constitutional liberties that were abridged, often brutally, by a military establishment and presidential administration that believed the war emergency gave to alleged imperatives of "military necessity" priority over all other values. In its administration of law and governance in Hawai'i, and to no less a degree in its litigation strategies, the army took full advantage of the president's and War Department's support to maintain a regime of martial law long after the course of actual events had rendered implausible the arguments about "necessity" that the army relied upon to justify that regime.

A Comparison with the Mainland Policies

In assessing the record of army rule in Hawai'i, it is useful, we think, to compare it with the much better known history of the wartime relocations and internments of Japanese Americans on the mainland—to consider whether the explanations that have been advanced to interpret the mainland policy may apply equally to the Hawai'i situation. Thirty-five years after the war, Congress authorized a Commission on Wartime Relocation and Internment of Civilians to review the wartime record. In its 1983 final report—which persuaded Congress to extend an official apology and to authorize payments to those who had been incarcerated—the commission stated that three forces had exercised a determinative influence on the actions of both the military and the civilian officialdom, from the White House down: "race prejudice, war hysteria, and a failure of political leadership."[5] Do these same three forces that shaped the dynamics of the mainland policies, as found in the commission's analysis, explain how and why the army was able to impose so successfully, and for so many years, its harsh regime in the Islands?

Racism and War Hysteria

First let us consider the interrelated factors of "race prejudice" and "war hysteria." The record of military rule in relation to racial prejudice, under Generals Emmons and Richardson in wartime Hawai'i, may best be described as mixed. The local political context of their decision making in Hawai'i differed significantly from that which framed and impelled the mainland command's policies that led to the mass removal and incarceration of 120,000 persons of Japanese ancestry.

In California and the West Coast states generally, where residents of Japanese descent were a tiny minority, there had long been a virulent strain of racist, anti-Japanese sentiment in society and in regional politics that reached a fever pitch with the bombing of Pearl Harbor.[6] "War hysteria" is a term that well describes the atmosphere of public opinion in the wake of the attack. Widespread rumors of spying and sabotage—all without basis in fact—were publicized in the press and attested to by leading elective officials. Racist concerns came to focus on the specific fear that Japanese forces would invade on the West Coast and be given support by large numbers of disloyal residents—both Issei and American citizens—in the Nikkei community. General John L. DeWitt, the regional commander, fiercely distrusted the loyalty of Japanese Americans, and he believed that sabotage and spying were palpable threats. Political leaders, prominently including Earl Warren as attorney general of California, advocated drastic measures to contain this alleged threat, and they sought a mass removal of all ethnic Japanese from the West Coast. Trading upon such demands from civilian politicians, DeWitt and his headquarters' staff, who were themselves also under pressure from numerous army legal officers, urged on the War Department the need for the removal and internment policies, insisting that nothing else would suffice to secure the region. The argument was wrapped in the doctrinal shroud of "military necessity" and then sold on that basis to President Roosevelt.

In Hawai'i, by contrast, where Japanese Americans were the largest ethnic group, many of the territory's political leaders were outspokenly committed to the ideal of a multiethnic society in which political equality and the rights of citizenship would be respected.[7] Although the Islands were by no means a paradise of universal interracial harmony—there was certainly evidence of considerable popular distrust of the Nikkei, and even some overt hatred—ugly expressions of racism, such as had been voiced freely at times in earlier decades, were no longer commonplace nor easily accorded any respectability in public discourse. Indeed, in the months leading up to the war, *haole* leaders had joined forces with the local FBI bureau director and with other respected leaders of the Chinese-American and Japanese-American communities to combat overt anti-Japanese sentiment. At the same time, Army Intelligence had taken the lead in a pro-America campaign among Japanese Americans.

The army command in Hawai'i was thus in a position to craft its policies as it saw best with regard to the Japanese-American population. Although myriad false rumors spread rapidly in the days following the attack on Pearl Harbor, the FBI and military authorities quickly denied them. Indeed, the local FBI chief, Robert Shivers, and the head of the Honolulu police espionage unit, John Burns, were instrumental in calming anti-Japanese sentiment both before the outbreak of hostilities and during the war itself. As a result of these factors, General Emmons did not have to contend with pervasive local racist pressures, or demands generated by hysteria, when he resisted the White House directions to prepare for a mass removal of the Nikkei population from Oʻahu. This is not to say that Emmons's decision for selective detention was met with universal acceptance; men like John A. Balch of the Mutual Telephone Company, the obsessively anti-Nikkei Acting U.S. Attorney Angus Taylor, and, in Washington, Secretary of the Navy Frank Knox continued to agitate for mass removals, but they were a relatively small, if vocal, faction.[8]

The army's policies under martial law appear, in retrospect, to have been *at least initially* both popularly supported and effective. The stringent controls imposed so comprehensively over civilian life and the initial closing of the courts were repressive, as martial law is intended to be, but no doubt they did serve the army's stated purpose of maintaining public confidence that security and public safety were assured in a time of pervasive uncertainty. Martial law also bought the time that was badly needed for shoring up the defenses against possible invasion.

Meanwhile, the command engaged in a kind of balancing act with regard to the Nikkei population. On the one hand, Emmons issued public statements—as would Richardson later on in the war—warning that any vigilante actions or personal violence against Japanese Americans would be severely punished by the provost courts. Emmons also assured the public that adequate measures had been put in place to protect against sabotage or espionage. On the other hand, the army and FBI pursued policies that involved the roundups, arrests, board hearings, and internments in which those suspected of disloyalty were roughly treated and in numerous cases unjustly incarcerated. There is no question that racial and cultural profiling was pervasive in the administrative process by which these actions went forward, with the result that an unwarranted measure of suffering was imposed on victims who were in practical terms powerless to obtain relief. Nevertheless, the fact remains that in Hawaiʻi, with the exception of its roundup of the Issei consular agents, priests, and language school teachers, the army did make some effort to distinguish between loyal and suspect Japanese Americans, rather than prejudging an entire ethnic population purely on the basis of race.

As to racism in the military itself, there was a huge contrast between the army's public posture in Hawaiʻi and that of General DeWitt and his command on the mainland. No doubt many individuals in the military in Hawaiʻi were to varying degrees skeptical about the loyalty and reliability of the Japanese Americans in the Islands. They included General Green, who remarked in his diary that the Nikkei were "vermin" who could not be understood by whites and certainly could not be trusted.[9] And racist prejudices and stereotypes often prevailed when army legal officers ruled on the findings of review boards that recommended internments or ruled upon prisoners' eligibility for parole or release. Yet the army command in Hawai'i never spoke out or wrote in public asserting the kind of vicious racist condemnations of the Nikkei population's loyalty such as DeWitt—author of the infamous "A Jap is a Jap" comment made in defense of his removal and internment policies—urged on the War Department from his headquarters on the West Coast.

On the whole, then, the army command in Hawai'i, including Green no less than his superiors Emmons and Richardson, was committed to preventing race prejudice from morphing into dangerous social tensions and interracial conflicts that could destabilize the governmental regime that the Office of the Military Governor (OMG) had imposed and thus interfere with the war effort. Indeed, the Morale Section was established within the OMG in part to work specifically to reduce racial tensions. Emmons went further in seeking to prevent wholesale infringement of the rights of the Nikkei: he tried to reassure Japanese Americans that they would be fairly treated; he sought assurances from the Roosevelt administration that those who were sent to mainland relocation centers would be provided with adequate housing, schools, and employment opportunities; and he successfully urged Secretary of War Stimson to approve the formation of a Nisei combat unit.

When it suited their purposes, however, both Emmons and Richardson proved willing to invoke the specter of subversion and disloyalty as a justification for the martial law regime. Moreover, the OMG made no response to the publication in 1943 in the conservative Honolulu *Advertiser* of featured articles contending that a "sinister influence has been at work in Hawaii for a generation and more. . . . Hawaii has been the focal point of Japanese propagandists, selfish Japanese commercial interests, and spies," and that the Nikkei population's "minds do not seem capable of publicly admitting that Japan is an enemy."[10] The army refrained from comment, declining to apply the censorship powers that it wielded on other occasions to mute or quash newspaper reports deemed unfavorable to its policies under the martial law regime. The army also posted broadsides throughout the Islands in September 1943, reprinting an *Advertiser* editorial that praised martial law, warned that Hawai'i is "not out of the war woods yet," and derided the army's critics as unrepresentative of public opinion.[11]

In resisting the demands that had built up by late 1942 to restore civilian control of government, jury trials, and the jurisdiction of the federal courts for hearing habeas petitions, the army commanders repeatedly insisted that "potential" disloyalty among the Nikkei remained a serious threat, making it imperative to keep martial law in place. In early 1944, even while conceding that the Nisei combat units had performed heroically in Italy, and that no evidence existed of any sabotage or espionage in the Islands, General Richardson defended his control over civilian life by citing the presence of the more than 160,000 residents of Japanese ancestry. "For the most part," he told the War Department, "of course, these Japanese appear to be loyal Americans. . . . [But] considering what we have at stake here, the loyalty of the many Japanese here must be subordinated to the questionable loyalty of the few." Any relaxation of "the security pressure we are able to exert against the entire Japanese community," he asserted, would make possible "intelligence leaks which might threaten any operation and might mean the defeat and loss of many men and ships."[12] This argument served as a constant theme in army policy-making councils and in the command's defense of the military government.

It was a kind of Catch-22 mantra of the commanders and the lawyers in their headquarters that there had been no incidents of sabotage or espionage *precisely because* martial law, including the exercise of provost court powers—reinforced by the army's periodic public warnings against disloyal behavior and its continuing arrests of suspects—had served so well to keep the Japanese-American population in line. The racial theme was always an essential element in that argument. Indeed, it was a dimension evident in the rationales that the generals set forth in defense of their policies down to the very last months of the war.

Failure of political leadership

In addition to race prejudice and war hysteria, the third factor cited by the Commission on Wartime Relocation and Internment was "failure of political leadership." Many of the high-ranking officials identified by the Commission as having failed in their responsibilities as civilian leaders when they permitted the mass violation of Japanese-American citizens' civil liberties on the West Coast were the same persons who had supervised the army regime in Hawai'i.

One must begin by taking the president's role into account, as it was similar in each arena: Roosevelt consistently took a pragmatic view, being concerned almost exclusively with the military security issue—and he accepted almost reflexively the recommendations of the War Department in this regard. He ordered modification of the Hawai'i military regime only when he was confronted with irreconcilable differences among his cabinet members (as when Biddle and Ickes prevailed in obtaining the agreement for partial restoration of civilian government in the December 1942 Washington meeting), or when, as happened in late 1944, he came under a spotlight of press criticism that threatened serious political damage. Harboring a strong personal distrust of all ethnic Japanese—of the Nisei no less than of the Issei—Roosevelt readily accepted the recommendations of the army, once they had been endorsed by McCloy and Stimson, for the West Coast removals in 1942 and similarly for the protracted extensions of martial law in Hawai'i until nearly the end of 1944. Indeed, in regard to Hawai'i, his authorization in early 1942 to evacuate all Japanese Americans from O'ahu went well beyond what the generals and War Department regarded as feasible. FDR clearly stated his acceptance of the "military necessity" rationale: *"I do not worry about the constitutional question. . . . The whole matter is one of immediate and present war emergency."*[13] Moreover, the reforms that the president did finally embrace did not represent anything close to a principled commitment that would have given constitutional values clear priority over the powers he accorded the army to impose arbitrary controls and hardships on citizens.

Withal, giving the army the benefit of the doubt was, for nearly three full years, the touchstone of FDR's wartime position on military government and civil liberties. One can easily imagine how the reports of deaths in combat of American troops and losses of American ships and aircraft that were reaching the president's desk in daily dispatches would have overshadowed the controversies over martial law in the ordering of priorities for his attention. Even his administration's most ardent critics of the Hawai'i military regime, Secretary Ickes and Attorney General Biddle, were reluctant to trouble Roosevelt with the martial law disputes. Although they were frustrated by his willingness to stand by the army on the Hawai'i issues, they also recognized that Roosevelt's energies were being taken up by the exhausting responsibilities of war and diplomacy. If Biddle failed to argue forcefully the issues of internment and widespread violation of individuals' constitutional rights, he did successfully bring to Roosevelt's attention in December 1942 the need to curb or reverse the military's usurpation of civilian government.

Assistant Secretary John McCloy's office was the crucial location in which a robust exercise of "leadership" (as the Commission used that word) might have had a salutary impact in requiring the army to balance civil liberties imperatives against the excesses of its Hawai'i regime. Secretary Stimson was of advanced age, and he found it necessary to restrict his hours in the office. He held to himself essentially full control over major decisions. And yet he systematically delegated important functions, assigning to McCloy responsibility for oversight of both the West Coast removal policies and the Hawai'i martial law issues.[14] McCloy therefore was the official who read the reports from the Hawai'i command; evaluated the policies pursued under martial law, including the strategies of litigation against the various suits for habeas in the courts; assimilated the consulting opinions of the judge advocate general and his staff lawyers; and, subject to review only on the most important policy issues, had to evaluate and approve the decisions made by Generals Emmons and Richardson. Within the Roosevelt administration councils, it was McCloy who also mainly carried the burden of dealing with the criticisms of the army's regime advanced by Ickes, Fortas, Biddle, Stainback, Samuel King, and Farrington. And it was McCloy who dealt with the coordination of litigation strategies to fend off the ACLU and the attorneys representing litigants in the habeas cases.

On what assumptions about the army, with what effectiveness, and with what degree (if any) of concern with constitutional principles did McCloy and the War Department discharge those responsibilities? Here again, there is a balance of considerations to be weighed. McCloy, acting for and in concert with his superior, Stimson, had many urgent assignments besides those concerned with Hawai'i and the fate of the mainland Japanese Americans. He was sent abroad, for example, in late 1943 on demanding missions to North Africa, Sicily, and Italy, and then in early 1944 to London to evaluate the military operations under General Eisenhower and to consult on planning for the D-Day invasion of France. The critical nature of these assignments, at the very heart of American military strategy and involving complex logistics and

Secretary of War Stimson (at left) bestowing the Distinguished Service Award on Assistant Secretary John J. McCloy (center) in recognition of wartime contributions, including oversight of the martial law regime in Hawai'i. At right is Robert Lovett, assistant secretary for air, receiving the same award, September 18, 1945. Credit: Department of War photo, in Henry L. Stimson Papers, Yale University Library.

politics, makes it to some degree understandable that he might have seen martial law issues as being by comparison of low priority. This consideration may have been even more applicable to Stimson himself, who was similarly engaged at times in arduous travel and on whom the president placed additional oversight responsibility for the massive operations of the top-secret atomic bomb project.[15]

As important as the depth and breadth of McCloy's other responsibilities, however, was his undeviating position, in all his negotiations with the Interior and Justice officials, regarding the army commanding general's proper role in Hawai'i: "The man on the ground," McCloy insisted, must not have his hands tied in determining what measures "military necessity" required.[16] This deferential view of the generals' responsibilities impelled McCloy to support his commanders adamantly. He hewed to that line in dealing with Ickes and others on the highest-level constitutional issues, including perpetuation of the suspension of habeas corpus, with regard to which he was in full agreement with the commanders' views. But he also deferred regularly to Emmons and Richardson on the few issues (such as their use of the title "Military Governor," and the OMG's control of labor late in the war) on which he nonetheless privately urged the generals to modify their policies.

Numerous officials in Interior and Justice who had regular contact with McCloy in discussions of the martial law policies deplored what they regarded as the core reality that McCloy and Stimson himself "did not," in Ennis's words, "do the job that constitutionally the civilian military authorities are supposed to do, namely, to examine what the uniformed military authorities ask for, and [then] determine independently whether it should be given to them."[17] Instead, they assumed the roles "of lawyers for a client."[18] Thus James Rowe, who was a top aide to the attorney general, wrote in a 1943 memorandum to Biddle that "Jack McCloy won't do anything [about the internment policy]. He is less afraid of the Attorney General than he is of Lieutenant Generals."[19] And after the war, Rowe recalled that it seemed "McCloy's main motives were to try to please the generals and make things easy for Stimson."[20] With the outcome of the war uncertain, however, neither McCloy nor Stimson regarded it as defensible in the circumstances to second-guess and flatly overrule, at the risk of weakening the war effort in the Pacific, what was presented to them as the generals' professional judgments.

In developing their wartime plans, both Stimson and McCloy seemed willing to compromise the rights of individuals—especially if those individuals were of Japanese ancestry. Thus, despite reservations initially expressed by Stimson, he and McCloy, at General DeWitt's urging, had encouraged Roosevelt to issue the controversial Executive Order 9066, calling for the removal of Japanese Americans from the West Coast. For McCloy, as for Roosevelt, military necessity clearly took priority over constitutional liberties: "[I]f it is a question of the safety of the country [and] the Constitution," McCloy stated, "... *why the Constitution is just a scrap of paper to me.*"[21]

While neither McCloy nor Stimson shared the blatant racism of DeWitt, they nevertheless regarded the Japanese as a race apart, inscrutable at best, and of unknown trustworthiness. Thus Stimson wrote in his diary on February 27, 1942, just after the decision to remove en masse and incarcerate the West Coast Nikkei population, that "their racial characteristics are such that we cannot understand or trust even the citizen Japanese."[22] Similarly, McCloy wrote in a private letter that he opposed the widespread release and dispersion of Japanese Americans from the camps run by the War Relocation Authority, since the camps would "afford a means of sampling their opinion and studying their customs and habits in a way that we have never before had possible." He continued: "I am aware that such a suggestion may provoke a charge that we have no right to treat these people as 'guinea pigs,' but I would rather treat them as guinea pigs and learn something useful than merely continue to treat them, or have them treated, as they have been in the past with such unsuccessful results."[23]

Such racial stereotyping doubtless influenced Stimson's and McCloy's receptiveness to the Hawai'i commanders' contention that because the Nikkei could not be trusted, the army's policies for martial law were essential for the defense of the Islands. Even during the imbroglio over the notorious General Orders No. 31 and the confrontation between General Richardson and Judge Metzger, McCloy and the War Department—now placed in an untenable position, with Judge Advocate General Cramer himself counseling them that there was no legitimate defense for the army command's action—sought to paper over the matter as best they could. They even went so far as withholding the order itself from publication in the *Federal Register*. McCloy also ardently pursued a presidential pardon for Richardson as part of the compromise ending that standoff. Similarly, when forced by the president's intervention to transfer General Green out of Hawai'i, McCloy and Stimson created a safe berth for him in Washington that was prelude to Green's appointment as judge advocate general—the post from which Green would orchestrate an elaborately staffed legal defense of his own record against civil damage suits that were sparked by the *Duncan* case decision.

Not easily defended, in any judgment on the quality of the War Department's supervision of Hawai'i policy, is McCloy's role when the army undertook in 1944 a publicity campaign designed to portray the termination of martial law—which in fact Richardson and his legal officers had opposed intransigently—as being the army's own idea. McCloy gave this cynical and self-serving effort his full cooperation. Even beyond that, he sought to frame the formal order ending martial law in specific terms that were intended to permit the generals and staff officers who had administered the wartime regime in Hawai'i to invoke an effective *respondeat superior* defense against any civil liability suits that might (and that did, in fact) ensue.

Finally, in assessing the failure of political leadership that enabled the military government to prevail for so long in Hawai'i, one must look at how that government came into being. The exact details of the deliberations between General Short and Governor Poindexter on that fateful day of December 7, 1941, may never be known definitively. There is no question, however, that Poindexter finally agreed, albeit reluctantly (as he testified later), to declare martial law and suspend the writ of habeas corpus. In doing so, he acted both in accordance with the provisions of the Organic Act establishing Hawai'i as a territory and with the approval of President Roosevelt. The Organic Act, however, gave the governor no authority to turn over to the army command essentially all the functions and powers of the civilian government. Nor is there any evidence that the president approved, or even saw, the text of Poindexter's proclamation that substituted military government for civilian government.

It is understandable that Poindexter, caught off-guard by the sudden attack on Hawai'i and fearing an imminent invasion, would be persuaded by the commanding general that martial law was necessary for the defense of the Islands. As General Short emphasized, the reaction of the large Japanese-American population to a Japanese invasion could not be known with any certainty. Furthermore, Poindexter apparently took at face value what he recalled as Short's assurances to him that martial law would be of short duration—a matter of days or month, if the threat of imminent invasion receded. Poindexter's declining health may also have contributed to what his detractors saw as his supine deference to the army in his willingness to accept the military takeover of civilian government.[24]

What is more puzzling is why Poindexter went so far beyond the authority granted to him in the Organic Act by delegating to the army judicial as well as executive powers. In essence, he abdicated his position and its legitimate powers; he subordinated his civilian government to the military, in contravention to the American tradition. His record of leadership was in sharp contrast to that of Ingram Stainback, who replaced Poindexter as governor in August 1942 and aggressively reasserted civilian government prerogatives—much to the consternation of the military authorities and the War Department.

Military Necessity, Accountability, and an "Occupation Mentality"

What remains as challenging to explain now as when Garner Anthony wrote on the issue sixty years ago is the question: Why should the generals in command in Hawai'i have carried things so far? Why should they have become so committed to the idea that military security would fail if the proven loyalty of the Nikkei population was acknowledged and the civil government's authority more fully restored? And why was it essential for internal safety that the banal embezzlement case of White the stockbroker, or a simple assault by Duncan that probably would have drawn a small fine in a civilian court, be tried in the provost courts, with harsh prison sentences imposed for their offenses? What possible threat to security was posed if either of these prisoners should serve a brief term and be released back into civilian life?

One must begin with the recognition that the commanders in Hawai'i lived with the specter of another Pearl Harbor disaster if they failed in sustaining a vigilant posture of defense for the Islands—a worry that was shared in the early months of the war by the civilian population at large and even by those who would later become some of the army's most insistent critics. After the passage of a few months, however, and especially after the Battle of Midway, many expert observers believed that the danger of another attack, let alone an invasion, was minimal. In addition, as Garner Anthony argued in his academic writings and as a public official and counsel to Duncan, an immediate re-imposition of martial law would have been fully justified—and above criticism—if evidence of a palpable threat did emerge.[25] Yet the commanders asserted throughout the war period that without a comprehensive control regime they could not fairly be held accountable for what might happen on their watch. As General Emmons testified in the postwar Zimmerman civil trial, he "took no chances"—and he believed that to have done less would have been a dereliction of duty.

The standard of accountability that Generals Emmons and Richardson had to keep in the forefront of policy calculus was explicitly set out by Stimson (then recently retired as secretary of war) in his testimony during the 1946 congressional hearings on the Pearl Harbor attack. In the military's lexicon, Hawai'i was an "outpost," far removed from the mainland with all the logistic disadvantages that distance imposed. Indeed the terms "outpost" and "fortress" appeared often in the War Department's correspondence with the Hawai'i command, as it also was invoked in legal argument and the Supreme Court dissenting opinion in *Duncan v. Kahanamoku*. The commander of an outpost, Stimson stated,

> is like a sentinel on duty in the face of the enemy. His fundamental duties are clear and precise. He must assume that the enemy will attack at his particular post, . . .

at the time and in the way in which it will be most difficult to defeat him. It is not the duty of the outpost commander to speculate or rely on the possibilities of the enemy attacking [elsewhere]. . . . It is his duty to meet him at his post at any time and to make the best possible fight that can be made against him with the weapons with which he has been supplied.[26]

General Short and Admiral Kimmel, held to this standard, had been removed from their commands immediately after the Pearl Harbor disaster. Their reputations were tarnished and their careers destroyed as the result of the official inquiries and congressional hearings that followed. Emmons and Richardson had to live every moment during their periods in command with the specter of another catastrophe of this sort happening on their watch.

In responding to the expectation of vigilance, however, the commanders placed the resident Japanese-American population squarely in the cross-hairs as a potential element of "the enemy" that might attack at any time—or at least be expected to aid and abet an attack. Thus the Nikkei became, for the commanding generals, an ever-present threat against which the Islands must be secured. And this internal "potential" threat posed by the ethnic Japanese residents—this "permanent enemy" as they were seen—required, as the army alleged, total control over the civilian institutions of governance and the justice system. What was an established ethos of accountability for the army thus became something qualitatively different in wartime Hawai'i: a regime that embraced final control, as we have seen, over every civilian institution and activity. Both in its position on the law and its explicit structure of powers, the regime came close to the model of a garrison state. To be sure, it was one in which elections of legislative officials continued to be held, and the administrative apparatus of the governor, as executive, was maintained; but the officials within that structure were all finally responsible, and effectively subordinated, to the military authorities in charge. The army's closure of the courts to habeas challenges that would protect fundamental liberties of American citizens was an essential part of the scheme.

The mentality in the OMG—and indeed the title of the office itself—thus was more appropriate to an occupying army than to the nation's military imposing a temporary suspension of normal constitutional guarantees. Secretary of War Stimson's experience as governor of the occupied Philippines, and his admiration for the army's record in the post-War of 1898 conquered areas, buttressed by his and McCloy's stereotyped views of the character of Japanese Americans, made him an invaluable asset to the commanders and their legal staffs in Hawai'i against challenges to the regime.[27] In addition, McCloy's view of the federal courts as a dangerous potential foe to the War Department's policies was a pivotal factor in maintaining martial law long past the time when an objective view of any danger from either the Japanese armed forces or internal subversion in Hawai'i warranted the regime as it was administered.

Personae

A word is needed with regard to the army personae involved, their individual personalities and biases being important to any explanation of why martial law and suspension of habeas were sustained for so long. General Emmons was, as we have seen, pragmatic in his approach to most martial law issues, even when faced with the critical emergency situation in the months following the Pearl Harbor attack. At the time, Emmons was not only organizing the defense of the Islands against the invasion threat, he was also overseeing the hasty buildup of airfields and fortifications and was successfully negotiating with Washington for priority in obtaining the aircraft, firepower, and personnel that would prove to be of decisive importance in winning the crucial Battle of Midway in June. He was also personally engaged in scouting, by dangerous, exploratory air flights, the remote Pacific islands that would serve as a "ferry service" infrastructure for supplying Allied forces in Australia.[28]

Under the circumstances, Green, as Executive, was given by Emmons the leeway to place his own personal stamp on the day-to-day operations of military rule. He did so in a style that Attorney General Biddle termed "autocratic, wasteful and unjust."[29] Green was confrontational and vindictive, scarcely hiding his contempt for critics, whom he was quick to condemn as acting out of motives verging on outright disloyalty. Officials in the Interior Department who sought modification of martial law were variously characterized by Green as liars, in one case as "an incorrigible Pinko," and more generally as either hostile to the military generally or else hopelessly naïve as to the security situation in Hawai'i.[30] Green thus provoked responses that understandably tended to escalate differences, as happened in Hawai'i with Anthony and Stainback, and in his personal encounters in Washington with Ickes, Fortas, and Biddle, prompting the attorney general to denounce Green to President Roosevelt as a "martinet" who should be immediately relieved of his duties as Executive.[31]

A focus on Richardson's period of command, beginning in mid-1943, a full year after the Battle of Midway, is of special relevance in probing the reasons for the prolongation of martial law. In Richardson's view, the inevitable delays of civilian courts, procedural maneuvering, and failure by judges to understand the need for keeping civilian society under control would introduce a dangerous weakness in defense of the Islands. Richardson spoke of civil liberties concerns as merely "academic" issues, admittedly an ornament of American law in peacetime but in fact a menace to maintenance of the security of an outpost "fortress" like Hawai'i in wartime. "The usual political factors that pervade civil enforcement agencies" were anathema to him, and trials in civil courts could not be expected to meet his standard for assured security: "The punishment must be swift; there is an element of time in it, and we cannot afford to let the trial linger and be protracted."[32] Richardson's full responsibilities of command embraced the supervision of army support operations, including oversight of training on Hawai'i of troops for the Saipan campaign and for the larger Pacific theater, and they eventually encompassed responsibilities crucial to all the army operations aimed at the expected invasion and planned defeat of Japan. In that context, he went so far as to claim that it risked great danger to security and the war effort—even in 1944—if he, as the commander, were to risk being "embarrassed" by an adverse review of *any* of his decisions in a civilian court's review, let alone what Judge Metzger had presumed to do in the *Duncan* habeas case.[33]

Richardson's determination to protect his prerogatives went beyond this hostility to the civilian courts. It was carried to an extreme in his tactics to discredit the opposition, including his manner of reporting to his civilian superiors in the War Department. He was highly selective in conveying information and was manipulative in interpreting it. He and the OMG legal staff under Morrison, on whom he no doubt depended heavily in this regard, consistently depicted the civilian population as wholly supportive of army rule—neglecting to admit that civilian compliance with the tough military regime was no doubt affected by surveillance through censorship of the mails and phone calls, to say nothing of the ever-present threat of provost court prosecutions. Moreover, OMG reports to Washington portrayed any criticism (such as was voiced by Anthony, Stainback, and other officials in Hawai'i, and a few liberal journalists) as being either idiosyncratic or else misguided because the critics failed to appreciate the essential role of martial law in assuring security of the Islands.[34]

Richardson and Morrison were quick to cite the advice and legal counsel of leading figures in Hawai'i politics who were supportive of the regime; but they suppressed or else blatantly sought to discredit the opinions of opponents who had to be acknowledged as "respectable" members of the Hawai'i social and professional elites. Morrison, for his part, was even more arrogant and vindictive than Green, most outrageously when he tried to sabotage Garner Anthony's legal practice by suggesting to the Islands' business leaders that they withdraw their business from Anthony's law firm.[35]

It is also relevant, we think, to ponder the suggestion voiced by some of the leading critics of the army regime that once in power "the individuals in this [OMG] office naturally enough resisted any change that would mean a liquidation of their jobs," to say nothing of the promotions in army rank that came so quickly in wartime.[36] In this same vein, Under Secretary of the Interior Abe Fortas complained that the Hawai'i command's resistance to terminating martial law in late 1944 was attributable to the selfish motives of many army officers in OMG "who have an interest and intellectual commitments in the functions which they exercised"—and whose defense of their authority was a symptom that they suffered from the common bureaucratic disorder "*jurisdictionitis.*"[37]

Enjoying the luxury of exercising final authority over civilian government and the media, as well as holding the reins of power in provost court procedures that initially were not subject to constitutional regulation or judicial appeals, the legal officers in OMG never ceased to argue that "potential danger" from within justified continuation of military control. Even in the closing days of 1944, as combat in the Pacific was thousands of miles away and the Hawai'i command had been formally downgraded by the War Department from "combat" to "support" status, Morrison and his legal staff sought to perpetuate the military regime. At a time when they were deplorably behind in processing papers for the release of Japanese-American internees found eligible for return to Hawai'i from mainland detention camps, they gave high priority to drafting proposed legislation for Congress that would transfer permanently the responsibility for governance of the territory from the Interior Department to the War Department.[38] Predictably, they were backed by Richardson, who uncritically echoed their legal views in all his dispatches to Washington, and who even as early as February 1944 had urged McCloy to seek White House approval to transfer control of the territory to the War Department—if for no other reason than for the "salutary effect" of making Secretary Ickes "content with the existing limited martial law setup."[39]

Chimerical as this scheme was, it indicated the extent to which the OMG had become a bureaucratic bubble seemingly oblivious to emerging political realities both in the War Department, where McCloy had begun in earnest pressing the army to permit the mainland detainees to return to their homes in the western states, and in the Roosevelt administration more generally.[40] Finally, President Roosevelt—confronted with the combat record of the Nisei units in the U.S. Army in Europe, pressed by Ickes and others in his administration to act, and aware that the decision in *Endo* was forthcoming—attested to the loyalty of Japanese Americans; he ordered the army and the relocation authorities to close the camps and begin the process of releasing the detainees from the camps.[41]

At the Hawai'i command headquarters, however, Morrison and his legal staff were still preoccupied (if not to say obsessed) with the perpetuation of a regime in which they enjoyed a heady level of power over others that they would never have experienced otherwise. In his 1946 report on his special investigation of the martial law regime, the Justice Department expert Frederick Wiener stated that in reviewing the legal staff's files in OMG, he found that "Every one, each letter that was selected at random and brought out, was discourteous. I haven't found a gracious letter in those files yet. You have a lot of small people clothed with a little authority, and it's the old saying of 'All power corrupts, and absolute power corrupts absolutely.'"[42] Withal, George Orwell's statement from *1984* was perhaps never more apt: "No one ever seizes power with the intention of relinquishing it."[43]

The Critics of Martial Law

The counsel that Generals Emmons and Richardson received from their legal staffs, starting with Green, was colored by the ethos of line-of-authority military norms. Green and Morrison were administrators as well as lawyers; and the likelihood of searching self-criticism on their part, let alone questioning the commander's preferences on important issues, was slender. The only considered criticism, either of law or of administration, came from outsiders; and the response of the command's legal staff was invariably defensive, often contemptuous, no matter how prestigious the credentials of the critics. In Washington, the widely respected lawyer, Judge Advocate General

Myron C. Cramer, who served in that capacity for nearly the entire wartime period, displayed an independence of mind that led him to counsel more self-restraint and respect for constitutional law than did the staff "on the ground" at the Hawai'i headquarters.[44] The only evidence of a similar concern for conscientious, principled lawyering during the period of Morrison's role as Executive was Richardson's decision in 1943 to undertake a systematic review of the files of internees and others who were being held by the army or sent to the camps in the mainland; and even this decision was made at the behest of the inspector general, who had found significant procedural irregularities in the handling of the detainees. In the review process that followed, as our analysis of the review records indicates, many manifestly unjust determinations were made on flimsy evidence or no evidence except that of stereotypical profiling, with the result that unwarranted imprisonment was prolonged. Not until they were caught up in civil indemnification suits after the war were generals who had shown a disregard for ordinary due process and the demands of equal justice suddenly converted to zealous champions of fair play.

In the early weeks of the war, however, criticism of the regime, both as to its legality and as to its fairness to the civilian population, was muted, indeed almost nonexistent. This apparent acceptance of martial law cannot be attributed to censorship alone. Even long after the danger of invasion had passed, there was considerable popular support for army rule. With the army allocating labor resources to their advantage and arranging "sweetheart deals" for the plantation owners, big business seemed to care little about civil liberties.[45] And while the labor controls resulted in severe inequities and harsh punishments from the provost courts, the unions did not openly protest; a combination of fear, patriotism, and high wages resulted in acquiescence until 1943.[46] In addition, the relatively good supply of food and other necessities, compared to the mainland's supply, contributed, as Garner Anthony pointed out, to the population's general tolerance of martial law.[47] Anthony, like Stainback, Farrington, and other leaders, became deeply concerned by what would be described by Senator Hiram Fong, in an interview years later, as civilian apathy owing to the population's becoming "too comfortable" with having the army in control.[48]

By late spring 1942, however, a few bold individuals had begun to raise their voices in opposition to the curtailment of constitutional liberties. In May, Garner Anthony published his searching, scholarly legal critique of the Hawai'i regime, setting forth the constitutional case against the army's curbs on the courts' jurisdictions and its seizure of control over civilian governmental institutions and powers. And by mid-year, administrative officials and lawyers in the Justice and Interior departments began to follow Anthony's lead, forthrightly placing civil liberties issues before their colleagues in government councils. Ickes, it might be noted, had a bureaucratic interest in regaining control of the Islands, his power having been wrested from him by the army. Yet there is no doubting Ickes's dedication to matters of constitutional principle, not least the vigilance he regarded as essential if rule of law was to be guarded successfully against the arbitrary rule by army officers, with the doctrine of "military necessity" overwhelming all other values. Ickes, Benjamin Thoron, Abe Fortas, and John P. Frank in the Interior Department, and Biddle, Ennis, and James Rowe, Jr., in the Justice Department advanced the arguments for restoration of civilian authority where army control was unnecessary and unwarranted by constitutional norm and statutory law.

Delegate King was equally outspoken in criticism of the regime, as was his successor in Congress, Joseph Farrington. Governor Stainback, too, was a consistent opponent of the usurpation of civilian government, although admittedly, like Ickes, he too had a special stake in restoration of civilian control. Judges Metzger and McLaughlin, presiding in the controversial habeas cases in district court, of course played pivotal roles in forcing the "judicialization" of the martial law issues, as the Justice lawyers had actually long wanted, framing the constitutional positions that ended in the appellate litigation and the Supreme Court's decision in the *Duncan* case.

Anthony's role, as time proved, was thus the classic one of an attorney pursuing fearlessly the cause of civil liberties in wartime—in his case, suffering some slanders from General Morrison along the way, and being denounced almost explicitly as doing harm to the war effort in his heated courtroom confrontation with General Richardson during the Duncan trial. Anthony's role was important politically as well, by dint of his correspondence with the ACLU and Delegate King in early 1942, sounding an urgent warning that the military was overreaching its proper role with its suspensions of due process and its wholesale takeover of government functions. In his published analyses and his letters, Anthony did much to define the agenda for the litigation over habeas that would follow. Ultimately he carried his arguments successfully into the courts with the *Duncan* case, the outcome of which largely vindicated his views. He received critical support from Roger Baldwin in bringing the American Civil Liberties Union into the litigation; and within the ACLU's internal councils, the brilliant Los Angeles labor lawyer A. L. Wirin, commencing with his role in the Zimmerman habeas case and continuing through the end of the war, contributed to the litigation his skilled lawyering and strong commitment to civil liberties. In the immediate postwar period, the attorney Wayne Collins of San Francisco advocated with similar dedication the cause of the renunciants who were imprisoned at Tule Lake and facing deportation.

Edward Ennis, though in government service, similarly played a classic lawyer's role in the contests over martial law. He was essentially a counselor to the situation, critical of Stimson and McCloy for their reflexive support of seemingly whatever Generals Emmons and Richardson wanted of them. Nonetheless, he met his obligations as the assigned counsel for the army in the habeas appeals, doing so, as he said, as a matter of "legal duty in a doubtful situation"; but he also stood up in the Duncan trial courtroom, and afterward in an eloquent public address, to defend Anthony against General Richardson's accusation that Anthony—by contending for Duncan's right to petition for habeas in federal court—was undermining the army's defense of the Islands. It was difficult for Ennis to walk the thin line between his duties as counsel and the pursuit of his constitutional responsibilities as an officer of the law. Although frustrated by the intransigence of the generals and the War Department in the habeas cases,

Ennis was finally successful in getting the government brief in the *Duncan* case before the Supreme Court to argue that it was a legitimate power of the Court to assess independently the facts that lay behind the army's blanket assertions as to "military necessity." This taking of "judicial notice" of the facts relating to "necessity" had been consistently opposed, of course, by the army's counsel in all the previous habeas cases.[49]

Charles Fahy, as U.S. Solicitor General, had a similarly ambiguous role. Convinced that Richardson had clearly overreached his authority in issuing General Orders No. 31, he urged McCloy to have it rescinded. And more generally, he tried to discourage the mooting of internee cases—the "flight from habeas" strategy—that was a key element in the army's legal efforts to prevent those cases from reaching the Supreme Court. Nevertheless, Fahy had presented the army's case very capably in the Zimmerman habeas appeal before the Ninth Circuit. On the other hand, over Ennis's objections, Fahy essentially suppressed evidence that would likely have favored Korematsu in the Supreme Court case on the mainland internment policy.[50]

The advocates of traditional constitutional values did win some victories in the cabinet-level policy decisions that led to limited reforms of martial law. But so long as American casualties were being taken in battle, it was extremely difficult to muster organized political support for termination of martial law from the public at large in Hawai'i, no matter how remote the combat areas might be geographically.[51] In the same way, persuading the White House to force a modification of the regime on General Richardson in 1943 and 1944 was a difficult challenge so long as the imperatives of pursuing total victory against Japan in the Pacific were the determinative factors in policy making.

Even when one recognizes, as fairness requires, that the commanders who took charge in the wake of the Pearl Harbor debacle "bore a very anxious and lonely trust,"[52] the evidence indicates that the military clearly went far beyond what the actual situation required, in a rational view, when it substituted military fiat over democratic governance so comprehensively, for so long a period, and with such grievous injustices done to civilians both in the internment processes and, with much wider impact, in the operations of the provost courts. The powers of governance and the administration of justice, once taken over by the army, were exercised with scant care for transparency and without a decent respect for constitutional imperatives that a democratic people deserve.

This prolonged suspension of constitutional rights in Hawai'i was an historic crisis of democratic government and the rule of law, one that serves to warn us of a dangerous kind of vulnerability in the fabric of American law and the structures of democratic governance, especially when a core strain of racially based discrimination is involved. The army's record in its administration of martial law illustrates well the grave dangers that inhere in a nontransparent system of military justice along with a displacement of civilian governance, entrenching in authority a military bureaucracy with a vested interest in maintaining its position of power. The martial law experience in Hawai'i stands as a reminder that systematic repression of civil liberties, in the name of "military necessity" or otherwise, exacts high costs to the liberty of individuals and to the constitutional order itself.

AFTERWORD

Although the Supreme Court's decision in *Duncan v. Kahanamoku* held that the army's trials of Hawai'i civilians in the provost courts had been illegal under the controlling statute, the justices had declined to cast the ruling in constitutional terms. As a consequence, taken together with the Court's majority opinions in the Japanese-American cases, there was no resolution of some fundamental questions that had been raised in the political and legal challenges to army rule in Hawai'i. Uncertainty remained in three regards: The first was as to whether, and for how long a time, the military might permissibly impose martial law whenever it deemed that "military necessity" required it. Second, there was no definitive ruling as to whether the arbitrary and indefinite detention of citizens—under the rubric of "preventive detention," or because of specific charges of "possibly dangerous," or otherwise—can ever be considered constitutional. Finally, there remained the important question as to whether, in any circumstances, the writ of the privilege of habeas corpus could be denied to citizens—by order of the president or by military commanders under martial law—when civilian courts were open or at least capable of functioning.

The surrender of Japan in 1945 did not suddenly render irrelevant these profound issues with regard to the constitutional limits of governmental power in cases involving claims of "military necessity"—or, more generally, in cases of alleged emergencies affecting national security, whether in wartime or otherwise. This legal opening did not go unnoticed by FBI Director J. Edgar Hoover or his top staff. Indeed, World War II had not even ended when Hoover, concerned about a new menace to American security, began developing an extraordinarily broad, detailed plan that would involve a wholesale suspension of civil liberties to meet potential threats in the emerging confrontation with the Soviet Union. Only a few weeks after President Roosevelt's death, Hoover abruptly informed President Truman that Roosevelt had secretly authorized the FBI to engage in wiretapping as part of its security program against espionage and sabotage in the war years. Hoover omitted to disclose to Truman, however, that Roosevelt's authorization had been for minimum wiretapping, limited, as far as possible, to resident aliens. Truman renewed that secret authority, but Hoover now used it to allow the FBI to engage in wholesale wiretapping, targeting citizens as well as aliens.[1]

This expansion of his authority was only one building stone, however, in the new surveillance and security structure that Hoover was designing. In May 1946, only a few weeks after *Duncan v. Kahanamoku* was decided, Hoover sent an extraordinary memorandum, marked "personal and confidential," to the president and to Attorney General Tom Clark, declaring that the FBI possessed evidence of "an enormous Soviet espionage ring in Washington." Among the "high Government officials" whom Hoover stated were "involved" in this ring were Dean Acheson, then serving as under secretary of state, and, incredible as it may seem, John J. McCloy, who as assistant secretary of war had overseen the army's regime for martial law in Hawai'i.[2] Nothing came of this memo for the moment. President Truman had become wary of Hoover by this time and was worried that the FBI had in mind what he termed "Gestapo" methods for the agency's security operations. Hence Hoover's implausible, if not to say manifestly paranoid, warning was filed without a White House response.[3]

Undeterred, Hoover continued to refine his plan on the lines already set out. For the next two years, his office worked on a "program for the detention of Communists," for which the selective detention plan (and concomitant invasion of civil liberties) that had occurred in wartime Hawai'i could almost have served as a blueprint. Hoover's strategy built upon the FBI's existing programs, which dated from the investigations in the 1930s of disloyalty of suspect Japanese Americans and of pro-Axis activities, resulting in the "ABC" detention lists.[4] The new plan called for interrogations to be conducted by the FBI, the army and the CIA, and for the "permanent detention" [*sic*] of thousands of suspects in federal prisons, with the overflow to be held in military facilities near New York, Los Angeles, and San Francisco.[5]

Hoover kept the scheme under wraps until July 7, 1950, shortly after the United States became engaged in the Korean War. He then sent a letter, marked "personal and confidential," to the National Security Council and to the president's special consultant on national security. The letter laid out "a plan of action for an emergency situation wherein it would be necessary to apprehend and detain persons who are potentially dangerous to the internal security of the country."[6] It went on to provide for a draft order that the president would issue in the event of an emergency, authorizing the apprehension of dangerous individuals and *suspending the writ of habeas corpus for those apprehended.* The attorney general, in turn, would issue a "master warrant" for the arrest initially of 12,000 persons, fully 97 percent of them citizens, who had already been investigated, identified by the FBI as "potentially dangerous," and listed on the FBI's secret Security Index.[7]

Hoover's plan stipulated that the prisoners would be brought before civilian hearing boards, and, as prevailed in Hawai'i under martial law, the hearing procedures would "not be bound by the rules of evidence." The hearing board, consisting of a state or federal judge and two citizens—all to be appointed by the attorney general—would recommend detention, parole, or release. The board's decision would be subject to review by the attorney general, whose decision would be final except for appeal to the president.[8]

The army's experience in Hawaiʻi served not only as a model, but also as a cautionary tale. Thus, the proposed suspension of habeas privileges for those apprehended as security risks would avoid the challenges that the army had faced in the district court in Hawaiʻi (and in the *Endo* challenge on the mainland), as well as the danger of judicial review of any assertions of "necessity" or "emergency situations." For Hoover, it appears, the internal threat of Communist sympathizers in the Cold War was explicitly comparable to the internal threat of potentially disloyal Nikkei as seen by the army command in Hawaiʻi during World War II; and he recommended similar action, albeit the hidden enemy in Hoover's scenario of subversion was defined by political rather than racial criteria.

Hoover's plan was never brought to light for nearly six decades, until 2007, when a collection of Cold War–era government documents was declassified. Despite the similarities between Hoover's plan and the actual treatment of suspects in wartime Hawaiʻi, however, the *New York Times,* in reporting on the Hoover document, stated that the "only modern precedent for Hoover's plan was the Palmer raids of 1920, . . . [which] swept up thousands of people suspected of being communists and rebels."[9] Not mentioned in the *Times* article was the nation's experience with the prolonged suspension of habeas corpus in Hawaiʻi and the nearly total (though geographically limited) curtailment then of constitutional protections of free speech, freedom of association, due process, and jury trials. This abrogation of civil liberties in Hawaiʻi was, and has long remained, largely unknown by the general public.

Although President Truman did not act on Hoover's proposal in 1950, Congress passed—over Truman's veto—the 1950 Internal Security Act (the McCarran Act), which contained an emergency detention provision, giving the president the authority to apprehend and detain "each person as to whom there is a reasonable ground to believe that such person probably will engage in, or probably will conspire with others to engage in, acts of espionage or sabotage."[10] This legislation followed the House Un-American Activities Committee's hearings in the late 1940s on Communist activities in Hollywood and the investigations involving Whittaker Chambers and Alger Hiss, which had heightened Cold War hysteria. The dramatic entrance on the national political scene of Senator Joseph McCarthy brought the debate on the proper balance between national security and individual liberties into high profile during the 1950s. The new "Red Scare," and the broadening of a repressive political movement against suspected "subversives," "fellow travelers," "loyalty risks," and (in the extreme case) "spies," alleged to be elements in a Communist conspiracy to subordinate U.S. government institutions and policies to the designs and interests of the USSR, cast a shadow on American constitutional liberties, even as the threat of nuclear destruction cast a shadow on the world.

Other crises of civil liberties would follow in the Vietnam War years, not long after the waning of the McCarthy-era Red Scare. Both the Nixon and Johnson administrations viewed opposition to government policy as the equivalent of "subversion" or even as outright treason. They therefore challenged the protesters' claims of freedom of speech and of the press, and they permitted the FBI and the other government agencies to invade on a vast scale the privacy of individuals and organizations that were targeted because of their opposition to the war. Whatever the provocations of radical political actions on the part of some groups that challenged the government in the 1960s and 1970s in their tactics of dissent, with some extreme elements resorting to violence, there is no gainsaying that a drastic diminution of traditional protections for civil liberties occurred as the result of the secret activities of the FBI, National Security Agency (NSA), Central Intelligence Agency (CIA), and even the Internal Revenue Service (IRS). In their efforts to collect intelligence, to identify individuals and groups for targeting, to infiltrate organizations they deemed subversive, and to punish the government's alleged "enemies," these agencies in a host of documented cases violated federal law and constitutional principles wholesale. As severe as the infringements of civil liberties were during the civil unrest of the Vietnam War period, there was, nevertheless, no serious consideration of the kind of mass detention of suspected subversives that FBI Director Hoover had proposed in 1950.

In response to the terrorist attacks of September 11, 2001, however, George W. Bush's administration immediately revived many of the features of Hoover's 1950 plan, which had in turn echoed Hawai'i's World War II experience with martial law. The measures taken as part of Bush's "War on Terror"—a war that was precipitated, like the United States' entry into World War II, by an attack on American citizens on American territory—included indefinite detention of suspects without formal charges being filed, virtually complete lack of due process under American law for individuals who were designated as "material witnesses" or "enemy combatants," and the denial of habeas corpus to such individuals.[11]

The controversy over such infringements of civil liberties and the limits to executive power has become more heated in this century's so-called War on Terror than it was when so few voices were raised against the government's massive violations of constitutional rights during World War II. Some of the current-day debate—in the popular forum, in Congress, and in the courts—has been over the government's resistance to constitutional or legal constraints in treating citizens and aliens alike who are designated as "enemy combatants" or as their allies. In addition, political controversy and legal battles have been intensified in response to revelations of comprehensive NSA electronic surveillance. The unconventional nature of the War on Terror, with no clear concept of either "the enemy" or a termination date, makes these issues all the more problematic, as witnessed by the decade or longer that many prisoners—including a large percentage against whom no charges have ever been heard in a court of law—have been held in the Guantanamo detention camp.

The stormy disputations and debates being heard today are but the latest manifestation of a series of recurring incidents of repressive programs, opposition responses, and constitutional debates that have roiled the waters in American society since the country's founding. Thus the tensions between constitutional freedoms and national security in wartime Hawai'i that are the subject of this book were but one episode—too often forgotten—in the history of the struggle to protect America's core constitutional values in times of extraordinary threats to the nation itself.

The recurrence of these crises of civil liberties is a deeply problematic feature of American political and legal culture. It reminds us of the fragility of constitutional protections that are afforded to individual freedoms when crises of national security (real or alleged) and claims of emergency requiring extraordinary repressive powers are arrayed against them.

NOTES

Preface

1. Proclamation 7463 of September 14, 2001, *Fed. Reg.* 66, No. 181 (September 18, 2001); *Authorization for Use of Military Force (AUMF)*, Pub. L. 107–140, 107th Cong., 2nd sess., September 18, 2001.

2. "Military Order-Detention, Treatment and Trial of Certain Non-Citizens in the War Against Terrorism." Executive Order dated November 13, 2001, Section 1(g), 66 *Fed. Reg.* 57833 (November 16, 2001).

3. Ibid., Section 1(f).

4. The Supreme Court of the United States, in *Hamdan v. Rumsfeld,* held that the president lacked the authority to establish such tribunals. *Hamdan v. Rumsfeld,* 548 U.S. 557 (2006). Congress subsequently authorized their establishment in the Military Commissions Act of 2006, which also prohibited detainees who were classified as enemy combatants from using habeas corpus to challenge their detention. (Pub. L. No. 109–366, 120 Stat. 2600 [October 17, 2006].) But in *Boumediene v. Bush,* the Supreme Court held the Military Commissions Act was unconstitutional because it suspended the right of habeas corpus. (*Boumediene v. Bush,* 553 U.S. 723 [2008].) It should be noted that in *Hamdi v. Rumsfeld,* the Supreme Court upheld the right of U.S. citizens accused as enemy combatants to the writ of habeas corpus, that is, a court hearing as to why they had been detained. (542 U.S. 507 [2004].)

Introduction

1. 71 U.S. 2 (1866). For a full discussion of the case and its background, see Charles Fairman, *Reconstruction and Reunion 1864–1888, Part One* (The Oliver Wendell Holmes Devise History of the Supreme Court of the United States, Vol. 6) (New York: Macmillan Company, 1971), 192–237; cf. Marl E. Neely Jr., *The Fate of Liberty: Abraham Lincoln and Civil Liberties* (New York: Oxford University Press, 1991), 160–184. See also William H. Rehnquist, *All the Laws but One: Civil Liberties in Wartime* (New York: Alfred A. Knopf, 1998), for a discussion of Lincoln's suspension of habeas corpus and of the *Milligan* case.

2. Habeas Corpus Suspension Act, 12 Stat. 755 (1863). This legislation also approved future suspensions of habeas for the remainder of the war. At the same time, it restricted the length of time a prisoner could be held without trial.

3. Four of the justices filed a concurring opinion but dissenting in part. *Ex Parte Milligan,* 71 U.S. 2 (1866).

4. See John P. Frank, "Ex Parte Milligan v. The Five Companies: Martial Law in Hawaii," *Columbia Law Review* 44 (1944): 639. Frank was a legal officer in the Department of the Interior in 1944.

5. See Charles Fairman, "The Law of Martial Rule and the National Emergency," *Harvard Law Review* 55 (1942): 1253 [hereinafter Fairman, "The Law of Martial Rule"] for a discussion of these cases. See also J. Garner Anthony, *Hawaii under Army Rule* (Stanford, CA: Stanford University Press, 1955). Cf. Christopher N. May, *In the Name of War: Judicial Review of the War Powers Since 1918* (Cambridge, MA: Harvard University Press, 1989).

6. Organic Act, Ch. 339, 31 Stat. 141, § 67 (1900).

7. See J. Garner Anthony, "Martial Law, Military Government and the Writ of Habeas Corpus in Hawaii," *California Law Review* 31 (1943): 478–479 [hereinafter Anthony, "Martial Law, Military Government"].

8. Of this number, some 37,000 were aliens, born in Japan and ineligible for citizenship, and approximately 121,000 were the children and grandchildren of Japanese immigrants, born in Hawai'i and therefore U.S. citizens, although some of these citizens had been registered with the Japanese consulate and held status as dual citizens under both Japanese and American law. See infra, p. 20. See, generally, Anthony, *Hawaii under Army Rule.* Population data are from Bureau of the Census, U.S. Department of Commerce, "Sixteenth Census of the United States: 1940."

9. Office of Internal Security, Territory of Hawaii, "Wartime Security Controls in Hawaii: 1941–1945," Part One, 3, Box 24, Richardson Papers, Hoover Institution Archives, Stanford University. Hawai'i was no stranger to martial law: the Islands had been subjected to rule by French and British military forces in the nineteenth century, and martial law was declared in 1895 when Queen Liliuokalani's supporters attempted to overthrow the Republic of Hawai'i.

10. 327 U.S. 304 (1946). The Court decided the *Duncan* case in a merged appeal with the case of *White v. Steer,* 327 U.S. 304 (1946).

11. The Court had agreed to hear the case two months earlier, in October, on the same day President Harry S. Truman formally terminated the last of the wartime measures for army control over civilian life in Hawai'i. John P. Frank has argued that it is the typical pattern for the Court in wartime civil liberties crises to act after the emergency is over. See John P. Frank, "Judicial Review and Basic Liberties," in *American Law and the Constitutional Order,* ed. Lawrence M. Friedman and Harry N. Scheiber (Cambridge, MA: Harvard University Press, 1978), 397–400.

12. See *Hirabayashi v. United States,* 320 U.S. 81 (1943); *Korematsu v. United States,* 319 U.S. 432 (1943). These cases involving the Nikkei internments are analyzed thoroughly in Peter Irons, *Justice at War: The Story of the Japanese-American Internment Cases* (New York: Oxford University Press, 1983) [hereinafter Irons, *Justice at War*], a work that upon its publication revealed on the basis of conclusive (and newly discovered) archival documentation that army officials on the West Coast had deliberately misrepresented the security threat allegedly posed by permitting the Japanese Americans to remain in their homes and jobs. Irons also presents a detailed accounting of how the War Department prevailed on the solicitor general to suppress information of these falsehoods when *Korematsu* and other cases were in progress in 1944. Irons's book does not deal with the Hawai'i situation, however, except with passing references to internments. See Roger Daniels, *The Japanese American Cases: The Rule of Law in Time of War* (Lawrence: University Press of Kansas, 2013) for a fresh review and analysis of the history of these cases.

13. See Eugene V. Rostow, "The Japanese-American Cases—A Disaster," *Yale Law Journal* 54 (1945): 489. But see also Fairman, "The Law of Martial Rule" (defending the internment policies at the time, seeing no constitutional objections and contending that the exigencies of war justified suspicion of the Japanese sufficient to warrant their removal and detention).

14. Gerald R. Ford, "Proclamation 4417, Confirming the Termination of the Executive Order Authorizing Japanese-American Internment During World War II," February 19, 1976. Available at http://www.fordlibrarymuseum.gov/library/speeches/760111p.htm.

15. Commission on Wartime Relocation and Internment of Civilians, *Personal Justice Denied* (Washington, DC: Government Printing Office, 1982) [hereinafter CWIRC, *Personal Justice Denied*], https://archive.org/details/Personal-Justice-Denied. For the *Korematsu* decision, see *Fred Korematsu v. United States of America,* 584 F. Supp. 1406, United States District Court, Northern District of California (April 19, 1984), and Peter Irons, ed., *Justice Delayed: The Record of the Japanese American Internment Cases* (Middletown, CT: Wesleyan University Press, 1989).

16. Public Law. 100–383, 100th Cong., 2nd sess. (August 10, 1988), 102 Stat. 903, http://www .internmentarchives.com/showdoc.php?docid=00172&search_id=32013 &pagenum=1. The legislation uses the terms "internment" and "internee" to refer to those who were forcibly removed from the restricted areas and incarcerated in WRA camps—a different definition from the one the authors have used. See supra, "A Note on Terminology," pp. xvii–xviii.

17. Peter Irons, "Race and the Constitution," in *[T]his Constitution: From Ratification to the Bill of Rights* (Washington, DC: American Political Science Association & American Historical Association, [1988]), 217, 227.

18. Korematsu received his medal in 1998, Hirabayashi in 2012, posthumously.

19. This was well known in official circles. Thus, in May 1943 Colonel Kendall Fielder, head of military intelligence in Hawai'i, made known his conclusion that "[t]here have been no known acts of sabotage, espionage or fifth column activities committed by the Japanese in Hawaii either on or subsequent to December 7, 1941." (Memorandum from Col. Kendall Fielder, May 17, 1943, the Japanese American Evacuation and Resettlement Records, Bancroft Library, University of California, Berkeley [hereinafter cited as JAERR].)

20. Gwenfread Allen, *Hawaii's War Years, 1941–1945* (Honolulu: University of Hawai'i Press, 1950), 263. This excellent study of social life and public policies in wartime Hawai'i is based upon extensive documentary materials in the Hawaii War Records Depository located at Hamilton Library, University of Hawai'i [hereinafter HWRD]. The Depository contains a vast and unique collection of printed materials, private correspondence, official papers of various Hawai'i organizations, and public documents from the war era that has been an invaluable source for the present study.

21. See Nanette Dembitz, "Racial Discrimination and the Military Judgment: The Supreme Court's Korematsu and Endo Decisions," *Columbia Law Review* 45 (1945): 175, 196. Even contemporary commentators critical of the internments made the same point. For example, an editorial in the *New Leader* deplored the stereotypes of Japanese Americans that were made by government counsel in the *Hirabayashi* case (in which they were characterized as unduly influenced by family ties to Japan, as isolated from the mainstream American society, etc.): "The obvious refutation of all these dangerous inferences based on race is Hawaii. . . . There, American citizens and aliens of Japanese ancestry constitute a full 37 percent of the population. . . . Hawaii, furthermore, is 1,500 miles [*sic*] closer to the enemy. . . . But Hawaii had no evacuation, no deliberately drummed up race hysteria, and instead, there, the citizens of Japanese origin are engaged in vital defense

work." John Dixon Ford, "Government Brief Invoked 'Race Doctrine' to Justify 'Jap-Crow' Evacuations," *New Leader,* June 12, 1943, p. 7.

22. Army and War Department insiders who during the war defended their mainland internment policies believed that it was precisely because martial law governed in Hawai'i that no espionage, sabotage, or vocal war dissent existed there. See infra, pp. 314, 319.

23. Some critics of martial law also argued, rhetorically at least, in policy debate—although the contention was not to our knowledge formally advanced in judicial proceedings—that the army's regime of coercive control of labor also violated the Thirteenth Amendment's prohibition of involuntary servitude.

24. Anthony, *Hawaii under Army Rule,* 98.

25. *Hamdi v. Rumsfeld,* 542 U.S. 507 (2004).

26. J. Garner Anthony, "Hawaiian Martial Law in the Supreme Court," *Yale Law Journal* 57 (1947–1948): 27.

Chapter 1: Prelude to Martial Law

1. "Territory of Hawaii: A Proclamation," December 7, 1941, reprinted in J. Garner Anthony, *Hawaii under Army Rule* (Stanford, CA: Stanford University Press, 1955), 127.

2. "Proclamation: United States Army," December 7, 1941, reprinted in ibid., 127–128. A controversy, still not resolved, emerged regarding whether Poindexter voluntarily undertook to suspend the writ of habeas corpus and declare martial law. See infra, chap. 3.

3. The "general orders" were the commands or regulations of the military governor, which were required to be published by the daily press at its own expense. See, inter alia, Office of the Chief of Military History, "United States Army Forces, Middle Pacific and Predecessor Commands during World War II, 7 December 1941–2 September 1945: Civil Affairs and Military Government," microfilm document, HWRD (Hawai'i War Records Depository), Hamilton Library, University of Hawai'i at Manoa, HI [hereinafter "Civil Affairs"]. See also Garner Anthony, "Report on the Status of Civil Government in Hawaii," September 20, 1943 (manuscript), Hawai'i and Pacific Collection, Hawai'i State Library [hereinafter Anthony Report]; oral history interview with Hon. Ernest Kapuamailani Kai, The Watumull Foundation Oral History Project, Honolulu, 1987; and General Thomas H. Green, Untitled manuscript, dated January 1961, Papers of General Thomas H. Green, Judge Advocate General's School Library, Charlottesville, VA (recounting Green's initiative in preparing detailed orders for martial law and military rule).

4. As noted earlier, the Organic Act provided that the governor "may, in case of rebellion or invasion, or imminent danger thereof, when the public safety requires it, suspend the privilege of the writ of habeas corpus, or place the Territory or any part thereof, under martial law until communication can be had with the President and his decision thereon made known." (Organic Act, Ch. 339, 31 Stat. 141, § 67 [1900].)

5. The phrase "the Japanese problem" was used, alternatively with "the Japanese menace," by the Hawai'i Emergency Labor Commission in its brief on "Hawaii and the Japanese" for congressional hearings in 1921. Testimony before Congress linked the Japanese problem with national security. "Hawaii and the Japanese," Governor Farrington Files, Territorial Departments, Labor Commission, Hawai'i State Archives. See also statement by Naval Intelligence Officer Lt. Cmdr. K. D. Ringle, infra at p. 127.

6. For a discussion of the decline of the indigenous population, see Ralph S. Kuykendall and A. Grove Day, *Hawaii: A History, From Polynesian Kingdom to American Statehood* (Englewood Cliffs, NJ: Prentice-Hall, 1976), 126ff.

7. Eleanor C. Nordyke and Richard K. C. Lee, "The Chinese in Hawai'i: A Historical and Demographic Perspective," *Hawaiian Journal of History* 23 (1989): 196–216. The Chinese government and the British government also took measures to restrict emigration of contract laborers from China and Hong Kong. See also Edward D. Beechert, *Working in Hawaii: A Labor History* (Honolulu: University of Hawai'i Press, 1985), chap. 5.

8. Ernest K. Wakukawa, *A History of the Japanese People in Hawaii* (Honolulu, HI: Toyo Shoin, 1938), provides a sympathetic account of its subject; it was written primarily for English-speaking Americans of Japanese ancestry. The first Japanese to arrive in Hawai'i, in the first half of the nineteenth century, were shipwrecked seamen. (Wakukawa, *A History of the Japanese People in Hawaii*, 4–12.) The first small group of Japanese contract workers arrived in Hawai'i in 1868. However, complaints soon arose from both planters and workers, and press coverage of exploitation created opposition in both Japan and Hawai'i to immediate further importation of Japanese laborers to Hawai'i. (See, in addition to Wakukawa, Ralph S. Kuykendall, *The Hawaiian Kingdom, 1854–1874* [Honolulu: University of Hawai'i Press, 1966], 183; and Beechert, *Working in Hawaii*, 70.)

9. "Japanese Immigration," *Planters' Monthly* 7 (January 1888): 7.

10. Beechert, *Working in Hawaii*, 88–89; Gavan Daws, *Shoal of Time: A History of the Hawaiian Islands* (Honolulu: University of Hawai'i Press, 1968), 180–181; Kuykendall and Day, *Hawaii: A History*, 157. For a detailed account of anti-Japanese sentiment in Hawai'i, see Gary Y. Okihiro, *Cane Fires: The Anti-Japanese Movement in Hawaii, 1865–1945* (Philadelphia: Temple University Press, 1991), 23ff. See also Eleanor C. Nordyke and Y. Scott Matsumoto, "The Japanese in Hawaii: A Historical and Demographic Perspective," *Hawaiian Journal of History* 11 (1977), 162–174.

11. "Japan's Hawaiian Protest," *New York Times,* June 25, 1897; Kuykendall and Day, *Hawaii,* 188–189. The protest was later remembered when Japan attacked Pearl Harbor, leading some to proclaim that Japan was reasserting its legal claim to ownership of Hawai'i. (John O'Donnell, "Capitol Stuff," *Washington Times-Herald,* March 16, 1942, copy in Samuel Wilder King Papers, Hawai'i State Archives [hereafter King Papers, HSA].)

12. U.S. Census Bureau, Campbell Gibson and Kay Jung, *Historical Census Statistics on Population Totals By Race, 1790 to 1990, and By Hispanic Origin, 1790 to 1990, For The United States, Regions, Divisions, and States* (2002), http://mapmaker.rutgers.edu/REFERENCE/Hist_Pop_stats .pdf. Nordyke and Matsumoto, "The Japanese in Hawaii," 163. Although close to 70,000 Japanese immigrants came to Hawai'i between 1885 and 1899, some returned to Japan, and others went to the mainland (Beechert, *Working in Hawaii*, 86; and Kuykendall and Day, *Hawaii: A History,* 157).

13. Beechert, *Working in Hawaii,* 89.

14. Franklin S. Odo, *No Sword to Bury: Japanese Americans in Hawaii during World War II* (Philadelphia: Temple University Press, 2004), 18–20.

15. For a discussion of Social Darwinism, the influence of Alfred Mahan, and racist attitudes of the time, including California's Alien Land Act, see Greg Robinson, *By Order of the President: FDR and the Internment of Japanese Americans* (Cambridge, MA: Harvard University Press, 2001), 15ff. More generally, see Walter LaFeber, *The New Empire: An Interpretation of American Expansion, 1860–1898* (Ithaca, NY: Cornell University Press, 1998); LaFeber, *The Clash: U.S.-Japanese Relations throughout History* (New York: W. W. Norton, 1997); and Richard Hofstadter, *Social*

Darwinism in American Thought (Boston: Beacon Press, 1992). Roger Daniels treats the "yellow peril" and anti-Japanese sentiment in *Concentration Camps USA: Japanese Americans and World War II* (New York: Holt, Rinehart and Winston, 1971), chap. 2.

16. The Japanese gained a strong foothold in carpentry, plumbing, fishing, small farming, barbering, tailoring, and retail trade. (Andrew W. Lind, "The Japanese in Hawaii under War Conditions," *American Council Paper* No. 5 [New York: American Council Institute of Pacific Relations, December 1942], 3.) Lind's paper and his subsequent book, *Hawaii's Japanese: An Experiment in Democracy* (Princeton, NJ: Princeton University Press, 1946) provide a detailed account by a University of Hawai'i professor of sociology of the Japanese in Hawai'i and attitudes toward them before and during the war.

In addition, some 20,000 Okinawans arrived in Hawai'i between 1900 and 1924. Nordyke and Matsumoto, "The Japanese in Hawaii," 164.

17. U.S. Department of Commerce and Labor, *Third Report of the United States Commissioner of Labor on Hawaii, 1905* (Washington, DC: Government Printing Office, 1906), 392.

18. *Takao Ozawa v. United States,* 260 U.S. 178 (1922); *Hidemitsu Toyota v. United States,* 268 U.S. 402 (1925).

19. Odo, *No Sword to Bury,* 36. For a broader discussion of the efforts of ethnic Japanese veterans to gain American citizenship, see Lucy Salyer, "Baptism by Fire: Race, Military Service, and U.S. Citizenship Policy, 1918–1935," *Journal of American History* 91, no. 3 (2004): 847–876.

20. See infra, chap. 9.

21. The value of Pearl Harbor as a military and commercial outpost had been discussed by the army as early as 1873. The Spanish-American War of 1898 emphasized the need for a major naval base in the Pacific and gave impetus to the move for annexation, and in 1908, Congress authorized the creation of a naval base at Pearl Harbor.

22. Lt. C. C. Windsor to Commandant Fourteenth Naval District, July 20, 1917, quoted in Michael Slackman, *Target: Pearl Harbor* (Honolulu: University of Hawai'i Press, 1990), 35.

23. *Farrington v. Tokushige,* 273 U.S. 284 (1927). The Merriam Report is discussed in Okihiro, *Cane Fires,* 103–105.

24. Wakukawa, *A History of the Japanese People in Hawaii,* chaps. 12, 16, and 19.

25. The HSPA was controlled by the "Big Five" sugar companies and factors: Castle & Cooke, Alexander & Baldwin, American Factors, C. Brewer & Co., and Theo H. Davies & Co.

26. The strike, protesting against low wages and poor living conditions, had been organized by the newly formed Japanese Federation of Labor and Filipino Federation of Labor. It lasted nearly six months and cost the planters nearly $12 million. For a detailed discussion of the strike and its aftermath, including the trial for an alleged Japanese conspiracy, see Masayo Umezawa Duus, *Japanese Conspiracy: The Oahu Sugar Strike of 1920* (Berkeley: University of California Press, 1999); and, among others, Beechert, *Working in Hawaii,* 169–174; Okihiro, *Cane Fires,* 45–53; and Wakukawa, *History of the Japanese People in Hawaii,* chap. 20, which also details the organization of the Japanese and Filipino unions. Yukiko Kimura presents the strike from the viewpoint of the Japanese in *Issei: Japanese Immigrants in Hawaii* (Honolulu: University of Hawai'i Press, 1988), 91–96.

27. January 27, 1920. The Japanese consul's opposition to the strike seemed not to influence the paper's conclusion.

28. February 13, 1920.

29. Lothrop Stoddard's *The Rising Tide of Color Against White World-Supremacy* (New York: Charles Scribner's Sons, 1920); Wallace Irwin's *Seed of the Sun* (New York: George H. Doran Company, 1921); and Peter Kyne's *The Pride of Palomar* (New York: Cosmopolitan Book Corporation, 1921) were among the books that fueled anti-Japanese prejudice.

30. Quotation cited in Okihiro, *Cane Fires,* 95. The commission was appointed to assess the need to import Chinese laborers to alleviate an alleged shortage of plantation workers following the strike. The commission found no labor shortage and recommended against importing foreign workers.

31. See Okihiro, *Cane Fires,* 109–111; and Slackman, *Target: Pearl Harbor,* 35–36.

32. Intelligence reports and the development of war plans in the 1920s and 1930s are detailed in Okihiro, *Cane Fires;* and Slackman, *Target: Pearl Harbor.*

33. Quoted in Slackman, *Target: Pearl Harbor,* 37.

34. Charles Pelot Summerall, *The Way of Duty, Honor, Country: The Memoir of General Charles Pelot Summerall* (Lexington: University of Kentucky Press, 2010), chap. 24.

35. Ibid., 180.

36. W. A. Bethel to Acting Assistant Chief of Staff, WPD, General Staff, June 28, 1923, RG 165, quoted in Okihiro, *Cane Fires,* 125–126. In contrast to the actual operation of martial law nearly two decades later, however, Bethel cautioned that the writ of habeas corpus could be suspended only for those arrested and held by the military government, not for the general population.

37. See infra, chap. 18.

38. George S. Simonds to Chief of Staff, July 29, 1931, RG 165, quoted in Okihiro, *Cane Fires,* 164.

39. The Fukunaga and Massie cases are graphically described in Ronald Kotani, *The Japanese in Hawaii: A Century of Struggle* (Honolulu: Hawai'i Hochi, Ltd., 1985), 71–84. For details of the Massie Affair, see, among others, David E. Stannard, *Honor Killing: How the Infamous "Massie Affair" Transformed Hawaii* (New York: Viking Press, 2005); Daws, *Shoal of Time,* 319–331; and Douglas O. Linder, "The Massie Trials: A Commentary," http://law2.umkc.edu/faculty/projects/ftrials/massie/massietrialsaccount.html.

40. Report quoted in Eric Muller, *American Inquisition: The Hunt for Japanese American Disloyalty in World War II* (Chapel Hill: University of North Carolina Press, 2007), 18.

41. Ibid.

42. Franklin D. Roosevelt, "Remarks in Hawaii, July 28, 1934," http://www.presidency.ucsb.edu/ws/?pid=14729#axzz1vFRUO2cq.

43. Copy, FDR Memorandum to Chief of Operations, U.S. Navy, August 10, 1936, President's Secretary's File, Box 106, Franklin D. Roosevelt Papers, Franklin D. Roosevelt Library, Hyde Park, NY [hereinafter PSF, FDR Papers, FDRL]. Emphasis added. The term "concentration camp" was forthrightly used by the administration in the early days of the war, although later, when news of the Nazi death camps began to surface, the term "relocation camp" was euphemistically used instead to describe the barbed wire enclosures to which Japanese Americans were forcibly removed. See A Note on Terminology.

44. Roosevelt also expressed concern about the ethnic Japanese population on the outlying islands, and especially about preventing them from being used as a base of operations against O'ahu. (PSF File, Box 106, FDR Papers, FDRL.)

45. Woodring to FDR, August 29, 1936, PSF Woodring File, Box 106, FDR Papers, FDRL.

46. The committee, which met with the secretary of the interior, included the secretaries of state, treasury, labor, navy and war, and the attorney general. (FDR, Memorandum for

Secretary Woodring, November 25, 1937, in PSF Confidential, "State Dept" files, FDR Papers, FDRL.)

47. Lewis Coren, Research and Historical Section, Office of Internal Security, "Memorandum of Interview with Lt. Col. Bryan M. Meurlott," March 9, 1945, RG 338, copy in folder 398, Japanese Internment and Relocation Files: The Hawai'i Experience 1942–1982, Hamilton Library, University of Hawai'i. [Hereafter cited as JIR.]

48. Quoted in Slackman, *Target: Pearl Harbor,* 38.

49. Michael Slackman, "The Orange Race: George S. Patton, Jr.'s Japanese-American Hostage Plan," *Biography* 7, no. 1 (June 24, 1984): 1–22.

50. As a territory, Hawai'i was headed by a governor who was appointed by a U.S. president for whom the residents of Hawai'i could not vote; further, Hawai'i residents were subject to taxes passed by Congress, where their delegate had no vote. For a study of the statehood movement in Hawai'i, see Roger Bell, *Last Among Equals: Hawaii Statehood and American Politics* (Honolulu: University of Hawai'i Press, 1984).

51. Kimura, *Issei,* 209.

52. Daws, *Shoal of Time,* 394. In 1934, Romanzo Adams, chair of the Sociology Department at the University of Hawai'i, had described the race mores of Hawai'i as those of race equality. (Romanzo Adams, "The Unorthodox Race Doctrines in Hawaii," in *Race and Culture Contacts,* ed. E. B. Reuter [New York: McGraw Hill, 1934].) Lind also cites the high rate of marriages across racial lines—roughly one-third of all marriages in Hawai'i—as contributing to the "melting pot" view of race relations. (Lind, *Hawaii's Japanese,* 19.)

53. Lind, "The Japanese in Hawaii Under War Conditions," 7.

54. Kimura, *Issei,* 208–210. According to Lind, the plantation strikes, language school controversy, and statehood hearings "served to touch off attitudes of hostility which had remained dormant under normal circumstances." (Lind, "The Japanese in Hawaii under War Conditions," 4.)

55. U.S. Congress, *Hearings before the Joint Committee on Hawaii Statehood,* 75th Cong., 2nd sess. (October 6–22, 1937), 247–263.

56. U.S. Congress, Testimony of Frank Midkiff, *Hearings Before the Joint Committee on Hawaiian Statehood,* 75th Cong., 2nd sess. (October 6–22, 1937), reprinted in Dennis M. Ogawa, *Kodomo no tame ni: For the Sake of the Children* (Honolulu: University of Hawai'i Press, 1978), 265–267. Midkiff had helped form a Japanese-American unit in the National Guard before World War I, and he was active in the New Americans Conference.

57. Among the most outspoken congressional critics of statehood was John Rankin of Mississippi, who remarked to Ernest Gruening, Director of the Division of Territories and Island Possessions, "Mah Gawd, if we give them folks statehood we're lahkley to have a senator named Moto" (Ernest Gruening, *Many Battles: The Autobiography of Ernest Gruening* [New York: Liveright, 1973], 230). Mr. Moto was a fictional Japanese detective/secret agent, created by John Marquand and portrayed by Peter Lorre in eight movies between 1937 and 1939.

58. For a discussion of the opposition to statehood, and the Roosevelt administration's determination to keep Hawai'i in territorial status as war with Japan loomed ever closer, see Bell, *Last Among Equals,* 67–75.

59. All Caucasians, including Portuguese immigrants, made up about 24.5 percent of the population in 1940. Of the total population of Hawai'i, 87.6 percent had been born in the United States or its territories. U.S. Census, 1940, http://www.census.gov/population/www/documentation/twps0056/tab26.pdf.

60. Ibid.

61. For a discussion of Japanese occupational structure, see Lind, *Hawaii's Japanese,* 17–18. See also U.S. Department of Commerce, Bureau of the Census, "Sixteenth Census of the United States: 1940," Series P-9, No. 8 and No. 9.

62. Office of Internal Security, Territory of Hawaii, "Wartime Security Controls in Hawaii: 1941–1945, A General Historical Survey," prepared for Lt. Gen. Robert C. Richardson Jr., (Honolulu, 1945), Part One: Historical Overview of the Internal Security Program in Hawai'i, 13–22, Box 24, Robert Charlwood Richardson Jr. Papers, Hoover Institution Archives, Stanford, California [hereinafter Richardson Papers, Hoover Institution]); Lind, *Hawaii's Japanese,* 24.

63. Estimates are that only 10 to 20 percent of the Nisei and Sansei born in Hawai'i after 1924 were so registered, but estimates from intelligence sources varied widely as to the *total* number of dual citizens. (Lt. Cmdr. M. C. Partello, District Intelligence Office, Fourteenth Naval District to Capt. E. B. Nixon, Office of Naval Intelligence, April 4, 1940, and attachment, "Report on the Nisei Situation in Hawaii," March 30, 1940, RG 165, NA.) This report examines several different estimates in drawing its conclusions that dual citizens constituted somewhat over 60 percent of the Nisei population or 17 percent of the total population of Hawai'i. Similarly, an attachment to a memorandum from G-2 for the chief of staff places the number of dual citizens in 1939 at 73,286, or 17.66 percent of the total population. ("Japanese Dual Citizens," attached to Memorandum from C. H. Mason for Chief of Staff, "Dual Citizenship," June 17, 1941, reproduced in Roger Daniels, ed., *American Concentration Camps,* vol. 1: *July 1940–December 31, 1941* (New York: Garland Publishing, 1989), n.p. Curiously, an FBI report of 1939 places the number of dual citizens at only 10,000–20,000—less than 5 percent of the total population. (J. Edgar Hoover to Asst. Sec. of State A. A. Berle, November 16, 1940, and attachment, "The Japanese in Hawaii," Box 1733, R.G. 165, NA.) Dennis Ogawa and Evarts Fox, citing the Office of the Chief of Military History, place the number of dual citizens at 68,000. (Dennis M. Ogawa and Evarts C. Fox Jr., "Japanese Internment and Relocation: The Hawaii Experience," in *Japanese Americans, From Relocation to Redress,* ed. Roger Daniels, Sandra C. Taylor, Harry H. L. Kitano, and Leonard J. Arrington [Salt Lake City: University of Utah Press, 1983].)

64. Daws, *Shoal of Time,* 337. See also Dorothy Ochiai Hazama and Jane Okamoto Komeiji, *Okage Sama De: The Japanese in Hawai'i, 1885–1985* (Honolulu, HI: Bess Press, 1986), 118–119. According to a 1934 War Department memo for the White House, the fact that only a relatively small number of Nisei expatriated was attributable "in part to inertia and in part to a greater loyalty to Japan." ("Memorandum for the Use of the President: War Department Information on the Hawaiian Islands, Requested by Letter of Mr. Stephen Early [Press Secretary to the President], dated May 31, 1934. Cover letter from J. W. Martyn to Mr. Early, June 6, 1934, FDRL.)

65. Hazama and Komeiji, *Okage Sama De,* 119, 144; Lind, "The Japanese in Hawaii under War Conditions," 5.

66. "Japanese Language Schools in the United States and the Territory of Hawaii," Report prepared by the Counter-Intelligence Section, Office of Naval Intelligence, February 4, 1942, copy in RG 165, NA. The plantation owners and public schools also sought to suppress the language schools, especially after the strike of 1920. For a discussion of the controversy over Japanese language schools in Hawai'i, see Noriko Asato, *Teaching Mikadoism: The Attack on Japanese Language Schools in Hawaii, California, and Washington, 1919–1927* (Honolulu: University of Hawai'i Press, 2005).

67. We have been unable to ascertain the exact number of Kibei who may have returned to Hawaiʻi from Japan and then undertaken the prescribed legal measures for expatriation through formal renunciation of the Japanese citizenship that had attached to them either by their registration in Japanese schools or by registration at birth with the Japanese consulate in Hawaiʻi. A memorandum, "Factors to be Considered in Investigations of Japanese Subjects," a document apparently prepared for Naval Intelligence, dated February 25, 1943, refers to the fact that "expatriation was a lengthy, complicated process" so that "sheer ignorance and apathy" might well explain a Kibei's maintaining of dual citizenship status. (File 5605, HWRD.)

68. It was common on the plantations for both parents to work, leaving no one to care for the children, who were therefore sent back to Japan to be cared for by the grandparents.

69. See Kinuko Maehara, "To Okinawa and Back Again: Okinawan Kibei Nisei Identity in Hawaii," master's thesis, University of Hawaiʻi, 2005. Although it pertains mainly to mainland Nikkei, see also Dorothy Swaine Thomas, "Some Social Aspects of Japanese-American Demography," *Proceedings of the American Philosophical Society* 94 (1950): 459–480, for an interesting discussion of social issues. See p. 459n46 infra, for the critical literature on Thomas's scholarship and the University of California project she directed during the war.

70. Maj. Louis F. Springer, Memorandum: "Interned American Citizens of Japanese Ancestry," December 31, 1943, Box 39, RG 494, NA.

71. Kibei were not distinguished from other Nisei in the census records, so it is difficult to know their precise numbers. The Office of the Chief of Military History estimated the number to be 5,000. Office of the Chief of Military History, *History of G-2 Section,* vol. 10, part 2 of *United States Army Forces Middle Pacific and Predecessor Commands during World War II* (1941–1942): 19, 24–25. One widely cited scholar, Andrew Lind, stated their numbers in Hawaiʻi to be 600, but this figure seems implausible. Lind, *Hawaii's Japanese,* 183. See also Robert L. Shivers, "Cooperation of the Various Racial Groups with Each Other and with the Constituted Authorities Before and After December 7, 1941" (Honolulu, HI: Territorial Emergency Service Committees, 1946), 2.

72. Lind, "The Japanese in Hawaii Under War Conditions," 5.

73. Americans of Japanese ancestry constituted 24.9 percent of registered voters and 19 percent of the teachers in the Territory of Hawaiʻi in 1938. (Ernest K. Wakukawa, *A History of the Japanese People in Hawaii* [Honolulu, HI: Toyo Shoin, 1938], 368, 370.)

Chapter 2: Final War Planning for Hawaiʻi, 1939–1941

1. Office of the Chief of Military History, "United States Army Forces, Middle Pacific and Predecessor Commands during World War II, 7 December 1941–2 September 1945: Civil Affairs and Military Government," microfilm document, HWRD (Hawaii War Records Depository), Hamilton Library, University of Hawaiʻi at Manoa, HI [hereinafter "Civil Affairs"].

2. President's Directive of September 6, 1939, reproduced in Federal Bureau of Investigation, "Memorandum on Pearl Harbor Attack and Bureau's Activities Before and After," December 6, 1945, Vol. 1, 212, Folder FBI-L, JIR [hereafter FBI, "Memorandum on Pearl Harbor Attack"]; copy also in AR19, Box 10, Folder 9, JCCH.

3. The Honolulu Office of the FBI increased in size with its increase in responsibilities, and by summer 1941 there were twelve investigative agents plus German and Japanese language translators. (Ibid.)

4. See A. A. Smyser, "He Saved Island AJAs from Mass Internment," *Honolulu Star-Bulletin,* December 6, 1979; Tom Coffman, *The Island Edge of America: A Political History of Hawai'i* (Honolulu: University of Hawai'i Press, 2003), chap. 4; and http://www.fbi.gov/news/stories/2009 /december/shivers_120709.

5. Shivers to FBI Director Hoover, December 4, 1941, copy, JCCH. President Roosevelt had authorized the army and navy intelligence services to engage in wiretapping and other methods of surveillance and detection with regard to labor disturbances as well as with regard to matters more directly related to military security. Attorney General Robert A. Jackson (later associate justice of the U.S. Supreme Court) in April 1940 resisted pressure from the War Department to have the FBI join in the operations regarding labor. Reflecting later on that episode, Jackson noted that Roosevelt "did not share the extreme position about civil rights that some of his followers have taken," and speculated that in the event of large-scale espionage or sabotage during the war years "Roosevelt would have taken the most ruthless methods to suppress it." (Robert H. Jackson, *That Man: An Insider's Portrait of Franklin D. Roosevelt,* ed. John Q. Barrett [New York: Oxford University Press, 2003], 71–73.) As the war threat intensified after mid-1940, given their broad mandate for covert surveillance and investigation, the military and naval intelligence services were able to provide a valuable store of information related to the threats of espionage and sabotage on which FBI operations had been focused (as was true of Shivers' FBI headquarters in Honolulu).

6. Jeffery M. Dorwart, *Conflict of Duty: The U.S. Navy's Intelligence Dilemma, 1919–1945* (Annapolis, MD: Naval Institute Press, 1983), 176.

7. Ibid.; Lt. Col. George W. Bicknell, "Security Measures in Hawaii during World War II," chap. 2, 17–18, Microfilm Reel 54, Item 5, HWRD [hereinafter Bicknell, "Security Measures in Hawaii"]. The details of the agreements among the three intelligence agencies can be found in FBI, "Memorandum on Pearl Harbor Attack." In October 1941, by mutual consent, the FBI and G-2 moved into adjacent offices in the Dillingham Building in downtown Honolulu. (Coren, "Memorandum of Interview with Lt. Col. Byron M. Muerlott," March 9, 1945, JIR.) See also U.S. Department of Justice, *The FBI: A Centennial History, 1908–2008* (Washington, DC: U.S. Government Printing Office, 2008), 34.

8. Stuart G. Brown, *John A. Burns Oral History Project, 1975–1976* (privately printed, n.d.),copy in possession of authors, Tape 2, p. 6 [hereinafter *Burns Oral History*].

9. Ibid., 6, 11–12. Burns would later object to a bill introduced by Rankin of Mississippi that would establish a commission form of government for Hawai'i.

10. Dan Boylan and T. Michael Holmes, *John A. Burns: The Man and His Times* (Honolulu: University of Hawai'i Press, 2000), 34.

11. Memorandum from FBI Honolulu Field Office, quoted in Memorandum from George W. Bicknell, G-2 Contact Officer, "Estimate of the Situation (Local Racial Elements)," January 1, 1942, RG 165, NA.

12. Gary Y. Okihiro, *Cane Fires: The Anti-Japanese Movement in Hawaii, 1865–1945* (Philadelphia: Temple University Press, 1991), 180–181. See infra, chap. 9, for further discussion of dual citizenship.

13. Federal Bureau of Investigation, Memorandum, November 15, 1940, FBI Records 65–286–61, rept. in CWIRC Papers, p. 19456 (Reel 17, p. 9), quoted in Okihiro, *Cane Fires,* 182, and Greg Robinson, *By Order of the President: FDR and the Internment of Japanese Americans* (Cambridge, MA: Harvard University Press, 2001), 62.

14. Ibid.

15. Bicknell, "Security Measures in Hawaii," chap. 2, 17–18, HWRD. See infra, chap. 8, for discussion of similar proposals and the conflict between Gen. Emmons and the Washington administration in 1942.

16. Bicknell, "Security Measures in Hawaii," chap. 2, 17–18, HWRD.

17. Lt. Cmdr. M. C. Partello, District Intelligence Office, Fourteenth Naval District, to Capt. E. B. Nixon, Office of Naval Intelligence, April 4, 1940, and attachment, "Report on the Nisei Situation in Hawaii," March 30, 1940, RG 165, NA.

18. Office of the Chief of Military History, "Civil Affairs," 2992.

19. Ibid., 2994.

20. For further discussion of the Americanization campaign, see Franklin S. Odo, *No Sword to Bury: Japanese Americans in Hawaii during World War II* (Philadelphia: Temple University Press, 2004).

21. John A. Rademaker, *These Are Americans: The Japanese Americans in Hawaii in World War II* (Palo Alto, CA: Pacific Books, 1951), 8.

22. Memorandum from C. H. Mason to Chief of Staff, "Dual Citizenship," June 17, 1941, reproduced in *American Concentration Camps*, vol. 1: *July 1940–December 31, 1941*, ed. Roger Daniels (New York: Garland Publishing, 1989). See infra, p. 198, for discussion of the 1944 Nationality Act.

23. Okihiro, *Cane Fires*, 198.

24. Gwenfread Allen, *Hawaii's War Years, 1941–1945* (Honolulu: University of Hawai'i Press, 1950), 68.

25. Reported in *Honolulu Advertiser,* October 10, 1940.

26. FBI, "Memorandum on Pearl Harbor Attack," JIR.

27. *Hawaii Sentinel,* July 31, 1941. Earlier in the month, the *Sentinel* detailed "documentary evidence" that "subversive agents," using Japanese language radio stations in Hawaii, were "working on the Japanese population, both alien and American born." *Hawaii Sentinel,* July 17, 1941.

28. *Honolulu Advertiser,* August 6, 1940.

29. Greg Robinson, *A Tragedy of Democracy: Japanese Confinement in North America* (New York: Columbia University Press, 2009), 53.

30. United Press release, July 6, 1941, clipping in King Papers, HSA.

31. Quoted in the *Honolulu Star-Bulletin,* August 18, 1941.

32. *Honolulu Star-Bulletin,* October 15, 16, and 17, 1941.

33. *Hawaii Sentinel,* editorial of August 8, 1941, clipping in King Papers, HSA.

34. King to Honorable Carl Vinson, July 17, 1941, copy in King Papers, HSA.

35. United Press Dispatch, July 16, 1941, copy in King Papers, HSA.

36. *Honolulu Advertiser,* August 9, 1941.

37. Telegram from George Waterhouse, President, Honolulu Chamber of Commerce to Delegate King, August 16, 1941, King Papers, HSA.

38. Hull to King, September 10, 1941, King Papers, HSA; Biddle to King, September 8, 1941, King Papers, HSA.

39. Biddle to King, September 8, 1941, King Papers, HSA.

40. Ickes to King, October 13, 1941, King Papers, HSA.

41. Tom Coffman, "Higedo Yoshida," *Densho Encyclopedia,* http://encyclopedia.densho.org /Shigeo_Yoshida. A similar, informal group, called the Committee for the Promotion of National

Unity, with parallel objectives and methods of operation, had overlapping membership with the Council for Inter-Racial Unity and was likely a predecessor organization. It was interested not only in promoting unity for national defense, but also in "the way the people of Hawaii are going to live together after the emergency is over." See Ellen Honda, Secretary to Charles F. Loomis, to Galen Fisher, September 16, 1941 and attachment, "Committee for the Promotion of National Unity," in JAERR, Reel 371, Bancroft Library, University of California, Berkeley.

42. Robert L. Shivers, "Cooperation of the Various Racial Groups with Each Other and with the Constituted Authorities Before and After December 7, 1941," Statement Presented before Sub-Committee on Statehood, U.S. House of Representatives, Iolani Palace, Honolulu, January 15, 1946 (Honolulu, HI: Chamber of Commerce of Honolulu, 1946), 5–8. The Council was instrumental in the formation of the Morale Section of the Office of the Military Governor (OMG), of which Hemenway was a member. See infra, pp. 138ff. For an exploration of racism during the war, including the Council and the related Morale Section of the OMG, see Tom Coffman's video production, "The First Battle: The Battle for Equality in War-time Hawaii," (San Francisco: Distributed by the Center for Asian American Media, 2006). The script is available at http://www.thefirstbattle.com /index.html. See also Tom Coffman, *How Hawai'i Changed America: The Campaign for Equal Treatment of Japanese Americans in the War Against Japan* (Honolulu, HI: EpiCenter, 2014).

43. Shivers, "Cooperation of the Various Racial Groups," 5.

44. *Honolulu Advertiser,* June 14, 1941.

45. *Honolulu Star-Bulletin,* July 19, 1941, July 21, 1941. For a discussion of the New Americans, see Dennis M. Ogawa, *Kodomo no tame ni: For the Sake of the Children* (Honolulu: University of Hawai'i Press, 1978), chap. 5.

46. Andrew W. Lind, *Hawaii's Japanese: An Experiment in Democracy* (Princeton, NJ: Princeton University Press, 1946), 132. See also Boylan and Holmes, *John A. Burns,* 33.

47. *Maui News,* June 2, 1941. Shivers's statements were reported in the text of an editorial supporting racial tolerance and urging its readers to "settle down to the important problem of civilian morale. The front lines can be no stronger than those built along the home defense front."

48. Quoted in *Honolulu Star-Bulletin,* November 1, 1941.

49. As it turned out, a Japanese-American citizen drew the No. 1 card in the prewar draft in Hawai'i, and immediately entered the service. *Honolulu Advertiser,* August 9, 1941.

50. Quotation from *Colliers' Weekly,* October 19, 1940, quoted by Samuel W. King and reproduced in *Honolulu Star-Bulletin,* June 11, 1941.

51. U.S. Army Pacific, "History, Commanding Generals—United States Army, Pacific," http:// www.usarpac.army.mil/history2/cg_herron.asp; see also, *Honolulu Star-Bulletin,* August 18, 1941. For a rich discussion of the Nisei in the Hawai'i Territorial Guard and the formation of the Varsity Victory Volunteers, see Odo, *No Sword to Bury.*

52. *Honolulu Star-Bulletin,* June 14, 1941.

53. *Honolulu Star-Bulletin,* July 19, 1941.

54. Ibid.

55. Short to Adjutant General, May 15, 1941, quoted in Michael Slackman, *Target: Pearl Harbor* (Honolulu: University of Hawai'i Press, 1990), 39.

56. Slackman, *Target: Pearl Harbor,* 40.

57. U.S. Congress Joint Committee on Pearl Harbor Attack, *Report by the Secretary of the Navy to the President, Hearings,* Exhib. 49, Part 24, 1750. The order to group the planes was issued on November 27, 1941. W. F. Craven and J. L. Cate, eds., *The Army Air Forces during World War II,* vol. 1:

Plans and Early Operations, January 1939–August 1942 (Chicago: University of Chicago Press, 1948), 194; Samuel Eliot Morison, *History of United States Naval Operations in World War II*. vol. 3, *The Rising Sun in the Pacific, 1931–April 1942* (1957, repr.; Urbana: University of Illinois Press, 2002), 123.

58. Robinson, *By Order of the President,* 57–58.

59. Memorandum by Secretary of the Navy to the President, October 9, 1940, President's Secretary File, quoted in Robinson, *By Order of the President,* 61.

60. CWIRC, *Personal Justice Denied,* chap. 11, http://www.archives.gov/research/japanese -americans/justice-denied/chapter-11.pdf.

61. Quoted in Robinson, *By Order of the President,* 65.

62. Stimson to Attorney General, March 7, 1941, War Records Group 407–3, copy in JCCH.

63. "Recommendations of Representatives of the War Department and of the Department of Justice for Cooperation Respecting Internment of Alien Enemies," March 26, 1941, copy in JIR and in AR 19 Box 8 Folder 3; "Joint Agreement of the Secretary of War and the Attorney General Respecting Internment of Alien Enemies," July 18, 1941, copy in AR 19, Box 8, Folder 4. For copies of the documents leading to this final agreement, see Daniels, *American Concentration Camps,* vol. 1.

64. Warren J. Draper, Acting Surgeon General, to Secretary of War, May 12, 1941, copy in JIR.

65. Short to Adjutant General, July 3, 1941, copy in JIR.

66. Norman M. Littell, *My Roosevelt Years* (Seattle: University of Washington Press, 1987), 11.

67. The Munson Report is reproduced in Daniels, ed., *American Concentration Camps,* vol. 1.

68. Ibid.

69. Ibid.

70. Curtis B. Munson, "Report on Hawaiian Islands," attached to Memo, John Franklin Carter to FDR, December 8, 1941, Carter File, FDRL. Also reproduced in Ogawa, *Kodomo No Tame Ni,* 299–303.

71. Ibid. For a detailed discussion of the Munson investigations, see also Robinson, *By Order of the President,* chaps. 2 and 3; and Michi Weglyn, *Years of Infamy: The Untold Story of America's Concentration Camps,* updated ed. (Seattle: University of Washington Press, 1996), chap. 1.

72. Quoted in Weglyn, *Years of Infamy,* 49.

73. See Weglyn, *Years of Infamy,* app. 10, p. 194, for Carter cover memo. It appears that the Munson Report was never released to the public until the postwar hearings on Pearl Harbor in 1946; what effect it might have had on the anti-Japanese hysteria on the West Coast can only be a matter for speculation.

74. Shivers, Memorandum to FBI Director Hoover, December 17, 1941, copy in JCCH. The plan actually listed three options, each dealing with a different scenario of the impact on Hawai'i of war with Japan. If there was no immediate threat to Hawai'i, the consular agents and a limited number of Buddhist and Shinto priests would be detained, subject to the results of hearing boards. If surprise raids against Hawai'i appeared likely, everyone on the detention lists would be interned, and the remaining Japanese population would be placed under surveillance. If Hawai'i was in imminent danger of invasion, martial law would be declared, and all persons on the detention list would be incarcerated, without benefit of review. (FBI, "Memorandum on Pearl Harbor Attack," JIR.) In actuality, the third plan was used—but with review procedures added.

75. Shivers, Memorandum to FBI Director Hoover, December 4, 194, FBI File No. 100-2-20, Section 2, copy in JCCH [hereinafter Shivers to FBI Director, "Custodial Detention"]. Emphasis added. Shivers's numbers differ slightly from official census data.

76. Ibid.

77. Ibid.

78. Office of Chief of Military History, "Civil Affairs," 2996.

79. Major General Thomas H. Green, "Martial Law in Hawaii, December 7, 1941–April 4, 1943," 35, http://www.loc.gov/rr/frd/Military_Law/pdf/Martial-Law_Green.pdf [hereinafter cited as Green, "Martial Law"].

80. "Meet General Green," *The Judge Advocate Journal* 2, no. 3 (1945): 5.

81. Ibid.

82. Ibid.

83. Office of the Chief of Military History, "Civil Affairs," 2997.

84. Green, "Martial Law," 41. The two lawyers were Deputy Attorney General Edward Sylva and Assistant Attorney General Rhoda Lewis.

85. J. Garner Anthony, *Hawaii under Army Rule* (Stanford, CA: Stanford University Press, 1955), 4; Office of Chief of Military History, "Civil Affairs," 2998.

86. Hawaii Senate Jour. (1941), Spec. Sess., 14, 15, quoted in Anthony, *Hawaii under Army Rule,* 4.

87. Hawaii Archives, Minutes, Senate Committee of the Whole (September 17, 1941), quoted in Anthony, *Hawaii under Army Rule,* 4. Emphasis added.

88. J. Garner Anthony, "Hawaiian Martial Law in the Supreme Court," *Yale Law Journal* 57 (1947–1948): 28.

89. Hawaii Defense Act (Act 24), 1941 Laws Terr. Haw. 1 (codified as amended at Rev. L. Haw. chap. 324 [1945]).

90. *Honolulu Star-Bulletin,* November 11, 1941.

91. *Honolulu Star-Bulletin,* November 10, 1941, and November 21, 1941. For John Burns's editorial opposition to the measure, see supra, p. 24.

92. *Honolulu Advertiser,* December 4, 1941, p. 1, and *Honolulu Star-Bulletin,* December 4, 1941, p. 1.

93. Green, "Martial Law," 49–50.

Chapter 3: Implementation of Martial Law and Military Government

1. Memorandum from Benjamin Thoron to Harold Ickes, May 12, 1942, Secretary of the Interior Records, Record Group 48, National Archives [hereinafter Ickes Files, NA] (reporting interview with Poindexter); report on statement by Poindexter, *Honolulu Star-Bulletin,* April 27, 1946. Allen writes that Gen. Short visited Poindexter at 12:10 to ask for martial law. Gwenfread Allen, *Hawaii's War Years, 1941–1945* (Honolulu: University of Hawai'i Press, 1950), 35.

2. Testimony in Federal district court, December 12, 1950, reported in the *Chicago Daily Tribune,* December 13, 1950; oral history interview with Hon. Ernest Kapuamailani Kai, The Watumull Foundation Oral History Project, 20–21. According to the army's official history, "Had war come by the normal processes of international law, the Hawaii Defense Act would probably have been adequate to meet the conditions for which it was designed. The situation on 7 December went far beyond all anticipations of those who had planned the Act and rendered it practically worthless." (Office of the Chief of Military History, "Civil Affairs," 2999.)

3. FBI, "Memorandum on Pearl Harbor Attack," JIR. According to this FBI file, Poindexter called Shivers about noon to ask if he should invoke the M-Day Act and received a positive reply. Poindexter contacted Shivers again at about 1:00 p.m. to ask if martial law should be declared, and Shivers responded that "by all means, martial law should be immediately declared." A different

version of Shivers's response to Poindexter's phone call is given by police captain John Burns, who says he was in Shivers's office when the call came. Recollecting that day many years later, Burns says that Shivers "avoided the question entirely," saying he "couldn't presume to tell the governor what to do." (*Burns Oral History,* Tape 4, 4.)

4. Diary of Charles M. Hite, quoted in Allen, *Hawaii's War Years,* 35.

5. Ibid.

6. *Chicago Daily Tribune,* December 13, 1950.

7. *Honolulu Star-Bulletin,* May 4, 1946, and Pearl Harbor Report, Part 23, p. 820, quoted in J. Garner Anthony, *Hawaii under Army Rule* (Stanford, CA: Stanford University Press, 1955), 9.

8. *Chicago Daily Tribune,* December 13, 1950.

9. Ibid.

10. Ickes to Henry Stimson, August 5, 1942, Assistant Secretary of War Files, War Department Records, Record Group 107, National Archives [hereinafter McCloy Files, NA]. In a memorandum for files, Green denied that Poindexter had been promised a termination of martial law "in thirty days maximum." (Notes made by General Thomas H. Green in Washington, DC, August 1942, [manuscript], Hawaii Military Government Records, Record Group 338, National Archives [hereinafter Green Notes].) Poindexter, however, claimed in the interview accounts of the incident only that "early" termination had been promised him. See *Chicago Daily Tribune,* December 13, 1950.

11. Diary of Harold Ickes, August 16, 1942, Harold L. Ickes Papers, Library of Congress, Washington DC [hereinafter Ickes Papers, LC]. The press coverage of the controversy over Poindexter's role in establishment of martial law is reviewed in James B. Lane, "Joseph B. Poindexter and Hawaii During the New Deal," *Pacific Northwest Quarterly* 62 (1971): 7, 14–15.

12. Thomas H. Green, "Martial Law in Hawaii, December 7, 1941–April 4, 1943," 35; http://www.loc.gov/rr/frd/Military_Law/pdf/Martial-Law_Green.pdf, 105. On a copy of the letter from Ickes to Stimson, August 5, 1942, there is a penciled notation that seems to be in General Green's hand, stating that on September 10, 1942, Poindexter "personally denied that he ever made such a statement to Mr. Ickes. . . ." It is on file in the Records of the Military Government of Hawaii, Record Group 338, National Archives [hereinafter cited as RG 338, NA].

13. Green's handwritten notes on a copy of Hite's diary entries for December 7, 1941. In a note added many years later, on September 22, 1970, Green wrote, "On rereading the above [notes] my views remain unchanged. Doubtless the diary of Hite will go down in history as the true facts. It has no basis in fact." Papers of General Thomas H. Green, Judge Advocate General's School Library, Charlottesville, VA [hereinafter Green Papers, JAGSL].

14. A Presidential Commission, chaired by Supreme Court Justice Owen Roberts, investigated the Pearl Harbor debacle and in January 1942 charged both General Short and Admiral Kimmel with errors of judgment and "dereliction of duty." Both officers were summarily relieved of their commands. Subsequent official investigations found that they were not given vital intelligence, and in 1999 the U.S. Senate passed a resolution exonerating them. (Philip Shenon, "Senate Clears 2 Pearl Harbor 'Scapegoats'," *New York Times,* May 26, 1999.) See p. 216 for discussion of Ickes's decision to remove Poindexter.

15. Oral history interview with Hon. Ernest Kapuamailani Kai, The Watumull Foundation Oral History Project, 21.

16. Text of proclamation is reprinted in Anthony, *Hawaii under Army Rule,* 127. Emphasis added.

17. Text of proclamation is also reprinted in ibid., 127–128.

18. See Green, "Martial Law," 107.

19. Biddle to Roosevelt, December 9, 1941 (copy), "Hawaii" file, Biddle Papers, FDRL; Anthony, *Hawaii under Army Rule,* 5 and appendix.

20. U.S. Army, *A Manual for Courts Martial,* quoted in J. Garner Anthony, "Martial Law, Military Government and the Writ of Habeas Corpus in Hawaii," *California Law Review* 31 (1943): 480. This article contains an excellent discussion of the distinction between martial law and military government. Similarly, in a 1945 summary of security measures taken in Hawai'i, the army's Office of Internal Security stated, "Military government is the government by military forces of territory occupied by a belligerent and is the consequence of war, constituting an exercise of the war power. Roughly speaking, military government involves military control of foreign territory; martial law concerns itself with military control of domestic territory." Office of Internal Security, Territory of Hawaii, "Wartime Security Controls in Hawaii: 1941–1945," Part One, 2, Box 24, Richardson Papers, Hoover Institution.

21. Anthony, *Hawaii under Army Rule.*

22. See infra, chaps. 11 through 14, for a discussion of the political and legal challenges to martial law and the military government.

23. For full discussion, see chap. 8, infra.

24. A total of 617 of the persons who would be interned in the Islands during the war were U.S. citizens, 570 of them being of Japanese ancestry, 42 of German ancestry, 2 of Italian ancestry, and 3 native-born Caucasian citizens. See Table 4, p. 196. (Office of Internal Security [Honolulu], Memorandum to War Department No. R73740, November 30, 1945, RG 338, NA.) These statistics differ slightly from those in Office of the Chief of Military History, "United States Army Forces Middle Pacific and Predecessor Commands during World War II, vol. 10, part 8, Appendix 1, Plans and Measures for the Control of Certain Elements of the Population," presented infra in chap. 7, note 8. See also chap. 10, note 116.

25. Andrew W. Lind, *Hawaii's Japanese: An Experiment in Democracy* (Princeton, NJ: Princeton University Press, 1946), 70–71 (quoting Emmons); on the Public Morale Section, see ibid., 81–83, and infra, pp. 138ff. On Emmons's reassurance to Japanese Americans and his statements re tolerance, see infra., chap. 8; see also Stetson Conn, Rose C. Engelman, and Byron Fairchild, *Guarding the United States and its Outposts,* U.S. Army, Center of Military History (Washington, DC: U.S. Government Printing Office, 1962), chapter 8 on The Hawaiian Defenses After Pearl Harbor.

26. Allen, *Hawaii's War Years,* 263–273 (discussing, in addition, combat service by the Engineers units); cf. Eileen O'Brien, "Making Democracy," *Paradise of the Pacific* 55 (December 1943), 42–45. See also discussion in chap. 7, infra.

27. http://www.foitimes.com/internment/Proc2525.html; http://www.nps.gov/tule/planyourvisit/upload/WWII_%20JA_timeline_2010.pdf. See infra, pp. 121ff., for discussion of Koreans in Hawai'i, who were initially classified as enemy aliens. See also Michael E. Macmillan, "Unwanted Allies: Koreans as Enemy Aliens in World War II," *Hawaiian Journal of History* 19 (1985): 179 (on the extension of prohibitions to residents of Korean ancestry, despite the suffering that their ancestor nation had undergone at the hands of Japanese imperial armies).

28. R. L. Shivers to Director, Federal Bureau of Investigation, "Custodial Detention and Apprehension of Japanese, German and Italian Aliens and Citizens of Those Races," December 17, 1941, copy in JCCH.

29. See infra, p. 46.

30. Allen, *Hawaii's War Years*, 39–46, 141, 351–352; Gary Y. Okihiro, *Cane Fires: The Anti-Japanese Movement in Hawaii, 1865–1945* (Philadelphia: Temple University Press, 1991), 204–267; Office of the Chief of Military History, "United States Army Forces, Middle Pacific and Predecessor Commands during World War II, 7 December 1941–2 September 1945: History of G-2 Section," HWRD, Hamilton Library, University of Hawai'i; Michi Weglyn, *Years of Infamy: The Untold Story of America's Concentration Camps,* updated ed. (Seattle: University of Washington Press, 1996), 49–52, 86–89.

31. *Burns Oral History,* Tape 2, 7.

32. Shivers to FBI Director, "Custodial Detention," December 17, 1941, JCCH.

33. Ibid.

34. Ibid.

35. Ibid.

36. Radiogram, from Adams (War Department) to Commanding General, Fort Shafter, December 11, 1941, U.S. District Court Case No. 730, Exhibit C, RG 21, National Archives, San Bruno, CA [hereinafter NASB].

37. FBI, Memorandum on Pearl Harbor Attack, JIR.

38. Karl R. Bendetsen, Major, J.A.G.D., Chief, Aliens Division, for Provost Marshal General Gullion, "Memorandum for the Adjutant General: Initiation of Internment Program," December 8, 1941. Copy in Folder 387, JIR.

39. The FBI had prepared plans before the war to apprehend *all* German and Italian aliens residing in Hawai'i, and they did so on December 8, excluding only the aged and the infirm. (Testimony of Robert Shivers, United States Congress, "Hearings before the Joint Committee on the Investigation of the Pearl Harbor Attack" [U.S. GPO, 1942] [hereinafter Roberts Commission], 663.)

40. FBI, Honolulu Field Division, Running Log, December 7–12, 1941, RG 65, NA.

41. FBI Memorandum, C. H. Carson to Ladd, December 9, 1941, File No. 100-2-20, Section 1, www.foitimes.com/internment/Honolulu1.pdf. An Alien Enemy Property Administrator's office was established, taking charge in 1942 of the holding and disposition of millions of dollars in land, businesses, and other property taken from the 120,000 who were sent away to the internment camps on the mainland. (Dillon S. Myer, *Uprooted Americans: The Japanese Americans and the War Relocation Authority during World War II* [Tucson: University of Arizona Press, 1971], 245–256.) In Hawai'i, because in most cases the families of those who were taken into custody or interned remained behind, so that they could maintain their homes and take care of possessions and often of businesses, the seizures of alien enemy property were of limited scope—though of great consequence, no doubt, to the relatively few individuals who were affected.

42. Newman A. Townsend, Acting Assistant Solicitor General, to Amberg, Special Assistant to Secretary of War, December 9, 1941, and Memorandum from Provost Marshal Allen Gullion to Secretary of War, "Confirmatory Warrants Covering F.B.I. Alien Enemy Apprehensions-Hawaii," January 14, 1942, copies in Folder 352, JIR. Emmons affirmed formally that the arrests were in accordance with his program and with his authority. (Radiogram, Emmons to Adjutant General, December 21, 1941, copy in Folder 352, JIR.)

43. Shivers to FBI Director, "Custodial Detention," December 17, 1941, JCCH.

44. Yasutaro (Keiho) Soga, *Life behind Barbed Wire: The World War II Internment Memoirs of a Hawai'i Issei* (Honolulu: University of Hawai'i Press, 2008), 25.

45. Garrett Hongo, *Volcano: A Memoir* (New York: Alfred A. Knopf, 1995), excerpted online at http://www.english.illinois.edu/maps/poets/g_l/hongo/volcano.htm.

46. Testimony by Mitsunobu Miyahira in Commission on Wartime Relocation and Internment of Civilians, *Personal Justice Denied* (Washington, DC: Government Printing Office, 1982) [hereinafter CWIRC, *Personal Justice Denied*].

47. Interview with Hisashi Fukuhara, Folder 232, JIR.

48. Transcript of Interview with Ella Tomita, interviewed by Kalei Ho and Mika Bailey, October 14, 2004, JCCH. Used with the kind permission of Ms. Tomita.

49. Allen, *Hawaii's War Years,* 137.

50. Interview with Joe Pacific, in Center for Oral History, *An Era of Change: Oral Histories of Civilians in World War II Hawai'i,* vol. 1 (Honolulu: Social Science Research Institute, University of Hawai'i, 1994), 163–189.

51. Doris Berg Nye, "Internment of a German-American Family in Hawaii," http://www.gaic.info/real_berg.html.

52. FBI, Honolulu Field Division, Running Log, December 7–12, 1941, RG 65, NA. Soon after December 7, the military governor formally banned possession by Nikkei of all such items, and searches of homes and business properties continued throughout the war years. (The board games may still be seen in the RG 494, NA files of provost court evidentiary materials.) The provost courts tried cases involving offenses under these prohibitions (Bicknell, "Security Measures in Hawaii," HWRD). See also Okihiro, *Cane Fires,* 210–214.

53. "Summary of FBI efforts to Combat Activities Inimical to the United States in the Hawaiian Islands," January 5, 1942, RG 65, Hawaiian Islands, NA, 7. There initially was a controversy in the government over the consular agents. The federal District Attorney Angus Taylor wanted them prosecuted en masse for violation of the foreign agents registration law, whereas the army and FBI resisted, only to intern them later. Taylor and Shivers discussed this history in testimony before the Roberts Commission. Shivers reported in his Roberts Commission testimony, as in his communications with FBI headquarters in Washington—and it was widely acknowledged—that before the Pearl Harbor attack the Japanese consulate had coordinated what in peacetime could be termed merely "intelligence gathering" (even though it involved observations of movements and defenses that any member of the public might see) but in war conditions would be termed instead "espionage." (Testimony of Robert Shivers, Roberts Commission.)

54. Reverend Yamada, "Struggling within a Struggle," (memoir of a Nisei Protestant minister's activities on Maui during the war period), 5–6, in JAERR, Reel 171, Bancroft Library, UC Berkeley.

55. Interview with Hisashi Fukuhara, Folder 232, JIR.

56. Thomas J. Hamilton, "Japanese Seizure Ordered by Biddle," *New York Times,* December 8, 1941, p. 6.

57. Karl R. Bendetsen to Assistant Chief of Staff, Memorandum, "Evacuation of Dangerous Enemy Aliens from Hawaii," January 30, 1942, in Roger Daniels, ed., *American Concentration Camps: A Documentary History of the Relocation and Incarceration of Japanese Americans, 1942–1945,* vol. 8: *Japanese of Hawaii* (New York: Garland, 1989), n.p.

58. Zimmerman's internment and appeal are discussed at length infra, pp. 253ff.

59. Bicknell, "Security Measures in Hawaii," chap. 5, 59, HWRD.

60. Office of the Chief of Military History, "History of G-2 Section, vol. 10 part 2 of United States Army Forces Middle Pacific and Predecessor Commands during World War II (1941–42)," 19, 24–25, HWRD.

61. FBI, Honolulu Field Division, Running Log, December 7–12, 1941, RG 65, NA.

62. R. L. Shivers, "Memorandum for the Bureau," December 18, 1941 and December 19, 1941, FBI File No. 100–2-20, "Custodial Detention."

63. Affidavit of Carl Magnus Torstan Arnfeld, read by the conservative radio commentator Fulton Lewis Jr., November 14, 1945, transcript, in Green Papers, JAGSL. (The Lewis transcript misspells his name.) Armfelt was picked up following reports from a civilian that there were photographs of airplane motors in the glove compartment of his car. (FBI, Honolulu Field Division, Running Log, December 7–12, 1941, RG 65, NA.)

64. By February 23, a total of 569 persons were being held in custody: 446 Japanese aliens, 38 Japanese-American citizens, 42 German aliens, 34 German American citizens, 7 Italian aliens, and 2 Italian-American citizens. In addition, several dozen had been interrogated and released. (FBI Radiogram, Honolulu to Director, February 24, 1942, and Shivers to FBI Director, February 11, 1942, FBI File No. 100–2-20 "Custodial Detention," http://www.foitimes.com /internment/Honolulu1.pdf.)

65. Statements by Gunther Herbert and Anna Walther, May 15, 1945, Edwin Norton Barnhart Papers, Box 7, Folder 15, Hoover Institution Archives, Stanford University. Upon their release, the Walthers, like Hans Zimmerman, refused to sign a statement absolving the government of all blame in their incarceration. They subsequently filed a civil suit against Emmons. See below, chap. 18. Honouliuli is discussed in chap. 10, infra.

66. Office of the Chief of Military History, "Civil Affairs," 3088. See infra, chap. 9.

67. McCloy to Richardson, October, 25, 1943, copy in Green Papers, JAGSL.

68. For the recollections of the Provost Marshal of Hawai'i, see "Oral History Interview with William 'Frank' F. Steer," by Mike Gordon, transcript available at https://jcch.follettdestiny.com /digitalresource/saas32_7500284/1421283849151_steer_william_frank.pdf.

69. Soga, *Life behind Barbed Wire*, 26. This firsthand account contains vivid descriptions of the indignities, hardships, and ennui of the various detention centers where this journalist was held throughout the war.

70. CWIRC, *Personal Justice Denied;* Office of the Chief of Military History, "United States Army Forces Middle Pacific and Predecessor Commands During World War II, 7 December 1941–2 September 1945." OCMH, SC No. 170007, vol. 24, pt. 2, copy in HWRD; Roland Kotani, *The Japanese in Hawaii: A Century of Struggle* (Official Program Booklet of the Oahu Kanyaku Imin Centennial Committee, 1985), 91; Allen, *Hawaii's War Years,* 136; Japanese Cultural Center of Hawaii, *Never Again: Executive Order 9066 to Honouliuli,* program commemorating the 65th Anniversary of Honouliuli, March 2, 2008 (pamphlet), 7.

71. Soga, *Life behind Barbed Wire,* passim. See infra, chap. 10, for further discussion of the detention centers.

72. Otokichi Muin Ozaki, radio script, original Japanese in AR1, Box 4, Folder 8, Script #5, JCCH, trans. reproduced in Gail Honda, ed., *Family Torn Apart: The Internment Story of the Otokichi Muin Ozaki Family* (Honolulu: Japanese Cultural Center of Hawai'i, 2012), 20. This book compellingly recounts the odyssey of an Issei language teacher who was arrested and incarcerated in a series of mainland camps, and his family's efforts to reunite with him. It is based on

letters, poetry, and radio scripts prepared by Ozaki for broadcast in 1949–1950. Used with permission of JCCH.

73. Interview with Jukichi Inouye, file 236, JIR.

74. Dennis M. Ogawa and Evarts C. Fox Jr., "Japanese Internment and Relocation: The Hawaii Experience," in *Japanese Americans, From Relocation to Redress,* ed. Roger Daniels, Sandra C. Taylor, Harry H. L. Kitano, and Leonard J. Arrington (Salt Lake City: University of Utah Press, 1983), 136.

75. Office of Internal Security, Territory of Hawaii, "Wartime Security Controls in Hawaii: 1941–1945, A General Historical Survey, Part Four: Security Regulations Affecting Alien Enemies and Dual Citizens" (Honolulu, 1945), 100–101, copy in Richardson Papers, Box 24, Hoover Institution, Stanford University.

76. Office of the Chief of Military History, "United States Army Forces Middle Pacific and Predecessor Commands During World War II, 7 December 1941–2 September 1945." OCMH, SC No. 170007, vol. 24, pt. 2, copy in HWRD.

Chapter 4: Life under General Orders

1. See, e.g., Gwenfread Allen, *Hawaii's War Years, 1941–1945* (Honolulu: University of Hawai'i Press, 1950), passim.

2. Vern Hinkley, *New York Times,* December 21, 1941.

3. Attorney General Francis Biddle and Acting Secretary of Interior Abe Fortas to John J. McCloy, December 19, 1942, McCloy Files, NA. See also J. Garner Anthony, "Hawaiian Martial Law in the Supreme Court," *Yale Law Journal* 57 (1947–1948): 29–32; and J. Garner Anthony, *Hawaii under Army Rule* (Stanford, CA: Stanford University Press, 1955), 14. See discussion of Provost Courts, infra, chap. 6.

4. Emmons address to Honolulu Chamber of Commerce, January 15, 1942, reported in *New York Times,* January 16, 1942, 2.

5. Emmons quoted in "Military Law Under Scrutiny," *Honolulu Star-Bulletin,* May 15, 1942.

6. These "security orders" were issued by the Office of Internal Security, which replaced the OMG in summer 1944.

7. Anthony to Governor Ingram M. Stainback, December 1, 1942, Papers of Governor Ingram M. Stainback, Hawai'i State Archives [hereinafter Stainback Papers, HSA]. Substantially the same position is expressed by a high-ranking member of the Department of the Interior hierarchy, in a letter from Benjamin Thoron to Harold Ickes, May 12, 1942, Ickes Files, NA; see generally Anthony, *Hawaii under Army Rule,* 12–45 and appendix E.

8. Lt. Gen. Robert C. Richardson Jr., "Hawaii—Fortress of the Pacific," *Army and Navy Journal* 82 (December 1944): 48.

9. Diary of Thomas H. Green, January 1, 1942, Green Papers, JAGSL.

10. Office of Internal Security, Territory of Hawaii, "Wartime Security Controls," Part One, 90, Box 24, Richardson Papers, Hoover Institution.

11. Thomas H. Green, "Martial Law in Hawaii, December 7, 1941–April 4, 1943," 35; http://www.loc.gov/rr/frd/Military_Law/pdf/Martial-Law_Green.pdf, 115.

12. Although Governor Poindexter seemed reluctant to challenge General Emmons's authority, his successor, Governor Stainback, strongly contested army rule.

13. Governor Stainback feared that the election of Japanese Americans would draw adverse publicity on the mainland and "would probably be used as an argument for continuing and possibly extending military government in the Islands." Stainback therefore intervened with party leaders, who persuaded the Nisei candidates to withdraw. (Stainback to Ickes, October 30, 1942, enclosed with Ickes to McCloy, November 7, 1942, McCloy Files, NA.)

14. Office of Internal Security, Territory of Hawaii, "Wartime Security Controls," Part Two, 131, Box 24, Richardson Papers, Hoover Institution.

15. On Oʻahu alone, there were seventeen divisions and subdivisions of the OCD. In February 1942, with the threat of an invasion seemingly still a real possibility, the territorial OCD employed more than 3,000 persons, with an additional 14,000 individuals serving as volunteers. By fall of 1942, both the size of the staff and the scope of its work had declined sharply, but in 1943 there were still some 27,000 volunteer workers. (Allen, *Hawaii's War Years*, 35, 166–171; Richardson Jr., "Hawaii—Fortress of the Pacific," 122.)

16. Ibid.

17. Stainback to Ickes, October 30, 1942, enclosed with Ickes to McCloy, November 7, 1942, McCloy Files, NA.

18. Stainback to Ickes, November 17, 1942, copy in McCloy Files, NA.

19. Anthony to Stainback, December 1, 1942, Stainback Papers, HSA.

20. Anthony, *Hawaii under Army Rule,* 191–195.

21. Ibid., 48–52; Office of Internal Security, Territory of Hawaii, "Wartime Security Controls," Part Two, 183–92, Box 24, Richardson Papers, Hoover Institution.

22. General Green's handwritten marginal notes, on manuscript, "Development of the Office of Military Governor" (draft chapter of an unpublished history, apparently prepared by army historians), Green Papers, JAGSL. See, however, text at note 11, supra.

23. Diary of Thomas H. Green, May 3, 1942, Green Papers, JAGSL. For Emmons's strikingly more modest assessment of Green's role, see p. 324.

24. See chap. 7 on Japanese Americans.

25. Anthony, *Hawaii under Army Rule,* 46–59; see also "Hawaii's Industry Goes to War," *Hawaii: A Magazine Of News And Comment,* July 18, 1942, p. 7; and Allen, *Hawaii's War Years.*

26. Richardson, "Hawaii—Fortress of the Pacific," 48.

27. *New York Times,* February 3, 1942, p. 5.

28. Green, "Martial Law," 120; Allen, *Hawaii's War Years,* 34.

29. Office of Internal Security, Territory of Hawaii, "Wartime Security Controls," Part Three, 18, Box 24, Richardson Papers, Hoover Institution.

30. Allen, *Hawaii's War Years,* 358; Dorothy Bond, "Christmas Letter from Oahu," *Washington Post,* December 10, 1942, p. 11; *Honolulu Star-Bulletin,* November 7, 1942.

31. Oral History Interview with Richard H. Y. Chun, April 1993, in *An Era of Change: Oral Histories of Civilians in World War II Hawaiʻi,* vol. 4 (Center for Oral History, Social Science Research Institute, University of Hawaiʻi at Manoa, 1994), 1127.

32. E. Long, Superintendent of Schools, Dept. of Public Instruction, to Col. T. H. Green, January 2, 1942, General Emmons Reading File, RG 338, NA.

33. General Orders No. 113, June 5, 1942.

34. One estimate was that only slightly more than half of the students who were enrolled prior to December 7 returned to school on February 2. *New York Times,* February 3, 1942, p. 5.

35. Office of Internal Security, Territory of Hawaii, "Wartime Security Controls," Part Two, 62–116, Box 24, Richardson Papers, Hoover Institution.

36. See Anthony, *Hawaii under Army Rule,* 137–184 (reprinting the general orders and discussing the regulations). See also Allen, *Hawaii's War Years,* passim.

37. Allen, *Hawaii's War Years,* 92; *New York Times,* January 11, 1942.

38. Vern Hinkley, "Honolulu Regains its Normal Poise," *New York Times,* December 21, 1941, p. 20.

39. The bulb, with a maximum of 25 watts and a one-inch aperture in the coating, was known as the "Emmons bulb." Office of Internal Security, "Wartime Security Controls," Part Two, 13, Box 24, Richardson Papers, Hoover Institution.

40. Ibid.; Dorothy Bond, "Life in Hawaii," *Washington Post,* December 26, 1943, p. B4; Allen, *Hawaii's War Years,* 112–114, 397.

41. Jan Jabulka, "Hawaii's Japanese," *Chicago Daily Tribune,* January 9, 1944, p. F2.

42. General Orders No. 31 is quoted in the exhibit, "Hawaiʻi under Martial Law: A Humanities Exhibit," Judiciary History Center, Honolulu, Hawaiʻi.

43. Jim A. Richstad, *The Press under Martial Law: The Hawaiian Experience* (Journalism Monographs, Association for Education in Journalism, No. 17, November 1970). Richstad, a former editorial writer and reporter for the *Advertiser,* draws on personal interviews with several of the key figures involved with the media and censorship for his detailed account of control of the media in Hawaiʻi during the war. He offers a more benign interpretation of censorship than does Garner Anthony. For a discussion of censorship and the press during World War II, see also George Chaplin, *Presstime in Paradise: The Life and Times of The Honolulu Advertiser, 1856–1985,* (Honolulu: University of Hawaiʻi Press, 1998), chap. 23; and Helen Geracimos Chapin, *Shaping History: The Role of Newspapers in Hawaii* (Honolulu: University of Hawaiʻi Press, 1996), chaps. 25 and 26.

44. Quoted in Richstad, *The Press under Martial Law,* 11.

45. Knox to G. E. Allen, *Hawaii Farm and Home,* December 31, 1940, copy in JIR.

46. Quoted in Theodore F. Koop, *Weapon of Silence* (Chicago: University of Chicago Press, 1946), 20. Koop was deputy director of the Office of Censorship and provides a lively, contemporary history of the office. See also Michael S. Sweeney, *Secrets of Victory: The Office of Censorship and the American Press and Radio in World War II* (Chapel Hill: University of North Carolina Press, 2001). Emphasis added.

47. Stetson Conn, Rose C. Engelman, and Byron Fairchild, *Guarding the United States and Its Outposts.* U.S. Army, Center of Military History (Washington, DC: U.S. Government Printing Office, 1962), 199.

48. Interview quoted in Richstad, *The Press under Martial Law,* 2. Joseph Farrington, president and general manager of the *Star Bulletin,* would serve as Hawaiʻi's delegate to Congress from 1942 to 1954.

49. *Honolulu Advertiser,* December 8, 1941.

50. Interview with Fielder in Richstad, *The Press under Martial Law,* 5.

51. Chaplin, *Presstime in Paradise,* 205.

52. Richstad, *The Press under Martial Law,* 7.

53. Riley Allen, "Memorandum on Newspaper Censorship in Hawaii as of June 5, 1944," copy in JIR, also in File 13, HWRD.

54. General Orders No. 14, reproduced in Anthony, *Hawaii under Army Rule,* 138.

55. Richstad, *The Press under Martial Law,* 16; Anthony, *Hawaii under Army Rule,* 40. There had been censorship by the U.S. Post Office during World War I, and editors were prosecuted under the Sedition Acts in 1798–1799, but these were not instances of military censorship. See Harry N. Scheiber, *The Wilson Administration and Civil Liberties, 1917–1921* (Ithaca, NY: Cornell University Press, 1960; reissued, New Orleans, LA: Quid Pro Books, 2003), chap. 3.

56. General Orders No. 40, December 22, 1941; General Orders No. 59, January 29, 1942.

57. Lili M. Kim, "How Koreans Repealed Their 'Enemy Alien' Status: Korean Americans' Identity, Culture, and National Pride in Wartime Hawai'i," in *From the Land of Hibiscus: Koreans in Hawai'i, 1903–1950,* ed. Yong-Ho Ch'oe (Honolulu: University of Hawai'i Press, 2007) [hereinafter Kim, "Enemy Alien Status"], 215–216. See chap. 7, infra, for discussion of the status of Koreans as enemy aliens.

58. Conn et al., *Guarding the United States,* 203.

59. General Orders 49. Soga's son, Shigeo Soga, took over as editor of the paper.

60. Samuel King to Cecil R. King (California assemblyman), May 21, 1941, King Papers, HSA. The *Nippu Jiji* had mistakenly sent the wrong King (Cecil) a copy of an article, leading to jocular remarks in the California Assembly.

61. Richstad, *The Press under Martial Law,* 10.

62. Quoted in Chapin, *Shaping History,* 182.

63. Kenneth J. Fielder, A.C. of S, G-2, to Chief of Military Intelligence Service, War Department, Washington, DC, "Report of Enemy Situation and Enemy Capabilities," August 22, 1942, RG 165, NA.

64. Ibid.

65. 56 Stat. 173 (18 U.S.C. 92a) and Title III of the Second War Powers Act, 1942, Section 2-i.

66. Anthony, *Hawaii under Army Rule,* 38, 40. It should be noted that Thurston's paper also had the lucrative contract to print a dozen military newspapers and magazines, including the *Stars and Stripes.* (Chaplin, *Presstime in Paradise,* 208.)

67. Thurston's appointment, like that of other civilian advisers, ended on March 10, 1943, with the partial restoration of civilian government. Richardson to McCloy, Radiogram 15652, May 9, 1944, McCloy Files, NA.

68. *Honolulu Advertiser,* September 4, 1942.

69. Chapin, *Shaping History,* 176.

70. Memorandum from Warner Gardner to Secretary Harold Ickes, December 10, 1942, Papers of James Rowe Jr., Franklin D. Roosevelt Library, Hyde Park, NY. Among the telephone calls that were recorded was one from Assistant Attorney General Tom Clark, who was visiting Hawai'i in August 1942, to Attorney General Biddle in Washington, DC. Clark gave a critical report on the provost courts and was immediately denounced by the OMG for meddling in Hawaiian affairs. ("Memo re the Military and Civil Governments," December 18, 1942, Papers of Delegate Joseph R. Farrington, Hawai'i State Archives [hereinafter Farrington Papers, HSA].)

71. See infra, chap. 12.

72. Allen, *Hawaii's War Years,* 146; Conn et al., *Guarding the United States,* 203.

73. Riley Allen, "Memorandum on Newspaper Censorship."

74. Ibid.

75. Lewis H. Jones, Lt. Col., J.A.G.D., Kauai District, to Office of the Military Governor, "Control of News Releases on Japanese Atrocities," February 4, 1944, RG 338, copy in Folder 157, JIR.

76. Riley Allen, "Memorandum on Newspaper Censorship."

77. Quoted in Richstad, *The Press under Martial Law,* 25.

78. Chapin, *Shaping History,* 172.

79. KGU began operating around the clock at the request of the military, providing a directional beam for pilots ferrying planes to Oʻahu. Chaplin, *Presstime in Paradise,* 205.

80. Allen, *Hawaii's War Years,* 146.

81. Richstad, *The Press under Martial Law,* 13.

82. H. R. Shaw to Gwenfread Allen, December 30, 1947, copy in File 13, HWRD.

83. H. R. Shaw, Foreword to "Censorship in Hawaii," by Willard Wilson, typescript, attached to letter to Gwenfread Allen, December 30, 1947, copy in File 13, HWRD.

84. Censorship Office, "Censorship in Hawaii," by Willard Wilson, typescript, copy in File 13, HWRD. This article was written in response to a request from Gwenfread Allen for an account of censorship during the war. See also "Oral History Interview with William 'Frank' F. Steer," by Mike Gordon, 3, transcript available at https://jcch.follettdestiny.com/digitalresource/saas32 _7500284/1421283849151_steer_william_frank.pdf. Dependents of military personnel who were not contributing directly to the war effort were shipped to the mainland. See infra, p. 76.

85. Wilson, "Censorship in Hawaii," File 13, HWRD.

86. Executive Order 9489, 9 Fed. Reg. 12831; also reproduced in Anthony, *Hawaii under Army Rule,* 134. Number of personnel is from Lt. Col. Louis Springer to Morrison, July 21, 1945, "Memorandum on Censorship Conference," RG 338, NA.

87. Ibid.

88. District Postal Censor, Office of Censorship, Honolulu, T.H., "General Information Summary, June 1–June 15, 1943," copy in JIR, Folder A-26.

89. Allen, *Hawaii's War Years,* 147–148.

90. District Postal Censor, "General Information Summary, June 1–June 15, 1943."

91. Judge J. Frank McLaughlin to Farrington, October 19, 1943, Farrington Papers, HSA.

92. The particular case in question involved a letter from Governor Stainback's office to the Interior Department. Abe Fortas's complaint, cited in text above, is from his letter to Byron Price, Director of Censorship, December 25, 1944, Under Secretary of the Interior Files (Fortas Files), RG 48, National Archives [hereinafter Fortas Files, RG 48, NA]. Similarly, a letter of June 1944 from Territorial Attorney General Tavares to District Attorney Crozier was intercepted and copied; the routing slip from G-2 to the commanding general, dated June 19, 1944, noted: "Since neither Mr. Crozier nor Mr. Tavares know that we have a copy of it we must keep it confidential. There is nothing we can do about it except perhaps prepare some counter statistics." (RG 338, NA.).

93. Thomas H. Green to Ruth Green, November 6, 1942, excerpted from manuscript collection of letters from Gen. Green in possession of Richard Hillenbrand, copy courtesy of JAG library, Charlottesville, VA.

94. H. R. Shaw, Foreword to "Censorship in Hawaii," by Willard Wilson, attached to letter to Gwenfread Allen, December 30, 1947, copy in File 13, HWRD. See also Allen, *Hawaii's War Years,* 148.

95. Shaw, Preface to "Censorship in Hawaii." This quote should not be taken to mean that B-29s based on Oʻahu could directly bomb Japan.

96. Even the Parker Ranch on the Big Island of Hawaiʻi, the second-largest cattle ranch in the United States, did not produce enough beef to meet the needs of the Islands' population. "Hawaii: Sugar-Coated Fort," *Fortune,* 1940, http://features.blogs.fortune.cnn.com/2011/12/11/hawaii -sugar-coated-fort-fortune-1940/; Green, "Martial Law," 114.

97. Donald M. Schug, "Hawaii's Commercial Fishing Industry: 1820–1945," *Hawaiian Journal of History* 35 (2001): 28–29.

98. Green, "Martial Law," 150.

99. The appointees were Alexander Budge, president of Castle and Cook, Director of Materials and Supplies; J. P. Winne, a member of the Mayor's Committee on Food, Director of Food Control; J. D. Bond, manager of the Ewa Plantation, Director of Labor Control; Ernest C. Gray, of the Hawaii Dredging Company, Director of Cargo and Passenger Control; Addison Kirk, president of the local bus company, Director of Land Transportation; and Frank Locey, Director of Civil Defense. Green, "Martial Law," 164–165.

100. General Orders reproduced in Anthony, *Hawaii under Army Rule,* appendix. See also "Hawaii's Industry Goes to War!" *Hawaii: A Magazine of News and Comment,* July 18, 1942, p. 7; see, generally, Allen, *Hawaii's War Years.*

101. "Memorandum Regarding the Military and Civil Governments in Hawaii," December 18, 1942, Farrington Papers, HSA [hereinafter "Memo re Military and Civil Governments"]. This memorandum is not attributed to an author but it was probably prepared by Warner W. Gardner, Solicitor, U.S. Department of the Interior, for Farrington because it contains some of the same language as Gardner Memorandum to Secretary of the Interior Ickes, December 10, 1942, Papers of James Rowe Jr., Box 36, FDRL.

102. Quoted in Allen, *Hawaii's War Years,* 157. Allen contains a detailed description of efforts at food production.

103. "Memo re Military and Civil Governments," December 18, 1942, Farrington Papers, HSA.

104. Allen, *Hawaii's War Years,* 157.

105. Dillingham was decorated by the army for his service as director of food production. According to Stainback, "a Japanese, Baron Goto, from the University of Hawaii, should be decorated if anyone should for his work with the local food production; Walter, at most, was a figure head and not particularly effective at that." (Stainback to Thoron, May 11, 1945, Office Files of Benjamin W. Thoron, Records of the Office of Territories, Department of the Interior, RG 126, NA [hereinafter Thoron Files, RG 126, NA].) Goto subsequently became director of the Extension Service, and in 1962 he became vice chancellor of the university's East West Center. In addition to his work with food production during the war, Goto was a member of the Morale Committee. He volunteered for military duty in 1944 and was assigned to the War Department's foreign morale section in Washington, DC (http://184.168.105.185/archivegrid/collection/data/663416378).

106. Robert W. Horton, Special Assistant to the Secretary, to Secretary of the Interior Harold L. Ickes, May 1, 1943, RG 107, McCloy Papers, NA.

107. Anthony, *Hawaii under Army Rule,* 108.

108. The federal Office of Price Administration (OPA) had been established as a division of the Office for Emergency Management in August 1941, several months before the war started; it became an independent agency in January 1942. (Records of the Office of Price Administration, RG 188, NA.)

109. Allen, *Hawaii's War Years,* 302–3; Dorothy Bond, "Life in Hawaii," *Washington Post,* December 26, 1943; Green, "Martial Law," 403–410.

110. The most complete accounts of prostitution in Hawaii during the war can be found in two works by Beth Bailey and David Farber: *The First Strange Place: Race and Sex in World War II Hawaii* (Baltimore: Johns Hopkins University Press, 1992), and "Hotel Street: Prostitution and the Politics of War," *Radical History Review* 52 (Winter 1992): 54–77. See also Green, "Martial Law,"

chap. 27; Ted Chernin, "My Experiences in the Honolulu Chinatown Red-Light District," *Hawaiian Journal of History* 34 (2000): 203–217; Richard Greer, "Dousing Honolulu's Red Lights," *Hawaiian Journal of History* 34 (2000): 185–202. For an account by Honolulu's most notorious prostitute, see Jean O'Hara, *My Life as a Honolulu Prostitute* (self-published, 1944), Hawai'i and Pacific Collection, University of Hawai'i at Manoa.

111. The White-Slave Traffic Act (the Mann Act) of 1910 made it a felony to engage in interstate or foreign commerce transport of "any woman or girl for the purpose of prostitution or debauchery, or for any other immoral purpose." (chap. 395, 36 Stat. 825; *codified as amended at* 18 U.S.C. §§ 2421–2424.) The May Act, signed into law in July 1941 as the United States was expanding its military forces, was designed to control venereal disease; it made it a federal offense to practice prostitution in areas designated by the secretaries of the army and the navy, that is, near military bases; federal agents were given authority to stamp out prostitution aimed at servicemen where local officials failed to do so.

112. Riley Allen, "The Fight on Prostitution Has Just Begun," Paper Given at the Meeting of the Social Protection Committee of the Honolulu Council of Social Agencies on Social Hygiene Day, February 7, 1945, copy in Gov. 9–37, HSA.

113. Hubert E. Brown, "The Effects of Closing Houses of Prostitution on the Community," Paper Given at the Meeting of the Social Protection Committee of the Honolulu Council of Social Agencies on Social Hygiene Day, February 7, 1945, copy in Gov. 9–37, HSA. According to Bailey and Farber, many of the prostitutes used drugs. (Bailey and Farber, *First Strange Place*, 107.)

114. The sources included prostitute Jean O'Hara and Col. Frank Steer. (See Greer, "Dousing Honolulu's Red Light," 192.) Green's memoir, "Martial Law," also refers to the rackets that were operating in prostitution.

115. Green, "Martial Law," chap. 27.

116. Steer did object, however, to the prostitutes raising their rates to $5/hour in response to increased demand, and the prostitutes backed down. Bailey and Farber, "Hotel Street," 435–436; and *The First Strange Place*, 120–121; Green, "Martial Law," chap. 27.

117. Green, "Martial Law," chap. 27.

118. Unsigned and undated report, but probably late summer 1942, in files of Governor Stainback, Gov. 9–37, HSA.

119. Green, "Martial Law," chap. 27.

120. Unsigned and undated report, but probably late summer 1942, in files of Governor Stainback, Gov. 9–37, HSA; Bailey and Farber, *The First Strange Place*, 124.

121. Anthony, *Hawaii under Army Rule*, 40.

122. The navy vehemently denied that it had ever stated its approval of the houses of prostitution. William R. Furlong, Acting Rear Admiral, U.S. Navy, to Honolulu Council of Social Agencies, September 24, 1944, copy in Gov. 9–37, HSA.

123. Bailey and Farber, *The First Strange Place*, 130.

124. The police had already closed the brothels on Maui and the Island of Hawai'i. Greer, "Dousing Honolulu's Red Light," 193–197.

125. Stainback to Richardson, September, 20, 1944, and Stainback to Nimitz, September 20, 1944, copies of both in Gov. 9–37, HSA.

126. It should be noted that the Police Commission of Kaua'i had already closed the houses of prostitution on that island in April 1944; the closure was followed by a decline in venereal disease. (Charles L. Wilbar, President of the Board of Health, T.H., "Effects of Closing of Houses of

Prostitution on Community Health," Paper Given at the Meeting of the Social Protection Committee of the Honolulu Council of Social Agencies on Social Hygiene Day, February 7, 1945, copy in Gov. 9–37, HSA.)

127. Allen, "The Fight on Prostitution."

128. After the houses of prostitution were closed, there were reports of prostitutes operating on their own and charging up to $100 per visit, of taxi drivers acting as procurers, and of hotels allowing prostitutes to operate on their premises. (Brown, "The Effects of Closing Houses of Prostitution.")

129. A total of some 20,000 army and navy dependents and 10,000 other women and children left Hawaiʻi for the mainland during the war. (Bailey and Farber, *The First Strange Place*, 12; Allen, *Hawaii's War Years*, 107; Conn et al., *Guarding the United States*, 202. See also *New York Times*, January 31, 1942.) See infra, p. 134, for impact of this evacuation on plans for large-scale removal of Japanese Americans from Hawaiʻi.

130. King to Roger Baldwin, February 14, 1942, King Papers, HSA.

131. Report of Stainback to Under Secretary [Fortas], September 7, 1942, quoted in Memorandum from W. Boardman: "The Territory of Hawaii Under Martial Law," May 1944, 12, Fortas Files, RG 48, NA [hereinafter Boardman Report].

132. Ickes to Stimson, September 28, 1942, quoted in Boardman Report, 13.

133. Fortas to Stainback, August 31, 1942, Gov. 9–22, HSA; Robert Patterson, Acting Secretary of War, to the Secretary of the Interior, October 7, 1942, copy in Gov. 9–22, HSA. .

134. R. A. Vitousek to Stainback, November 12, 1942; Stainback to Fortas, November 16, 1942, Gov. 9–22, HSA.

135. *Honolulu Advertiser,* November 20, 1942.

136. Joint Policy Governing Transportation of Civilians to the Hawaiian Area from the Mainland, 12 April 1943, Gov. 9–30, Transportation file, HSA. Copy also in folder 43, JIR.

137. Memorandum from J. [John] Frank to Under Secretary Fortas, March 31, 1944, Fortas Files, RG 48, NA; see also Allen, *Hawaii's War Years*, 346–348; and Frank Midkiff to Admiral E. S. Land, October 16, 1943, Farrington Papers, HSA. See also chap. 16, infra.

138. Stainback to Fortas, February 25, 1944 and Stainback to Ickes, February 25, 1944, copies of both in Stainback files, Gov. 9–22, HSA; Bailey and Farber, *The First Strange Place*, 108 (this book contains an extended discussion of prostitution in Hawaiʻi).

139. *Asia,* March 1939.

140. Col. George W. Bicknell, "Security Measures in Hawaii During World War II," 82, HWRD.

141. Edward D. Beechert, *Working in Hawaii: A Labor History* (Honolulu: University of Hawaiʻi Press, 1985), 280. For a general discussion of race issues in Hawaiʻi during the war, see Bailey and Farber, *The First Strange Place.*

142. Memorandum from Lawrence M. Judd Sr., December 1943, File IV.D, Papers of Lawrence M. Judd Sr., HSA.

143. See Lt. R. J. Hoogs to Maj. R. H. Johnston (an officer on active service in the Pacific), November 17, 1943, Judd Papers, File IV.D, HSA (denying passage to Johnston's wife on grounds of lack of sufficient time in residence prior to evacuation).

144. The director of the Central Identification Bureau in the OMG claimed that all civilians wanting to return to Hawaiʻi had been accommodated by mid-April 1944, and that ships returning to Hawaiʻi were not filled to capacity. (Meeting Summary and Transcript, "Provost Court

Judges in Conference at the Office of the Military Governor" 22 [May 26, 1944], RG 338, NA [here-inafter Provost Court Judges in Conference Transcript].) However, as of July 1945, an estimated 3,000 Islanders were still stranded on the mainland. (Allen, *Hawaii's War Years,* 401.)

145. The "exiles" phrase is from Boardman Report, Fortas Files, RG 48, NA.

146. B. W. Thoron to R. Keith Kane, Special Assistant to the Secretary of the Navy, January 29, 1945, Thoron Files, RG 126, NA.

147. Allen, *Hawaii's War Years,* 330; see also Bailey and Farber, *The First Strange Place,* 33.

148. *Honolulu Advertiser,* January 31, 1945. The *Advertiser* placed a paid message in the *Washington Post* and the *Washington Star* to "Wake Up Washington" to the housing crisis in Honolulu. Allen, *Hawaii's War Years,* 329–330.

149. See Allen, *Hawaii's War Years,* 327–335. On the other hand, the special assistant to the secretary of the interior reported that in early 1943, there were huge supplies of building materials in the hands of the military, much of which was being consumed by termites. (Horton to Ickes, May 1, 1943, RG 107, McCloy Papers, NA.)

150. Thoron to Robert T. Williams, Williams Equipment Co., Honolulu, January 3, 1945, Thoron Files, RG 126, NA; Ickes to Harold D. Smith, Director, Bureau of the Budget, January 8, 1945, ibid.

151. Criticism was also directed at the army for its failure to deal effectively with the severe housing shortages that developed. See U.S. Congress, 79th Cong., 1st Sess., House Committee on Naval Affairs, Congested Areas Subcommittee, *Investigation of congested areas: A report on the Pearl Harbor-Honolulu Area (1945).*

Chapter 5: Control of Labor

1. U.S. Census, 1940, Hawai'i, Characteristics of the Population.

2. *New York Times,* January 10, 1942.

3. General Orders No. 38, December 20, 1941, RG 338, NA.

4. Thomas H. Green, "Martial Law in Hawaii, December 7, 1941–April 4, 1943," http://www.loc.gov/rr/frd/Military_Law/pdf/Martial-Law_Green.pdf, 392.

5. Anthony to Stainback, December 1, 1942, reproduced as appendix E in J. Garner Anthony, *Hawaii under Army Rule* (Stanford, CA: Stanford University Press, 1955).

6. General Orders No. 56, January 26, 1942.

7. Moon-Kie Jung, *Reworking Race: The Making of Hawaii's Interracial Labor Movement* (New York: Columbia University Press, 2006), 134.

8. Office of Internal Security, Territory of Hawaii, "Wartime Security Controls in Hawaii," Part Six, 4, Box 25, Richardson Papers, Hoover Institution. J. D. Bond was replaced by his deputy, John R. Mead, in March 1943. (Green, "Martial Law," 389, 395.)

9. General Orders No. 56, January 26, 1942; Gwenfread Allen, *Hawaii's War Years, 1941–1945* (Honolulu: University of Hawai'i Press, 1950), 310. Nearly 5,000 men and 700 women registered under this order, but since no top age limit had been designated, some of the registrants were unemployable. (Ernest May, "Hawaii's Work in Wartime, *Honolulu Star-Bulletin,* May 27, 1945.)

10. General Orders No. 152, November 5, 1942; *Honolulu Advertiser,* November 12, 1942; Allen, *Hawaii's War Years,* 307. More than 62,500 women registered, of whom slightly more than one-half were already working. Nearly 6,700 of those not then employed stated that they were available for work. (May, "Hawaii's Work in Wartime.")

11. Hawai'i Employers Council, *Employment and payrolls of civilian employees in Hawaii, 1940–1949* (Honolulu, 1950), 17. The total number of civilian workers in Hawai'i (excluding small farm workers, the self-employed, and domestic employees) increased by about 45 percent. (Ibid.)

12. General Orders No. 38 (December 20, 1941) and No. 91 (March 31, 1942), copies in HWRD. General Orders Nos. 38 and 91 are also reproduced in Anthony, *Hawaii Under Army Rule*, 141, 155; see also ibid., 42–45.

13. Provost Court Judges in Conference Transcript; "Daily Newspaper Report of Provost Court Sentences for Absenteeism among Labor Under Military Control," Provost Court file, Gov. 9, HSA. The estimate for wages is for defense workers, who received upward of $1.50 an hour and worked more than 48 hours per week. Plantation workers earned a minimum of 41 or 42 cents an hour. The average family income in Honolulu in 1943 was $450 per month. (Allen, *Hawaii's War Years*, 245, 310, 324.) See infra, pp. 84–85, for discussion of plantation labor.

14. Provost Court Dispositions, Hawaiian Islands, RG 338, NA; Provost Court Prosecutions, RG 338, NA; Office of Internal Security, Territory of Hawaii, "Wartime Security Controls," Part Six, 25, 43, Box 25, Richardson Papers, Hoover Institution; Gary Y. Okihiro, *Cane Fires: The Anti-Japanese Movement in Hawaii, 1865–1945* (Philadelphia: Temple University Press, 1991), 313n54. See also chap. 6, infra, on provost courts.

15. Provost Court Judges in Conference Transcript.

16. Ibid. (quoting Captain John Wickham, Provost Court Commissioner).

17. Fortas to McCloy, May 30, 1944, McCloy Files, NA.

18. Gavan Daws, *Shoal of Time: A History of the Hawaiian Islands* (Honolulu: University of Hawai'i Press, 1968), 360–361.

19. Richardson to McCloy, February 10, 1944, McCloy Files, NA.

20. Ibid. In an interview with a provost judge in early 1942, a similar attitude with respect to racial and ethnic stereotyping is evident: Willard Brown, "Has Solomon Role," *Paradise of the Pacific,* February 1942, 24–25. General Orders barred alien Japanese from working on the docks. (Daws, *Shoal of Time,* 361.)

21. Christina Lam, "Problems of Defense Workers in Post-War Hawaii," *Social Process in Hawaii* 11 (May 1947): 65. Contract workers who were dismissed as the result of absenteeism often required assistance from the Department of Public Welfare. (Ibid.)

22. Allen, *Hawaii's War Years,* 310; Edward D. Beechert, *Working in Hawaii: A Labor History* (Honolulu: University of Hawai'i Press, 1985), 287. See supra, p. 13, for discussion of cooperation between the HSPA and military intelligence.

23. The HSPA claimed the figure exceeded 500,000 man-days (Hawaiian Sugar Planters' Association, *The War Record of Civilian and Industrial Hawaii: A Documentary History of the Assistance extended to the Armed Forces by the Civilian Community and the Sugar Plantations* 24 [1945], copy in File 1.03 of the HWRD). The army claimed it was 195,000 man-days, and that the practice was greatly reduced in response to complaints by the plantation owners that their production was declining from the diversion of labor. (Office of Internal Security, Territory of Hawaii, "Wartime Security Controls," Part Six, 25, Box 25, Richardson Papers, Hoover Institution.)

24. Beechert, *Working in Hawaii,* 287.

25. Allen, *Hawaii's War Years,* 311. Women workers on the plantations were paid slightly less than the men were paid. (Advertisements for workers in Dole Corporation Archives, Hawaiian and Pacific Collections, Hamilton Library, University of Hawai'i.)

26. Beechert, *Working in Hawaii,* 287; Jung, *Reworking Race,* 138–139.

27. *Honolulu Advertiser,* August 6, 1943; *Honolulu Star-Bulletin,* August 17, 1943.

28. *Honolulu Advertiser,* January 25, 1942.

29. Richardson to McCloy, February 10, 1944, McCloy Files.

30. Provost Court Judges in Conference Transcript, 22.

31. Frank E. Midkiff to Emmons, December 24, 1942, Delos Carleton Emmons Papers, "Martial Law" folder, Hoover Institution Archives, Stanford University [hereinafter Emmons Papers].

32. Wire from Leslie A. Hicks, President, Chamber of Commerce, and Lawson H. Riley, President, Retail Board to President Roosevelt, Attorney General Biddle, Delegate Farrington, Secretary of Interior Ickes, Secretary of Navy Knox, Secretary of War Stimson, Governor Stainback, and Eric Johnston (U.S. Chamber of Commerce), copy in Emmons Papers, "Martial Law" folder, Hoover Institution Archives; also reproduced in Anthony, *Hawaii under Army Rule,* 28–29.

33. Anthony to Farrington, January 26, 1943, Farrington Papers, HSA.

34. Farrington to Riley Allen, editor of the *Honolulu Star-Bulletin,* December 31, 1942, Farrington Papers, HSA.

35. See infra, pp. 218, 258.

36. Boardman Report, May 1944. It was General Green's private view that Ickes and his top aides in Interior were (as he wrote of Fortas, the under secretary) "completely prejudiced against local [Hawai'i] business, whom he thinks is hand and glove with the military because the military have obtained its cooperation." (Marginal notes in Green's hand on copy of a letter from Green to McCloy, December 19, 1942, Green Papers, JAGSL [notes referred to Fortas and to Attorney General Francis Biddle].)

37. Bernard W. Stern, *Rutledge Unionism: Labor Relations in the Honolulu Transit Industry* (Honolulu: University of Hawai'i Center for Labor Education and Research, 1986), http://www.hawaii.edu/uhwo/clear/Pubs/RutledgeUnionism.html.

38. Okihiro, *Cane Fires,* 240.

39. Quoted in Gerald Horne, *Fighting in Paradise: Labor Unions, Racism and Communists in the Making of Modern Hawai'i* (Honolulu: University of Hawai'i Press, 2011), 49, 62. See also Beechert, *Working in Hawaii,* 288; and Roland Kotani, *The Japanese in Hawaii: A Century of Struggle* (Honolulu: Hawaii Hochi, Ltd., 1985), 126–127. As its title implies, Horne's book deals extensively with the role of the Communist Party in building the labor unions and in shaping the modern state of Hawai'i.

40. Stern, *Rutledge Unionism,* chap. 3.

41. Anthony, *Hawaii under Army Rule,* 44–45. For a detailed account, see Paul R. Van Zwalenburg, "Hawaiian Labor Unions under Military Government," master's thesis, University of Hawai'i, 1961. See also Allen, *Hawaii's War Years,* 377; Beechert, *Working in Hawaii,* 287–295; Daws, *Shoal of Time,* 360ff.; Okihiro, *Cane Fires,* 240–243. On March 2, 1942, John Owens, the territorial representative of the AFL, wrote General Green, enclosing a copy of a letter from the president of the AFL, pledging not to strike. (Office of Internal Security, Territory of Hawaii, "Wartime Security Controls," Part Six, 15, Box 25, Richardson Papers, Hoover Institution.)

42. Clifford O'Brien to Harry Bridges, February 4, 1942, ILWU, Organizing Files, Hawaii, quoted in Beechert, *Working in Hawaii,* 288.

43. Bicknell, "Security Measures in Hawaii," chap. 5, 81, HWRD.

44. Ibid., chap. 5, 82, HWRD.

45. General Orders No. 91, March 31, 1942; Richardson to McCloy, February 10, 1944, McCloy Files, NA.

46. Anthony, *Hawaii under Army Rule,* 43; Hawaii Employers Council, *Employment and Payrolls.*

47. Ickes to Stimson, January 27, 1943, copy in McCloy Files, NA.

48. See infra, chap. 12.

49. Proclamation by the Governor of Hawaii, February 8, 1943, reproduced in Anthony, *Hawaii under Army Rule,* 129–131.

50. Telegram from Secretary of the Interior to Stainback, February 27, 1943, Gov. 9–37, Hawai'i State Archives.

51. Allen, *Hawaii's War Years,* 312.

52. Telegram, Stainback to Secretary of the Interior, no date, but in reply to Ickes telegram to Stainback of February 27, 1943, Gov. 9–37, HSA.

53. Garner Anthony to Stainback, February 26, 1943, and enclosed draft of "Hawaii Defense Act Providing for the Control of Employment in Essential Industries," Gov. 9–37, HSA; Robert W. Beasley, Chairman, Hawaii Manpower Board to Stainback, April 5, 1943, Gov. 9–37, HSA.

54. [Territory of Hawai'i], War Manpower Commission Committee, Minutes of meetings of May 3, 10, and 17, in War Manpower Board Records, HWRD. NB: The nomenclature in the Board's records is confusing, the "Committee" herein named being comprised of the Board's appointed members but with additional participants (including Garner Anthony). In its own minutes and in newspaper reports, it was often referred to as both "War Manpower Board" and "Hawaii Manpower Board."

55. Beasley to Stainback, April 5, 1943, Gov. 9–37, HSA.

56. Ibid.

57. General Orders No. 10, reproduced in Anthony, *Hawaii under Army Rule*, 175.

58. Memorandum from A. J. Coughlin, n.d., in Governor's Papers, Gov. 9–37, HSA. Coughlin was a supervisor in one of the employment agencies under General Orders No. 10.

59. Ibid.

60. Stainback circular letter, May 4, 1943, Box 439, OCD files, HSA.

61. [Territory of Hawai'i], War Manpower Commission Committee, Minutes of meeting of May 17, 1943, War Manpower Board Records, HWRD.

62. Ibid.

63. Ibid., Minutes of meetings of April 28 (McNutt's position stated) and June 14, 1943.

64. Ibid., Minutes of meetings, May 3–June 14, passim.

65. Ibid., Minutes of meetings of April 28, 1943, and (on management representatives' posture) Minutes of April–September, 1943, meetings, passim.

66. Arthur A. Rutledge, Secretary, Central Labor Council, to Richardson, June 18, 1943, copy in Gov. 9–37, HSA. Rutledge's continuing political role as an anti-Communist labor leader and "stalwart of the Stainback wing of the Democratic Party" is treated in T. Michael Holmes, *The Specter of Communism in Hawaii* (Honolulu: University of Hawai'i Press, 1994), 72, 124.

67. *Honolulu Advertiser* and *Honolulu Star-Bulletin,* June 30, and July 10, 1943.

68. Richardson to Stainback, June 29, 1943, copy in Stainback Papers, HSA.

69. Office of Internal Security, Territory of Hawaii, "Wartime Security Controls," Part Six, 50, Box 25, Richardson Papers, Hoover Institution.

70. Daws, *Shoal of Time,* 361–62; "A History of HEC," http://hecouncil.org/about/history.

71. The Territorial Director of Labor and Industrial Relations, L. Q. McComas, wrote to Governor Stainback, "By the recent formation of the Employer's Council a strong economical force

has been mobilized to counter-balance the economical strength afforded by the growth of labor organizations." (McComas to Stainback, February 24, 1944, copy enclosed with letter from Stainback to Ickes, February 25, 1944, Ickes Files, NA.) Three cases were brought before the National Labor Relations Board in 1947 by the Gasoline and Oil Drivers, Warehousemen and Helpers Union, Local 904, affiliated with the AFL, against the Hawaii Employers Council and Shell Oil, Union Oil, and Tide Water Oil. The NLRB's trial examiner found that during the war, the Employers Council had engaged in delay tactics in negotiating with the unions, had fought wage increases, and had pressured the member firms not to negotiate contracts with the unions except through the Council. (NLRB, Cases No. 23-C-40, 23-C-43, and 23-C-44, File 38.98, HWRD.)

72. Stainback to Ickes, October 4, 1943, Ickes Files, NA. Secretary Ickes apparently sent Stainback's letter to the War Department, and McCloy responded on October 14, 1943, "You can be sure that if there is a concerted effort on the part of any faction to effect a complete restoration of military government there, neither the War Department nor the Commanding General will encourage it. From all I can learn, the military authorities there are satisfied with the controls they now exercise." (McCloy to Secretary of the Interior, October 14, 1943, McCloy Files, NA.)

73. All quotations in this paragraph are from Radio W81110 from Richardson to General George C. Marshall, December 18, 1943, McCloy Files, NA.

74. Ibid. Emphasis added. Richardson specifically singled out Arthur Rutledge of the AFL as the leader of the radicals; Rutledge tried, unsuccessfully, to join with Jack Kawano of the ILWU in 1943 to form a single union for the sugar industry. Rutledge's efforts to organize the plantation workers were unsuccessful, but the ILWU under Kawano's leadership made great strides in 1944 and 1945. (Daws, *Shoal of Time,* 362.) Rutledge led the Teamsters Union protest of 1944, discussed below. (Beechert, *Working in Hawaii,* 288.) Rutledge headed more than 200 strikes and was arrested multiple times during the course of his union leadership. He died in 1997. (*New York Times,* September 27, 1997.)

75. Richardson to McCloy, January 27, 1944, McCloy Files, NA.

76. L. Q. McComas to Stainback, February 24, 1944, quoted in the Boardman Report.

77. [Territory of Hawai'i], War Manpower Commission Committee, Minutes of meeting of May 17, 1943, in War Manpower Board Records, HWRD.

78. Ibid.

79. Reported in ibid., Minutes of Meeting of September 3, 1943.

80. Morrison to McCloy, radiogram marked "Top Secret," June 28, 1944, RG 338, NA.

81. Richardson to McCloy, June 24, 1943, RG 338, NA.

82. Allen, *Hawaii's War Years,* 313.

83. Report to the Secretary of the Interior from Governor Stainback, January 15, 1944, quoted in the Boardman Report, 14. Emphasis added.

84. J. D. Coates, WMC, to William H. Davis, NWLB, February 8, 1944; Beasley to Stainback, February 24, 1944, Thoron Files, RG 126, NA.

85. Letter from Col. Morrison and Major Krim to McCloy, May 5, 1944, reported in Office of Internal Security, Territory of Hawaii, "Wartime Security Controls," Part Six, 73, Box 25, Richardson Papers, Hoover Institution.

86. Allen, *Hawaii's War Years,* 326.

87. These included disputes between the International Brotherhood of Electric Workers and management, the Marine Engineers and Dry Dock Workers and the Inter-Island Steam Navigation Co., the Streetcar Workers and the Honolulu Rapid Transit Co., and the Marine Engineers

and Dry Dock Workers and the Hawaii Tuna Packers. (Office of Internal Security, Territory of Hawaii, "Wartime Security Controls," Part Six, 84–91, Box 25, Richardson Papers, Hoover Institution.)

88. See Beechert, *Working in Hawaii,* 289–295. John Burns, a Honolulu police officer at the time and later governor, states in his oral history: "Martial law, it really opened up the way to union movement"—in part because the military showed that there could be people in authority other than the Big Five, who had opposed unionism. (Stuart G. Brown, *John A. Burns Oral History Project, 1975–1976* [n.d., privately printed], copy in possession of authors, Tape 5.) Between January 1944 and January 1945, ILWU membership increased from 970 to 6,610. The NLRB ruled in January 1945 that more than half of the plantation workers were classified as industrial workers whose collective bargaining rights were protected by the National Labor Relations Act, and in May of that year the Territorial legislature extended collective bargaining rights to all agricultural workers in Hawaii. As a consequence, the ILWU boasted 33,000 members by the end of 1945. Kotani, *The Japanese in Hawaii,* 130; Horne, *Fighting in Paradise,* 81. Jung, *Reworking Race,* has a detailed discussion of the organization of the sugar, pineapple, and dock workers and of the role of race and class ideologies (pp. 140ff.).

89. Richardson to International Longshoremen and Warehousemen's Union, March 31, 1944, included with memorandum from Capt. Adrian S. Fisher to Assistant Secretary of War McCloy, September 27, 1944, McCloy Files, NA.; Kotani, *The Japanese in Hawaii,* 128–129; Beechert, *Working in Hawaii,* 291.

90. Richardson to International Longshoremen and Warehousemen's Union, March 31, 1944, cited in previous note.

91. John P. Frank Memorandum for the Under Secretary, "Summary of Memorandum on Military Control of Hawaiian Labor," April 15, 1944, Fortas Files, RG 48, NA [hereinafter "Memorandum on Military Control of Hawaiian Labor"].

92. Ibid. See also Allen, *Hawaii's War Years,* 326. Union leadership regarded this case as further proof that the army was on the side of business.

93. Frank, "Memorandum on Military Control of Hawaiian Labor," Fortas Files, RG 48, NA. See also T. Michael Holmes, *The Specter of Communism in Hawaii* (Honolulu: University of Hawai'i Press, 1994), 34.

94. See chap. 16 for discussions on terminating martial law.

95. Frank, "Memorandum on Military Control of Hawaiian Labor," Fortas Files, RG 48, NA.

96. Ickes to McCloy, April 20, 1944. Ickes Papers, LC.

97. Memorandum from Lt. Col. Harrison to Capt. Colclough, June 6, 1944, McCloy Files, NA.

98. Fortas to William H. Davis (c/o Governor Stainback), May 30, 1944, RG 48, NA.

99. "Suggested Plan for Civilian Control of Labor Situation in Hawaii, as Discussed in McCloy's Office, June 14, 1944," enclosed in Fortas to Ickes, June 16, 1944, Ickes Files, NA; copy also in Fortas Files, RG 48, NA. The meeting was also attended by B. W. Thoron and Capt. Fisher.

100. McCloy to Richardson, June 27, 1944, Cable WAR 56672, McCloy Files, NA. Emphasis added.

101. Cable, Richardson to McCloy, June 28, 1944, RG 338, NA.

102. Ibid. Emphasis added.

103. Ibid.

104. Richardson to McCloy, July 7, 1944, McCloy Files, NA.

105. Fortas Memorandum to Secretary Ickes, July 19, 1944, Fortas Files, RG 48, NA.

106. "Richardson Sees Availability of Labor Becoming Acute Shortly," *Honolulu Advertiser,* April 12, 1944.

107. Ibid.

108. Anthony, *Hawaii under Army Rule,* 43–44.

109. *Honolulu Advertiser,* August 15, 1944, clipping in McCloy Files, NA.

110. Allen, *Hawaii's War Years,* 323; McCloy to Wm. H. Davis, Chairman, National War Labor Board (Washington), August 11, 1944, McCloy Files, NA.

111. Honolulu *Advertiser,* August 15, 1944.

112. Allen, *Hawaii's War Years,* 324.

Chapter 6: "Drum-head Justice"?

1. J. B. Poindexter, Proclamation, Territory of Hawai'i, December 7, 1941, reproduced in J. Garner Anthony, *Hawaii under Army Rule* (Stanford, CA: Stanford University Press, 1955), 127.

2. Walter C. Short, Proclamation, United States Army, December 7, 1941, reproduced in Anthony, *Hawaii under Army Rule,* 127.

3. General Orders No. 4, reproduced in ibid., 137.

4. Emmons to McCloy, July 1, 1942, RG 338, NA.

5. Ibid.

6. Green to Col. Archibald King, July 18, 1942, Green Papers, JAGSL. In notations Green made after the war—apparently as late as the early 1960s—on copies of wartime correspondence, he indicated again his view that to have permitted ethnically mixed juries would have been "ruinous to Japanese Americans" (presumably defendants). (Green's handwritten notations on copy of letter from Abe Fortas to John J. McCloy, December 19, 1942, Green Papers, JAGSL.) According to Green's diaries, federal district judge Metzger agreed with the decision against permitting jury trials, but on different grounds: Metzger was concerned that jury service would divert too many persons from essential war work. (Diary of Thomas H. Green, July 27, 1942, Green Papers, JAGSL.)

7. Office of Internal Security, Territory of Hawaii, "Wartime Security Controls," Part Eight, 6–8, Box 25, Richardson Papers, Hoover Institution.

8. The military commission was created by General Orders No. 3, December 7, 1941, reproduced in Anthony, *Hawaii under Army Rule,* 137. The civilian members were James Coke, former chief justice of the Supreme Court of Hawai'i; Alva Steadman, former circuit judge, and Angus Taylor, acting U.S. District Attorney. (Ibid.)

9. Green, "Martial Law," 118.

10. Anthony, *Hawaii under Army Rule,* 11–12.

11. Diary of Thomas H. Green, October 20, 1942, Green Papers, JAGSL. See also Office of the Chief of Military History, "United States Army Forces, Middle Pacific and Predecessor Commands during World War II, 7 December 1941–2 September 1945: Civil Affairs and Military Government," microfilm document, HWRD (Hawai'i War Records Depository), Hamilton Library, University of Hawai'i at Manoa, HI [hereinafter "Civil Affairs"].

12. For discussion regarding concern about civil liability, see infra, pp. 299, 304, 321ff.

13. General Orders No. 25, December 14, 1941, reproduced in Anthony, *Hawaii under Army Rule,* 140. In addition to Anthony and Green, see Office of the Chief of Military History, "Civil Affairs," 3217, for a discussion of how the commission, initially appointed in December 1941, was superseded shortly afterward by an all-military commission.

14. Howard T. Fereb, Secretary to the Governor, to B. W. Thoron, Department of the Interior, December 4, 1942, Gov. 9–22, HSA.

15. In addition to the two cases discussed below, the commission tried the following cases: Andres Balderman Peralde, accused of murder, found not guilty; Yoshinji Sugai, accused of unlawful sexual intercourse, sentenced to life imprisonment but paroled in 1944; Joseph Marcial, accused of robbery, sentenced to ten years at hard labor, sentence reduced to seven years; Aceslo Manuel, accused of murder, sentenced to twenty years at hard labor, sentence reduced to fifteen years; Haruo Iwamoto, manslaughter, found not guilty; and Rosendo Sedeno, attempted murder, found guilty of assault and battery with a dangerous weapon and sentenced to eighteen months at hard labor. (Office of the Chief of Military History, "Civil Affairs," 3219–3223.)

16. R. L. Shivers to Director, FBI, January 7, 1942, FBI records, Kuehn File, http://vault.fbi.gov/bernard-julius-otto-kuehn/bernard-julius-otto-kuehn/view.

17. Radiogram, Hoover to Special Agent in Charge, January 15, 1942. FBI Records, Kuehn File.

18. Hoover, Memorandum for Attorney General, January 19, 1942, FBI Records, Kuehn File.

19. Wendell Birge, Assistant Attorney General, to Hoover, February 4, 1942, and Assistant Secretary Breckinridge Long to Hoover, January 27, 1942, FBI records, Kuehn file. For a discussion of the exchange of consular agents and other civilians between Japan and the United States, see P. Scott Corbett, *Quiet Passages: The Exchange of Civilians between the United States and Japan during the Second World War* (Kent, OH: Kent State University Press, 1987).

20. FBI Record, File No. 65–4, February 7, 1942. FBI Records, Kuehn File. See infra, pp. 157ff., for discussion of hearing boards.

21. Shivers to Hoover, February 23, 1942, FBI Records, Kuehn File; Green, "Martial Law," 302.

22. J. Edgar Hoover, Memorandum to the Attorney General, February 23, 1942, FBI Records, Kuehn File.

23. D. M. Ladd (FBI), Memorandum for Director, FBI, Re: Bernard Julius Otto Kuehn, April 30, 1942, FBI Records, Kuehn File.

24. Oscar Cox, Assistant Solicitor General, to J. Edgar Hoover, Memorandum, October 10, 1942, FBI Records, Kuehn File. The case was *Ex parte Quirin* 317 U.S. 1 (1942).

25. Quoted in Richard J. Ellis, *Judging Executive Power: Sixteen Supreme Court Cases that Have Shaped the American Presidency* (Lanham, MD: Rowman and Littlefield Publishers, 2009), 113.

26. *Ex parte Quirin* 317 U.S. 1 (1942). The other two prisoners, including Dasch, who had notified the FBI of the plot, were sentenced to life in prison; in 1948 they were granted clemency and returned to Germany. For a discussion of the constitutional issues raised in *Quirin*, see Louis Fisher, *Nazi Saboteurs on Trial: A Military Tribunal and American Law*, 2nd ed., revised and abridged (Lawrence: University Press of Kansas, 2005).

27. H. M. Kimball, Memorandum for Mr. Ladd re Bernard Julius Otto Kuehn, November 24, 1942, FBI Papers, Kuehn file.

28. FBI Report, "Bernard Julius Otto Kuehn," December 15, 1942, FBI Papers, Kuehn file. According to the army history, Attorney General Biddle had expressed his opinion that Kuehn should not receive more than the fifty years' maximum imprisonment for espionage during peacetime because the offense was committed before war was declared. (Chief of Military History, "Civil Affairs," 3221.) Kuehn was deported to Germany in 1948.

29. Thomas H. Green, "Martial Law in Hawaii, December 7, 1941–April 4, 1943," http://www.loc.gov/rr/frd/Military_Law/pdf/Martial-Law_Green.pdf, 300ff.

30. Anthony, *Hawaii under Army Rule,* 20–21.

31. Police Department, County of Maui, Arrest and Disposition Record, Case of Saffery Brown, RG 338, NA.

32. A. S. Spencer to Samuel W. King, May 5, 1942, King Papers, HSA. Spencer was the chief executive officer of the County of Maui Board of Supervisors.

33. Pia Cockett to King, May 8, 1942, and King to Maj. Gen. James A. Ulio, May 15, 1942, King Papers, HSA.

34. Ickes to King, May 13, 1942; Stimson to King, May 13, 1942; King to Pia Cockett, June 30, 1942, all in King Papers, HSA.

35. See infra, pp. 218ff., for further discussion of King's and Anthony's opposition to martial law. Brown's case was reviewed on February 2, 1944 by the Military Commission and Provost Court Reviewing and Parole Board, which recommended that Brown's sentence be reduced to a period of thirty years. General Richardson ordered the reduced sentence on February 17, 1944. (Saffery Brown Case records, RG 338, NA; Office of the Chief of Military History, "Civil Affairs," 3222.)

36. Office of Censorship, Report on Civilian Morale, October 21, 1942, RG 165, NA. One must use caution in evaluating such reports, since correspondents were well aware that their mail was censored and might likely be reluctant to criticize openly the martial law regime.

37. Midkiff to Ickes, May 28, 1942, Papers of Governor Poindexter, Public Morale Section Records, HSA.

38. Garner Anthony to Samuel W. King, June 10, 1942, King Papers, Miscellaneous Subject Correspondence, HSA.

39. Office of the Chief of Military History, "Civil Affairs," 3224.

40. General Orders No. 29, December 16, 1941, and General Orders No. 57, January 27, 1942, reproduced in Anthony, *Hawaii under Army Rule,* 140, 148. Emphasis added.

41. See infra, chap. 12, for an account of the meetings.

42. Fortas to Stainback, August 20, 1942, Gov. 9–22, "Interior," HSA.

43. General Orders No. 133, August 31, 1942, and General Orders No. 135, September 4, 1942, reproduced in Anthony, *Hawaii under Army Rule,* 159–160, 162; Stainback to Fortas, September 17, 1942, Gov. 9–22, "Interior," HSA (reporting Green's intransigence).

44. See supra, chap. 5.

45. Office of the Chief of Military History, "Civil Affairs," 3226.

46. Green, "Martial Law," 279; Office of the Chief of Military History, "Civil Affairs," 3226.

47. Anthony, *Hawaii under Army Rule,* 38–39, 46–59; Office of the Chief of Military History, "Civil Affairs," passim; Willard Brown, "Has Solomon Role," *Paradise of the Pacific,* February 1942, 24–25.

48. Provost Court Judges in Conference transcript. See also Judge McLaughlin's ruling in the Spurlock habeas case, that the prisoner had been the victim of gross denial of due process, infra, pp. 279–280.

49. "Provost Courts Opposed," *Honolulu Star-Bulletin,* April 7, 1944, pp. 1, 6.

50. Office of the Chief of Military History, "Civil Affairs," 3226.

51. Official Army History, 94, draft version in Green Papers, JAGSL.

52. Robert C. Richardson Jr., "Hawaii—Fortress of the Pacific," *Army and Navy Journal* (December 1944): 48.

53. Office of the Chief of Military History, "Civil Affairs," 3226, 3227–3247, and passim.

54. Green Notes, Green Papers, JAGSL.

55. See supra, p. 100.

56. Office of the Chief of Military History, "Civil Affairs," 3244.

57. Oral History interview with Ernest Kapuamailani Kai, 25.

58. Memorandum from Warner W. Gardner to Harold Ickes, December 10, 1942, Ickes Files, NA.

59. Provost Court Judges in Conference Transcript, 16 (quoting Lt. Col. Slattery).

60. Ibid., 15–16.

61. Gen. Robert Richardson to the Judge Advocate General, December 4, 1945, McCloy Files, NA. Commanding General Mid Pacific to War Department, December 4, 1945, (Radio RJ 73740) Green Papers, JAGSL. See also Green, "Martial Law," 288. The estimate of 60,000 comes from the authors' examination of Provost Court Dispositions, copy in RG 65, Hawaiian Islands, NA.

62. W. A. Gabrielson, chief of police, "Crime Trends Under Martial Law and Blackout Conditions," not dated but early 1943, HWRD; Provost Court Dispositions, RG 65, Hawaiian Islands, NA.

63. See Transcript of Record, *Duncan v. Kahanamoku,* U.S. Supreme Court, October Term, 1945, 467 [hereinafter *Duncan* Transcript]; Anthony, *Hawaii under Army Rule,* 52–53.

64. "'Kangaroo' Trials Charged to Army," *New York Times,* July 2, 1944.

65. Richardson to Judge Advocate General, December 4, 1945, McCloy Files, NA.

66. Radio RJ73740, Commanding General Mid Pacific to War Department, December 4, 1945, Green Papers, JAGSL.

67. "Extract from Report of the Attorney General, Territory of Hawaii, to the Governor on the Crime Situation in the Territory of Hawaii, and on Civilian-Military Relations" (not dated, but July 1944), copy in "Hawaii" file, Box 9, Papers of Samuel Rosenman, FDRL [hereinafter Tavares Report] (on 67 prisoners in civilian jails and 123 in O'ahu Military Prison serving time between six months and life, as of June 30, 1943); Office of the Chief of Military History, "Civil Affairs," 3230–3231 (on juveniles tried in provost courts); Gwenfread Allen, *Hawaii's War Years, 1941–1945* (Honolulu: University of Hawai'i Press, 1950), 183; Anthony, *Hawaii under Army Rule,* 48 (on fines paid), 50–52; May, "Hawaii's Work in Wartime," *Honolulu Star-Bulletin,* May 18, 1944.

68. Official Army History, 96, draft in Green's notes, Green Papers, JAGSL.

69. Office of the Chief of Military History, "Civil Affairs," 3250.

70. *Honolulu Star-Bulletin,* December 24, 1941, 2; Lt. Frederick Simpich Jr., "Life on the Hawaii 'Front,'" *National Geographic Magazine,* October 1942, p. 545.

71. Anthony, *Hawaii under Army Rule,* 18, 54–58; Office of the Chief of Military History, "Civil Affairs," 3232–3236 (on policy and implementation regarding reviews for clemency); Green, "Martial Law," 281 (on bond purchases and blood donations). Several persons interviewed by the authors referred to a "blood book" in which the courts recorded forced blood donations, but our search in the Ft. Shafter court records did not discover it. Neal Franklin, who presided over the O'ahu Provost Court, stated that he never sentenced anyone to forfeit blood, but "rather a sentence was adjudged and in part remitted if a blood donation was made to blood bank." (Neal Franklin, Notes Relative to Part Eight of "Wartime Security Controls in Hawaii, 1941–1945, a General Historical Survey," copy in Green Papers, JAGSL.)

72. In 1942 alone, nearly 1,700 persons were sent to county jail or the O'ahu penitentiary. (Anthony, *Hawaii under Army Rule,* 52–54.)

73. Memorandum from Warner Gardner to Secretary Ickes, December 10, 1942, Ickes Files, NA. Anthony quotes other passages from this memorandum, a copy of which he examined from Department of the Interior files. (Anthony, *Hawaii under Army Rule,* 26.)

74. Green Notes, Green Papers, JAGSL.

75. Richardson to McCloy, February 10, 1944, McCloy Files, NA.

76. Quoted in Office of the Chief of Military History, "Civil Affairs," 3238. Martial law ended on October 24, 1944.

77. Radio No. R72230 from Richardson to McCloy, December 7, 1944, McCloy Files, NA.

78. Office of the Chief of Military History, "Civil Affairs," 3236–3238; Statement of Major Louis Springer, Provost Court Judges in Conference Transcript, 26.

79. Springer, ibid., 27. Statistics on African-American defense workers are from Beth L. Bailey and David Farber, *The First Strange Place: Race and Sex in World War II Hawaii* (New York: Free Press, 1992), 225n3.

80. Green Notes, Green Papers, JAGSL.

81. Col. Neal Franklin, Judge Advocate General Division, "Notes relative to Part Eight of 'Wartime Security Controls in Hawaii, 1941–1945,'" undated manuscript, Green Papers, JAGSL.

82. Provost Court Judges in Conference Transcript, 27. See discussion of censorship, chap. 4.

83. Stainback to Ickes, September 2, 1942, Secretary's Files, Ickes Papers, LC, quoted in Boardman Report, Appendix, p. xi.

84. Diary of Thomas H. Green, January 4, 1942, Green Papers, JAGSL. This entry was apparently in the original diary, differentiated from handwritten commentaries and emendations apparently made by Gen. Green in later years. Such obviously retrospective additions and emendations will be noted as such in this book's citations.

85. Ibid. Entries from early January 1942.

86. W. A. Gabrielson, "Crime Trends Under Martial Law and Blackout Conditions," not dated but early 1943, HWRD.

87. Biddle and Fortas to McCloy, December 19, 1942, McCloy Files, Box 32, NA.

88. Proclamation by the Governor of Hawaii, February 8, 1943, and Proclamation by the U.S. Army (Delos Emmons), February 8, 1943, both reproduced in Anthony, *Hawaii under Army Rule,* 129–132. See infra, chap. 12, for further discussion of the Washington negotiations and the partial restoration of civilian government.

89. Tavares Report, Rosenman Papers, FDRL. For discussion of the legality of the provost courts, see infra, chap. 14.

90. Transcript, "Oral Report Made by Mr. Frederick B. Wiener, 11 May 1946" [to Maj. Gen. Moore et al.], 10, Richardson Papers, Hoover Institution [hereinafter Wiener Report].

91. *Ex parte Duncan,* 66 F. Supp. 976, 980 (Metzger, J.).

Chapter 7: "An Extreme Degree of Fear"

1. See pp. 39–40, 43.

2. Gwenfread Allen, *Hawaii's War Years, 1941–1945* (Honolulu: University of Hawai'i Press, 1950), 350; Yukiko Kimura, *Issei: Japanese Immigrants in Hawaii* (Honolulu: University of Hawai'i Press, 1988), 217. See also infra, pp. 123–124. According to Military Intelligence, the ethnic Japanese feared that "the Filipinos would take matters into their own hands should any major disasters occur in the Philippine Islands." Both the plantations and the Filipino subsection of the army's G-2 intelligence office made efforts to restrain anti-Japanese sentiment among the Filipinos from erupting into hostile actions, for example, by increasing surveillance by G-2 and separating the workforces by ethnicity on some plantations. (Memorandum from George W. Bicknell, G-2

Contact Officer, "Estimate of the Situation [Local Racial Elements]," January 1, 1942, RG 165, NA.) See also supra, p. 100, for Green's concerns about ethnic conflict.

3. General Orders No. 5, reproduced in Thomas H. Green, "Martial Law in Hawaii, December 7, 1941–April 4, 1943," http://www.loc.gov/rr/frd/Military_Law/pdf/Martial-Law_Green.pdf, 120. Emphasis added.

4. Ibid.

5. See Note on Terminology, supra. For a further discussion of terminology used in reference to the removal and incarceration of Japanese Americans by the leading expert on the subject, see Roger Daniels, "Words Do Matter: A Note on Inappropriate Terminology and the Incarceration of Japanese Americans," in *Nikkei in the Pacific Northwest: Japanese Americans and Japanese Canadians in the Twentieth Century,* ed. Louis Fiset and Gail Nomura (Seattle: University of Washington Press, 2005), 183–207.

6. Office of the Chief of Military History, "United States Army Forces Middle Pacific and Predecessor Commands during World War II," vol. 10, part 8, appendix 1, "Plans and Measures for the Control of Certain Elements of the Population," 16 (ms., microfilm copy), HWRD [hereinafter "Plans and Measures for the Control of Certain Elements of the Population"]. Since 50,000 of the 158,000 Japanese Americans in Hawaiʻi were under the age of sixteen, the adult population was approximately 108,000. Estimates of number of children are from Samuel W. King article, *Honolulu Advertiser,* March 1941, quoted in Yukiko Kimura, *Issei,* 209. See infra, p. 130, for discussion of Nisei already serving in the army and the National Guard.

7. Commission on Wartime Relocation and Internment of Civilians, *Personal Justice Denied* (Washington, DC: Government Printing Office, 1982) [hereinafter CWIRC, *Personal Justice Denied*], chap. 11; Gwenfread Allen, *Hawaii's War Years,* 134.

8. The difference between internment and evacuee status is explained below at p. 144. According to the G-2 History of the United States Armed Forces, 1,579 persons in Hawaiʻi were apprehended, of whom 1,466 were of Japanese extraction, 114 German, 17 Italian, and 2 French. Of this number, 617 were paroled or released, 67 excluded, 313 relocated, and 97 repatriated. Thirteen died. There were still 494 in custody in Hawaiʻi when the war ended. ("Plans and Measures for the Control of Certain Elements of the Population," 16.)

9. Bicknell, "Security Measures in Hawaii," chap. 5, 72, HWRD.

10. For the impact of these and other regulations in the early days of the war, see Allen, *Hawaii's War Years,* esp. 40–41, 109–110, and 141–142; and Kimura, *Issei,* chap. 14.

11. Everett R. Ferris, Special Agent, CIC, Memorandum: Japanese Phonograph Record Project, January 5, 1943, RG 338, NA.

12. Midkiff to Green, March 11, 1943, and attached Interstaff Routing Slip, Headquarters Hawaiian Department, RG 338, NA, copy in folder 190, JIR.

13. On this and related regulations impacting Japanese Americans, see Andrew W. Lind, "The Japanese in Hawaii under War Conditions," *American Council Paper* No. 5 (New York: American Council Institute of Pacific Relations, December 1942); Andrew W. Lind, *Hawaii's Japanese: An Experiment in Democracy* (Princeton, NJ: Princeton University Press, 1946); Office of the Chief of Military History, "United States Army Forces, Middle Pacific and Predecessor Commands during World War II, 7 December 1941–42 September 1945: History of G-2 Section" (on file in HWRD). See also, *inter alia,* Bicknell, "Security Measures in Hawaii," HWRD.

14. Erma Cull, compiler, Territorial Office of Defense Health and Welfare Services, "The Japanese Population of the Territory of Hawaii—Its Relationship to the War Effort," May 21, 1942

(confidential typescript report), JAERR, Reel 371, Bancroft Library, UC Berkeley. See also Lind, *Hawaii's Japanese*, 83.

15. Social Security Board, "Labor Market Report, July 15–August 15, 1942," Reel 27. HWRD.

16. The authors have examined dozens of petitions for permits for weddings and funerals in the correspondence of the Executive, RG 338, NA.

17. Harold W. Rice (Maui) to Stainback, February 4, 1944, Gov. 9–22, HSA. In forwarding the letter to Ickes, Stainback commented: "It is difficult enough to fight our local fascists without having one in California impose his orders upon us. Besides, we need every pound of food that can be produced locally." (Stainback to Ickes, February 5, 1944, copy, Gov. 9–22, Hawai'i State Archives.)

18. Lind, *Hawaii's Japanese*, 176.

19. Quoted in Lind, *Hawaii's Japanese*, 63–64; see also Lind, "The Japanese in Hawaii Under War Conditions," 14. Executive Order 8802 was signed by Roosevelt on June 25, 1941, in response to pressure from African-American leaders who were protesting against segregated facilities in the defense industry. (Office of Federal Contract Compliance, U.S. Department of Labor, "History of Executive Order 11246," http://www.dol.gov/ofccp/about/History_EO11246.htm.)

20. Lili M. Kim, "How Koreans Repealed Their 'Enemy Alien' Status: Korean Americans' Identity, Culture, and National Pride in Wartime Hawai'i," in *From the Land of Hibiscus: Koreans in Hawai'i, 1903–1950*, ed. Yong-Ho Ch'oe (Honolulu: University of Hawai'i Press, 2007) [hereinafter Kim, "Enemy Alien Status"] 197–198. Although some of the Koreans had come to Hawai'i prior to Japan's annexation of the country in 1910, no distinction was made for purposes of military rule. For a discussion of the army's policies toward Koreans in Hawai'i, so fraught with irony, see, in addition to Kim, Michael E. Macmillan, "Unwanted Allies: Koreans as Enemy Aliens in World War II," *Hawaiian Journal of History*, 19 (1985): 179–203. See Richardson's statement, infra, p. 122, regarding similarities in appearance between Koreans and Japanese.

21. Stimson to Rev. Peong Koo Yoon, undated, cited by Kim, "Enemy Alien Status," 200.

22. Indeed, in December, the anti-Japanese Sino-Korean Peoples League sent a message to President Roosevelt, pledging support and predicting a Korean revolt against Japanese forces. (*New York Times*, December 29, 1941, p. 3.) The Sino-Korean People's League was formed in the late 1930s in opposition to the conservative Syngman Rhee; it worked to foment anti-Japanese sentiment in Hawai'i. The anti-Japanese movement among Korean immigrants is treated in Wayne Patterson, *The Ilse: First Generation Korean Immigrants in Hawaii, 1903–1973* (Honolulu: University of Hawai'i Press, 2000).

23. Kim, "Enemy Alien Status," 198–200; Macmillan, "Unwanted Allies," 183.

24. Quote from *Honolulu Star-Bulletin*, July 27, 1943, p. 8.

25. "General Emmons Asked to Alter Korean Status," *Honolulu Star-Bulletin*, May 18, 1943, p. 1. Gillette also appealed directly to President Roosevelt. (Kim, "Enemy Alien Status," 202.)

26. *Korean National Herald-Pacific Weekly*, February 25, 1942, quoted in Kim, "Enemy Alien Status," 198.

27. "Time to Correct an Injustice," *Honolulu Star-Bulletin*, May 6, 1943, p. 8 (editorial); see also May 8, 1943, letter to the editor.

28. "Provost Court Rule on Koreans to be Appealed," *Honolulu Star-Bulletin*, May 5, 1943, p. 5.

29. "Koreans Here to Remain as Enemy Aliens," *Honolulu Star-Bulletin*, June 2, 1943, p. 1 (reporting on the appeal of the curfew violation conviction of Syung Woon Sohn).

30. Kim, "Enemy Alien Status," 205; Macmillan, "Unwanted Allies," 193.

31. Memorandum, Strong to chief of staff, 29 June 1943, tab 1, AG 014.311 (4–30–42), quoted in Macmillan, "Unwanted Allies," 196–197.

32. Memorandum of Interview: Major Edward Walker, March 9, 1945, conducted by A. F. Newkirk and Lewis Coren in the Office of the Research and Historical Section, 17, copy in folder 397, JIR [hereinafter Walker Interview].

33. Kimura, "Some Effects of the War Situation upon the Alien Japanese in Hawaii," 18.

34. Hatsuno Mihara to Brig. Gen. Donald J. Myers, March 23, 1944, and Wm. R. C. Morrison to Office of the Representative of the Military Governor, Maui District, April 24, 1944, copies in AR 19, Box 9, Folder 31, JCCH.

35. Kimura, *Issei*, 225, 217. See also Gary Y. Okihiro, *Cane Fires: The Anti-Japanese Movement in Hawaii, 1865–1945* (Philadelphia: Temple University Press, 1991), 229–232, for a description of the social impacts of martial law.

36. Lind, *Hawaii's Japanese*, 102.

37. Bicknell, "Security Measures in Hawaii," chaps. 3, 4, HWRD. The contemporary observer Lind also noted: "The understandable tendency among the Japanese to seek protection in silence naturally stimulated the growth of fantastic myths about them." Lind, *Hawaii's Japanese*, 7.

38. Bicknell, "Security Measures in Hawaii," chaps. 3, 4, HWRD.

39. Green, "Martial Law," 120.

40. Kimie Kawahara and Yuriko Hatanaka, "The Impact of War on an Immigrant Culture," *Social Process in Hawaii* 8 (November 1943): 38.

41. "Matsuju Miyashiro: That's what my life is all about," Transcript of interviews by Sayuri Oshiro, 1991. The interviews were conducted as part of a directed reading and research program guided by Dr. Franklin Odo, Ethnic Studies Program, University of Hawai'i at Manoa.

42. Testimony of Robert Shivers, *Roberts Commission*, 669. The commission, appointed on December 18, 1941, was headed by U.S. Supreme Court Associate Justice Owen Roberts; other members of the Commission were Adm. Joseph M. Reeves, Adm. William H. Standley, Gen. Frank R. McCoy, and Gen. Joseph T. McNarney. The commission, which held hearings in Washington and Hawai'i, made its report to Congress on January 28, 1942. For a summary of its findings, see http://www.ibiblio.org/pha/pha/roberts/roberts.html.

43. Interview with Hisashi Fukuhara, folder 232, JIR.

44. FBI, Honolulu Field Division, Running Log, December 7–December 12, 1941, RG 65, NA.

45. Testimony of Sally Tsuneishi, reproduced in Patricia (Kirita) Nomura, ed., no title [a collection of experiences of Hawai'i residents incarcerated in Jerome, Arkansas, likely prepared for a reunion], n.d., but probably 1985.

46. Quoted in Kimura, *Issei*, 226.

47. Ibid.

48. In the first two months of the war, the American Friends Service Committee provided assistance to some 159 families (600 to 700 persons); 18 of them were families of detainees and many of the others were families of fishermen. ("Report of the American Friends Service Committee, February 26, 1942," AR19, Box 8, Folder 21, JCCH.)

49. Robert Freund, Hawaiian Department Alien Processing Center, to Green, July 20, 1942, copy in folder 338, JIR; Allen, *Hawaii's War Years*, 138; Erma Cull, compiler, Territorial Office of Defense Health and Welfare Services, "The Japanese Population of the Territory of Hawaii—Its Relationship to the War Effort," May 21, 1942 (confidential typescript report), JAERR, Reel 371, Bancroft Library, UC Berkeley.

50. Gustav W. Olson, vice-consul of Sweden, to Hatsumo Honda, July 24, 1942, Samuel King Papers, HSA.

51. Ibid. See P. Scott Corbett, *Quiet Passages: The Exchange of Civilians between the United States and Japan during the Second World War* (Kent, OH: Kent State University Press, 1987), for a discussion of the exchange repatriation. The United States was a signatory to the Geneva Convention that provided for a neutral country to be appointed as a "protecting power" of a combatant and to safeguard the interests of prisoners of war and others residing in the hostile country; Switzerland assumed this role for the United States, and Spain assumed this role for Japan, except in Hawai'i, where Sweden was assigned for Japan. However, Japan's Diet had not ratified the convention; hence Japan was not bound by its provisions.

52. B. M. Bryan, Chief, Aliens Division, to Department of Welfare, Territory of Hawaii, July 3, 1942, King Papers, HSA.

53. M. G. Fox, Agent, Department of Public Welfare, Territory of Hawaii, to Samuel W. King, August 7, 1942, King Papers, HSA.

54. Allen W. Gullion, Provost Marshal General, to Samuel Wilder King, August 25, 1942, King Papers, HSA. In point of fact, the question of repatriation to Japan of Japanese citizens (including dual citizens) from Hawai'i was the subject of difficult and protracted negotiations, beginning in the summer of 1942, among various agencies within the U.S. government and between the United States and Japan. Assistant Secretary of the Navy James Forrestal protested to Secretary of State Hull that Japanese from Hawai'i were undoubtedly familiar with local defenses and to repatriate them could compromise national security. The Military Intelligence Division (MID) in the War Department, the Office of Naval Intelligence (ONI) in the Navy Department, the Alien Enemy Control Unit in the Justice Department, and the FBI had similar objections; the repatriation of Japanese fishermen from Hawai'i was of particular concern, but they agreed that the State Department should have the final say. As the negotiations dragged on, Gen. Emmons and Secretary of War Stimson weighed in against repatriation of Hawai'i residents. To exclude certain Japanese residents from Hawai'i, however, from the lists requested by Japan would be a breach of the exchange agreements between Japan and the United States to which Japan refused to acquiesce. The repatriation policy was further complicated by the issue of forced repatriation of persons against their wishes. It was not until September 1943 that a compromise was reached and the *Gripsholm* set sail for Japan with 1,340 Japanese on board. (Corbett, *Quiet Passages*, 72–95.) For Emmons's policies of repatriation of residents from Hawai'i, see infra, p. 151.

55. Memorandum from Edward H. Hickey to James Rowe, April 6, 1943, "Summary of FBI Reply to Angus Taylor's Memorandum," Papers of James Rowe Jr., FDRL [hereinafter Summary of FBI Reply to Angus Taylor's Memorandum]. See also Lind, *Hawaii's Japanese*, chap. 3.

56. For discussion of rumors, see Bicknell, "Security Measures in Hawaii," chap. 5, 67 (attributing some of the rumors to the evacuated women); Allen, *Hawaii's War Years*, 47–56; and Roland Kotani, *The Japanese in Hawaii: A Century of Struggle* (Honolulu: Hawai'i Hochi, Ltd., 1985), 87–88. Lind argues that these rumors were instrumental in the decision for the mass evacuation of Japanese from the West Coast of the mainland. (Lind, *Hawaii's Japanese*, chap. 3.) See also "Fifth Column in U.S.—Fighting the Foe Within," *United States News,* February 27, 1942.

57. Quoted in *New York Times,* January 10, 1942.

58. Kimmel is quoted in Otto Friedrich, "A Time of Agony for Japanese Americans," *Time Magazine*, December 2, 1991.

59. *Honolulu Star-Bulletin,* December 15, 1941. On Secretary Knox and his campaign for evacuation and his allegations of sabotage on December 7, see Roger Daniels, *Prisoners without Trial: Japanese Americans in World War II,* rev. ed. (New York: Hill & Wang, 2004), 37 et passim. The Norwegian reference is to the assistance given to the German invasion by Nazi-sympathizers under the leadership of Vidkun Quisling in 1940.

60. *New York Times,* December 23, 1941. Emphasis added.

61. U.S. Department of the Navy, Ringle Report on Japanese Internment, Serial No. 01742316, January 26, 1942, copy in folder 54, JIR.

62. Ibid. Emphasis and paragraph break added.

63. See discussion of Munson Report, supra, pp. 32ff.

64. Curtis Munson, December 20, 1941, quoted in Michi Weglyn, *Years of Infamy: The Untold Story of America's Concentration Camps,* updated ed. (Seattle: University of Washington Press, 1996), 49.

65. Petrie informed the Tolan Committee that he had "no personal information substantiating the fact that acts of sabotage may have been committed on Dec seventh and since." (Radiogram for Delegate King, March 15, 1942, in King Papers, HSA.)

66. Quoted in Lind, *Hawaii's Japanese,* 47.

67. Roberts Commission, 663.

68. Memorandum from Hoover to Assistant Attorney General James Rowe Jr., March 16, 1942, Papers of James Rowe Jr., FDRL (attached to a Memorandum for the Attorney General dated April 20, 1942).

69. Bicknell, "Security Measures in Hawaii," chap. 5, 67, HWRD.

70. See supra, p. 124.

71. The 14th Naval District Intelligence Office report, quoted in Richard B. Frank, "Zero Hour in Nihau," *World War II* (October 2010), http://www.historynet.com/zero-hour-on-nihau.htm. The pilot was killed by the islanders, and the Nisei killed himself. The Nisei's wife, suspected of being a Japanese spy, was held in a military prison on Oʻahu until late 1944. U.S. attorney for Hawaiʻi Angus Taylor was among those who viewed the incident as evidence that the ethnic Japanese in Hawaiʻi would join with the enemy if Japan were to invade. (Ibid.) For other accounts of the Niʻihau incident, see Allan Beekman, *The Niihau Incident* (Honolulu, HI: Heritage Press of the Pacific, 1982); William Hallstead, "The Niihau Incident," *World War II* (November 2000), http://www.historynet.com/the-niihau-incident-htm/2. See also Allen, *Hawaii's War Years,* 44–46; and Dorothy Ochiai Hazama and Jane Okamoto Komeiji, *Okage Sama De: The Japanese in Hawaiʻi, 1885–1985* (Honolulu, HI: Bess Press, 1986), 131–132.

72. Memorandum from FBI Honolulu Field Office, quoted in Memorandum from George W. Bicknell, G-2 Contact Officer, "Estimate of the Situation (Local Racial Elements)," January 1, 1942, RG 165, NA.

73. Herman Phleger to Hon. Samuel W. King, March 6, 1942, in King Papers, HSA.

74. "Fifth Column in U.S.—Fighting the Foe Within," *United States News,* February 27, 1942.

75. Rev. Masao Yamada, 1942, quoted in "Kauai Morale Committee," Exhibit, April 2009, Kauaʻi Museum, Lihue, Kauaʻi. Yamada, a Nisei, led the Kauai Emergency Service Committee until 1943, when he became the first Japanese-American chaplain after volunteering to serve in that capacity with the 442nd Regimental Combat Team. Although wounded in action, he continued to minister to the troops and then helped the Nisei soldiers readjust to life in Hawaiʻi after the

war before resuming his civilian ministry. See Michael Markrich, "Masao Yamada," http://www
.100thbattalion.org/history/veterans/chaplains/masao-yamada/2/.

76. Diary of Thomas H. Green, February 3, 1942, Green Papers, JAGSL.

77. Ibid.

78. Franklin S. Odo, *No Sword to Bury: Japanese Americans in Hawaii during World War II*
(Philadelphia: Temple University Press, 2004), 108, 112–113, 126; Allen, *Hawaii's War Years,* 149;
Ted T. Tsukiyama, "Ted's Corner, Pearl Harbor Aftermath: From Tragedy to Triumph," http://
442sd.org/other-news/teds-corner-pearl-harbor-aftermath-from-tragedy-to-triumph [hereinafter
"Ted's Corner, Pearl Harbor"]. Odo provides a lively discussion with firsthand accounts of the
ROTC, Varsity Victory Volunteers, and Japanese Americans in the military.

79. Franklin Odo interview with Ted Tsukiyama, quoted in Odo, *No Sword to Bury,* 110, 108,
112–113; Allen, *Hawaii's War Years,* 149. Tsukiyama went on to join the 442nd Regimental Combat Team and then was assigned to the Military Intelligence Service. He subsequently earned his
law degree and practiced in Honolulu. He has collected a substantial archive, deposited in Hamilton Library, University of Hawai'i, about the VVV, the 442nd, the Military Intelligence Services
(MIS), and Hawai'i in World War II. The authors have benefited from several conversations with
him regarding the war period in Hawai'i.

80. Tsukiyama, "Ted's Corner, Pearl Harbor."

81. See, in addition to Odo, Yutaka Nakahata, *The Volunteer,* a 40-page illustrated booklet
about the history, activities, and membership of the VVV edited by one of its members, JAERR,
Bancroft Library, UC Berkeley (http://digitalassets.lib.berkeley.edu/jarda/ucb/text/cubanc6714
_b317w02_0467.pdf); and *New York Times,* February 26, 1942, p. 4. Tsukiyama attributed the idea
of forming a labor battalion to Hung Wai Ching, secretary of the University YMCA and a member of the OMG's Morale Section. See pp. 138ff.

82. Tuskiyama, "Ted's Corner, Pearl Harbor."

83. For a brief account of Nisei soldiers before and during World War II, including their contributions to the Military Intelligence Service, see Ted Tsukiyama's "Ted's Corner, The Nisei Soldiers of
World War II," http://442sd.org/other-news-teds-corner-the-nisei-soldiers-of-world-war-ii.

84. Roland Kotani, *The Japanese in Hawaii: A Century of Struggle* (Honolulu: Hawai'i Hochi,
Ltd., 1985), 108.

85. Hazama and Komeiji, *Okage Sama De,* 149–151; Kimura, *Issei,* 232–235; CWIRC, *Personal
Justice Denied.* The petition to serve in combat is discussed in Cecil Henry Coggins, "The Japanese-
Americans in Hawaii," *Harper's Magazine,* June 1943, pp. 75–83.

86. Oahu Local Board No. 5 to Stainback, October 2, 1941, Gov. 9–22, Interior, HSA.

87. Memorandum from Edwin G. Arnold, Special Assistant to the Director, to Dillon S. Myer,
War Relocation Authority, December 16, 1942, Box 3, RG 210, NA.

88. Stainback to Ickes, October 31, 1942, Gov. 9–22, Interior, HSA.

89. Masayo Duus, trans. Peter Duus, *Unlikely Liberators: The Men of the 100th and the 442nd*
(Honolulu: University of Hawai'i Press, 2006), 56. This book, based on archival research and in-
terviews, provides a lively account of the origins and extraordinary combat history of the Japanese-
American fighting units.

90. Transcript of telephone conversation between General DeWitt and Mr. McCloy, Asst. Sec.
of War, Washington, DC, January 18, 1943, http://www.the442.org/activation.html.

91. Duus, *Unlikely Liberators,* 57–58.

92. For a concise history of the 100th Battalion, see F. Odo, "100th Infantry Battalion," *Densho Encyclopedia*, http://encyclopedia.densho.org/100th%20Infantry%20Battalion/.

93. Lind, *Hawaii's Japanese*, 155, 160–161. Nisei women also answered the call to service: twenty-six of the fifty-nine women in Hawai'i who joined the Women's Army Corps in late 1944 were of Japanese ancestry. (Ibid., 190.)

Chapter 8: Selective Detention and Removal

1. *Honolulu Star-Bulletin*, December 22, 1941; *Honolulu Advertiser*, December 22, 1941; *Los Angeles Times*, December 23, 1941, p. 3; *New York Times*, December 23, 1941. Ironically, the *New York Times* summarized his speech in the same column as the report from the War Department on the arrest of 273 Japanese Fifth Columnists. (See supra, p. 126.) See also Yukiko Kimura, *Issei: Japanese Immigrants in Hawaii* (Honolulu: University of Hawai'i Press, 1988), 222; Commission on Wartime Relocation and Internment of Civilians, *Personal Justice Denied* (Washington, DC: Government Printing Office, 1982) [hereinafter CWIRC, *Personal Justice Denied*].

2. Dorothy Ochiai Hazama and Jane Okamoto Komeiji, *Okage Sama De: The Japanese in Hawai'i, 1885–1985* (Honolulu, HI: Bess Press, 1986), 140; Andrew W. Lind, *Hawaii's Japanese: An Experiment in Democracy* (Princeton, NJ: Princeton University Press, 1946), 69–70.

3. See A Note on Terminology. In his opinion for the Ninth Circuit in the Abo Case, Judge Denman would specifically compare the layout of the facilities at the Tule Lake camp, including the gun turrets and barbed wire, to the Nazi camps. See infra, p. 332.

4. Presumably, this request from Knox prompted Attorney General Biddle to inquire of FBI Director Hoover about plans to move the Japanese from O'ahu to another island, and Hoover called Shivers on December 20. Shivers assured Hoover that the alien Japanese would remain at their current places of confinement: the Immigration Station and Sand Island, and the other facilities on Kaua'i, Maui, and Hawai'i. (Shivers to FBI Director Hoover, "Movement of Enemy Aliens from Honolulu to Adjacent Island," December 26, 1941, FBI File No. 100–2-20 "Custodial Detention," NA.)

5. CWRIC, *Personal Justice Denied*, n.p.; Tetsuden Kashima, *Judgment without Trial: Japanese American Imprisonment during World War II* (Seattle: University of Washington Press, 2003), 76.

6. Edward A. Tamm, Memorandum for the Director, December 22, 1941, FBI File 100–2-20, "Custodial Detention," NA. Tamm was assistant director of the FBI.

7. Arthur Lerch, Deputy Provost Marshal General, Memorandum for the Adjutant General, January 10, 1942, with text of secret radiogram to be sent to Commanding General, Hawaiian Department, copy in JIR; see also Radiogram (Provost Marshal General's Office) to Commanding General, Hawaiian Dept., January 10, 1942, in Roger Daniels, ed., *American Concentration Camps*, vol. 8: *Japanese of Hawaii* (New York: Garland Publishing, 1989), n.p.

8. Radiogram, Emmons to Adjutant General, January 12, 1942, copy in Folder A-5, JIR. Emphasis added.

9. Address to Chamber of Commerce reported in the *New York Times*, January 16, 1942.

10. Radiogram, Emmons to Adjutant General, January 12, 1942, copy in Folder A-5, JIR. It is likely that Emmons reached these conclusions based on briefings from Col. Thomas Green, Executive for the OMG, and from the FBI and intelligence service heads.

11. Adams to CG, Hawaiian Dept., January 17, 1942, in Daniels, ed., *American Concentration Camps*.

12. Stetson Conn, Rose C. Engelman, and Byron Fairchild, *Guarding the United States and Its Outposts.* U.S. Army, Center of Military History (Washington, DC: U.S. Government Printing Office, 1962), 208.

13. Radiogram 2071, Emmons to Adj. General, February 4, 1942, in Daniels, ed., *American Concentration Camps.*

14. Ibid. Emphasis added.

15. A total of 485 "enemy aliens and dangerous citizens of enemy extraction" were being detained in Oʻahu as of the end of January 1942. (L. T. Gerow, Asst. Chief of Staff, War Dept. to Chief of Staff, "Evacuation of Dangerous Japanese from Hawaii," January 31, 1942, RG 107, copy in folder 337, JIR.)

16. Memorandum from George W. Bicknell, G-2 Contact Officer, "Estimate of the Situation (Local Racial Elements)," January 1, 1942, RG 165, NA.

17. See John J. Stephan, *Hawaii under the Rising Sun: Japan's Plans for Conquest after Pearl Harbor* (Honolulu: University of Hawaiʻi Press, 1984).

18. Radio No. 2166, Emmons to Adjutant General, February 9, 1942, in Daniels, ed., *American Concentration Camps.*

19. Ibid.

20. Radio No. 2193, Emmons to Adjutant General, February 10, 1942, copy in Folder A-8, JIR.

21. Joint U.S. Chiefs of Staff, Hawaiian Defense Forces, JCS 11, February 12, 1942, copy in FDRL, also in Folder A-10, JIR. Emphasis added.

22. Knox to Roosevelt, February 23, 1942, PSF Confidential file, FDR Papers, FDRL.

23. Memorandum, President to the Secretary of the Navy, February 26, 1942, PSF Confidential File, FDR papers, FDRL. Emphasis added. Executive Order 9066, signed February 19, authorized the exclusion of persons from prescribed military areas and their removal to relocation centers. It was the basis for the exclusion of some 110,000 ethnic Japanese from the West Coast of the United States and their forced relocation and incarceration. Roosevelt's choice of one of the other Hawaiian islands for a concentration camp for the ethnic Japanese was similar to his suggestion in 1941 of a detention camp for alien enemies from Central America "on one of the uninhabited Galapagos Islands. It is really true that the climate of the Galapagos is delightful all the year round. Food and tents and clothing and cooking utensils would be the only cost." (Roosevelt to Cordell Hull, April 24, 1941, quoted in Thomas Connell, *America's Japanese Hostages: The World War II Plan for a Japanese Free Latin America* [Westport, CT: Praeger, 2002], 5.)

24. H. R. Stark to President Roosevelt, March 11, 1942, FDRL. Cf. p. 135. Copy also in Folder A-10, JIR. Emphasis added.

25. According to General Dwight D. Eisenhower, assistant chief of staff, it was the president who made this modification. General Dwight D. Eisenhower, "Memorandum for the Assistant Secretary of War, Subject: Evacuation of Japanese from Hawaii," n.d. but in response to McCloy's memo to Eisenhower of March 28, 1942, copies of both memoranda in Folder A-12, JIR.

26. Greg Robinson, *By Order of the President: FDR and the Internment of Japanese Americans* (Cambridge, MA: Harvard University Press, 2001), 151; Conn et al., *Guarding the United States,* 210.

27. Memorandum from Eisenhower for Adjutant General for dispatch to Commanding General, Hawaiian Dept., March 18, 1942, in Daniels, ed., *American Concentration Camps.* Emphasis added.

28. Emmons reply quoted in memo from Eisenhower to McCloy, April 3, 1942, copy in folder A-12, JIR.

29. Army officials also expressed fear of widespread conflagrations in case of bombings or incendiary raids if all ethnic Japanese residents were evacuated and entire neighborhoods were depopulated. (Bicknell, "Security Measures in Hawaii," chap. 5, 73, HWRD.)

30. Ibid., chap. 5, 74, HWRD.

31. Midkiff to Emmons, February 22, 1942, JAERR, Reel 371, Bancroft Library, University of California, Berkeley [hereafter UC Berkeley].

32. Erma Cull, compiler, Territorial Office of Defense Health and Welfare Services, "The Japanese Population of the Territory of Hawaii—Its Relationship to the War Effort, May 21, 1942," (confidential typescript report), JAERR, Reel 371, Bancroft Library, UC Berkeley.

33. Memorandum from Edwin G. Arnold, Special Assistant to the Director, to Dillon S. Myer, War Relocation Authority, December 16, 1942, RG 210, NA. See also Allen, *Hawaii's War Years,* 310–326; Gary Y. Okihiro, *Cane Fires: The Anti-Japanese Movement in Hawaii, 1865–1945* (Philadelphia: Temple University Press, 1991), 253–260.

34. Linton Collins, Memorandum for Mr. Rowe, April 22, 1942, Papers of James Rowe Jr., FDRL. Collins was summarizing a report by Charles Pietsch, formerly chairman of the Hawaii Housing Authority, who was in Washington, delivering a message from, and expressing the views of, U.S. Attorney Angus Taylor.

35. Ennis to Rowe, April 27, 1942, Papers of James Rowe Jr., FDRL.

36. Green, Manuscript Recollections, Green Papers, JAGSL. In this retrospective view, Green also wrote that the proposed plan for mass removal of all Japanese from Oʻahu and their internment elsewhere was "illegal, unjust, and, of even more importance, it was impractical" in light of shipping, maintenance, and other logistical needs. (Ibid.)

37. Statement of Jack Wakayama, January 3, 1942, Reel 371, JAERR, Bancroft Library, UC Berkeley.

38. See Tom Coffman, *How Hawaiʻi Changed America* (Honolulu, HI: EpiCenter, 2014).

39. Robert L. Shivers, "Cooperation of the Various Racial Groups with Each Other and with the Constituted Authorities Before and After December 7, 1941" (Honolulu: Territorial Emergency Service Committees, 1946), 8–9.

40. Morale Section, Office of Civilian Defense, April 14, 1942, Box 440, HSA.

41. Ibid., December 22, 1941.

42. See Franklin S. Odo, *No Sword to Bury: Japanese Americans in Hawaii during World War II* (Philadelphia: Temple University Press, 2004), 134–137.

43. The Kauai Morale Committee was appointed in May, the Maui Emergency Committee in August, the Lanai Emergency Service Committee in January 1943, and the Hawaii AJA Morale Committee in April 1944. (Allen, *Hawaii's War Years,* 144.)

44. Office of the Military Governor, Morale Section, Emergency Service Committee, *Final Report of the Emergency Service Committee* (Honolulu: n.p., 1946), 1, quoted in http://encyclopedia .densho.org/Emergency%20Service%20Committee/.

45. Bicknell, "Security Measures in Hawaii," chap. 5, 76, HWRD; Lind, *Hawaii's Japanese,* 82.

46. Tom Coffman, *The Island Edge of America: A Political History of Hawaiʻi* (Honolulu: University of Hawaiʻi Press, 2003), 69.

47. "Kauai Morale Committee," Exhibit, April 2009, Kauaʻi Museum, Lihue, Kauaʻi.

48. Ibid.

49. Ibid.; Bicknell, "Security Measures in Hawaii," chap. 5, 80, HWRD; Kelli Nakamura, "Emergency Service Committee," *Densho Encyclopedia,* http://encyclopedia.densho.org /Emergency%20Service%20Committee. See also Kimura, *Issei,* 227–229.

50. "Kauai Morale Committee," poster displayed in exhibit, April 2009, Kaua'i Museum, Lihue, Kaua'i.

51. "Report of the Conference of Americans of Japanese Ancestry," September 12, 1943, JAERR, Bancroft Library, UC Berkeley.

52. "Report of Second Oahu Conference of Americans of Japanese Ancestry," January 28, 1945, JAERR, Bancroft Library, UC Berkeley.

53. Ibid.

54. Headquarters Hawaiian Dept. to Adjutant General, February 8, 1942 in Daniels, ed., *American Concentration Camps.*

55. Included in the initial transport were 156 Issei and 16 Nisei, along with 20 Germans, 1 Norwegian, 1 Dane, 2 Italians, and 2 Caucasian U.S. citizens. The army considered the non-Japanese internees to be pro-Nazi and dangerous. (Provost Marshal General to Chief of Staff, War Dept., February 28, 1942, U.S. Army, Records of the Provost Marshal General's Office, RG 407, NA; Office of the Chief of Military History, "Plans and Measures for the Control of Certain Elements of the Population," 2–3; Kashima, *Judgment without Trial,* 78.) A second ship bearing 166 internees departed on March 19 and a third with 109 internees on May 23. (Yasutaro [Keiho] Soga, *Life behind Barbed Wire: The World War II Internment Memoirs of a Hawai'i Issei* [Honolulu: University of Hawai'i Press, 2008], 226.)

56. Office of the Chief of Military History, "Civil Affairs," 3090; Walker interview, JIR, 16–17.

57. Lerch to Adjutant General, March 3, 1942, in Daniels, ed., *American Concentration Camps.*

58. Stimson to Roosevelt, April 15, 1942, RG 107, copy in Folder 78, JIR.

59. Ibid. This British legislation and the World War II internments under its terms are discussed in A. W. Brian Simpson, *In the Highest Degree Odious: Detention without Trial in Wartime Britain* (Oxford: Clarendon Press, 1992).

60. Stimson Diary, April 7, 1942, Yale University Library (microfilm), also quoted in CWIRC, *Personal Justice Denied.*

61. Office of the Chief of Military History, "Plans and Measures for the Control of Certain Elements of the Population," 3.

62. Col. B. M. Bryan, Chief, Aliens Division, Office of the Provost Marshal General, to Commanding General, Western Defense Command, July 29, 1942, copy in Folder A-17, JIR; CWIRC, *Personal Justice Denied.*

63. "Dr. Kazuo Miyamoto's Story," Former internee, quoted in Patricia (Kirita) Nomura, ed., no title (Experiences of Hawaiians incarcerated in Jerome, Arkansas), no date, but probably 1985. Educated at Stanford University and Washington University Medical School, Miyamoto had pursued advanced medical study in Japan, where he published his observations of the Sino-Japanese war— allegedly the cause of his arrest by the FBI on December 7, 1941. Upon his return to Sand Island in summer 1942, he began writing his historical novel, *Hawaii: End of the Rainbow.* He returned to the mainland with his family in November 1943, first to Jerome, Arkansas, and then to Tule Lake, where he was a staff physician. He resumed his practice in Hawaii following the war, and in 1951 he was appointed as a medical consultant by the Surgeon General of the Air Force. See Kelly Y. Nakamura, "Kazuo Miyamoto," *Densho Encyclopedia,* http://encyclopedia.densho.org/Kazuo_Miyamoto/.

64. U.S. Army, *History of the U.S. Army MIDPAC,* quoted in Allen, *Hawaii's War Years,* 138.

65. William Gordon, "WW II Internment Camp Revisited," *Honolulu Advertiser* website, http://the.honoluluadvertiser.com/article/2008/Mar/03/ln/hawaii803030363.html (includes video of the return of a small group of survivors of the internment to the site, being surveyed for designation as a park or monument). The internees called the camp "Hell Valley," because of the intense heat that characterized the weather in the local area. (Ibid.) Some Japanese prisoners of war were also held there in a separate but adjacent section of the camp.

66. See next section, "Additional Removals," infra.

67. The Special Division of the State Department, in an effort to avoid forced repatriation of Japanese aliens, asked the WRA to survey those being held in the relocation centers. According to the surveys, conducted in July and the fall of 1942, only one-third to one-half of the aliens wanted to be repatriated to Japan. However well intentioned, the surveys resulted both in rumors of forced repatriation and in tensions within the WRA centers between those wanting to be repatriated ("Japanese sympathizers") and the rest of the detainees. Myer, the director of the WRA, thought the potential repatriates should be separated in their own camp, and in the summer of 1943 Tule Lake was designated for such a purpose. (P. Scott Corbett, *Quiet Passages: The Exchange of Civilians between the United States and Japan during the Second World War* [Kent, OH: Kent State University Press, 1987], 129.) For a discussion of the Tule Lake camp, see infra, pp. 197ff.

68. Memo, "Evacuation of Japanese from Hawaii," Mr. McCloy for Gen. Eisenhower, March 28, 1942, RG 107, Office of the Secretary of War, copy in folder 360, JIR.

69. Ibid.

70. Notes, War Council meeting, March 23, 1942, quoted in Conn et al., *Guarding the United States,* 211.

71. Memo, OPD for ASW, April 3, 1942, quoted in Conn et al., *Guarding the United States,* 211.

72. Quoted in Conn et al., *Guarding the United States,* 211.

73. Memorandum from Knox to Roosevelt, April 20, 1942, JIR, citing an excerpt from a report by Commander John Ford. Ford, a navy reservist, left his position as a Hollywood director and went on active duty in September 1941; he was one of Colonel Bill Donovan's operatives in special intelligence and operations.

74. McCloy to Emmons, May 18, 1942, in Daniels, ed., *American Concentration Camps.*

75. Emmons to McCloy, June 15, 1942, in ibid.

76. Conn et al., *Guarding the United States,* 212. Emphasis added.

77. Thomas Handy, Memorandum for War Dept. for transmittal to Emmons, June 27, 1942, in Daniels, ed., *American Concentration Camps.* See infra, pp. 192ff., for further discussion. The War Relocation Authority was created by President Roosevelt on March 18, 1942, to "provide for the removal from designated areas of persons whose removal is necessary in the interests of national security." (Executive Order 9102, quoted in Dillon S. Myer, *Uprooted Americans: The Japanese Americans and the War Relocation Authority during World War II* [Tucson: University of Arizona Press, 1971], appendix C, 309.) Initially designed for the evacuees from the West Coast of the mainland, the WRA centers subsequently received Nikkei from Hawai'i who were sent to the mainland as evacuees and excludees, as well as alien internees who were released from Department of Justice internment camps.

78. J. R. Deane, General Staff, to McCloy, July 17, 1942, RG 389, Provost Marshal's Office Records, copy in folder 363, JIR. Also, paraphrased in radiogram from Marshall to Commanding Gen-

eral, Hawaiian Department, July 20, 1942, RG 389, Provost Marshal's Office Records, copy in ibid. The memorandum was based on a draft.

79. Ibid.

80. E[rnest] J. King, Commander-in-Chief, U.S. Fleet, and G[eorge] C. Marshall, Chief of Staff, "Memorandum for the President," July 15, 1942, on which is written, "OK, F.D.R." Copy in Japanese Evacuation, FDRL4, JIR.

81. Kendall J. Fielder, Assistant Chief of Staff, G-2 to Chief, Military Intelligence Service, August 17, 1942, folder 67, JIR. As of early January, this group was still being held in North Carolina. (Gustaf Olson, Vice Consul to Col. Erik de Laval, Royal Legation of Sweden, January 4, 1943, RG 407, copy in folder 343, JIR.)

82. Conn et al., *Guarding the United States,* 214.

83. Emmons, paraphrase of radiogram dated October 2, 1942, in Daniels, ed., *American Concentration Camps.*

84. Marshall, paraphrase of secret War Dept. radiogram, October 7, 1942, copy in Folder A-16, JIR; also in Daniels, ed., *American Concentration Camps.*

85. Diary of Thomas H. Green, October 1, 1942, October 3, 1942, Green Papers, JAGSL.

86. Memorandum from Maj. G. S. Eckhardt, Chief, Central Pacific Section, OPD to Col. Scobey, executive to Assistant Secretary of War, "Japanese Problem in Hawaii," October 21, 1942, Folder A-21, JIR.

87. Stimson to Roosevelt, October 28, 1942, FDR Papers, War Department File, FDRL; Copy also in Folder A-22, JIR. See also Michi Weglyn, *Years of Infamy: The Untold Story of America's Concentration Camps,* updated ed. (Seattle: University of Washington Press, 1996), 87–89nn23–30.

88. White House Memorandum initialed "F.D.R.," November 2, 1942, Folder A-22, JIR.

89. General Delos Emmons to Secretary Henry Stimson, November 2, 1942, Folder A-22, JIR.

90. This quotation as to the program's intentions and details is taken from a December 1942 report written by Edwin Arnold, who was sent by the War Relocation Authority to Hawai'i. (Memorandum from Edwin G. Arnold, Special Assistant to the Director, to Dillon S. Myer, War Relocation Authority, December 16, 1942, RG 210, NA.) The report attaches a memorandum from Capt. Blake of the Contact Office of the Military Intelligence Division of army headquarters in Honolulu to Lt. Col. Bicknell, "Review of Evacuee Transfer," December 1, 1942. According to Arnold, Blake and Bicknell, along with Col. Fielder, were responsible for the evacuation policy.

91. Blake to Bicknell, Memorandum, "Review of Evacuee Transfer," December 1, 1942, Box 3, RG 210, NA.

92. Office of the Chief of Military History, "History of G-2 Section, vol. 10 part 2 of United States Army Forces Middle Pacific and Predecessor Commands during World War II (1941–42)," 137 (HWRD).

93. Community Analysis Section, War Relocation Authority, Tule Lake Center, Newell, California, "Field Report #18: Problems Connected with Internal Security: Three Sample Interviews," Interview with the Assistant to the former Chief of Internal Security, October 26, 1943, RG 210, copy in folder 108, JIR. See infra, pp. 195ff, for further discussion of these Kibei.

94. Ibid.

95. Ibid.

96. "Consent to Internment in Family Internment Camp," RG 338, copy in folder 204, JIR.

97. Richardson to Commander in Chief, Pacific Ocean Area, "Return of Hawaiian Evacuees to Homeland," Draft Memorandum, March 18, 1945, RG 494, NA. Ogawa and Fox state that the

shipments were as follows: November 23: 107 individuals; December 28: 443 individuals; January 26: 261 individuals; March 2: 226 individuals. (Dennis M. Ogawa and Evarts C. Fox Jr., "Japanese Internment and Relocation: The Hawaii Experience," in *Japanese Americans, From Relocation to Redress,* ed. Roger Daniels, Sandra C. Taylor, Harry H. L. Kitano, and Leonard J. Arrington [Salt Lake City: University of Utah Press, 1983], 137.) These numbers total 1,037, the same number used by Michi Weglyn in *Years of Infamy,* 88.

98. WRA, Department of the Interior, *The Evacuated People: A Quantitative Description* (Washington, DC: n.p., n.d.), 206. This source reports 493 children under age 19 and 217 adult women (of whom 137 were Nisei), including 21 single women.

99. Ibid. See discussion, infra, at pp. 151–152.

100. Memo, McFadden to Bendetsen, November 19, 1942, RG 338, NA, quoted in CWRIC, *Personal Justice Denied.*

101. "Testimony of Sally Tsuneishi at the L.A. Reparations Hearing," quoted in Patricia (Kirita) Nomura, ed., untitled [book on experiences of Hawaiians incarcerated in Jerome, Arkansas, n.d., but probably 1985].

102. Ibid. For other firsthand accounts of internment, see Gail Honda, ed., *Family Torn Apart: The Internment Story of the Otokichi Muin Ozaki Family* (Honolulu: Japanese Cultural Center of Hawai'i, 2012), and Soga, *Life behind Barbed Wire.* See also collections of oral histories in JIR and JCCH.

103. This later program, which had the same intent and much the same practical impact on Kibei and their families, is discussed infra, pp. 152ff. Other firsthand accounts of internment are in the JCCH and JIR collections.

104. Memorandum from Edwin G. Arnold, Special Assistant to the Director, to Dillon S. Myer, War Relocation Authority, 16 December 1942, RG 210, NA. Taylor, who was virulently anti-Japanese, was Acting U.S. Attorney for the District of Hawai'i.

105. Robert W. Horton, Special Assistant to the Secretary, to Ickes, May 1, 1943, copy in McCloy Files, NA.

106. "Removal of Isle Japanese Urged by J.A. Balch," *Hawaii Times,* January 18, 1943, p. 1.

107. Ibid.; see also "Japanese Peril to Future of Hawaii, Balch Contends," *Honolulu Star-Bulletin,* June 24, 1943, p. 1.

108. Memorandum from Edward Hickey to James Rowe Jr., "Memorandum for Mr. Rowe: Summary of Taylor Memorandum on Internal Situation in Hawaii," April 3, 1943, Papers of James Rowe Jr., FDRL.

109. Memorandum from James Rowe Jr. to Francis Biddle, "Memorandum for the Attorney General: The Japanese in Hawaii," April 10, 1943, Papers of James Rowe Jr., FDRL.

110. Summary of FBI Reply to Angus Taylor's Memorandum. Despite the lack of evidence of sabotage, Emmons himself remained concerned, in spring 1943, as to the possibilities of Japanese sabotage of water and food supplies. (Robert W. Horton, Special Assistant to the Secretary, to Ickes, May 1, 1943, RG 107, McCloy Papers, NA.)

111. McCloy had special reference to the litigation that was then ongoing in Judge Metzger's court over habeas corpus hearings. (John McCloy, *Diaries,* entry of September 17, 1943, John J. McCloy Papers, Amherst College.)

112. Knox to Roosevelt, August 19, 1942, FDRL (copy in Folder FDRL-5, JIR).

113. Ibid.

114. Kendall J. Fielder, December 14, 1942, RG 338, NA.

115. Fielder, "Democracy and Military Necessity in Hawaii," address to University of Hawaii Convocation, April 15, 1943, 7–8, quoted in Lind, *Hawaii's Japanese,* 76–77.

116. Reported in letter from Joseph R. Farrington to Riley Allen, March 8, 1943, Delegate Farrington Papers, HSA.

117. Col. Kenneth Fielder, memorandum to OMG, November 21, 1943, describing the Navy Intelligence officer's recommendations, RG 494, NA.

118. Fielder, ibid.

119. Edwin Arnold, Memorandum from Edwin G. Arnold, Special Assistant to Myer, 16 December 1942, RG 210, NA.

120. Radiogram No. 954, Emmons to Provost Marshal General, June 21, 1942, copy in Folder A-18, JIR.

121. OPD 014.31, July 16, 1942 (Paraphrase of Outgoing Message), Copy in Folder A-18, JIR. The navy also opposed repatriation of Japanese from Hawai'i. (James Forrestal to Secretary of State, August 5, 1942, copy in Folder A-18, JIR.)

122. McCloy to Commanding General, Hawaiian Department, December 30, 1942, copy in Folder A-23, JIR.

123. As early as November 1942, military officials were suggesting that separate camps might have to be constructed on the mainland for Hawaiian evacuees, but this idea apparently gained little traction because of the costs involved and the delays in timing of evacuations. (Memorandum from Col. William Scobey to Dillon S. Myer, Director, War Relocation Authority, December 31, 1942, RG 210, NA.)

124. Memorandum from Jerome Relocation Center to Charles Ernst, Project Director at Central Utah Relocation Center, February 26, 1943, RG 210, NA.

125. Myer to McCloy, February 27, 1943, in Daniels, ed., *American Concentration Camps.* Question 28 asked those being held in the WRA camps if they would swear unqualified allegiance to the United States and forswear allegiance to the Japanese emperor or any foreign government. See infra, pp. 171ff.

126. Paul Taylor to Myer, February 28, 1943, and attachment, "Hawaiian Evacuees," RG 210, NA.

127. Myer to McCloy, February 27, 1943, in Daniels, ed., *American Concentration Camps.*

128. Conn et al., *Guarding the United States,* 214.

129. WRA, *The Evacuated People,* 206. The reduced, but apparently unwelcome, flow of new evacuees throughout 1943 led Dillon Myer of WRA to complain to OMG in 1944: "At the present time, we find it very undesirable to accept additional residents at the Tule Lake Segregation Center," and he requested that the OMG discourage voluntary evacuees from applying for family reunification in mainland WRA centers. (Memorandum from Dillon S. Myer, Director, War Relocation Authority, to Brig. Gen. William R. C. Morrison, January 20, 1944, RG 494, NA.)

130. Gustaf W. Olson to Col. Erik de Laval (Legation of Sweden, Washington, DC), June 19, 1943, file JDRO-1, JIR.

131. See infra, chaps. 13 and 14, for discussion of legal challenges and the controversy over habeas petitions. See chaps. 11 and 12 for discussion of political challenges leading to termination of martial law.

132. Richardson to McCloy, February 2, 1944, copy in folder A-30, JIR.

133. Memorandum from Myer to Morrison, January 20, 1944, RG 494, NA.

134. John Hall, Office of Asst. Secretary of War McCloy, to Commanding General, Central Pacific, February 2, 1944, McCloy Files, NA.

135. Recorded telephone conversation between Lt. Col. Slatterly and Col. Morrison in Hawaii, 1345–1400, August 25, 1944, McCloy Files, NA.

136. Richardson to McCloy, February 10, 1944, McCloy Files. For more on Richardson's attitude toward the courts, see infra, pp. 214, 264ff.

137. Richardson to McCloy, June 16, 1944, copy in Rosenman Papers, "Hawaii file," Box 9, FDRL.

138. McCloy to Richardson, Radio W27874, September 1, 1944, McCloy Files, NA.

139. Executive Order No. 9489, October 18, 1944, 9 Fed. Reg. 12831, reprinted in Anthony, *Hawaii under Army Rule,* 134.

140. Memorandum to Brig. Gen. William R. C. Morrison from Maj. Robert B. Griffith, "Exclusion Procedure in the Territory of Hawaii Military Area," November 13, 1945, RG 494, NA. Public Proclamation Number One is reproduced in Anthony, *Hawaii under Army Rule,* 135. Richardson's proclamation was modeled closely on documents solicited from the Western Defense Command and Eastern Defense Command that were used in the mass removal of the ethnic Japanese from the West Coast and selected areas in the eastern United States. (Memorandum from Maj. Chas. A. Middleton to Col. William R. C. Morrison, "Individual Exclusion Order Procedure," September 11, 1944 [forwarding two copies of Individual Exclusion Order Procedure, Headquarters Western Defense Command and Fourth Army, as of September 1, 1942], RG 494, NA.) N.B. On July 21, 1944, the Office of Military Governor became the Office of Internal Security. (General Orders No. 63, reprinted in Anthony, *Hawaii under Army Rule,* 183.)

141. "Dual Citizens Selected for Exclusion from Territory of Hawaii Military Area," October 23, 1944, RG 494, NA.

142. Office of Internal Security, Territory of Hawaii, "Wartime Security Controls in Hawaii," Part Four, 197–199, Box 24, Richardson Papers, Hoover Institution.

143. "Sailing List of Seventy-One Hawaiian Excludees," November 8, 1944, RG 494, NA.

144. Memorandum from Dillon S. Myer to Assistant Secretary of War Davidson Sommers, August 3, 1945, RG 494, NA; Office of Internal Security, Territory of Hawai'i, "Wartime Security Controls in Hawaii," Part Four, 176–177, Box 24, Richardson Papers, Hoover Institution. Sixty-seven excludees were in the first group, with an additional six arriving in July 1945.

145. Headquarters Central Pacific Base Command, Office of the Assistant Chief of Staff for Military Intelligence, Counter Intelligence Division, *Weekly Counter Intelligence Division Summary, re: Period ending 24 March,* dated March 24, 1945 (marked "Confidential"), RG 338, NA.

146. Ibid.

Chapter 9: Determining Loyalty

1. See, among other sources, Yukiko Kimura, *Issei: Japanese Immigrants in Hawaii* (Honolulu: University of Hawai'i Press, 1988); Dennis M. Ogawa, *Kodomo no tame ni: For the Sake of the Children* (Honolulu: University of Hawai'i Press, 1978); and Yasutaro (Keiho) Soga, *Life behind Barbed Wire: The World War II Internment Memoirs of a Hawai'i Issei* (Honolulu: University of Hawai'i Press, 2008). For an interesting discussion of identity and the different reactions to the war within the Hirabayashi family, one of whose members refused to comply with orders against Japanese Americans and appealed his case to the Supreme Court, see James A. Hirabayashi, "Four Hirabayashi Cousins: A Question of Identity," in *Nikkei in the Pacific Northwest: Japanese Americans and Japanese Canadians in the Twentieth Century,* ed. Louis Fiset and Gail M. Nomura

(Seattle: University of Washington Press, 2005), 146–170. Although the family was not from Hawaiʻi, the issues they confronted transcended specific locales.

2. See infra, pp. 163ff. Although it does not deal specifically with Hawaiʻi, a detailed discussion of attempts to determine the loyalty of the Nikkei can be found in Eric Muller, *American Inquisition: The Hunt for Japanese American Disloyalty in World War II* (Chapel Hill: University of North Carolina Press, 2007). Defining "loyalty" is a challenging exercise in any event, whatever the target group under suspicion; and in fact, on the mainland, the authorities in charge of internment used professional psychologists to classify evidences of loyalty and disloyalty in what became an elaborate pseudo-scientific exercise, the impact of which, Muller shows, carried over to the postwar period of the loyalty oaths and McCarthyism. Muller calls the government loyalty machinery "a system of legalized racial oppression"; Fiset and Nomura (*Nikkei in the Pacific Northwest,* 10) refer to the treatment of Japanese Americans as "oppressive legalized racism and discrimination."

3. Radiogram, Adams (War Department) to CG Fort Shafter, TH, December 10, 1941. (*Exhibit "B," Admitted December 7, 1952, Case No. 730, U.S. District Court, Dist. of Hawaii*), RG 21, NASB.

4. Radiogram, Adams (War Department), for Gullion, to CG Fort Shafter, TH, December 11,1941. (*Exhibit "C," Admitted December 7, 1952, Case No. 730, US District Court, Dist. of Hawaii*), RG 21, NASB. Emphasis added.

5. Walker interview, 1–6, Folder 397, JIR.

6. "Hawaiian Department Alien Processing Center," undated report, author unknown, from Records of the U.S. Army Command 1942–, Military Government of Hawaii, Office of Internal Security, Research and Historical Section, RG 338, NA., copy in Folder S-16, JIR. Hereinafter cited as "Hawaiian Department Alien Processing Center." This report contains details of what was involved in "processing," i.e., forms to be filled out, data to be collected, fingerprinting, photographing, etc. See also Office of the Chief of Military History, "Civil Affairs," 3086.

7. "Hawaiian Department Alien Processing Center." See also E. E. Walker to Provost Marshal M. L. Craig, Hawaiian Department, "Coordinated Plan for the Handling of All Persons Detained or Captured in the Hawaiian Department," January 29, 1942, RG 338, copy in folder 187, JIR.

8. "Draft Memorandum for Director, Security and Investigations Division, OPMG, Thru Military Clearance Branch, Subject: Hawaiian Japanese," no date, but handwritten notation, given to Roper by phone, July 11 [1945], copy in Folder 387, JIR; Office of the Chief of Military History, "History of G-2 Section, vol. 10 part 2 of United States Army Forces Middle Pacific and Predecessor Commands during World War II (1941–42)," 24 (HWRD). In the interest of readability, and because the great majority of detainees were male, the authors generally use the male pronoun rather than "he or she," but the same procedures applied to the relatively few women who were detained.

9. Ibid., 6–8.

10. Ibid., 8–9.

11. Office of the Chief of Military History, "Civil Affairs," 3086.

12. Gary Y. Okihiro, *Cane Fires: The Anti-Japanese Movement in Hawaii, 1865–1945* (Philadelphia: Temple University Press, 1991), 245–246.

13. Control of Civilian Internees and Prisoners of War in the Central Pac. Area, n.d., OMG, RG 338, copy in folder 212, JIR.

14. See listing of board members in "Hawaiian Department Alien Processing Center." The contemporary author Gwenfread Allen reported the boards were civilian (*Hawaii's War Years, 1941–1945* [Honolulu: University of Hawaiʻi Press, 1950], 135), but in fact, the case files of hearings

(in RG 338) show that military officers actively participated. According to the official history of the G-2 Section, "Each person was brought before a hearing board made up of representatives from the CIC, the FBI, and the ONI. If this board decided that someone should be interned, his case was placed before a Civilian Hearing Board made up of two army officers and three civilians. Its recommendations were reviewed by the Intelligence Review Board. . . ." (Office of the Chief of Military History, "History of G-2 Section, vol. 10 part 2," 24.)

15. Case of S. U., Minutes of the Military Governor's Reviewing Board, June 1943, RG 338, NA. Initials used to protect individual's privacy.

16. Shivers to Director, FBI, December 17, 1941, "Custodial Detention," FBI File 100–2-20.

17. "Deposition of Delos Emmons," May 18, 1949 deposition, San Francisco, examined by A. L. Wirin and Col. Hughes. Records of U.S. District Court for Hawaii, Zimmerman Civil Suit File, NASB.

18. Ibid., Testimony of December 8, 1950.

19. Control of Civilian Internees and Prisoners of War, JIR; "Hawaiian Department Alien Processing Center," JIR.

20. "Hawaiian Department Alien Processing Center," JIR; Office of Internal Security, Territory of Hawaii, "Wartime Security Controls in Hawaii," Part Four, 110–111, Box 24, Richardson Papers, Hoover Institution.

21. Ibid., 112.

22. Quoted in Allen, *Hawaii's War Years,* 135.

23. Control of Civilian Internees and Prisoners of War in the Central Pacific Area, RG 338, copy in folder 212, JIR.

24. Affidavit of Carl Armfeld, reported by Fulton Lewis Jr., November 15, 1945; transcript of Fulton Lewis Jr. broadcast in Green Papers, JAGSL.

25. Allen, *Hawaii's War Years,* 135.

26. Samuel Wilder King to Edward J. Ennis, August 24, 1943, King Papers, HSA.

27. Walker interview, 9, JIR; "Hawaiian Department Alien Processing Center."

28. Walker interview, 12, JIR.

29. Control of Civilian Internees, JIR.

30. Soga, *Life behind Barbed Wire,* 43.

31. Testimony by Mitsunobu Miyahira in CWIRC, *Personal Justice Denied.*

32. Interview with Minosuke Hanabusa, folder 234, JIR.

33. Testimony of Kwantoku Goya, in CWIRC, *Personal Justice Denied.*

34. "Summaries of the Activities of Persons of Japanese Ancestry, since Arriving on the Mainland after Evacuation from Hawaii, Who Are Now Residing at the Tule Lake Center, Newell, California," July 2, 1945, RG 210, NA.

35. U.S. Congress, Joint Committee on the Investigation of the Pearl Harbor Attack, 79th Cong., 1st and 2nd sess., 1946, part 35, p. 570, quoted in Allen, *Hawaii's War Years,* 134.

36. These lists of adverse and positive factors are drawn from the authors' investigation of scores of cases of internees, reported in the Minutes of the Internee Review Board, Military Governor's Reviewing Board, June 1943–December 1944, RG 338, NA. The Review Board documentation summarizes the findings of earlier interviews and hearings. Quotation is from the case of a branch manager of a Japanese language newspaper, who had a son in the army; he was paroled on the mainland after being interned for eighteen months.

37. Professor Okihiro came to the same conclusions on the basis of his examination of an unspecified number of internee case files. Okihiro, *Cane Fires*, 245.

38. Cases of M. M., M. F., and T. M., summaries attached to Memorandum from Major Louis F. Springer to Colonel Morrison, Executive, "Interned American Citizens of Japanese Ancestry," December 31, 1943, Box 26, Richardson Papers, Hoover Institution.

39. Lt. Col. Eugene J. Fitz Gerald to Green, February 13, 1942, RG 338, NA.

40. Green to Fitz Gerald, February 18, 1942, RG 338, NA.

41. Memorandum from Green to Fitz Gerald, "Subject: Disloyal Citizens," February 17, 1942, RG 338, NA.

42. Thomas H. Green to Provost Marshal, Hawaiian Department, Fort Shafter, T.H., "Instructions Governing Release or Parole of Detainees," May 30, 1942, RG 338, NA.

43. Office of Chief of Military History, "Civil Affairs," 3089.

44. Memorandum from E. H. Bryan, "Factors to Be Considered in Investigations of Japanese Subjects," February 25, 1943, File 56.05, HWRD.

45. Ibid. Emphasis added.

46. Manual prepared for persons attached to the District Intelligence Office, Fourteenth Naval District, RG 389, NA. The manual bears no date, but its internal references to the earlier manual and to events and memoranda make it likely that it was issued in August 1943. [Hereinafter cited as "Navy DIO manual, August 1943."]

47. In fact, transcripts of various interrogations that led to internment decisions that we have examined in course of this research are riddled with stereotyping of precisely the sort that the navy's manual expresses.

48. The manual's authors also relied upon Hearn for a long discussion of the patriarchal structure of the Japanese family, and for assertions as to the allegedly unwavering deference of Japanese youth to their elders. The manual did, however, acknowledge the increasing disintegration of Japanese family patterns, particularly in the urban areas, and a certain degree of role reversal between the Nisei and their Issei parents after the beginning of the war. (Navy DIO manual, August 1943.)

49. Navy DIO Manual, August 1943, 60. Emphasis added.

50. Ibid., 52.

51. Interview with Iwao Kasaka, File 237, JIR.

52. See, for example, Case of M. F., August 5, 1943; Case of R. N., December 9, 1943; Case of K. H., December 16, 1943, all in Minutes of the Meeting of the Internee Review Board, April 1944–August 1944, RG 338, NA. Initials used to protect privacy of individuals.

53. Greg Robinson, *By Order of the President: FDR and the Internment of Japanese Americans* (Cambridge, MA: Harvard University Press, 2001), 182. "There isn't such a thing as a loyal Japanese and it is just impossible to determine their loyalty by investigation—it just can't be done," DeWitt told the Provost Marshal General. (Telephone transcript January 14, 1943, quoted in Muller, *American Inquisition*, 33.) DeWitt was notorious for his public statement "A Jap is a Jap," with regard to the alleged danger posed by the Nikkei on the West Coast.

54. Memorandum from Major Louis F. Springer to Colonel Morrison, Executive, "Interned American Citizens of Japanese Ancestry," December 31, 1943, Box 26, Richardson Papers, Hoover Institution.

55. Provost Court Judges in Conference Transcript.

56. Richardson to McCloy, February 2, 1944, in Roger Daniels, ed., *American Concentration Camps,* vol. 8: *Japanese of Hawaii* (New York: Garland Publishing, 1989).

57. R. W. Flournoy to Hackworth, Disloyal Japanese Americans: Proposed Measures for Their Expatriation and Deportation, Conference with Colonel King and Colonel Slattery, September 6, 1944, Box 148, Record Group 494, NA.

58. Office of Internal Security, Territory of Hawaii, "Wartime Security Controls in Hawaii," Part One, 10, Box 24, Richardson Papers, Hoover Institution.

59. Memorandum from Major Louis F. Springer to Colonel Morrison, Executive, "Interned American Citizens of Japanese Ancestry," December 31, 1943, and Louis F. Springer, "Review of Cases by the Military Governor's Reviewing Board," February 17, 1944, Box 26, Richardson Papers, Hoover Institution.

60. Memorandum for Chief, Japanese American Branch, Office of the Provost Marshal General, from Captain Stanley D. Arnold, "Hawaiian-Japanese," June 4, 1945, RG 389, NA. Emphasis added.

61. When the army called for Nisei volunteers in 1943, 40 percent of Nisei men between the ages of 18 and 35 tried to register. Of the nearly 32,200 men inducted in Hawai'i by the Selective Service, half were Nisei. (Allen, *Hawaii's War Years,* 263–273.) Of the 2,000–3,000 Nisei used in Army Intelligence as translators, 40 percent were from Hawai'i. (Dorothy Ochiai Hazama and Jane Okamoto Komeiji, *Okage Sama De: The Japanese in Hawai'i, 1885–1985* [Honolulu, HI: Bess Press, 1986], 167.)

62. The report, approved September 14, 1942, is quoted in CWRIC, *Personal Justice Denied,* chap. 7.

63. CWRIC, *Personal Justice Denied,* chap. 7.

64. Ibid. See also Robinson, *By Order of the President,* 163–169.

65. Memo for the record, Office of Provost Marshal General, January 9, 1943, quoted in CWRIC, *Personal Justice Denied,* chap. 7.

66. U.S. Department of the Interior, War Relocation Authority, *Impounded People: Japanese Americans in Relocation Centers* (Washington, DC: Government Printing Office, 1946), 100.

67. Donald E. Collins, *Native American Aliens: Disloyalty and the Renunciation of Citizenship by Japanese Americans during World War II* (Westport, CT: Greenwood Press, 1985), chap. 3; Dillon S. Myer, *Uprooted Americans: The Japanese Americans and the War Relocation Authority during World War II* (Tucson: University of Arizona Press, 1971), 71–72; CWRIC, *Personal Justice Denied,* chap. 7; Robinson, *By Order of the President,* 168–169; Tetsuden Kashima, *Judgment without Trial: Japanese American Imprisonment during World War II* (Seattle: University of Washington Press, 2003), 161; Muller, *American Inquisition,* chap. 5.

68. For further discussion of these issues, see sources cited in previous note.

69. Myer, *Uprooted Americans,* 72.

70. CWRIC, *Personal Justice Denied,* chap. 7.

71. War Relocation Authority, "Summaries of the Activities of Persons of Japanese Ancestry, Since Arriving on the Mainland after Evacuation from Hawaii, Who Are Not Residing at Tule Lake Center, Newell, California, April 24, 1945," Box 280, RG 210, NA.

72. Ibid. We have used initials rather than names to protect the privacy of individuals.

73. Minoru Kiyota, *Beyond Loyalty: The Story of a Kibei* (Honolulu: University of Hawai'i Press, 1997), 97. Although Kiyota was from the mainland, his conflicted feelings undoubtedly prevailed among many of the Kibei from Hawai'i as well.

74. Interview of Takejiro Higa, "The Hawai'i Nisei Story: Americans of Japanese Ancestry During World War II," University of Hawai'i, 2006–2007, http://nisei.hawaii.edu/page/home. Higa, it should be noted, was not interned, but the conflicted feelings he expressed likely pertained to many Kibei of draft age, however loyal. Higa had left Japan to avoid conscription into the Japanese Army, but he nonetheless chose to volunteer for the U.S. Army. He served in Military Intelligence.

75. War Relocation Authority, "Summaries of the Activities of Persons of Japanese Ancestry, Since Arriving on the Mainland after Evacuation from Hawaii, Who Are Not Residing at Tule Lake Center, Newell, California, April 24, 1945," Box 280, RG 210, NA.

76. See "Kibei Hearings," Final Report: Manzanar Relocation Center, vol. 1, Bancroft Library, UC Berkeley.

77. CWRIC, *Personal Justice Denied,* chap. 7; Myer, *Uprooted Americans,* 73.

78. Ibid. Of the total, 5,300 answered "no," and more than 4,600 refused to answer or qualified their answer. It is noteworthy that in Hawai'i, where there had not been mass forced relocation, nearly 10,000 Nisei—about one-third of draft-age men—volunteered for the army. This expression of patriotism was in marked contrast to that of the evacuated Nisei. See Jacobus tenBroek, Edwin N. Barnhart, and Floyd W. Matson, *Prejudice, War and the Constitution* (Berkeley: University of California Press, 1968), 170 (noting that only 1,165 Nisei then in the camps, or 6 percent of all eligibles in that group, volunteered; the army had hoped for 3,500.)

79. See infra, pp. 197ff.

80. See Muller, *American Inquisition,* 36.

81. For details of the JAJB, and the dissension among its members, see Muller, *American Inquisition.*

82. "Analysis Chart of Special Questionnaire Relating to Citizens of Japanese Ancestry Who Make Application for Voluntary Induction into the Army of the United States for Service with the Combat Team," RG 389, copy in folder 276, JIR.

83. Quoted in Myer, *Uprooted Americans,* 75.

84. Myer to Stimson, June 8, 1943, quoted in Myer, *Uprooted Americans,* 173.

85. Ibid., 76.

86. War Relocation Authority, "Summaries of the Activities of Persons of Japanese Ancestry, Since Arriving on the Mainland after Evacuation from Hawaii, Who Are Not Residing at Tule Lake Center, Newell, California, April 24, 1945," Box 280, RG 210, NA.

87. The total of 340 included 165 single persons and 155 in family groups; 327 (260 males and 67 females) were Nisei. Myer to Farrington, November 22, 1943, Box 280, RG 210, NA.

88. "Segregant Population of Tule Lake as of July 1944 by Area of Pre-War (1 December 1941) Residence Compared to 1940 Census of Japanese, and by Place from Which Segregated," WDC-CAD-Research Branch, September 4, 1944, copy in JAERR files, Reel # 170, Bancroft Library, UC Berkeley.

89. Case of S. K., June 22, 1944, Minutes of the Meeting of the Internee Review Board, April 1944–August 1944, RG 338, NA. Initials used to protect the privacy of individuals.

90. War Relocation Authority, "Summaries of the Activities of Persons of Japanese Ancestry, since Arriving on the Mainland after Evacuation from Hawaii, Who Are Now residing at Tule Lake Center, Newell, California, July 2, 1945," Box 280, RG 210, NA; records of affidavits in Wayne Collins Papers, Bancroft Library, UC Berkeley.

91. "Minutes of the Meetings of the Internee Review Board, June 1943–April 1944," Box 327, RG 338, NA. In three of the fifteen decisions documented in these Minutes, the board was willing

to grant parole on the explicit condition: "if no resentment shown"! (Ibid.) Reviewers cited "evasiveness" as sufficient reason for an adverse finding in many of the several dozens of individual loyalty review files for 1943 and 1944 that the authors have examined.

92. Case of F. K., June 15, 1944, Minutes of the Meetings of the Internee Review Board, June 1944, Box 328, RG 338, NA. Initials used to protect privacy of individuals.

93. Interview with Iwao Kasaka, File 237, JIR.

94. "Minutes of the Meetings of the Internee Review Board, June 1943–April 1944," RG 338, NA.

95. Eric Muller provides an informative discussion of the theoretical and practical perplexities associated with loyalty assessment. Minimal fairness, he states, requires "a welter of information about an individual's past conduct, environment, and psychology. Hinging a prediction of a person's future risk of dangerous or illegal behavior on one or two rudimentary facts about him is unthinkable. And when those facts are a person's ancestry and cultural practices and ties, the prediction is uniquely dangerous. . . . Focus on a person's ancestry and cultural practices is far more likely to corrupt an inquiry into his loyalty and dangerousness than to enhance it." (Muller, *American Inquisition,* 143–144.)

96. "Hawaiian Department Alien Processing Center," RG 338, NA, quoted in Okihiro, *Cane Fires,* 245.

97. Minutes of Meetings of the Internee Review Board, June 1943–April 1944, RG 338, NA. Emphasis added.

98. Case of M. O., June 26, 1944, Minutes of Meetings of the Internee Review Board, June 1944, RG 338, NA. Initials used to protect privacy of individuals.

99. Slattery to Military Governor's Reviewing Board, June 15, 1944, Subject: Consideration of the cases of B. B. . . . and A. B. . . . and proposal to grant rehearings to Internees in Hawaii, RG 338, NA. Initials used to protect privacy of individuals.

100. Ibid.

101. Deposition of Gen. Delos Emmons, taken at San Francisco, May 18, 1949, in *Zimmerman v. Poindexter et al.,* in Box 157, Case Files for the U.S. District Court for the District and Territory of Hawaii, NASB [hereinafter Zimmerman Civil Suit File]. See infra, pp. 253ff., for discussion of trial.

102. Ibid.

103. Bicknell, "Security Measures in Hawaii," chap. 5, 73, HWRD.

104. MID report, February 11, 1942, in Minutes of the Meetings of the Internee Review Board, April 1944–August 1944, RG 338, NA. Emphasis added.

105. MID memo, September 17, 1943, ibid.

106. May 18, 1944, report on review, ibid.

107. Emmons deposition in *Zimmerman v. Poindexter et al.,* Zimmerman Civil Suit File, NASB. In the 1943–1944 board review of earlier decisions on individual internees, we have found in our examination of summaries of action as well as of individual files that at least a fourth of the favorable initial recommendations had been overridden by the military and intelligence officers who made final recommendations to the commanding general to continue incarceration.

108. These factual statements and others that we have given with regard to the procedures and decisions on loyalty are based, unless otherwise specifically noted, upon our examination of scores of individual files in the intelligence and army records held in the National Archives and the Bancroft Library, UC Berkeley, and material in the Japanese Cultural Center of Hawaiʻi collections.

109. War Relocation Authority, *The Evacuated People,* 192. Of the 136 from Hawai'i in the WRA camps who requested transfer to Japan, 125 were evacuees, 10 were excludees, and 1 had been released and was on parole. Allen gives the *total* number of those from Hawai'i who requested repatriation to Japan as 248. (Allen, *Hawaii's War Years,* 141.) Presumably, this larger number includes those who were in Department of Justice camps as well as others who were never in custody, including family members of those who elected to return to Japan. See infra, pp. 197ff., for discussion of Tule Lake and renunciation.

Chapter 10: The Fate of the Detainees

1. The Alien Enemies Act of 1798. The United States first used internment during the War of 1812, when some British citizens were removed from the coast and interned. In World War I, some 8,000 enemy aliens were arrested, of whom about 2,300, mostly German, were interned. For a concise summary, see Roger Daniels, "Internment, Wartime," *Dictionary of American History,* http://www.encyclopedia.com/doc/1G2-3401802122.html.

2. Data from R. L. Shivers to Hoover, Director, FBI, March 30, 1942, FBI File No. 100-2-20. Summarized in Tetsuden Kashima, *Judgment without Trial: Japanese American Imprisonment during World War II* (Seattle: University of Washington Press, 2003), 78.

3. See supra, pp. 140–143.

4. Shivers to Director, FBI, "Custodial Detention," December 17, 1941.

5. Office of the Chief of Military History, "Civil Affairs," 3090.

6. A. M. Tollefson, Provost Marshal General's Office, "Persons Evacuated from the Territory of Hawaii Military Area Presently Residing on the Mainland," October 9, 1945, RG 494, NA. See p. 373n24 supra re discrepancy of statistics.

7. JCCH, "Never Again," 7.

8. Louis F. Springer, "Treatment of Japanese Civilian Internees at Sand Island," no date, but in response to Cablegram of December 23, 1942, from the Japanese Imperial Government to the U.S. government through the Swedish Legation, available at http://www.hawaiiinternment .org/static/downloads/rb_section2.pdf.

9. Otokichi Ozaki, Radio Script, "Memories of Four Years Behind Barbed Wire: Body Searches," original Japanese in Otokichi Ozaki's Archival Collection, AR1, Box 4, Folder 8, script #5, JCCH, translation published in Gail Honda, ed., *Family Torn Apart: The Internment Story of the Otokichi Muin Ozaki Family* (Honolulu: Japanese Cultural Center of Hawai'i, 2012), 19–20.

10. Affidavit of Carl Arnfeld [Armfelt], in radio broadcast by Fulton Lewis Jr., November 14, 1945, transcript in Green Papers, JAGSL.

11. Yasutaro (Keiho) Soga, *Life behind Barbed Wire: The World War II Internment Memoirs of a Hawai'i Issei* (Honolulu: University of Hawai'i Press, 2008), 30.

12. Interview with Kaetsu Furuya, n.d., folder 233, JIR.

13. Various obituaries, including Dennis McLellan, "Carl Eifler, 95; Ran OSS Unit in WWII," *Los Angeles Times,* April 21, 2002. For a full biography, see Thomas N. Moon, *The Deadliest Colonel* (New York: Vantage Press, 1975).

14. Draft of form letter, March 13, 1942, and "Memorandum to Friends and Relatives of Detainees," Folder 189, JIR.

15. Concerned about the treatment of Americans being held by the Japanese, the Special Division of the U.S. State Department arranged a series of visits to detention centers by the

International Red Cross to demonstrate that Japanese and Japanese-American internees being held by the United States were being well treated. (P. Scott Corbett, *Quiet Passages: The Exchange of Civilians between the United States and Japan during the Second World War* [Kent, OH: Kent State University Press, 1987], 113.)

16. Report of M. J. Sulzer, International Red Cross Committee, transmitted to the Office of Military Governor, March 31, 1943, copy in RG 338, NA. Copy in French, "Revue Internationale de la Croix-Rouge, Mars 1943," in Folder 220, JIR. The fact that Sulzer specified the white races—presumably Italian and German detainees—may imply that the Japanese were not as well treated as the others. [Hereinafter Sulzer Report.]

17. See, for example, Doris Berg Nye's account, "Internment of a German-American Family in Hawaii," available at www.gaic.info/real_berg.html; and Kelly Y. Nakamura, "Kazuo Miyamoto," *Densho Encyclopedia,* http:// http://encyclopedia.densho.org/Kazuo_Miyamoto/. The diminished likelihood of an invasion by Japan following the U.S. victory at Midway in June 1942 undoubtedly contributed to the relaxation of the conditions imposed at Sand Island.

18. Springer, "Treatment of Japanese Civilian Internees at Sand Island."

19. Sulzer Report, March 31, 1943, RG 338, NA.

20. Soga, *Life behind Barbed Wire,* 226.

21. In all, seventeen sites were used to confine the detainees. For a complete listing of the sites, as well as a proposal to include Honouliuli in the National Park system, see National Park Service, "Honouliuli Gulch and Associated Sites, Draft Special Resource Study and Environmental Assessment, May 2014" (Washington, DC: U.S. Department of the Interior, 2014). In 2009, Congress authorized the National Parks Service to undertake a study of Honouliuli and other World War II internment sites in Hawaii to determine their suitability for inclusion in the National Park System. This draft report, issued for comments in May 2014, is the result of that study. [Hereinafter, National Park Service, *Honouliuli Gulch.*] See infra, p. 188, for designation of Honouliuli as a National Monument.

22. George Hoshida, "Life of a Japanese Immigrant Boy in Hawaiian America: From Birth Through World War II, 1907–1945" (ms., JCCH Resource Center, n.d.). Hoshida produced hundreds of watercolors and drawings that document his experience as an internee as he was transferred from Kilauea to Sand Island, and then to Department of Justice camps at Lordsburg and Santa Fe, New Mexico, and finally to WRA camps in Jerome, Arkansas, where he was reunited with his family, and Gila River, Arizona. Many of his works, which were donated to the Japanese American National Museum in Los Angeles, can be viewed online at http://www.janm.org /collections/george-hoshida-collection/.

23. "Big Island [Hawai'i] Internment Sites, Kilauea Military Camp," JCCH Resource Center; Jeffery F. Burton and Mary M. Farrell, *World War II Japanese American Internment Sites in Hawai'i* (Tucson, AZ: Trans-Sierran Archaeological Research, 2007), 15.

24. Marc Peter, Delegate of the International Red Cross Committee, to Office of the Military Governor, March 31, 1943, RG 338, NA; National Park Service, *Honouliuli Gulch,* 32.

25. "An American Experiment," n.d., RG 338, JIR.

26. It appears likely that some seventy-five internees were held in Kaua'i and were later transferred to Sand Island. "Kauai Internment Sites," JCCH Resource Center.

27. National Park Service, *Honouliuli Gulch,* 32–33.

28. Ibid., 38; Sulzer Report, March 31, 1943.

29. Office of Internal Security, Territory of Hawaii, "Wartime Security Controls in Hawaii," Part Four, 102–3, Box 24, Richardson Papers, Hoover Institution.

30. According to the National Park Service Study, the move from Sand Island to Honouliuli was prompted in part to allow expansion of the Embarkation Port facilities on Sand Island. (National Park Service, *Honouliuli Gulch,* 8.)

31. Louis F. Springer, "Control of Civilian Internees and Prisoners of War in the Central Pacific Area," n.d., OMG, RG 338, copy in folder 212, JIR. For a concise history of Honouliuli, see Alan Rosenfeld, "Honouliuli," *Densho Encyclopedia,* http://encyclopedia.densho.org/Honou liuli_%28detention_facility%29/; and "The Internment Camp in West Oahu's Backyard," http:// www.hawaii.edu/malamalama/2011/10/honouliuli/.

32. For text of the proclamation, see https://www.whitehouse.gov/the-press-office/2015/02 /24/presidential-proclamation-establishment-honouliuli-national-monument. The site will be administered by the National Park Service.

33. Ibid.; Olson to de Laval, June 19, 1943, Folder 248, JIR; Springer, "Control of Civilian Internees and Prisoners of War."

34. http://archives.starbulletin.com/2004/06/02/news/story1.html.

35. Col. William C. Morrison, Executive, to Maj. Robert B. Griffith, June 3, 1943, Case of K. T., RG 338, copy in Folder 210, JIR. (Initials used to protect the privacy of individuals.) The internees' requests were handled by the Swedish consulate.

36. Office of the Chief of Military History, "Civil Affairs," 3091; Office of Internal Security, Territory of Hawaii, "Wartime Controls in Hawaii," Part Four, 152–173, Box 24, Richardson Papers, Hoover Institution.

37. Brian Niiya, "Journey to Honouliuli," April 17, 2008, http://www.discovernikkei.org/en /journal/2008/4/17/journey-to-honouliuli/. See also Soga, *Life behind Barbed Wire,* appendix 4.

38. Angus M. Taylor to Commanding General, Central Pacific Base Command, March 1, 1945, "Monthly Cumulative Report on Internees," RG 338, NA.

39. Office of Internal Security, "Statistical Data on Civilian Internees Held Within the Area of the Central Pacific Base Command," October 1, 1945, RG 338, NA.

40. Rosenfeld, "Honouliuli," *Densho Encyclopedia,* http://encyclopedia.densho.org /Honouliuli_%28detention_facility%29/.

41. The total number of U.S. citizens was 617: 570 were Nisei, 42 were naturalized citizens of German ancestry, two were naturalized citizens of Italian ancestry, and three were native-born Caucasians. (General Richardson to Adjutant General, December 4, 1945, copy in Green Papers, JAGSL.)

42. "Abe Detained in Hawaii," *New York Times,* September 8, 1942.

43. Military Governor's Reviewing Board, Case of Sanji Abe, January 20, 1944, Alien Processing Center, RG 338, Internee Case Files, AR19, Box 4, Folder 45, JCCH; copy also in Folder 219, JIR.

44. Ibid.

45. Military Governor's Reviewing Board, Case of Sanji Abe, March 2, 1944, Alien Processing Center, RG 338, Internee Case Files, AR19, Box 4, Folder 45, JCCH; copy also in Folder 219, JIR.

46. Case of Sanji Abe, copy in AR19, Box 4, Folder 45, JCCH and Folder 219, JIR.

47. See Emmons postwar testimony, cited above, p. 178.

48. See supra on "voluntary evacuees," pp. 145–148.

49. Soga, *Life behind Barbed Wire,* 53.

50. Interview with Minosuke Hanabusa, folder 234, JIR.

51. Otokichi Ozaki, Radio Script: "Life behind Barbed Wire," original Japanese in Otokichi Ozaki Archival Collection, AR1, Box 4, Folder 13, #B, JCCH, translation published in *Family Torn Apart,* ed. Honda, 66–67.

52. Otokichi Ozaki, Radio Script, "Memories of Four Years Behind Barbed Wire: Body Searches," in *Family Torn Apart,* ed. Honda, 19–20.

53. Ozaki's Archival Collection, JCCH.

54. See, for example, interviews with Hanabusa and Fukuhara, JIR.

55. Hideko Ozaki, Letter to husband, June 3, 1942, original in Otokichi Ozaki Archival Collection, AR1, Box 1, Folder 1, JCCH, reproduced in *Family Torn Apart,* ed. Honda, 90–91.

56. Hideko Ozaki, Letter to husband, January 19, 1943, original Japanese and English translation in Otokichi Ozaki's Archival Collection, AR1, Box 1, Folder 5, JCCH.

57. Reverend Naitoh's journal entries from the Gladys Naitoh Archival Collection (AR4), JCCH.

58. Transcript of Interview with Ella Tomita, Interviewed by Kalei Ho and Mika Bailey, October 14, 2004, "Voices of WWII," booklet compiled by Linda Kay Smith, copy in JCCH Resource Center. Reproduced with permission of Ms. Tomita.

59. Ibid.

60. Ibid.

61. Office of Internal Security, Territory of Hawaii, "Wartime Security Controls in Hawaii," Part Four, 132–45, Box 24, Richardson Papers, Hoover Institution; recollections of former internees and evacuees in oral histories archived in the JCCH; and letters from internees, evacuees, and family members asking for the army's or elected officials' permission to rejoin their family members. The Hawaii Command records, RG 338, NA, also contain correspondence from families seeking reunification with loved ones in the camps or incarcerated persons seeking early return to their families in Hawai'i.

62. Kashima, *Judgment without Trial,* 86. The Crystal City camp was also used to detain Latin American Japanese who were being held in the United States pending repatriation to Japan in exchange for Americans being held by the Japanese government. See Thomas Connell, *America's Japanese Hostages: The World War II Plan for a Japanese Free Latin America* (Westport, CT: Praeger, 2002), chap. 11; and Jan Jarboe Russell, *The Train to Crystal City* (New York: Scribner, 2015).

63. Records in the WRA database show 324 Kibei were held in WRA centers. See p. 373n24, supra.

64. Stanley D. Arnold to Commanding General, Western Defense Command, Third Report, Capt. Arnold, May 7, 1945, Provost Marshal General Office Records, RG 389, NA. For a description of Arnold's assignment to review the security measures involving Hawai'i Nikkei, see p. 204.

65. Office of Internal Security, Territory of Hawaii, "Wartime Security Controls in Hawaii," Part Four, 97, Box 24, Richardson Papers, Hoover Institution.

66. Office of the Chief of Military History, "Civil Affairs," 3089; Michi Weglyn, *Years of Infamy: The Untold Story of America's Concentration Camps,* updated ed. (Seattle: University of Washington Press, 1996), 88. German Americans were also forced to sign such waivers. See chap. 18 for discussion of postwar civil suits for false imprisonment.

67. "Release," RG 338, copy in Folder 205, JIR. Emphasis added.

68. Emmons deposition, San Francisco, May 18, 1949, in *Zimmerman v. Poindexter et al.,* in Box 157, Case Files for the U.S. District Court for the District and Territory of Hawaii, RG 21, NASB. In the Zimmerman case, the army backed down and withdrew its demand for the waiver.

69. Transcript, "Oral Report Made by Mr. Frederick B. Wiener, 11 May 1946" [to Maj. Gen. Moore et al.], 10, Richardson Papers, Hoover Institution [hereinafter Wiener Report]. Prisoners of war in Manchuria, including American soldiers, were subjected to slave labor and atrocities at the hands of the Japanese; it was this cruelty to which Wiener was referring in speaking of "hosts in Manchuria."

70. Chief of Military History, "Civil Affairs," 3089.

71. Hank Sato, "Honouliuli Camp," *Honolulu Star-Bulletin,* March 18, 1976, quoted in Kashima, *Judgment without Trial,* 85.

72. Edgar C. McEvoy, "Interview with a Hawaiian Kibei," Jerome Community Analyst Report No. 113, September 8, 1943, RG 210, NA, quoted in Weglyn, *Years of Infamy,* 88–89.

73. War Relocation Authority, "Summaries of the Activities of Persons of Japanese Ancestry, since Arriving on the Mainland after Evacuation from Hawaii, Who Are Not Residing at Tule Lake Center, Newell, California," April 24, 1945, Box 280, RG 210, NA.

74. Weglyn, *Years of Infamy,* 88.

75. Bicknell to Bendetsen, February 11, 1943, RG 338, NA, copy in folder 131, JIR.

76. Bendetsen to Bicknell, February 25, 1943, RG 338, NA, copy in folder 131, JIR. For a discussion of Bendetsen's role in the incarceration of persons of Japanese ancestry, see, inter alia, Peter Irons, *Justice at War: The Story of the Japanese-American Internment Cases* (New York: Oxford University Press, 1983), chaps. 1–3; and Klancy Clark de Nevers, *The Colonel and the Pacifist: Karl Bendetsen, Perry Saito, and the Incarceration of Japanese Americans during World War II* (Salt Lake City: University of Utah Press, 2004).

77. Reverend Kyojo Naitoh's Journal, Gladys Naitoh Archival Collection, AR4, Box 5, Folder 6, JCCH. Spelling has been corrected but not the grammar.

78. The history of the Tule Lake Center and the disturbances that occurred there are well documented, beginning with contemporary analyses undertaken by the WRA itself and by the University of California, Berkeley group of social scientists who studied the removal and internments. (Dorothy Swaine Thomas and Richard S. Nishimoto, *The Spoilage: Japanese-American Evacuation and Resettlement during World War II* [Berkeley: University of California Press, 1969].) A convenient recapitulation of the facts, and a concise accounting of the resistance and the renunciations, is provided in Donald E. Collins, *Native American Aliens: Disloyalty and the Renunciation of Citizenship by Japanese Americans during World War II* (Westport, CT: Greenwood Press, 1985). See also Barbara Takei, "Legalizing Detention: Segregated Japanese Americans and the Justice Department's Renunciation Program," *Journal of the Shaw Historical Library* 19 (2005): 75–105.

79. See discussion of renunciants below, pp. 198–200. On the litigation, see infra, pp. 330ff.

80. 18 U.S. Code Annotated, sec. 801 (1940), 58 Stat. 677 (amended 1944). The initiative for this legislation came from Edward Ennis, Francis Biddle, and the Department of Justice, who were eager to solve the problem of what to do with the most pro-Japanese and potentially dangerous detainees at Tule Lake after the relocation camps were closed and the exclusion order rescinded. See discussion in John Christgau, "Collins versus the World: The Fight to Restore Citizenship to Japanese American Renunciants of World War II," *Pacific Historical Review* 54 (1985): 1–31; Collins, *Native American Aliens,* 5–6 and passim; Takei, "Legalizing Detention"; and see Jacobus tenBroek, Edwin N. Barnhart, and Floyd W. Matson, *Prejudice, War and the Constitution* (Berkeley: University of California Press, 1968), 315–317.

81. Takei, "Legalizing Detention," 88–89.

82. Copies of relevant administrative correspondence reflecting the confusion are in Reels 170 and 171, JAERR files, Bancroft Library. See especially WRA Director [Myer] to H. Coverley, Project Director, Tule Lake Relocation Center, February 26, 1943; id. to id., February 27, 1946 (stating: "I am sorry we got you out on a limb regarding the arrests"); see also Myer, *Uprooted Americans,* 72–80; and, for an account critical of the administrators' actions, on the intensive cycle of tense confrontations later in 1943 that culminated in the army's declaring martial law in the Center, Thomas and Nishimoto, *The Spoilage,* 113–146.

83. Harry L. Black (former Assistant Project Director, Tule Lake Center), Affidavit, [1946], reprinted in Collins, *Native American Aliens,* 136.

84. Biddle Cabinet Notes, Papers of Francis Biddle, FDRL.

85. McGrath v. Abo, 186 F.2nd 766 at 768. See also tenBroek et al., *Prejudice, War, and the Constitution,* 316–321. See infra, pp. 331ff., for discussion of the Ninth Circuit case.

86. A full discussion of the registration campaign, and the resistance to it, sparked by the resentment and confusion engendered by the notorious questionnaire with its Questions 27 and 28, is provided in Eric Muller, *American Inquisition: The Hunt for Japanese American Disloyalty in World War II* (Chapel Hill: University of North Carolina Press, 2007), 31–106.

87. Paul A. Taylor to Myer, with attachment, "Hawaiian Evacuees," February 28, 1943, RG 210, copy in AR19, Box 9, Folder 7, JCCH.

88. Thomas and Nishimoto, *The Spoilage,* chap. 6 (on martial law imposed from November 13, 1943, to January 15, 1944); tenBroek et al., *Prejudice, War and the Constitution,* 164–166.

89. Dillon S. Myer, *Uprooted Americans: The Japanese Americans and the War Relocation Authority during World War II* (Tucson: University of Arizona Press, 1971), 243–244.

90. Ibid., 63. Myer incorrectly refers to the Japanese-American leader as Kurihari. For more on Kurihara, see his autobiography, an unpublished typescript, in JAERR, Bancroft Library, UC Berkeley; Eileen Tamura, "Joe Kurihara," *Densho Encyclopedia,* http://encyclopedia.densho.org /Joe_Kurihara/; and Eileen Tamura, *In Defense of Justice: Joseph Kurihara and the Japanese American Struggle for Equality* (Urbana-Champaign: University of Illinois Press, 2013).

91. Community Analysis Section, War Relocation Authority, Tule Lake Center, Newell, California, "Field Report #18: Problems Connected with Internal Security: Three Sample Interviews," Interview with the Assistant to the former Chief of Internal Security, October 26, 1943, Box 24, RG 210, copy in folder 108, JIR.

92. Ibid.

93. The principal "agitators," he wrote, "rarely come out into the open themselves but used the young Kibei, with whom they were well supplied, to do the dirty work." (Tony O'Brien to Glick, March 17, 1945, in Reel No. 70, JAEER files, Bancroft Library.)

94. "Segregant Population of Tule Lake as of July 1944," WDC-CAD-Research Branch, 4 September 1944, copy in Reel No. 170, JAERR files, Bancroft Library. Eight men from Hawai'i were among sixty-seven segregants who, having renounced their American citizenship, were therefore removed from Tule Lake in February 1945 to await processing in another federal facility for repatriation to Japan. Two of the eight were alleged to have participated in violent and "subversive" activities. ("Appendix Fd: Departures for Klamath Falls," [February 1945], copy in JAERR collection, Reel #170, Bancroft Library.)

95. More than a quarter of the Nikkei (from Hawai'i and the mainland) being held in WRA camps were relocated between January 1943 and January 1945. Meyer, *Uprooted Americans,* 334.

96. Minutes of Meeting of the Military Governor's Reviewing Board, December 1943, RG 338, NA. Emphasis added. Initials used to protect the privacy of the individual.

97. Case of K. H., December 7, 1941, Commanding General's Internee Review Board, RG 338, NA. Initials used to protect the privacy of individuals.

98. S. Sgt. Y. M. to Attorney General, Territory of Hawaii, August 16, 1943, Minutes of the Meeting of the Internee Review Board, June 1943–April 1944, RG 338, NA. Attorney General Garner Anthony passed on this letter to General Richardson. Slattery recognized that the internee was "torn between two loves," but recommended against parole.

99. *Ex parte Endo,* 323 U.S. 283 (1944). For further discussion of *Endo,* see pp. 309ff.

100. The OIS was successor to the OMG organization.

101. Memorandum from Brig. Gen. Morrison, OIS, to Office of the Provost Marshal General, "Japanese Civilian Internees from the Territory of Hawaii with Sons in the Armed Forces of the United States," December 9, 1944, RG 494, NA.

102. Tollefson to Commanding General, Pacific Ocean Area, March 6, 1945 and April 7, 1945, RG 494, NA.

103. "Japanese Civilian Internees from the Territory of Hawaii with Sons and Daughters in the Armed Forces of the United States," Memorandum to General Morrison, January 12, 1945, RG 389, NA.

104. Memorandum from Ickes to Stimson, February 14, 1945, RG 494, NA. Ickes also noted that OMG had initially led the federal authorities to believe that the Hawai'i Japanese evacuees did not pose a security risk to the mainland, but that in practice many received exclusionary orders from Western Defense Command, and some (such as the former war workers who OMG demanded be kept separate from other Japanese seeking repatriation) were designated for segregation.

105. Memorandum from Richardson to the Adjutant General, War Department, "Return of Hawaiian Evacuees to Homeland," April 17, 1945, RG 494, NA. The priority group system would give preference to individuals with sons or daughters in the armed forces of the United States, the aged, the infirm, and to "persons deserving of such consideration because of unusual circumstances." (Ibid.)

106. John Frank to Abe Fortas, March 31, 1944, memorandum in Fortas Files, RG 48, NA.

107. Memorandum from Richardson to the Adjutant General, War Department, "Return of Hawaiian Evacuees to Homeland," April 17, 1945, RG 494, NA.

108. Memorandum from Dillon S. Myer, War Relocation Authority, to Maj. Davidson Sommers, Office of the Assistant Secretary of War, August 3, 1945, RG 494, NA.

109. For further details, see Harry N. Scheiber, Jane L. Scheiber, and Benjamin Jones, "Hawai'i's Kibei under Martial Law: A Hidden Chapter in the History of World War II Internments," *Western Legal History* 22 (2009): 1–102.

110. Interview with Kiyoshi Yoshimura, quoted in Dorothy Ochiai Hazama and Jane Okamoto Komeiji, *Okage Sama De: The Japanese in Hawai'i, 1885–1985* (Honolulu, HI: Bess Press, 1986), 168–169.

111. "Return of Japanese to Hawaii," Memorandum for Col. Alton C. Miller from Maj. Clarence R. Harbert, January 17, 1945, Provost Marshal General Office Records, RG 389, NA.

112. Memorandum for the Adjutant General from Col. A. B. Johnson, Assistant to the Provost Marshal General, "Temporary Duty Orders outside Continental Boundaries," April 6, 1945, RG 389, NA. On the organization and functions of the Japanese American Branch, and the

Japanese American Joint Board, each of which played an important role in loyalty determination processes, see Muller, *American Inquisition,* 39–65.

113. Draft Memorandum, "Hawaiian Excludees and Personnel Security Program," Spring 1945, RG 389, NA.

114. Memorandum from Capt. Stanley J. Arnold to Chief, Japanese-American Branch, Office of the Provost Marshal General, "Hawaiian Japanese," June 4, 1945, RG 389, NA.

115. Ibid.

116. Memorandum from Col. Louis F. Springer to Gen. William R. C. Morrison, "Evacuees of Japanese Ancestry Approved for Return to Territory of Hawaii," May 25, 1945, RG 494, NA. Springer stated that a total of 705 aliens had been interned on the mainland, and 1,040 citizens and aliens had been evacuated to Relocation Centers, for a total of 1,745. As with previous sets of figures, however, these numbers conflicted with documents prepared by the mainland authorities. An August 10, 1945, memorandum from WRA's Dillon Myer to Maj. Davidson Sommers stated that WRA originally received 1,136 ethnic Japanese evacuees from Hawai'i, in addition to the 73 excludees sent to Tule Lake between 1944 and July 1945. As of August 10, Myer reported that only 4 of the 1,136 evacuees had returned to Hawai'i, with 65 others designated for inclusion in an early movement. Six hundred twenty-eight individuals were located in Tule Lake, while 319 evacuees were located in other camps, including Gila River, Granada, Central Utah, Heart Mountain, and Rohwer. Additionally, Myer noted that 65 individuals had relocated permanently to the mainland, and 55 individuals had died, been interned, or repatriated to Japan. (Memorandum from Dillon S. Myer to Maj. Davidson Sommers, August 10, 1945, RG 494, NA.) These figures from Myer's memorandum differ from the official WRA report, *The Evacuated People,* 191. Kashima states that a total of 2,092 Japanese Americans, including 875 aliens shipped to the Department of Justice camps, were sent to the mainland. (Kashima, *Judgment without Trial,* 86.) Kashima's source is James Okahata, ed., *A History of Japanese in Hawaii* (Honolulu: United Japanese Society of Hawai'i, 1971), 265.

117. The WRA notified OMG of this financial problem in an August 13 memorandum, exhorting General Richardson to expedite action for return of the evacuee population before WRA funding dried up. (Memorandum from Harrison A. Gerhardt, Executive to Assistant Secretary of War, to Richardson, August 13, 1945, RG 494, NA.)

118. These orders had been issued under Presidential Proclamation No. 2525 (invoking the Enemy Aliens Act) and Presidential Executive Order No. 9489 (designating a military commander for the Territory of Hawai'i, and authorizing him to prescribe the territory as a military area).

119. Radio from OMG McCloy, August 27, 1945, RG 494, NA; Memorandum from McCloy to Richardson, September 8, 1945, RG 494, NA.

120. Internees List, August 29, 1945, RG 494, NA.

121. Parolees List, August 31, 1945, RG 494, NA.

122. Radio to Provost Marshal General's Office from General Richardson, September 14, 1945, RG 494, NA. A total of 248 individuals from Hawai'i asked for repatriation. Allen, *Hawaii's War Years,* 141. A separate storm was brewing throughout the course of September 1945 over the continued internment in Honouliuli, O'ahu, of three Kibei seeking to renounce their U.S. citizenship and repatriate to Japan. The legal authority for their continued detention after the termination of martial law was doubtful. The matter was resolved when the attorney general allowed them to renounce their American citizenship, and the three were eventually transferred to Tule Lake. Extensive correspondence on this episode is archived in RG 494, NA.

123. Message from Provost Marshal General's Office to Richardson, October 27, 1945, RG 494, NA.

124. Message from Richardson to Commanding General, Army Port and Service Command, October 22, 1945, RG 494, NA.

125. See supra, pp. 76–79.

126. Memorandum from USAT *Shawnee* to Commanding General, Mid Pacific, December 1945, RG 494, NA; *Honolulu Advertiser,* November 14, 1945, pp. 1–2, 5; *Honolulu Star-Bulletin,* November 14, 1945, p. 4; *Honolulu Star-Bulletin,* December 10, 1945, pp. 1, 4.

127. WRA, Department of the Interior, *The Evacuated People: A Quantitative Description* (Washington, DC: U.S. Government Printing Office, n.d.), 55.

128. Allen, *Hawaii's War Years,* 141; WRA, *The Evacuated People,* 55.

129. Weglyn, *Years of Infamy,* 88.

130. Office of the Chief of Military History, "Civil Affairs," 305–306.

131. Weglyn, *Years of Infamy,* 88 (quoting a November 9, 1942, transcript of a telephone conversation between Lt. Col. W. F. Durbin and Col. Fielding).

132. Richardson to McCloy, February 11, 1944, McCloy Files, RG 107, NA.

133. Ibid.

134. Memorandum included with Richardson to McCloy, August 19, 1944, McCloy Files, RG 107, NA.

135. Thus the Ninth Circuit, in several appeals of habeas cases from the district court in Hawai'i, and also the dissenters in *Duncan* in the U.S. Supreme Court, regarded the allegedly dangerous presence of the Japanese-American population as a major factor justifying martial law and military government. These decisions and opinions are considered, *inter alia,* infra, parts 5, 7. In addition, the *Korematsu* and *Hirabayashi* cases turned, for the Supreme Court's majority, on the dual premises that the ethnic Japanese population posed a danger and that the army was the best judge of security issues.

Chapter 11: Alarms and Responses

1. Hearings, Joint Committee on the Investigation of the Pearl Harbor Attack, 79th Cong., S. Con. Res. 27, Part 28, 1444. See also J. Garner Anthony, *Hawaii under Army Rule* (Stanford, CA: Stanford University Press, 1955), 107; and Fred Israel, "Military Justice in Hawaii, 1941–44," *Pacific Historical Review* 36 (1967): 251–259 (an overview of the debate at the Cabinet level during 1942 over Hawai'i martial law issues).

2. See supra, pp. 36–38.

3. Hawaii Defense Act (Act 24), section 15, 1941 Laws Terr. Haw. 1, 16–17, codified as amended at Rev. L. Haw. chap. 324 (1945) (addressing challenges to the constitutionality of the Act).

4. See supra, p. 39.

5. Testimony of General Richardson and Admiral Nimitz in Duncan trial court, *Duncan* Trial Record, 1030–1031, April 17, 1944 (copy in Case File #10, 763), NASB.

6. Radio No. 284 from Emmons to McCloy, January 3, 1943, McCloy Files, NA.

7. Radio No. 1224 from Emmons to McCloy, July 2, 1942, RG 338, NA. Much of the language is also reproduced in "Paraphrase of Secret Radiogram No. 1224 dated July 2, 1942, from the Commanding General, Hawaiian Dept., to Mr. John J. McCloy," attached to letter from J. L. Mckee to R. H. Tate, July 10, 1942, McCloy Files, NA.

8. Radio No. 1224 from Emmons to McCloy, July 2, 1942, RG 338, NA. This theme was also voiced in the testimony of Gen. Richardson in *Duncan* Trial Record, 1027–1030, a point that drew comment from the Supreme Court when it ruled in favor of Duncan on appeal in 1946.

9. *Honolulu Star-Bulletin,* January 16, 1942, p. 1.

10. Emmons to McCloy, December 15, 1942, McCloy Files, NA.

11. Ibid. Emphasis added.

12. Memorandum from E. K. Burlew to the Secretary of the Interior, May 25, 1942, Green Papers, JAGSL (reporting Green's view). Emphasis added.

13. Green Notes, RG 338, NA.

14. Green to McCloy, September 15, 1942, McCloy Files, NA.

15. Gen. Thomas H. Green, Manuscript (untitled memoir of the war years), Green Papers, JAGSL.

16. Judge Delbert Metzger to Green, March 4, 1943, Green Papers, JAGSL. Ironically, only a few months later, Judge Metzger would contend, quite to the contrary, that army rule was illegal and unconstitutional. See discussion of the *Glockner* case, infra, pp. 263ff.

17. Notation on manuscript, "Development of the Office of Military Governor," Green Papers, JAGSL.

18. Gen. Thomas H. Green, Memorandum for Chief, Bureau of Public Relations, War Department (no date, but late 1945), Green Papers. JAGSL.

19. Richardson to McCloy, February 10, 1944, McCloy Files, NA.

20. Memorandum from Col. E. V. Slattery to Col. William R. C. Morrison, February 17, 1944, accompanying a draft bill (untitled), copy in RG 338, NA.

21. Memorandum from Solicitor Nathan Margold, June 8, 1942, King Papers, Miscellaneous Subject Correspondence, HSA. (A copy is enclosed with a letter from Harold Ickes to Samuel W. King dated June 15, 1942.) The conclusion of this report focused upon the decisions of the military commission in two capital cases.

22. Memorandum from E. K. Burlew to McCloy, May 28, 1942, McCloy Files, NA.

23. Ickes to Stimson, November 20, 1942, Green Papers, JAGSL.

24. On President Roosevelt's view, at least in the early months of the war, see p. 135.

25. Ickes to Donald Nelson, Chairman, War Production Board, June 3, 1942, Ickes Papers, LC. Ickes named in particular Messrs. Budge, president of Castle and Cooke, Russell, executive of Theo. H. Davies & Co., and Carden, a high executive of the Bank of Hawai'i, as three of the Hawai'i business executives in the "Five Companies" or "Big Five" group. (Ibid.)

26. Ibid. See pp. 84–85 for a discussion of the special relationship between the military and the plantation owners.

27. Thoron would serve under Ickes as director of Territories from October 1942 through June 1945.

28. T. H. Watkins, *Righteous Pilgrim: The Life and Times of Harold L. Ickes, 1874–1952* (New York: Henry Holt, 1990), 784 (quoting a February 7, 1942, diary entry).

29. Memorandum from B. W. Thoron to the Secretary of the Interior, Report No. 2, March 29, 1942, Ickes Papers, LC.

30. Memorandum from B. W. Thoron to the Secretary of the Interior, "Civilian Defense and Military Government in Hawaii, Report No. 4," May 25, 1942, Ickes Papers, LC.

31. Ibid.

32. Watkins, *Righteous Pilgrim,* 784. There was a cabinet discussion in April 1942 about the possibility of seeking legislation from Congress to eliminate the requirement that the governor of Hawai'i be a resident of the Islands, but the idea was abandoned since Ickes and President Roosevelt agreed that "such a move could easily be used by the Axis powers for propaganda purposes to show that America was eating up the small countries." (Diary of Francis Biddle, April 24, 1942, Papers of Attorney General Francis Biddle, FDRL, Hyde Park, NY.)

33. Diary of Thomas H. Green, February 16, 1942, Green Papers, JAGSL.

34. Littell to Marvin McIntyre (White House aide), November 14, 1941, Secretary's Files, Ickes Papers, LC.

35. Interestingly enough, Ickes was not enthusiastic about appointing Stainback and was considering as alternative choices some Democratic Party rising stars on the mainland. It seems likely that Ickes's decision was heavily influenced by the probability of opposition from Hawai'i's Democrats if he chose a mainland figure rather than appointing a prominent person from the Islands. (Ickes to McIntyre, November 28, 1941, and other correspondence on the governorship issue, March–May 1942, Ickes Papers, LC.)

36. Memorandum for the files from Archibald King, June 16, 1942 (reporting conversation with Stainback), McCloy Files, NA.

37. Ibid.

38. Ibid. Col. King, it should be noted, was no stranger to the legal and constitutional issues surrounding the martial law controversy, since he was probably at that very time preparing a rejoinder to a law review article by Garner Anthony that challenged army rule in Hawai'i on both statutory and constitutional grounds. See discussion of the academic debate infra, pp. 222ff.

39. Office of Internal Security, Territory of Hawaii, "Wartime Security Controls," Box 24, Richardson Papers, Hoover Institution; Anthony, *Hawaii under Army Rule,* 22.

40. "Memo re Military and Civil Governments," December 18, 1942, Farrington Papers, HSA.

41. Stainback to Ickes, September 2, 1942, cited in Boardman Report, Fortas Files, RG 48, NA; and Stainback to Ickes, July 25, 1943, Ickes Papers, LC.

42. Stainback to Ickes, November 17, 1942, McCloy Files, NA.

43. King to Ickes, June 17, 1942, Miscellaneous Subject Correspondence, King Papers, HSA.

44. King to Garner Anthony, July 6, 1942, King Papers, HSA. On King's earlier involvement with statehood, see supra, p. 18. On the statehood fights, especially the vicious and unrestrained racism of Representative John Rankin of Mississippi, directed against the Hawai'i Japanese, see United Press release, June 3, 1943 (reporting Rankin press conference), copy on file in the Farrington Papers, HSA. Rankin later would oppose the army's formation of a Japanese-American combat unit; in this instance, too, he couched his views in an especially virulent racist rhetoric. ("Quit Coddling the Japs: Speech of Hon. John E. Rankin of Mississippi," *Congressional Record,* February 3, 1943.)

45. King to Henry Holstein, May 14, 1942, King Papers, HSA.

46. King to Anthony, July 6, 1942, ibid. Anthony's article is discussed infra, pp. 222–223.

47. King to Henry Holstein, May 14, 1942, King Papers, HSA.

48. Farrington to Riley Allen, January 25, 1943, Farrington Papers, HSA. Farrington reported that the transition went smoothly with King's full cooperation, and noted that King was immediately preoccupied with reestablishing his family in Hawai'i, several members apparently having just returned from the mainland. (Ibid.)

49. Anthony, *Hawaii under Army Rule,* 28 (quoting a December 21, 1942, public announcement by Farrington).

50. Ickes and Stimson clashed directly on this issue. See discussion infra, pp. 246–247.

51. Judd to Farrington, August 22, 1942, Farrington Papers, HSA. Judd was involved at the time with the strandee issue and was frustrated by the army's policies. (Ibid.)

52. Anthony, *Hawaii under Army Rule,* 28 (for Farrington's views); Garner Anthony to Joseph R. Farrington, August 27, 1943, Farrington Papers, HSA; cf. J. Garner Anthony, "Martial Law, Military Government and the Writ of Habeas Corpus in Hawaii," *California Law Review* 31 (1943): 477–514 passim. In this respect, it may be said, Anthony and Farrington simply wanted a strict application of *Milligan* standards. Governor Stainback told the press that if the army treated Hawai'i as a military district, as was done on the West Coast, a declaration of martial law might always be made anew in a serious emergency. ("Governor Expects Hawaii to Become Military District," *Honolulu Star-Bulletin,* April 8, 1944, p. 1.)

53. Ickes to Stimson, August 5, 1942, in McCloy Files, NA.

54. Ibid.

55. "Memo re Military and Civil Governments," December 18, 1942, copy in Farrington Papers, HSA. Emphasis added.

56. Ickes to Stimson, November 30, 1942, copy in Green Papers, JAGSL.

57. Numerous references to his frustration with the president on this score appear in the Diary of Harold Ickes (e.g., entries of August 10, 1942, August 16, 1942), Ickes Papers, LC.

58. Anthony, "Martial Law in Hawaii," *California Law Review* 30 (1942): 374.

59. Ibid., 376.

60. Ibid., 381 (quoting *Ex parte Milligan,* 71 U.S. 2, 127 [1866]). Anthony regretted Judge Metzger's closing of his court and unwillingness to hear a petition for writ of habeas corpus in the *Zimmerman* case, on which see chap. 13.

61. Anthony, "Martial Law in Hawaii." Writing after the war, Anthony observed that when he here suggested that Congress might establish combat areas that would "give the military authorities any needed powers," he was unaware that Congress had already enacted such a measure, *viz.,* the Act of March 21, 1942, 56 Stat. 173, 18 U.S.C. 97(a), under terms of which the legislative branch had in effect given its authorization for the removal under executive order of the Japanese-American population from the West Coast on the mainland. (Anthony, *Hawaii under Army Rule,* 61n2, 4.)

62. Anthony, "Martial Law in Hawaii," 387. Later Anthony wrote: "Neither the President with Congress, nor the President alone, have authorized a military government for Hawaii." (Anthony, "Martial Law, Military Government," 479.)

63. Anthony, "Martial Law in Hawaii," 388. See also Fairman, "The Law of Martial Rule." When the Supreme Court finally ruled on the legality of the Hawai'i martial law regime, Justice Black took the same position as Anthony's on the difficulty of defining "martial law," whereas Chief Justice Stone insisted that the term "martial law" as used in the Organic Act was not "devoid of meaning." (*Duncan v. Kahanamoku,* 327 U.S. 304 at 319 [Black], 335 [Stone].)

64. Anthony, "Martial Law in Hawaii," 390.

65. Archibald King, "The Legality of Martial Law in Hawaii," *California Law Review* 30 (1942): 599. For discussion between King and Stainback, see p. 218.

66. Ibid., 624.

67. Ibid., 625.

68. Ibid., 633.

69. See pp. 234ff., infra.

70. Charles Fairman, "The Law of Martial Rule and the National Emergency," *Harvard Law Review* 55 (1942): 1253–1302.

71. Ibid., 1295, 1296, 1299.

72. Ibid., 1301–1302.

73. Ibid.

74. Ibid., 1259. Emphasis added.

75. Ibid., 1287. Fairman published a second edition of his treatise on martial law in 1943, incorporating into it nearly verbatim the concluding section of his article. But in his book *Reconstruction and Reunion* (written two decades after his wartime role), Fairman, by then professor of law at Harvard, took a quite different view of the constitutional mandate deriving from *Milligan;* see p. 217.

76. Anthony, *Hawaii under Army Rule,* 109 (quoting Emmons).

77. Ibid., 109–110 (quoting Emmons).

78. Anthony to King, June 10, 1942, King Papers, HSA.

79. Radio No. 1224 from Emmons to McCloy, July 2, 1942, RG 338, NA. Emphasis added.

80. Radio from Emmons to McCloy, July 1, 1942, Files of Gen. Thomas H. Green, RG 338, NA.

81. Ibid. It should be noted that this response was written nearly a month after the U.S. victory over the Japanese fleet at the Battle of Midway.

Chapter 12: "Delineation" and Restoration, 1942–1943

1. See supra, p. 217.

2. E. K. Burlew to John J. McCloy, July 15, 1942, McCloy Files, NA; Green Notes, RG 338, NA; Memorandum from Jaretski to McCloy, June 5, 1942, McCloy Files, NA.

3. Radio No. 2338 from General Emmons to Green, August 19, 1942, Green Files, RG 338, NA (referring to "report[s] from usual source" and detailing material in Stainback's correspondence and the correspondence of Samuel Clark of the Justice Department). The army archives contain, for example, a copy of a confidential report by the territorial attorney general on the subject of military rule, together with a questionnaire that the territorial attorney general sent to the U.S. District Attorney in Honolulu. It is marked that the addressee "is unaware of our possession of the letter." (Notation on a form letter from Attorney General Tavares [questionnaire], date illegible, but June or July 1944, copy filed with Memorandum from Fowler Harper to Abe Fortas [copy], August 17, 1944, RG 338, NA.)

4. Green Notes, RG 338, NA.

5. Ibid.

6. Ickes to Stimson, August 5, 1942, copy, Green Notes, RG 338, NA.

7. Memorandum from Thoron to Ickes, May 12, 1942, Ickes Papers, LC.

8. Memorandum from Thoron to the Secretary of the Interior, "Civilian Defense and Military Government in Hawaii, Report #4," May 25, 1942, copy in Green Papers, JAGSL.

9. General Orders No. 133, HWRD, also in J. Garner Anthony, *Hawaii under Army Rule* (Stanford, CA: Stanford University Press, 1955), 159–160.

10. [Gen. Thomas H. Green], Memorandum, "Notes Regarding Issuance of General Orders Nos. 133 and 135," September 24, 1942, in Green Papers, JAGSL.

11. General Orders No. 135, HWRD; also in Anthony, *Hawaii under Army Rule,* 162.

12. [Gen. Thomas H. Green], Memorandum, "Notes Regarding Issuance of General Orders Nos. 133 and 135," September 24, 1942, Green Papers, JAGSL.

13. Ibid.

14. Stainback's angry response to the order is described in a memorandum dated September 25, 1942, attached to a letter from Green to John J. McCloy, in McCloy Files, NA; also in the Green Papers, JAGSL. Green reported such conflicts with the governor to the War Department in a way that served to discredit Stainback, e.g., writing that the governor "on many occasions . . . has gotten very angry over the matter. However, I know him quite well and have discounted his fits of anger as a thing that is usual with him." (Green to McCloy, September 15, 1942, McCloy Files, NA.) See also Anthony, *Hawaii under Army Rule,* 23–27. General Green made a regular practice of consulting civilian judges and former judges in matters of army legal policy. Although the judge who was consulted by Green in this instance is identified in the Memorandum only as a "district judge," it is unlikely that it was U.S. District Court Judge Delbert E. Metzger; rather, we think it was a Hawai'i territorial judge. Still, it is noteworthy that at a later date Metzger praised General Green for his having had the "wisdom to use nearly all the established functions of local government" in the military government plan, and especially his not chancing any loss of "time or efforts through dual governmental managements, and no possibility of division of authority, or division of responsibility" that would have hampered the effectiveness of the army just after the Pearl Harbor disaster. (Metzger to Green, March 3, 1943, Green Papers, JAGSL.) If the advice regarding Order No. 135 did in fact come from Judge Metzger, it would have been ironic, since it was Metzger's court that struck the first solid blow against continuation of martial law in the habeas corpus cases of mid-1943, on which see pp. 264ff., infra.

15. Draft copy of proposed letter (not sent) from the Attorney General and Secretary Ickes to the President (apparently prepared by James Rowe and Sam Clark), October 7, 1942, and Memorandum from Rowe to Clark, October 5, 1942, in Papers of James Rowe Jr., FDRL.

16. Memorandum from the Solicitor of the Department of the Interior to the Secretary (not dated, but September or October 1942), Rowe Papers, FDRL.

17. Memorandum from Major General Cramer (the judge advocate general) to the Assistant Secretary of War, "Change in General Order 135, Office of the Military Governor of Hawaii, September 4, 1942," October 23, 1942 (Confidential), McCloy Files, NA.

18. Ibid.

19. Governor Stainback angrily charged that the army had rushed to issue its General Orders No. 135 before its terms could be properly analyzed and the civilian government's reaction obtained. All this Green denied. ([Thomas H. Green], "Memorandum: Notes Regarding Issuance of General Orders Nos. 133 and 135," September 25, 1942 [attached to a letter from Green to McCloy dated September 25, 1942], McCloy Files, NA; also in Green Papers, JAGSL.)

20. Authors' interview of Mrs. Garner Anthony, Honolulu, April 1994; "Anthony Dies—Argued against Isle Martial Law," *Honolulu Advertiser,* November 3, 1982. See also Kelli Nakamura, "J. Garner Anthony," *Densho Encyclopedia,* http://encyclopedia.densho.org/J._Garner_Anthony/.

21. [Green], "Memorandum: Notes Regarding Issuance of General Orders Nos. 133 and 135," September 24, 1942 (attached to a letter from Green to McCloy dated September 25, 1942), McCloy File, NA; also in Green Papers, JAGSL.

22. See pp. 100-101, supra.

23. Two versions exist as to what transpired in this confrontation in the office Green occupied, one Green's own (in Green's diary, Green Papers, JAGSL), and the other a desk memorandum that Anthony wrote immediately after returning to his own office from the meeting with Green (original copy in the possession of Mrs. Garner Anthony). We think that the differences in factual detail are not as important as the clear documentation both versions offer that the men had come to a difficult pass in their personal relationship. Anthony clearly was dubious about Green's integrity and deplored his absolutism. Green, for his part, resented the independence of mind that Anthony displayed on the issues of martial law's constitutionality and on the need to respect the prerogatives of the civilian government—a characteristic of mind that Green viewed as dangerous to the unity of the war effort.

24. Anthony, *Hawaii under Army Rule,* 25.

25. J. Garner Anthony, "Martial Law in Hawaii," *California Law Review* 30 (May 1942): 371–396. His December 1 report is in the Stainback Papers, HSA, and is reprinted in Anthony, *Hawaii under Army Rule,* appendix E, 191–199.

26. Anthony, *Hawaii under Army Rule,* 191–197.

27. Ibid., 199.

28. Ibid., 24.

29. Ickes to James Rowe Jr. (assistant to the attorney general), December 14, 1942, Ickes Papers, LC.

30. Our account of the intense negotiations in December has been pieced together from General Green's diary, in the Green Papers, JAGSL; from the relevant departmental archival records; from the John J. McCloy Diaries, McCloy Papers, Archives and Special Collections, Amherst College Library, available at https://www.amherst.edu/media/view/390251/original/McCloy _diary_1942.pdf. [hereinafter McCloy Diaries, Amherst College]; and from personal correspondence in the Farrington Papers, HSA.

31. Farrington to Anthony, August 27, 1943 and September 10, 1943, Farrington Papers, HSA. See also Anthony, *Hawaii under Army Rule,* 105–106; "Military Rule Here Modified," *Honolulu Star-Bulletin,* September 2, 1942, p. 1 (civil courts restored).

32. Diary and personal memoranda of Thomas H. Green, December 1942, Green Papers, JAGSL.

33. Ickes to Stimson, November 20, 1942, copy, Green Papers, JAGSL.

34. Ickes to Stimson, November 30, 1942, copy, Green Papers, JAGSL.

35. Diary of Henry L. Stimson, January 9, 1943, Yale University Library, New Haven, CT (microfilm).

36. McCloy to Harry Hopkins, October 19, 1942, McCloy Files, NA.

37. See infra, p. 241.

38. Biddle to Roosevelt, December 17, 1942 (confidential), Papers of Francis Biddle, FDRL. It should be noted that Biddle, despite his misgivings about the violation of mainland Japanese Americans' civil liberties in the evacuation and internment policies, in the end deferred to the military and took the position that it was an army problem, not the Justice Department's. (Peter Irons, *Justice at War: The Story of the Japanese-American Internment Cases* [New York: Oxford University Press, 1983], 17–18, 52–54.)

39. Biddle to Roosevelt, December 17, 1942 (confidential), Papers of Francis Biddle, FDRL.

40. Ibid. The army command cannot possibly have been unaware that criticism was blunted and dissent chilled under martial law. As an example, an army intelligence report of mid-1942

stated: "Never was there any public frontal attack on martial law *as such* or on the Governor's action [in turning the government over to the army] *per se.* . . . Some competent observers have confided that had it not been for . . . reluctance to offend the military authorities, the criticism would have been much more blunt and open." ("Political Report to Kendall J. Fielder, G-2: The Governorship of Hawaii, July 31, 1942," Green Papers, JAGSL.)

41. Letters from James Rowe to the Attorney General, December 26, 1942, April 10, 1943, and August 27, 1943, all in the Rowe Papers, FDRL.

42. Biddle and Fortas to McCloy, December 19, 1942, McCloy Files, NA.

43. Samuel O. Clark Jr., "Memorandum for the Attorney General, In re: Military Government in Hawaii, December 9, 1942," Rowe Papers, FDRL. One has to think that Acting District Attorney Angus Taylor had little influence on the outcome of the meeting, in which his superiors in the Justice Department decided the departmental position—especially since Taylor had been a strong advocate, earlier in the year, for internment and expulsion of large numbers of Japanese Americans in Hawai'i, and for tougher security measures, leading Justice officials and McCloy to doubt the value of his judgment. See supra, p. 149.

44. Biddle and Fortas to McCloy, December 19, 1942, copy in Green Papers, JAGSL.

45. Ibid. The language is also in the December 9, 1942, memorandum from Samuel O. Clark to the Attorney General, cited supra, note 43, Rowe Papers, FDRL.

46. Biddle recorded in his notebooks that he handed his letter directly to Roosevelt's secretary for the president's personal attention, and that FDR had acted promptly upon it. Biddle Notebooks, not paginated, Papers of Francis Biddle, FDRL.

47. See supra, p. 135.

48. Francis Biddle, *In Brief Authority* (New York: Doubleday, 1962), 219.

49. Memorandum from Roosevelt to Biddle, December 13, 1942, Francis Biddle Papers, FDRL.

50. Ibid.

51. McCloy to Emmons, January 6, 1943, copy in Green Papers, JAGSL. President Roosevelt also instructed Secretary Stimson and Biddle to discuss the possibility of replacing Green with a prominent Democratic politician, William O'Dwyer of New York City, then serving as a lieutenant colonel in the army. (Biddle to Roosevelt, December 17, 1942, and Roosevelt to Biddle, December 18, 1942, Biddle Papers, FDRL [stating that O'Dwyer "would be an excellent man to clean this thing up."]). McCloy wrote to Emmons a few weeks later to tell him that O'Dwyer might be sent out not as Green's replacement but instead as a second-in-command to Green's successor. (McCloy to Emmons, January 6, 1943, Emmons Papers, Hoover Institution.) Later that week, McCloy spoke by phone with O'Dwyer about this proposed assignment. (McCloy Diaries, entry of January 10, 1943, Amherst College.) For reasons that are not clear to us from the available documentation, the idea was dropped; and when Green was relieved of his position and transferred to Washington, his own top aide, Col. (later Gen.) William R. C. Morrison, was named to succeed him. Dwyer was later mayor of New York, 1946–1950.

52. McCloy to Harry Hopkins, October 19, 1942, McCloy Files, NA. This was the very time that the judge advocate general was preparing an analysis for McCloy that would find most of the content of General Orders No. 135 unacceptable on policy grounds, and some of it on legal grounds.

53. Biddle and Fortas to McCloy, December 19, 1942, McCloy Files, NA. McCloy's diary for January reveals the intensity of negotiations, with entries on nearly every day, and on several days up to four conferences and phone discussions. (McCloy Diaries, Amherst College.)

54. McCloy to Harry Hopkins, October 19, 1942, McCloy Files, NA.

55. Green to Emmons, January 1, 1943, Emmons Reading File, RG 338, NA.

56. James Rowe, in the Justice Department, received a phone call on the day that a December Drew Pearson article appeared. He was called by a Washington lawyer, Lee Warren, "to express outrage" and to urge "that we talk to General Green to get the other side of the story, that Governor Stainback and 'his henchmen' were nothing but a bunch of politicians . . . [and that] it was of the utmost importance that the Military continue its rule." Pressed by the office secretary who took the call, Rowe reported, Warren admitted he was the Washington attorney for one of the most powerful figures in the Hawai'i business establishment, Walter Dillingham. (Memorandum from James Rowe to the Attorney General, December 26, 1942, Rowe Papers, FDRL.) Dillingham was one of the territory's wealthiest men and among the army's most trusted civilian advisers, a staunch public defender of martial law and military governance, who later would be appointed to head the army's wartime control of food supply.

57. Pearson column in the *Washington Post,* December 26, 1942; Ickes quotation from Diary of Harold Ickes, December 27, 1942, LC.

58. *Ex parte Quirin* 317 U.S. 1 (1942). See p. 238, supra.

59. Ibid., 6. This passage was quoted by Gov. Stainback from the Court's advanced sheets, in letter from Stainback to Ickes, November 17, 1942, copy in McCloy Files, NA.

60. Stainback to Ickes, November 17, 1942, ibid.

61. Ibid.

62. Radio No. 1995 from Green to Morrison, December 23, 1942, RG 338, NA.

63. Radio from Green to Emmons, December 25, 1942, RG 338, NA; Radio No. 040321 from Admiral Nimitz to Admiral King, December 4, 1942, copy in ibid; and McCloy Diaries, entry of December 30, 1942, Amherst College.

64. Emmons to McCloy, December 15, 1942, McCloy Files, NA.

65. See supra, chap. 6.

66. See supra, p. 239; Gwenfread Allen, *Hawaii's War Years, 1941-1945* (Honolulu: University of Hawai'i Press, 1950), 263-273; cf. Eileen O'Brien, "Making Democracy Work," *Paradise of the Pacific,* December 1943, 42-45.

67. Emmons to McCloy, December 15, 1942, McCloy Files, NA.

68. Ibid.

69. Emmons to McCloy, December 15, 1942, McCloy Files, NA. Emphasis added.

70. Ibid.

71. McCloy Diaries, Entries of December 15-16, 24, and 28, 1942, Amherst College.

72. Ibid., Entry of December, 30, 1943. Biddle also noted in his memoir that Roosevelt "grew infinitely tired of the continual bickering between department heads" as the war continued. (Biddle, *In Brief Authority,* 186.)

73. Green to Emmons, January 1, 1943, Emmons Reading File, RG 338, NA.

74. McCloy Diaries, Entries of January 3, 4-10, 13-16, and 20, 1943, Amherst College.

75. A highly detailed account of the inside negotiations in Washington and the resulting agreement appeared in testimony during the *Duncan* case in the U.S. District Court in 1944. The proclamations of the governor and commanding general that promulgated the final agreement, both dated February 8, 1943, are reprinted in Anthony, *Hawaii under Army Rule,* 129-132. On the troubled history of argument between the civilian government and army for the control of Honolulu's red-light district and its denizens, see supra, pp. 73-75, and Beth L. Bailey and David Farber, *The First Strange Place: Race and Sex in World War II Hawaii* (New York: Free Press,

1992), passim. Later, in 1943, Judge Metzger, in *Ex parte Glockner,* read the language of the pre-amble to the agreement (a "whereas" clause stating that martial law was "in effect" and habeas corpus "remains suspended") as being merely an historical statement of fact rather than an af-firmation that martial law was being continued. All the parties directly associated with the nego-tiations, however, were in agreement that Metzger was in error on this important point. Far-rington, who had been involved in the Washington negotiations of the agreement, wrote: "Certainly [Metzger] has not interpreted correctly the understanding prevailing at the time the [restoration] agreement was reached." (Farrington to Garner Anthony, August 27, 1943, Far-rington Papers, HSA.) On the judge's misreading of the Restoration Agreement of 1943, see also Garner Anthony, "Martial Law, Military Government and the Writ of Habeas Corpus in Ha-waii," *California Law Review* 31 (1943), 494. See chap. 13, infra, on *Glockner* and the related habeas cases.

76. Anthony, *Hawaii under Army Rule,* 129–32

77. Green to Emmons, January 1, 1943, RG 338, NA.

78. Green to Emmons, January 7, 1943, RG 338, NA.

79. Memorandum from McCloy to Stimson, December 16, 1942, McCloy Files, NA.

80. Diary of Henry Stimson, Entry of December 28, 1942, Yale University Library (microfilm).

81. Ibid.

82. Diary of Harold Ickes, January 9, 1943, Ickes Papers, LC.

83. Emmons to McCloy, January 3, 1943, McCloy Files, NA.

84. Green to Morrison, January 3, 1943, RG 338, NA.

85. Roosevelt to Stimson, February 1, 1943, McCloy Files, NA.

86. Quotations in text are from two communications of same date, McCloy to Emmons, Jan-uary 24, 1943, copies in McCloy Files, NA.

87. McCloy Diaries, Entries of January 30 and February 10, 1943, Amherst College. The imme-diate problem that McCloy was charged with concerned the still unsettled realignment of the free French forces with the U.S. and British armies.

88. Radio No. 1716, from Emmons to Chief of Staff (U.S. Army), March 14, 1943, McCloy Files, NA.

89. "John Public Has Cause for Worry!" *Hawaii: A Magazine of News and Comment,* Febru-ary 1943, 1, 8.

90. Notation in Diary of Thomas H. Green, Green Papers, JAGSL.

91. William Ewing, "A Unique Experience in Government," *Paradise of the Pacific,* April 1943, 2 (describing the ceremonies); Office of Internal Security, Territory of Hawaii, "Wartime Secu-rity Controls in Hawaii," Part One, 140, Box 24, Richardson Papers, Hoover Institution; Riley H. Allen to Delegate Joseph R. Farrington, February 18, 1943, Farrington Papers, HSA, commenting on the "tremendous amount of rearrangement and adjusting" that had to be done before "what might be called E-Day (E for emancipation)."

92. Anthony to Stainback, September 20, 1943, "Anthony Report," copy in Hawai'i and Pa-cific Collection, Hawai'i State Library [hereinafter Anthony Report].

93. On the end of martial law in 1944, see infra, chap. 16.

94. Diary of Thomas H. Green and personal memoranda, Green Papers, JAGSL.

95. Green to Morrison, January 5, 1943, Green Papers, JAGSL.

96. Green to Morrison, January 9, 1943; and Diary of Thomas H. Green (entries of December 1942–January 1943), both in the Green Papers, JAGSL.

97. See Anthony, *Hawaii under Army Rule.* McCloy had arranged as early as January to transfer Green to the judge advocate general's staff in Washington. (McCloy to Emmons, January 6, 1943, Emmons Papers, Hoover Institution.) Green's promotion to major general and his appointment as judge advocate general of the army were done in a quiet manner, Anthony has written: "Not until after the Senate had acted did the public in Hawaii realize that his name was under consideration." (Anthony, *Hawaii under Army Rule,* 116.) A former chief justice of the territorial high court, James L. Coke, denounced Green's appointment on grounds that he was "not fit for the position in view of his record in Hawaii." (Quoted in ibid.) *Contra,* in Green's personal correspondence (Green Papers, JAGSL), there are numerous letters of congratulation on his appointment from former associates, including civilians, in the military government, praising his performance of duties during military rule in Hawai'i.

98. The plan that Richardson authored in 1941 did not need to be put into effect in the immediate circumstances of the coal miners' strike, which was ended by mediation arranged by the president and placed under Secretary Ickes's direction. (John H. Ohly, *Industrialists in Oliver Drab: The Emergency Operation of Private Industries in World War II* [Washington, DC: Center of Military History, U.S. Army, 2000], 13, 57–58, and appendix G-7.) Documents on Richardson's role in the famous Gary strike are in a folder titled "Legal Aspects," Box 6, Richardson Papers, Hoover Institution.

99. See discussion of the *Glockner* habeas hearing and Richardson's General Orders threatening a federal judge, infra, pp. 263ff.

100. Ironically—in light of the declaration by Ickes and other critics such as Anthony, that only a conquered nation should be ruled as the army was ruling in Hawai'i—General Green believed that one important "reward" that would be reaped from the experience of martial law in Hawai'i was that it would provide "a proving ground for the Military government of Japan"! (Green to General E. C. McNeil, July 9, 1942, Green Papers, JAGSL.)

101. Ickes to Stimson, January 27, 1943, copy in McCloy Files, NA.

102. Stimson to Ickes, January 29, 1943, copy in McCloy Files, NA.

103. Ibid.

104. Ibid. On Stimson's role in the Philippines, see Geoffrey Hodgson, *The Colonel: The Life and Wars of Henry Stimson, 1867–1950* (New York: Knopf, 1956), 134–141.

105. Ickes to Stimson, February 4, 1943, copy in Green Papers, JAGSL.

106. Ibid.

107. On McCloy's central role in the internments policy, see Irons, *Justice at War,* passim; and Hodgson, *The Colonel.*

108. McCloy to Biddle, December 23, 1942, McCloy Files, NA.

109. Ibid. Emphasis added.

110. McCloy to Fortas, January 24, 1943, McCloy Files, NA.

111. McCloy to Biddle, December 23, 1943, McCloy Files, NA.

Chapter 13: The Habeas Corpus Cases

1. The army, as we shall see, maintained that everything within the "fortress" of Hawai'i was related to the war effort and the security of the Islands.

2. Radio No. 284 from Emmons to McCloy, January 3, 1943, McCloy Files, NA.

3. See text supra at pp. 144–145, 153.

4. For discussion of the Supreme Court's decision, see infra, chap. 17.

5. Green to Col. Archibald King, September 24, 1942; and King to Green, September 4, 1942, (stating that the evidence "is no part of the record and has no bearing on your legal right to hold him in custody"), Green Papers, JAGSL.

6. See supra, text at p. 48.

7. FBI, File on Dr. Hans Zimmerman, "alias Fritz Kuhn", No. 5–106, January 28, 1942, copy in Zimmerman Suit records, *Zimmerman v. Poindexter et al.*, Box 157, Case Files for the U.S. District Court for the District and Territory of Hawaii, RG 21, NASB [hereinafter Zimmerman Civil Suit File, RG 21, NASB].

8. Extract from December 30, 1940, FBI report, filed under "33.8—GERMANS (Binder 1)" one-page photostat filed with other evidence in the postwar Zimmerman Civil Suit File, RG 21, NASB. A strange feature of the FBI study is that while it was being compiled, the FBI was apparently working on the theory, entirely lacking in factual support, that Zimmerman had used the alias "Fritz Kuhn"—the name of the leader of the German American Bund, and a name similar to that of Otto Kuehn, the only person ever to be prosecuted for espionage in wartime Hawai'i. (See supra, chap. 6, for discussion of the Otto Kuehn case.) None of the available FBI archival documents indicates that it was ever claimed by the agency's informants or others that Zimmerman ever associated socially or otherwise with Kuehn.

9. Zimmerman made such a claim in a letter to Secretary of War Stimson, March 21, 1942, copy in Zimmerman Civil Suit File, RG 21, NASB. As mentioned below, p. 257, Judge Delbert Metzger, in private correspondence with Zimmerman, encouraged this view of a conspiracy of rivals.

10. Quoted in FBI File No. 65–106, January 28, 1942 (photostatic copy), 3, filed in Zimmerman Civil Suit File, RG 21, NASB.

11. Emmons's deposition in the Zimmerman Civil Suit File, 17, 19-21, 27, RG 21, NASB.

12. Ibid.

13. Frank Thompson, Attorney to Dr. Hans Zimmerman, Sand Island, January 5 [1942], transcript in [Military Government] Office of Censorship [marked incorrectly as dated January 1943], copy Exhibit "TT" in Zimmerman Civil Suit File, RG 21, NASB.

14. Metzger ruling, Zimmerman Suit File, NASB. The precise chronology of the petition and Judge Metzger's action is in the briefs filed in the appeal of Metzger's decision to the Ninth Circuit, and collected in the file for Case #10,093, In re Application of Clara Zimmerman for and on behalf of Hans Zimmerman, for a Writ of Habeas Corpus, Zimmerman Civil Suit File, RG 21, NASB. See also J. Garner Anthony, *Hawaii under Army Rule* (Stanford, CA: Stanford University Press, 1955), 61–64.

15. A chronology of the army command's actions in this regard is included in a detailed memorandum of the Office of the Assistant Chief of Staff for Military Intelligence, Headquarters Hawaiian Department, "Memorandum for the Officer in Charge, Subject: Hans Zimmerman," dated March 18, 1943, copy in Zimmerman Civil Suit File, RG 21, NASB.

16. In late March, there were thirteen internees being held at Camp McCoy as enemy aliens who claimed to be U.S. citizens. (F. R. Gosby, Asst. Adj. General to Adjutant General, "Alien Enemies Claiming American Citizenship," March 27, 1942, copy in Folder 343, JIR.) Two of these internees, G. Herbert Walther and Alfred B. M. Smith, would later sue Gen. Emmons for wrongful detention, as would Zimmerman. See chap. 18, infra.

17. McCloy to Roger Baldwin, Telegram, June 30, 1942, in McCloy Files, NA; copy also in ACLU Records, Seeley G. Mudd Manuscript Library, Princeton University.

18. Ibid.; Roger Baldwin to McCloy, June 30, 1942; Arthur G. Hays and Roger Baldwin to McCloy, July 2, 1942, all in ACLU Records, Seeley G. Mudd Manuscript Library, Princeton University.

19. A transcript of this letter, the original being dated March 13, 1942, was cleared for release by the office of the Cable and Radio Censor, Honolulu, and was released by OMG with Judge Metzger's permission on August 14, 1943, to the *Chicago Tribune*. Metzger also referred to Zimmerman's "sworn enemies" as a factor in generating rumors of his disloyalty, an element of the situation leading to his internment that Zimmerman and his wife had suspected (as noted above) but for which we have found no hard evidence in the files. Judge Metzger was reported in 1943 by the army's counterintelligence division as having been a personal friend of Zimmerman before the war. (Memorandum from Special Agent Charles Slabaugh for the Officer in Charge, Subject: Delbert E. Metzger, August 25, 1943, copy in Richardson Papers, Hoover Institution.) This counterintelligence report may well have been instigated by Richardson in his confrontation with Metzger. However, there is no explicit statement in the War Department and army archives indicating that this information had an influence either way on the army's tactical decisions in the earlier litigation.

20. FBI Files No. 65-106, January 28, 1942 (photostatic copy), p. 3, filed in Zimmerman Civil Suit File, RG 21, NASB.

21. See infra, p. 263.

22. See infra, pp. 264ff.

23. King to Roger N. Baldwin, March 21, 1942, in "Hawaii Files," ACLU Records, Princeton University. The Zimmerman Case was already being discussed among the ACLU's leaders, as evidenced in letter from Baldwin to A. L. Wirin, February 20, 1942, ibid. See also Clifford Forster to Wirin, January 18, 1942, ibid.

24. Anthony, "Martial Law in Hawaii," *California Law Review* 30 (1942), discussed above.

25. Baldwin to Anthony, May 18, 1942, and reply, June 3, 1942, Hawaii files, ACLU Records.

26. See infra, p. 272.

27. Anthony to Baldwin, June 3, 1942, Hawaii files, ACLU Records, Princeton University.

28. W. Wade Boardman to Arthur Garfield Hays, June 16, 1942, ACLU Records, Princeton University.

29. Emmons deposition, 33–34, in Zimmerman Civil Suit File, RG 21, NASB.

30. Col. B. M. Bryan, Memorandum, Subject: ACLU Letter of July 2, 1942, July 11, 1942, McCloy Files, NA. No intervention by the White House is mentioned in the cited documents, but Attorney General Biddle states in his memoir of the period that "the legality of detaining evacuated American citizens against their will was extremely dubious, and, after a few conflicting policy decisions, and the President had declared his unwillingness to suspend the writ of habeas corpus in the [mainland] United States, the few citizen internees who had been brought over were returned to Hawaii." (Francis Biddle, *In Brief Authority* [Garden City, NY: Doubleday, 1962], 223.) See discussion of return of citizen internees to Hawai'i, supra, chap. 8.

31. Roger Baldwin to McCloy, marked USW014311, September 4, 1942; McCloy to Baldwin, September 6, 1942; JMH [Hughes] to McCloy, September 5, 1942 (conveying Gen. Gullion's wish not to disclose location of the internees), all in McCloy Files, NA.

32. Quotation from Judge J. Frank McLaughlin, address at the Social Science Association of Honolulu, May 6, 1946, transcript in Richardson Papers, Hoover Institution; and reproduced in the *Congressional Record,* July 31, 1946, *Appendix,* A4931. [hereinafter McLaughlin Speech].

33. Brief for the United States in *Zimmerman v. Walker,* 132 F.2nd 442 at 446 (9th Cir. 1942), *cert. denied,* 319 U.S. 744 (1943). The lead signature on the government brief was that of Solicitor General Charles Fahy, who had taken this role at the behest of the War Department—which had been asked by General Richardson to seek the highest possible visibility of representation by the Justice Department. (Oscar Cox to Solicitor General Charles Fahy, July 20, 1942, Papers of Charles Fahy, FDRL.)

34. *United States v. Carolene Products,* 304 U.S. 114, 152 n.4 (1935).

35. ACLU and defendant's briefs, *Zimmerman v. Walker,* 132 F.2nd 442, 446 (9th Cir. 1942), *cert. denied,* 319 U.S. 744 (1943) (No. 10,093), Case Files, Hawaii, Record Group 21, NASB.

36. In Warren's testimony to the Tolan committee, he made much the same arguments as in the amicus brief in the Zimmerman appeal, declaring that there was proof of fifth-column activity and naming Japanese-American organizations on which he had evidence of subversive activities. (Charles Wollenberg, "'Dear Earl': The Fair Play Committee, Earl Warren, and Japanese Internment," *California History,* 89 [2012], 22–55.) This episode and the broader roles of Warren and Wenig in contending that espionage and sabotage were immediate threats to security in California and the other West Coast states, and in coordinating with pressure groups hostile to the Nikkei to agitate for evacuation and removal policies, are documented in Peter Irons, *Justice at War: The Story of the Japanese-American Internment Cases* (New York: Oxford University Press, 1983), 212–214 passim.

37. Brief of the State of California as Amicus Curiae, filed November 12, 1942, in *Zimmerman v. Walker* 132 F.2nd 442, 446 (9th Cir. 1942), *cert. denied,* 319 U.S. 744 (1943) (No. 10,093), Case Files, Hawaii, RG 21, NASB. Quotations at 40–41, and 8–9 (relying on article in the *San Francisco Chronicle,* November 6, 1942, 6, in asserting possibility of 161,000 Hawai'i Nikkei being removed to mainland).

38. Brief of the State of California (Ibid., 9). Emphasis added.

39. See especially Wollenberg, "'Dear Earl,'" 22–55.

40. Brief of the State of California as Amicus Curiae, filed November 12, 1942, in *Zimmerman v. Walker,* RG 21, NASB, 40. Emphasis added. The army was concerned that this aspect of Warren's brief might weaken their argument.

41. *Zimmerman v. Walker,* ibid.

42. See text, infra, at p. 263.

43. Memorandum from General Myron Cramer to Assistant Secretary John J. McCloy, "Release of Hans Zimmerman," January 3, 1943, Green Papers, JAGSL. This memorandum indicates that Gen. Green was not against the parole of Zimmerman, but that the Army Intelligence office and the board that examined Zimmerman were opposed to his parole. (Ibid.) Gen. Green apparently had favored parole for Zimmerman before the decision in the Ninth Circuit appeal was filed: "Since the decision in his [Zimmerman's] case is so favorable [the army] suggests that consideration be given to paroling him." (Radiogram No. 2006 from Green to Col. William R. C. Morrison, December 24, 1942, RG 338, NA.)

44. McCloy to General Myron Cramer, January 14, 1943, Green Papers, JAGSL.

45. See Zimmerman Civil Suit File, and Zimmerman to Farrington, November 26, 1942, Farrington Papers, HSA. In a letter to Farrington reviewing her futile efforts to obtain information

about the charges against her husband and to prevent his repeated transfers to and from the main-land, Zimmerman's wife stated that Dr. Zimmerman "would prefer vindication in the eyes of the public instead of just release because of the ending of the war." (Clara Zimmerman to Farrington, February 15, 1943, Delegate Farrington Papers, HSA.) The postwar civil suit is discussed in chap.18, infra.

46. Historical memoir, manuscript, Green Papers, JAGSL. Green gave testimony in the post-war *Zimmerman* suit that "the security people" had believed Zimmerman was a spy (research notes on file in the Edward Norton Barnhart Papers, Hoover Institution Archives). But the army's top security officer in Hawai'i during 1941–1943, Col. Fielder, testified that he had "had nothing to do with the decision." (Ibid.)

47. Zimmerman to Farrington, November 26, 1942, Farrington Papers, HSA.

48. Anthony, *Hawaii under Army Rule,* 64.

49. Diary of Thomas H. Green, entry of July 27, 1942, Green Papers, JAGSL.

50. See *Ex parte Seifert,* No. 296 (D. Haw. 1943); *Ex parte Glockner,* No. 295 (D. Haw. 1943). Both case files, including briefs and transcripts, are on file in the U.S. District Court for Hawaii Records, NASB.

51. Diary of Thomas H. Green, entry of April 7, 1942, Green Papers, JAGSL.

52. Ibid., entry of January 27, 1942, Green Papers, JAGSL.

53. "Annex No. 2 to G-2 Periodic Report, No. 61 (marked "Secret"), Office of the Command-ing General, Hawaiian Department, August 28, 1943, RG 338, NA.

54. Ibid.

55. See Anthony, *Hawaii under Army Rule,* 64–77, for detail of the cases and the incidents that surrounded the hearings before Judge Metzger in the district court.

56. Richardson to Judge Brian Montague, September 2, 1943, Richardson Papers, Hoover Institution.

57. August 17, 1943, Cable JAG 9, for General Marshall to Richardson, August 17, 1943, copy in McCloy Files, NA.

58. *Honolulu Star-Bulletin,* August 18, 1943 (late afternoon edition).

59. Anthony to Farrington, August 27, 1943, Farrington Papers, HSA.

60. Assistant Secretary McCloy's office had become involved in discussion of the Hawai'i situation with Justice Department officers as early as August 25, when McCloy telephoned Solici-tor General Fahy to discuss Judge Metzger's rulings. In the following three days, McCloy spoke by phone several more times with Fahy and also with Fortas and Generals Emmons and Green; and he and Fahy agreed that they should "try to get Judge to withdraw contempt order." (McCloy Diaries, entries of August and September 1942, Amherst College.)

61. Transcript of Record, *Ex parte Glockner,* No. 295 (D. Haw. 1943), copy in Habeas Case Files, Hawaii Files, NASB.

62. Annex No 2 to G-2 Periodic Report, No. 61 (marked "Secret"), Office of the Command-ing General, Hawaiian Department, August 28, 1943, RG 338, NA.

63. Charles W. Slabaugh, Special Agent, CIC, "Memorandum for Officer in Charge (Gen. Holmes), Counter Intelligence Division, Subject: Delbert E. Metzger," August 25, 1943, Richardson Papers, Hoover Institution; H. Brett Melendy, "Delbert E. Metzger, Hawaii's Liberal Judge," *Ha-waiian Journal of History* 35 (2001): 54. In fact, Metzger had a degree from the Indiana Law School and had passed the Hawai'i bar exam in 1923.

64. Anthony, *Hawaii under Army Rule,* 66.

65. General Orders No. 31, August 25, 1943, reprinted in Anthony, *Hawaii under Army Rule*, 179. Andrew Jackson, Commanding General in the War of 1812, declared martial law in New Orleans after occupying the city; he arrested a judge who issued a writ of habeas corpus for release of a prisoner who had been arrested for sedition. See Matthew Warshaver, *Andrew Jackson and the Politics of Martial Law* (Knoxville: University of Tennessee Press, 2007).

66. Judge J. Frank McLaughlin, Address at the Social Science Association of Honolulu, Hawaii, May 6, 1946, transcript in the Richardson Papers, Hoover Institution. Judge McLaughlin's speech was later published in the *Congressional Record,* appendix, July 31, 1946, A4931. See also the story as recounted later by Judge Claude McColloch, "Now It Can Be Told: Judge Metzger and the Military," *American Bar Association Journal* 35, no. 5 (1949): 365. Metzger and McLaughlin seldom took the same position on controversial issues. See Melendy, "Delbert E. Metzger," 56–59.

67. Transcript, "Oral Report Made by Mr. Frederick B. Wiener, 11 May 1946" [to Maj. Gen. Moore et al.], 10, Richardson Papers, Hoover Institution [hereinafter Wiener Report].

68. Wiener Report, 15–16 (also pointing out that Col. Morrison at this time "went around trying to get Garner Anthony's clients to boycott their lawyer").

69. Green to Harry Hassock, September 8, 1943, Green Papers, JAGSL.

70. Radio No. 5283, from Richardson to McCloy, August 27, 1943, McCloy Files, NA.

71. Ibid. The later appellate litigation is considered infra, pp. 283–284.

72. Memorandum from Capt. John A. Hall to Capt. Horan, Subj: Publication in Federal Register of Hawaiian Military Governor's General Orders 31 and 38, November 23, 1943 (apparently forwarded for McCloy's attention), in McCloy Files, NA. See also Anthony, *Hawaii under Army Rule,* 68–69 (describing how special measures had to be taken by the military to protect Gen. Richardson from service of court papers during a visit to Honolulu of Under Secretary of War Patterson).

73. McCloy to Richardson, September 24, 1943, McCloy Files, NA.

74. McCloy to Richardson, Radio No. 6316, August 31, 1943, McCloy Files, NA.

75. Richardson to McCloy, September 3, 1943, McCloy Files, NA.

76. Richardson to McCloy, September 5, 1943, RG 338, NA.

77. Ibid.

78. Ickes to McCloy, August 30, 1943, Ickes Papers, LC.

79. Garner Anthony, who worked behind the scenes trying to bring Judge Metzger around to a compromise position, wrote privately that neither he nor many other experts agreed with Metzger as to the claim that the partial restoration in March had tacitly involved the termination of martial law. Anthony to Farrington, August 27, 1943, Farrington Papers, HSA. See supra, p. 267, and infra, p. 278.

80. Ickes to McCloy, August 30, 1943, Ickes Papers, LC.

81. McCloy to Charles Fahy, September 30, 1943, McCloy Files, NA.

82. Ickes to Stimson, October 1, 1943, McCloy Files, NA.

83. Fahy to McCloy, September 29, 1943, McCloy Files, NA.

84. Fortas to Walter P. Armstrong, October 15, 1943, copy in Ickes Papers, LC.

85. Ibid.

86. Ibid.

87. Memorandum from Edward J. Ennis to General Robert Richardson, "Habeas Corpus Proceedings," [no date, but August 1943], copy in the Richardson Papers, Hoover Institution.

88. Ibid.

89. All quotations that follow in this paragraph are from ibid. Ennis's view about the status of civil liberties in the United Kingdom was, in fact, too sanguine. For a scholarly history of British policy, see A. W. Brian Simpson, *In the Highest Degree Odious: Detention without Trial in Wartime Britain* (Oxford: Clarendon Press, 1992).

90. Memorandum from Edward J. Ennis to General Robert Richardson, "Habeas Corpus Proceedings," [no date, but August 1943], copy in the Richardson Papers, Hoover Institution.

91. Ibid.

92. Richardson to General Julius Ochs Adler, October 8, 1943, RG 338, NA. Richardson had been adamant that the fine should be quashed altogether. He left no doubt that he was disappointed in having been forced to back down. "It is a personal, punitive fine, as far as I am concerned," he wrote, suggesting that the president himself ought to remit the $5,000, thus "showing that he was back of the military in this case." (Ibid.). Edward Ennis agreed with Richardson that if the president paid the fine, he would consequently legitimize the army's stand. For this reason, Ennis opposed such a move and wrote, "A pardon or a remission of fines is . . . undesirable because it is not normally used until the judicial remedy has been exhausted and it might appear to validate the military action and rebuke an independent court." (Report [author unknown], "Summary of Ennis Report," October 1943, Fortas Files, RG 48, NA.)

93. See Ennis to McCloy, August 7, 1943, McCloy Files, NA.

94. Ibid.

95. Ibid.

96. Radio 102251Z from Colonel Hughes (Fort Shafter) to McCloy, October 14, 1943, McCloy Files, NA.

97. Ibid. That the effect of a full-dress trial would not necessarily be wholly damaging to the army was indicated in correspondence between Delegate Farrington and Garner Anthony in September. Farrington noted that the confrontation between Richardson and the court had attracted a great deal of attention in Washington. "It will interest you to know," he reported further, "that the comment of Senator Reynolds, Chairman of the Senate Military Affairs Committee, was that any controversy of this nature should be resolved in favor of the military." (Farrington to Anthony, September 10, 1943, Farrington Papers, HSA.) Farrington also predicted that if the president should instruct Richardson to revoke his order against the court, it might inspire "a counter-proposal in Congress, emanating from War Department sources, to establish military government in the Islands by law." (Ibid.)

98. Wiener Report, 10. See also McCloy to Richardson, August 15, 1943, RG 338, NA.

99. Richardson to McCloy, October 13, 1943, McCloy Files, NA.

100. Anthony to Stainback, September 20, 1943, "Anthony Report," copy in Hawai'i and Pacific Collection, Hawai'i State Library.

101. Ibid., 3. On the Organic Act and its terms, see supra, pp. 1, 21.

102. Anthony to Stainback, September 20, 1943, "Anthony Report," 7, 9.

103. Ibid., 12–14.

104. See supra, p. 238.

105. Anthony Report, 15–22. Exclusion was, indeed, the plan that was implemented when martial law was ended, but without incorporating Anthony's insistence on due process. See supra, p. 154.

106. Ibid., 22. N.B. This report was also used by Anthony as the principal basis for his second *California Law Review* article in 1943, supra, chap. 11, note 52.

107. J. Garner Anthony, "The University in a Free Society," University of Hawaiʻi Occasional Paper No. 42, June 1943 [hereinafter Anthony, "Free Society"].

108. Authors' interview of Mrs. Garner Anthony, Honolulu, April 1994; and Lynda Mair, interview of J. Garner Anthony, Honolulu, November 12, 1971, Oral History Project of the Watumull Foundation, Honolulu, copy in Hawaiʻi State Library.

109. Ickes to Biddle, December 18, 1943, Fortas Files, RG 48, NA.

110. Ibid. When Anthony resigned in December 1943, in the face of appeals from Joseph R. Farrington and others that he remain as attorney general, he expressed confidence that his successor, Nils Tavares, would continue to work effectively in that office, including presumably work in the cause of restoration of civilian government. (Anthony to Farrington, December 24, 1943, Farrington Papers, HSA.)

111. Radio No. 102251Z from Colonel Hughes (Fort Shafter) to Assistant Secretary John J. McCloy, October 14, 1943, McCloy Files, NA. ("[A] Japanese American case would clearly be [the] best test case of internment power which could probably be won on [the] basis of [the] *Hirabayashi* case which the Judge [Metzger] here agrees with.")

112. Radio No. 102251Z from General Robert Richardson to Assistant Secretary John J. McCloy, October 13, 1943, McCloy Files, NA.

Chapter 14: New Habeas Cases

1. *Ex parte Duncan,* 66 F. Supp. 476 (D. Hawaii 1944); *Ex parte White,* 66 F. Supp. 982 (D. Hawaii 1944); *Ex parte Spurlock,* 66 F. Supp. 997 (D. Hawaii 1944).

2. *Honolulu Star-Bulletin,* April 8, 1944, p. 6; Transcript of Record, *Duncan v. Kahanamoku,* U.S. Supreme Court, October Term, 1945, 467 [hereinafter *Duncan* Transcript].

3. *Duncan* Transcript.

4. See *Duncan* Transcript, and Nimitz testimony in the government's brief for appellant, filed June 17, 1944, in *Steer v. White,* copy in Case File No. 10,774, U.S. 9th Circuit Court of Appeals, RG 276, National Archives, San Bruno. Contemporary newspaper accounts in the *Honolulu Star-Bulletin* and in the *Honolulu Advertiser* were also quite complete, day-by-day, as the testimony was presented. General Richardson's testimony is extensively quoted in Dorothy Benyas, "Richardson Says Martial Law Is Valid," *Honolulu Advertiser,* April 12, 1944, p. 1; "Habeas Case Verdict to Be Issued Today," *Honolulu Advertiser,* April 13, 1994, p. 1; and Nimitz's as well, in "Testimony of General Richardson, Admiral Nimitz in Habeas Corpus Case," *Honolulu Star-Bulletin,* April 15, 1944, p. 8.

5. In addition to the *Duncan* Transcript, detailed accounts of Stainback's testimony are in Dorothy Benyas, "Governor Speaks For Civilian Rule," *Honolulu Advertiser,* April 8, 1944, p. 1; and "Text of Governor Stainback's Testimony in Habeas Corpus Case," *Honolulu Star-Bulletin,* April 18, 1944, p. 7.

6. *Duncan* Transcript; the judges' testimony was also cited as important evidence on the point of "necessity" by Judge McLaughlin in his habeas order in *Ex parte Spurlock*.

7. "Richardson and Anthony in a Spirited Exchange," *Honolulu Star-Bulletin,* April 11, 1944, 6.

8. Transcript, "Oral Report Made by Mr. Frederick B. Wiener, 11 May 1946" [to Maj. Gen. Moore et al.], 11–12, Richardson Papers, Hoover Institution [hereinafter Wiener Report]. General Morrison "is the one who went around trying to get Garner Anthony's clients to boycott their lawyer." (Ibid., 15.) In correspondence with Farrington just after a decision came down in the *Duncan*

hearing, Anthony wrote: "I would like you to know that Colonel William R. C. Morrison, the executive of the 'military governor,' has attempted to intimidate me by getting at some of the leading clients of [my] firm." (Anthony to Farrington, March 23, 1944, Delegate Farrington Papers, HSA.)

9. "A Comment From Mr. Ennis," *Honolulu Star-Bulletin,* April 17, 1944, p. 4 (editorial). Emphasis added.

10. *Ex parte Duncan,* 66 F. Supp. 976.

11. Ibid., 980. All quotations of Judge Metzger's opinion, in text following here, are from ibid., 980, 981.

12. Ickes to McCloy, August 30, 1943, McCloy Files, NA.

13. Telephone conversation between Abe Fortas and Capt. Hall, August 18, 1943, transcription in McCloy Files, NA. It was Edward Ennis's interpretation that under the 1943 Restoration Agreement martial law remained in effect and the writ was suspended, "but civilian agencies resumed specified functions. In addition, judicial proceedings, with the exception of criminal actions against members of the armed forces and criminal prosecutions for violations of military orders, were returned to the courts." (Staff Memorandum, "Summary of Ennis Report," October 1943, Fortas Files, RG 48, NA.) Unlike the War Department and army command, however, Ennis at this time apparently regarded it as remaining within the authority of the civilian territorial governor to determine whether and when the privilege of the writ of habeas corpus might be restored—rather than regarding the December 1941 proclamation of martial law as having surrendered this question to the entire discretion of the commanding general. (Ibid.)

14. *Duncan* Transcript. The case went up on appeal as *Kahanamoku v. Duncan,* 146 F.2nd 576 (9th Cir. 1945). The transcripts of record of the Duncan and White habeas hearings in the District Court are available in full in the case files, NASB. (See note 4, supra.)

15. *Ex parte White,* 66 F. Supp. 982, 984 (D. Haw. 1944).

16. Ibid., 988.

17. Richardson to McCloy, Radio R-16621, May 18, 1944, copy in Richardson Papers, Hoover Institution.

18. *Ex parte Spurlock,* 66 F. Supp. 997 (1944). Richardson's views are quoted from a radiogram of Richardson to McCloy, May 18, 1944; and Morrison for Richardson in a radiogram from himself to Gen. Cramer and McCloy, May 23, 1944, both in McCloy Files, NA.

19. Richardson to McCloy, May 18, 1944 (Radio R. 1662), and Morrison for Richardson to Cramer and McCloy (Radio RJ 17077), copies in Richardson Papers, Hoover Institution.

20. *Ex parte Spurlock,* 66 F. Supp. 997, 1006.

21. Ibid., 1004.

22. Ibid., 1006.

23. Slattery to Morrison, February 17, 1944, RG 338, NA. Slattery was chief of the Legal Section in the Office of the Military Governor and had himself presided over many of the hearings of the Military Governor's Reviewing Board.

24. Ibid.

25. Earlier, it will be recalled, Zimmerman, Glockner, and Seifert were asked to sign damage waivers; Zimmerman refused, but the other two did agree to the procedure in order to gain their freedom, upon agreeing also to withdraw from litigation of the appeals. The Japanese-American internees were similarly asked to sign waivers before being "released" on parole to the mainland WRA camps.

26. Col. W. J. Hughes to Morrison, February 13, 1945, copy, RG 338, NA.

27. Radio No. R-71951 from Robert Richardson to Judge Advocate General T. H. Green, October 15, 1945, Richardson Papers, Hoover Institution.

28. Ennis to Angus Taylor, October 13, 1942, Criminal Files, Zimmerman Case File, Dept. of Justice Records, RG 118, NASB. "I intend to restrict the argument of this [Zimmerman] appeal very closely to the limited point involved and to avoid the more controversial aspects of martial law." (Ibid.)

29. Ennis to Biddle, April 10, 1943, Dept. of Justice Records, RG 118, NASB.

30. "Writ Privilege Denied Only in Military Cases," *Honolulu Advertiser,* October 23, 1943, 1.

31. Memorandum from Edward Ennis to the Solicitor General, January 21, 1944, Papers of Charles Fahy, FDRL. The purpose of this memorandum was to persuade the Justice Department not to moot the *Endo* case, which was going up on appeal. Ennis referred to the mooting strategy as one that might also be applied in the *Duncan* and *White* cases (as had happened already with the *Zimmerman, Seifert,* and *Glockner* cases) with the unfortunate result of preventing the high court from ruling on the "probably unconstitutional" actions of the army regime in Hawaiʻi. (Ibid.)

32. Memorandum from Lt. Col. Harrison to Capt. Colclough, June 6, 1944, McCloy Files, NA.

33. Ibid. Urging that the military authorities take a different approach in Hawaiʻi, Col. Harrison also contended that "the major arguments used under martial law have not dealt with the question of the military necessity for such martial law but have tended to become arguments for the maintenance of control of the labor forces in Hawaiʻi. In this problem both the Army and Navy are seriously concerned." (Ibid.)

34. Authors' telephone interview with John P. Frank, Esq., August 1990. There is correspondence between Frank and Fortas as to the most effective arguments that might be advanced in briefs for the appellants in the *White* and *Duncan* appeals to the Supreme Court. There is also some evidence that the Department of the Interior lawyers considered, at least briefly, seeking permission to file an amicus brief in the Duncan litigation, on the side of the appellants and against the army. (Memorandum from John P. Frank to the Under Secretary, June 12, 1944, copy in the Fortas Files, RG 48, NA.)

35. *Ex parte Duncan,* 146 F.2nd 576 (9th Cir. 1944), *rev'd sub nom., Duncan v. Kahanamoku,* 327 U.S. 304 (1946); *White v. Steer,* 146 F.2nd 576 (9th Cir. 1944); *Steer v. Spurlock,* 146 F.2nd 652 (9th Cir. 1944).

36. 146 F.2nd, 581, 583–584.

37. Ibid., 580, 581.

38. Ibid., 586 (Wilbur, J., concurring). Moreover, the concurring opinion also quoted Governor Stainback's own proclamation announcing partial restoration, in which Stainback declared that "it was agreed that martial law should be continued" but with partial restoration of authority to the civilian government. (Ibid.)

39. Ibid., 589 (Wilbur, J., concurring).

40. *Ex parte White,* 66 F. Supp. 982, 988 (D. Haw. 1944)

41. See supra, p. 279.

42. *Duncan,* 146 F.2nd at 580.

43. *Steer v. Spurlock,* 146 F.2nd 652 (9th Cir. 1944).

44. One may speculate that Stephens held back from releasing it because of ill feeling on the Ninth Circuit bench that had been directed against one of his fellow judges, William Denman,

when the latter had written a heated protest against a certification procedure, rushing a case to the Supreme Court rather than ruling on the Japanese-American appellants' suits in the famous "test cases" challenging the curfew and removal orders. (This was in the *Hirabayashi, Korematsu,* and *Yasui* cases on appeal.) Peter Irons discusses this incident and the decision to block publication of Denman's dissent in *Justice at War: The Story of the Japanese-American Internment Cases* (New York: Oxford University Press, 1983), 182–185. Notoriously erratic and unpredictable, Denman in April 1944 vigorously pursued an end-run around the government lawyers in the *Endo* case, this time to advance the precise certification procedure he had so bitterly opposed earlier. (Ibid., 263–265.) See also Roger Daniels, *The Japanese American Cases: The Rule of Law in Time of War* (Lawrenceville: University Press of Kansas, 2013), 40–46.

45. On mooting of *Ex parte Spurlock* see 324 U.S. 868 (1945); and J. Garner Anthony, *Hawaii under Army Rule* (Stanford, CA: Stanford University Press, 1955), 81. See also Louis Fisher, *Military Tribunals: Historical Patterns and Lessons,* Congressional Research Service Report for Congress, No. RL32458 (Washington, DC: Congressional Research Service, 2004), 51.

46. The six cases to which we refer were those of Zimmerman, Glockner, Seifert, White, Duncan, and Spurlock.

Chapter 15: Rising Protests

1. *Chicago Daily Tribune,* August 28, 1943.

2. "What Need for Martial Law in Hawaii?" *Louisville Courier-Journal,* April 15, 1944, reprinted in "Press Comment on Habeas Corpus Case: Mainland Newspapers Discuss Decision," *Honolulu Star-Bulletin,* May 18, 1944, p. 4.

3. Editorial, *San Francisco Daily News,* (n.d.) reprinted in "Civil Rights in Hawaii Upheld: Mainland Newspaper Views on Martial Law," *Honolulu Star-Bulletin,* May 13, 1944, p. 4.

4. Editorial, *San Francisco Chronicle* (n.d.) reprinted in ibid.

5. "'Invasion' in Hawaii," *Boston Herald,* (n.d.) reprinted in ibid.

6. Merlo Pusey, "War vs. Civil Rights," *Washington Post,* May 9, 1944, p. 9.

7. Newspaper clipping attached to letter from Fortas to J. V. Forrestal, July 12, 1944, in Fortas Files, RG 48, NA.

8. The lack of progress in the talks, which centered heavily on control of labor, is reported in Memorandum from Fortas, July 19, 1944, in Fortas Files, RG 48, NA. The memorandum reports that after numerous conferences on the subject, McCloy now had informed him "that it was not contemplated that we 'civilian officials' should have any functions under the civilian labor control plan." On July 12, 1944, Solicitor Fowler Harper reported that the negotiations had "apparently broken down." (Harper to Fortas, July 12, 1944, in Fortas Files, RG 48, NA.)

9. Fortas to McCloy, July 12, 1944, Fortas Files, RG 48, NA. See also Laura Kalman, *Abe Fortas: A Biography* (New Haven, CT: Yale University Press, 1990), 79–80.

10. Quotation of Representative Roy O. Woodruff, "Congress Hears Speech on Civil Rights in Hawaii in Wartime," *Honolulu Star-Bulletin,* June 1, 1944. On concern in Congress regarding conditions under martial law in Hawai'i, see, e.g., "Don't Rock the Boat," *Honolulu Advertiser,* March 29, 1944, p. 6.

11. Representative Jed Johnson of Oklahoma, quoted in *Honolulu Star-Bulletin,* April 26, 1944.

12. "Provost Courts Opposed," *Honolulu Star-Bulletin,* April 7, 1944, p. 1. A prominent member of the bar told the press that "everything which has been accomplished under martial law

could also be accomplished under promulgation of defense regulations as provided under [the] act of congress adopted in 1942 permitting the president and secretary of war and military commanders to prescribe military areas." (J. Russell Cades, quoted in ibid., 6.)

13. Green to E. C. McNeil, July 9, 1942, in Green Papers, JAGSL. Some civilian supporters of the army's regime shared the view voiced by one apologist for martial law, that "Hawaiian tin-pot attorneys, abetted by Ickes, Thoron, and such," along with Governor Stainback, were responsible for making martial law an issue of unfortunate controversy. (Harry Hassock to Green, August 14, 1942, in ibid.)

14. McCloy to Harry Hopkins, October 19, 1942, McCloy Files, NA.

15. Richardson to John A. Matthewman, January 25, 1946, copy in the Richardson Papers, Hoover Institution.

16. "Lawyers Hit at Provost Courts," *Honolulu Star-Bulletin,* April 7, 1944, pp. 1, 6. Ennis knew, of course, that in the *Hirabayashi* case, for example, concurring opinions by Justices Murphy and Rutledge had expressed serious doctrinal differences with the majority on the legitimacy of the army's claims to authority to suspend the constitutional rights of civilians on the mainland. (*Hirabayashi v. United States,* 320 U.S. 81, 88, 99, 112–14 [1943].)

17. "Bourbon Platform Urges Earliest Termination of Martial Law Here," *Honolulu Star-Bulletin,* May 1, 1944, p. 7. The national Republican platform called for statehood for Hawai'i but did not mention martial law.

18. "Extract from Report of the Attorney General, Territory of Hawaii, to the Governor on the Crime Situation in the Territory of Hawaii, and on Civilian-Military Relations" (not dated, but July 1944), copy in "Hawaii" file, Box 9, Papers of Samuel Rosenman, FDRL [hereinafter Tavares Report].

19. "Memorandum from Governor Stainback: Desirability of Terminating Martial Law and the Suspension of the Privilege of the Writ of Habeas Corpus by Executive Proclamation" (not dated, but July or August 1944 as determined by internal evidence), reporting Stainback's comments, Papers of Samuel Rosenman, FDRL.

20. Ibid. Similarly Farrington saw Garner Anthony's campaign to restore civilian control of civilian affairs as part of the larger cause of "perpetuation of a sound system of local self-government in the Islands." (Farrington to Anthony, December 30, 1943, Farrington Papers, HSA.)

21. [Staff] Memorandum to Kendall J. Fielder, "Political Report: The Governorship of Hawaii," dated July 31, 1942, copy in Green Papers, JAGSL.

22. Farrington to Anthony, December 30, 1943, Farrington Papers, HSA.

23. Anthony to Stainback, September 20, 1943, "Anthony Report," copy in Hawai'i and Pacific Collection, Hawai'i State Library.

24. Ibid., 22.

25. Quotations are all from J. Garner Anthony, "The University in a Free Society," University of Hawai'i Occasional Paper No. 42, June 1943.

26. Bill Castle to Farrington, March 13, 1944, Farrington Papers, HSA. Mr. Castle was a law partner of Garner Anthony.

27. Morrison, Memorandum on martial law for Gen. Richardson, January 20, 1944, Richardson Reading File, RG 338, NA. The official U.S. Army history, published after the war, documented the fact that Richardson and his legal staff, anticipating further attacks on martial law from Stainback and Ickes, "felt that the Commanding General should be prepared not only with a good defense, but might also launch an offensive by suggesting a few plans which might give

those who were then opposed to martial law cause for thought." (Office of the Chief of Military History, "Civil Affairs," 3341n87.)

28. Richardson to McCloy, February 10, 1944, RG 338, NA.

29. McCloy to Richardson, May 17, 1944, McCloy Files, NA.

30. C. Nils Tavares, an attorney practicing in Hawai'i, had previously served as the territorial special deputy attorney general for war matters, 1941–1942, and then under Garner Anthony as territorial assistant attorney general, 1942–1943. He returned to private practice in 1947, and in 1960 he was appointed judge, U.S. District Court, District of Hawai'i, a position he held until his death in 1976. Federal Judicial Center, History of the Federal Judiciary, http://www.fjc.gov/servlet/nGetInfo?jid=2343&cid=999&ctype=na&instate=na.

31. Tavares Report, 8.

32. Stainback to Ickes, January 26, 1944, Ickes Papers, LC (enclosing clipping from the *Honolulu Star-Bulletin,* January 24, 1944).

33. J. Garner Anthony, *Hawaii under Army Rule* (Stanford, CA: Stanford University Press, 1955), 58–59, 103; Gwenfread Allen, *Hawaii's War Years, 1941–1945* (Honolulu: University of Hawai'i Press, 1950), 113–114.

34. Richardson relied for his rejoinder on "Memorandum from Provost Courts Commissioner John F. Wickham to Brig. Gen. William R. C. Morrison," September 23, 1944, RG 338, NA.

35. Tavares Report, 11.

36. Richardson to McCloy, August 13, 1944, McCloy Files, NA. (This was essentially the same consideration as moved the War Department to announce the termination of internments just before the *Endo* decision was issued.) See Peter Irons, *Justice at War: The Story of the Japanese-American Internment Cases* [New York: Oxford University Press, 1983], 344–345, and infra, p. 309.)

37. Richardson to McCloy, August 13, 1944, McCloy Files, NA.

38. See supra, p. 272.

39. Richardson to McCloy, June 19, 1944, copy, Papers of Samuel Rosenman, FDRL.

40. Ernest May, "Hawaii's Work in Wartime, Part II: Our Government of Today," *Honolulu Star-Bulletin,* May 16, 1944, p. 8; Ernest May, "Hawaii's Work in Wartime, Part XXIII: War Labor Board," *Honolulu Star-Bulletin,* June 12, 1944, p. 9; Richardson to McCloy, April 14, 1944, McCloy Files, NA (proposing in general terms a way of turning manpower allocation issues back to civilian agencies). In his *Duncan* trial testimony, however, Stainback charged that the army had done practically nothing to reduce the reach of its significant powers in regulation of civilian life and the economy.

41. McCloy to Richardson, February 2, 1944, McCloy Files, NA (citing Stainback's complaint).

42. Radio No. 1224 from Emmons to McCloy, July 2, 1942, McCloy Files, NA; copy also in the Green Papers, JAGSL.

43. Ibid. With regard to the quality of Richardson's legal counsel from Morrison and staff, in a statement issued by him in court but not published until 1949, Judge Metzger stated that "it appears quite certain that he [General Richardson] was not competently advised locally" in the army's role in the *Glockner* case and the imbroglio surrounding the general order that threatened a federal judge with imprisonment and a fine. (Memorandum from Delbert Metzger, quoted at length in Claude McColloch, "Now It Can Be Told: Judge Metzger and the Military," *American Bar Association Journal* 35, no. 5 [1949]: 365, 368 [stating, in addition, that the legal counsel given Richardson placed the general in the position of "what appeared at the time to be flagrant willful defiance of and disrespect to the Court"].)

44. Fortas to McCloy, April 6, 1944, McCloy Files, NA. Evidence of McCloy's recommendation to the Hawai'i command is in a letter from McCloy to Ickes, August 27, 1943, Ickes Papers, LC. Signs of McCloy's softening of views on this issue were earlier reported in Memorandum from Harold Ickes to Benjamin Thoron, June 2, 1943, Ickes Papers, LC (reporting, in addition, that Richardson, just appointed to succeed Emmons, had agreed to reconsider the need for the military governor title).

45. McCloy to Ickes, August 27, 1943, Ickes Papers, LC.

46. Adler to Richardson (marked "Secret"), October 1, 1943, RG 338, NA.

47. Ibid; McCloy Diaries, entry of October 5, 1943, Amherst College. Adler's advice came despite the fact that General Richardson had sent Adler, a member of the family that owned the *New York Times,* a long memorandum condemning the actions by Judge Metzger in the *Glockner* habeas proceeding and asserting the absolute necessity of military rule in the Islands; he suggested that Adler might place his memorandum in hands of "the right editors." (Richardson to Adler, September 8, 1943, Richardson Papers, Hoover Institution.) Ten days later Secretary Ickes complained to the War Department that the *Times* of September 18 had published a long article on the confrontation in the federal court in Honolulu that hewed so closely in its content to the army position that he believed it obvious that "the article was prepared . . . if not in collaboration with the military authorities, at least with their active cooperation." (Ickes to McCloy, September 18, 1943, McCloy Files, NA.)

48. McCloy to Ickes, February 2, 1944, Ickes Papers, LC (stating that Richardson had never actually agreed to discontinue use of the title, and that Richardson "has felt, I believe on the advice of his lawyers, that as long as martial law existed that term [military governor] was necessary").

Chapter 16: The Termination of Martial Law

1. Francis Biddle, *In Brief Authority* (New York: Doubleday, 1962), 219.

2. Robert E. Sherwood, *Roosevelt and Hopkins: An Intimate History* (New York: Harper & Brothers, 1948), 270–278, 296–300 et passim, is the classic, highly detailed, recounting of the terrific challenges facing Roosevelt and the U.S. armed forces in 1940–1941. See also Attorney General Jackson's earlier comments on what was for the president "the very dark prospect" at the outset of America's combat role in the war: Robert H. Jackson, *That Man: An Insider's Portrait of Franklin D. Roosevelt,* ed. John Q. Barrett (New York: Oxford University Press, 2002), 103–105.

3. President of the United States, *Proclamation of Unlimited National Emergency, May 2, 1941,* Department of State Bulletin, May 31, 1941, http:ibiblio.org/pha/policy/1941/410527a.html.

4. "Roosevelt to Lead Fight On Espionage," *New York Times,* August 5, 1940, 1. Meanwhile he was also authorizing the FBI to engage in wiretapping and other covert measures in the national security area, as recalled in Jackson, *That Man,* 103–105.

5. Biddle, *In Brief Authority,* 226. Emphasis added. Late in 1942, Roosevelt's closest adviser in the White House, Harry Hopkins, sent to the War Department what seems to have been a clear signal that the president was not deeply concerned about, or at least not giving priority to, the civil liberties issues in the Islands. Agreeing to pass on to FDR information of the concerns about the army's overreaching in the martial law regime, Hopkins wrote: "I don't want you to think that I am proposing any change in military control." (Harry Hopkins to John J. McCloy, October 20, 1942, McCloy Files, NA.)

6. Ickes, as was noted earlier, did introduce the issue repeatedly in cabinet meetings, but even he explained that his prime motive in yielding on some important points in the December

1942–January 1943 negotiations was to protect the president's time and energy. (Ickes to Stimson, January 27, 1943, McCloy Files, NA.) By early August, however, Ickes had decided to appeal directly to Stimson. (See supra, p. 267.)

7. Richardson to McCloy, August 1, 1944, McCloy Files, NA.

8. Richardson to McCloy, August 8, 1944, McCloy Files, NA. Emphasis added.

9. The mission assigned to Rosenman is documented in the conference reports and the correspondence in the Hawaii File, Samuel Rosenman Papers, FDRL, passim.

10. Extract from Report of the Attorney General, Territory of Hawaii, to the Governor on the Crime Situation in the Territory of Hawaii, and on Civilian-Military Relations" (not dated, but July 1944), copy in "Hawaii" file, Box 9, Papers of Samuel Rosenman, FDRL [hereinafter Tavares Report], 2.

11. Ibid.

12. Memorandum from Governor Ingram Stainback, "Desirability of Terminating Martial Law and the Suspension of the Privilege of the Writ of Habeas Corpus by Executive Proclamation" (n.d. but ca. July 1944 as determined by internal evidence), Papers of Samuel Rosenman, FDRL. On the *Chicago Daily Tribune* editorial, see p. 287, supra.

13. Richardson's report of his meetings with the president and with Rosenman is in Richardson to McCloy, August 1, 1944, McCloy Files, NA.

14. Ibid.

15. Richardson to McCloy, August 8, 1944, McCloy Files, NA. Emphasis added.

16. Slattery to Morrison, July 25, 1944, RG 338, NA. Slattery was Morrison's top aide, then back in Washington attending talks with the War Department officials and judge advocate general lawyers. Slattery's letter reported that as the proposed draft Executive Order then stood, the provision for transfer of Hawai'i from Interior to War still remained under consideration, though Gen. Green and Col. Hughes (both in the office of the judge advocate general) had not yet committed themselves to it entirely. Slattery stated further: "Colonel Hughes feels that maybe at a later date [in negotiations with Interior and Justice] we might again insert it in the [draft] order for the sake of bargaining and to excite the Department of Interior a little." (Ibid.)

17. Memorandum from Fortas to Ickes, July 19, 1944, Ickes Papers, LC.

18. Richardson to McCloy, August 8, 1944, McCloy Files, NA. Emphasis added. See supra, chap. 5, for discussion of unified labor control.

19. Radio No. R25730 from Richardson to McCloy, August 13, 1944, McCloy Files, NA. Emphasis added. Of course, Richardson wanted the executive order to incorporate no language that cast doubt upon the hierarchy of authority during wartime conditions.

20. "No Cause for Jubilation," *Hawaii: A Magazine of News and Comment,* October 17–31, 1944, 7. Emphasis added.

21. Slattery to Morrison, July 25, 1944, RG 338, NA.

22. Memorandum from Col. William J. Hughes to Col. Harrison Gerhardt, August 31, 1944, McCloy Files, NA.

23. The disagreement remained unresolved even at the end of August. Thus Under Secretary of Interior Fortas contended that "termination should be handled in the same way as the original proclamation," which was issued by the then-governor, Poindexter: "What we were going to do was send it over to him [the president] for approval," but it would be "Stainback's proclamation." The conversation ended with discussion of the alternative of having Stainback and the president

simultaneously issue orders for termination of martial law. (Telephone conversation between Col. Gerhardt and Fortas, August 31, 1944, [transcript], McCloy Files, NA.)

24. *Respondeat superior* (Latin, "Let the master answer") is the legal doctrine that holds an employer liable for the actions of an employee if the action is performed within the scope of his or her employment.

25. Col. Hughes, JAGD, Memorandum for the Secretary of War: "Reasons Why Martial Law in Hawaii Should Be Terminated by Proclamation of the President, Not of the Governor," August 1, 1944, McCloy Files, NA. (This document was also attached to copy of a letter from Ickes to FDR, August 5, 1944, in ibid.). In forwarding to Richardson a draft of the termination proclamation, McCloy explicitly emphasized the desirability of having the president issue the order, so that "in event of any civil suits instituted in Hawaii against Gen. Richardson et al., it would then be possible to plead respondeat superior in courts." (McCloy to Richardson, September 8, 1944, radio WA 2748, RG 338, NA, also copy in McCloy Files, NA.) And, in fact, after the war, General Green used precisely this *respondeat superior* defense in his public statements on martial law in Hawai'i. For example, in an address, "The Dilemma of a General," Green declared: "The Army had nothing [*sic*] to do with martial law in Hawaii except as the agency of the President, and, I might also add, the agency of the civil government of Hawaii." (Undated speech by General Green, manuscript on file in Box 16 of the Green Papers, JAGSL.)

26. Gen. Myron C. Cramer to McCloy, August 25, 1944, McCloy Files, NA; Telephone Conversation between Gerhardt and Hughes, August 25, 1944, 4:30 p.m. (transcript), McCloy Files, NA.

27. Ickes to Roosevelt, August 5, 1944, copy in McCloy Files, NA.

28. Ibid.

29. Ibid.

30. See McCloy Files and Fortas Files (RG 48, NA), August and September 1944, for correspondence and transcripts of telephone calls relating to drafts of the executive order to terminate martial law.

31. Executive Order No. 9489, October 18, 1944, 9 Fed. Reg. 12831; reprinted in J. Garner Anthony, *Hawaii under Army Rule* (Stanford, CA: Stanford University Press, 1955), 134.

32. Presidential Proclamation 2627, dated October 19, 1944, 9 Fed. Reg. 12, and proclamations by Governor Stainback and Gen. Richardson, both dated October 24, 1944. Copies of all three proclamations are in the HWRD, and are also reproduced in Anthony, *Hawaii under Army Rule*, 134–136.

33. See p. 294, supra, re Brig. Gen. Adler's suggestion to Richardson in October 1943 that Richardson create a bureau under a different title from that of military government; Adler's approach was essentially adopted in the plan made effective in late 1944.

34. Territory of Hawaii, Office of Internal Security, "Wartime Security Controls in Hawaii," Part One, 88, Box 24, Richardson Papers, Hoover Institution. In October 1944, with the end of martial law, Morrison became the "Executive of the Military Commander of the Territory of Hawaii Military Area." (Ibid.)

35. Slattery to Morrison, July 25, 1944, RG 338, NA.

36. Radio from Richardson to McCloy, July 21, 1944, McCloy Files, NA.

37. Roosevelt to Stimson, February 1, 1943, copy in McCloy Files, NA.

38. See, e.g., Ickes to Roosevelt, August 5, 1944, and Stimson to Harold Smith (n.d., but marked August 17, 1944), copies of both in McCloy Files, NA (indicating, in addition, that the army was

particularly reluctant to cede a meaningful measure of control over labor exclusively to civilian agencies, as it feared the effect of absenteeism on logistics).

39. See Anthony, *Hawaii under Army Rule,* 103, for further discussion of the termination of martial law.

40. Fortas to McCloy, November 16, 1944, McCloy Files, NA; Judge Adv. Gen. Cramer to McCloy, November 23, 1944, McCloy Files, NA.

41. Richardson to McCloy, December 2, 1944, McCloy Files, NA.

42. McCloy to Fortas, December 11, 1944, McCloy Files, NA. The term "jurisdictionitis" had been used in Fortas's letter of November 16, in which Fortas warned: "Just as soon as the Commanding General assumes another title which has civil connotations, and just as soon as he sets up a separate staff to perform the civil functions vested in him, his aides begin to get jurisdictionitis and conflicts begin to appear between the military and the civilian authorities." (Fortas to McCloy, November 16, 1944, McCloy Files, NA.)

43. Gwenfread Allen, *Hawaii's War Years, 1941–1945* (Honolulu: University of Hawai'i Press, 1950), 113–114; Anthony, *Hawaii under Army Rule,* 103–104 and passim. Richardson issued Security Order No. 3, reaffirming the curfew, on October 24, 1944, the very day that martial law was lifted. The order is reproduced in ibid, 187–189.

44. *Honolulu Star-Bulletin,* July 2, 1945. The Chamber of Commerce meeting at which lifting the curfew was opposed was held in March. Allen, *Hawaii's War Years,* 114.

45. Lynda Mair, Interview of J. Garner Anthony; see also Anthony, *Hawaii under Army Rule,* 28–30, 103.

46. Reference is to Security Order No. 4 in December 1944, quoted in letter drafted by Abe Fortas for Harold Ickes to Henry Stimson (not dated, but attached to note dated December 15, 1944), Fortas Files, RG 48, NA.

47. Ibid.

48. Ibid.

49. *Honolulu Star-Bulletin,* August, 28, 1945, p. 1. The OIS did not close until the end of October. *Honolulu Advertiser,* October 27, 1945, p. 2.

50. Transcript, "Oral Report Made by Mr. Frederick B. Wiener, 11 May 1946" [to Maj. Gen. Moore et al.], 11–12, Richardson Papers, Hoover Institution, [hereinafter Wiener Report]. See also pp. 322–323 for further criticism of Morrison. On General Orders No. 31 and the Metzger-Richardson confrontation, see pp. 263ff.

51. Wiener Report, 12.

52. Ibid.; Memorandum from Richardson to Maj. Gen. George F. Moore, Re: Personnel in Office of Civil Affairs, March 14, 1946; and Memorandum from Richardson to the Secretary of War, May 3, 1946, both in the Richardson Papers, Hoover Institution.

53. Richardson to Commander-in-Chief, Army Forces Pacific, Tokyo, January 15, 1946 (Radiogram-74561), Box 26, Richardson Papers, Hoover Institution.

Chapter 17: The *Duncan* and *White* Cases

1. Ennis to Fahy, April 13, 1944, Attorney Records, Criminal Files, Record Group 118, NASB. See also "Interior, Justice Departments Seek Martial Law Tests," *Honolulu Star-Bulletin,* May 2, 1944.

2. Radio No. RJ 17077 from General R. C. Morrison (for General Richardson) to General Myron Cramer and Assistant Secretary John J. McCloy, April 24, 1944, Richardson Papers, Hoover Institution.

3. A concise biographical reference is available at waikiki.com/dukekahanamoku.html.

4. Draft Memorandum from Stimson to President Roosevelt, December 13, 1944, JAERR, Bancroft Library, UC Berkeley. See also Peter Irons, *Justice at War: The Story of the Japanese-American Internment Cases* (New York: Oxford University Press, 1983), chap. 10.

5. McCloy to Representative Clarence F. Leal, December 6, 1944, JAERR.

6. *Ex parte Endo,* 323 U.S. 283 (1944). For a discussion of the litigation tactics on appeal in this case, and for the president's resistance to the release prior to the elections even though Stimson had indicated at the May 26 cabinet meeting that incarceration of Japanese Americans could be ended "without danger to defense considerations," see Irons, *Justice at War,* 269–72; and Roger Daniels, *The Japanese American Cases: The Rule of Law in Time of War* (Lawrence: University Press of Kansas, 2013), 63–79.

7. The significance of the Court's deliberations in the *Endo* proceeding for the prospective outcome of the *Duncan* appeal is discussed infra, pp. 312–313.

8. Irons, *Justice at War,* 345.

9. Col. Harrison A. Gerhardt, "Memorandum for Mr. McCloy," September 18, 1945, and McCloy to Attorney General Tom Clark, September 18, 1945, both in folder 107–14, JIR.

10. Interview with Edward Ennis, U.S. Attorney, December 20, 1972, JAERR [hereinafter Ennis Interview, JAERR]. See infra, p. 320, for Ennis's own assessment of his role in the *Duncan* and *White* cases.

11. Ibid.

12. Ennis memo prepared for Biddle to be sent to FDR, December 30, 1943, ibid.

13. Memorandum from Edward Ennis to the Solicitor General, January 21, 1944, Papers of Charles Fahy, FDRL. Emphasis added.

14. Ibid.

15. Ibid.

16. Ennis interview, JAERR. It should be recalled that despite knowing that the army report on "necessity" for the West Coast evacuations had been inaccurate in its assertions regarding alleged espionage and sabotage, Ennis, after objecting but being overruled by Solicitor General Fahy, nonetheless had participated as counsel for the government in the *Korematsu* case. (Daniels, *The Japanese American Cases,* 67–70.)

17. Brief for Petitioner at 39–40, 44–45, *Duncan v. Kahanamoku,* 327 U.S. 304 (1946) (Nos. 14, 15).

18. Ibid.

19. Authors' interview with the late John P. Frank. In an interview with Warner W. Gardner by Prof. Laura Kalman (excerpts from interview provided to authors by Prof. Kalman), Gardner, too, recalls that Anthony was given access to the Department of the Interior files.

20. Brief of Nils C. Tavares, Attorney General of Hawaii, and the Bar Association of Hawaii Amicus, at 11, *Duncan v. Kahanamoku,* 327 U.S. 304 (1946) (Nos. 14, 15).

21. Brief for Amicus ACLU, at 29, *Duncan v. Kahanamoku,* 327 U.S. 304 (1946) (Nos. 14, 15).

22. Brief for the United States, at 58, *Duncan v. Kahanamoku,* 327 U.S. 304 (1946) (Nos. 14, 15).

23. Ibid., 55–57, 58–59.

24. See discussion of arguments in that case on appeal, supra, chap. 13.

25. Ibid. The army's absolutist position has been termed the "blanket view" of the martial law power—as opposed to the "qualified view," which admits that the military's judgment can be reviewed on the facts by the civilian courts. See J. Garner Anthony, *Hawaii under Army Rule* (Stanford, CA: Stanford University Press, 1955), 64; cf. Frank, "Ex parte Milligan," 650 (proposing a distinction between "*qualitative*" and "*punitive* or *absolute*" martial law, the former regarding temporary emergency takeovers of authority by the military in emergency conditions, the latter denoting the kind of complete displacement of civil authority such as the army instituted in the Islands).

26. Moreover, the opinion in *Hirabayashi* and the majority in *Korematsu* technically had been concerned only with the initial actions of the army for evacuation, amidst the emergency conditions in the weeks just following Pearl Harbor.

27. *Ex parte Endo,* 323 U.S. 283 (1944). For an illuminating discussion of *Endo* in the context of the exclusion cases, see Howard Ball, "Judicial Parsimony and Military Necessity Disinterred: A Reexamination of the Japanese Exclusion Cases, 1943–44," in *Japanese Americans: From Relocation to Redress* edited by Roger Daniels, Sandra C. Taylor, Harry H. L. Kitano, and Leonard J. Arrington (Salt Lake City: University of Utah Press, 1983). See also Joel B. Grossman, "The Japanese-American Cases and the Vagaries of Constitutional Adjudication in Wartime," *University of Hawai'i Law Review* 19 (1997); and Patrick O. Gudridge, "Remember 'Endo'?" *Harvard Law Review* 116 (May 2002–2003). A comprehensive study of the wartime Court is provided in William M. Wiececk, *The Birth of the Modern Constitution: The United States Supreme Court, 1941–1953* (History of the Supreme Court of the United States, Vol. 12) (New York: Cambridge University Press, 2006), passim.

28. General Orders No. 57, January 27, 1942, in Anthony, *Hawaii under Army Rule,* 148–149. See Charles Fairman, "The Supreme Court on Military Jurisdiction: Martial Rule in Hawaii and the Yamashita Case," *Harvard Law Review* 59 (1946): 833, 855–856 [hereinafter Fairman, "Military Jurisdiction"].

29. Executive Order No. 9066, 7 Fed. Reg. 1407, 1407 (1942) (stating "the successful prosecution of the war requires every possible protection against espionage and against sabotage"); Public Proclamation No. 17 Fed. Reg. 2320, 2321 (1942) (setting the evacuation process in motion, and declaring the entire Pacific Coast to be "subject to espionage and acts of sabotage, thereby requiring the adoption of military measures necessary to establish safeguards against such enemy operations"). These two statements of the rationale for evacuation and internment were quoted in Douglas's first draft, dated November 1, 1944, of the *Endo* majority decision. (Draft opinion, copy in the Papers of William O. Douglas, Library of Congress.) In the final published version the statements were also central to Douglas's argument that espionage and sabotage were not relevant to the *Endo* release.

30. Reed to Douglas, November 9, 1944, Papers of Justice Douglas, LC (regarding irrelevance of espionage and sabotage).

31. Ibid.

32. Memorandum from Justice Douglas to Chief Justice Stone, November 28, 1944, ibid., regarding *Endo.*

33. Ibid.

34. Justice Douglas's draft majority opinion, *Ex parte Endo,* October 27, 1944, Douglas Papers, LC (annotated in handwriting and marked "OK for Printer, 11/1,"; the published opinion contained nearly identical language).

35. Ibid.

36. *Ex parte Endo,* 323 U.S. 283, 310 (1944) (Roberts, J., concurring).

37. *Korematsu v. United States,* 323 U.S. 214, 233 (1944) (Murphy, J., dissenting). Peter Irons points out that Black's majority opinion in *Korematsu,* probably in response to Murphy's attack, insisted that there was "a factual foundation of record" that supported the detention program: Black wrote that "the government's action was predicated not on racial prejudice, but upon the compelling urgencies of national defense." (Irons, *Justice at War,* 339.) It was late in the day, however, for the Court's majority to be backing off from its very explicit endorsement of the idea that all residents, including citizens, of Japanese ancestry could be regarded as potentially dangerous in the context of possible espionage and sabotage.

38. See p. 128 for reference to the Niʻihau incident, which was sometimes cited, despite its unique circumstances, as an example of aiding the enemy.

39. *Duncan* Trial Transcript (Richardson testimony discussing the army's ascribing lack of espionage to martial law).

40. Stone to Black, January 17, 1946, Papers of Justice Hugo Black, LC. Stone wanted Black to frame his argument so as to leave the door open, for example, for the executive to authorize the use of military courts for ordinary justice in a situation in which "the [civil] courts were unable to function for a long period of time, say two or three years." (Ibid.) Mr. Justice Black's Papers have been consulted and cited with the generous permission of Hugo Black Jr., Esq., of Miami.

41. Black to Stone, January 18, 1946, Black Papers, LC. All quotations following are from ibid.

42. Ibid.

43. 327 U.S. 304, 316–317. See Anthony, "Hawaiian Martial Law," 37–53 (providing a perceptive discussion of Black's opinion). A highly critical view of the opinions is in Edward S. Corwin, *Total War and the Constitution* (New York: Alfred A. Knopf, 1947), 100–105.

44. 327 U.S., 324.

45. 327 U.S., 335 (Stone, C. J., concurring).

46. Ibid.

47. Ibid., 337.

48. 327 U.S. 304, 332 (Murphy, J., concurring).

49. Ibid.

50. Ibid., 334.

51. Notes of Justice Murphy on the *Duncan* and *White* cases conference (not dated), Papers of Justice Frank Murphy, University of Michigan Library (summarizing Justice Frankfurter's views).

52. Irons, *Justice at War,* 340–341.

53. 327 U.S. 304, 341 (Burton, J., dissenting).

54. Justice Murphy's notes on December 18 conference, Murphy Papers, University of Michigan Library.

55. 327 U.S. 341.

56. Ibid., 344.

57. Fairman, "Military Jurisdiction," 855.

58. General Green's office in Hawaiʻi had ordered a large number of reprints of Fairman's earlier *Harvard Law Review* article contesting Garner Anthony's criticism of the military regime, with the intent of giving them wide distribution in Hawaiʻi. Also, Fairman had been involved personally

in some of the discussions of the Hawai'i policy—and specifically with the delineation issues—in the offices of the general staff and judge advocate general in Washington during the war.

59. Fairman, "Military Jurisdiction," 857.

60. Ibid.

61. Ibid., 858. The Latin phrase *pro tanto* means "for so much," or "to such an extent." This view was, essentially, the burden of Chief Justice Stone's position in his *Duncan* concurring opinion. See *Duncan v. Kahanamoku,* 327 U.S. 304, 335 (Stone, C. J., concurring).

62. Fairman, "Military Jurisdiction," 858–859.

63. Ibid., 859. Emphasis added.

64. Ibid., 858. See supra, pp. 224–225, for discussion of Fairman's wartime position.

65. Ennis interveiw, JAERR.

66. See Judge J. Frank McLaughlin, address at the Social Science Association of Honolulu, May 6, 1946, transcript in Richardson Papers, Hoover Institution; and reproduced in the *Congressional Record,* July 31, 1946, *Appendix,* A4931, 33–35 [hereinafter McLaughlin Speech].

67. Ibid.

68. See Fairman, "Military Jurisdiction," 857.

69. "They Did It—And We Liked It!," *Honolulu Advertiser,* March 16, 1946, p. 18.

70. McLaughlin Speech.

Chapter 18: War's Aftermath and the Courts

1. Green to Morrison, January 2, 1943, RG 338, NA.

2. Col. William Hughes Jr., JAGD, Memorandum for the Secretary of War: "Reasons Why Martial Law in Hawaii Should Be Terminated by Proclamation of the President, not of the Governor," August 1, 1944, in McCloy Files, NA; copy also in RG 338, NA.

3. Resume of Frederick Bernays Wiener, http://www.relocationarchives.com/showdoc.php?docid=00181&search_id=42415&pagenum=3.

4. See supra, p. 303.

5. Richardson, Memorandum for Secretary of War, marked "Approved by Secretary Robert Patterson," May 3, 1946, copy in Richardson Papers, Hoover Institution.

6. Green to Harry Hassock, March 24, 1948, Green Papers, JAGSL.

7. "Memorandum for General Green, Subject: Martial Law in Hawaii—Contents of Mr. McCloy's Files," March 14, 1946, Green Papers, JAGSL.

8. Emmons was by reputation very gracious in personal relationships, in contrast with the imperiousness of Richardson, Green, and Morrison. He was more inclined than the other three to credit Stainback, Ickes, and other critics for honorable intentions. But he, too, had been insistent on the full extent of his authority once the Office of the Military Governor was functioning under his command. It will be recalled that it was his position in December 1942, a year into the war and well after victory in the Battle of Midway, that "the civil governor must, in the last analysis, be subordinate to the Military Governor." (Emmons to McCloy, December 15, 1942, McCloy Files, NA.)

9. Copies of the broadcasts are in the Green Papers, JAGSL.

10. *Congressional Record,* appendix A, 1699, March 25, 1946. The original draft manuscript is in the Green Papers, JAGSL.

11. Ibid. Emphasis added.

12. Anthony, *Hawaii under Army Rule,* 98.

13. Green, "Memorandum for Chief, Bureau of Public Relations, War Department," n.d., copy in Green Papers, JAGSL.

14. Ibid.

15. Emmons testimony, Zimmerman Civil Suit File, transcript, NASB.

16. Richardson refers to "a number of suits already filed" for damages by May 1946. Memorandum, Richardson to Chief of Staff, "Legislation to Cover Hawaiian Damage Suits," May 29, 1946, Richardson Papers, Hoover Institution.

17. The Walthers had refused to sign a waiver upon their release from internment. Their suit was still pending in 1949, causing General Emmons to evade a marshal trying to serve him a summons when he was visiting Hawai'i. (*Honolulu Star-Bulletin,* October 13, 1949.) Also filing suit against the same five defendants, in March 1946, was Alfred B. M. Smith, a German-born citizen naturalized in 1940, who had been arrested on December 7, 1941, and held in internment until paroled in July 1943. (*Honolulu Star-Bulletin,* March 12, 1946.) The relevant court documents include U.S. District Court, District of Hawaii case files Civil #711, Petrowski v. United States et al. March 2 1946; Civil #719, Walther v. Short et al. December 29, 1950, writ marked as "*returned unexecuted*" on grounds that the defendants Generals Emmons, Richardson, Green, and Morrison had been granted "immunity and protection from service on all processes issued by any Court within the District and Territory of Hawaii," pursuant to an "Order Protecting Witnesses [in the Zimmerman civil suit]" issued on September 6, 1950, by Judge Paul J. McCormick, who had presided in the Zimmerman civil case; and Civil #713, Smith v. Short et al. (marked as discontinued, April 4, 1957), NASB; and also documents relating to Civil Suits #717, #719, and #720, Reel #47, HWRD Collection, University of Hawai'i Library.

18. H.R. 861, 80th Congress, 1st session, January 13, 1947.

19. According to the Wiener Report, Anthony had drafted the indemnity statute "for the sole purpose of permitting these internees to clear their names." (Transcript, "Oral Report Made by Mr. Frederick B. Wiener, 11 May 1946" [to Maj. Gen. Moore et al.], 6, Richardson Papers, Hoover Institution, [hereinafter Wiener Report], 6.)

20. Memorandum from Richardson to the Secretary of War, "Legislation to Cover Hawaii Damage Suits," May 8, 1946, Richardson Papers, Hoover Institution.

21. In 1950, the bill was still pending; at the time, the district court in Honolulu was trying the civil suit brought by Zimmerman against General Emmons, and the judge charged the jury to disregard in its deliberations the possibility that Congress might in future vote compensation to Zimmerman and others. (Zimmerman Civil Suit File, transcript, NASB; "Testimony in Zimmerman Damage Suit Concluded," *Honolulu Star-Bulletin,* December 20, 1950.) Ultimately, the bill failed to pass, although Congress did pass another measure in 1948, providing payment for property losses incurred as a result of evacuation or exclusion from Hawai'i. (Gwenfread Allen, *Hawaii's War Years, 1941–1945* [Honolulu: University of Hawai'i Press, 1950], 369.)

22. Emmons correspondence with the War Department, 1946–1950, Delos C. Emmons Papers, Hoover Institution Archives, Stanford University; Richardson correspondence with the War Department and individuals, 1946–1951, Richardson Papers, Hoover Institution.

23. Richardson to James V. Forrestal, Secretary of National Defense, January 30, 1948; Memorandum from Richardson to the Secretary of War, "Legislation to Cover Hawaii Damage Suits," May 8, 1946, Richardson Papers, Hoover Institution.

24. After his release to the mainland, Zimmerman had spent the rest of the war years in Chicago, where he unsuccessfully sued local hospitals for denying him staff privileges because he lacked the M.D. degree. He later was convicted of conducting surgery without a proper license. (Various FBI reports, Zimmerman Civil Suit File.)

25. Zimmerman Civil Suit File, transcript, passim, NASB. The trial was also followed daily in the Honolulu newspapers. See *Honolulu Star-Bulletin,* May 8, 1946.

26. After hearings in Honolulu, the case was moved temporarily for preliminary proceedings to Judge McCormick's court in Los Angeles. (*Honolulu Star-Bulletin,* November 6, 1947.) Zimmerman then brought a similar suit, against the same defendants, in the U.S. District Court in Washington, DC, a jurisdiction that covered both General Green and Captain Mayfield. (*Honolulu Star-Bulletin,* June 27, 1946.) Unable to serve papers on Emmons, Zimmerman brought suit against General Emmons in Huntington, West Virginia, Emmons's home, and subsequently in San Francisco, when Emmons retired to San Mateo. (*Honolulu Star-Bulletin,* December 21 1947, and July 11, 1949.)

27. *Honolulu Star-Bulletin,* December 15, 1950. The judgment sought was also lowered to $322,647.22. (Summary in *Zimmerman v. C. Emmons,* 225 F.2d 97, August 1, 1955.)

28. Zimmerman Civil Suit File, transcript, NASB. See discussion supra, chap. 13, on the Zimmerman internment and appeals.

29. *Honolulu Star-Bulletin,* December 22, 1950.

30. Ibid., December 22, 1950; "Dr. Zimmerman Loses Suit," ibid., December 23, 1950.

31. Authors' interview with Senator Fong, Honolulu, August, 1999.

32. *Zimmerman v. Emmons,* 225 F.2d 97, (August 1, 1955); *Zimmerman v. Emmons,* 350 U.S. 932 (1956). See also "Court of Appeals Upholds Verdict in Zimmerman Case," *Honolulu Star-Bulletin,* August 3, 1955.

33. "Top Court Rejects Zimmerman Suit," *Honolulu Star-Bulletin,* January 9, 1956.

34. Lynda Mair, interview of J. Garner Anthony, Honolulu, November 12, 1971, Oral History Project of the Watumull Foundation, Honolulu, copy in Hawai'i State Library. Reference above is to his book, *Hawaii under Army Rule* (Stanford, CA:, Stanford University Press, 1955).

35. Notations, some of them added in 1969 and other years, and memoranda, in Diary of Thomas H. Green, Green Papers, JAGSL.

36. Originally known as the Hawaiian Department, the command became U.S. Army Forces, Central Pacific Area in 1943, then U.S. Army Forces, Middle Ocean Areas, in August 1944, and U.S. Army Forces, Middle Pacific, in July 1945. For discussion of Richardson's "pompous" and "finicky" personality, and his "carping" in his relationships with the Navy and the Marine Corps commands, see Stephen Taaffe, *Marshall and His Generals: U.S. Army Commanders in World War II* (Lawrence: University Press of Kansas, 2011), 148–157.

37. Dr. Zimmerman and his wife established the Hans and Clara Zimmerman Foundation to provide financial aid to individuals in Hawai'i wishing to become teachers or to pursue education in a health field. Assets that went to the foundation at his death made it one of the largest scholarship funds in Hawai'i.

38. Yukiko Kimura, *Issei: Japanese Immigrants in Hawaii* (Honolulu: University of Hawai'i Press, 1988), 253–255. For firsthand accounts of several Japanese Americans who went to the mainland as children to join their fathers in relocation camps, see Center for Oral History,

University of Hawai'i, "Unspoken Memories: Oral Histories of Hawai'i Internees at Jerome, Arkansas," www.oralhistory.hawaii.edu/pages/historical/jerome.html. See also collections of oral histories at JCCH and JIR.

39. American Japanese Evacuation Claims Act (Pub. L. No. 80–886, ch. 814, 62 Stat. 1231 [codified as amended at 50 U.S.C.A. app. § 1981 (1982)]); Gwenfread Allen, *Hawaii's War Years, 1941–1945* (Honolulu: University of Hawai'i Press, 1950), 369.

40. CWIRC, *Personal Justice Denied;* Japanese American Evacuation Cases, http://legal-dictionary.thefreedictionary.com/Japanese+American+Evacuation+Cases.

41. Kimura, *Issei,* 229. For several years after the war, however, rumors persisted among a small minority of the Issei and Kibei that Japan had won the war, and as late as 1948 some members of the Hissho Kai (Absolute Victory Club) still believed in Japanese invincibility. (Dorothy Ochiai Hazama and Jane Okamoto Komeiji, *Okage Sama De: The Japanese in Hawai'i, 1885–1985* [Honolulu, HI: Bess Press, 1986], 172–173; Allen, *Hawaii's War Years,* 364.)

42. The Immigration and Nationality Act of 1952 (The McCarran-Walter Act) declared that "the right of a person to become a naturalized citizen of the United States shall not be denied or abridged because of race or sex," thus eliminating the ineligibility of Asians to become citizens. *The Immigration and Naturalization Act of 1952,* Public Law 414, 66 Stat., Title III, Ch. 2, Sec. 311, June 7, 1952. Truman vetoed the bill, despite the fact that, as he said, he had "long urged that racial or national barriers to naturalization be abolished," because it maintained discriminatory quotas against the nations of Southern and Eastern Europe and it applied a political litmus test. In his veto message to Congress, he wrote: "I want all our residents of Japanese ancestry, and all our friends throughout the Far East, to understand . . . I cannot take the step I would like to take, and strike down the bars that prejudice has erected against them, without, at the same time, establishing new discriminations against the peoples of Asia and approving harsh and repressive measures directed at all who seek a new life within our boundaries." (Harry S. Truman, "Veto of Bill to Revise the Laws Relating to Immigration, Naturalization and Nationality, June 25, 1952," www.presidency.ucsb.edu/ws/?pid=14175.)

43. See Kimura, *Issei,* chaps. 14 and 15; Hozami and Komeiji, *Okage Sama De,* 173 and chap. 8; Franklin S. Odo, *No Sword to Bury: Japanese Americans in Hawaii during World War II* (Philadelphia: Temple University Press, 2004), Conclusion.

44. Shivers had been forced by poor health in 1943 to seek a less arduous post on the mainland. The following year, however, he secured an appointment as a customs inspector so he could return to the Islands. He died in 1950.

45. D. S. Myer (Director, WRA), to Ray West (Project Director, Tule Lake Center), March 22, 1945, and copies enclosed with it of letters from Myer directly to Tule Lake prisoners informing them that their wives could not be given permission to join them as "it is contrary to the policy of the WRA to admit persons to the Tule Lake Center who are not already in centers. Hence your request must be denied at this time." (D. S. Myer, Director, WRA, to Tule Lake prisoner Shomei Kaneshiro, Copy stamped "March 22, 1945," RG 210, NA.) The authors have seen in government and personal papers, as well as in the Hawaii Command/OMG records, scores of poignant letters from spouses and other family members separated in this way, and, in several cases, letters from sons who were serving in combat with the 442nd or with the army in the Pacific Theater, pleading that their parents be reunited when the father was incarcerated and the mother left behind in Hawai'i.

46. The account we offer here of the renunciants' status and the litigation that followed is heavily based on analysis in Donald E. Collins, *Native American Aliens: Disloyalty and the Renunciation of Citizenship by Japanese Americans during World War II* (Westport, CT: Greenwood Press, 1985), passim, and John Christgau, "Collins versus the World: The Fight to Restore Citizenship to Japanese American Renunciants of World War II," *Pacific Historical Review* 54 (1985): 1–31. Precise numbers are very difficult to ascertain, since applicants for renunciation recanted in so many cases, and even files on original applications are difficult to trace. As Roger Daniels indicates in his analysis of recently published research, more than 5,500 petitions for renunciation were approved by the attorney general, and half of the petitioners were released or relocated. See Roger Daniels, *The Japanese American Cases* (Lawence: University Press of Kansas, 2013), 122–124; see also Barbara Takei, "Legalizing Detention: Segregated Japanese Americans and the Justice Department's Renunciation Program," *Journal of the Shaw Historical Library* 19 (2005), also in nine parts at https://www.facebook.com/TuleLakeNPS/posts/539669362744875. A perceptive contemporary interpretation (published in 1954, when the last stage of the litigation was still in progress), still very useful, is provided by Jacobus tenBroek, Edwin N. Barnhart, and Floyd W. Matson, *Prejudice, War and the Constitution* (Berkeley: University of California Press, 1968), 175–184. See also Patrick O. Gudridge, "The Constitution Glimpsed from Tule Lake," *Law and Contemporary Problems* 68 (2005): 81–118, a study that also gives attention to the UC Berkeley project (the JERS) and its critics.

47. The government was unyieldingly determined, it became clear, to deport all the renunciants and other prisoners they could, to stay a step ahead of legal proceedings that would impede the program, and to accomplish deportations speedily. The posture taken by the Department of Justice, in defending against renunciants' legal claims as they did, over so long a time, provoked charges from some defenders of the Japanese Americans and from civil liberties groups that it amounted to a campaign to get rid of Japanese residents in the largest numbers possible.

48. Earlier in the war, Judge Goodman had been the only federal judge to dismiss the government's case against Japanese Americans who in 1944, while incarcerated in various WRA camps, had resisted the draft. The case of twenty-six draft resisters from Tule Lake came up before his court. "It is shocking to the conscience," Goodman wrote, "that an American citizen be confined on the ground of disloyalty, and then while so under duress and restraint, be compelled to serve in the armed forces, or be prosecuted for not yielding to such compulsion." Although the Tule Lake draft resisters were not sent to prison, as were those from other camps, they remained incarcerated at Tule Lake. See Eric Muller, *Free to Die for Their Country: The Story of the Japanese American Draft Resisters in World War II* (Chicago: University of Chicago Press, 2001), 143.

49. The other reasons that would warrant denial of petition were that the person had voluntarily chosen to enter the Tule Lake Center in order to reunite with family there; or that the person had been assigned to the center as a prisoner "because of a negative answer to question 28, or because of a denial by the WRA of leave clearance." See tenBroek, *Prejudice, War and the Constitution,* 182. That a large number who refused to answer the questions were given "no, no" status by order of the officials in charge further complicated, if not to say corrupted, the procedure, as explained in Daniels, *The Japanese American Cases,* 94–97.

50. Final order, Judgment and Decree, April 12, 1949, quoted in Christgau, "Collins versus the World," 27.

51. Ibid.

52. Quoted from petition text template prepared by Attorney Collins and incorporated in petitions to U.S. Attorney General Tom Clark, Tule Lake, February 1946, in the Wayne Collins Papers, Bancroft Library, U.C. Berkeley.

53. *McGrath v. Abo et al., McGrath v. Furuya et al.,* 186 F.2nd 766, 773.

54. The decision did grant immediate and full relief, with restoration of citizenship, to 899 Nisei who had been under the age of 21 when they had renounced, for 8 persons declared mentally incompetent, and for 58 renunciants whose appeals for restoration had been denied by the Department of Justice solely on grounds that "they went to Tule Lake to be with family members" [*sic*]. See Collins, *Native American Aliens,* 137–138.

55. *Acheson v. Murakami,* http://id.findacase.com/research/wfrmDocViewer.aspx/xq/fac .19490826_0001.C09.htm/qx. The opinion also included quotations from interviews of Tule Lake prisoners that had been published recently in the book on relocation and internment, *The Spoilage,* which, with a companion volume, *The Salvage,* were, as was noted earlier (p. 198n78) the products of the U.C. Berkeley JERS project. (Dorothy Swaine Thomas and Richard S. Nishimoto, *The Spoilage* [Berkeley: University of California Press, 1946]; and Dorothy Swaine Thomas et al., *The Salvage* [Berkeley: University of California Press, 1952].)

56. 186 F.2nd 766, 772.

57. The Wayne Collins Papers, Bancroft Library, UC Berkeley, contain the full records of Attorney Collins' filings and pleadings, his correspondence with the litigants and the organization that was formed to support their efforts, and billing records. Data on final numbers of litigants are from Christgau, "Collins versus the World," 30–31.

58. The 4,978 included 1,327 of the Nikkei who had already been sent back to Japan in 1945 and 1946, some 347 of the latter group having been denied restoration of their citizenship. (Ibid.)

59. Ibid. An especially ironic aspect of this final day in court was that the named government defendant was Attorney General Ramsey Clark. His father, Tom Clark (later a U.S. Supreme Court justice), then attorney general, was the named defendant in the initial filing of the suit in the U.S. district court nearly a quarter century earlier.

Conclusion

1. Earl Warren, "The Bill of Rights and the Military," *New York University Law Review* 37 (1962): 182.

2. In two other World War II cases, *Korematsu* and *Hirabayashi,* the Court ruled against the Japanese-American petitioners and upheld the government's claim of military necessity; in *Endo,* the Court upheld the rights of individual citizens whose loyalty had been affirmed by the government itself. These three cases were all decided while the war was still in progress, but, unlike in the Hawai'i case of *Duncan,* the courts were open and available to the plaintiffs.

3. John P. Frank, "Judicial Review and Basic Liberties," in *American Law and the Constitutional Order,* edited by Lawrence M. Friedman and Harry N. Scheiber (Cambridge, MA: Harvard University Press, 1978), 397–407.

4. Three of those convicted for violating military orders during the West Coast curfew and evacuation conducted by the army in 1942—Gordon Hirabayashi, Minoru Yasui, and Fred Korematsu—some forty-one years later filed in the federal district courts three separate petitions of *coram nobis* (a rarely invoked procedure for reversal of a conviction on grounds of factual errors on which judgment had relied). They presented documentation of the sordid manipulation

and suppression of evidence, and the crude racist premises, that General DeWitt's command had deployed in order to justify the removals policy. They also documented how Solicitor General Fahy had determined to avoid presenting to the Supreme Court, in the *Japanese-American Cases,* the evidence that would have discredited much or all of the army's case. The hearing on Yasui's petition was mooted on his death in 1986; in the other two cases, the district courts, and on appeal the Ninth Circuit, ruled that the convictions of Hirabayashi and Korematsu should be vacated. The Reagan administration's Justice Department declined to appeal those rulings to the Supreme Court, so that the definitive constitutional ruling that the litigants sought—that is, explicit repudiation of the decisions in the *Japanese-American Cases*—was not (and still has not been) obtained from the Court. Meanwhile, in several subsequent opinions, individual justices of the Supreme Court have referred to those decisions as being, among other things, perverse violations of the equal protection guarantee, "invidious," and "presumptively unconstitutional." (A full account of the *coram nobis* litigation, reprinting the key documents, is in Peter Irons, *Justice Delayed: The Record of the Japanese American Internment Cases* [Middletown, CT: Wesleyan University Press, 1989].) It should also be noted that the Civil Liberties Act of 1988 "acknowledge[d] the fundamental injustice of the evacuation, relocation, and internment of United States citizens and permanent resident aliens of Japanese ancestry during World War II" and provided for redress. (Public Law 100–383 [1988].) See generally Peter Irons, *Unfinished Business: The Case for Supreme Court Repudiation of the Japanese American Internment Cases,* http://lawprofessors.typepad.com/files/case -for-repudiation-1.pdf.

5. CWIRC, *Personal Justice Denied,* Part Two: *Recommendations,* 5. See also Peter Irons, *Justice at War: The Story of the Japanese-American Internment Cases* (New York: Oxford University Press, 1983), 362; and Leslie T. Hatamiya, *Righting a Wrong: Japanese Americans and the Passage of the Civil Liberties Act of 1988* (Stanford, CA: Stanford University Press, 1993).

6. Ethnic Japanese constituted approximately 0.1 percent of the mainland population, 1 percent of the population of the West Coast states, and less than 3 percent of the California population. (U.S. Census, 1940.) The anti-Japanese sentiment was driven in part by economic rivalry and in part by fears based on racial stereotypes of the "yellow peril." See CWIRC, *Personal Justice Denied,* Summary. See also Roger Daniels, *The Politics of Prejudice: The Anti-Japanese Movement in California and the Struggle for Japanese Exclusion* (Berkeley: University of California Press, 1962); Carey McWilliams, *California: The Great Exception,* new ed. (Berkeley: University of California Press, 1999); and, with regard especially to Earl Warren's role in the agitation for mass removal, Charles Wollenberg, "'Dear Earl,'" *California History* 89 (2012): 24, 28–32.

7. There had been serious overt prejudice and racial antagonisms, as well as open strife in labor disputes, in earlier periods of the century in Hawai'i, as referred to in chap. 1, supra. By the 1930s, however, prominent leaders in territorial politics and public discourse—including, for example, Delegate Samuel King and publisher Joseph Farrington, Garner Anthony, the *Star-Bulletin* editor Riley Allen, Judge Delbert Metzger (who as a labor lawyer had represented immigrant plantation workers), Honolulu Police official John Burns, and Hiram Fong, then a young lawyer and acknowledged spokesman for the Chinese-American community—were not only committed to equality of opportunity and political rights for the Japanese Americans and other ethnic groups, but also regarded racial equality in Hawai'i (what Farrington termed "the American Way") as a model for race relations and protection of civil rights for all in the mainland states. These were the very things that the rabid segregationists in the U.S. Congress responded to as the *danger,* rather than as a source of hope, if Hawai'i were to be granted statehood. (Authors' interviews with

Mrs. Garner Anthony, April 1994, and with Senator Hiram Fong, August 1999.) See also Stuart G. Brown, *John A. Burns Oral History Project, 1975–1976* (n.d., privately printed); and J. Garner Anthony, "The University in a Free Society," University of Hawai'i, Occasional Paper No. 42, June 1943. In 1921 Metzger, then magistrate in the Hilo court on the Big Island, had intervened dramatically to stop a sheriff's force from ambushing a group of Filipino plantation workers' strike leaders; in 1924, as counsel in a Hanapepe court, he won acquittal, on grounds of their rights of free speech, for leaders of a strike of Filipino field workers. (Ruth Tabrah, *Hawaii: A History* [New York: W. W. Norton, 1984], n.p.; John E. Reinecke, *The Filipino Piecemeal Sugar Strike, 1924–25*, vol. 3 [Honolulu: University of Hawai'i Press, 1996], 62.)

8. See supra, p. 149.

9. Diary of Thomas H. Green, February 1, 1942, Green Papers, JAGSL.

10. Earl Albert Selle, "The Emperor Is the Enemy," *Honolulu Advertiser,* March 19, 1943, p. 12. The *Honolulu Advertiser* also ran a series of signed editorial columns by Selle in which Japanese Americans were stereotyped in a great variety of uncomplimentary ways, raising questions about their reliability in wartime. (Selle, "The Floor Is All Theirs," *Honolulu Advertiser,* March 8, 1943, p. 10.) See also "Begin on Japanism Now," *Honolulu Advertiser,* March 5, 1943, p. 10; "Thin-Skinned and Thick-Headed or Discrimination—A Basis for It," *Honolulu Advertiser,* March 12, 1943, p. 12.

11. *Honolulu Advertiser,* September 12, 1943. It must be noted that this was a period in which the army had begun to draw heavy criticism for General Richardson's aggressive confrontation with Judge Metzger in the habeas imbroglio.

12. Richardson to McCloy, February 10, 1944, McCloy Files, NA.

13. Memorandum, President to the Secretary of the Navy, February 26, 1942, PSF Confidential File, FDR papers, FDRL. Emphasis added.

14. Godfrey Hodgson, *The Colonel: The Life and Wars of Henry Stimson, 1867–1950* (New York: Alfred A. Knopf, 1990), discusses Stimson's policy roles and McCloy's responsibilities.

15. On McCloy's involvement in crucial military matters in Europe during 1943–1944, see Kai Bird, *The Chairman: John J. McCloy and the Making of the American Establishment* (New York: Simon and Schuster, 1992), 172–186. On the intensity of combat and heavy U.S. casualties (creating heavy pressure of the War Department planners and administration) in the period of McCloy's involvement in civilian oversight of the army in combat operations, see Rick Atkinson, *The Day of Battle: The War in Sicily and Italy, 1943–1944* (New York: Henry Holt, 2007). On Stimson's role in oversight of the A-bomb's development, see Hodgson, *The Colonel: The Life and Wars of Henry Stimson,* 292–341.

16. See supra, pp. 247–248.

17. Interview with Edward Ennis, December 20, 1972, transcript in JAERR Collection, Bancroft Library, UC Berkeley.

18. Quotation from Edward Ennis in private interview and public testimony before the CWIRC, quoted in Peter Irons, *Justice at War,* 350.

19. Rowe, "Memorandum for the Attorney General," April 16, 1943, Box 33, Rowe Papers, FDRL.

20. Rowe, quoted in Walter Isaacson and Evan Thomas, *The Wise Men: Six Friends and the World They Made* (New York: Simon and Schuster, 1986), 199.

21. February 1, 1942, responding to Biddle's objections to the forced removal. Quoted in Roger Daniels, *The Japanese American Cases: The Rule of Law in Time of War* (Lawrence: University Press of Kansas, 2013), 9. Emphasis added.

22. Stimson Diary, February 27, 1942, Yale University Library (microfilm); also quoted in Hodgson, *The Colonel,* 259.

23. McCloy to Alexander Meiklejohn, September 30, 1942, copy to Dillon Myer, JAERR, Bancroft Library, UC Berkeley.

24. Diary of Charles M. Hite, December 7, 1941, quoted in Gwenfread Allen, *Hawaii's War Years, 1941–1945* (Honolulu: University of Hawai'i Press, 1950), 35; Testimony in federal district court, December 12, 1950, reported in the *Chicago Daily Tribune,* December 13, 1950, and in "Poindexter Tells about Martial Law," *Honolulu Star-Bulletin,* December 12, 1950.

25. J. Garner Anthony, "Martial Law in Hawaii," *California Law Review* 30 (1942), 371–396.

26. *Hearings before the Joint Committee on the Investigation of the Attack on Pearl Harbor,* 79 Cong, 2nd Sess. (1946), Part I: 5428.

27. For Stimson's admiration of the U.S. administration of the territories following 1898, see supra, pp. 246–247.

28. The folder on "Medal citations, clippings, and correspondence" in the Emmons Papers, Hoover Institution, contains information on Emmons's illustrious career as champion of long-range bomber operations, special representative of the U.S. Armed Forces in initial discussions in England of joint command planning in 1940, and other matters.

29. Confidential memorandum, Biddle to the President, December 17, 1942, Biddle Papers, Box 2, FDR Library.

30. Diary of Thomas H. Green, entries of March 9, April 6, and July 23, 1942; and January 1943, Green Papers, JAGSL.

31. See supra, pp. 246–247.

32. Richardson testimony in *Duncan* trial case, in "Court Record of Richardson's Testimony," *Honolulu Star-Bulletin,* April 14, 1944.

33. Ibid. Richardson referred, in his testimony, to some cases on the mainland in which federal judges had granted habeas relief to internee prisoners.

34. Richardson to McCloy, June 24, 1943, McCloy Files, NA (stating that Stainback and Anthony were opposing measures vital to the success of the war effort).

35. Wiener Report; see also supra, pp. 235, 244.

36. Anthony to Roger M. Baldwin, February 28, 1944, copy in Farrington Papers, HSA.

37. Fortas to John J. McCloy, November 16, 1944, marked "Personal and Confidential," McCloy Files, NA. See supra, p. 302, for McCloy's reply with reference to the "jurisdictionitis" syndrome.

38. Numerous draft versions of proposed executive orders and statutes are archived in the legal files of the Military Governor and (later) Office of Internal Security files, RG 338, NA.

39. Richardson to McCloy, February 10, 1944, McCloy Files, NA.

40. On McCloy's efforts to persuade commanders who succeeded DeWitt in the western mainland area—the first, ironically, being Emmons, then General Charles Bonsteel—to authorize and oversee the early return of internees and others who had been evacuated, see Eric L. Muller, *American Inquisition: The Hunt for Japanese American Disloyalty in World War I* (Chapel Hill: University of North Carolina Press, 2007), 86–98.

41. Ibid. (This was at the same time as he also formally terminated martial law in the Islands, though approving the new "military area" scheme by which the army retained emergency powers. Supra, p. 300.)

42. Wiener Report, 10.

43. George Orwell, *1984* (London: Secker and Warburg, 1949; Plume Printing, 1983), 234.

44. This was most dramatically evident when Cramer strongly criticized General Richardson for defying Judge Metzger and threatening imprisonment of the judge if his court agreed to hear habeas cases. See above, p. 262.

45. See supra, p. 84.

46. See supra, pp. 86–87.

47. J. Garner Anthony, *Hawaii under Army Rule* (Stanford, CA: Stanford University Press, 1955), 108. Honolulu's Mayor Petrie wrote in January 1943 that "in some respects we have been favored by martial law. The [army] . . . has brought food shipments into the islands with dispatch that could hardly have been hoped for otherwise. Sugar and coffee have not been rationed here, and our gasoline and tire restrictions are no more burdensome than they are elsewhere in the United States." ("The Mayor Speaks," *Honolulu Advertiser,* January 10, 1943.)

48. Authors' interview of Senator Fong, Honolulu, August 1999.

49. For a critical appraisal of some of Ennis's performance in other aspects of his position in the Justice Department, see Roger Daniels, *The Japanese American Cases: The Rule of Law in Time of War* (Lawrence: University Press of Kansas, 2013).

50. Fahy's role as counsel for the government in the Korematsu litigation thus revealed another side to his personality and lawyering style. In contrast to his determination to submit the martial law issues to judicial review in the Hawai'i habeas cases, he effectively withheld, in presenting his brief and in oral argument, some important evidence (made known to him by Ennis and others on the staff) of a serious misrepresentation of facts in the army's report justifying the internments and incarceration policy on the mainland, at issue in the Court's consideration of Korematsu's appeal. Ironically, Fahy's associate in the litigation, Herbert Wechsler, who supported that misrepresentation in the face of Ennis's objections, was the army's choice of counsel for the *Duncan* litigation in the Court; but Ennis, whose reservations about the constitutionality of the regime of martial law were well known to the army, received the assignment nonetheless. See supra, p. 309. See also Irons, *Justice at War,* 287–292 and passim; and see again Daniels, *The Japanese-American Cases,* 51–52.

51. It should be noted, however, that the Hawaiian Democratic convention in 1944 called for the termination of martial law.

52. Charles Fairman, "The Supreme Court on Military Jurisdiction, Martial Rule in Hawaii and the Yamashita Case," *Harvard Law Review* 59 (1946): 857.

Afterword

1. Tim Weiner, *Enemies: A History of the FBI* (New York: Random House, 2012), 135.

2. Ibid., 144. McCloy would go on to become president of the World Bank in 1947, and then, two years later, the high commissioner for the occupation in Germany.

3. Ironically, the Justice Department and the White House had also disregarded a November 1945 memorandum from Hoover, "Soviet Espionage in the United States," warning that Alger Hiss, among others, was engaged in spying for the Soviet Union. (Weiner, *Enemies,* 138–139.) Two years later, in 1947, Truman did issue the country's first loyalty order to guard against Communist infiltration of the government. See, inter alia, Athan Theoharis, *Seeds of Repression: Harry S. Truman and the Origins of McCarthyism* (Chicago: Quadrangle Books, 1971).

4. In 1939, Hoover had instituted a Custodial Detention Program, ordering his agents throughout the United States to prepare a list of persons to be detained in case of a threat to national security. See supra, pp. 22–23.

5. Letter from the Director of the FBI (Hoover) to the President's Special Consultant (Souers), marked "personal and confidential: by special messenger," Washington, July 7, 1950, in U.S. Dept. of State, Office of the Historian, *Foreign Relations of the United States, 1950–1955: The Intelligence Community, 1950–1955,* Document No. 16. See discussion of this document in Weiner, *Enemies,* 160–161.

6. Hoover to Souers, July 7, 1950.

7. Ibid.

8. Ibid.

9. Tim Weiner, "Hoover Planned Mass Jailing in 1950," *New York Times,* December 23, 2007. A Pulitzer Prize–winning reporter, Weiner subsequently has published the highly acclaimed book *Enemies,* cited above. For a discussion of the Palmer Raids and other infringements of civil liberties during World War I and its aftermath, see Harry N. Scheiber, *The Wilson Administration and Civil Liberties, 1917–1921* (Ithaca, NY: Cornell University Press, 1960), reissued, 2013 by Quid Pro Books.

10. 64 Stat. 987 (Public Law 81–831). Congress also secretly appropriated funds to construct six detention centers. Weiner, *Enemies,* 161.

11. Congress enacted a provision denying habeas corpus in 2006, but in 2008 the Supreme Court held this provision unconstitutional. (*Boumediene et al. v. Bush,* 542 U.S. 466 [2008].) See also *Ashcroft v. Al-Kidd,* 563 U.S. 131 (2011), in which the Supreme Court ruled that the U.S. Attorney General was immune from suits for his role in the detention of an American citizen as a material witness.

A NOTE ON SOURCES

Materials for the documentation of how martial law operated, in terms of both its dynamics as a bureaucratic military entity and its actual impact on the civilian population, are richly abundant in the several archival collections that we have cited in the chapter endnotes of this book. The National Archives (NA) in College Park, Maryland, administers the vast store of records of the Military Government (RG 338), overlapping in subject categories with the files of the army's Hawaii Department (RG 494). The authors have worked in detail through the commanding generals' and Executive's subject-matter and correspondence files. They contain a variety of records that pertain to all aspects of the military's policy and administration in Hawai'i, including the entire range of the civilian activities and institutions that operated under army supervision and control. They incorporate the materials documenting the policies that so vitally affected the Nikkei and others suspected of disloyalty, including the records of scores of individual interrogations and hearings, and case reviews of internees and others incarcerated in the Islands or the mainland. The files also contain records relating to the provost court operations; litigation in the federal courts, including legal staff's functions more generally; and the administration of censorship, resources allocation, prisons, transportation, labor control, propaganda, and morale efforts.

For the War Department's role in overseeing the martial law regime, the files of Assistant Secretary John J. McCloy (RG 170, also in the College Park facility) are an indispensable source, being comprehensive as to his correspondence with the command in Hawai'i, with general staff and judge advocate general officers, and with the cabinet-level and other major officials in the Department of the Interior and Department of Justice. McCloy's revealing wartime diaries, part of the collection of his papers held at Amherst College Library, are now available as a web-based resource. Also of special significance is the large collection of General Thomas H. Green Papers, held at the Judge Advocate General School's library in Charlottesville, Virginia. His diaries, correspondence, manuscripts of postwar speeches and lectures, and other materials provide valuable insights regarding his role as Executive for the Office of the Military Governor (OMG), his attitudes as to race and civil liberties, and his relationships with his army colleagues and the civilian officials in both the territorial government's ranks and in Washington. His personal account of "Martial Law in Hawaii" is now available online. The private papers of Green's successor as Executive, General William Morrison, apparently have never been deposited in a research library; but his memoranda and official correspondence, archived in RG 338, are a useful resource as to his operation and provision of legal counsel. The Papers of General Delos Emmons and the Papers of General Robert Richardson, both held in the Hoover Institution Archives at Stanford University, also contain materials that usefully complement these other sources.

Other material from the National Archives that proved important to this study are found in the records of the military and naval intelligence organizations, the War Relocation Authority (WRA), the FBI, and the Department of Justice, all in the College Park facility. The Japanese American Internee Data File is available online and provides detailed information on the Nikkei who were incarcerated in WRA camps. The files of the Office of Territories and those of Under Secretary of the Interior Abe Fortas, in the Department of the Interior records group, also in NA at College Park, are of special importance for documentation of the department's perspective and interests that shaped the protracted conflicts over delineation of civilian and military functions—and bore finally on the termination of martial law.

A major source on the habeas corpus cases and the ensuing constitutional litigation is the set of case file records for the U.S. District Court, Hawai'i, and for the appeals of the habeas cases in the Ninth Circuit Court of Appeals, along with Department of Justice administrative correspondence and criminal case files of relevance, that are housed in the National Archives at San Francisco, located in San Bruno (NASB). An especially important source for this aspect of our study is the enormous Transcript of Record for *In re Duncan,* including General Richardson's extensive testimony, later the subject of keen attention by the U.S. Supreme Court.

Complementing the archived case files and the army and Justice Department correspondence for the legal issues regarding the "military necessity" doctrine, the *Japanese-American Cases,* and *Duncan v. Kahanamoku,* are the conference notes and other materials in the Papers of Justice Hugo L. Black and Papers of Justice William O. Douglas, both of them in the Library of Congress; and the Papers of Justice Frank Murphy, in the Bentley Historical Library of the University of Michigan, Ann Arbor. In the Seeley G. Mudd Manuscript Collection of the Princeton University Library are the American Civil Liberties Union Papers; they include the important correspondence of Roger Baldwin, Garner Anthony, and the attorney A. L. Wirin regarding the legality of provost court justice and the constitutional issues in the treatment of the Nikkei and in the habeas litigation involving Zimmerman, Duncan, and White.

In the Franklin D. Roosevelt Library, in Hyde Park, New York, the president's own files on a variety of subjects relating to the Hawai'i situation and to national security more generally were of special significance, of course, in evaluating FDR's political and executive decisions with regard to martial law. Four other manuscript collections valuable to our research and housed in the FDR Library are the Papers of Attorney General Francis Biddle, of Assistant Attorney General James H. Rowe Jr., of Solicitor General Charles Fahy, and of presidential advisor Samuel Rosenman. The Harold L. Ickes Papers in the Library of Congress, together with the Henry L. Stimson diaries in the Yale University Library, were important sources for our reconstruction of the cabinet-level disputes over the constitutional questions raised by the martial law regime and for insights into these individuals whose stance was so central to the course and duration of martial law.

To represent accurately the full scope of the legal, military-administrative, and social history of the martial law years, fortunately for historical scholarship the Hawai'i State Archives, the University of Hawai'i at Manoa, and the Japanese Cultural Center of Hawai'i (JCCH), all in Honolulu, have devoted impressive efforts to documenting the World War II experience in the Islands. The Hawai'i State Archives house the very full subject-matter files of Governor Stainback and of Congressional Delegates Samuel King and Joseph Farrington. In all of them are found correspondence with the OMG generals and staff and with the top officials in the departments of Justice and Interior, letters from constituents (including internees or others who were incarcerated and their families), as well as documentation on labor control, prostitution, and bureaucratic issues such as financing through fines, liquor licensing, and the like. Also included are materials on political campaigns and controversies, statistical and policy reports, and hundreds of newspaper clippings.

The Hawai'i War Records Division (HWRD) collection in the University of Hawai'i's library is the product of a remarkable project undertaken intensively during the war itself, augmented in subsequent years by further collecting of documentary materials, that includes interviews, photographic images, committee reports, plantation and other business records, newspaper and journal files and clippings, and other sources of information on wartime government as well as the daily life and travails of the civilian population under army rule. In recent years, the HWRD collection has been augmented with a set of records called "The Japanese Internment and Relocation Files: The Hawai'i Experience" (cited as JIR), collected under the direction of Professor Dennis Ogawa. It consists of photocopied materials, many of them from RG 338 and other agency or department records in the National Archives, as well as oral history transcripts, that relate to the ethnic Japanese population and the policies of internment, removal, and incarceration endured by the Nikkei during the war.

Also invaluable as a repository for materials on the Nikkei—including copies of the documents compiled by Professor Ogawa—is the JCCH, whose staff and volunteers have collected voluminous materials, including letters and memoirs that they have translated from the original Japanese. The JCCH also took a major role in pursuing research on the Honouliuli camp, and in disseminating information that inspired public support for creation of a National Parks Service historic site or monument there, approved in 2015.

Finally, the Bancroft Library of the University of California, Berkeley, has a massive holding, "The Japanese American Evacuation and Resettlement Collection"—a portion of which is in the process of digitalization—that proved invaluable to us as a source of evidentiary materials on manifold issues on which the governmental and military archives provided a very different, bureaucratic perspective. This magnificent Bancroft collection includes detailed reports, correspondence, interviews, and other materials that were archived by the famous wartime UC Berkeley-led project that documented the fate of the West Coast Nikkei; it has been supplemented with additional acquisitions since the war. Also in the Bancroft Library are the papers of the civil liberties lawyer Wayne M. Collins, documenting his research, interviewing, and litigation on behalf of the internee renunciants and other incarcerated Nikkei who sought to have their American citizenship restored.

INDEX

241; and the "liberation" of Hawai'i, 214–218; military reactions to, 214, 227, 235, 239, 245, 302, 324; opposition to General Orders No. 31, 231, 268; opposition to martial law, 110, 113, 222, 226, 282, 288, 311; opposition to military control of labor, 80, 83, 85, 87–88, 95–96; negotiations with Green, 228, 229, 235; relations with military, 235; and restoration of civilian rule, 106, 268, 277, 288–289, 299–300. *See also* Frank, John P.; Fortas, Abe (Under Secretary of the Interior); and Ickes, Harold (Secretary of the Interior)

Department of Justice (DOJ): asserting civilian authority, 87–88, 113, 211; calls for modified martial law, 105; citizens refused in camps, 142; custody transfer to War Department, 31; detention under, 45, 174; domestic surveillance, 22; and exclusion, 152; habeas efforts, response to, 160; handling "enemy aliens," 182; internment camps under, 31, 32, 50, 118, 194; opposition to General Orders No. 31; prosecution of consular agents 30; skepticism of anti-Japanese claims, 149; Special Defense Unit, 31. *See also* Biddle, Francis (U.S. Attorney General); Department of the Interior: Justice-Interior memorandum; Department of the Interior: and restoration of civilian rule; FBI; internment: selective

Department of Labor, U.S.: 1905 report on Japanese immigration, 12; investigation of Hawai'i conditions, 91

Department of the Navy, 299. *See also* Knox, Frank (Secretary of the Navy)

Department of War, 46, 216, 217; assertion of final authority, 5, 291; anti-Japanese prejudice in, 126; authority over shipping traffic, 77; and civil suits, 325; civilian authority, growing favor for, 222; detention centers, 32; and dual citizens, 26, 102, 205, 207; and *Duncan* and *White* cases, 309, 322; and *Endo,* 309; and enemy aliens, 102, 129, 205, 207; "fifth columnist" concerns, 126; "fortress" mentality 344; General

Orders No. 31, 233; and Hawaii Bar Association, 289; habeas cases, 259–260, 265, 266, 269–270, 283, 288, 298, 324; and internment, 50, 152, 169, 208, 304; and Japanese Americans, 29, 130, 143; and Justice Department, 32; knowledge of civil rights violations, 4; and loyalty questionnaires, 173; and mass removal, 133, 135, 137, 141, 144; and "military necessity" argument, 343–344; release program, 309; restoration of civil authority, 105–106, 228–229, 234–246, 270, 277–278, 290, 292, 294; support for martial law regime, 235, 282, 335. *See also* Green, Thomas H. (General, OMG Executive); labor: army control of; McCloy, John J. (Assistant Secretary of War); Nationality Act; Richardson, Robert C. (Commanding General, military governor); Stimson, Henry L. (Secretary of War)

deportation: of ethnic Japanese to Japan, 330, 331, 350. *See also* mass removal of ethnic Japanese

detainees, 3, 44, 118–119, 163, 182; assistance to, 125, 139; camp conditions, 118, 185–190, 192–201; custody, 158; defined, xvii; family notification, 124; final disposition withheld, 51; guilt, presumption of, 176; habeas pleas, 175, 251–252; hearings, 160–166; individual accounts, 46–47; logistical and legal difficulties, 152; morale, 192, 199; numbers of, 181–184, 196, 424n116; processing, 143, 159, 173, 349; release, 201, 204–207, 309. *See also* evacuees; excludees; internees; loyalty questionnaires; selective removals; renunciants

detention lists, 34–35, 44–46. *See also* "ABC List"

DeWitt, John L. (General), 245; anti-Japanese sentiment, 168, 245, 332, 336, 338, 342, 460–461n4; prejudice against Kibei, 168, 174; prewar martial law planning, 15

Dillingham, Walter, 72, 211, 382n105, 433n56

Director of Labor Control (OMG), 81–84, 88, 91

ABOUT THE AUTHORS

Harry N. Scheiber is Chancellor's Professor of Law and History, Emeritus, in the School of Law, University of California, Berkeley. He also directs the School's Institute for Legal Research and its Law of the Sea Institute, and is former director of its Sho Sato Program in Japanese and U.S. Law. Previously he was professor of history at Dartmouth College and at the University of California, San Diego.

A leading authority on constitutional and legal history, Scheiber is a Fellow of the American Academy of Arts and Sciences and past president of the American Society for Legal History. He has been a Distinguished Fulbright Lecturer, the Wallace Fujiyama Distinguished Visiting Professor of Law at the University of Hawai'i, and twice a Guggenheim Fellow. He is author or editor of fourteen books, including *The Wilson Administration and Civil Liberties, 1917–1921*, recently republished; *Earl Warren and the Warren Court; The State and Freedom of Contract; American Law and the Constitutional Order; Ohio Canal Era*: and *New Concepts of Rights in Japanese Law*. Other books include *Federalism and the Judicial Mind*, and, most recently, several books on ocean law. He has published more than one hundred articles in journals of history, law, and the social sciences.

Jane L. Scheiber is a research associate in the Center for the Study of Law and Society, School of Law, University of California, Berkeley. She was previously a longtime member of the academic and senior professional staffs at the University of California, San Diego, and UC Berkeley, and director of the Public Affairs Laboratory at Dartmouth College.

She has published ten books, including *America and the Future of Man; In Search of the American Dream; American Issues: The Molding of American Values;* and *Crime and Justice in America*. Recently she served as coeditor of *U.S. Law and Courts in the Pacific: A Special Issue of Western Legal History*. Other scholarly work includes several studies of civil rights and civil liberties in wartime, which have appeared in *Western Legal History, University of Hawai'i Law Review, Labor History,* and *Legal Affairs*.